Shenonda Gad
The Annex Village Campus
116 Madison Ave,
Toronto, Ont.

Physics

THE FUNDAMENTAL SCIENCE

1 mile = 1760 Yrs
= 5280 ft

Barton • Raymer

ISBN 0-03-922282-9

Printed in Canada
    7   8   76

TO THE STUDENT

Ours is an age of spectacular scientific accomplishment. The harnessing of atomic energy, the orbiting of earth satellites, trans-world television, and the fantastic capabilities of modern electronic computers—all these achievements, which today seem almost commonplace, were hardly more than wild dreams to the ordinary citizen even a quarter century ago.

These developments belong to the ever-expanding field of physics, which is the study of the physical laws governing the universe. To understand and make good use of the rapidly-developing technology of our modern world, it is of increasing importance that we, as students, equip ourselves with the knowledge necessary to appreciate its significance.

This book has been written to provide you with your first detailed study of this fascinating science. It is a book that is meant to be read; do not treat it merely as an exercise book.

Suppose we scan through it now—

In the opening chapter you will note that much space is given to a description of the slide rule. Although this is not essential to an understanding of the course, a few hours spent in mastering the slide rule can save you much time in mathematical calculations, and you will find it a fascinating tool.

The sequence of topics in this book follows the chronological development of physics. The first several chapters are concerned with that branch of physics called mechanics. This subject has been well understood for several hundred years, and much of it was welded together by one man—Sir Isaac Newton.

Very likely you have already made a basic study of sound and light. We will pursue these topics more deeply with particular emphasis on their behaviour as *waves*. In recent years wave theory has become increasingly important in the description of other physical phenomena.

The latter half of the book is devoted to the study of electricity and its applications, and to "modern physics"—the study of the atom.

An extremely important part of your study of physics is the experimental work, of which there is much in this book. Exercise care in the performing and recording of each experiment, making each measurement as accurately as your apparatus allows. You will be rewarded with a deeper understanding and appreciation of the phenomenon being investigated.

And now, good luck!

O. C. BARTON
R. J. RAYMER

ACKNOWLEDGMENTS

The authors express their gratitude to all who assisted them in the writing and evaluation of this book. Special mention and thanks are due the following persons: Mr. C. K. Duff, of the Faculty of Applied Science and Engineering, University of Toronto, whose careful checking of the problems and constructive criticism of the text contribute much to the accuracy and validity of the work; Mrs. J. E. Dean, whose original problems add wider scope to the book. The advice of Mr. E. G. Micklewright of Stark Electronic Instruments Ltd., was most helpful in the preparation of a number of experiments. Thanks are also due the artists whose work appears in the book: Mr. Gastone Fantuz and Mr. Antony Bradshaw. The photographs to illustrate the experiments in Chapters 2, 3 and 4 were taken by Mr. Clifford Heckel. Many of the remaining photographs were taken by Mr. Raymer. Finally, to those institutions and individuals who have made available photographs, and to all others who have contributed time and effort to the work, the authors convey their gratitude.

O.C.B.
R.J.R.

Owen C. Barton is Head of the Physics Department of Central Technical School, Toronto.

Ronald J. Raymer is Head of the Physics Department of Oakwood Collegiate Institute, Toronto.

Contents

Physics
THE FUNDAMENTAL SCIENCE

Prologue

Matter and Energy

> *"We are such stuff*
> *As dreams are made on, and our little life*
> *Is rounded with a sleep."*
>
> Shakespeare, The Tempest, IV. 1, 60-63

From the beginning of time, man has marvelled about his environment—about the earth, the sun, the moon, the stars. Through the ages a ray of light would appear when a sage revealed some order in the nature of things to dispel the superstition which results from awe and the fear of the unknown.

Much was written by the early Greeks concerning the nature of our universe, but unfortunately their ideas were not subjected to the purifying fire of experimentation. Scientific studies embraced the entire spectrum of knowledge: an educated man was expected to glean all that was recorded in the realm of knowledge. For centuries scientists who studied the physical world called themselves *natural philosophers*.

In many ways a student of physics is still a natural philosopher, for physics is *the fundamental science*. No sharp line of demarcation exists between physics and the other sciences, for physics is basic to, and encroaches upon, all the other sciences. As the study of nuclear physics proceeds, it spills over into the realm of chemistry, medicine, biology, mineralogy, and mathematics.

Many famous names have left their indelible imprint on the pages of physics. In earlier times, Thales, Pythagoras, Aristotle, and Democritus awakened man to serious study. Later Galileo clarified the ideas concerning motion, and Newton recorded the laws governing motion throughout our solar system, even setting out the principles that predict the clocklike movements of the heavenly bodies.

In modern times, knowledge in the field of physics is bursting forth at an ever-expanding rate. Einstein, the greatest of the moderns, described the interrelation between an exchange of matter and energy. Compton, DeBroglie, Bohr, J. J. Thomson, and many others have expanded our concepts of wave mechanics, nuclear forces and structure.

1. PHYSICS IN THE MODERN WORLD

Today, physics should never be a dull procession of facts to be memorized and spewed forth at examination time. Have we lost entirely our childhood desire to explore and wonder, to question and dream? As the story of this science unfolds, its

2

day-by-day revelation of new frontiers to conquer and its accomplishments in the field of engineering, together with its application of modern methods to medical research, industry, and the arts should stimulate us to probe many aspects of its fundamental relationships.

To understand our world and the laws that govern it, a student must subject himself to disciplines. Thus, the immense distances of outer space and the minute measurements of nuclear physics require a knowledge of number manipulation in the form of indices, logarithms, and the slide rule. The rotation of satellites and the revolution of planets require an understanding of motion and the forces concerned with the motion. Energy transmission and the relationship between matter and energy necessitate a study of wave theory and wave mechanics. However, as our study progresses, do not let our disciplines hide the true nature of our voyage on the sea of knowledge: an understanding of the world in which we live, preparation for further study in all fields of science, and the satisfaction to be derived from finding the key to revelations yet to come.

2. THE CONCEPT OF MATTER

Since physics is a study of inanimate things we begin our story with the meaning of matter. The Greek atomists believed matter to be composed of atoms or combinations of atoms, a concept similar to that prevailing today. Modern theory and experimentation have pictured the atom itself as a combination of particles in various configurations that reveal some of the characteristics peculiar to each atom.

All atoms are comprised of a central nucleus containing a number of particles, or nucleons, the remainder of the atom being composed of electrons that circle the nucleus in orbits confined to several regions known as electron shells or energy levels. Each region possesses a characteristic amount of energy. The low-energy particles occupy orbits close to the nucleus and those of higher energy occupy orbits farther out from the nucleus.

3. THE NUCLEUS

The nucleus of an atom consists of protons and neutrons which together make up virtually the entire mass of an atom. The number of protons in the nucleus determines the *atomic number* of the atom. The symbol Z is used to designate the atomic number of a naturally occurring material composed of molecules formed of like or similar atoms. For oxygen $Z=8$; for hydrogen $Z=1$; for uranium $Z=92$.

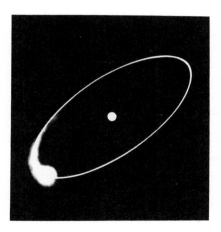

Fig. 1: *The hydrogen atom: an electron orbits a nucleus consisting of one proton. What is the atomic number of hydrogen? What is its mass number?*

The symbol N is reserved for the number of neutrons in the nucleus of an atom. The sum of the number of protons and neutrons, that is, $Z+N$, is equal to, or constitutes, the *mass number* of an atom. The most abundant type of uranium atom contains 92 protons and 146 neutrons to give it a mass number of 238 and an atomic number of 92.

3

Since atomic structure is outlined in more detail in a later chapter, only a brief reference is made to it at this time.

Fig. 2: *The oxygen atom: 8 electrons orbit a nucleus consisting of 8 protons and 8 neutrons. What is the mass number and atomic number of oxygen?*

Similar or dissimilar atoms may combine to form molecules; for example, two atoms of oxygen combine to form one molecule of oxygen, but two atoms of hydrogen combine with one atom of oxygen to form one molecule of water (Figure 3).

Table 1 lists the atomic structure of a few atoms. Protium, deuterium, and tritium are *isotopes* of hydrogen. Isotopes are atoms whose nuclei contain the same number of protons but a different number of neutrons.

4. MATTER AND ENERGY

Our study of physics is largely an investigation of the changes produced in matter by energy. Unlike matter, energy does not possess mass, nor does it occupy space. Energy is a basic concept so fundamental that it is difficult to describe. Since it performs work when it affects matter, it is measured by its ability to do work. When

Table 1

Isotope	Nuclear particles	Atomic number	Atomic mass	Mass number
Protium	1 proton	1	1.007826	1
Deuterium	1 proton 1 neutron	1	2.014102	2
Tritium	1 proton 2 neutrons	1	3.016049	3
Carbon-12	6 protons 6 neutrons	6	12. (exactly) (by definition)	12
Carbon-13	6 protons 7 neutrons	6	13.003357	13
Carbon-14	6 protons 8 neutrons	6	14.003249	14
Uranium-234	92 protons 142 neutrons	92	234.039893	234
Uranium-235	92 protons 143 neutrons	92	235.043007	235
Uranium-238	92 protons 146 neutrons	92	238.049781	238

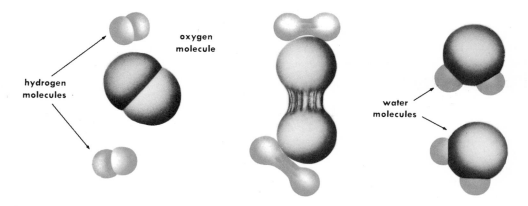

Fig. 3: *The formation of two molecules of water results from each of the two oxygen atoms in the oxygen molecule combining with two atoms from each of the two hydrogen molecules.*

some forms of energy are recognized as heat, light, electricity, magnetism, sound, chemical energy and mechanical energy, some understanding of the difference between mass and energy may be achieved.

Frequently one form of energy is changed to another in some appliance or machine. Such an interchange occurs when electrical energy is used to produce heat in a toaster or chemical energy to produce heat as a log is burnt. The chemical changes that resulted from the log's burning did not involve any change in the atoms taking part but only in their combinations.

Energy can be released in large amounts by a nuclear or atomic change of matter. Albert Einstein (1879-1955) predicted the relationship involved in the conversion of matter to energy, or vice versa, in the equation $E = mc^2$, where E represents the amount of energy, m the mass, and c is the velocity of light. When a log is burnt, the heat and light energy produced can be converted to the mass equivalent; thus, when 6 tons of carbon combine with 16 tons of oxygen, the heat and light energy released is equivalent to 0.00007 ounce of matter. Even in the most violent chemical reactions, the amount of energy released is equivalent to an unbelievably small amount of matter.

5. CHANGE IN MATTER

The changes in matter brought about by energy can be classified into three categories:

    (1) physical
    (2) chemical
    (3) nuclear.

In a *physical* change the identity of the substance is not lost; the composition remains the same, but the form of the substance changes. A physical change of matter occurs when ice becomes water or water becomes water vapour.

As previously indicated, in a *chemical* change the composition of the substance is altered and new substances with new properties are produced. In a chemical change, the combinations of atoms may change but the atom itself remains the same.

In a *nuclear* reaction, new materials are formed by changes in the identity of the atoms themselves. Nuclear changes occur spontaneously in nature when unstable nuclei such as those of radium gradually change to nuclei of lead. Atomic and hydrogen bombs owe their energy to nuclear changes. Beneficial nuclear transformations have given us atomic power, the cobalt bomb for medicinal purposes, and a new understanding of plant and animal life.

Chapter 1

Measurement

1. SYSTEMS OF MEASUREMENT USED IN PHYSICS

The object of physics is to give a detailed description of the physical world. This description not only involves the inter-relation of physical phenomena in a general way but it also involves the magnitudes of physical quantities.

The quantities essential for precise rocket calculations, determination of astronomical distances, and many other types of measurement, require agreement concerning the unit to be used in each case. The fundamental quantities which require measurement in physics are *length, mass,* and *time.* (Later we shall need to include *temperature* and *electrical charge.*) These three quantities are called fundamental because others such as speed, velocity, acceleration, and so forth, are combinations of these three. The units chosen for scientific work are the *metre* as the unit of length, the *kilogram* of mass, and the *second* of time. The system is briefly referred to as the MKS system.

Engineers in the English-speaking countries more commonly use a system in which *length, force* (weight), and *time* are chosen as the fundamental quantities. Here, the *foot* is the unit of length, the *pound* of force, and the *second* of time. This is known as the British Engineering System of units. In English-speaking countries students of physics and allied subjects must learn to live with both these systems.

(a) The Metric System—an absolute system

Historically, the fundamental units in the metric system were thought to have some basic significance. The metre, for example, was intended to be one ten-millionth of the distance along the meridian through Paris from the Equator to the Pole. Further determination of the length of this portion of the meridian has shown that the metre is not precisely one ten-millionth of it, and in any event its accuracy now seems irrelevant. The unit of length, the metre, is, in fact, quite arbitrary and was defined as the distance between two microscopic scratches on a bar of platinum-iridium which is kept at the International Bureau of Weights and Measures at Sèvres in France. Copies of this standard are kept at the laboratories of the National Research Council, Ottawa, as well as at other national laboratories.

A further protection of the unit of length has been provided by determining the number of wavelengths of the very pure orange light given out by krypton atoms. There are 1,650,763.73 of these wavelengths in the metre; thus this number of wavelengths of the orange light from krypton is essentially the new and indestructible unit of length, and was so adopted in 1960.

The kilogram, the unit of mass, is likewise arbitrarily chosen as the mass of a piece of platinum-iridium kept at Sèvres. It is actually in the form of a cylinder about 0.015 metre in diameter and 0.015 metre high. Copies of this model or pattern are to be found in national physics laboratories throughout the world.

The unit of time, the second, is defined as $\frac{1}{86,400}$ of the average interval of time, taken throughout the year, between successive instants at which the sun is at its highest point—an interval that we know as the mean solar day.

This system of units, the MKS system, is an absolute system since the basic units chosen (and in particular the unit of mass) are independent of position on the surface of the earth. It has the great advantage that the unit of length and the unit of mass can be duplicated to a very high order of precision—about one part in ten million. Astronomical measurements of the mean solar day can also be reproduced to a remarkable degree of precision. The use of platinum-iridium for the units of length and mass avoids rapid chemical deterioration.

(b) The British Engineering System— a gravitational system

The standard of mass, in the English-speaking countries, was for many years a carefully preserved block of metal known as the *pound mass.* In 1959, these countries reached agreement in redefining the pound mass to be an exact fraction of the kilogram standard:

1 pound mass = 0.45359237 kg

The unit of length, the foot, in this system of measurement was originally defined to be one third of the standard yard, preserved at the National Physical Laboratory in Teddington, England. More recently this unit of length has been redefined to be an exact fraction of the standard metre:

1 foot = 0.3048 m

The British unit of length is thus tied to the indestructible unit of length referred to on the previous page.

The unit of time, as in the MKS system, is the second.

This system is referred to as a *gravitational system,* because of the manner in which the unit of force is defined. The gravitational pull of the earth on a one-pound mass, at a location at sea level and 45° North Latitude, is referred to as a *pound force.* It is necessary to specify the location in this definition because of the slight variation in gravitational pull at different points on the earth's surface.

(c) The CGS System—an absolute system

A system of measurements in which the units of length and mass are submultiples of the metre and the kilogram has long been in use in scientific work but is gradually being discarded for the preferable MKS system. In this system, commonly called the CGS system, the unit of length is the centimetre and the unit of mass is the gram.

Table 1-1

CONVERSION FACTORS FOR COMMON UNITS	
British System	*Metric System*
Length: 1 inch*	2.54 centimetres (cm)
39.37 inches	1 metre (m)
Volume: 1 quart (Imperial)	1.14 litres (l)
0.88 quart (Imperial)	1.00 litre (l)
Weight: 1 pound	454 grams (g)
2.20 pounds	1.00 kilogram (kg)

*Exactly by definition

2. PRECISION IN MEASUREMENT

The tremendous growth of man's knowledge during the past few centuries is in direct

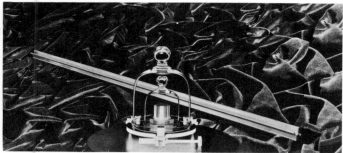

Fig. 1-1: *The platinum-iridium cylinder, shown under the bell jars, is the standard of mass for one kilogram. The H-shaped bar behind it is also of platinum-iridium alloy, and the distance between the two lines scratched on it served for many years as the standard of length for one metre. Now the metre is defined in terms of the wavelength of a krypton-86 spectral line.*

relation to his ability to measure the phenomena he observes. Newton, in measuring the acceleration of an object when acted upon by various forces, found that a simple relationship existed between these quantities, and from this he formulated one of the most basic laws of physics.

Quite often, however, in order to prove or disprove a scientific theory, experiments must be devised and measurements made. An outstanding example of this has occurred in recent times. In 1905 Albert Einstein shook the scientific world with the publication of his general theory of relativity. This work contained many radically new concepts which for many decades to follow were not completely accepted by the scientific community. Only in the last few years have experimental techniques been devised which have enabled investigators to verify the predictions contained in this theory.

It is important for the student to realize that there is always some margin of error in every measurement. *Some difference will always exist between the true value of a quantity being measured and the value of that quantity given by the measuring device.* The smaller this difference is, the more *precise* we say the measurement is. A machinist using a micrometer is quite capable of determining the diameter of a steel rod to the nearest 0.001 cm. If he were asked to perform the same measurement with an ordinary ruler, he could, with assurance, determine it only to the nearest 0.1 cm. We can say, then, that the micrometer is an instrument of higher precision than the standard ruler.

In general, it is true that the precision of a measurement is determined by the means by which it was made; that is, by the measuring device and the skill of the person using it.

Because a number arising from a measurement does not represent the exact value of the quantity being measured, it is often referred to as an *approximate number*, to distinguish it from *exact numbers* which are arrived at by a counting process.

To illustrate, consider the measurement of a student's desk, made by means of a metre stick calibrated in millimetres. Using this instrument, the student sees that the length lies between 97.7 cm and 97.8 cm, but closer to the latter figure. If he estimates the length to lie eight-tenths of the distance between the .7 and .8 readings, the measurement would be recorded as 97.78 cm, or 0.9778 m. This number, representing a measured quantity, is an approximate number. If the student then counts the number of desks in the room and records it as 36, this number is an exact number since it exactly represents the quantity it describes. Other examples of exact numbers are the number of days in January, and the value in dollars of a 25-cent piece.

In performing computations with approximate numbers, it is important that certain simple rules be adhered to. These will be discussed in Section 5 of this chapter.

3. SIGNIFICANT DIGITS

An examination of the table measurement 0.9778 m reveals the following information: in this measurement the 9, 7, and 7 are actual divisions on the scale and are certainly known. The 8, on the other hand, arises from an estimate of the fraction of the smallest division on the scale, in this case millimetres. This figure implies that the measurement might have been 0.9777 or 0.9779, but the experimenter believes that 0.9778 is the closest estimate. The figure, however, has an element of doubt. We say that the four digits in this measurement are *significant**: i.e., they have a meaning in the measurement. It is usual in physical measurements to retain the first doubtful figure in a measurement. A zero in a measurement may be a significant figure. Suppose that the second seven of our measurement had coincided, as nearly as could be judged, with the edge marking one end of the table; then the next digit would have been no-tenths of the smallest division and the recording would be 0.9770 metres, a measurement with four significant figures. If the measurement had been recorded as 0.977 metres, it would have been understood that the digit, this second 7, was in doubt and this measurement would have been less precise than 0.9770 metres.

A set of detailed rules is sometimes set up for determining whether zeros in a measurement are significant, but it is much better to use one's judgment. For example, in the measurement 0.000683, it is clear that the zeros merely indicate the position of the decimal point and are not significant. On the one hand, in the measurement 0.0006830, the zero to the right of the 3 is significant, for it signifies that this zero digit is an estimate of the number of tenths of the smallest division on the scale used. On the other hand, to record a large distance as 268,000 miles, really gives no indication as to how many figures are significant unless one has some knowledge of the instruments and technique used in making the measurement and can therefore judge the order of precision involved.

The *accuracy* claimed by a measurement is indicated by the number of significant digits used to express it.

4. SCIENTIFIC NOTATION

To avoid these uncertainties in respect to significant figures, as well as to express very large and very small quantities in a form easily understood and handled, scientific notation is used. In this notation a number has the form

$$M \times 10^n$$

— Index or Exponent
— Base is 10

where M is a number between 1 and 10 and n is a positive or negative integer.

To change a number into scientific notation:

(a) Determine the number M by moving the decimal point so that you leave only one nonzero digit to the left of it.

(b) Determine the index n by counting the number of places you have moved the decimal point; if moved to the left, n is positive; if moved to the right, n is negative.

The following examples will illustrate:

(1) The velocity of light is 29,979,280,000 cm per second. This measurement is known to seven significant figures. This degree of accuracy is not evident in the form in which the measurement is recorded here, but written in scientific notation it becomes 2.997928×10^{10} cm/sec and at once the number of significant figures becomes evident.

(2) The mass of the electron is 0.000,000,-000,000,000,000,000,000,000,910,83 g and is known to five significant figures. This fact, of course, is evident from the way it is written above; but the form is quite inconvenient, for it is difficult from this form to appreciate the magnitude of the mass. In scientific notation, however, it becomes 9.1083×10^{-28} g.

---

*The terms *significant digit* and *significant figure* are used interchangeably.

5. CALCULATIONS INVOLVING MEASURED QUANTITIES

Most physical experiments involve several direct measurements. These, in turn, must be combined in a series of additions, subtractions, multiplications, or divisions. Sometimes these quantities must be raised to some power, or some root must be extracted. It becomes important that we do these calculations in such a way that the final answer will not contain more than one doubtful figure, for of course the final answer could not be more accurate than the least accurate of the direct measurements which were used to calculate the answer.

The following examples will illustrate the rules for arithmetic processes involving significant figures:

Addition and Subtraction

Suppose we have three measurements of length which must be added. Let them be 4.8 m; 16.56 m; and 0.483 m. Since the least precise measurement, 4.8 m, is uncertain in the tenths place, the sum should not be expressed to better than a tenth of a metre. To maintain the precision required, the other numbers, 16.56 and 0.483, are rounded to the hundredths place. Before the addition, therefore, we round the measurement 0.483 to

Table 1-2

METRIC UNITS OF LENGTH Fundamental Unit: 1 metre (m)				
Name and Abbreviation	*Fundamental Unit Equivalent*	*Scientific Notation*	*Submultiple Equivalent*	*Scientific Notation*
*1 megametre	1,000,000 m	1×10^6m		
1 kilometre (km)	1000 m	1×10^3m		
1 metre (m)	1 m			
1 decimetre (dm)	0.1 m	1×10^{-1}m		
1 centimetre (cm)	0.01 m	1×10^{-2}m		
1 millimetre (mm)	0.001 m	1×10^{-3}m	0.1 cm	1×10^{-1}cm
1 micron (μ)	0.000001 m	1×10^{-6}m	0.001 mm or 0.0001 cm	1×10^{-3}mm or 1×10^{-4}cm
**1 millimicron (mμ)	0.000000001 m	1×10^{-9}m	0.0000001 cm	1×10^{-7}cm
1 Ångström (Å)	0.0000000001 m	1×10^{-10}m	0.00000001 cm or 0.0001 μ	1×10^{-8}cm or $1 \times 10^{-4}\mu$
1 fermi (f)	0.000000000000001 m	1×10^{-15}m	0.00001 Å	1×10^{-5} Å

Mega means "great", and in physics is 1,000,000 times a given unit. It is in general use in electronics. For example, *megacycle* may be used in television to identify the frequency of a television station. Channel 6 (Toronto) broadcasts in the region of 85 Mc (megacycles per second) or 8.5×10^7 cycles/sec. *Megohm* is a large unit of electrical resistance equal to 1,000,000 or 1×10^6 ohms. Resistors in the megohm range are used as part of the "grid leak" circuit in radios. The equivalent unit of length, the *megametre* mentioned in the table above, is not in common use.

**The prefix "nano" is commonly used to denote the fraction one-billionth. Thus, one millimicron is one *nanometre.*

0.48 and use 16.56 as it stands. The addition then yields 21.84 m which, when properly rounded, gives 21.8 m. A similar procedure is followed in subtraction.

Multiplication and Division

Let us suppose that an area, such as the top of a rectangular table, is to be measured. There will be two direct measurements involved—the length and the width of the table top. The operator uses MKS units and makes the measurements as described in Section 2. He obtains as length 1.467 m, as width 0.748 m. Each measurement contains one doubtful figure, 7 in the length and 8 in the width. Suppose we multiply these by the usual process of multiplication and keep track of the doubtful figures by circling them. We note that any figure multiplied by a doubtful figure leaves a result in doubt. Thus:

$$
\begin{array}{r}
1 . 4\,6\,⑦ \\
0 . 7\,4\,⑧ \\
\hline
1\,①\quad ⑦③⑥ \\
5\,8\quad 6\,⑧ \\
1\ 0\,2\,6\quad ⑨ \\
\hline
1 . 0\,9\,⑦\quad ③①⑥
\end{array}
$$

The result has seven digits, at least four of which are in doubt. These four must be discarded, and it will thus be appreciated that considerable time and effort have been wasted in getting figures which in the end must be thrown away. For this reason the above product should be stated as 1.09 or 1.10.

In general, *the product of two or more measured quantities should be stated to the same number of significant figures as the least accurate factor.* The reader will recall that the least accurate factor is the one with the least number of significant figures.

When measured quantities are divided, similar caution should be observed, namely: *the quotient should be expressed to the same number of significant figures as the least accur-*

ate of the numbers involved. For example, in the quotient $26.34 \div 7.3$ (both measured quantities), the result should be expressed to two-digit accuracy as 3.6.

There are short ways of multiplying which will avoid carrying all these useless digits, but a most convenient and rapid method is the use of a slide rule.

To work with large and small numbers, a recollection of the Laws of Indices is useful:

1. Law of Multiplication $x^m \times x^n = x^{m+n}$

   e.g., $10^6 \times 10^2 = 10^8$

2. Law of Division $x^m \div x^n = x^{m-n}$

   e.g., $10^6 \div 10^2 = 10^4$

3. Law of Powers $(x^m)^n = x^{mn}$

   e.g., $(2^2)^3 = 2^6$

4. Power of a Product $(xy)^m = x^m y^m$

   e.g., $(2 \times 3)^2 = 2^2 \times 3^2$

EXAMPLE 1

1. Add 14.75 g, 24.6 g, and 6.489 g.
   Solution: $14.75 + 24.6 + 6.49$ yields **45.8 g**.

2. Add 6.85×10^2 km and 5.42×10 km.
   Solution: $(6.85 + 0.542) \times 10^2$ yields **7.39×10^2 km**.

3. Subtract 46.7 g from 96 g.
   Solution: $96 - 46.7$ yields **49 g**.

4. Subtract 6.40×10^{-2} m from 1.39×10^2 m.
   Solution: $(1.39 - 0\ 000640) \times 10^2$ yields **1.39×10^2 m**.

5. Multiply 3.66×10^6 cm by 3.7×10^{-2} cm.
   Solution: $(3.66 \times 3.7)\ (10^4) = 13.542 \times 10^4$
   Properly rounded: **1.4×10^5 cm**.

6. Divide 8.83×10^4 cm by 1.35×10^{-3} cm.
   Solution: $(8.83 \div 1.35) \times (10^4 \div 10^{-3}) =$ **6.54×10^7 cm**.

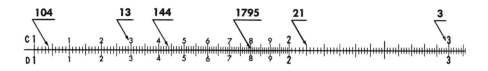

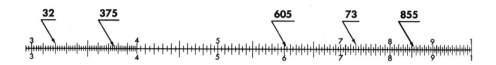

Fig. 1-2: *Reading numbers on a slide rule. Numbers can be read to 3-figure accuracy with the last digit estimated in most cases. More accurate readings can be made at the left end of the rule than at the right end.*

6. USING THE SLIDE RULE

The slide rule permits rapid calculations to an accuracy of at least 3 significant figures. Only slide-rule operations helpful in making calculations in physics will be described.

Of the scales provided, attention will be confined to the C, D, and A scales only. Locate these scales on your slide rule. The C scale is on the bottom of the slide with the D scale immediately below it; the A scale is at the top of the rule. A moveable transparent runner is provided with an index line (hairline).

Reading the Scales

The C and D scales are used to multiply and divide, whereas the A and D are used in calculating squares and square roots.

Examine the C and D scales positioned with the 1 of the C scale coinciding with the 1 of the D scale. The two scales will be identical.

Refer to Figure 1-2 and check the reading of numbers. Note that the scale does not provide decimal points and that therefore the reading 144 can represent 14.4, 1.44, .00144, etc. In multiplication, the scale lengths of the two numbers are added together; in division, the scale length of the divisor is subtracted from the scale length of the dividend.

Multiplying Two Numbers

EXAMPLE 2

1. Multiply 2 by 4:

    (*a*) Set the large 1 at the left end of C opposite 2 on D.

    (*b*) Move the hairline over the large 4 on C.

    (*c*) Read the answer **8** on D underneath the hairline.

Check the manipulation by reversing the multiplication order, that is, multiplying **4** by **2**.

2. Multiply 2 by 7:

    Proceeding as above, the hairline cannot reach the 7 on the C scale; hence it is necessary to use the large 1 of the C scale at the right-hand end of the slide. This time move the hairline to the left over the 7 on the C scale. Read the answer **14** where the hairline crosses the D scale.

Multiplying More than Two Numbers

EXAMPLE 3

1. Multiply 2×3×4:

   (a) Set the large 1 at the left end of C opposite 2 on D.

   (b) Move the hairline over the large 3 on C. (It is not necessary to read the answer on D, which you will observe is 6.)

   (c) Now move the slide to the left to place the large 1 (right-hand side) of C under the hairline.

   (d) Move the hairline over the large 4 on C. (This operation multiplies the answer to step (b), which is 6, by 4.)

   (e) Read the answer, which is the hairline setting on D, namely, **24**.

2. Multiply 2×6×7:

   (a) The large 1 at the right end of C is set opposite the 2 on D and the hairline moved over the 6 on C.

   (b) Move the slide to the right to place the large 1 at the left of C under the hairline (which retained the sub-answer.)

   (c) Find the answer on D by sliding the hairline over 7 on C, giving **84**.

Dividing

EXAMPLE 4

Divide 84 by 2:

   (a) Place the hairline at 84 on D.

   (b) Move the slide to place the large 2 on C under the hairline.

   (c) Move the hairline over the large 1 on C.

   (d) The hairline indicates the answer **42** on D.

These operations are just the reverse of those used to multiply two numbers.

Combined Multiplication and Division

EXAMPLE 5

1. $196 \times \dfrac{744}{784}$:

   (a) Set the hairline over 196 on D. Move the slide to place 784 on C under the hairline. (The sub-answer is opposite the large 1 on C; hence the slide is set to multiply the sub-answer.)

   (b) Move the hairline to 744 on C. Read the answer recorded on D by the hairline, namely, **186**.

2. $45 \times \dfrac{273}{293} \times \dfrac{732}{760}$:

   (a) *Division:* Set the hairline above 45 on D. Move the slide to place 293 on C under the hairline.

   (b) *Multiplication:* Move the hairline to 273 on C.

   (c) *Division:* Move the slide to place 760 on C under the hairline.

   (d) *Multiplication:* Move the hairline to 732 on C. Read the answer below the hairline on D, namely, **40.4**.

Placing the Decimal Point

The proper location of the decimal point for simple problems can be obtained by inspection, but other methods are required for more complex calculations. A recommended procedure is shown on the following page.

EXAMPLE 6

$$\frac{0.00275 \times 31 \times 5650}{43 \times 0.0094}:$$

Number	Scientific Notation	Approximation by Scientific Notation
0.00275	2.75×10^{-3}	3×10^{-3}
31	3.1×10^{1}	3×10^{1}
5650	5.65×10^{3}	6×10^{3}
43	4.3×10^{1}	4×10^{1}
0.0094	9.4×10^{-3}	9×10^{-3}

Numerical factors

$$\frac{3 \times 3 \times 6}{4 \times 9} = 1.5$$

Exponential (index) Factors

$$\frac{10^{-3} \times 10^{1} \times 10^{3}}{10^{1} \times 10^{-3}} = \frac{10^{1}}{10^{-2}}$$

$$\left(\frac{x^{m}}{x^{n}} = x^{m-n}\right) = 10^{3}$$

Approximate answer: 1.5×10^{3}

The digits obtained by slide-rule manipulations are 1190.

If the original numbers are exact numbers, the answer can be stated as 1190 or 1.190×10^{3}. However, if the original numbers were obtained by measurement, the answer should be quoted as 1.2×10^{3}, since the least accurate of the quantities involved has 2 significant digits.

Squaring a Number

The A scale is used with the D scale to square a number or to find the square root of a number. The A scale is similar to the C and D scales, but the scale divisions are only half the length. To square a number, set the hairline over the number on the D scale and find the answer by reading the number under the hairline on the A scale. Usually before squaring it is advisable to express the number in scientific notation.

The following example will illustrate the procedure.

EXAMPLE 7

Find the square of 135:
$135 = 1.35 \times 10^{2}$. Set the hairline on 135 of the D scale and read 182 on the A scale. Thus the square of 1.35 should be 1.82: also the square of 10^{2} is 10^{4}.
The answer thus becomes $\mathbf{1.82 \times 10^{4}}$.

Obtaining the Square Root of a Number

(a) Rewrite the number in exponential form (base 10) so that the index is an *even number* and the numerical part has one or two digits before the decimal point.

(b) If the numerical factor has only *one* digit before the decimal point, set the hairline to that number on the left-hand A scale. If the numerical factor has *two* digits before the decimal point, set the hairline to that number on the right-hand A scale.

(c) The digits for the square root are located under the hairline on the D scale.

(d) Multiply this result by the power of 10 whose index is half that of (a).

EXAMPLE 8

1. Find $\sqrt{900}$:
   $\sqrt{900} = \sqrt{9 \times 10^{2}}$ (Since 9 is a one-digit number, use the left A scale and halve the index.)
   $\therefore \sqrt{900} = 3 \times 10^{1} = \mathbf{30}$ (Answer).

2. Find $\sqrt{0.0090}$:
   $\sqrt{0.0090} = \sqrt{90 \times 10^{-4}}$ (Since 90 is a two-digit number, use the right half of the A scale and halve the index.)
   $\therefore \sqrt{0.0090} = 9.48 \times 10^{-2} = \mathbf{9.5 \times 10^{-2}}$.

THREE SYSTEMS OF MEASUREMENT: The three systems of measurement used in physics are: the MKS, CGS, and British Engineering.

ACCURACY: Every measurement possesses some margin of error. The *accuracy* claimed by a measurement is indicated by the number of significant digits used to express it.

SCIENTIFIC NOTATION serves two useful purposes:

        (*a*) it indicates the number of significant digits in a measurement

        (*b*) it is a method of recording very large or very small numbers.

PRECISION: The *precision* of a measurement is determined by the smallest unit recorded in the measurement.

EXERCISE A

1.

(*a*) Rapidly examine each numbered set of figures shown. Then answer the following questions. Each question refers to the correspondingly numbered figures.

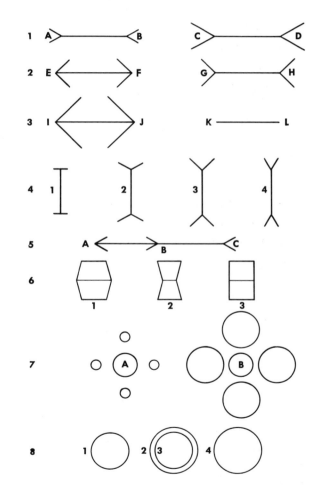

    1. Which is longer: *AB* or *CD*?

    2. Which is longer: *EF* or *GH*?

    3. Which is longer: *IJ* or *KL*?

    4. Which vertical line is longest: 1, 2, 3, or 4?

    5. Which line is longer: *AB* or *BC*?

    6. Which base line is longest: 1, 2, or 3?

    7. Which circle is larger: *A* or *B*?

    8. (i) Which circle is larger: 1 or 3?

       (ii) Which circle is larger: 2 or 4?

(*b*) With the aid of a ruler, measure the length of the lines and the diameters of the circles carefully. Check your answers to part (*a*) against your measurements in part (*b*).

15

(c) What conclusions do you reach about the role of measurement in making observations?

(d) Which part of the ruler is least reliable as a starting point for making a measurement?

2. Name the three fundamental quantities discussed in this chapter.

3. (a) Name the three systems of measurement commonly used by physicists. (b) Give the basic units of each system.

4. What factors determine the precision of a measurement?

5. What are the rules for adding, subtracting, multiplying, and dividing with measured quantities?

6. List the value of four metric-system prefixes as a power of 10 (e.g., deci $= 10^{-1}$).

7. State the number of significant digits in each of the following measured quantities: (a) 2400 g, (b) 3.00×10^{10} cm/sec, (c) 5808 Å, (d) 0.0803 m.

8. What is a conversion factor?

9. The measurements of two different lengths were recorded as 5.4 cm and 226 cm. Which is the more precise measurement? Which measurement has the higher degree of accuracy?

10. Using library research sources, prepare a report on the historical development of the metric system. What circumstances were favourable to its adoption?

EXERCISE B

1. In your notebook, convert each of the following quantities to the required smaller unit:

(a)	15 metres	= ?	decimetres (dm)
(b)	14.7 centimetres	= ?	millimetres (mm)
(c)	2.3 kilograms	= ?	grams (g)
(d)	6.576 grams	= ?	milligrams (mg)
(e)	7.8 kilolitres	= ?	litres (l)
(f)	9.37 litres	= ?	millilitres (ml)
(g)	1.25 kilograms	= ?	decigrams (dg)
(h)	62.54 centigrams	= ?	milligrams (mg)
(i)	0.23 kilometre	= ?	centimetres (cm)
(j)	0.034 kilogram	= ?	milligrams (mg)

2. In your notebook, convert each of the following quantities to the required larger unit:

(a)	937 decimetres	= ?	metres (m)
(b)	125 millilitres	= ?	litres (l)
(c)	2.3 millimetres	= ?	centimetres (cm)

(d) 3125 decigrams   = ? grams (g)

(e) 62.5 grams   = ? kilograms (kg)

(f) 627 milligrams   = ? centigrams (cg)

(g) 867 centimetres   = ? kilometres (km)

(h) 489 milligrams   = ? grams (g)

(i) 0.23 millilitre   = ? centilitres (cl)

(j) 5.178 millilitres   = ? kilolitres (kl)

3. In your notebook, convert each of the following quantities to the required British units:

(a) 2.0×10 metres   = ? inches (in)   = ? feet (ft)

(b) 1.270×10^3 centimetres   = ? inches (in)

(c) 4.60 litres   = ? quarts (qt)

(d) 227 grams   = ? pounds (lb)

(e) 2.2 kilograms   = ? pounds (lb)

4. In your notebook, convert each of the following quantities to the required metric units:

(a) 1.5 inches   = ? centimetres (cm)   = ? metres (m)

(b) 19.685 inches   = ? metres (m)

(c) 2.640 quarts   = ? litres (l)

(d) 3.5 pounds   = ? grams (g)

(e) 15.4 pounds   = ? kilograms (kg)

5. (i) Express the following numbers in scientific notation:

(a) 56   (b) 789

(c) 4   (d) 3210 (4 significant digits)

(e) 186,000 (3 significant digits) (f) 30,000,000,000 (1 significant digit)

(g) 0.70   (h) 0.0012

(i) 0.000403   (j) 0.00000000000000000000000000009107

(ii) Express the following in other than scientific notation:

(a) 5×10^1 (b) 6.2×10^3 (c) 7.4×10^0

(d) 9.1×10^2 (e) 4.3687×10^5 (f) 1×10^{-1}

(g) 4.3×10^{-2} (h) 8.94×10^{-5} (i) 3.076×10^{-3}

(iii) Simplify the following:

(Express parts (j) to (o) in scientific notation.)

(a) $10^1 \times 10^1$ (b) $10^2 \times 10^3$ (c) $10^{-1} \times 10^4$

(d) $10^2 \times 10^{-5}$ (e) $10^4 \div 10^2$ (f) $10^5 \div 10^3$

(g) $10^{-5} \div 10^2$ (h) $10^{-4} \div 10^{-3}$ (i) $10^2 \div 10^{-2}$

(j) $1.2 \times 10^2 \times 3 \times 10^1$ (k) $2.5 \times 10^3 \times 2 \times 10^{-2}$ (l) $6 \times 10^{-4} \times 3 \times 10^{-2}$

(m) $4 \times 10^6 \div (2 \times 10^3)$ (n) $6 \times 10^{-2} \div (3 \times 10^{-4})$ (o) $2.4 \times 10^3 \div (3 \times 10^{-4})$

6. In your notebook, convert each of the following quantities to the required larger unit:

   (Express each answer in scientific notation.)

   (a) A wavelength of visible light:
   5432 Ångströms (Å) = ? microns (μ)

   (b) Calculated radius of an electron:
   2.82 fermis (f) = ? Ångströms (Å)

   (c) Radius (covalent) of the hydrogen atom:
   0.28 Ångström (Å) = ? centimetres (cm)

   (d) Wavelength of ultraviolet light:
   225 Ångströms (Å) = ? metres (m)

   (e) Frequency of radio station CBL:
   740 kilocycles/sec = ? megacycles/sec

7. In your notebook, convert each of the following quantities to the required smaller unit:

   (Express each answer in scientific notation.)

   (a) A wavelength of visible light:
   4.50×10^2 millimicrons (mμ) = ? Ångströms (Å)

   (b) Radius (covalent) of the carbon atom:
   0.77 Ångström (Å) = ? fermis (f)

   (c) A wavelength of infrared radiation:
   0.0925 centimetre (cm) = ? microns (μ)

   (d) The mass of an electron (try to express answer exponentially):
   9.11×10^{-31} kilogram (kg) = ? gram (g)

   (e) The size of an atomic nucleus:
   0.0001 Ångström (Å) = ? fermis (f)

   The following questions are provided for slide rule practice.

8. Multiplication of Two Numbers:

   (a) 2×3 (b) 3×5 (c) 2×35 (d) 3×3.2

   (e) 4×0.55 (f) 0.42×0.23 (g) 11×2 (h) 14×7

9. Multiplication of Three Numbers:

   (a) $2 \times 3 \times 2$ (b) $3 \times 4 \times 5$ (c) $4 \times 2 \times 7$

   (d) $2 \times 2.3 \times 6$ (e) $1.2 \times 3 \times 5$ (f) $3 \times 0.44 \times 6$

   (g) $0.23 \times 0.35 \times 4$ (h) $0.14 \times 0.46 \times 0.50$ (i) $0.32 \times 0.54 \times 0.67$

10. Division:

   (a) $75 \div 3$ (b) $66 \div 5$ (c) $57 \div 4$

   (d) $3 \div 5$ (e) $7 \div 9$ (f) $17 \div 12$

   (g) $76 \div 9$ (h) $142 \div 63$ (i) $337 \div 123$

   (j) $227 \div 725$ (k) $635 \div 8.2$ (l) $78.9 \div 345$

   (m) $5.67 \div 7.65$ (n) $0.452 \div 0.014$

11. Successive Operations: Solve—

(a) $24 \times \dfrac{25}{75}$ (Hint: After the first division, bring the hairline over the 1 at the right side of C; then move the left 1 on C to hairline before multiplication.)

(b) $31 \times \dfrac{17}{42}$

(c) $46 \times \dfrac{79}{13}$ (Hint: After division bring hairline to left on C; then move right 1 on C to hairline before multiplication.)

(d) $57 \times \dfrac{66}{17}$ (Hint: As in Problem 11c.)

(e) $65 \times \dfrac{34}{55}$

(f) $\dfrac{6.25 \times 7.32}{81}$

(g) $\dfrac{54.6 \times 0.724}{2.47}$

(h) $\dfrac{2 \times 5 \times 7}{3 \times 9}$

(i) $\dfrac{31 \times 42 \times 65}{57 \times 78}$

(j) $\dfrac{75 \times 21 \times 58}{15 \times 29}$

(k) $345 \times \dfrac{323}{273} \times \dfrac{760}{800}$

12. Evaluate the following to slide-rule accuracy:

(a) $\dfrac{4.3 \times 5.6}{8.1}$

(b) $\dfrac{6.2 \times 0.45}{5}$

(c) $\dfrac{75 \times 0.32}{0.043}$

(d) $\dfrac{0.094 \times 720}{4.4}$

(e) $\dfrac{2.64 \times 3.78}{0.612}$

(f) $\dfrac{0.832 \times 14.7}{765}$

(g) $\dfrac{1.750 \times 1.355}{0.1085}$

(h) $\dfrac{48.4 \times 6.25}{0.394 \times 0.0313}$

(i) $\dfrac{150 \times 710 \times 273}{760 \times 288}$

(j) $\dfrac{432 \times 3.68 \times 0.0564}{71.6 \times 0.00247}$

13. Evaluate the following with the use of the slide rule:

(a) 3^2

(b) 16^2

(c) 123^2

(d) 2.4^2

(e) 0.11^2

(f) 7.05^2

14. Evaluate the following with the use of the slide rule:

(a) $\sqrt{4}$

(b) $\sqrt{7}$

(c) $\sqrt{49}$

(d) $\sqrt{77}$

(e) $\sqrt{255}$

(f) $\sqrt{0.255}$

(g) $\sqrt{0.64}$

(h) $\sqrt{0.2}$

(i) $\sqrt{0.05}$

Chapter 2

Motion

1. THE MEANING OF MOTION

In a crucial hockey game a defending forward chases his opposite number at the same speed along the boards and behind the net where both skate in an arc of a circle about the goalkeeper. If both players travel at the same speed along the same **straight** path, they are not in motion with respect to each other; but they are both in motion with respect to the goalkeeper even when they remain at the same distance from his position as they circle behind the net. The players are also in motion with respect to other moving players as well as to the stationary spectators.

How can one find an answer to the meaning of motion from a confused situation such as this? The answer lies in what is known as a frame of reference. As far as the defending forward is concerned, he is not changing his position relative to his opponent. In physics we say that in his frame of reference the straight line (rectilinear) distance between the players is not changing in *magnitude* (size) or *direction*; hence they are not in motion with respect to each other. As they circle the goalkeeper, they are in motion with respect to *him*, for the rectilinear distance joining each to the goalkeeper is changing in *direction* (but not in size).

By the above description, **an object is in motion with reference to another object if** the straight line joining them changes in magnitude (size) or direction.

2. TYPES OF MOTION

When an object such as our hockey player is moving in a *straight line* at a *steady rate* (covering equal distances in the same time) the motion is described as **uniform motion**. The following examples illustrate uniform motion:

(a) a raindrop falling when it has reached a steady rate of fall (terminal velocity)

(b) light travelling in outer space.

Nonuniform motion occurs in the following situations:

(a) a spacecraft as it starts its journey toward earth just after the firing of the retro rockets

(b) a motorist slowing after observing a radar trap

(c) a skier starting down a slope

(d) the motion of the earth about the sun.

3. VECTOR AND SCALAR QUANTITIES

A study of motion requires a knowledge of vector and scalar quantities. To specify a *scalar quantity*, only the magnitude of the quantity and its unit need be stated. For example, 10 kg of water specifies completely the mass of the water; thus mass is a scalar quantity. On the other hand, to specify a force by saying 10 units of force is to leave the statement incomplete since the effect of a force depends upon its direction as well as upon its magnitude. To refer to a force of 10 units acting northwest is to specify the force completely. Force, therefore, is a *vector quantity*.

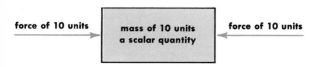

Fig. 2-1: *Mass is a scalar quantity because it possesses no directional characteristic. Force is a vector quantity because it possesses both magnitude and a directional characteristic.*

A scalar quantity is one which requires for its complete specification a number and a unit only. It has no directional property whatsoever. On the other hand, a vector quantity is one which requires a number, a unit, and a direction for its complete specification.

4. DISPLACEMENT—A VECTOR QUANTITY

A runner training for a meet attempts to improve his time for the mile event by practising on a banked circular ½-mile track. The starting line is marked at the east side of the track. When the runner has completed ¼ of a lap, he has travelled a distance of ¼ of 2640 ft, or 660 ft, to arrive at the north end of the track. At this point he has changed his position by an amount of 594 ft from the starting point; that is, as we say in physics, he has been *displaced* 594 ft in a northwesterly direction. When the runner is halfway round the track he has travelled a distance of 1320 ft with a displacement of 840 ft (diameter) westward. At the end of a

lap the distance covered has increased to 2640 ft (½ mile), but the displacement is now zero since his position is the same as at the start. At this point the trainer clocks the time as exactly 2 minutes or 120 seconds.

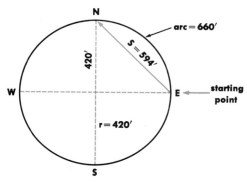

Fig. 2-2: *In going from point E to point N, the runner has travelled a distance of 660 ft. His displacement, however, is 594 ft, northwest.*

The motion of the runner can be indicated in terms of the distance travelled in a given time or by the displacement in a given time. Since the distance travelled is executed in a constantly changing direction, direction has no meaning when one is describing the motion in terms of the distance covered, except in a general way as anticlockwise; hence *distance is a scalar quantity*. On the other hand, the displacement from the starting point at any point considered in the lap has a direction; hence *displacement is a vector quantity*.

5. VELOCITY—A VECTOR QUANTITY; SPEED—A SCALAR QUANTITY

Although it is most improbable, let us consider the number of laps made by the runner in a given time to remain constant; hence ¼ of a lap would take 30 seconds, ½ a lap 60 seconds, and a full lap 120 seconds.

When $\frac{1}{4}$ of a lap has been completed *the time rate of change of distance* is $\frac{660}{30}$ or 22 ft/sec; that is, the *average speed* of the runner is 22 ft/sec. At this point the *time rate of change of displacement* is $\frac{594}{30}$ or 19.8 ft/sec northwest; that is, the *average velocity of the miler is 19.8 ft/sec NW.*

We can conclude that **speed is a scalar quantity equal to the time rate of change of distance; whereas velocity is a vector quantity equal to the time rate of change of displacement.**

It should be noted that the average speed as half a lap is completed is $\frac{1320}{60}$ or 22 ft/sec, with a corresponding velocity of $\frac{840}{60}$ or 14 ft/sec W. When the runner has lapped the track his average speed for the entire lap is unchanged at 22 ft/sec, *but the average velocity is zero since at that moment his displacement is zero.*

A study of Figure 2-3 should aid in the understanding of speed and velocity.

EXAMPLE 1

A man drives from Brantford to Kitchener via Woodstock and Shakespeare. It is 27 miles from Brantford to Woodstock, 16 miles from Woodstock to Shakespeare, 20 miles from Shakespeare to Kitchener. As the crow flies Kitchener is 24 miles North of Brantford. The man makes the trip in 1 hour and 48 minutes.

    (a) What is his final displacement?

    (b) What was his average speed?

    (c) What was his average velocity?

Solution:

    (a) His displacement is **24 mi N.**

    (b) Average speed $= \dfrac{20+16+27}{1.8} = 35$ mi/hr.

    (c) Average velocity $= \dfrac{24 \text{ mi N}}{1.8 \text{ hr}} = 13$ mi/hr **North**.

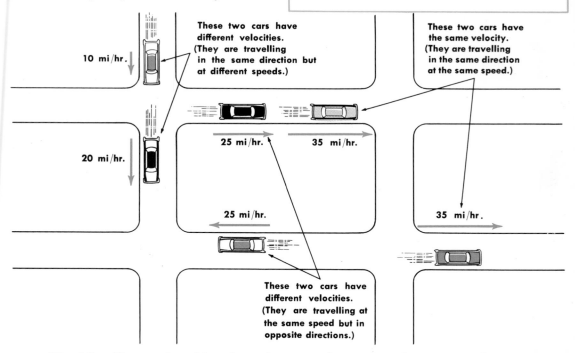

10 mi/hr.

These two cars have different velocities. (They are travelling in the same direction but at different speeds.)

These two cars have the same velocity. (They are travelling in the same direction at the same speed.)

20 mi/hr.

25 mi/hr.　　35 mi/hr.

25 mi/hr.　　35 mi/hr.

These two cars have different velocities. (They are travelling at the same speed but in opposite directions.)

Fig. 2-3: *Two moving objects have the same velocity when they move in the same direction at equal speeds.*

EXAMPLE 2

An athlete runs around a circular race track that is 420 feet in radius. He starts from the north side of the track and when he passes the south end of the diameter, 66 seconds have elapsed.

(a) What was his average speed during the 66 seconds?

(b) What was his average velocity during the 66 seconds?

(c) If he maintains his speed until he returns to the north side of the track, what will have been his average velocity?

Solution:

(a) Average speed $= \dfrac{\pi r}{66} = $ **20 ft/sec** (2 significant digits).

(b) Average velocity $= \dfrac{2r}{66} = $ **13 ft/sec South**.

(c) Average velocity **0 ft/sec**.

6. A STUDY OF MOTION BY THE GRAPHICAL METHOD

In order that we may analyse economic trends, variations in sales or production, and innumerable other data, a suitable and modern method is to study the data graphically. Motion also can be conveniently studied by this method.

Uniform Motion: The table records the distance travelled in intervals of 1 second by a runner on a straight track when running with a constant speed of 20 ft/sec.

Table 2-1

Time (seconds)	Displacements as distance travelled (feet)
0	0
1	20
2	40
3	60
4	80
5	100

Figure 2-4 illustrates the motion when the motion is plotted as a graph.

The result of the plot produces a straight line, which provides the information that the

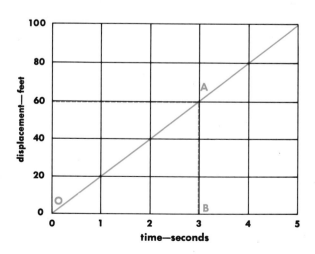

Fig. 2-4: *Displacement—time graph for a runner moving with uniform motion.*

23

distance travelled (also the displacement in this case) varies directly as the time taken; i.e., when the time has doubled the displacement has likewise doubled.

The magnitude of the velocity can be found by dividing the displacement by the corresponding time or $\dfrac{AB}{OB}$ for the example shown. Hence the uniform velocity is $\dfrac{60}{3}$ ft/sec or 20 ft/sec in the direction taken by the runner. The ratio AB/OB is known as the *slope* of the line AO.

Nonuniform Motion: The table lists the displacements (vertical) covered by a parachutist for each second of fall for the 5 seconds before the pull cord is operated.

Table 2-2

Time-seconds	Displacement-feet
0	0
1	16
2	64
3	144
4	256
5	400

The result of this plot as illustrated by Figure 2-5 is a curved line.

The graph indicates that the parachutist did not fall the same distance for each second of time. Since the graph shows that the velocity is not uniform, the motion can be expressed in this way. However, it is best to study nonuniform motion in more detail.

From a consideration of point A on the graph, we find that the jumper has fallen 400 ft in 5 secs, indicating an *average velocity* for the five-second interval of $\dfrac{400}{5}$ or 80 ft/sec downward. However, the parachutist is falling much faster than 80 ft/sec after 5 seconds of fall.

7. INSTANTANEOUS VELOCITY

The jumper's actual velocity at any instant of time is termed the *instantaneous velocity* at that instant.

An examination of a shorter time interval, such as that designated B to D, reveals that the displacement is $256-64$ ft for a time interval of $4-2$ secs; hence the average velocity for this 2-second interval is $\dfrac{192}{2}$ or 96 ft/sec.

If the time interval under consideration becomes shorter and shorter, the average velocity for that interval approaches what is termed the instantaneous velocity at that time. The instantaneous velocity at any

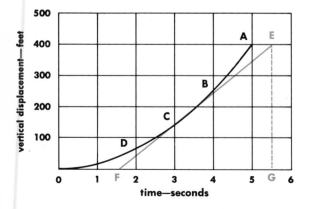

Fig. 2-5: *Displacement—time graph for a parachutist falling with nonuniform motion.*

time can be found graphically by drawing a tangent to the displacement-time curve at the particular time under consideration. To find the instantaneous velocity at the 3-second mark, the tangent to the curve at point C is drawn (Figure 2-5) and the slope of this tangent gives the instantaneous velocity at that time. This slope is the ratio $\frac{EG}{FG}$, where E and F are any points on the tangent. Thus the instantaneous velocity at the 3-second mark is approximately $\frac{400}{5.5-1.5}$ or 100 ft/sec downward.

A comparison with Figure 2-4 will show that the instantaneous velocity is found from the tangent in the same way that the average velocity was obtained from our straight-line graph of uniform velocity.

8. ACCELERATION—A VECTOR QUANTITY

Acceleration is a term used to specify how rapidly the instantaneous velocity of an object is changing. When the velocity changes at a constant rate the acceleration is a uniform or constant acceleration. Since velocity itself is a vector quantity, acceleration is also a vector quantity.

The instantaneous velocity of the parachutist of Section 7 for each second of fall is tabulated in Table 2-3.

Table 2-3

Elapsed time— seconds	Velocity downward (ft/sec)
0	0
1	32
2	64
3	96
4	128
5	160

From the table the student will note that during each second the velocity increases by 32 ft/sec; thus the acceleration of the jumper is 32 ft/sec/sec. Note that the acceleration is found by dividing the change in velocity by the corresponding time interval or, in symbols, $a = \frac{v-u}{t}$ where u and v represent the initial and final velocities respectively for a time interval of t seconds.

As an illustration of the manner in which this formula is used, let us find the acceleration of an automobile which starts from rest and attains a velocity of 60 ft/sec in 10 seconds:

$$u = 0 \text{ ft/sec}$$
$$v = 60 \text{ ft/sec}$$
$$t = 10 \text{ sec}$$

Hence: $a = \dfrac{v-u}{t} = \dfrac{60-0 \text{ ft/sec}}{10 \text{ sec}}$
$$= 6.0 \text{ ft/sec/sec} = 6.0 \text{ ft/sec}^2 .$$

This important formula, $a = \dfrac{v-u}{t}$, is frequently written in the form:
$$v = u + at.$$

9. REPRESENTATION OF VECTOR QUANTITIES

At this stage in our work we have already encountered several vector quantities: displacement, velocity, and acceleration. Later we shall meet still other vector quantities; consequently, it is important that we study their characteristics.

We must first agree upon a method of representing a vector quantity. Since a vector quantity involves both a number and a direction, it is convenient to represent the quantity by a straight line with an arrowhead. The length of the line represents the numerical value, according to some chosen scale, and the arrowhead shows the direction of the vector quantity. Thus, if a car is moving at 60 mi/hr East, this velocity would be represented by a line segment whose length, according to any convenient scale, represents 60 mi/hr and whose direction is East as indicated by an arrowhead pointing to the right as in Figure 2-6.

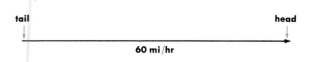

tail   head

60 mi/hr

Fig. 2-6: *A vector is a directed line segment representing, in magnitude and direction, a vector quantity. Here a velocity vector is shown.*

Such a line segment with its arrowhead representing a *vector quantity* is called simply a *vector*. **A vector is thus a directed line segment which represents a vector quantity.**

We may get an idea of how to add such quantities by considering displacements. Let us suppose that a man walks across a street from one side to the other. The street is 80 feet wide. He then walks along the sidewalk for a distance of 60 feet. It is clear from

Figure 2-7(*a*) and from the meaning of displacement, that the man's displacement is made up of two parts, or *components* as we say, namely, 80 feet across the street, and at right angles to this a second *component* displacement of 60 feet along the sidewalk.

But again, by our understanding of displacement, his total displacement is 100 feet, making an angle with the direction of the street of approximately 53 degrees. The two component displacements can be made one after the other or simultaneously, but the final result is the same. The man could have acquired his final displacement by first crossing the street and then walking along the sidewalk; or by walking along the sidewalk on the first side for 60 feet and then crossing, Figure 2-7(*b*); or by walking 100 feet along the line AC. Thus the displacement AC may replace the two displacements AB and BC. If one had not seen the man crossing the street one could not have told by which method he acquired the displacement AC. The displacement AC is thus called the *sum* or *resultant* of the two displacements AB and BC. Such a method of addition of displacements applies to all vectors.

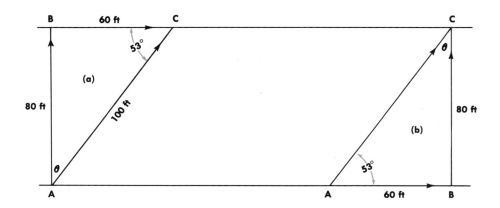

Fig. 2-7: *The resultant displacement AC of a man crossing a street is made up of two component displacements. In (a) and (b) the street is crossed by two different methods, but the resultant displacements are equivalent.*

26

10. RULES FOR VECTOR ADDITION AND SUBTRACTION

In the previous section we have seen how two individual vectors, in this case displacement vectors, were added to form an overall, or resultant, displacement.

In many branches of physics the use of vector quantities is a powerful tool and certain fundamental rules apply in all situations where similar vector quantities are added. These rules are as follows:

1. A vector remains unchanged if it is moved *parallel* to itself, provided its length is unchanged.

2. To add two vectors, the tail of one vector is placed at the head of the other. The sum of the two vectors is then represented by the line which completes the triangle. The direction of the resultant is from the tail of one vector to the head of the other vector. Thus in (a) and (b) of Figure 2-8 vectors A and B are added. In (a), vector B has been moved parallel to itself so that its tail is at the head of vector A. The resultant vector A+B is represented by the third side of the triangle with its direction as indicated by the arrow. In (b), the addition is carried out by moving vector A parallel to itself

and placing its tail at the head of vector B. The resultant A+B is equal to that obtained in (a) *because it is of the same magnitude and pointing in the same direction.*

Before considering how vectors might be subtracted, let us see what meaning, if any, can be attached to a negative vector. A clue is provided by the algebraic identity that $A + (-A) = 0$. If we consider A and $-A$ to be vectors, then $-A$ can be interpreted as a vector which nullifies the effect of vector A; accordingly, $-A$ must be a vector equal in magnitude but opposite in direction to A.

The process of vector subtraction can be considered as one of vector addition, using the relationship $A - B = A + (-B)$. Thus in Figure 2-8(c) where B is to be subtracted from A we first draw the vector $-B$ equal in length but opposite in direction to that of vector B. Vector $-B$ is then added to vector A according to the rules of addition outlined above. The result gives vector $A-B$. Similarly, in Figure 2-8(d) vector A is subtracted from vector B thereby giving the resultant vector $B-A$. Note that vector $B-A$ is equal in magnitude but opposite in direction to vector $A-B$.

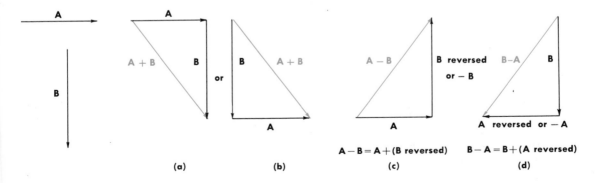

Fig. 2-8: *The vectors A and B are added in (a) and in (b) to give identical resultants A + B. In (c) vector B is subtracted from vector A by adding to A the vector B reversed. In (d) vector A is subtracted from B by adding to B the vector A reversed.*

EXAMPLE 3

A man can row a boat at a speed of 3.0 ft/sec in still water. He heads directly East across a river which flows South at the rate of 3.0 ft/sec. Determine the magnitude and direction of his resultant velocity.

Solution:

The man and his boat are subject to two velocities which are represented below by vectors V_B (velocity of boat) and V_S (velocity of stream).

The resultant velocity V_R is found by adding the vectors. From the diagram we see that $V_R = \sqrt{3.0^2 + 3.0^2} = $ **4.2 ft/sec E45°S.**

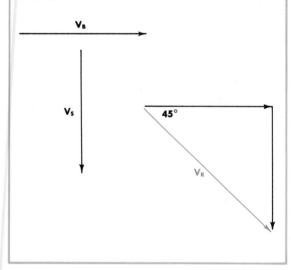

11. RELATIVE MOTION

The velocity of an object is usually specified by considering its motion relative to the earth's surface, which is taken as a fixed frame of reference. It is well to realize, however, that the earth itself is in motion, as is the sun around which it revolves. It readily becomes apparent that *all motion is relative to what we arbitrarily choose as a reference.*

Let us suppose that there are two cars, which for convenience we shall call A and B, travelling on a straight level highway, A ahead of B (Figure 2-9). Suppose car A is moving at 40 mi/hr while B is moving at 60 mi/hr and that an observer is in car B. His observation will be that car A seems to approach at 20 mi/hr. This is the velocity of car A with respect to or relative to car B. This relative velocity could be considered as the velocity which A appears to have when viewed from B, with B assumed to be stationary.

It is interesting to note that if we imagine these two cars to be moving on a large platform which itself is capable of motion, let us say the deck of an aircraft carrier, any motion of the platform in the same or in the opposite direction (or indeed in any direction) to that of the cars does not alter the velocity of A relative to B. Putting the statement in algebraic language, we may add any common velocity to both A and B and this will not alter their relative velocity. In particular, if we added B's reversed velocity to both A and B, then B would be at rest and A would move with a velocity which is equal in magnitude and direction to A's velocity relative to B (20 mi/hr toward B). But to add B's reversed velocity (60 mi/hr) to that of A is merely to subtract the velocity of B from that of A. *The process of calculating a relative velocity is thus a simple process of subtraction.*

Further, a little thought will show that the relative velocity of A to B is numerically the same as the relative velocity of B to A, but is *opposite in direction.* Thus, if the two cars in question are both moving east with the velocities specified, the velocity of A relative to B is given by subtracting the velocity of B from that of A and its value is 20 mi/hr West. On the other hand, the velocity of B with respect to A is given by subtracting A's velocity from that of B and its value is 20 mi/hr East.

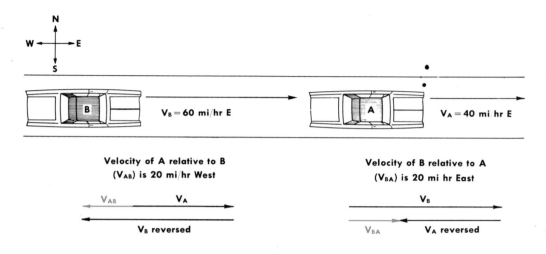

$V_B = 60$ mi/hr E

$V_A = 40$ mi. hr E

Velocity of A relative to B
(V_{AB}) is 20 mi/hr West

Velocity of B relative to A
(V_{BA}) is 20 mi hr East

V_{AB} V_A

V_B reversed

V_B

V_{BA} V_A reversed

Fig. 2-9: *The velocity of a moving object is dependent on what we consider as a frame of reference. Relative to the earth, Car A has a velocity of 40 mi/hr E. Relative to car B, its velocity is 20 mi/hr W.*

EXAMPLE 4

Two cars, A and B, are moving eastward on a straight level highway. A moves at 60 mi/hr and B at 35 mi/hr.

(*a*) Calculate the velocity of A relative to B.

(*b*) Calculate the velocity of B relative to A.

Solution:

We have seen that relative motion is simply a matter of subtraction and that the velocity of A relative to B is simply the vector difference (velocity of A minus velocity of B). We therefore add B's reversed velocity to that of A.

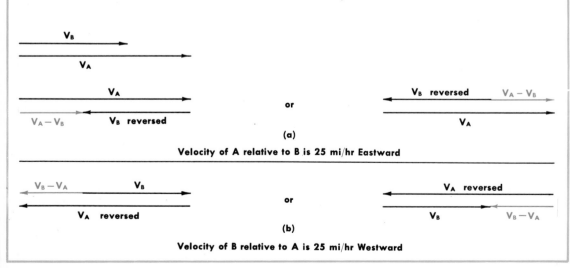

V_B

V_A

V_A

$V_A - V_B$ V_B reversed

or

V_B reversed $V_A - V_B$

V_A

(a)

Velocity of A relative to B is 25 mi/hr Eastward

$V_B - V_A$ V_B

V_A reversed

or

V_A reversed

V_B $V_B - V_A$

(b)

Velocity of B relative to A is 25 mi/hr Westward

29

EXAMPLE 5

The cars referred to in Example 4 are moving in opposite directions, A to the West and B to the East.

(a) Calculate the velocity of A relative to B.

(b) Calculate the velocity of B relative to A.

Solution:

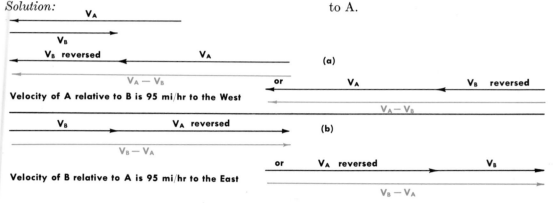

Velocity of A relative to B is 95 mi/hr to the West

Velocity of B relative to A is 95 mi/hr to the East

In the foregoing discussion we have determined the velocity of one object relative to another which moves in the same straight-line path. When the objects are not moving in the same straight-line path, the velocity of one with respect to the other is found by a similar approach. Example 6 illustrates such a situation.

EXAMPLE 6

The cars referred to in the two previous examples are moving, A southward at 60 mi/hr, and B on a crossroad moves eastward at 35 mi/hr.

(a) Calculate the velocity of A relative to B.

(b) Calculate the velocity of B relative to A.

Solution:

The vector triangles for the subtracton of the velocity of B from that of A are shown below. The difference may be obtained by scaling or calculation.

By Pythagorean theorem:
$$(V_A - V_B) = \sqrt{60^2 + 35^2} = 70 \text{ mi/hr S30°W.}$$

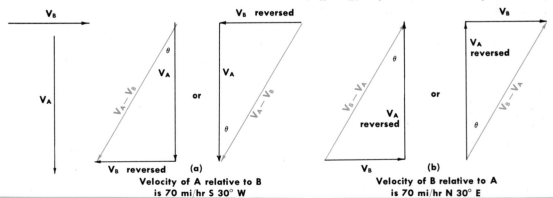

(a) Velocity of A relative to B is 70 mi/hr S 30° W

(b) Velocity of B relative to A is 70 mi/hr N 30° E

MOTION: An object is in motion with reference to another object if the straight line joining them changes in magnitude or in direction.

VECTOR QUANTITY: A quantity which requires a number, a unit, and a direction for its complete specification.

SCALAR QUANTITY: A quantity which requires only a number and a unit for its complete specification.

DISPLACEMENT: A vector quantity representing a change in position.

AVERAGE VELOCITY: A vector quantity equal to the time rate of change of displacement.

$$\overline{v} = \frac{s}{t}$$

where s represents displacement
$\overline{v}$ average velocity
t time .

SPEED: A scalar quantity equal to the time rate of change of distance. Speed $= \dfrac{d}{t}$.

INSTANTANEOUS VELOCITY: The average velocity over an extremely short time interval.

ACCELERATION: The time rate of change of velocity.

EXERCISE A

1. When is a blocking football player in motion with respect to his running mate?

2. In what way does a scalar quantity differ from a vector quantity?

3. What kind of variation is represented by a straight line graph?

4. Which of the following are vector quantities and which are scalar?
   (a) the list price of a television set at $198.98
   (b) the force exerted by a pile driver
   (c) 50 mph
   (d) the mass of an electron: 9.108×10^{-31} kg
   (e) the acceleration due to gravity: 9.8 m/sec²
   (f) the speed of sound in air at 0°C: 331.4 m/sec .

5. If the length of the hour hand on a city-hall clock is 10 ft and zero time is midnight, what is the displacement and distance moved by the pointer end of the hour hand at:
   (a) 3 a.m.   (b) 6 a.m.   (c) 9 a.m.   (d) 12 noon?

6. What does the graph in each of the following cases indicate about the motion taking place?

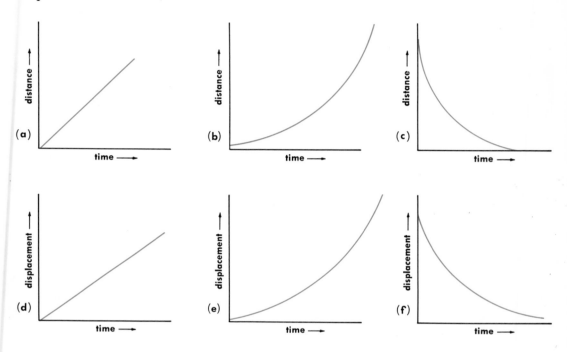

7. A Canadian family decides to leave town and have lunch at a picnic ground 20 miles away. There is an ice-cream stand 5 miles from town. The highway has no turns. The family sets out by car in a westerly direction. Describe the motion of the car from the following graph:

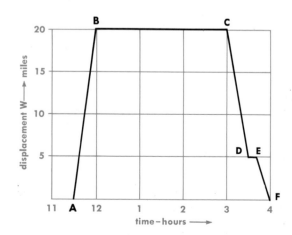

8. How can you find the relative velocity between two moving objects?

9.

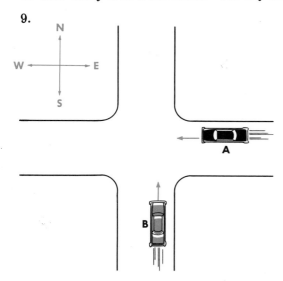

Car A is approaching the intersection at 20 mi/hr and car B is approaching at 30 mi/hr. Draw vectors to find the velocity of:

(a) B relative to A

(b) A relative to B.

10. As an Air Canada passenger who is eager to get home for Christmas, are you more interested in the air speed or the ground speed of the plane? Why?

11. In outer space what would Earthlings use for a northerly bearing? Why not use a compass?

EXERCISE B

Note: All measured data in the following problems are to be considered accurate to the number of digits quoted.

1. To determine that sound travels at a uniform speed, students were stationed in a straight line at intervals of 100 metres. The students were each provided with a stop watch and instructed to start the watch as the gun flashed at the starting point and to stop the watch when each heard the report of the gun. The results were recorded in a table as follows:

Distance in metres	100	200	300	400	500	600	700	800	900	1000
Time in seconds	0.3	0.6	0.9	1.2	1.5	1.8	2.1	2.4	2.7	3.0

(a) Plot a distance-time graph with time as the horizontal axis and distance travelled as the vertical plot. If standard $\frac{1}{10}$th-inch graph paper is used, make the distance plot end at the top of the graph and the time terminate one inch from the end.

(b) Was the speed constant? How did your graph indicate this?

(c) From your graph find the speed of sound and record it as metres/second. Indicate on the graph how your answer was obtained.

33

2. While preparing his runners for a two-mile race, a trainer times them for 7 laps of 500 yards. The times for runners A, B, and C are listed in the following table:

Laps	1	2	3	4	5	6	7	
	secs	secs	secs	secs	secs	secs	secs	
Elapsed time at	60	110	193	275	367	451	542	Runner A
the end of each	66	133	212	284	367	431	495	Runner B
lap in secs.	75	115	254	335	405	468	530	Runner C

(a) Plot a distance-time graph of the results on standard $\frac{1}{10}$th-inch graph paper. Turn the graph to place the long side as the horizontal time plot. Start with 50 seconds at the left and use a scale of 2 inches as equivalent to 100 seconds. Using a scale of 1 lap = 1 inch, plot the distance in lap intervals on the vertical scale.

(b) Which runner runs with nearly uniform speed?

(c) Which runner would do best in a race of: (i) 1000 yards, (ii) 440 yards?

(d) Which two runners would the trainer enter in the one-mile event?

(e) When did B pass A?

(f) When did C pass B?

3. A destroyer tracking a submarine travelled 40 miles N, then 25 miles NE, and then 30 miles SW:

(a) Estimate the distance from its final position to its starting point.

(b) If the search took 5.0 hours, what was: (i) the average speed of the destroyer, (ii) its average velocity?

4. An express train travels directly from Argon City (A) to Energy City (E). A local train joins these cities, too, but goes by way of the towns Brent (B), Calamity (C), and Deadwood (D). The local goes SW from Argon to Brent, a distance of 28 miles, thence 44 miles S to Calamity, 12 miles E to Deadwood, and finally 30 miles SE to Energy City:

(a) How far is it from Argon City to Energy City?

(b) What direction does the express train travel from Argon City to Energy City?

(c) Find the displacement in miles for each train.

(d) If the express train takes 1.50 hours to go from Argon to Energy and the local takes 6.0 hours, what is: (i) the average speed of each train, (ii) their average velocity?

5. An outboard motor can push a small boat at 7.0 mi/hr in calm water. How fast would it travel upstream against a current of 3.0 miles an hour? How fast would it travel downstream?

6. If the velocity of an automobile is 20 mi/hr North and changes to a velocity of 40 mi/hr North in 6.0 secs, what is its acceleration?

7. If a parachutist drops for 10.0 secs without opening his parachute and acquires a downward velocity of 97.8 m/sec, what is the acceleration due to gravity?

8. An ocean liner is moving at a speed of 30 knots (with reference to the bottom of the ocean); a passenger is taking a brisk morning walk around the deck at a speed of 4.00 knots. What is his speed relative to the bottom of the ocean:

   (a) (i)   when he walks toward the bow?
   (ii) when he walks toward the stern?
   (iii) when he makes a right-angled turn and heads for the dining-room?

   (b) Assume that 30.0 knots is the ship's speed in calm water but that she is now bucking a tide of 7.00 knots which meets her head on while a following wind blowing straight against her stern is strong enough to add 2.00 knots to her speed. Considering these factors, answer questions (i), (ii), and (iii) of part (a).

9. Record the following observations by referring to the diagram below (measure all angles clockwise from North):

   (a) What direction is the helmsman steering? What is the ship's velocity relative to the water?

   (b) What is: (i) the direction, (ii) the velocity, of the tide?

   (c) Find the direction of the course made good.

   (d) Find the velocity of the ship relative to the ocean bottom.

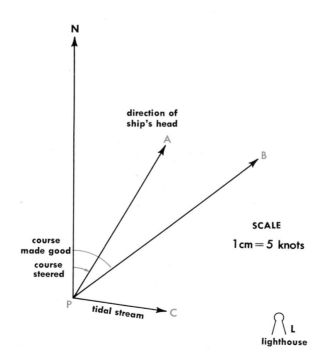

The following problems are to be solved by vector diagrams. The student is free to choose whatever scale seems suitable but is advised to make the diagrams quite large in order to reduce percentage errors.

10. An airplane is climbing at an angle of 20.0° to the horizontal. Observed from two positions on the ground, its horizontal speed is found to be 150 mi/hr. How long does it take to climb 1200 feet?

11. A man can swim at the rate of 1.50×10^2 ft per minute. He swims at right angles to the current across a river 2.00×10^2 ft wide with the current flowing at 100 ft/min:
    (a) How far below the starting point will he land?
    (b) At what angle would he have to swim in order to land directly opposite the starting point?

12. Two canoeists can paddle 7.0 miles an hour in still water. They paddle across a straight river that is a mile wide and has a current of 3.0 mi/hr:
    (a) How much farther downstream will they be than when they started?
    (b) How far will they have travelled?
    (c) In what direction should they have headed in order to arrive exactly where they meant to arrive by the shortest possible route?

13. A pilot in a fighter plane leaves an aircraft carrier and flies W for one hour, a distance of 200 nautical miles. As he is about to turn back, he is advised by radio that for the past hour the carrier has been steaming N at a speed of 20 knots (a knot is a speed of 1 nautical mile per hour) and will maintain this velocity:
    (a) What course will the pilot plot to arrive at the carrier in one hour?
    (b) How far must he travel?

14. If there are no passengers to get on or off at a railway flag station, the mail bag is thrown off while the train is still moving. If the bag is thrown due West at 11 ft/sec while the train is travelling North at 30 mph:
    (a) What path will the mail bag follow along the platform?
    (b) What path would it have taken if it had been thrown at an angle of: (i) 45° forward, (ii) 45° backward?

15. The S.S. Princess leaves port A at midnight to sail East at 20 knots. At midnight H.M.S. Huron also leaves port B, which is 60 nautical miles S of port A, but she has a velocity of 30 knots NE:
    (a) How far apart will the ships be at: (i) 1.00 a.m., (ii) 2.00 a.m.?
    (b) How far apart are they when the Huron crosses the course of the Princess?
    (c) Does the man on watch at 3.00 a.m. on the Huron see the Princess' starboard light or her port light?
    (d) Which light did he see when he first sighted the Princess?
    (e) What might have happened if the Huron had to slow up for some reason on her first hour out?

16. The Whistlewing and the Plucky are two fishing boats that leave harbour together at noon. The Whistlewing heads N for two hours at 16.0 mi/hr, when she develops trouble in one of her engines and anchors to repair the damage. The Plucky runs NE for 2.50 hrs at 10.0 mi/hr and stops to lift her pond nets. At 2:45 p.m. the Whistlewing radios the Plucky that she is in trouble and is travelling back, cutting her one engine speed to 8.00 mi/hr and asking the Plucky to keep on the lookout for her on the way home. At 4.00 p.m. when the pond nets are lifted fog has set in:

(a) Where is the Whistlewing at 4.00 p.m.?

(b) How far is the Plucky from the course of the Whistlewing at 4.00 p.m.?

(c) At what time will the Plucky arrive at the Whistlewing's course if she travels West?

(d) Where will the Whistlewing be at this time?

(e) Anxious to get his fish to port quickly, the owner of the Plucky makes some fast calculations and decides to travel on a bearing 245° clockwise from N. When he reaches a point due N of the harbour, how far away is the Whistlewing, and in what direction?

17. (a) If you take the circumference of the earth through the poles as 25,000 miles, how many miles of circumference represent one degree at the centre of the earth (2 significant figures)?

(b) If you divide your answer by 60, you get the length on the earth's surface subtended by one minute of arc. This is what is called a nautical mile. How long is it compared to a mile as recorded on a car's speedometer?

(c) Arvex is a (fictitious) town on the 45th parallel of N latitude. An airplane pilot leaves from a position 414 miles S of Arvex and flies on a northerly bearing with the wind blowing 40 mi/hr from the West:

(i)   From what degree of latitude did he leave?

(ii) What is his ground speed if his air speed is 300 mi/hr?

(iii) What course should he have flown to land at Arvex without having to change course?

Chapter 2

Motion

▶ ## Experiment 1

To determine the period and frequency of a recording timer.

The recording timer offers a simple means of illustrating many of the concepts involved in the study of motion.   It will be used extensively in later experiments to determine the velocity, acceleration, and energy of moving objects.   This experiment is designed to familiarize us with the operation of the timer.

Recording timer kit

D-c supply (1.5 volt or 6 volt)

Rheostat (approximately 20 ohms maximum resistance)

Stop watch

C-clamp

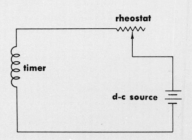

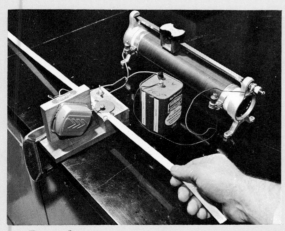

Procedure

1. Clamp the timer firmly to the table as illustrated in the photograph.

2. Place one end of a length of tape in the timer, with the carbon disk over the tape, face down.

3. Make the electrical connections shown in the circuit diagram.   If necessary, adjust the timer for smooth operation of the clapper.

4. Practice pulling the tape through the timer at such a rate that each dot is clearly separate from its adjacent dots.

5. To determine the period and frequency of the timer, it is necessary to measure the time required for a number of dots to be formed.   To do this, feed one end of another length of tape (about 2 metres) into the timer, and allow the clapper to make a heavy initial dot on the tape.   Hold the stop watch in one hand and depress it at the instant you begin pulling the tape with the other hand.

6. When the other end of the tape is a few inches from the clapper, simultaneously depress the watch and cease pulling the tape.

The most important consideration in the above steps is that the tape be pulled quickly enough that the dots do not overlap, and yet slowly enough that many separate dots are formed. It is not necessary that the tape be pulled at constant speed.

You may wish to repeat steps 5 and 6 to achieve better co-ordination with the stop watch. Alternatively, you may prefer that your partner operate the watch while you pull the tape.

Analysis

1. Record the elapsed time indicated by the stop watch.

2. Count the total number of dots that were formed during this time.

3. The *frequency* of the timer is defined as the number of dots formed per second. The *period* is the time interval between each dot.
Determine each of these quantities for your particular timer.

Question

To how many significant digits should you determine these quantities? Why?

Experiment 2

To study Motion.

> Recording timer
>
> D-c supply (1.5 volt or 6 volt)
>
> Rheostat (approximately 20 ohms)
>
> C-clamp
>
> Metre stick

Procedure

1. Clamp the timer to the desk as illustrated in Experiment 1.

2. Insert in the timer one end of a length of tape approximately 2 metres long.

3. Set the timer in operation, and pull the tape through the timer with as uniform a speed as you are able to judge.

Analysis

1. Using the initial dot on your tape as a starting point, mark off (in pencil) consecutive groups of 10 dots.

2. Measure the distance from each tenth dot to the starting point. These

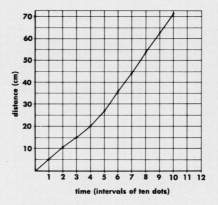

are the displacements s_1, s_2 . . . . s_8 shown in the diagram.

3. Using as a unit of time (the time required for 10 dots to be formed), construct a table giving total displacement in cm vs. total elapsed time. The elapsed time for displacement s_1 will be 1 unit, for displacement s_2 will be 2 units, etc. It is not necessary to know these time values in seconds.

4. Plot a graph of displacement vs. elapsed time, using the vertical axis for displacement. Connect the points by a smooth curve.

5. From your graph determine at what time the velocity was (i) the least, (ii) the greatest, (iii) the most constant. When was the acceleration the greatest?

Chapter 3

Motion With Constant Acceleration—Uniformly Accelerated Motion

1. UNIFORM AND NONUNIFORM ACCELERATION

The meaning of acceleration was given in Chapter 2 as the time rate of change of velocity, and, like velocity, it was shown that acceleration is a vector quantity.

In this chapter we will pursue a more detailed study of accelerated motion, but we will restrict our analysis to that of motion along a straight-line path, that is, *rectilinear motion*. Analogous to velocity, acceleration may be uniform or nonuniform, and we begin our study with a simple illustration of each of these.

(a) Nonuniform Acceleration

Car A, proceeding East from an intersection, increases speed in the manner shown in Table 3-1. A velocity-time graph for the car's motion is given in Figure 3-1.

In this example the increase in velocity during successive equal time intervals is not constant, and the acceleration is said to be nonuniform acceleration.

(b) Uniform Acceleration

Car B, travelling East, increases speed in the manner shown in Table 3-2. The corresponding velocity-time graph is shown in Figure 3-2.

From Table 2 we see that during each second the velocity of the car increases by 8 ft/sec, and we observe that the resulting graph is a straight line. Motion in which the change in velocity during successive equal time intervals is constant, is referred to as *uniformly accelerated motion*, and the acceleration is said to be *uniform acceleration*.

2. AVERAGE ACCELERATION AND INSTANTANEOUS ACCELERATION

Let us compute the acceleration of car A and of car B referred to earlier. Since each car has attained a velocity of 40 ft/sec East in a time of 5 seconds, their average acceleration during this time is given by:

$$\bar{a} = \frac{\text{change in velocity}}{\text{elapsed time}}$$

$$= \frac{40 \text{ ft/sec} - 0 \text{ ft/sec}}{5 \text{ sec}} \text{ East}$$

$$= 8 \text{ ft/sec/sec East}$$

or simply 8 ft/sec^2 E.

If we now determine the average acceleration of car A during smaller time intervals, we find that during the first second the average acceleration is 5 ft/sec^2 E, and successive intervals of 1 second give accelerations of 10 ft/sec² E, 1 ft/sec² E, 8 ft/sec² E, and 16 ft/sec² E. (Verify these figures.) The average acceleration for the whole period has no relationship to the accelerations existing for shorter intervals, when nonuniform acceleration exists.

For car B, however, we find that during each second the acceleration is 8 ft/sec² E. (Verify this.) This is a value equal to the average acceleration over the entire interval.

If we take shorter intervals of time, say tenths of seconds, and determine the average acceleration for these time intervals, we would arrive at the same value, 8 ft/sec² E.

The value of average acceleration when an extremely short interval of time is considered, is called *instantaneous acceleration.* From our earlier study of the motion of car B, we see that *for uniformly accelerated motion, instantaneous acceleration and average acceleration are equal quantities.*

Table 3-1

time—sec	velocity East, ft/sec
0	0
1	5
2	15
3	16
4	24
5	40

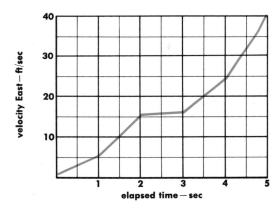

Fig. 3-1: *Velocity — time graph illustrating nonuniform acceleration.*

Table 3-2

time—sec	velocity East, ft/sec
0	0
1	8
2	16
3	24
4	32
5	40

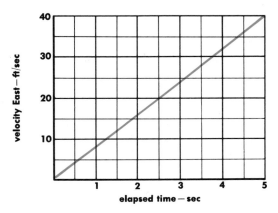

Fig. 3-2: *Velocity — time graph for uniform acceleration.*

The symbol used in this book to denote instantaneous acceleration is the letter a. (Recall that $\bar{a}$ represents average acceleration.) Furthermore, since we will henceforth consider only the case of uniform acceleration, where average acceleration and instantaneous acceleration have the same value, we can now write the following formulas for uniformly accelerated motion:

$$\bar{a} = \frac{v-u}{t} \text{ or } v = u + \bar{a}t$$

$$a = \frac{v-u}{t} \text{ or } v = u + at \qquad (1)$$

EXAMPLE 1

In taking off, an airplane accelerates uniformly from rest and attains a take-off speed of 90 mi/hr (132 ft/sec) in 12 seconds. Determine its average acceleration for the 12-second interval, and its instantaneous acceleration 5 seconds before take-off.

Solution:

$$a = \frac{v-u}{t} = \frac{132-0}{12} \ \frac{ft}{sec^2}$$

$$= \ \textbf{11 ft/sec}^2 \text{ in the}$$

direction of motion.

The instantaneous acceleration 5 seconds before take-off will also be **11** ft/sec², since the acceleration is uniform.

In the foregoing example it is quite correct to express the acceleration either as 90 mi/hr per **12** seconds, or 7.5 mi/hr per second (7.5 mi/hr/sec), but it is generally preferred to use the same unit of time in the measurement of change of velocity and of elapsed time.

EXAMPLE 2

A tennis ball strikes a racquet with a velocity of 30 ft/sec, and rebounds with a velocity of 70 ft/sec in the opposite direction. If the racquet and ball are in contact for 0.5 seconds, determine the acceleration of the ball.

Solution:

In this problem the velocity vectors differ not only in magnitude but also in direction.

To indicate this difference in direction we shall assign a positive sign to vectors which act in one direction and a negative sign to vectors which act in the opposite direction. Proceed as follows:

Let vectors acting in the initial direction of the ball be positive. Then:

$$u = +30 \text{ ft/sec}$$

$$v = -70 \text{ ft/sec}$$

$$t = 0.5 \text{ sec}$$

$$\text{and } a = \frac{v-u}{t} = \frac{-70-(+30)}{0.5} \ \frac{ft}{sec^2}$$

$$= -2 \times 10^2 \textbf{ ft/sec}^2 .$$

The negative sign in our value for acceleration is of great significance; it indicates the direction of the acceleration to be that of the motion of the ball *after* impact.

EXAMPLE 3

An automobile, travelling South, slows down uniformly from a speed of 30 ft/sec to a speed of 18 ft/sec in an interval of 6 seconds.

(*a*) Determine the car's acceleration.

(*b*) In what direction is the car's acceleration?

Solution:

(a) $u = 30$ ft/sec S

$v = 18$ ft/sec S

$t = 6$ sec

and $a = \dfrac{v-u}{t} = \dfrac{(18-30)}{6} \dfrac{\text{ft}}{\text{sec}^2}$ S

$= -2$ **ft/sec² S** .

(b) The negative value of acceleration obtained in (a) indicates that the acceleration acts in the direction opposite to that of the initial and final velocities, to which positive signs were attached. The acceleration thus acts in the direction of North even though the car is travelling South.

3. DISPLACEMENT DURING UNIFORM ACCELERATION

In Chapter 2, displacement was related to average velocity by the relationship:

$$\text{displacement} = \frac{\text{average}}{\text{velocity}} \times \text{elapsed time}$$

or, algebraically:

$$s = \bar{v}t \, .$$

We may now ask, "What is the average velocity of an object which accelerates uniformly from an initial velocity of u to a final velocity of v?" A student quick to answer might say "$\dfrac{u+v}{2}$", which is simply the arithmetical average of the initial and final velocities for the interval. The answer is, in fact, true, although the reason is not quite as simple as it might appear. It is *not* true, in general, when the acceleration is nonuniform. Thus, for uniform acceleration:

$$\bar{v} = \frac{u+v}{2} \qquad (2)$$

If we substitute this value for average

velocity into the fundamental equation for displacement, we have:

$$s = \left(\frac{u+v}{2}\right)t \qquad (3)$$

Figure 3-3 shows a velocity-time graph for an object uniformly accelerating from velocity u to velocity v in t seconds. The average velocity is indicated on the graph.

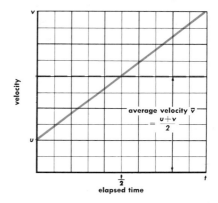

Fig. 3-3: *Velocity — time graph for an object accelerating uniformly for t seconds Note that the instantaneous velocity at the half-time (t/₂ seconds) is equal to the average velocity for the t seconds.*

EXAMPLE 4

A subway car accelerates uniformly from 5 ft/sec to 45 ft/sec in a time of 8 seconds. Determine the average velocity of the car during this time, and its displacement.

Solution:

$$u = 5 \text{ ft/sec}$$
$$v = 45 \text{ ft/sec}$$
$$t = 8 \text{ sec}$$

Then average velocity $\bar{v} = \dfrac{(5+45)}{2} = 25$ **ft/sec**

and displacement $\dfrac{(u+v)}{2} t = 25 \times 8$ ft

$= 2.0 \times 10^2$ **ft** (in the direction of motion)

4. ACCELERATION DUE TO GRAVITY

Experiments have shown that all objects, regardless of their mass or shape, if allowed to fall in a vacuum, have the same acceleration. This acceleration, which is called the *acceleration due to gravity*, varies slightly from one geographical location to another. The symbol g is used for this acceleration. In the neighborhood of Toronto g has a value of 32.2 ft/sec² or 9.80 m/sec².

An object which is subject only to the force of gravity and negligible air resistance, is referred to as a freely falling object. A few examples of free fall will help to clarify the meaning of this term:

(1) a stone dropped from rest from a height
(2) a ball thrown directly upward
(3) a ball thrown horizontally
(4) a football which has been kicked
(5) a stone thrown directly downward.

Of these illustrations the first, second, and fifth illustrate rectilinear motion. Items 3 and 4 illustrate that a freely falling object, in addition to its vertical motion, may also have motion in a horizontal direction.

EXAMPLE 5

An object is dropped from a building and hits the ground after 3.00 seconds of fall.

(a) Determine the speed of the object when it hits the ground.
(b) How high is the building?

Solution:

(a) $u = 0$ ft/sec
$a = 32.2$ ft/sec²
$t = 3.00$ sec
then $v = u + at = 0 + 32.2 \times 3.00 = $ **96.6 ft/sec.**

(b) $s = \left(\dfrac{u+v}{2}\right)t = \dfrac{0+96.6}{2} \times 3.00 = 144.9$ ft,

thus the building is **145 ft high**.

EXAMPLE 6

A stone is thrown vertically upward with a velocity of 49 m/sec. How high will it rise?

Solution:

At the peak of its ascent, the velocity of the stone is zero.
Hence: $v = 0$.
Because the initial velocity and the acceleration are vector quantities acting in opposite directions, we indicate this as follows:
Let downward vectors be positive. Then:

$$u = -49 \text{ m/sec}$$
$$a = +9.8 \text{ m/sec}^2$$
$$v = 0 \text{ m/sec}.$$

Using the equation $v = u + at$, we are able to find the length of time the stone is rising:

$$v = u + at$$
$$0 = -49 + (9.8)t$$
$$t = \frac{49}{9.8} = 5.0 \text{ sec}.$$

Now, by means of equation (3):

$$s = \frac{(u+v)}{2}t = \frac{(-49+0)}{2} \times 5.0$$
$$= 1.2 \times 10^2 \text{ m}.$$

Thus the stone will rise to a height of 120 metres. Note that two separate steps were necessary in the solution.

5. TERMINAL VELOCITY

In point of fact, no body falls freely since the air is always in contact with all falling bodies and presses upward upon them with a force that increases with their speed of fall. Thus, as the body falls with increasing speed, there comes a time when the upward resisting force of the air is equal to the downward pull of the earth and from this moment onward the body falls with zero acceleration or at a constant velocity. This velocity we call the *terminal velocity* of the body. Should a large terminal velocity be desired, the falling body must be designed so as to have minimum air resistance; consequently, when the force due to air resistance equals the force or pull of the earth, the velocity is great. Conversely, if a low terminal velocity is desired, arrangements must be made to give the body a very high air resistance. This is the case when a parachutist opens his parachute and thus greatly increases the resist-ance to his passage through the air. He will, in this way, reduce his terminal velocity from about 120 mi/hr with an unopened parachute to about 14 mi/hr, a terminal velocity which makes a landing reasonably safe. Raindrops fall from a considerable height and by the time they have nearly reached the earth they have attained their terminal velocity.

NONUNIFORM ACCELERATION: Motion in which the change in velocity during successive equal-time intervals is not constant.

UNIFORM ACCELERATION: Motion in which the change in velocity during successive equal-time intervals is constant.

AVERAGE ACCELERATION: $\bar{a} = \dfrac{\text{change in velocity}}{\text{elapsed time}} = \dfrac{v - u}{t}$.

INSTANTANEOUS ACCELERATION: The value of the average acceleration when an extremely short interval of time is considered.

For uniformly accelerated motion, instantaneous acceleration and average acceleration are equal quantities.

In this case $\bar{a} = a = \dfrac{v-u}{t}$ and $v = u + at$.

DISPLACEMENT DURING UNIFORM ACCELERATION:

Displacement = average velocity × elapsed time

$s = \bar{v}t$.

For uniform acceleration $\bar{v} = \dfrac{u+v}{2}$,

hence $s = \left(\dfrac{u+v}{2}\right)t$.

ACCELERATION DUE TO GRAVITY: All objects, regardless of their mass or shape, falling in a vacuum have the same acceleration: the acceleration due to gravity. At Toronto $g = 32.2$ ft/sec^2 or 9.80 m/sec^2.

EXERCISE A

1. When an object undergoes acceleration, is the motion uniform or nonuniform? What is the distinction between uniform motion and uniform acceleration?

2. What is the difference between uniformly accelerated motion and nonuniformly accelerated motion?

3. What is meant by a freely falling body?

4. How can the value of the terminal velocity of a falling object be: (a) increased, (b) decreased?

5. When a straight line results from a velocity-time graph, how would you describe the motion?

6. What type of motion is illustrated when a nonlinear graph is obtained for the velocity-time plot of the motion?

EXERCISE B

In the following problems use acceleration due to gravity: $g = 32.0$ ft/sec², 9.80 m/sec². Assume each of the digits quoted in the measured quantities to be significant.

1. A Toronto subway train takes 11 seconds to brake down to a stop from 60 mi/hr. What is its acceleration?

2. When passing on the highway, a motorist accelerates uniformly from a speed of 40 mi/hr to 60 mi/hr in 5.0 seconds:
   (a) Find his average velocity in mi/hr and in ft/sec.
   (b) How far does the car move in the 5.0 seconds?
   (c) What is the acceleration of the car in ft/sec²?

3. A stunt parachutist jumping from an airplane delays opening his parachute until a terminal velocity of 120 mi/hr is reached:
   (a) Express the terminal velocity in ft/sec.
   (b) How long does it take the parachutist to reach the terminal velocity?
   (c) How far does he drop in this time?

4. A skier levels off at the foot of a hill and just slides to a stop. If his speed at the foot of the hill was 1500 metres per minute, and he came to a stop in 2.0 minutes, what was his average acceleration?

5. A curler was practising on a pond covered with smooth ice. He delivered his rock with a velocity of 150 metres per minute and it took 25 seconds for it to stop. How far did he have to walk before he could throw the rock again?

6. Two cars were side by side at a stop light and began to move ahead at the same time. They accelerated uniformly at 4.0 ft/sec² and 6.0 ft/sec² respectively:
   (a) How long did it take each car to reach the speed of 44 ft/sec?
   (b) What does a speed of 44 ft/sec represent in mi/hr?

7. When the brakes were applied to a car travelling 30 mi/hr, the car came to a stop in 6.0 seconds. What was the speed at the end of each second assuming uniform acceleration?

8. A body starts with a velocity of 90 ft/sec and loses a third of its velocity each second. When will it come to rest? Describe its acceleration.

9. A boy got on his bicycle at the top of a hill and rode downhill. After 16.0 seconds he was at the bottom travelling at a speed of 640 cm/sec:
   (a) What was his average acceleration?
   (b) What distance did he travel downhill if we assume his acceleration was uniform?

10. A stone is thrown upward over a lake with an initial velocity of 128 ft/sec:
    (a) How long will it ascend?
    (b) How high will it rise?
    (c) What will be its velocity when it hits the water? (Assume that the time to descend is the same as in (a).)

11. A train is travelling 60 mi/hr during a fog. As the train comes out into a clear stretch, the engineer suddenly sees a car stalled on the track 0.30 mile away. He applies the brakes, which are capable of giving the train an acceleration of -3.0 ft/sec^2:
    (a) How long will it take the train to stop?
    (b) Will a collision occur?

12. A particle has an initial speed of 20 cm/sec and receives an acceleration of 8.0 cm/sec^2. What distance will it travel in 15 seconds?

13. Through what distance must a body fall to acquire a velocity of 80.0 ft/sec?

14. An object moves to the left with an initial velocity of 40 cm/sec, and is subject to a constant acceleration of 5.0 cm/sec^2 to the right. Determine its velocity and displacement at the end of 4.0, 8.0 and 12.0 seconds respectively, and interpret your answer.

15. A stone is thrown down a deep well with an initial velocity of 1200 cm/sec:
    (a) What will be its velocity at the end of 5.00 seconds?
    (b) If it hits the water 7.00 seconds after it was thrown, how far down is the surface of the water?

16. A stone is dropped from a high cliff. Two seconds later another stone is dropped. How many feet apart will the stones be after the second one has been falling 3.00 seconds?

17. A locomotive is running at 72.0 km/hr:
    (a) What acceleration must be produced by the brakes to bring it to a full stop in 16.0 seconds?
    (b) What distance did it cover in coming to a full stop?
    (c) If it is accelerated at 75.0 cm/sec^2, how long will it take to reach its original speed?
    (d) What distance did it travel before it gained its original speed?

18. If a ball falls for 3.00 secs and breaks a pane of glass which makes it lose $\frac{1}{3}$ of its velocity, find the total distance it will have fallen in 4.00 secs after being dropped.

19. A vehicle moves with a constant velocity of 50 ft/sec E for 5.00 secs:
    (a) Draw a velocity-time graph for the vehicle.
    (b) What displacement has it undergone in this time?
    (c) Determine the area under the velocity-time graph for the 5-second interval.
    (d) What conclusion might you arrive at regarding the relationship between displacement and area under a velocity-time graph?
    (e) Test this conclusion using a velocity-time graph for the subway car in Example 4.

20. Using the procedure outlined in Question 19, attempt to find the displacement in t sec from Figure 3-3.

Motion with Constant Acceleration — Uniformly Accelerated Motion

▶ **Experiment 3**

To study accelerated motion.

> Recording timer kit
>
> 1-kg mass
>
> D-c source (1.5 volt or 6 volt)
>
> Rheostat—approximately 20 ohms
>
> C-clamp
>
> Metre stick

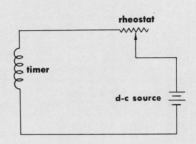

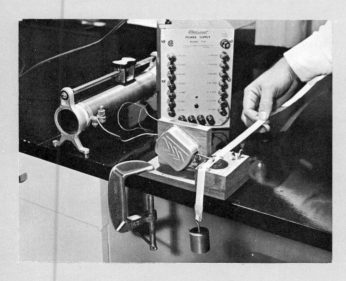

Procedure

1. Clamp the timer firmly to a table.

2. Set one end of a piece of timer tape approximately two metres long in the timer.

3. Reinforce this end with Scotch tape, and securely fasten the kilogram mass to this end.

4. Set the timer in operation, adjusting the rheostat so that the clapper operates smoothly with no bounce.

5. Allow the mass to hang from the side of the table. The mass should be suspended immediately below the edge of the table.

6. Release the tape, permitting the mass to fall to the floor.

Analysis

1. Examine the tape. Using the heavy initial dot as a starting point, mark off, with pencil, consecutive groups of 6 dots each as shown in the illustration on page 49. The elapsed time for each group of 6 dots will be used as a unit of time.

2. Determine the displacements s_1, s_2, s_3 etc., and construct a table showing *total displacement* vs. *elapsed time*, i.e., displacement s_1 occurs in 1 unit of time, s_2 in 2 units of time, etc.

3. From this table, plot *total displacement* vs. *elapsed time*.

To determine the acceleration of the falling mass, it will be necessary to determine the velocity of the mass at various instants. The instants we will choose are those indicated as a, b, c . . . These are the *mid-time* instants of each 6-dot interval used above. Proceed as follows:

4. Determine the average velocity over the displacement s_1. This is the displacement s_1 in cm divided by the elapsed time (one unit of time). The *average velocity* over this interval is s_1 cm per unit time. This is equal in value to the *instantaneous velocity* at time a.

Next, determine the average velocity over the second 6-dot interval. This is $(s_2 - s_1)$ cm per unit time, and is the instantaneous velocity at time b.

5. By a similar process, the instantaneous velocity can be determined for the mid-time instants of each 6-dot interval.

6. Construct a table showing instantaneous velocity vs. elapsed time.

7. Plot the values listed in the table of step 6 in order to obtain a velocity—time graph. As illustrated, you can use the same graph sheet as that used for the displacement—time graph. The plotted points on the velocity—time graph should fall approximately on a straight line. Draw the best straight line through these points, as illustrated.

8. Determine the slope of this straight

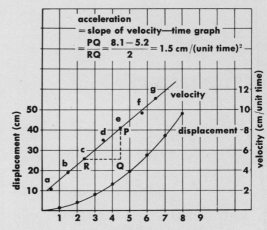

line. The unit for this slope is $\dfrac{\text{cm/unit time}}{\text{unit time}}$ or cm/(unit time)^2, and its value gives the acceleration of the falling mass.

Questions

1. What factor, or factors prevent us from considering the 1-kg mass as a freely falling object?

2. What assumption is made when we draw the best straight line through the points plotted for velocity vs. time?

The foregoing procedure may be followed to determine the acceleration due to gravity. The timer, however, should be mounted vertically as shown on page 94. Why? The only additional step required is that of finding the period of the timer, and hence the number of seconds in a 6-dot interval. The value of g (in cm/sec^2) can then be determined.

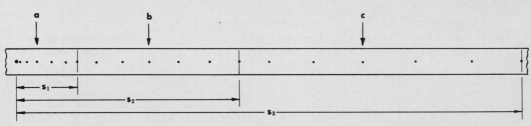

Chapter 4

The Concept of Force

1. NEWTON'S FIRST LAW OF MOTION—INERTIA

In all the previous discussions concerning the various types of motion, no thought was given to the agent or agents producing the motion. Suppose the agent is a shove given to a box at rest on the floor. If the shove is vigorous enough, it may start the box moving; the box will continue to move for a time and then come to rest again. The box was accelerated since its velocity was increased in the first part of the motion and decreased in the second part. The initial acceleration was caused by the shove given the box, perhaps with the hand; the latter acceleration was given by the friction between the floor and the box. *This simple illustration leads us to associate force with the change of motion of bodies.* Two things must be noticed about these forces that act on the

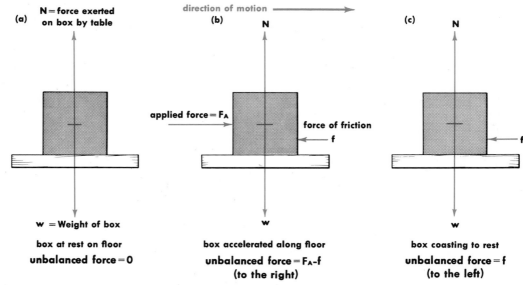

Fig. 4-1: *In (a) no unbalanced force acts on the box, and it maintains its state of motion. In (b) and (c) the presence of an unbalanced force produces acceleration.*

box. In the first place, in order to have a force acting on the box, some material thing must have been in contact with the box. One had to touch the box with the hand or a stick or a rope before one could exercise a force upon it; i.e., the force was an *external force*. In the second place, we notice that the acceleration of the box was *in the same direction as the force exerted upon it.*

When one pushes a box at rest or pulls it with a rope, sometimes there is no acceleration; or, in common language, we say that the box does not move. This is because the friction between the box and the floor just balances the push or pull given to the box. As a result there is no *unbalanced* or *net* force on the box at all. Nevertheless, the push or pull on the box tends or tries to give it an acceleration. Looking at the situation from another point of view, when we observe that the box has no acceleration, we conclude that there is no unbalanced force on the box.

Force may be defined as that agent which produces or tends to produce change of motion of a body; or, force is the agent which produces or tends to produce acceleration of a body.

From the point of view of the body, it appears that unless an unbalanced force, external to the body, acts upon it, its motion will remain unchanged.

This property of bodies to resist a change of motion is called inertia.

The word *inertia* has not the same meaning in physics as in ordinary usage. Inertia customarily implies a degree of sluggishness or inactivity. The term as used in physics also indicates a degree of inactivity since it implies that a force is required to move an object if it is initially at rest; but in addition, the body having been given its motion, it is just as great a problem to take it away. Specifically, an external unbalanced force is required to move a body if at rest and likewise to stop it once it is in motion.

The relationship between inertia and motion was stated by Sir Isaac Newton (1642-1727) in what has since been called his **First Law of Motion,** sometimes referred to as the *law of inertia.* **A body continues in its state of rest or uniform motion unless an external unbalanced force acts on it.**

One might assume from the shove given a box to produce acceleration that all forces must touch an object in order to act. However, a magnet can attract certain objects some distance removed, electrical

Fig. 4-2: *A simple illustration of inertia.*

forces can attract or repel electrons, and the force of gravity can pull on objects with no material connection to provide the accelerating force.

2. MASS: THE MEASURE OF INERTIA

In the previous section we have defined inertia as that property possessed by all objects by which they tend to maintain their state of motion. We know from experience that some objects possess more inertia than others—that is, some objects offer greater resistance than others to the effect of forces applied to them. **The amount of inertia possessed by an object is termed its mass.**

The terms mass and weight are often taken as identical, but, as will be shown in Chapter 5, there is a fundamental difference between the two. The mass of an object is invariable—a fixed value which is independent of the location of the object on the earth or elsewhere. On the other hand, the weight of that same object, as we shall see, is totally dependent upon its location and mass.

A fundamental demonstration to illustrate the concept of mass is shown in Figure 4-3. Two objects A and B, resting on a smooth horizontal surface, are joined by a coil spring, or heavy elastic band. When tension is set up in the spring, *equal*

and *opposite* forces act on the objects. If the tension is now allowed to act, the objects accelerate at a rate dependent upon their inertia. That which accelerates least is said to have the higher mass.

3. NEWTON'S SECOND LAW OF MOTION

It was Newton who investigated the exact relationship between the acceleration undergone by a mass, and the force causing that acceleration.

We shall begin our own investigation by defining, for the MKS system, the unit of force as that force which, acting on a 1-kg mass, produces an acceleration of 1 m/sec². This unit of force is called the *newton*. If two such forces were applied in the same direction to the kilogram mass, we would find the acceleration to be twice as great, that is 2 m/sec². Similarly the application of other values of applied force would cause a proportional increase in the acceleration of the kilogram mass, leading us to Table 4-1.

We conclude that *the acceleration produced varies directly as the unbalanced force acting on the mass.*

Let us now consider the acceleration produced by a constant unbalanced force when allowed to act on various masses. We know from our considerations above that an unbalanced force of 10 nt acting on a

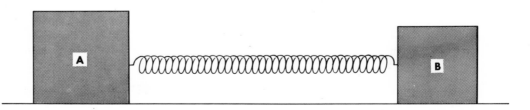

Fig. 4-3: *A fundamental demonstration of the meaning of mass. Equal forces, acting on A and B, cause A to accelerate at a lesser rate than B. We say that A has greater mass than B.*

mass of 1 kg will impart to it an acceleration of 10 m/sec². We also know that the same unbalanced force, applied to a mass twice that magnitude will, because of the increased inertia, result in a smaller acceleration. But how much smaller will it be?

Newton's experiments showed that doubling the mass resulted in an acceleration one half the former value. Further investigation of the accelerations produced on other masses by this same unbalanced force leads us to Table 4-2.

We see that *the acceleration produced is inversely proportional to the mass of the object.*

A study of Tables 4-1 and 4-2 leads us to the mathematical relationship between unbalanced force, mass, and acceleration.

$$\text{unbalanced force} = \text{mass} \times \text{acceleration}$$
$$F_u = ma$$

It should be stressed at this time that F_u (read "F unbalanced" or "F sub u") in this equation represents the *unbalanced* force

Table 4-1

Acceleration produced by various forces on a 1-kg mass

Unbalanced Force	Mass	Acceleration	Direction of Acceleration
1 nt	1 kg	1 m/sec²	direction of unbalanced force
2 nt	1 kg	2 m/sec²	direction of unbalanced force
5 nt	1 kg	5 m/sec²	direction of unbalanced force
12 nt	1 kg	12 m/sec²	direction of unbalanced force

Table 4-2

Acceleration produced by a given force acting on various masses

Unbalanced Force	Mass	Acceleration	Direction of Acceleration
10 nt	1 kg	10 m/sec²	direction of unbalanced force
10 nt	2 kg	5 m/sec²	direction of unbalanced force
10 nt	5 kg	2 m/sec²	direction of unbalanced force
10 nt	10 kg	1 m/sec²	direction of unbalanced force

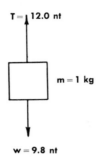

T = 12.0 nt

m = 1 kg

w = 9.8 nt

Fig. 4-4: *A force diagram is an important device in the solution of problems involving Newton's Second Law. Shown here is a force diagram for a 1-kg mass that is being accelerated by a string with a tension of 12.0 nt. The unbalanced force is 2.2 nt upward.*

acting on the object in question. This is of particular importance when considering the motion of an object when acted upon by more than one force.

The results of these findings are known as **Newton's Second Law of Motion**, which may be stated as follows: **the acceleration of an object takes place in the direction of the external unbalanced force acting on it, and varies directly as the unbalanced force and inversely as the mass.**

An important particular case exists when an object undergoes no acceleration, that is when an object maintains a state of rest or of uniform motion. From the Second Law of Motion we would conclude that no unbalanced force acts on the object, a fact already stated in the First Law of Motion. Hence Newton's First Law is really a particular case of the more general Second Law of Motion.

EXAMPLE 1

(a) What unbalanced force, in newtons, is required to accelerate a small cart of mass 15 kg at the rate of 5.0 m/sec² in an eastward direction along a level road?

(b) If the frictional force opposing the motion is 1.0 nt, what applied force will be required?

Solution:

(a) $F_u = ma$
$= 15 \text{ kg} \times 5.0 \text{ m/sec}^2$ East
$= 75 \text{ kg m/sec}^2$ or 75 nt East
The unbalanced force required is **75 nt East.**

(b) In all problems involving objects acted upon by more than one force, the student is strongly advised to draw a *force diagram* indicating the forces.

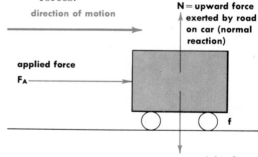

direction of motion

N = upward force exerted by road on car (normal reaction)

applied force
F_A —

f

w = weight of car

We note there are two forces perpendicular to the road that are exerted on the cart. Since the cart does not accelerate in the vertical direction, these forces balance each other. In the horizontal direction the net force, or unbalanced force is $F_A - f$.

$$F_u = F_A - f$$

and from part (a) $F_u = 75$ nt eastward

$$F_A - f = 75 \text{ nt}$$
$$F_A = 75 + f = 76 \text{ nt eastward}.$$

EXAMPLE 2

(a) The acceleration due to gravity is 9.8 m/sec² on the earth's surface. What is the force of gravity (i.e., the weight) acting on a mass of 1.0 kg?

(b) What is the weight of a mass of m kg at a location where the acceleration due to gravity is g m/sec²?

Solution:

(a) Let us consider the 1.0 kg mass in a situation in which the only force acting on it is the force of gravity, that is, in a state of free fall.

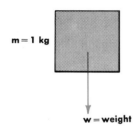

w = weight

$$F_u = ma$$
$$= 1.0 \text{ kg} \times 9.8 \text{ m/sec}^2 = 9.8 \text{ nt.}$$

Hence the weight of a 1-kg mass is **9.8 nt** (but only when the acceleration due to gravity is 9.8 m/sec²).

(b) Similar to part (a)

$$F_u = ma$$
$$= mg$$

∴ The weight of a mass of m kg is **mg newtons.**

e.g.:

The weight of a 25.0 kg object at a position on the earth where g, the acceleration due to gravity, is 9.83 m/sec² would be

$$25.0 \times 9.83 \text{ nt}$$
$$= 2.46 \times 10^2 \text{ nt.}$$

EXAMPLE 3

(a) The tension in the cable of an elevator is measured as 1.00×10^4 nt. If the mass of the elevator and its passengers is 8.00×10^2 kg, what is the direction and magnitude of the acceleration?

(b) In what direction is the elevator moving?

Solution:

(a) A force diagram of the elevator is shown. The weight of elevator and passengers is

$$w = 8.00 \times 10^2 \times 9.8 \text{ nt}$$
$$= 7.84 \times 10^3 \text{ nt}$$

Then $F_u = (1.00 \times 10^4 - 7.84 \times 10^3)$ nt upward

$$= 2.16 \times 10^3 \text{ nt upward.}$$

and $a = \dfrac{F_u}{m} = \dfrac{2.16 \times 10^3 \text{ nt}}{8.00 \times 10^2 \text{kg}}$

$$= \textbf{2.70 m/sec}^2 \textbf{ upward.}$$

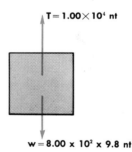

T = 1.00 × 10⁴ nt

w = 8.00 x 10² x 9.8 nt

(b) Although we know the acceleration of the elevator is upward, we cannot conclude from this that the elevator is necessarily *moving* upward. We can only conclude that either it is moving upward with increasing velocity, or it is moving downward with decreasing velocity. In either case, an upward unbalanced force is required, producing an upward acceleration.

4. UNITS FOR NEWTON'S SECOND LAW OF MOTION

The solution of problems involving the application of Newton's Second Law requires that the proper units of mass, force, and acceleration be used.

In the MKS system, we have already defined these units as the kilogram, newton, and metre/sec², respectively. From Newton's Second Law, we have 1 newton = 1 kilogram ×1 metre/sec² or 1 nt = 1 kg m/sec².

In the CGS system, the unit of force, the *dyne*, is that unbalanced force which, acting on a mass of one gram, causes an acceleration of 1 cm/sec². Thus, 1 dyne = 1 g cm/sec².

In applying the equation $F_u = ma$, using the British Engineering System, a new unit of mass, the *slug*, must be used.

1 slug = 32.1740 pounds mass

The unit of force is the pound force, as defined in Chapter 1, and the unit of acceleration is ft/sec².

5. FORCE, A VECTOR QUANTITY

An important part of Newton's Second Law of Motion, a part too often forgotten, is that the acceleration produced by a force is in the same sense (direction) as the force. It is agreed that we recognize the presence of a force by the acceleration that it produces, or that it tends to produce. It follows that the *direction* of a force is as important

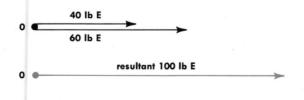

Fig. 4-5: *The vector addition of two forces acting in the same direction.*

as its magnitude. Force is, therefore, a vector by our definition. Force vectors are added in the same way that we add displacement, velocity, and acceleration vectors.

Suppose that a boy pulls on a rope with a force of 40 lb and that a second boy pulls on the same rope, in the same sense, with a force of 60 lb. The vector addition of these two forces is shown in Figure 4-5 and the sum is 100 lb.

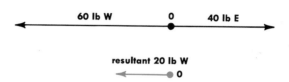

Fig. 4-6: *The vector addition of two forces acting in opposite directions.*

On the other hand, if one of the boys pulls with a force of 40 lb East and the second boy pulls with a force of 60 lb West, the sum of the forces, as shown in the vector diagram, Figure 4-6, is 20 lb West.

Suppose that one force of 10.0 nt acts on a body at 0, Figure 4-7, in an easterly direction, while at the same time a second force of 15.0 nt acts at the same point in a southerly direction. It is clear that the force OE tends to move the object along the line OE, whereas the second force tends to move it along the line OS. The net result is that the body tends to move along some line such as OR. The force OR, the magnitude and direction of which may be obtained by making the diagram to scale, is the sum of the two forces OE and OS. Since the line SR is equal to and parallel to OE, the sum of the forces, OR, has been obtained by the vector addition of OE and OS in the same way as displacement and velocity vectors were added.

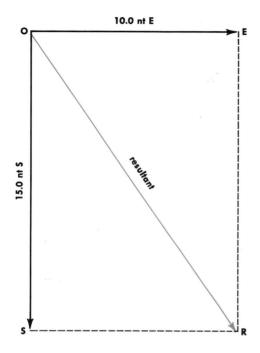

10.0 nt E

15.0 nt S

resultant

O · · · · · · · · E

S · · · · · · · · R

Fig. 4-7: *The vector addition of two forces that are not in a straight line.*

table top, which is the only material object in contact with the book, pushes up on the book with a force equal in magnitude to the weight of the book, but in the opposite sense.

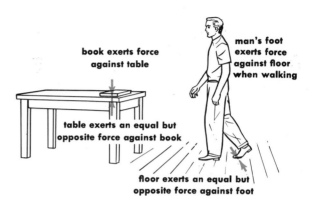

book exerts force against table

table exerts an equal but opposite force against book

man's foot exerts force against floor when walking

floor exerts an equal but opposite force against foot

Fig. 4-8: *Examples of action and reaction forces.*

The statement that the force OR is the sum of the forces OE and OS means that the forces OE and OS may be completely replaced by the single force OR. The effect of the single force OR upon the motion, or tendency to motion, of the body at O is exactly the same as the effect on the body of the two forces OE and OS acting simultaneously.

6. NEWTON'S THIRD LAW OF MOTION

If a book rests on a solid table top, the book is not accelerated; it follows that there is no unbalanced force acting upon it. Because of its weight, the book exerts a downward force on the table top; therefore the

The driving wheels of an automobile are forced to turn, and, by means of the friction between tire and roadway, to push backward on the road. Since the car is moving forward, we must conclude that there is a force exerted by the roadway on the tire, opposite in direction to the force exerted by the tire upon the road. This is the tractive force exerted upon the car.

Two things are to be noted about these situations. First, forces always appear in pairs; secondly, these two forces always *act upon different bodies*. The reader is advised to think of situations in which forces are involved and verify the fact that, indeed, forces do always appear in pairs and that the two elements of these pairs act upon different bodies.

These pairs of forces are usually referred to respectively as the *acting force* and the

10 lb   10 lb

Fig. 4-9: *A demonstration of Newton's Third Law. Can you identify three pairs of equal and opposite forces?*

reacting force, or *action* and *reaction.* Which is the acting force and which is the reacting force depends upon our point of view. Usually the force in which we are primarily interested is referred to as the action and the other as the reaction.

These observations are summed up in **Newton's Third Law of Motion,** thus:

Whenever one body exercises a force upon a second body, the second body always exerts upon the first a force opposite in direction and equal in magnitude.

The law can be illustrated as follows: Fasten one spring balance to a solid post and hook another spring balance to the first one, as shown in Figure 4-9.

If we pull steadily, we find that both balances read the same. The pull of the first balance on the second is equal in magnitude and opposite in direction to the pull of the second on the first. And further, the pull of the first on the post is equal in magnitude and opposite in direction to the pull of the post on the first balance. Similarly, the pull of the second balance on the hand is equal in magnitude and opposite in direction to the pull of the hand on the second balance. Indeed, it is by a series of pairs of forces, action and reaction, that the force is transmitted from the post to the hand.

EXAMPLE 4

A box of mass 2.0 kg is pushed by hand along a smooth table, resulting in an acceleration of 1.0 m/sec² to the right.

(a) What average force does the hand exert on the box?

(b) What average force does the box exert on the hand?

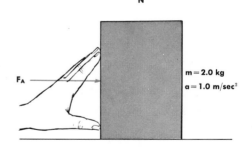

N

$m = 2.0$ kg
$a = 1.0$ m/sec²

F_A

w

Solution:

(a) To solve part (*a*) we employ Newton's Second Law: the unbalanced force is the applied force in the horizontal direction (since we are neglecting friction).

Then $F_u = F_A = ma$
$$= 2.0 \text{ kg} \times 1.0 \text{ m/sec}^2$$
$$= 2.0 \text{ nt (to the right)}.$$

Thus, the hand exerts a force of **2.0 nt** to the *right* (F_A).

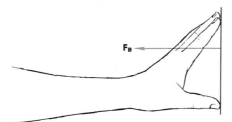

Employing Newton's Third Law, the force exerted on the hand by the box, is equal in magnitude and opposite in direction to that found in (*a*).

The box thus exerts on the hand a force of **2.0 nt** to the left (F_B).

Illustrations of Newton's Third Law of Motion

(*a*) Rowing a boat: The oars exert a force on the water; the water exerts a force on the oars.

(*b*) Propellers of an aircraft or boat: The propeller exerts a force on a fluid; the fluid exerts a force in the opposite direction on the propeller.

(*c*) Gun carriage: The force of the gun on the bullets produces the muzzle velocity of the bullets; the force of the bullets on the gun provides the recoil force on the gun (Figure 4-10).

Fig. 4-10: *Force exerted by bullets acting on the gun accelerates it to the right. This is the reaction to the force exerted on the bullets by the gun.*

(*d*) Jet and rocket engines: The jet velocity of the gases is comparable to the muzzle velocity of the bullets (force of engine on gas). The force of the gases on the engine provides the thrust forward (Figure 4-11).

National Defence Photograph

Fig. 4-11: *Jet and rocket propulsion are other illustrations of Newton's Third Law.*

FORCE: *Force* is a *vector quantity* and may be defined as that which tends to produce an acceleration. The *acceleration* of an object is determined by the *net* or *unbalanced* force that acts on it, and also by the *mass* of the object.

MASS: The *mass* of a body is a measure of how great is its *resistance to a change in motion,* a property possessed by all objects, called *inertia.* The mass of a body is a *fixed quantity,* independent of the location of the body.

NEWTON'S FIRST AND SECOND LAWS: The mathematical relationship between force, mass, and acceleration was stated by Newton in his *Second Law of Motion,*

$$F_u = ma$$

This law is a further extension of the *First Law of Motion,* which states that an unbalanced force is necessary to produce a change in motion.

WEIGHT: The weight of an object is the *force of gravity* which acts upon it and is *dependent upon* the *mass* of the object and the *acceleration due to gravity.* Because the latter is dependent upon location, so also is weight.

UNITS OF FORCE: The basic unit of force in the MKS system is the *newton*—that force which imparts to a mass of 1 kilogram an acceleration of 1 metre/sec². In the CGS system, a *dyne* is that force required to produce an acceleration of 1 cm/sec² on a mass of 1 gram. In the British System, the unit of force is the pound, as defined in Chapter 1. The amount of mass to which a 1-pound force imparts an acceleration of 1 ft/sec² is called a *slug.*

NEWTON'S THIRD LAW: Experience shows that whenever a force acts, another force is produced, equal in magnitude and opposite in direction. These *action* and *reaction* forces each act on *different* objects, and each influences the motion of only the object it acts *upon.* This observation forms Newton's *Third Law of Motion.*

EXERCISE A

1. What is the terminology used to describe the force that produces acceleration?

2. State what is meant by the inertia of an object.

3. (*a*) Which of Newton's laws is known as the Law of Inertia?
   (*b*) State the law.

4. What is the value of the unbalanced force that acts on an automobile travelling with uniform motion?

5. Name three units of force that are used in the equation $F_u = m\,a$.

6. List four vector quantities involved in the study of motion.

7. Newton's Third Law states that the reaction force is equal in magnitude to the action force. In what respect do these two forces differ?

8. Name the reaction force to each of the following action forces; indicate the object on which the force acts:

 (*a*) the gravitational pull of the sun on the planet Mars

 (*b*) the force of attraction of an electron on a proton

 (*c*) the force exerted by the north pole of a magnet on the south pole of a magnetic compass

 (*d*) the force of the air on the walls of an inflated tire.

9. If twice the force gives twice the acceleration, why does a 10-kg stone not fall twice as fast as a 5-kg stone?

10. A boy jumps down from a platform with a pound weight on his upturned hand. What will happen to the force on his hand: (*a*) while he is in the air, (*b*) when he lands on the ground?

11. If a suitcase falls from a luggage rack of a fast-moving train, will it fall on the passenger in the seat in front, in the seat below, or in the seat behind?

12. Unidentified flying objects (flying saucers) were perplexing since they seemed to be able to make angular turns without changing speed. What physical law did they seem to violate?

13. If you release the air from an inflated toy balloon as you suddenly let go of it, what happens? Why?

14. The acceleration of a train running on a level track can be judged by hanging a short pendulum from the ceiling and measuring the angle it makes with the vertical. Explain.

15. To tighten a sledge hammer or a pick on its handle, you pound on the end of the handle. Explain.

16. If two men were dropped together by helicopter on to the middle of a completely frictionless surface, how could they get off? Could one man have got off if he were dropped alone?

17. A girl steps from the seat of a small boat expecting to step on to the dock. Instead she lands in the water. Which law of physics did she ignore?

18. In the famous Von Guericke's experiment with the Magdeburg hemispheres, it took two teams of horses pulling in one direction and two teams pulling in the opposite direction to pull the hemispheres apart. If one hemisphere had been anchored to something substantial enough, how many teams would have been required to break the partial vacuum?

19. Why can you remove the snow from your shoes by stamping your feet?

20. A girl with a kilogram weight suspended from a spring balance that is capable of weighing up to 2 kilograms, steps into an elevator. How will the pointer move

 (*a*) when the elevator starts up?

 (*b*) when it stops?

 (*c*) when it starts down?

21. A man is slowly lowered at constant speed down the side of a building by another man standing on the roof. In what direction does the tension in the rope act:
(a) from the point of view of the man being lowered?
(b) from the point of view of the man on the roof?
(c) Why do these two forces not cancel each other?

EXERCISE B

Use $g = 32.0$ ft/sec² or 9.80 m/sec². Assume all numerical data to be correct to the number of digits shown.

1. What is meant by an acceleration of one g? How many g's are represented by an acceleration of 320 ft/sec²?

2. If a force of 1.00 newton causes an object to accelerate at the rate of 4.00×10^{-1} m/sec², what is the mass of the object?

3. An object moving West with an acceleration of 8.0 m/sec² has a mass of 6.0 kg. What is the unbalanced force acting on the object?

4. The unbalanced force acting on a ball of mass 0.25 kg is 16 newtons to the right. Find the acceleration of the ball.

5. A mass of 1.00 kg is given an acceleration of 1.00 m/sec².
(a) Find the unbalanced force acting on the mass.
(b) Change the mass and acceleration to CGS units and express the unbalanced force in dynes.
(c) How many dynes are equivalent to one newton?

6. Calculate the force needed to give a 25.0-kg mass an acceleration of 5.00 m/sec².

7. A stone of mass 1.0 kilogram sinks to the bottom of a lake with an acceleration of 5.00 m/sec².
(a) Why did the stone not sink with an acceleration of 9.8 m/sec²?
(b) Draw a force diagram showing the forces exerted on the stone while sinking.

8. A 10.0-kg block rests on a horizontal surface. What constant horizontal force is required to give it a velocity of 4.0 m/sec in 2.0 secs, starting from rest, if the friction force between the block and the surface is constant and equal to 5.0 newtons?

9. An elevator has an upward acceleration of 1.0 m/sec². With what force will the elevator floor push upward on a 82-kg passenger?

10. A cage weighing 520 kg is being lowered down a mine by a cable. Find the tension in the cable:
(a) when the speed is increasing at the rate of 2.0 m/sec²
(b) when the speed is uniform
(c) when the speed is diminishing at the rate of 2.0 m/sec².

11. A 1.00×10^2-gram weight is suspended from a spring balance and carried in a balloon. What will be the reading on the balance:

    (a) when the balloon is ascending with a uniform acceleration of 2.00 m/sec²?

    (b) when it is descending with an acceleration of 4.00 m/sec²? (Assume that in each case the acceleration is in the direction of motion.)

12. After re-entry, an astronaut of mass 75 kilograms is rescued at sea on the end of a rope attached to a helicopter. When the helicopter accelerates upward at 0.50 m/sec² what tension must the rope withstand?

13. A young lady who weighs 5.80×10^2 nt plans to elope by sliding down an improvised rope made of nylon stockings. The maximum force the stockings can withstand without tearing is 4.00×10^2 nt.

    (a) Can the girl slide down with uniform velocity?

    (b) What is the minimum acceleration with which she can slide down the rope?

14. Although the kilogram is a unit of mass, the word kilogram is quite commonly used to specify forces. A *kilogram force* is the weight of a kilogram mass, and will vary with location, whereas a newton force is constant.

    What is the value of a kg force, in newtons:

    (a) at the earth's surface? ($g = 9.8$ m/sec²)

    (b) on the moon? ($g = 1.6$ m/sec²)

15. A crate has a mass of 192 pounds and is acted upon by an unbalanced force of 12 pounds.

    (a) What is the mass of the crate, in slugs?

    (b) What acceleration will the crate receive?

16. The crate referred to in question 15 is subjected to the pull of two ropes. The tension in one rope is 45 pounds, acting in a northeasterly direction, and in the other the tension is 75 pounds, acting in an easterly direction.

    (a) Determine, by vector diagram, the unbalanced or resultant force.

    (b) Determine the acceleration of the crate under these circumstances.

17. A 88-kg aviator during free fall acquires a speed of 46 m/sec before opening his parachute. Ten seconds after the chute opens, his speed has been reduced to 6.6 m/sec.

    (a) Find the average acceleration of the aviator after the parachute opened.

    (b) Calculate the average force provided by the parachute.

    (c) What average force does the man exert on the parachute during this time?

18. An automobile travelling North at 12.0 m/sec is brought to a stop in 3.00 secs by the application of the brakes. Calculate the average retarding force exerted on the automobile if its mass is 1.00×10^3 kg.

19. A 100-kg football player in motion at 10.0 m/sec South is tackled and brought to a stop in 2.0 secs.

    (a) Find the average horizontal force exerted *by* the tackler.

    (b) What average horizontal force is exerted *on* the tackler?

Chapter 4

The Concept of Force

▶ Experiment 4

To study the relationship between acceleration and unbalanced force applied to a constant mass.

Dynamics kit

Recording timer kit

C-clamp

Metre stick

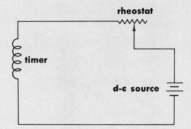

The dynamics kit consists basically of a cart, the mass of which can be altered by placing on it one or more bricks. In this experiment the mass of the moving cart will be kept constant by using one brick. Various forces will be applied to the cart by using, in turn, one, two, and three rubber bands stretched by equal amounts. In each case, acceleration of the cart will be determined by means of the method used in Experiment 3.

Procedure

1. Clamp the timer to one end of the table so that the tape will feed along the length of the table. (The table should be at least 6 ft in length.)

2. Feed one end of about 10 ft of tape through the timer, and attach the tape to the cart by means of Scotch tape.

3. Using tape or chalk, make a fixed reference point on the ruler. This mark will be used to maintain the tension in the rubber bands at a constant value while the cart is being accelerated.

4. Have your partner set the timer in operation, and with the cart at the timer end of the table, place one rubber band over the peg at the front of the cart. Using the metre stick, stretch the rubber band until the peg and the reference point are lined up. It will be necessary for your partner to hold the cart steady.

5. When the cart is released, maintain the tension in the rubber band as the cart accelerates along the table. Another member of your party, located at the other end of the table, will ensure that the cart does not crash to the floor.

6. Save the tape from step 5. Repeat the experiment twice, using two rubber bands, and then three bands. In each case, maintain the same tension used for the single band.

Analysis

1. Using the first tape, divide the dots into groups of six, starting from the initial heavy dot. (Count the first dot after the initial heavy dot as dot number 1.) The elapsed time for the formation of 6 dots will be used as a unit of time.

2. Plot a velocity—time graph as outlined in steps 4-7 of Experiment 3. Determine the acceleration in cm/(unit time)^2.

3. Repeat this procedure for each of the other two tapes. Plot both velocity—time graphs on the same paper that was used for the plot of the first tape.

4. Let us refer to the tension in the first rubber band as F_1. The unbalanced force acting on the cart in the three trials will then be F_1, $2F_1$, and $3F_1$, respectively. (What assumption are we making here?) Let us call the corresponding accelerations a_1, a_2, and a_3.

Determine the ratios $\dfrac{a_2}{a_1}$, $\dfrac{a_3}{a_1}$ and $\dfrac{a_3}{a_2}$.

Compare these ratios with the corresponding ratios of unbalanced forces.

What conclusion can be made regarding the acceleration of an object, and the unbalanced force acting on it?

Chapter 5

Universal Gravitation

1. WEIGHT AND ITS MEASUREMENT

In Chapter 4 the weight of an object was defined as the force of attraction exerted on it by the earth, and it has been mentioned that this force varies slightly, depending on the location of the object. For example, precise measurements made on a mass of 1 kilogram show that its weight at sea level in Bermuda is 9.798 newtons, whereas at sea level in Greenland it weighs 9.825 newtons. Were observations made at different altitudes we would find a similar variation in weight, the weight progressively decreasing with altitude.

Weight and mass are related to each other as follows:

weight = mass × acceleration due to gravity

or $w = mg$

a result obtained directly from Newton's Second Law.

The direct measurement of weight is obtained by using a spring balance, such as that shown in Figure 5-1. The extension of a spring is proportional to the force causing the extension, a law first stated by Robert Hooke in 1678 and known now as Hooke's Law. Accordingly, a spring which is extended 2.0 in. by a force of 1.5 pounds will undergo an extension of 4.0 in. when this force is doubled. This simple law holds provided

Fig. 5-1: *The spring balance records the gravitational force exerted by the earth on the object suspended from it. Its reading will vary with its location.*

the elastic limit of the spring is not exceeded. The equal-arm balance (Figure 5-2) is used in the measurement of mass, by comparing the weights of different masses at the *same* location. It does *not* give a direct measurement of weight.

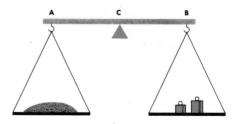

Fig. 5-2: *The equal-arm platform balance measures mass. Once balanced, it will remain balanced at all locations.*

66

2. NEWTON AND THE UNIVERSAL LAW OF GRAVITATION

Sir Isaac Newton published the *Mathematical Principles of Natural Philosophy* in 1687. In this treatise he described the solar system as a precise mechanism the parts of which move in relation to one another because of a universal force—the force of gravity. This force acts on thrown baseballs, rockets, and all objects on the earth, as well as upon the heavenly bodies; they all obey the same law.

Bodies free to move near the surface of the earth will always fall. In more precise language they are accelerated towards the centre of the earth. Moreover our experience is that they all fall with the same acceleration. Since they are thus accelerated, there must be an unbalanced force pulling them in the direction of this acceleration. The unbalanced force is, of course, the pull of the earth on the body in question. Appealing to Newton's Third Law of Motion, we must conclude that the reaction to this force is the pull of the body in question upon the earth. This mutual attraction is called *gravity*. Newton extended the concept of the attraction between bodies and the earth to that of a mutual attraction between all material bodies. In this more general sense, this mutual attraction is called *gravitation*. Ordinarily we do not notice this force of attraction between bodies since it is very small, unless one or both of the bodies has a great mass, such as that of the earth. Two one-pound masses separated by a foot have a mutual attraction of 3.3×10^{-11} lb only.

The discovery of the universal law of gravitation arose, as did the discovery of many other important physical laws, from an intelligent "hunch". While thinking of the phenomenon of bodies falling towards the earth, Newton conjectured that this force of attraction might extend throughout all planetary space. The classic story of Newton and the falling apple is not without

British Information Services

Fig. 5-3: Isaac Newton was born in Lincolnshire, England, in 1642. As a rather frail boy of quiet manner, he enjoyed tinkering with mechanical gadgets. At the age of 19 he entered Cambridge University where he excelled as a student. By the astonishingly young age of 24 he had made most of his profound discoveries in mathematics (the binomial theorem and differential calculus) and in physics (his theory of colours, and his laws of motion).

foundation. The initial stages of his argument were, in general, as follows:

The Test of Gravitation: The Apple and the Moon

Newton predicted that the force of attraction between any two objects in the universe would be proportional to the product of their masses and inversely proportional to the square of the distance between their centres of mass. Accordingly, the acceleration of the apple at the earth's surface and the acceleration of the moon should bear a ratio equal to the reciprocal of the ratio of the squares of their respective distances from the earth's centre.

The apple in free fall had an acceleration of approximately 32 ft/sec². Since the apple is 4.00×10^3 miles from the earth's centre and the moon 2.39×10^5 miles, the ratio of these distances is approximately $\dfrac{4 \times 10^3}{24 \times 10^4}$ or 1/60 (Figure 5-4). Accordingly, Newton should find the acceleration of the moon to be $\dfrac{32}{60^2} = 8.9 \times 10^{-3}$ ft/sec². When Newton obtained the acceleration by calculation it was found to be 8.9×10^{-3} ft/sec².

It remained to test the effect of the masses of the attracting bodies upon the force of attraction. The problem was formidable since the attraction is very small and direct experiments are very difficult to perform with any precision. Nevertheless, Mitchell and Cavendish as early as 1798 were able to test the law directly and obtained a result in close agreement with the most modern experiments. The **law of gravitation**, initially conjectured, and finally tested by experiment is this:

The mutual attraction of particles of matter is directly proportional to the product of the masses of the attracting particles and inversely proportional to the square of the distance separating the particles.

Expressed algebraically this becomes:

$$F = \frac{Gm_1m_2}{d^2}$$

in which

G is the constant of gravitation;
m_1, m_2 are the respective masses;
d is the distance between the masses.

This law refers strictly to what we usually call *point* masses, that is bodies which are very small compared with the distances separating them. Newton later proved that it could be applied to uniform spheres at any distance apart, provided the distance referred to is the distance between the centres of the spheres.

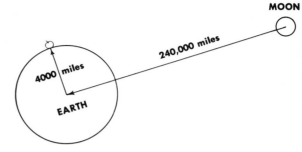

Fig. 5-4: *Newton postulated that the force required to hold the moon in its orbit was the same force that causes objects to fall. His comparison of the moon's acceleration with the value of g on earth led to his Law of Universal Gravitation.*

When the force of attraction was measured in newtons, the two masses in kilograms, and the separating distance in metres, the value of G was found to be 6.67×10^{-11} **nt m²/kg²** (MKS units).

EXAMPLE 1

Find the gravitational force between two metal spheres placed 2.0 cm apart if their masses are 6.0×10^{-3}kg and 1.0×10^{-2}kg.

Solution:

$$F = \frac{Gm_1m_2}{d^2}$$

$$= \frac{6.67 \times 10^{-11} \times 6.0 \times 10^{-3} \times 1.0 \times 10^{-2}}{(2.0 \times 10^{-2})^2}$$
newtons

$$= \frac{40.0 \times 10^{-16}}{4.0 \times 10^{-4}} \text{ newtons}$$

$$= \mathbf{1.0 \times 10^{-11} \ newtons} .$$

---

3. VARIATION IN WEIGHT

We may use the Law of Universal Gravitation to determine the weight of an object at points remote from the earth.

Let us consider a mass of m kg at A on the

earth's surface, a distance d_1 from the earth's centre, and the same mass of m kg located in space at point B, a distance d_2 from the earth's centre (Figure 5-5).

Then, the force of gravity F_1 acting on the mass at A is mg_1, and the force of gravity F_2 acting on the mass at B is mg_2, where g_1 and g_2 are the accelerations due to gravity at points A and B respectively.

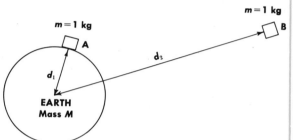

Fig. 5-5: *The weight of an object varies inversely as the square of its distance from the earth's centre.*

These forces, expressed in terms of Newton's Law of Gravitation, are:

$$F_1 = \frac{GMm}{d_1^2}$$

and $F_2 = \dfrac{GMm}{d_2^2}$.

$$\therefore \frac{F_2}{F_1} = \frac{\dfrac{GMm}{d_2^2}}{\dfrac{GMm}{d_1^2}} = \frac{GMm}{d_2^2} \times \frac{d_1^2}{GMm} = \frac{d_1^2}{d_2^2} .$$

$$\therefore \frac{mg_2}{mg_1} = \frac{d_1^2}{d_2^2}$$

or $\dfrac{g_2}{g_1} = \left(\dfrac{d_1}{d_2}\right)^2 .$

The ratio of the weights of mass at two locations is equal to the inverse square of the ratio of their distances from the earth's centre.

EXAMPLE 2

What is the value of g at a distance 8,000 miles above the earth?

Solution:

Consider a mass m at each of these two locations:

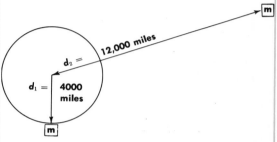

Here, $d_1 = 4,000$ mi
$d_2 = 12,000$ mi
$g_1 = 32$ ft/sec^2

then $\dfrac{mg_2}{mg_1} = \left(\dfrac{d_1}{d_2}\right)^2 = \left(\dfrac{4,000}{12,000}\right)^2$

$$= \frac{1}{9} .$$

$\therefore \dfrac{g_2}{g_1} = \dfrac{1}{9}$ and $g_2 = \dfrac{1}{9}g_1$

or $g_2 = \dfrac{32}{9}$ ft/sec^2

$$= 3.6 \text{ ft/sec}^2 .$$

On the following page (Figure 5-6) the weight of an astronaut is given for various distances from the earth.

By a similar approach, the weight of an object on another planet may be determined. The example below illustrates the method:

EXAMPLE 3

(a) The radius of the earth is 4.0×10^3 miles while that of Mars is 2.1×10^3 miles. If the mass of Mars is 0.108 that of the earth, what would a 100-lb student weigh on the surface of Mars?

(b) What is the acceleration due to gravity on Mars?

Solution:

(a) Let m = mass of student
F_E = his weight on the earth
F_M = his weight on Mars
r_E = radius of earth
r_M = radius of Mars
M_E = mass of earth
M_M = mass of Mars

Then $F_E = \dfrac{G m M_E}{r_E{}^2}$ $\qquad$ $F_M = \dfrac{G m M_M}{r_M{}^2}$

$$\frac{F_M}{F_E} = \frac{\dfrac{G m M_M}{r_M{}^2}}{\dfrac{G m M_E}{r_E{}^2}} = \frac{G m M_M}{r_M{}^2} \times \frac{r_E{}^2}{G m M_E}$$

$$= \left(\frac{M_M}{M_E}\right)\left(\frac{r_E}{r_M}\right)^2.$$

Now $\dfrac{M_M}{M_E} = 0.108$

and $\dfrac{r_E}{r_M} = \dfrac{4.0 \times 10^3}{2.1 \times 10^3} = \dfrac{4.0}{2.1}$

$\therefore \dfrac{F_M}{F_E} = 0.108 \times \left(\dfrac{4.0}{2.1}\right)^2 = 0.39$

$\therefore F_M = 0.39 F_E$, and the weight of the student on Mars is 0.39×100 lb = **39 lb.**

(b) g on Mars = 0.39 g on earth
$= 0.39 \times 32$ ft/sec^2 = **12 ft/sec^2.**

It will be noted that in this example, as in the previous example, it was unnecessary to substitute the value of G. This is true in most problems involving the Law of Universal Gravitation.

The change in weight becomes more apparent when one goes out into space. The illustration Figure 5-6 shows graphically how a man's weight decreases as he ascends from the surface of the earth. The reader should verify these figures.

4. THE MASS OF THE EARTH

Now that Newton had extended the concept of gravitation to include all bodies in the universe, the physicist was presented with a tool by which the mass of the earth could be found.

By Newton's Second Law the weight or force produced by gravity on a body of mass m is given by $w = mg$ ($F_{(u)} = ma$); also, the weight of the same mass m according to Newton's Universal Law of Gravitation is given by

$$w = \frac{G m M}{r_E{}^2}$$

Mass of Earth — Radius^2 of Earth

$$\therefore \frac{G m M}{r_E{}^2} = mg \text{ or } M = \frac{g r_E{}^2}{G}.$$

Since $r_E = 6.37 \times 10^6$ m,

$$M = \frac{(9.80)\,(6.37 \times 10^6)^2}{6.67 \times 10^{-11}} = 5.96 \times 10^{24} \text{ kg.}$$

5. THE EQUAL-ARM BALANCE THE COMPARISON OF MASSES BY WEIGHING

Figure 5-2 illustrates the equal-arm balance. The beam, AB, of the balance is carefully constructed to be light and rigid so that it will not bend under the loads imposed upon it. It rests on a knife-edge agate bearing at the mid-point of the beam C. When balance pans of equal weight are added at each end of the beam, the centre of gravity of the beam system is at the knife edge C.

An object of unknown *mass* is placed on the left-hand balance pan and standard known *masses* are placed on the right-hand pan until the beam is balanced. The weight of the balance arm itself is equally disposed on either side of the knife edge and so balances out. Since the total clockwise force is equal to the total anticlockwise force when the beam is balanced, it follows that the force of gravity on the unknown mass, or its weight, is equal to that on the known masses. But the acceleration of gravity is the same for both the unknown and the known masses since they are essentially at the same point on the earth's surface. It follows, therefore, that the *masses* are the same. When one is "weighing" with an equal-arm balance, one is really measuring *mass*.

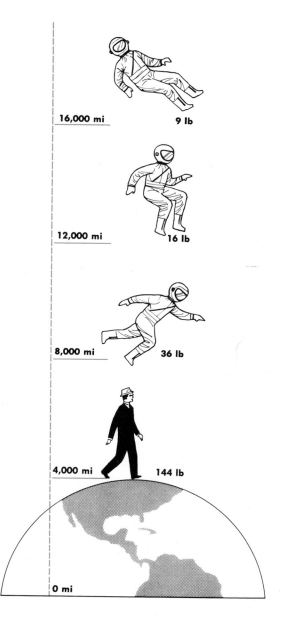

16,000 mi — 9 lb

12,000 mi — 16 lb

8,000 mi — 36 lb

4,000 mi — 144 lb

0 mi

Fig. 5-6: *Variation in weight at various distances from the earth's centre is shown in this diagram. The term "weightless" is often used to describe the condition of an astronaut when orbiting a few hundred miles above the earth. The actual force of gravity acting on him, however, has diminished by only a few pounds as this illustration indicates, and his "apparent weightlessness" stems from the fact that both he and the satellite are in a state of free fall. The high forward velocity of the satellite, combined with the acceleration downward caused by gravitational attraction, combine to produce a curved orbit around the earth.*

LAW OF GRAVITATION:

Newton postulated that every object exerts a gravitational force of attraction on every other object, and that this force is proportional to the product of the masses of the two objects and inversely proportional to the square of the distance separating them.

$$F = \frac{Gm_1 m_2}{d^2}.$$

The weight of an object is the gravitational attraction exerted on this object by the earth.

$$w = m_1 g. \quad \text{Thus:} \quad \frac{Gm_1 M}{d^2} = m_1 g.$$

71

It is this gravitational force which is responsible for the orbital motion of planets about the sun, and satellites about the earth.

The constant G is known as the Universal Constant of Gravitation and in the MKS system is $6.67 \times 10^{-11} \frac{\text{nt m}^2}{\text{kg}^2}$.

Because of the inverse square relationship, the weight of an object varies with its location.

EXERCISE A

1. Newton extended one of his laws to formulate the law of gravitation. Name the law which was extended.

2. If Newton's universal law of gravitation is true, namely: that the mutual attraction between any two objects is proportional to the product of their masses, why do objects of different mass fall at the same rate when dropped from a height?

3. Explain how the orbiting of the moon can be used as a clock.

4. If any two bodies in the universe mutually attract each other, what evidence indicates that the moon attracts the earth?

5. What are the two laws given by Newton which can be used to find the mass of the earth?

6. When we "weigh" an object on an equal-arm balance, what are we actually measuring?

7. The earth, rather than being a perfect sphere, is an ellipsoid; that is, it bulges at the Equator. How would the weight of an object at the North Pole compare with the weight of the same object at the Equator?

8. Suppose sugar sells for 50 cents a pound at the North Pole, and also at the Equator. Which purchase represents the better value:
   (a) if a spring balance is used for measuring the sugar
   (b) if an equal-arm balance is used?

EXERCISE B

(Consider all measured quantities correct to the digits stated.)

1. If an object weighing 36.0 newtons were taken to the moon where g is $\frac{1}{6.0}$ that on earth:
   (a) what would it weigh on the moon?
   (b) what would its mass be on the moon?

2. If G is 6.67×10^{-11} nt m^2/kg^2, calculate the force of attraction between two 200 kg masses when they are 2.00 m apart.

3. The mass of the earth is 6×10^{24} kg and the mass of the sun is 2×10^{30} kg. What is the ratio of the mass of the sun to that of the earth?

4. The instrument-carrying pay-load of a rocket weighs 100 lb on the earth's surface. What does it weigh at an altitude of 2.0×10^4 miles above the surface of the earth? The average radius of the earth is 4.0×10^3 miles.

5. If the earth were to remain the same size but its average density were twice what it is, what would be the value of g in ft/sec²?

6. A space explorer who is 2 billion miles distant from a star finds that its gravitational force on his spaceship is 200 lb. What will its force be on his spaceship when the explorer is 1 billion miles from the star?

7. Consider a 1000-lb satellite in space 4000 miles above the earth's surface.
   (a) If the radius of the earth is 4000 miles, how much farther from the centre of the earth is the satellite than when it was on the earth's surface?
   (b) What is its weight at this location?

8. The mass of Mars is 10% of that of the earth; yet its surface gravitation is 38% of the earth's gravitation.
   (a) Why is its gravitational force as high as this?
   (b) What would a 100-kg man weigh on Mars?
   (c) What would the acceleration due to gravity be in m/sec²?

9. Venus has a radius of 3.85×10^3 miles and a mass 0.81 of the earth's mass. What would be the acceleration due to gravity on Venus in ft/sec²?

10. The force of gravity on the planet Jupiter is about 2.6 times as great as it is on the surface of the earth. What would be the velocity of an object which fell for 10 seconds on Jupiter?

11. If we compare the earth with the moon, we get these ratios: radii 4:1, volume 64:1, density 10:1.
    (a) If the moon had been as large as the earth and only the densities different, what would have been the acceleration due to gravity on the moon in ft/sec²?
    (b) If the earth had been as small as the moon and kept its own density, what would have been the value of g on the earth?
    (c) Would a rocket need as much thrust to get into outer space from the moon as from the earth? Explain.

12. Find the gravitational force between an electron and a proton in the hydrogen atom using the following data:

mass of the electron	9.11×10^{-31} kg
mass of proton	1.67×10^{-27} kg
radius of orbit of electron	5.29×10^{-11} metres
$G = 6.67 \times 10^{-11}$ nt m²/kg²	

Chapter 6

Work, Energy, Power

1. THE CONCEPT OF WORK

Work is a term used by everyone, and with a wide variety of meanings. In Figure 6-1, a warehouseman loading boxes onto a truck thinks of himself as doing work. Here the idea of work is associated with the fact that he is physically exerting himself to do the job. We might ask on what conditions the amount of work depends. Obviously, the weight of the box and the height that it is lifted determine the work done, if we gauge work by the physical exertion required.

Quite often, however, the term work is used to describe effort where no motion takes place. The workman might support one of the boxes on his shoulder while his partner makes room for it on the truck. Does this motionless effort constitute work? If so, does the length of time during which he supports the box tend to increase the amount of work? Further, if he carries the box on his shoulder from one truck to another, is work done? The answers to these questions depend on how we define work.

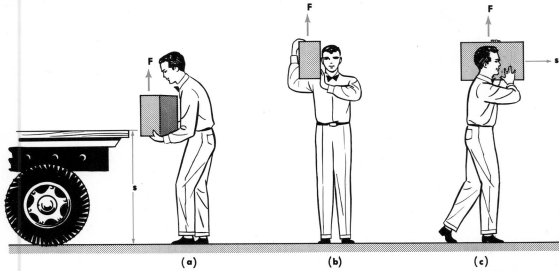

Fig. 6-1: *The man is performing work in only one of the above illustrations. Which one is it?*

In physics we will be very definite in what we consider as work. We will think of work being done only when an object moves as a result of an applied force. Specifically, our definition of work is as follows: **Work is done by a force acting on a body when the body undergoes a displacement parallel to the force. The work done by the force is equal to the product of the force and the parallel displacement undergone while the force acts.**

Algebraically, $W = F \cdot s$ (where F and s are parallel).

Let us re-examine the situations referred to earlier and see which, according to the above definition, constitute work. The warehouseman certainly performs work when lifting the boxes on the truck because he applies to each box an upward force and displaces the box upwards. However, with the box motionless on his shoulder no work is done even though the force applied to the box is considerable, because there is no displacement parallel to the applied force. Similarly, when he walks along the floor while supporting the box, no work is done on the box.

Units of Work

In our definition, work is the product of force and displacement, two vector quantities. Work, itself, is considered a scalar quantity for reasons which will be more apparent later on.

In the MKS system, a force of one newton, producing a displacement of one metre, does an amount of work which we may call *one newton-metre*. A more common term for this amount of work is the *joule*, named after the English physicist James Joule (1818-1889).

1 joule (j) = 1 newton-metre (nt-m)

In the British system of units, the work done by a force of 1 pound for a displacement of 1 foot, is 1 *foot-pound* (ft-lb).

EXAMPLE 1

In Figure 6-1, the weight of the box is 25 nt, and it is lifted 1.4 m above the floor. What work does the man do on the box?

Solution:

The average force exerted by the man in lifting the box = weight of box = 25 nt.

$$\text{Work done} = Fs = 25 \text{ nt} \times 1.4 \text{ m}$$
$$= 35 \text{ nt-m}$$
$$= \textbf{35 j.}$$

EXAMPLE 2

A man applies a horizontal force of 50.0 lb to a box for a distance of 4.0 ft, and the box coasts for an additional 11 ft. The frictional force resisting the motion of the box is 8.0 pounds.

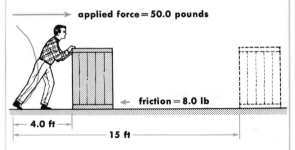

applied force = 50.0 pounds

friction = 8.0 lb

4.0 ft

15 ft

(a) What is the work done by the man?

(b) What is the work done by the force of friction?

Solution:

(a) Work done by man
$$= 50.0 \text{ lb} \times 4.0 \text{ ft}$$
$$= \textbf{2.0} \times \textbf{10}^2 \textbf{ ft-lb.}$$

(b) Frictional force = 8.0 lb.
Displacement of box while frictional force acts = 4.0 + 11 = 15 ft
∴ Work done by frictional force =
8.0 lb × 15ft = **1.2 × 10² ft-lb.**

It is interesting to note that in (a) the force is in the direction of the displacement, whereas in (b) the force is in the direction opposite to the displacement. In each case, force and displacement are parallel.

Does a force do work on an object if the force is not parallel to the resulting displacement? According to our definition the answer would be no, but the following example is included to illustrate that *work is done if the force has a component parallel to the displacement.*

EXAMPLE 3

A man pulls his son in a sleigh by pulling on a rope with a force of 36 lb inclined at an angle of 60° to the level ground. What work is done in moving the sleigh 4.0 ft.?

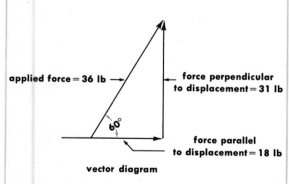

applied force = 36 lb →   ← force perpendicular to displacement = 31 lb

force parallel to displacement = 18 lb

vector diagram

Solution:

The pulling force is shown as performing two functions. It has a horizontal component parallel to the displacement, which accounts for the forward motion of the sleigh,

and a vertical component which tends to lift the sleigh. Work is done by the horizontal component. The magnitude of the horizontal component may be determined by a vector diagram. This component has a magnitude of 18 lb.

Work done = 18 lb × 4.0 ft = **72 ft-lb** .

The vertical component of the applied force, being perpendicular to the displacement, performs no work.

2. ENERGY

In physics the concepts of work and energy are inseparable. When work is done on an object a change takes place in the condition of the object. A bowling ball, Figure 6-2, initially at rest, has work done on it when it is thrown. As a result of the work done on it, the ball attains a rather high speed. We may think of the ball as having absorbed the work done on it. As a consequence of this absorbed work, the ball is capable of doing work on another object or system of objects, in this case the bowling pins.

Because the ball has absorbed work, or alternatively, because the ball is capable of performing work, we say it possesses energy.

The energy of a system is the amount of work absorbed by it, or the amount of work it is capable of performing.

In Figure 6-2, page 77, the work absorbed by the ball causes the ball to move and we say the ball possesses energy of motion or *kinetic energy.* Absorbed work, however, does not always show up as energy of motion. Our warehouseman of Example 1 does 35 joules of work in lifting a box from the floor to the truck. In absorbing this 35 joules of work, the box is capable of giving back the same amount of work, provided we allow it to fall. Because the energy of the elevated box is potentially available to us, we say it has potential energy. **The energy possessed by an object, due to its elevated position, is**

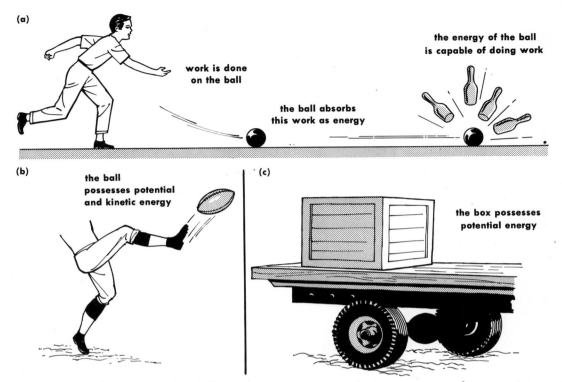

(a)

work is done
on the ball

the ball absorbs
this work as energy

the energy of the ball
is capable of doing work

(b)

the ball
possesses potential
and kinetic energy

(c)

the box possesses
potential energy

Fig. 6-2: (*a*) *An example of the transformation of work into energy and energy into work.* (*b*) *Transformation of work into two forms of mechanical energy.* (*c*) *An elevated object possesses potential energy because work has been done on it.*

called **gravitational potential energy.** Kinetic energy and gravitational potential energy are each a form of *mechanical energy.* It is quite easy to conceive of an object as possessing both of these forms of energy simultaneously. One example would be a football, just after kick-off. We will study in detail both of these forms of energy later in this chapter.

3. FORMS OF ENERGY

We are familiar with many of the other forms which energy may take: chemical energy derived from food sustains all forms of life, and electrical energy is the very foundation of modern technology. Matter itself can now provide us with almost unimaginable quantities of nuclear energy. Other forms of energy, to name but two, are heat energy and magnetic energy. Many

forms will be studied at appropriate points in the text.

Were we to analyse the many forms of energy in relation to their capacity for doing work, we would find that transformation from one form to another is commonplace. In our simple example of the bowling ball, some of the kinetic energy of the ball is transformed into heat produced by the friction between it and the floor.

Heat energy contained in the sun's radiation causes the evaporation of huge quantities of water from our oceans, and this water reappears later as snow and water at higher elevations, thus representing tremendous amounts of gravitational potential energy. The gravitational potential energy possessed by the water in the upper Niagara River becomes kinetic energy at the base of the falls, capable of rotating huge generators which supply us with electrical energy. This electrical energy, in turn, may be transformed into mechanical energy by means of electric motors, or to heat and light energy by other devices.

The kinetic energy possessed by a moving automobile is derived from a transformation of the chemical energy inherent in the gasoline. This chemical energy is available to us only if we ignite the fuel, and we can think of this chemical energy as *potential energy*. Similarly, a battery possesses potential electrical energy, because the energy becomes available to us when we connect the terminals and permit electrical charges to flow. In general, **we may think of potential energy as energy possessed by an object or substance by virtue of its position, condition, or chemical nature.** As we progress in our study of physics we will see that we are largely involved with the interchange of potential and kinetic energy, and their effects on material things.

Units of Energy

Because energy is defined as the ability to do work, units of energy are the same as the units of work. In the MKS system, the unit of energy is the *joule*, and in the British system it is the *foot-pound*. Sometimes in defining extremely small quantities of energy the *erg* is used.

$$1 \text{ erg} = 10^{-7} \text{ joule (exactly)}$$

Energy, in general, cannot be assigned a directional characteristic, and is considered a scalar quantity, as is the work from which it is derived, and the work which it is capable of performing.

4. CONSERVATION OF ENERGY

It was James Joule who showed that whenever one newton-metre of mechanical energy is converted entirely into heat energy, the amount of heat produced is constant. Initially his experiments were carried out by allowing a falling mass to rotate a series of paddle wheels submerged in water, the loss in gravitational potential energy of the mass being converted to heat energy in the water (Figure 6-3). He also found that the same quantity of heat energy was obtained by passing one newton-metre of electrical energy into the water. (We shall find in our study of electricity that electrical energy is measured in newton-metres, or joules). Later experiments showed that when this same amount of heat energy is used to perform mechanical work, one newton-metre of work is done.

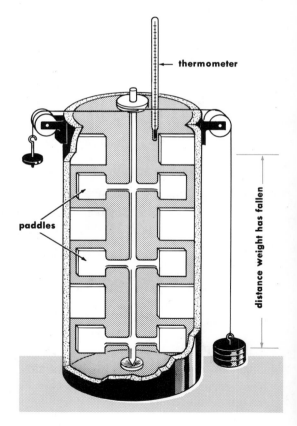

Fig. 6-3: *Apparatus used by Joule to determine the relationship between mechanical work and heat energy.*

The conclusion reached by Joule and his contemporaries was that in an energy transformation, the total energy involved remains constant—none is destroyed nor is additional energy created. Later experiments by others, involving widely different forms of energy, gave added evidence to this effect.

This principle of conservation of energy has come to be accepted as universally true for any interchange of energy, and although no formal proof is possible, no situation has arisen where it has been disproved. As usually stated, the law of conservation of energy is as follows:

Energy can be neither created nor destroyed. In any transformation of energy the total amount of energy is preserved.

For our present purposes we will make use of this law as stated above, but it is important to appreciate that in the present century revolutionary discoveries have necessitated a radical revision of this conservation theory. In 1905, Albert Einstein predicted in his theory of relativity the direct conversion of matter into energy. Years later the prediction was verified in the laboratory and led to the development of the atomic bomb during World War II. Einstein's equation relating mass and energy, referred to in the prologue, is $E = mc^2$, where E is the energy released by the annihilation of a mass m, and c is the speed of light.

The tremendous amount of energy radiated by the sun and other stars is accounted for by this conversion of matter into energy. Each second over four million tons of the sun's mass is converted into energy, which is radiated into space. This conversion of matter into energy has been a continuous process for many billions of years, yet the sun is sufficiently massive (about 2.0×10^{30} kg) that it can continue to lose mass at this rate for more than 10 billion years!

The creation of energy from matter is not in agreement with our earlier statement of the **law of conservation of energy,** which can now be stated in its more general form:

The total amount of energy plus mass in the universe remains unchanged.

Fig. 6-4: *Each second over 4 million tons of the sun's mass is converted into energy. A solar eclipse is shown here.*

Dept. of Mines and Technical Surveys

5. GRAVITATIONAL POTENTIAL ENERGY

In Example 1 the warehouseman has done 35 joules of work in lifting the box to its new position. Because of its elevation the box now possesses gravitational potential energy. We can think of this potential energy as a storage of the work done on it, or alternatively we may think of it as the source of kinetic energy that it develops if it is allowed to fall.

More generally let us consider a mass of m units raised through a vertical distance of h units (Figure 6-5). Then:

work done in lifting box

$\quad$ = lifting force × displacement

$\quad$ = $mg \times h$

$\quad$ = mgh

$\quad$ = potential energy in elevated position

$P.E. = mgh$.

In this formula the quantity mg represents the weight of the object. This weight is expressed in newtons in the MKS system, and in pounds in the British system. The corresponding units of potential energy are joules and foot-pounds, respectively.

Clearly, the potential energy possessed by an elevated object depends upon the level from which we measure its height, this level being called the level of zero potential or simply the reference level. For instance the box of Example 1 possesses 35 joules of potential energy relative to the floor immediately below. Relative to the basement floor, however, its potential energy is much greater because more work would be required to lift it to its present height from that position. In addition, the box would develop greater kinetic energy in falling to that level. *In any statement concerning gravitational potential energy, it is important that the reference level be given or clearly implied.*

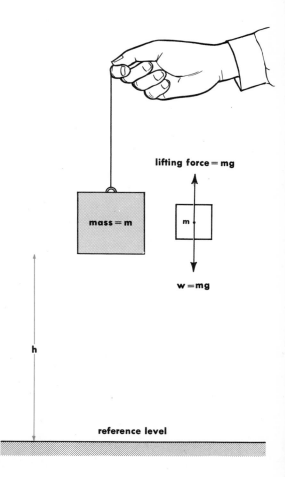

Fig. 6-5: *The gravitational potential energy of the mass is mgh because this is the work done in elevating it.*

EXAMPLE 4

What is the potential energy of the box in Example 1, if it is referred to the basement floor 5.0 metres below the main floor?

Solution:

$\quad mg = 25$ nt

$\quad h = 1.4 + 5.0 = 6.4$ m

$\quad P.E. = mgh = 25 \times 6.4 = 1.6 \times 10^2$ **joules** .

Fig. 6-6: *The gravitational potential energy of the water at the top of Niagara Falls is a vast source of electrical energy. What intermediate transformation of energy takes place?*

EXAMPLE 5

A mass weighing 2.5×10^2 lbs is used on a construction project to drive steel columns into the ground.

(a) What potential energy does it have prior to being dropped from a point 35 ft directly above the top of the column? Consider the top of column as reference level.

(b) What kinetic energy does it possess when it reaches the column?

Solution:

(a) $P.E. = wh$
$$= 2.5 \times 10^2 \times 35 = 8.8 \times 10^3 \text{ ft-lb}.$$

(b) When the mass reaches the column, its gravitational potential energy, using the top of the column as reference level, will be zero. Complete transformation to other forms of energy will have taken place. During its fall, a small amount of its initial potential energy will be transformed to heat energy, caused by friction with air molecules. For practical purposes we may consider this heat energy as negligible, and the kinetic energy just before impact with the column will be 8.8×10^3 ft-lb.

6. KINETIC ENERGY

Any moving object is capable of doing work. A carpenter, in driving a nail, utilizes the kinetic energy of the hammer to overcome the resistive force between nail and wood. A plunging fullback can drive his way through the defence, and we are aware that the greater his speed and mass, the more effective he is in doing this.

It is rather obvious that the amount of work which can be performed by a moving object will be dependent upon its mass, and its velocity. However, the exact relationship is by no means apparent.

We wish now to derive a formula for kinetic energy, and we will make use of our understanding that the kinetic energy of a moving object is derived from work which was done on it.

Consider a box of m kg initially at rest, being pushed by an applied force of F newtons through a distance s metres. After t seconds it will have a velocity v m/sec (Figure 6-7). The frictional force of f newtons between floor and box will offer resistance to the motion.

The man has done Fs joules of work, which now appears as energy in two forms (*i*) heat energy developed due to friction and (*ii*) kinetic energy possessed by the moving box.

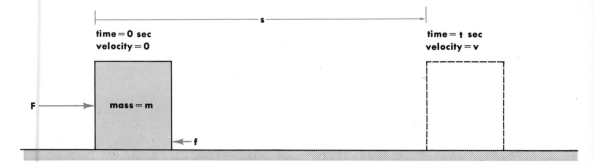

time = 0 sec
velocity = 0

time = t sec
velocity = v

F

mass = m

f

Fig. 6-7: *A mass set in motion possesses kinetic energy equal to the work done on it less any loss due to friction.*

total work done = work done against friction + kinetic energy developed by the box

or,

kinetic energy (K.E.) of box = total work done − work done against friction

$$= Fs - fs = (F-f)s.$$

We shall now make use of the following formulas developed earlier:

$$F_u = ma$$

$$a = \frac{v-u}{t}$$

$$s = \frac{(u+v)}{2}t.$$

In this case, we see that $F_u = F - f.$

Also, since $u = 0$, we have $a = \frac{v}{t}$ and $s = \left(\frac{v}{2}\right)t$

∴ we may write $K.E. = (F-f)s$

$\qquad = ma \cdot s$ where a is the acceleration of the mass

$$= m\left(\frac{v}{t}\right)\left(\frac{v}{2}\right)t$$

$$= \frac{mv^2}{2}.$$

This latter expression gives the work absorbed by the moving box, in terms of its mass and velocity, and is a convenient formula for the kinetic energy of any object.

$$K.E. = \tfrac{1}{2}mv^2$$

This formula gives the kinetic energy in joules, when m is in kg and v is in m/sec.

82

EXAMPLE 6

An automobile of mass 1.0×10^3 kg is travelling at 4.0 m/sec. What is its kinetic energy?

Solution:

$$K.E. = \tfrac{1}{2}mv^2 = \tfrac{1}{2}(1.0 \times 1.0^3)\ (4.0)^2$$
$$= 8.0 \times 10^3 \text{ joules}.$$

EXAMPLE 7

An object of mass 5.0 kg is dropped from a height of 12.0 m. What is its velocity when it strikes the ground?

Solution:

This problem may be solved by using the law of conservation of energy. The initial gravitational potential energy of the box will be transformed entirely into kinetic energy when the object reaches the ground. (We are neglecting the small amount of energy converted to heat by friction with the air.)

$P.E.$ at height of 12.0 m $= mgh$

$$= 5.0 \times 9.80 \times 12.0 \text{ j}.$$

$K.E.$ at ground level $= \tfrac{1}{2}\ mv^2$

$$= \frac{5.0 \times v^2}{2}\ \text{j}.$$

∴ $5.0 \times 9.80 \times 12.0 = \dfrac{5.0 \times v^2}{2}$ \qquad (1)

$$v^2 = 9.80 \times 12.0 \times 2 = 235.$$

Therefore:

$$v = \sqrt{235}$$
$$= 15.3 \text{ m/sec}$$
$$\text{or } \textbf{15 m/sec}$$
(to two significant digits).

Note that the mass of the object (5.0 kg) is a factor on both sides of the equation (1), and does not enter into our final calculation of v. This is in agreement with our findings in Chapter 3, that the velocity of a falling object is independent of its mass.

7. CONSERVATION OF ENERGY IN FLUID FLOW—BERNOULLI'S PRINCIPLE

Interesting illustrations of the law of conservation of energy are provided by certain phenomena that occur as a result of the flow of a fluid, either liquid or gas.

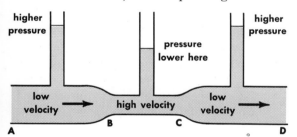

Fig. 6-8: *Pressure variations exist in a liquid when velocity variations are present.*

The Swiss physicist Daniel Bernoulli (1700-1782) was the first to investigate in detail the flow of a liquid through a pipe of variable diameter, such as that shown in Figure 6-8. The vertical pipes, called man-ometers, are indicators of fluid pressure, the level of liquid in each manometer being a measure of the pressure at that point in the pipe. Bernoulli observed that at the narrow portions of the pipe the pressure was lower than it was at the wider portions.

A simple explanation of this behaviour, using the law of conservation of energy, rests on an understanding of the following two points:

(1) Because the liquid is incompressible, the quantity of water leaving at point D each second must equal the quantity which enters at point A in that time. Hence the water must *increase* in velocity while passing through the narrow tube BC, much as the water from a wide river speeds up as it empties into a narrow gorge.

(2) *Water, under pressure, possesses potential energy.* This can be seen by considering Figure 6-9 (a). Here, a piston exerts a force on the liquid in the closed container, causing an increased pressure in the fluid, which in turn is transmitted to the walls of the container.

If allowed to flow, as in Figure 6-9 (b), the water would be ejected in a stream with rather high velocity, and correspondingly high kinetic energy. Simultaneously, the pressure in the fluid would decrease causing a decrease in the potential energy of the fluid. *The kinetic energy is obtained at the expense of the potential energy due to pressure.*

Returning now to Figure 6-8, a mass of water entering at point A possesses kinetic energy due to its motion, and potential

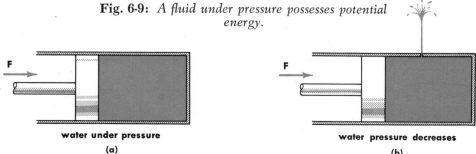

Fig. 6-9: *A fluid under pressure possesses potential energy.*

water under pressure
(a)

water pressure decreases
(b)

83

energy due to its pressure. From A to B each of these components of energy will remain constant (we are assuming that frictional effects are negligible). On entering section BC, however, this mass of water speeds up, with a corresponding increase in kinetic energy, at the expense of its potential energy, the total energy of the mass remaining constant. The pressure in section BC, an indication of the water's potential energy, therefore drops accordingly.

This relationship between the velocity and pressure of a smoothly flowing fluid is called **Bernoulli's Principle** and may be stated as follows:

When a fluid undergoes an increase in velocity, its pressure decreases, and conversely a decrease in velocity is accompanied by an increase in pressure.

An understanding of pressure variations in a tube such as that of Figure 6-8 can also be had using Newton's Laws of Motion as follows:

The pressure at any point in a fluid is a measure of the forces exerted on a particle at that point, by the particles surrounding it. Figure 6-10 illustrates a particle in each of three different positions. In Figure 6-10(a) a particle moving from left to right in section AB, does so at constant speed; hence no unbalanced force acts on it. The fluid behind the particle exerts on it a force F_1, equal and opposite to the force F_2 exerted on it by the fluid in front of it. (We are neglecting the friction encountered by the particle.)

In Figure 6-10(b) the particle enters the narrow section BC and, as we have seen,

speeds up. This acceleration to the right indicates the presence of an unbalanced force acting in this direction. Hence the force behind the particle (F_1) exceeds the resisting force in front of it, F_3.

In Figure 6-10(c) the particle enters the wide portion CD and slows down, that is, it undergoes an acceleration to the left. An unbalanced force acts on the particle, to the left, indicating that the resisting force F_5 exceeds the force F_4 acting to the right.

The force vectors in Figure 6-10 can be considered vectors of pressure, since pressure is merely force per unit area. We see that pressure is a minimum in the section BC, where the velocity is greatest.

Applications of Bernoulli's Principle

1. *The Airfoil*: An airplane has great masses of air driven across its wings by a propeller, or by the forward thrust given to it by its jet engine. Figure 6-11 shows the cross-section of an aircraft wing (airfoil), with the air moving from left to right relative to the wing. The curvature of the upper surface of the wing produces a pronounced "narrowed-tube" effect similar to the portion BC of Figure 6-8. Consequently, the air along this surface increases in velocity, compared to the velocity of the air passing along the lower surface. This increase in air velocity is attended by a decrease in the pressure it exerts, and as a consequence the total force exerted upwards against the lower surface exceeds that exerted downwards against the upper surface.

In the diagram the vector R represents the unbalanced force caused by these differences

Fig. 6-10: *Newton's Laws of Motion can be used to predict pressure variations in a tube of nonuniform cross-section. The horizontal forces acting on a fluid particle are shown here for three locations of the particle.*

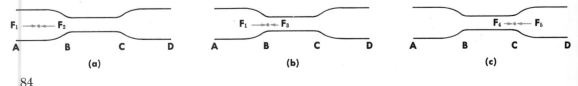

84

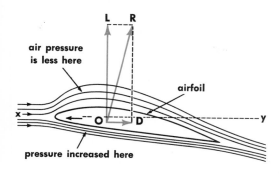

Fig. 6-11: *Reduced pressure on the upper surface of an airfoil results in an upward force (L) that tends to lift the aircraft.*

in pressure exerted on the wing's surfaces. The force is not a vertical force, but can be thought of as composed of a vertical lift (*L*) and a horizontal drag (*D*). It is when the force *L* exceeds the weight of the plane that the aircraft will rise.

What relationship would the lift have to the weight of the aircraft when in level flight?

Why is the aircraft wing tilted upwards when in takeoff position? The angle created by the wing's lower surface and the horizontal is called the "angle of attack".

2. Curve of a ball due to spin: A good tennis player will deliberately impart a top spin to a strong forehand drive in order to keep it in the court. At other times an underspin given the ball allows him an extra split-second to get back into position while the ball curves upwards.

Similarly, a ball thrown by a pitcher can be very deceptive to the batter when it curves away from the plate, or curves in a vertical plane.

An understanding of why a spinning ball curves can be had by considering the motion of air relative to the ball. In Figure 6-12 the spinning ball is moving to the right and, relative to the ball, air is passing over it from right to left. The upper surface of the

ball is spinning in the same direction as the air current is moving, causing an increase in the air speed of this surface. Hence, the air pressure on this surface is relatively low.

The lower surface, however, is moving counter to the air current, resulting in a lower air speed for this surface, with attendant higher pressure.

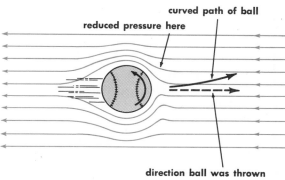

Fig. 6-12: *A spinning ball provides an interesting illustration of Bernoulli's Principle.*

The force exerted on the lower surface exceeds that on the upper surface, and the ball, in this case, curves upwards as shown.

There is another value to the spin of a ball, not directly related to Bernoulli's Principle. A ball moving through the air has a wall of air in front of it and a partial vacuum immediately behind it, and the tendency of the ball is to stop due to this backward force. If the ball is spinning, and has other than a perfectly smooth surface, some of the air in front of the ball will be carried around behind it, partially equalizing the pressure on the front and rear surfaces of the ball, thereby resulting in far greater "distance." This is a major reason for the dimples on a golf ball.

Industrial applications of Bernoulli's Principle are numerous. One such application is the spray gun, a simple form of which is

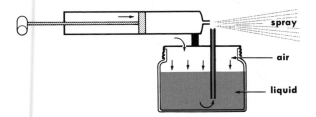

shown in Figure 6-13. Liquid in the container is under normal atmospheric pressure. A high-speed jet of air is blown over the upper opening of the vertical tube, reducing the pressure in this tube. The liquid is forced up this tube where, at the opening, it is broken into a fine spray by the air jet.

8. THE SIMPLE PENDULUM

The simple pendulum provides an example of continuous transformation from gravitational potential energy to kinetic energy, and vice versa. Such a pendulum is illustrated in Figure 6-14, in each of three different positions. The bob is pulled from its rest position B to position A, thus raising it a vertical distance h. In this position, the bob possesses potential energy mgh (referred to its initial position) where m is the mass of the bob. If allowed to vibrate the bob will attain kinetic energy which will be a maximum at position B. In passing from B to C, this kinetic energy will be transformed to potential energy, which will be a maximum at point C.

Were there no energy losses, the vibrations would continue indefinitely, with the bob rising each time to the same height h. In practice some of the energy of the system is lost in friction at the support and in the air, and the vibrations gradually diminish in amplitude.

How would you determine the velocity at B, if you were given the value of h? Example 7 will provide a clue.

9. POWER

The student will have noted that our definition of work does not involve the time interval during which the work was performed. A similar statement holds for

Fig. 6-14: *A simple pendulum in three positions.*

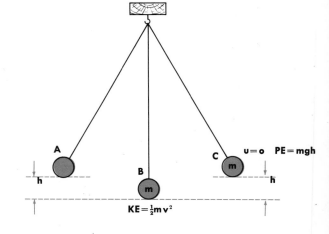

energy. Work and energy are independent of time; the loading of one box onto the truck, in Example 1, required 35 joules of work regardless of how quickly or slowly the box was lifted.

When we consider the time required to do the work, we are then concerned with the *rate* of doing work, a concept called power. **Power is the rate of doing work, or the rate of using energy.** If 3.0 seconds are required to do 35 joules of work, the rate at which the work is done is 11.7 or 12 joules per second.

$$\text{Power} = \frac{\text{work done}}{\text{elapsed time}}$$

or:

$$\text{Power} = \frac{\text{energy used}}{\text{elapsed time}}.$$

Units of Power

In the MKS system, the unit of power is the joule per second, usually referred to as a *watt*, in honour of the Scottish engineer James Watt (1736-1819).

1 watt = 1 joule/sec .

A larger unit of power is the *kilowatt* (kw), equivalent to 1000 watts.

In the British system, the basic unit of power is the *foot-pound per second* but a larger unit, *the horsepower* (hp), is in more common use. The horsepower is defined as being equivalent to 550 ft-lb/sec.

1 hp = 550 ft-lb/sec .

The kilowatt and the horsepower are very common units of power, and it is frequently necessary to convert from one to the other. Their relationship is:

1 hp = 0.746 kw .

EXAMPLE 8

A rope tow pulls 30 skiers averaging 1.50×10^2 lb up a hill in 25 seconds. If the hill is 225 ft high determine the power of the engine which operates the tow.

Solution:

Work done in 25 seconds

$$= P.E. \text{ gained by skiers}.$$

$$mgh = (1.50 \times 10^2) \times 30 \times 225 \text{ ft-lb}.$$

$$\text{Power} = \frac{1.50 \times 10^2 \times 30 \times 225}{25} \text{ft-lb/sec}$$

$$= 4.05 \times 10^4 \text{ ft-lb/sec}$$

$$= \frac{4.05 \times 10^4}{550} \text{ hp}$$

$$= \textbf{74 hp}.$$

This power represents the rate at which the engine is supplying energy to the rope tow.

The engine itself would have to be supplied with energy at a greater rate than 74 hp because of frictional losses in the machine. The ratio of output power to input power is called the *efficiency* of the machine. In this example, if the electrical energy input was at the rate of 100 hp, the efficiency of the engine would be 74%.

$$\text{Efficiency} = \frac{\text{energy output}}{\text{energy input}} = \frac{\text{power output}}{\text{power input}}.$$

The efficiency of machines is expressed as a percentage.

EXAMPLE 9

A pump is required to lift 1.8×10^3 kg of water per minute from a well 4.0 m deep and eject it at a speed of 4.0 m/sec:

(a) What is the work done per second in lifting the water?

(b) What is the work done per second in ejecting the water?

(c) What input horsepower to the motor is required assuming its efficiency is 60%?

Solution:

(a) Mass lifted per second $= \dfrac{1.8 \times 10^3}{60}$ kg

$$= 30 \text{ kg} .$$

Work done in lifting this water

$$= mgh$$
$$= 30 \times 9.8 \times 4.0 = 1176 \text{ j}$$
$$= \mathbf{1.2 \times 10^3 \text{ j}}$$

(to **2** significant digits) .

(b) Each second a mass of 30 kg of water is given a speed of 4.0 m/sec.

$$K.E. = \tfrac{1}{2}mv^2 = \tfrac{1}{2} \times (30) \times (4.0)^2$$
$$= 240 \text{ j}$$
$$= \mathbf{2.4 \times 10^2 \text{ j}}$$

(to **2** significant figures) .

(c) Total work per second $= 1176 + 240$
$$= 1416 \text{ joules}$$
or **1.4×10^3 joules**

(to **2** significant digits) .

$\therefore$ power $= 1.4 \times 10^3$ watts $= 1.4$ kw

$$= \frac{1.4}{.746} \text{ hp} = 1.9 \text{ hp} .$$

$\therefore$ input power required for pump

$$= \frac{1.9}{0.6} \text{ hp} = \mathbf{3.2 \text{ hp}}$$

(to **2** significant digits) .

From the relationship

$$\text{power} = \frac{\text{energy}}{\text{elapsed time}}$$

we may write

$$\text{energy} = \text{power} \times \text{time} .$$

Thus, energy units may be expressed as the product of units of power and time. For example:

$$1 \text{ joule} = 1 \text{ watt-second} .$$

In specifying electrical energy, the kilowatt hour is extensively used.

1 kilowatt hour (kwh)

$$= 1000 \text{ watts} \cdot 3600 \text{ seconds}$$
$$= 3.6 \times 10^6 \text{ watt-seconds}$$
$$= 3.6 \times 10^6 \text{ joules}$$
$$\mathbf{1 \text{ kwh} = 3.6 \times 10^6 \text{ j} .}$$

WORK: The product of force and the displacement parallel to this force.

$$W = Fs$$

ENERGY: The ability to do work.

GRAVITATIONAL POTENTIAL ENERGY: The energy possessed by an object by virtue of its elevated position.

$$P.E. = mgh$$

where mg = weight of object

h = the height of the object measured from some reference level .

KINETIC ENERGY: The energy possessed by an object by virtue of its motion.

$$K.E. = \tfrac{1}{2}mv^2$$

where m = mass of object
v = velocity of object

UNITS OF WORK AND ENERGY: In the MKS system: the joule. In the British system: the foot-pound.

1 joule = 1 newton-metre
= 1 watt-second.
1 kilowatt hour (kwh) = 3.6×10^6 watt-secs or joules.

LAW OF CONSERVATION OF ENERGY: Energy can be neither created nor destroyed. In any transformation of energy, the total amount of energy is preserved.

BERNOULLI'S PRINCIPLE: When a fluid undergoes an increase in velocity, its pressure decreases, and conversely, a decrease in velocity is accompanied by an increase in pressure.

POWER: The rate of doing work, or the rate of using energy.

UNITS OF POWER: In the MKS system: joules/sec = watts.
In the British system: ft-lb/sec.

550 ft-lb/sec = 1 hp.

Conversion relationship:

1 hp = 0.746 kw.

EXERCISE A

1. Define the term work, as it is used in physics.

2. (*a*) What becomes of the work performed on a system?

   (*b*) Under what conditions will an applied force perform no work on an object?

3. (*a*) State the equivalent value of the joule in terms of MKS units of force and displacement.

   (*b*) Express this in terms of the fundamental MKS units (mass, length, time).

4. List the type of potential energy possessed by the following systems: (*a*) fuel oil, (*b*) transistor radio, (*c*) water approaching Niagara Falls, (*d*) an atomic pile, (*e*) a star, (*f*) a weight lifter (human), (*g*) a piece of lodestone, (*h*) a piece of pie, (*i*) an infra-red lamp, (*j*) a puck held by a referee during a face-off, (*k*) a stretched rubber band.

5. What type of energy is associated with (*a*) motion?

   (*b*) elevation?

6. Describe the energy transformations produced by a swinging pendulum.

7. State the meaning of the Law of Conservation of Energy.

8. What additional information is needed when one is calculating the power developed from the work accomplished?

9. What is the relationship between horsepower and kilowatts.

10. A weekend employee of a supermarket erects a pyramid of tins containing tomato juice. Can you name three forms of energy possessed by the top tin?

11. Mountain roads are usually designed to wind around the hill gradually rather than go straight up.   Explain why.

12. Explain, in terms of work and energy, how a child can pump a swing from rest position to a height almost that of the crossbar, or greater.

13. A rubber ball is dropped from a height of 4 ft and bounces to a height of 3 ft.
    (a) What change has taken place in the gravitational potential energy of the ball?
    (b) How is this accounted for?

14. A spring is kept compressed by means of a wire joining its ends.   The spring is placed in an acid where it dissolves.
    (a) What name would you give to the energy possessed by the spring while compressed?
    (b) What do you think becomes of this energy after the spring dissolves?

15. Predict what will occur in each of the following cases, and explain:
    (a) Two ping-pong balls are each suspended by pieces of thread affixed to them by wax. The balls are held two inches apart and air is blown through the space separating them.
    (b) A sheet of paper is held on the palm of the hand and air is blown over the top surface.

16. An accumulation of ice on the wings of an aircraft can create difficulty in maintaining altitude even though the weight of the ice is small compared with that of the plane. Explain.

17. (a) What spin should be imparted to a golf ball in order to attain maximum distance?
    (b) A right-handed golfer "slices" the ball when it curves to his right.   A curve to the left is called a "hook".   Analyse these trajectories in terms of spin of the ball and deduce how they could be corrected.

EXERCISE B

Consider all numerical data to be accurate to the number of digits shown.

1. A force of 75 lb is required to push a piano weighing 800 lb.   How much work is done in pushing the piano 12 ft along the floor?

2. A trunk weighs 150 lb and a force of 30 lb is required to slide it on a level floor:
   (a) How much work is required to slide it 5.0 ft?
   (b) What work is required to lift it 5.0 ft?

3. What is the potential energy of a 1600-lb elevator at the top of the Empire State Building, 1248 ft above street level?

4. A honeybee requires a force of 1.0×10^{-4} N to drag a dead drone a distance of 1.5×10^{-1} m outside the entrance to the beehive
   (a) Calculate the work done by the honeybee.
   (b) The drone's mass is 5.0×10^{-4} kg and the hive platform is 1.0×10^{-1} m above the ground. Find the potential energy of the drone just as he is shoved off.
   (c) What is the drone's kinetic energy on reaching the ground as a result of the honeybee's shove?

5. A construction worker weighing 180 lb carries a 100-lb bag of cement on his back and climbs a 20-ft ladder in 20 sec to the floor 10 ft above. Find:
   (a) the total work done by the man
   (b) the rate at which the work is done.

6. Calculate the potential energy possessed by 20.0 ft³ of water at the top of Niagara Falls. (One ft³ of water weighs 62.4 lb and Niagara Falls is 167 ft high.)

7. A pendulum 1.0 m long is pulled aside to the position where the bob has been raised vertically a distance of 10 cm. If the bob weighs 100 grams, calculate:
   (a) the potential energy of the bob before release
   (b) the kinetic energy of the bob at its lowest position
   (c) the velocity of the bob at the lowest position.

8. When construction firms wreck old buildings, a large pendulum arrangement is frequently used. If the ball of the equipment suspended on a cable weighs 1000 kg and is raised 3.0 metres vertically when it is pulled to one side, find:
   (a) the kinetic energy of the ball as it strikes the building
   (b) the velocity of the ball on impact
   (c) the work done by the building in stopping the ball
   (d) the force exerted by the wall if the ball penetrates the stone 5.0 cm.

9. An electron has a mass of 9.1×10^{-31} kg. It moves in a vacuum tube at a speed of 1.0×10^{4} m/sec. Calculate its kinetic energy.

10. What is the difference in energy possessed by a puck of mass 0.20 kg travelling along the ice at 15 m/sec, and one propelled by a slap shot travelling at the same speed but 2.0 metres above the ice?

11. A 12-volt storage battery rated at 30 ampere-hours possesses 1.3×10^{6} joules of potential chemical energy. If all of this energy could be completely converted to mechanical energy, to what height could it raise a 10-kg mass?

12. A projectile of mass 14 kg is fired from a mortar whose length is 3.0 m. It leaves the barrel of the mortar with a muzzle velocity of 630 m/sec. Calculate:

    (*a*) the kinetic energy of the projectile as it leaves the barrel

    (*b*) the average force in newtons acting on the shell as it was fired.

    (Remember that the total work, disregarding friction, is equal to the energy attained.)

13. An object sliding along the floor possesses the same amount of energy as does a stationary ball of the same mass, elevated 1.0 m above the floor. What is the speed of the sliding object? (Let the mass of each object be m kg.)

14. An object of mass 50 g is raised a height of 2.5×10^{-1} m in 0.50 sec. Calculate the power developed.

15. An automobile engine is rated at 320 horsepower:

    (*a*) Calculate its power in kilowatts.

    (*b*) Find the work done in 15 minutes when the engine is working at its rated power. Express your answer in both MKS and British units.

16. (*a*) What is the minimum horsepower required of an engine which raises 500 gallons of water per minute from a depth of 160 feet (1 gallon weighs 10 lb)?

    (*b*) What input power is required if the engine is 25% efficient.

17. An electric heater is rated at 2000 watts when used on a 220-volt supply:

    (*a*) What is the equivalent rating in hp?

    (*b*) If the appliance were left on for one hour, how many joules (watt secs) of energy would be used?

18. How long would it take a 150 hp motor to raise 1.0 ton of ore from the bottom of a mine shaft 1100 ft deep?

19. If energy costs 5 cents per kwh, what does it cost to operate a 10 hp motor for 8.0 hr?

20. Using the method of Example 7, derive a formula for the velocity at ground level attained by an object when allowed to fall from a height *h* (neglect air resistance).

21. In the illustration, the 2.0 kg mass is allowed to fall:

    (*a*) What was its initial gravitational potential energy?

    (*b*) What will be the gravitational potential energy of the 1.0 kg mass when the 2.0 kg mass reaches the floor?

    (*c*) What does the difference of these energies represent?

    (*d*) Determine the speed of the masses when the 2.0 kg mass hits the floor.

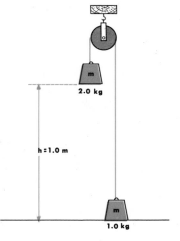

For the following questions: speed of light $= 3.00 \times 10^8$ m/sec .

22. How much energy would be produced if 1.00 kg of matter could be entirely converted into energy?

23. If the sun possesses 2.0×10^{30} kg of matter, calculate the energy available due to the conversion of matter into energy.

24. When high-velocity hydrogen nuclei are fired at a certain isotope of lithium, sometimes they enter the lithium nucleus and the result is the formation of two helium nuclei. In this process, for each hydrogen nucleus combining with each lithium atom, there is a loss of mass of 3.06×10^{-23} kg. Calculate the energy released.

Chapter 6

Work, Energy, Power

▶ Experiment 5

To determine the kinetic energy of a falling object at a given instant, and its loss in potential energy up to that instant.

Recording timer kit

6-volt d-c source with rheostat

C-clamp

1 kilogram mass

Stop watch

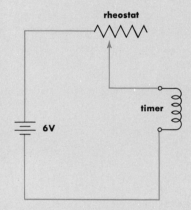

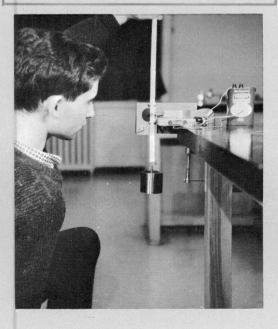

Procedure

1. Clamp the recording timer to the side of the table so that the tape can feed through it vertically.

2. Reinforce one end of the timer tape with Scotch tape and firmly attach this end to the 1 kg mass. Cut off about 6 ft of the tape and set it in the timer as shown.

3. Hold the tape vertically, with the mass immediately below the timer. Have your partner set the timer in operation, and allow a heavy initial dot to be made on the tape.

4. Release the tape. After the impact of the mass with the floor, set the tape aside. *Do not adjust the rheostat.*

5. Following the procedure outlined in Experiment 1, Chapter 2, determine the period of vibration of the timer.

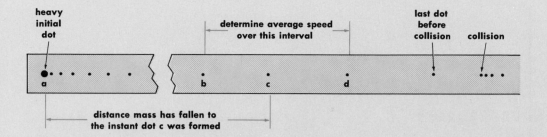

heavy
initial
dot

determine average speed
over this interval

last dot
before
collision

collision

a   b   c   d

distance mass has fallen to
the instant dot c was formed

Analysis

1. Examine the tape. What type of motion is represented by the pattern of dots up to the moment of impact? Determine which dot was the first to occur *after* collision.

2. Choose three *consecutive* dots which occurred just prior to impact. We will refer to these dots as *b, c, d* respectively, and to the heavy initial dot as *a*. (Do not choose the dot that occurred immediately prior to impact).

3. Determine the *average speed* of the tape during the time interval $b-d$. (If necessary, refer to Experiment 2.) This is equal to the *instantaneous speed* of the tape, and hence the instantaneous speed of the falling mass, at the instant dot *c* was formed.

4. Determine the kinetic energy possessed by the mass at the instant dot *c* was being formed.

5. When dot *c* was being formed, the mass had fallen a distance equal to that between dots *a* and *c*. Use this distance to determine the loss in potential energy of the mass up to that instant.

6. Compare the two values of energies determined above. How do you account for the difference? Express this difference as a percentage of the loss of potential energy. If it is less than 10%, your results are good.

7. This analysis can be repeated, using another set of three consecutive dots.

Chapter 7

Machines

1. PARALLEL FORCES

Up to this point in our study of mechanics, we have been involved with the effects of forces acting at a single point. We are now prepared to study the effect of one or more forces acting on an object at different points. We will confine our study to the more common situation where the forces acting on the object are *parallel forces.*

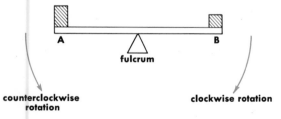

Fig. 7-1: *The load at each end of the beam tends to produce rotation about the fulcrum. Rotational equilibrium exists when these tendencies balance.*

A simple case of a body acted upon by parallel forces is shown in Figure 7-1. Here, a bar is subjected to a downward force at each end, and is supported at an intermediate point. As we shall see later in the chapter, such a device is called a *lever of the first class.* Quite likely our first encounter with this simple machine is a playground seesaw.

The effect of the load at each end of the lever is to tend to produce rotation about the point of support, or *fulcrum.* That is, the load at *A* tends to produce *counterclockwise rotation*, while that at *B* tends to produce *clockwise rotation.* If each of these tendencies is equal in magnitude, the lever will not rotate, and the system is said to be in *rotational equilibrium.*

2. MOMENT, OR TORQUE

The turning effect produced by a force acting on an object free to rotate about a point of support, is called its *moment* about that point or *torque*. The magnitude of this moment depends on two factors: the magnitude of the force, and its distance from the point of support. For this reason the moment of a force is defined as the product of these two factors.

$$\frac{Moment\ of\ a\ force}{about\ a\ point} = \frac{Force \times distance\ of\ the\ force}{from\ the\ point}$$

The unit to be used in describing a moment, will be the product of units of force and distance. Most commonly the pound-foot and the metre-newton are used. You will note that these are the same units used in describing work, but the concepts of work and turning moment are quite different. The joule, which is equivalent to a newton-metre of work, must never be used in connection with moments.

EXAMPLE 1

A 75-lb boy is located 8.0 ft from the fulcrum of a seesaw, which is supported at its centre. On the opposite side of the fulcrum, and located 6.0 ft from it, is a boy of 120 lb.

(a) What is the moment of each boy, about the fulcrum?

(b) In what direction will the seesaw rotate?

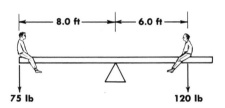

Solution:

(a) Moment of 75-lb boy about fulcrum
$$= 75 \times 8.0 = 6.0 \times 10^2 \text{ lb ft (counterclockwise)}.$$
Moment of 120-lb boy about fulcrum
$$= 120 \times 6.0 = 7.2 \times 10^2 \text{ lb ft (clockwise)}.$$

(b) Because the clockwise moment is the greater, the seesaw will rotate clockwise, as viewed in our diagram.

In this problem, we have not taken the weight of the seesaw into consideration. This factor will be considered later.

3. CONDITIONS FOR EQUILIBRIUM

The method of Example 1 can be extended to an object acted upon by any number of parallel forces. It is apparent that if the object is free to rotate, no rotation will take place if the sum of all clockwise moments about the point of rotation is equal to the sum of all the counterclockwise moments about that point.

EXAMPLE 2

In the diagram, what is the value of x such that rotational equilibrium exists?

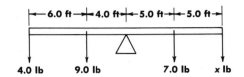

Solution:

Taking moments about the point of support:

Counterclockwise moments:
$$= (4.0 \text{ lb} \times 10 \text{ ft}) + (9.0 \text{ lb} \times 4 \text{ ft}) = 76 \text{ lb ft}.$$

Clockwise moments:
$$= (7.0 \text{ lb} \times 5.0 \text{ ft}) + (x \text{ lb} \times 10 \text{ ft})$$
$$= 35 + 10x \text{ lb ft}.$$

For rotational equilibrium: $35 + 10x = 76$
$$10x = 41$$
$$x = \textbf{4.1 lb.}$$

In the drawing accompanying Example 2, the bar is shown as acted upon by four downward forces totalling 24.1 lb. Obviously the point of support must be exerting an equal force upward to prevent the bar from falling in a downward direction. In other words, in accordance with Newton's First Law, the unbalanced force acting on the bar is zero, since it is in a state of rest. The upward force of 24.1 lb, exerted by the fulcrum, has no rotational effect on the bar, since this force passes through the point of support.

Because the bar is moving neither upward nor downward, it is said to be in *translational equilibrium*. The word translation here indicates movement from one place to another.

When a body is neither moved nor rotated by the forces acting on it, we say it is in equilibrium.

A body can be in equilibrium only under the following conditions:

(1) *The sum of the forces pulling the body in any direction must equal the sum of the forces pulling the body in the opposite direction (translational equilibrium).*

(2) *The sum of the clockwise moments about any point must equal the sum of the counterclockwise moments about that point (rotational equilibrium).*

A given body may possess both of these conditions, one of them, or perhaps none. Describe the state of equilibrium in each of the following cases:

(a) the propellor blade of an aircraft warming up before take-off

(b) a football shortly after being kicked end-over-end

(c) a person jumping from the second floor of a burning building.

4. CENTRE OF GRAVITY

In Examples 1 and 2, the weight of the suspended beam has not been taken into consideration. Quite often, however, it is necessary to do so.

Let us consider a uniform bar, such as a metre stick. We may think of it as being made up of a very large number of particles of wood, each particle having its own weight. If we suspend the metre stick at its midpoint, we find that it balances. The rotational effect of the particles to the left of the midpoint counteracts the rotational effect of the particles on the other side. We may think of the entire weight of the stick as concentrated at that point, since the entire stick can be kept in equilibrium by supporting it at that point.

The point at which the entire weight of a body may be considered to act, is called the centre of gravity of the body. For a uniform object, such as the metre stick, the centre of gravity is located at the geometric centre.

For nonuniform objects, the exact position of the centre of gravity is not obvious, but may be located approximately by finding the point of balance as for the metre stick.

An interesting method for finding the centre of a thin irregular object such as that shown in Figure 7-2, is as follows:

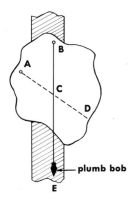

Fig. 7-2: *Determining the centre of gravity of a thin irregularly-shaped object.*

(1) Drill a small hole at *B*, near the edge of the object, and using a nail suspend it from that point.

(2) By means of a plumb bob suspended from the nail, determine the line *BE*. The centre of gravity must lie somewhere along this line, because the sum of the moments about point *B* of all the particles to the right of *BE* is equal and opposite to the sum of the moments of the particles to the left of *BE*.

(3) Repeat the process for another small hole, thus determining another line *AD*, along which the centre of gravity lies. The intersection of these two lines allows us to determine point *C*, the centre of gravity.

It is interesting to note that the centre of gravity of a body may lie entirely apart from the body. The simplest example would be that of a doughnut. Here the centre of gravity is located near the geometric centre. Similarly in the case of a tennis ball, the centre of gravity is located inside the object at a point where none of the mass is actually located.

The following example illustrates the use of the concept of centre of gravity.

EXAMPLE 3

Two hunters carry a lion from the jungle, using a 14 ft uniform rod that weighs 25 lb. If the lion weighs 175 lb and is supported 6.0 ft from one end of the rod, how much of the total load is shared by each hunter?

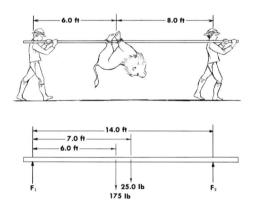

Solution:

The system has two points of support. For our purpose we may consider either one as a fulcrum about which rotational equilibrium exists. Taking moments about the point of support at the left:

Clockwise moments $= (175 \times 6.0) + (25 \times 7.0)$
$$= 1225 \text{ lb ft}.$$

Counterclockwise moments $= 14F_2$, where F_2 is the upward force applied by the hunter at the right.

$$\therefore \ 14F_2 = 1225$$
and $\quad F_2 = 87.5 \text{ lb or } \textbf{88 lb}.$

Notice that we have not taken into account the force F_1. The reason is that F_1 does not produce any rotational effect about the left support, since its line of action passes through this point.

Because the total system is in translational equilibrium, the sum of F_1 and F_2 must equal the sum of the downward forces, 200 lb.

$$\therefore \ F_1 = 200 - 88 = 112 \text{ lb}$$
$\qquad\qquad$ or **110 lb** to two significant
$\qquad\qquad\qquad\qquad\qquad$ digits.

Similar results would have been obtained by taking moments about the support at the right. The student should check this.

5. USE OF MACHINES

Machines are devices used to *transform energy* from one form to another. Thus, an electric generator transforms mechanical energy to electrical energy. Machines are also used to *transfer energy* from place to place. Belts and pulleys, connecting rods and crank shafts of prime movers, and driving shafts, together with their accompanying gear, are examples of such machines. Still another use of machines is to *multiply force*. Examples are the automobile jack that multiplies the lifting force by a large factor and any system of pulleys arranged to multiply force. In some cases it is desirable that the force be decreased in order to increase speed. A simple example is the bicycle drive. The conservation of energy does not allow both an *increase of speed* and an increase of force, as a little thought on the part of the reader will confirm. Machines are also used merely to *change the direction* of a force. A single pulley aloft is an example. The pulley allows a downward pull on a rope to exercise an upward pull upon the load without multiplication of the force.

6. MECHANICAL ADVANTAGE

The *force applied* to the machine is understood to be the force that the operator applies to make the machine work. This force is frequently called the *effort*. Such a force or effort is supplied by the machine to raise or move a weight, stretch a spring, or move a conductor through a magnetic field. The force moved is referred to as the *load* or *resistance*.

During the operation of the machine, both the applied force and the load are displaced. Let the displacements of the applied force and the load be S_E and S_R. The *ideal mechanical advantage*, IMA, of a machine is the ratio of the distance that the applied force moves, to the distance that the load moves, or $\dfrac{S_E}{S_R}$. Since friction results from the contact of moving parts, the actual mechanical advantage is somewhat less than this ideal mechanical advantage. The *actual mechanical advantage*, AMA, can be determined as the ratio of the load to the applied force, or $\dfrac{F_R}{F_E}$.

7. EFFICIENCY OF MACHINES

The fundamental purpose of any machine is to do useful work. In order that a machine should do work, it is necessary to supply work or energy to operate the machine. Because of friction and other nonideal features of actual machines, some of the energy supplied to operate the machine is always wasted and never appears as useful work done by the machine. The *efficiency* of machines is evaluated as the ratio of the useful work done by a machine in a given time to the work (or energy) supplied to operate the machine in the same time. Expressing this algebraically:

$$\text{Efficiency} = \frac{\text{useful work done by the machine}}{\text{work done on the machine}}$$
$$= \frac{\text{work output}}{\text{work input}}.$$

It is understood that the output and input work are found for the same period of time. It follows that the efficiency is sometimes more conveniently expressed as:

$$\text{Efficiency} = \frac{\text{useful power delivered by the machine}}{\text{power supplied to operate the machine}}$$
$$= \frac{\text{power output}}{\text{power input}}.$$

Using the notation which was used in discussing the mechanical advantage, we find that the output work is $F_R S_R$ and the input work $F_E S_E$; so the efficiency is given by:

$$\text{Efficiency} = \frac{F_R S_R}{F_E S_E} = \frac{\dfrac{F_R}{F_E}}{\dfrac{S_E}{S_R}} = \frac{\text{AMA}}{\text{IMA}}.$$

That is, a special expression for the efficiency is the ratio shown by the fraction: the actual mechanical advantage over the ideal mechanical advantage. This expression must *not* be taken as the definition of efficiency.

8. FUNDAMENTAL TYPES OF MACHINES

Machines, regardless of their complexity, can usually be considered as combinations of six fundamental types: *lever, pulley, wheel and axle, inclined plane, wedge,* and *screw*.

As we shall see, the pulley and wheel and axle are adaptations of the lever, while the wedge and screw are derived from the inclined plane. Hence, we may regard the lever and the inclined plane as the most basic of the simple machines.

9. THE LEVER

A lever is a rigid bar which is free to turn about a fixed point called the *fulcrum*. The lever in its simplest form is illustrated in Figure 7-3. The applied force is at the left-hand end, whereas the load lies on the right-hand end of this lever. When the force is applied, the lever is moved as shown in the illustration. If the angle through which it is moved is small, the arc S_E and the arc S_R

become straight lines and the work supplied to the lever in this small displacement is $F_E S_E$, while the useful work done (the raising of the load in this case) is $F_R S_R$. The IMA is $\dfrac{S_E}{S_R}$, whereas the actual mechanical advantage is $\dfrac{F_R}{F_E}$. From similar triangles it is evident in the illustration that $\dfrac{S_E}{S_R}$ is equal to $\dfrac{l_E}{l_R}$; therefore the IMA can be found as $\dfrac{l_E}{l_R}$.

In the lever shown in Figure 7-3 the fulcrum lies between the load and the applied force. This need not be the case and Figure 7-4 shows the lever arrangements which are classified as first, second, and third class.

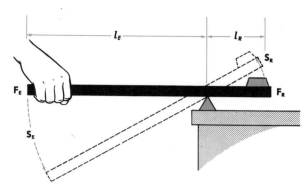

Fig. 7-3: *When the effort force (F_E) moves through a distance S_E, the resistance (F_R) moves a distance S_R. Neglecting frictional losses, the work done by the effort force is equal to that done against the resistance.*

Fig. 7-4: *Examples of levers of the first, second, and third class. Note the relative position of effort, resistance, and fulcrum for each class.*

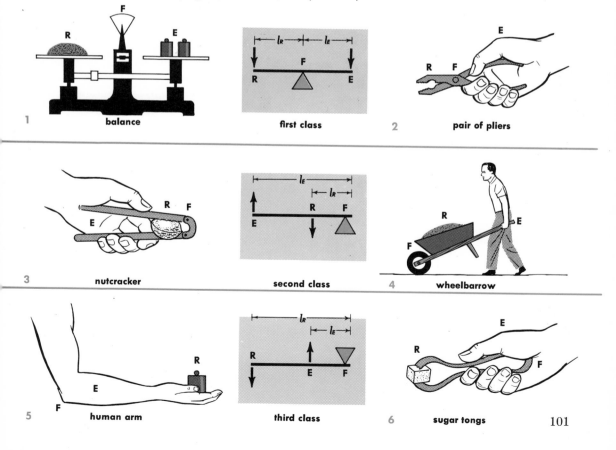

101

Classes of Levers

First Class: The fulcrum of a first-class lever is between the resistance F_R and the effort F_E. Examples are the equal-arm balance and the playground seesaw. The mechanical advantage can be equal to, greater than, or less than one.

Second Class: The resistance this time is between the effort and the fulcrum. The wheelbarrow is a good example of a second-class lever. The ratio $\frac{l_E}{l_R}$ or IMA will always be greater than one.

Third Class: The effort is situated between the resistance and the fulcrum in a third-class lever. A familiar third-class lever is the human forearm. The IMA in this case is always less than one, but third-class levers increase the load displacement.

EXAMPLE 4

The Lever

A screwdriver is used as a first-class lever to pry the lid from a can of paint. The distance from the edge of the blade to the pivot point against the rim of the can is 1.00 cm. A force of 19.6 nt is exerted 20.0 cm from this pivot point. Calculate the force applied to the lid of the can.

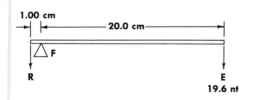

Solution:

Clockwise moments about $F=$ counterclockwise moments about F

$$E\times20.0=R\times1.00$$

$$R=\frac{E\times20.0}{1.00}=19.6\times20.0=\textbf{392 nt}\cdot$$

EXAMPLE 5

A fishing rod is 10.0 ft long, weighs 4.0 lb and has its centre of gravity 1.5 ft from the handle. You place one hand at the end of the rod to act as a fulcrum and place the other hand 2.0 ft away to act as the effort force.

(a) What class of lever is being used?

(b) Calculate the force required to pull an 8.0-lb fish out of the water.

(c) Calculate the force at the fulcrum and determine the direction of this force.

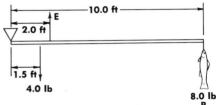

Solution:

(a) This is a lever of the third class, because the effort force is situated between the fulcrum and resistance.

(b) Taking moments about the fulcrum: Total clockwise torque = total counterclockwise torque

$$4.0\times1.5+8.0\times10.0=E\times2.0$$

$$E=\frac{4.0\times1.5+8.0\times10.0}{2.0}=\textbf{43 lb}\cdot$$

(c) For parallel forces in equilibrium: The total upward force = the total downward force
Letting $x=$ the force at the fulcrum: then 43 lb $=4.0+8.0+x$ lb

$$x=\textbf{31 lb downward}\cdot$$

The force at the fulcrum must be downwards since the arms apply forces in opposite directions to produce the turning motion or torque.

Note: Part (c) could be solved by considering the torques about the centre of gravity of the rod.

Counterclockwise torque = clockwise torque

$$x\times1.5+43\times0.5=0\times4.0+8.0\times8.5$$

$$x=\frac{46.5}{1.5}=\textbf{31 lb}\cdot$$

102

10. THE PULLEY

The *pulley* is a special case of the lever. A pulley is simply a wheel that turns on an axle mounted in a frame. A device consisting of one or more pulleys mounted in a frame is often called a *block*. A series of pulleys with attached chain or rope is called a *block and tackle*.

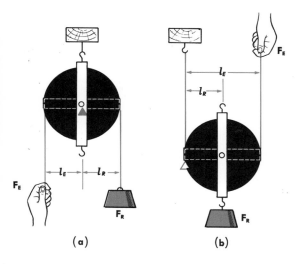

Fig. 7-5: *The single fixed pulley in (a) is basically a lever of the first class. How might you classify the single movable pulley in (b)?*

Figure 7-5(a) shows a single fixed pulley; it is simply a lever in which l_R equals l_E, and the ideal mechanical advantage is unity. If we neglect friction, an applied force of 1 lb pulling downward through a distance of 1 ft raises a load of 1 lb through a distance of 1 ft. Thus, a single pulley is an equal-arm, first-class lever. This machine provides no gain of force or speed, such a pulley merely serving to change the direction of the force; however, this is often very useful.

A single movable pulley is shown in Figure 7-5(b). The applied force is at the end of the arm l_E, which is the diameter of the pulley. The fixed hook to which the rope is attached is the fulcrum. The load is on the end of the arm, l_R, which is the radius of the pulley. This arrangement of a single pulley has an ideal mechanical advantage of two; when the applied force moves 2 ft the load is lifted 1 ft.

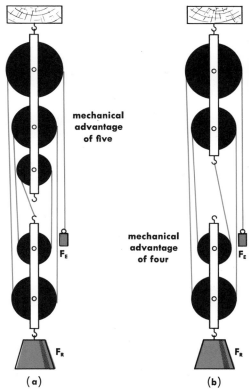

Fig. 7-6: *Block-and-tackle arrangements with an IMA of 5 and 4 respectively. Note that the IMA is equal to the number of strands supporting the resistance.*

Figure 7-6(a) illustrates a block and tackle consisting of two blocks with the load end of the continuous rope fastened to the movable block. In this system the applied force must be displaced 5 ft in order to raise the load 1 ft. This is because each of the five strands supporting the movable block will also move up 1 ft, with the end of the rope moving down 5 ft. Therefore, $\frac{S_E}{S_R}$ is equal to five, or the IMA is five. Note that this is precisely the number of strands of the rope that supports the movable block, i.e., the number of resistance strands. The strand to which the force is applied is not counted since it does not support the movable block. The upper pulley in the fixed block does not contribute to the mechanical advantage but merely changes the direction of the applied force. Because of the inevitable friction, the ratio $\dfrac{F_R}{F_E}$, which is the AMA, will be less than $\dfrac{S_E}{S_R}$.

Figure 7-6(b) illustrates a similar block and tackle consisting of four pulleys, two per block. In this arrangement the movable block is supported by only four strands; therefore the ideal mechanical advantage of this system is four.

In any block, the pulleys of the block are mounted on a common shaft, but have been shown separately in Figure 7-6 for greater clarity.

A pulley wheel is commonly referred to as a *sheave*. Thus, in Figure 7-6(a), the upper block is a triple-sheave block, while the lower is a double-sheave block.

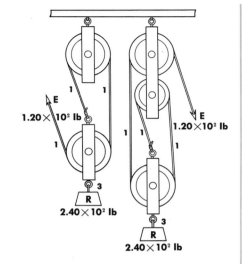

(c) $\text{AMA} = \dfrac{F_R}{F_E} = \dfrac{2.40 \times 10^2 \text{ lb}}{1.20 \times 10^2 \text{ lb}} = 2.00$

(d) $\text{Efficiency} = \dfrac{\text{AMA}}{\text{IMA}} \times 100\%$
$= 67\%$

EXAMPLE 6

A pulley system is used by a workman to raise a weight of 2.40×10^2 lb a vertical distance of 24 ft. The workman's effort of 1.20×10^2 lb moves through a distance of 72 ft.

(a)   Calculate the IMA.

(b)   Make two diagrams that represent pulley systems with this IMA.

(c)   Calculate the AMA.

(d)   Calculate the efficiency.

Solution:

(a) $\text{IMA} = \dfrac{S_E}{S_R} = \dfrac{72 \text{ ft}}{24 \text{ ft}} = 3.0$.

(b)   To produce an IMA of 3.0, the possible arrangements are

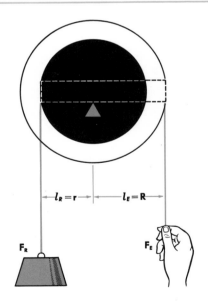

Fig. 7-7: *The wheel and axle. Like the pulley, this machine is derived from the lever.*

11. WHEEL AND AXLE

The *wheel and axle* illustrated in Figure 7-7 is another example of the lever, usually first class. This device consists of two wheels of different diameter which must rotate together on the same axle. A crank is sometimes substituted for the larger wheel. If the circumference of the larger wheel is C ft and that of the smaller wheel is c ft, and the applied force F_E is displaced downward a distance equal to C, the load moves up a distance c, so that the ratio S_E/S_R, the IMA, is equal to C/c. When the wheel and the axle together are considered as a lever, the IMA becomes the ratio of the radii R/r or the diameter D/d. Friction in the system once more makes the AMA less than the IMA.

EXAMPLE 7

A carpenter uses a screwdriver with a handle diameter of $1\frac{1}{8}''$ and blade width $\frac{1}{4}''$. When exerting a force of 45 lb on the handle the blade exerts a force of 192 lb on a screw.

(a) Calculate the IMA of the screwdriver.

(b) Find the AMA of the screwdriver.

(c) Calculate the efficiency of the system.

Solution:

(a) $\text{IMA} = \dfrac{D}{d} = \dfrac{\frac{9}{8}}{\frac{2}{8}} = \textbf{4.5}.$

(b) $\text{AMA} = \dfrac{F_R}{F_E} = \dfrac{192}{45} = 4.27$ or $\textbf{4.3}.$

(c) $\text{Efficiency} = \dfrac{\text{AMA}}{\text{IMA}} \times 100\% = \dfrac{4.27}{4.5} \times 100$

$\qquad\qquad = \textbf{95}\%$

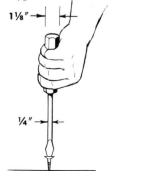

12. THE INCLINED PLANE

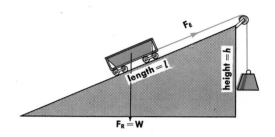

Fig. 7-8: *The inclined plane. The resistance in this machine is the weight of the load, and acts through a distance h equal to the vertical rise of the plane.*

Figure 7-8 shows an *inclined plane* or *ramp*. The purpose of this machine is to displace an object such as the cart through a *vertical distance* equal to that of the height of the plane. This is done by applying an effort force F_E parallel to the plane. While the effort force F_E moves through a distance equal to the length of the plane, the resistance force, which is the weight W of the object, is moved vertically a distance h.

Then, work done on car (work output)

$$= Wh = F_R h$$

and work done by applied force (work input)

$$= F_E l.$$

If we assume a frictionless surface, then work output = work input,

and $F_R h = F_E l$

$$\frac{F_R}{F_E} = \frac{l}{h}$$

$$\therefore \ \text{IMA} = \frac{l}{h} .$$

As is the case with all machines, the AMA of the inclined plane $= \dfrac{F_R}{F_E}$.

EXAMPLE 8

The coal car of Figure 7-8 is raised 3.0 ft above the ground by moving it 15.0 ft along the incline. If the car and contents weigh 4320 lb and the effort force required is 2150 lb, calculate (a) the work output, (b) the IMA, (c) the efficiency, (d) the work done against friction, and (e) the effort force used in overcoming friction.

Solution:

(a) the work output $4.32 \times 10^3 \times 3.0$ ft lb
$$= 1.3 \times 10^4 \text{ ft-lb}.$$

(b) $\text{IMA} = \dfrac{l}{h} = \dfrac{15 \text{ ft}}{3.0 \text{ ft}} = 5.0.$

(c) $\text{Efficiency} = \dfrac{\text{Work output}}{\text{Work input}} \times 100$
$$= \dfrac{1.30 \times 10^4 \text{ ft lb}}{2.15 \times 10^3 \times 15 \text{ ft lb}} \times 100\%$$
$$= \dfrac{1.30 \times 10^4}{3.22 \times 10^4} \times 100\%$$
$$= 40\%.$$

(d) The work input = work output + work against friction
$$W_i = W_o + W_f$$

$$W_f = W_i - W_o = 3.22 \times 10^4 - 1.30 \times 10^4 \text{ ft-lb}$$
$$= 1.92 \times 10^4 \text{ ft-lb}$$
$$= 1.9 \times 10^4 \text{ ft-lb}.$$

(e) From (d) $W_f = fs$
$$f = \dfrac{W_f}{s} = \dfrac{1.9 \times 10^4}{15.0}$$
$$= 1.3 \times 10^3 \text{ lb}.$$

13. THE WEDGE

The wedge may be a single or a double inclined plane. In the case of the inclined plane, the load moves; but in the case of the wedge, it is more usual to have the plane move with respect to the load; that is, the wedge is usually pushed or hammered under the load. The force applied is thus more nearly parallel to the base of the plane and friction is usually great; accordingly, the IMA is of little significance. A wedge that is long in proportion to its thickness is easier to drive than a thick wedge; so the mechanical advantage of a wedge depends upon the ratio of thickness to length.

Common examples of the wedge are cutting tools, such as a knife or axe. The cam, used in operating the valves of an automobile engine, is basically a wedge (Figure 7-9).

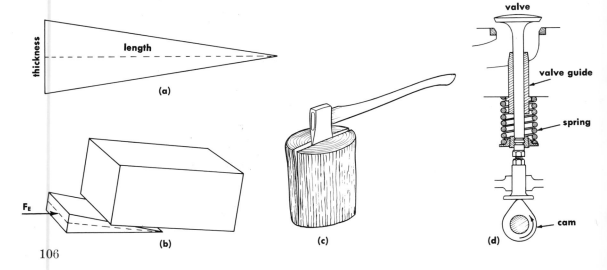

Fig. 7-9: *The wedge in (a) is a double inclined plane that moves against a fixed resistance, as in (b) and (c). The cam in (d) is a rotating inclined plane used to overcome the resistance of the compressed valve-spring. It can be considered a wedge.*

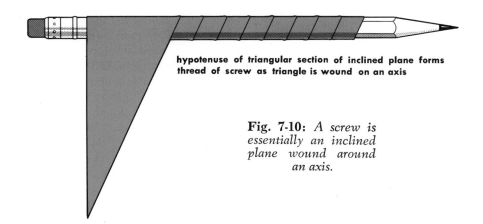

hypotenuse of triangular section of inclined plane forms thread of screw as triangle is wound on an axis

Fig. 7-10: A screw is essentially an inclined plane wound around an axis.

14. THE SCREW

A screw is essentially a wedge wound round a cylinder as illustrated in Figure 7-10. A sheet of paper cut into the form of a right angle is wound round a pencil, making evident the *threads* of the screw. The distance between threads, measured along the axis of the screw, is called the *pitch* of the screw. The wedge is pushed under the load by rotating the screw. This operation may be carried out by applying a tangential force to the handle of a screwdriver, or by using a lever in the form of a wrench.

Both these arrangements provide the advantage of the wheel and axle for the system since the *E*ffort is applied at the wheel (screwdriver handle) and the *R*esistance force acts against the turning of the screw (axle). In one turn or revolution of the screwdriver, the *E*ffort has moved a distance $2\pi r$, where r is the radius of the wheel (screwdriver handle or wrench). Since one turn of the wheel also turns the screw one revolution, the load is moved one thread higher or the pitch of the screw. Thus the IMA $=\dfrac{2\pi r}{p}$, where p is the pitch of the screw. As in the case of the wedge, the friction here is considerable; consequently, the IMA is usually much greater than the AMA.

The screw is used widely in applications such as the jackscrew (Example 9). Bolts, nuts, and wood screws are other applications of this simple machine. For precise measurements of length, the screw is made use of in such instruments as the micrometer.

EXAMPLE 9

The jackscrew illustrated has a handle 25 inches long. The pitch of the screw is 0.25 in. What force must be applied to the handle in order that a force of 1500 lb may be applied to the bumper of an automobile? (Neglect friction.)

Solution:

$$\text{IMA of screw} = \frac{2\pi r}{p} = \frac{6.28 \times 25}{.25}$$
$$= 628 \text{ or } 6.3 \times 10^2.$$

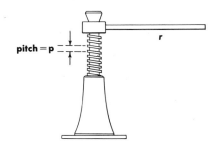

pitch = p

r

$$\therefore \quad \frac{F_R}{F_E} = 6.3 \times 10^2$$

But $F_R = 1500$ lb.

$$\therefore \quad F_E = \frac{1500}{6.28 \times 10^2} = \textbf{2.4 lb}.$$

Because of the large amount of friction encountered, the actual effort required will be considerably greater than 2.4 lb.

15. COMPLEX MACHINES

Many complicated machines are merely combinations of simple machines. The crank of a kitchen food-chopper works on the principle of the wheel and axle. The crank turns a screw, which forces the food through small holes, where it is chopped off by the wedge action of a cutting disk.

Figure 7-11 illustrates a compound machine, a combination of an inclined plane and a block and tackle. The box, which is raised a height of 4 ft, weighs 4000 lb. The inclined plane, or ramp, upon which the box moves, is 20 ft long. The IMA of the plane is 20/4, or 5. Neglecting friction, we still need to apply parallel to the plane, a force of $\frac{4000}{5}$ lb, or 800 lb. If now the movable block of a block

and tackle is fastened to the box, as shown in Figure 7-11 we gain a further IMA of 5, so that the men at the top of the plane must pull with a force of 800/5, or 160 lb. The IMA of this compound machine is thus 4000/160, or 25. It is the product of the IMA of the individual components of the compound machine. *In nearly all cases of compound machines, the total IMA is the product of the separate mechanical advantages.*

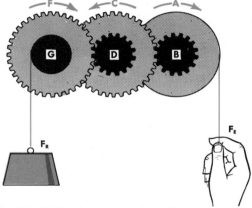

Fig. 7-12: *A compound machine consisting of a wheel and axle separated by two pairs of spur gears. Each pair of gears act basically as a wheel and axle.*

Fig. 7-11: *A compound machine consisting of an inclined plane and block and tackle. The IMA of this system is 25.*

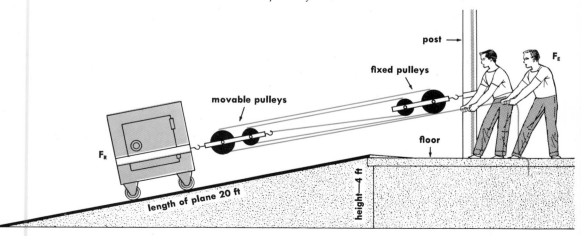

Figure 7-12 shows a wheel and axle, A and G, with an intervening set of gearwheels. It can be shown that the IMA of this compound system is given by:

$$\frac{\text{(radius of A)}}{\text{(radius of G)}} \times \frac{\text{(number of cogs in C)}}{\text{(number of cogs in B)}} \times \frac{\text{(number of cogs in F)}}{\text{(number of cogs in D)}}$$

Figure 7-13 illustrates a worm wheel. This is essentially a wheel and axle with an intervening worm and gearwheel. The wheel, at the rim of which F_E acts, causes the worm to rotate. Each time the worm rotates once, the gear rotates through the angle between two consecutive teeth. But for the intervening worm and gear, the IMA would be that of the wheel and axle alone, namely, R/r, where R and r are, respectively, the radius of the wheel and of the axle. If there are n teeth, the IMA is $n(R/r)$.

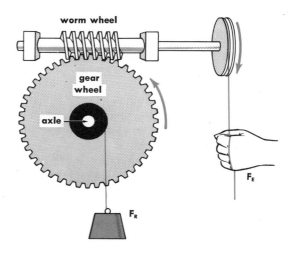

Fig. 7-13. *This worm-drive mechanism is used to transfer rotational energy from one shaft to another shaft at right angles to it. The combination of screw with wheel and axle produces a high mechanical advantage.*

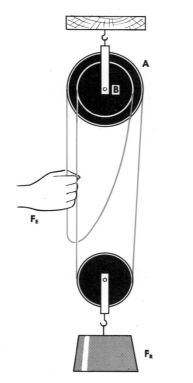

Fig. 7-14: *The differential pulley is a combination of a single movable pulley and a wheel and axle. Wheels A and B, in conjunction with the endless chain, act as a wheel and axle of very high mechanical advantage.*

Figure 7-14 illustrates a *differential pulley* and the equivalent commercial chain hoist. This compound machine has two wheels of unequal diameter that are fastened together and turn on the same axle. An endless chain is wound around the two wheels and movable pulley. In the commercial chain hoist, the endless chain is a link chain, the links of which fit into grooves in the pulleys and thus prevent slipping. As the effort F_E moves a distance C equal to the circumference of A, the chain is unwound by an amount c equal to the circumference of B. Thus the chain is shortened by the difference between the circumferences of A and B, namely $C-c$.

Since the lower pulley moves upwards a distance equal to one half the chain movement, S_R for the differential pulley is $\frac{1}{2}$ $(C-c)$ for $S_E=C$. Therefore the IMA is $\frac{2C}{C-c}$. Because the circumference of each of the pulleys is proportional to its diameter,

the IMA is conveniently given by the formula $\text{IMA} = \dfrac{2D}{D-d}$, where D is the diameter of the large pulley, and d the diameter of the small pulley.

It follows from this formula that the smaller this difference in radii, the greater the IMA will be.

EXAMPLE 10

A differential pulley has a large pulley of 8.0 inch diameter, and a smaller pulley of 7.5 inch diameter. Determine its IMA.

Solution:

$$\text{IMA} = \frac{2D}{D-d} = \frac{16}{8.0-7.5} = 32.$$

The AMA would be somewhat less than this because of friction between the pulleys and chain.

MOMENT OF A FORCE ABOUT A POINT: the product of the force and the perpendicular distance from the point to the line of action of the force.

CONDITIONS FOR EQUILIBRIUM OF A BODY:
  (i) The sum of the clockwise moments and of the counterclockwise moments about any point in the body must be numerically equal (rotational equilibrium).
  (ii) The sum of the forces acting on the body in any one direction must equal the sum of the forces acting in the opposite direction (translational equilibrium).

CENTRE OF GRAVITY: the point at which the entire weight of an object may be considered to act.

A MACHINE: a device generally used to transfer or transform energy.

EFFORT: the input force applied to a machine [F_E].

RESISTANCE: the output force produced by the machine [F_R] or the force overcome by the machine.

IDEAL MECHANICAL ADVANTAGE (IMA)
$$= \frac{\text{displacement of effort}}{\text{displacement of resistance}} = \frac{S_E}{S_R}.$$

ACTUAL MECHANICAL ADVANTAGE (AMA)

$$= \frac{\text{resistance}}{\text{effort}} = \frac{F_R}{F_E}.$$

Efficiency of any machine $= \dfrac{\text{work output}}{\text{work input}} = \dfrac{\text{AMA}}{\text{IMA}}.$

THE SIX SIMPLE MACHINES:

1. Lever: 1st class: fulcrum located between effort and resistance
   2nd class: resistance located between effort and fulcrum
   3rd class: effort located between resistance and fulcrum

$$\text{IMA} = \frac{\text{effort arm}}{\text{resistance arm}} = \frac{l_E}{l_R}.$$

2. Pulley: IMA = number of strands supporting the resistance .

3. Wheel and Axle:

$$\text{IMA} = \frac{\text{radius of wheel}}{\text{radius of axle}} = \frac{R}{r}.$$

4. Inclined Plane:

$$\text{IMA} = \frac{\text{length of plane}}{\text{height of plane}} = \frac{l}{h}.$$

5. Wedge: an inclined plane which moves against the resistance .

6. Screw: $\text{IMA} = \dfrac{2\pi r}{p}$

   where $r =$ effort arm
   $p =$ pitch of screw.

DIFFERENTIAL PULLEY:

$$\text{IMA} = \frac{2D}{D-d}$$

where $D =$ diameter of large pulley
$d =$ diameter of smaller pulley.

COMPOUND MACHINE: a machine composed of a combination of two or more simple machines.

For a compound machine,

IMA = product of the mechanical advantages of the individual components.

EXERCISE A

1. Give the position of the applied force, the load, and the fulcrum in each of the following:
   (a) a clawhammer when used to pull a nail
   (b) the oar of a rowboat
   (c) forceps of a chemical balance when handling small weights
   (d) an equal-arm balance
   (e) a pair of scissors when cutting
   (f) a wheelbarrow.

2. (a) Draw a diagram of a lever in which the weight of the lever aids the applied force.
   (b) Draw a diagram of a lever in which the weight of the lever opposes the applied force.

3. For a lever, how would you determine the following?
   (a) the ideal mechanical advantage
   (b) the actual mechanical advantage.

4. Under what condition does a first-class lever have a mechanical advantage greater than one?

5. Why is the mechanical advantage of a second-class lever always greater than one?

6. (a) Why is the mechanical advantage of a third-class lever always less than one?
   (b) Of what benefit is this characteristic of a third-class lever?

7. A tinsmith's shears have long handles and short blades, while a tailor's shears have short handles and long blades.   Explain.

8. Show by a diagram how you would connect two double-sheave blocks to obtain the highest mechanical advantage.   What is the IMA of this arrangement?

9. Why is it impractical to calculate the IMA for a wedge?

10. What will be the ratio of the number of teeth in the gearwheel attached to the second hand of a watch, and the number of teeth in the gearwheel attached to the minute hand?

11. Write, in terms of the dimensions of the machine, the ideal mechanical advantage of (a) the lever, (b) the wheel and axle, (c) the inclined plane, (d) the differential pulley, (e) the jackscrew.

12. Can the same machine be used to gain both force and speed at the same time? Explain why.

13. How could you use the same machine to gain force in one instance, and speed in another instance?

EXERCISE B

Assume measured quantities are accurate to the number of digits quoted.

1. A 120-lb boy sits 4.0 ft from the fulcrum of a seesaw.   How far from the fulcrum must an 80-lb boy sit, in order to balance the board?

2. When a mass of 1.50×10^2 gram is placed at the 10.0 cm mark of a metre stick, and an unknown mass is placed at the 75.0 cm mark, the metre stick balances when supported at its midpoint. Determine the value of the unknown mass.

3. A truck and its contents have a total weight of 6200 lb. The truck stops 25 ft from the end of a bridge which is 60 ft long. How much of the total weight of the truck is supported by each pier of the bridge?

4. A nonuniform bar, weighing 35 lb, has a length of 21 ft. When it is supported at its mid point, it is found that equilibrium is obtained when a load weighing 14 lb is placed at one end. Determine the location of the centre of gravity of the beam.

5. A father and his son carry a deer weighing 120 lb by means of a uniform pole 10 ft in length, weighing 12 lb. Where should the deer be placed so that the father supports two thirds of the total load?

6. A 10.0 foot beam is used as a first-class lever to lift a rock that weighs 388 lb. A fulcrum is provided by a log 2.00 ft from the rock.
   (a) What is the IMA of this lever?
   (b) If the machine is 100% efficient, what effort is needed to lift the rock?

7. The beam of question six is used to loosen a tree root by fastening a wire around the root, 2 ft from the end of the beam. This end rests on a flat rock and the cottager raises the far end with a force of 45 pounds.
   (a) What type of lever is being used?
   (b) Calculate the IMA of the lever.
   (c) What force will be applied to the root if the machine is 90% efficient?

8. The centre of gravity of a wheelbarrow and its load is 18.0 inches from the centre of the wheel. The wheelbarrow and its load weigh 125 lb and a gardener grips the handles 4.00 ft from the wheel centre.
   (a) What type of lever is the machine?
   (b) Calculate the IMA of the lever.
   (c) Calculate the force that must be applied to each handle to lift the legs off the ground assuming 100% efficiency.

9. A right-handed man lifts 10.0 lb of snow with its centre of gravity 6.0 in. from the end of a 4.0 ft shovel. His left hand is 2.0 ft from the handle.
   (a) What type of lever is employed?
   (b) Calculate the IMA of the lever. (Neglect the weight of the shovel.)
   (c) Assuming 100% efficiency, what effort is used by the man?

10. In Figure 7-5 (a) of the text, the single pulley is of 8-in diameter and the load is 20.0 lb.
    (a) What is the IMA of this machine?
    (b) What is the AMA and the efficiency of this machine, if the applied force is 20.0 lb?

11. In Figure 7-5 (b) of the text, the single pulley shown is 8.00 in. in diameter and weighs 2.00 lb.   The load is 30.0 lb.

    (a) What is the IMA of this system?

    (b) In practice the applied force is found to be 16.8 lb.   Calculate the AMA of this system.

    (c) What is the applied force used to overcome the friction of the pulley?

    (d) When the applied force moves through 2.00 ft, how far has the load moved?

12. The block and tackle shown in Figure 7-6 (a) of the text consists of light smooth pulleys and is loaded with 160 lb.

    (a) What applied force is required to operate it?

    (b) What is the pull in each part of the rope?

    (c) In order to raise the load 10 inches how far must the applied force be moved?

    Note: The expressions *smooth* and *light* always signify that the friction in the moving parts is negligible and that the weight of the pulleys and rope in comparison with the load, may be neglected.

13. Make the same calculations as in the problem above for the block and tackle shown in Figure 7-6 (b) when it is loaded with 160 lb, assuming that the pulleys in the block are smooth and light.

14. A block and tackle is to be used to raise a load of 1.00×10^3 lb.   If the maximum force which can be applied to the block and tackle is 220 lb, how many strands of rope must support the movable block?   Sketch the arrangement which you suggest.

15. A force of 100 lb is exerted on the rope of a block and tackle, and the rope is pulled in 30.0 ft.   This work causes a weight of 500 lb to be raised 5.00 ft.   Calculate:

    (a) the AMA and the IMA of the machine

    (b) the efficiency of the machine.

16. (a) What horsepower must be developed in order to pull 100 ft of rope from a block and tackle with a force of 55.0 lb in 5.0 seconds?

    (b) If *four* strands support the movable block in this block and tackle and the weight raised is 165 lb, what is the efficiency of the block and tackle?

17. A force of 50 lb on the crank handle of a windlass can raise a load of 600 lb.   What is the efficiency of the windlass if the length of the crank handle is 10 in and the diameter of the axle is 1.0 in?

18. A wrench is used to turn a bolt of diameter 0.25 in.   The centre of the bolt head is 8.0 in from the application of the force.

    (a) Calculate the IMA of the machine.

    (b) If the efficiency of the system is 50%, determine the AMA of the machine.

19. A jackscrew having 5 threads per inch has a lever arm of 2.5 ft.   To raise a load of 3000 lb, it is found that a force of 30 lb must be applied to the end of the lever arm.   Calculate the IMA, the AMA, and the efficiency of this machine.

20. A house-mover's jackscrew exerting a force of 11 tons on a house, can raise one corner 0.50 ft in 10 minutes. If the efficiency of the jackscrew is 30%, what is the horsepower input?

21. The higher end of a ramp 12 ft long, is 3.0 ft higher than the lower end.
    (a) If the friction is neglected, what force is required to push a box weighing 120 lb up the plane?
    (b) If a force of 50 lb is actually required, determine the efficiency of the plane.

22. The large wheel of a differential pulley has a circumference of 0.60 m; the small wheel has a circumference of 0.55 m:
    (a) What is the IMA of this differential pulley?
    (b) If a force of 45 lb is required to raise a motor block weighing 765 lb, what is the AMA?
    (c) Calculate the efficiency.

23. A 2.00-ton safe is pulled up a 20.0-ft ramp on to a platform 4.00 ft high. A block and tackle having an IMA of 5.0 is attached to the safe. If two men each pulling with a force of 125 lb move the safe, what is the efficiency of this system?

24. A cottager purchases a winch to lift his 625-lb boat and motor out of the water. The small gear has 12 teeth and the large one 60 teeth. The crank handle is 6.0 in long and the axle about which the wire is wound, is 0.50 in in diameter.
    (a) Calculate the IMA of the machine.
    (b) If the winch is 75% efficient, calculate the effort force required to lift the boat and motor.

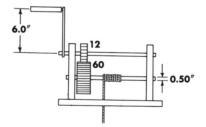

25. A worm drive such as is shown in Figure 7-13, has 90 teeth in the gearwheel. If the radius of the drive wheel is 0.40 m and the radius of the axle is 0.020 m, what load can be lifted by a force of 10.0 lb, the efficiency being 65%?

26. The worm wheel system shown in Figure 7-13 of the text has an axle 2.00 in. in radius and a gearwheel 12 in. in radius. The worm wheel has a pitch of 0.25 in. The small wheel round which the rope to the applied force is wrapped is 6.00 in. in radius. To raise a load of 2260 lb requires an applied force of 10.0 lb. Determine:
    (a) the IMA of the worm drive (consider it as a screw)
    (b) the IMA of the gear wheel and axle
    (c) the IMA of the compound machine
    (d) the AMA of the compound machine
    (e) the efficiency of the machine.

Machines

▶ Experiment 6

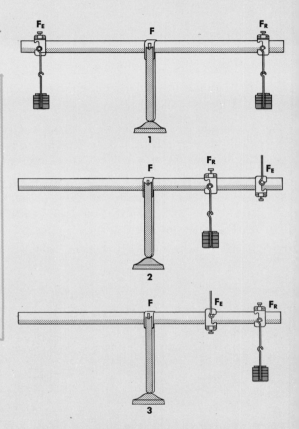

To study the three classes of levers.

> Metre stick
>
> Metre stick knife edge and support
>
> 2 metre-stick clamps
>
> 2 weight hangers
>
> Slotted weights
>
> 1 500-gram spring balance
>
> 1 250-gram spring balance
>
> Triple beam or platform balance
>
> (Twine and hooked weights can replace the slotted weights)

Procedure

First-Class Lever

1. Support the metre stick at its centre of gravity (illustration 1) with the knife edge resting on the support.

2. Suspend two weight hangers from metre-stick clamps arranged near each end of the metre stick.

3. Load the hanger marked F_R to produce a total mass of approximately 200 g for the hanger plus weights. Move F_R to a distance of 20 cm from F.

4. Similar to instruction 3, suspend a total mass of 150 g as F_E and move F_E along the lever until equilibrium occurs.

5. Record the distances of F_R and F_E from F as l_R and l_E respectively.

6. Weigh each clamp on a balance and determine the total value of F_R and F_E.

7. Calculate the IMA, the AMA, and the efficiency of the lever.

8. Repeat the experiment using different values for F_R and l_R.

Second-Class Lever

1. Arrange a second-class lever as indicated in illustration 2.

2. Conduct two trials similar to those outlined for the first-class lever. F_E this time will be recorded on a spring balance.

3. In the case of the second-class lever, the metre stick must be in the correct position at equilibrium. What is the correct position?

4. Calculate the IMA, AMA, and efficiency of the second-class lever.

Third-Class Lever

1. Refer to illustration 3 to arrange a third-class lever.

2. Obtain two sets of measurements in a manner similar to those obtained previously.

3. In the case of the third-class lever it may be necessary to tie the knife edge to its support with twine. Why?

4. Calculate the same values as before.

It is recommended that the measurements and results of calculations made concerning this experiment and the experiments to follow be summarized in a table. A suitable table for this experiment is shown below:

Class	Trial	F_E	F_R	l_E	l_R	F_El_E	F_Rl_R	IMA l_E/l_R	AMA F_R/F_E	Efficiency
First	1									
	2									
Second	3									
	4									
Third	5									
	6									

SAMPLE ONLY

Experiment 7

To study the wheel and axle.

Wheel and axle

Support stand and clamps

Strong thread or fish line

1 weight hanger

Slotted weights

1 metric ruler

1 250-gram spring balance

Calipers

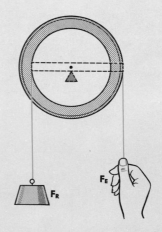

Procedure

1. Clamp the wheel and axle to the support stand.

2. Use the calipers and metric ruler to make the measurements required to determine the IMA of the wheel-and-axle combinations.

3. Suspend a mass of 200 grams consisting of the hanger plus weights as shown in the illustration on page 107.

4. Measure F_E on the spring balance.

5. Move F_E a measured distance S_E and record the corresponding movement of F_R as S_R.

6. Calculate the IMA, AMA, work input, work output, and efficiency of the machine.

7. Conduct two more trials in a similar manner using a different wheel-and-axle for each trial.

8. Summarize your results in a suitable table and list your conclusions.

Experiment 8

To study the characteristics of a single fixed pulley, a single movable pulley, and pulley combinations.

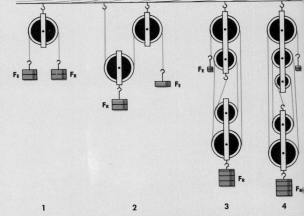

Pulley support frame or stands

2 or 3 single pulleys

4 pulleys with 2 or 3 sheaves each

Strong thread or fish line

2 weight hangers

Slotted weights

1 250-gram spring balance

1 500-gram spring balance

1 metre stick

1 balance

Procedure

Single Fixed Pulley

1. Suspend a combined mass of 200 grams to provide the resistance force F_R.

2. Add weights to the F_E weight hanger until F_R rises without acceleration if given a slight start. Fine adjustments may be made to F_E by adding available light objects such as paper clips. If such adjust-

ments are made, record their combined weight on the balance.

3. Use the metre stick to measure a suitable movement of F_E. Record this distance as S_E and measure the corresponding movement S_R of the force F_R.

4. Calculate the IMA, AMA, work input, work output, and efficiency of the pulley.

Single Movable Pulley

1. Arrange the single movable pulley as indicated in the illustration.

2. Suspend a mass of 250 grams or other suitable mass as F_R and determine F_E as before.

3. Determine the values listed for the single fixed pulley.

Pulley Combinations

1. Assemble two pulley combinations as suggested in illustrations 3 and 4.

2. Determine the IMA, AMA, work input, work output, and efficiency for these systems.

Tabulate the measurements and results of calculations and list the main conclusions that may be derived from this experiment.

Experiment 9

To study the characteristics of the inclined plane.

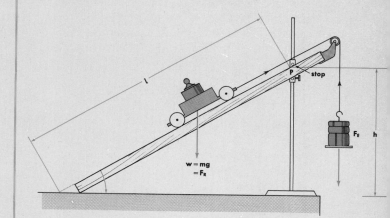

Inclined plane

Inclined plane support

1 weight hanger

Slotted weights

1 500-gram mass

Cart

1 balance

1 metre stick

Strong thread or fish line

Procedure

1. Assemble the plane as indicated in the illustration with the angle of the plane approximately 10°.

2. Load the cart with a 500-gram mass.

3. Add slotted weights (masses) to the hanger until the cart will move up the plane without acceleration after an initial start. Small adjustments for F_E can be made using paper clips or other suitable materials.

4. Determine the mass of any unmarked additions to F_E by means of the balance.

5. With the metre stick, measure the distance l along the plane and the vertical height h to the same common point P.

6. Conduct two more trials using a different inclined-plane angle for each trial.

7. For each trial calculate the IMA, AMA, work input, work output, and efficiency.

8. Record the measurements and calculations in a suitable table, and list the important conclusions.

Question

In what manner do the efficiency and AMA of the machine change when the angle of the inclined plane is increased?

Chapter 8

Liquids at Rest

In this chapter we shall be studying the forces exerted on objects completely or partially submerged in a fluid. Let us first review the basic concepts of density and pressure, both of which are closely related to what is to follow:

1. DENSITY AND SPECIFIC GRAVITY

One of the most fundamental physical concepts is that of density. The density of a substance is defined as the mass per unit volume of the substance.

$$\text{density} = \frac{\text{mass}}{\text{volume}}$$

$$\text{or } D = \frac{m}{V}$$

It is customary to express density in grams per cubic centimetre (g/cm³), or kilograms per litre (kg/l). Very often, units of weight per unit volume are used to express density. For example, the density of water is expressed as 62.4 pounds per cubic foot (lb/ft³). Because a choice of units is available, it is important that these units be stated when specifying the density of a material.

The unit of mass, the gram, was originally defined as the mass of 1 cm³ of water at a temperature of 4°C.

$$\text{density of water} = 1 \text{ g/cm}^3$$
$$1 \text{ g/cm}^3 = 62.4 \text{ lb/ft}^3.$$

A concept closely related to density is that of *specific gravity*.

specific gravity (s.g.) =

$$\frac{weight \ (or \ mass) \ of \ a \ substance}{weight \ (or \ mass) \ of \ an \ equal \ volume \ of \ water}$$

The specific gravity of a substance is a pure number, without units. This number merely represents the ratio of two weights (or masses). For example, 1 cm³ of mercury has a mass of 13.6 g, whereas an equal volume of water has a mass of 1 g. The specific gravity of mercury is, therefore, $\frac{13.6 \text{ g}}{1 \text{ g}} = 13.6$. Its density is 13.6 g/cm³.

Note that density, when expressed in g/cm³, or in kg/l, is *numerically* equal to specific gravity. This is not so when density is expressed in lb/ft³.

The density and specific gravity of common substances are listed in Table 8-1 on page 129.

EXAMPLE 1

A block of wood is 12.0 cm long, 3.0 cm wide, and 1.0 cm thick. It has a mass of 27.0 g. Determine

(a) the density of the wood in g/cm³

(b) its specific gravity

(c) its density in lb/ft³

(d) the volume of 1.50×10^2 g of the wood.

Solution:

(a) $D = \dfrac{m}{V} = \dfrac{27.0 \text{ g}}{12.0 \times 3.0 \times 1.0 \text{ cm}^3}$

$\qquad = \textbf{0.75 g/cm}^3$.

(b) $\quad$ s.g. $= \textbf{0.75}$.

(c) $\quad$ 0.75 g/cm³ $= 0.75 \times 62.4$ lb/ft³

$\qquad\qquad\qquad = 46.8$ lb/ft³ or **47 lb/ft³**.

(d) $\quad V = \dfrac{m}{D} = \dfrac{1.50 \times 10^2 \text{ g}}{0.75 \text{ g/cm}^3} = \textbf{2.0} \times \textbf{10}^2 \textbf{ cm}^3$.

2. KILOGRAM FORCE AND GRAM FORCE

Basically, the terms kilogram and gram are units of *mass*. By the following definitions, however, the term may be used to indicate force:

1 kilogram force (kgf) is the weight of a 1-kilogram mass.

1 gram force (gf) is the weight of a 1-gram mass.

We know from Chapters 4 and 5 that the weight of any given mass is dependent upon its location. Thus, unlike the newton which is an absolute force unit, the kilogram force is a gravitational force unit, and varies with location. On the earth's surface, where g is 9.8 m/sec², the kilogram force is equivalent to 9.8 newtons.

Throughout this chapter, the use of the kilogram force and gram force will be extensive in specifying the weights of objects. The letter f in the abbreviations kgf and gf will serve to remind us that a force is being referred to.

The pound mass and the pound force, in the British system of units, have already been defined (Chapter 1). However, the general use of the term pound is becoming more and more restricted to the specification of forces only, mass being expressed in slugs. For this reason, we too will follow this accepted procedure.

3. PRESSURE

Pressure is defined as force per unit area

$$\text{pressure} = \frac{\text{force}}{\text{area}}$$

$$\text{or } p = \frac{F}{A}$$

It is obvious from the definition of pressure that a small force is capable of exerting a great pressure if the area over which it is distributed is small. Similarly, a large force may exert little pressure if spread over a wide area. For example, the total weight of the earth's atmosphere is 6×10^6 tons. Distributed over the entire surface of the earth, the pressure produced is about 15 lb/in². Contrast this with the pressure of 10 tons/in² that is produced on a long-playing record by the phonograph needle.

In this chapter we are particularly interested in the pressure produced by a liquid, at any point beneath the surface of the liquid. Let us illustrate some fundamental concepts by an example.

EXAMPLE 2

A thin rectangular sheet of wood, measuring 2.0 ft by 3.0 ft is held in a horizontal plane 1.0 ft below the surface of a lake. Determine:

(a) the total force exerted by the water on the surface of the sheet

(b) the pressure exerted on this surface.

Solution:

(a) The force applied to the surface of the wood is produced by the weight of water immediately above it.

Volume of water above sheet
$$= 2.0 \times 3.0 \times 1.0 \text{ ft}^3 = 6.0 \text{ ft}^3.$$

∴ Weight of water above sheet
$$= 6.0 \text{ ft}^3 \times 62.4 \text{ lb/ft}^3 = \mathbf{3.7 \times 10^2 \text{ lb.}}$$

(b) Area of surface $= 2.0 \times 3.0 \text{ ft}^2 = 6.0 \text{ ft}^2$

$$\therefore \ p = \frac{F}{A} = \frac{3.7 \times 10^2 \text{ lb}}{6.0 \text{ ft}^2} = \mathbf{62 \text{ lb/ft}^2.}$$

The liquid pressure at a point below the surface of a liquid is dependent upon two factors: the *depth of the point*, and the *density of the liquid.*

EXAMPLE 3

Determine the liquid pressure in a gasoline storage tank at a depth of 5.0 metres. The density of gasoline is 0.69 g/cm³.

Solution:

Consider an area of 1.0 cm² at this depth. Volume of gasoline above this area
$$= 5.0 \times 10^2 \text{ cm} \times 1.0 \text{ cm}^2$$
$$= 5.0 \times 10^2 \text{ cm}^3$$

∴ mass of fluid acting on this area
$$= 5.0 \times 10^2 \text{ cm}^3 \times 0.69 \text{ g/cm}^3$$
$$= 3.45 \times 10^2 \text{ g}$$

∴ pressure $= 3.45 \times 10^2 \text{ gf/cm}^2$
or $\mathbf{3.4 \times 10^2 \text{ gf/cm}^2.}$

This pressure could also be stated as
$$\mathbf{3.4 \times 10^3 \text{ kgf/m}^2.}$$

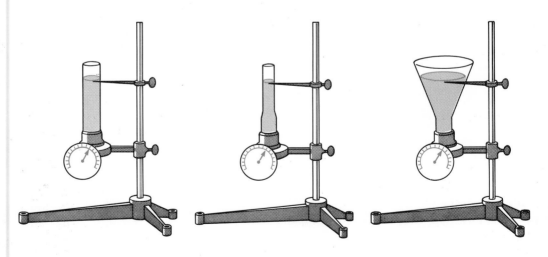

Fig. 8-1: *Pressure at a point within a liquid is dependent upon the depth of the point, and the density of the liquid, but is independent of the volume of the liquid.*

An important property of liquid pressure was first stated by the French philosopher and scientist Blaise Pascal (1623-1662), and known as Pascal's Principle. **When the pressure in a confined liquid is changed at any point, this change in pressure is transmitted equally throughout the entire liquid.**

Important examples of the application of this principle are to be found in the hydraulic press and the lift pump.

Figure 8-1 illustrates that pressure at a point below the surface of a liquid is determined by the depth of the liquid but not by its volume.

The apparatus shown in Figure 8-2 can be used to indicate that *fluid pressure acts not only downward, but, at a given depth, is exerted equally in all directions.*

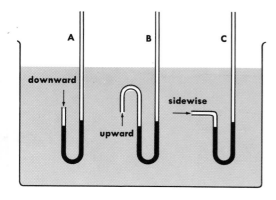

Fig. 8-2: *At a given point in a liquid, pressure is exerted equally in all directions.*

4. BUOYANT FORCE

Everyone is familiar with the apparent decrease in weight undergone by a solid object when immersed in water. This phenomenon, first investigated by Archimedes (287-212 B.C.), can be understood by considering the forces due to liquid pressure, acting on the surfaces of the submerged object.

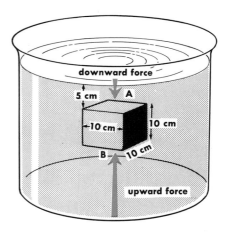

Fig. 8-3: *A cube submerged in a fluid. The resultant of the upward and downward forces is called buoyant force. When this resultant exceeds the gravitational pull on the object, it will float.*

Figure 8-3 illustrates a cube, each side of which measures 10 cm. It is held under water so that its upper surface is 5.0 cm below the surface. The pressure on the upper surface of the cube is 5.0 gf/cm², and

total force acting on upper surface $= pA$
$$= 5.0 \text{ gf/cm}^2 \times 1.0 \times 10^2 \text{ cm}^2$$
$$= 500 \text{ gf}$$
$$= 5.0 \times 10^2 \text{ gf}.$$

The pressure at the lower surface is equal to the weight of water above 1 cm² of area at that depth (15 cm), and is 15 gf/cm².

Total force acting on lower surface $= pA$
$$= 15 \text{gf/cm}^2 \times 1.0 \times 10^2 \text{ cm}^2$$
$$= 1.5 \times 10^3 \text{ gf}.$$

The force of 500 g on the upper surface is a downward force, while that on the lower surface is an upward force, because *liquid pressure acts at right angles to all surfaces.*

The resultant of these two forces in this example is (1500-500) gf or 1000 gf upward, and is called the buoyant force. **The buoyant force exerted on a solid partially or** completely submerged in a fluid, is the resultant of the forces exerted by the fluid due to pressure variations within it.

If the object's weight in air exceeds this buoyant force, the object will sink. Otherwise the object will float. In either case, the object will appear to lose weight by an amount equal to the buoyant force. The difference between the object's weight and the buoyant force is called the *apparent weight* of the object in the fluid.

Note that if the cube in our example is placed at a greater depth, the forces on both the upper and lower surfaces would increase proportionally. However, the buoyant force, which is the difference between these forces, would remain the same. *The buoyant force acting on a submerged solid is independent of the depth of the solid.* The student can verify this by determining the buoyant force on the cube of Figure 8-3 when the upper surface is at a depth of, say, 15 cm.

5. ARCHIMEDES' PRINCIPLE

A further interesting fact arises from our discussion in the last section. The volume of the cube is 1000 cm³ and it displaces 1000 cm³ of water. The weight of this displaced liquid is 1000 gf, which is precisely the value of the buoyant force (or apparent loss of weight).

This fact, true for any object submerged in any fluid, is known as *Archimedes' Principle*.

An object submerged in a fluid undergoes an apparent loss of weight equal to the weight of the fluid displaced.

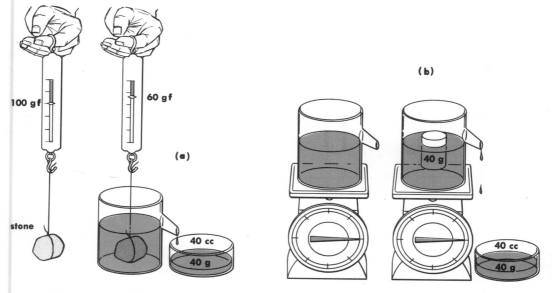

Fig. 8-4: (a) The apparent weight of the stone in the fluid is 60 gf, indicating a buoyant force of 40 gf. This buoyant force is equal to the weight of the fluid displaced. (b) The apparent weight of the floating object is zero, indicating a buoyant force of 40 gf. This buoyant force is again equal to the weight of the fluid displaced. A floating object always displaces its own weight.

The apparent weight of a floating object is zero for the following reason. Since the object moves neither upward nor downward, the buoyant force acting upward must exactly counterbalance the true weight of the object acting downward. We would then expect the weight of fluid displaced to equal the weight of the object in air. This fact is referred to as the *Law of Flotation*. **A floating object displaces an amount of fluid equal to the weight of the object in air.**

Figure 8-4 portrays both of the above principles.

EXAMPLE 4

A man weighing 215 lb and having a volume of 3.00 ft³ jumps into the ocean.

(*a*) Will he float? The density of sea water is 64.0 lb/ft³.

(*b*) On his next jump, the man wears a life preserver, which has a volume of 1.00 ft³ and weighs 5.0 lb. Will he float?

Solution:

(*a*) buoyant force = weight of fluid
$$\text{displaced}$$
$$= 3.00 \text{ ft}^3 \times 64.0 \text{ lb/ft}^3$$
$$= 192 \text{ lb} .$$

Because the buoyant force is less than the weight of the man, he will sink. Let's hope he can swim.

(*b*) Suppose the man and life preserver are completely submerged.

volume of fluid
$$\text{displaced} = 4.00 \text{ ft}^3$$
weight of fluid
$$\text{displaced} = 4.00 \text{ ft}^3 \times 64.0 \text{ lb/ft}^3$$
$$= 256 \text{ lb}$$
$$\therefore \text{ buoyant force} = 256 \text{ lb} .$$

Because the buoyant force now exceeds the total weight of man and preserver (220 lb), the man will rise to the surface.

EXAMPLE 5

A block of wood has a surface measuring 12.0 cm by 8.00 cm and has a uniform thickness of 5.00 cm. Its specific gravity is 0.70.

(*a*) To what depth will it sink when placed in water?

(*b*) What is the smallest mass that can be placed on it so that the upper surface will be submerged?

Solution:

(*a*) Total volume
$$\text{of wood} = 12.0 \times 8.00 \times 5.00 \text{ cm}^3$$
$$= 4.80 \times 10^2 \text{ cm}^3$$
$$\text{mass of wood} = DV = 4.80 \times 10^2 \times 0.70 \text{ g}$$
$$= 336 \text{ g}$$
$$\therefore \text{ mass of water}$$
$$\text{displaced} = 3.36 \times 10^2 \text{ g}$$
and volume of
$$\text{water displaced} = 3.36 \times 10^2 \text{ cm}^3 .$$

Let x = depth to which block sinks
$$\therefore \ 12.0 \times 8.0 \times x = 336$$
$$x = \textbf{3.50 cm} .$$

(*b*) To cause the remainder of the block to sink:

additional volume of water to be displaced = $12.0 \times 8.0 \times 1.5 \text{ cm}^3 = 144 \text{ cm}^3$
weight of additional water
$$\text{displaced} = 144 \text{ gf}$$
$$\therefore \text{ minimum mass required} = \textbf{144 g} .$$

6. MEASURING SPECIFIC GRAVITY BY THE USE OF ARCHIMEDES' PRINCIPLE

1. *Solids*

(*a*) *Solids more dense than water*

Figure 8-4(*a*) illustrates a convenient method for determining the density of an object more dense than water. The solid is first weighed in air, and then weighed when totally immersed in water. The apparent loss in weight (found by subtracting these two readings) enables us to find the weight of water displaced. This displaced water is equal in volume to that of the solid. In this illustration:

$$\text{buoyant force} = 40 \text{ gf}$$
$$\therefore \text{ weight of water displaced} = 40 \text{ gf}.$$

The volume of this water is equal to that of the submerged solid.

$\therefore$ Specific gravity

$$= \frac{\text{weight of solid}}{\text{weight of equal volume of water}}$$

$$= \frac{\text{weight of solid}}{\text{apparent loss of weight in water}}$$

$$= \frac{100 \text{ gf}}{40 \text{ gf}} = 2.5.$$

(b) *Solids less dense than water*

The method in (a) is unsuitable. A satisfactory method, illustrated in Figure 8-5, is to attach a sinker to the object and proceed as follows:

(i) Weigh the object in air.

(ii) Attach the sinker below the solid and submerge only the sinker in water. Reweigh as illustrated.

(iii) Submerge both object and sinker. Make a final weighing.

The difference recorded between the second and third weighings is due solely to the buoyant force produced by the water displaced by the object, since the sinker was submerged in both cases.

As before

specific gravity

$$= \frac{\text{weight of object in air}}{\text{apparent loss of weight in water}}$$

$$= \frac{10 \text{ nt}}{(30-5) \text{ nt}} = 0.4.$$

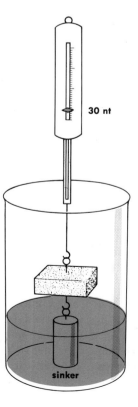
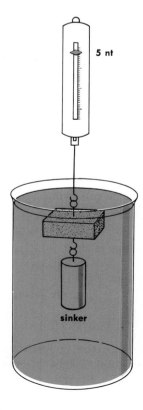

Fig. 8-5: *The sinker method for determining the density of a solid of low density.*

2. Liquids

(a) Buoyancy method

The specific gravity of a liquid may be obtained by comparing the buoyant force it exerts on any submerged object with the buoyant force exerted on that object by water.

Consider an object whose weight in air is 4.0 lb. When weighed in water, its apparent weight is 2.0 lb, and when weighed in the second liquid, the apparent weight is 2.5 lb. The weight of displaced water is 2.0 lb, and an equal volume of the other liquid weighs 1.5 lb.

$$\therefore \text{Specific gravity of liquid} = \frac{1.5}{2.0} = 0.75.$$

(b) The specific gravity bottle

This is a bottle of special design, which ensures that equal volumes of the liquid and water are weighed. The empty bottle is weighed first: then it is filled with the liquid and weighed once more. Another weighing is made when the bottle is filled with water. By subtracting the weight of the empty bottle from each of these values, the specific gravity of the liquid can be determined.

(c) Specific gravity by the commercial hydrometer

Figure 8-6 illustrates the commercial hydrometer, which consists of a glass container to provide a large bulk and a lower bulb weighted with shot or mercury. The hydrometer floats upright in a liquid to a depth determined by the density of the liquid and the weighted material in the bulb. The specific gravity is read on a calibrated scale at the mark where the liquid surface meets the scale. Some hydrometers are designed to measure the specific gravity of liquids less dense than water, while others are used for liquids more dense than water.

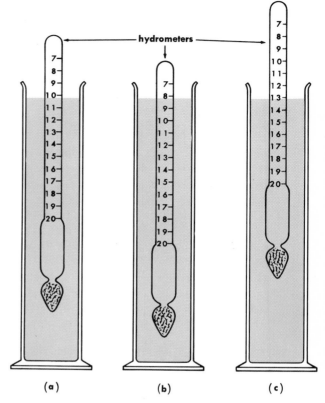

Fig. 8-6: *The hydrometer provides the most convenient method for measuring specific gravity. Which of these liquids is water?*

Commercially, the hydrometer is used by the service-station attendant to find the percentage of sulphuric acid in the electrolyte of a car battery. The specific gravity of the sulphuric acid reads 1.30 when the battery is fully charged and 1.15 if nearly completely discharged. The attendant also checks the percentage of antifreeze in the radiator of an automobile by the same method in order to ensure adequate winter protection.

7. BUOYANCY OF BALLOONS AND SUBMARINES

It is clear from Archimedes' Principle that if a body is less dense than water, the buoyant force on it will be equal in magnitude to its weight before it is completely submerged; that is, it will float. A ship floats when the weight of the water that it displaces is equal to the weight of the ship. When a wooden block is well submerged in water, the buoyant force is greater than its weight; hence the unbalanced upward force accelerates it upward and it rises to the surface. A balloon inflated with a light gas such as hydrogen or helium will have a buoyant force acting on it greater than the weight of the balloon, and so the balloon is accelerated upward by this unbalanced force. As it rises, the balloon may come to equilibrium, either because some gas has been allowed to escape or because of the decreasing density of the air as the balloon rises.

A submarine dives because water is allowed to flow into appropriate tanks in the ship, thereby increasing its weight until the buoyant force is less than its weight. When it rises again, it does so because compressed air is forced into its water tanks, thereby displacing the water and decreasing the weight of the craft. It is clear that the adjustments of air and water in its tanks may be such as to cause it to lie submerged in equilibrium.

A point about flotation is sometimes overlooked, namely, that in order that a liquid exert its buoyant force on a submerged body, the liquid must surround the body at the bottom. A submarine that sinks until its bottom is in the mud, the water not completely surrounding the bottom, loses the buoyant force due to the water and will not rise. This has often happened in the history of submarines. In order to raise such a submerged submarine from the sea floor, it is necessary to get water under the bottom of the submarine; otherwise, the entire weight of water above it holds it down.

This point may be demonstrated by the simple device shown in Figure 8-7. The beaker shown is filled with water and a piece of plate glass P lies at the bottom of the beaker. A cork, C, has a small piece of plate glass, p, waxed to its lower side so that cork and glass float. If this cork-and-glass object is pushed down under the water, it will, of course, bob up again because of the buoyant force. If the object is pressed down and the water squeezed out from between the faces of the glass plates p and P, the cork and glass p will remain at the bottom. However, the smallest wedge of water that is allowed to get between p and P, will at once supply sufficient buoyant force to cause the cork C and the glass plate p to bob up to the surface again.

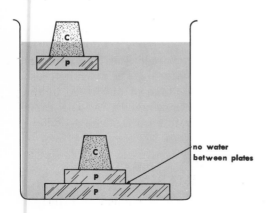

no water
between plates

Fig. 8-7: *Demonstration to illustrate that no buoyant force exists if liquid is not underneath the submerged object.*

Table 8-1

Density (g/cm³) and Specific Gravity of Common Substances (at 20°C)

Solids	Density (g/cm³) or Specific Gravity	Liquids	Density (g/cm³) or Specific Gravity
Aluminum	2.70	Carbon tetrachloride	1.60
Brass	8.5	Chloroform	1.50
Copper	8.9	Ether	0.73
Cork	0.24	Ethyl alcohol	0.81
Gold	19.3	Gasoline	0.68
Ice	0.92	Kerosene	0.82
Iron	7.6	Mercury	13.6
Lead	11.3	Olive oil	0.92
Platinum	21.4	Sea water	1.03
Silver	10.5	Turpentine	0.87
Wood, elm	0.57	Water	1.00
Wood, pine	0.42		
Zinc	7.1		

DENSITY: mass per unit volume of a substance.

SPECIFIC GRAVITY: the ratio of the weight of a substance to the weight of an equal volume of water.

KILOGRAM FORCE (kgf) AND GRAM FORCE (gf) are gravitational units of force, equal to the weight of a kilogram mass and gram mass, respectively.

PRESSURE: force per unit area. The pressure at a point in a liquid is dependent upon the depth of the point and the density of the liquid, but is independent of the volume of the liquid.

BUOYANT FORCE: the resultant upward force exerted on an object by the fluid, due to a greater pressure at its lower surface. It is equal to the apparent loss of weight of the object while in the fluid.

ARCHIMEDES' PRINCIPLE: the apparent loss of weight of an object immersed in a fluid is equal to the weight of fluid displaced. The law of flotation is a particular case, in which a floating object, with apparent weight zero, displaces its entire weight.

> In problems involving buoyant force it is well to recall three quantities that are always equal in value:
>
> buoyant force = apparent loss in weight = weight of displaced fluid .

EXERCISE A

1. What two factors determine the pressure exerted by a liquid?

2. Name the factors that determine the force exerted by the water against the side wall of a swimming tank.

3. (a) What is meant by buoyant force?
   (b) Upon what does the magnitude of the buoyant force depend?

4. How is specific gravity converted to mass density in: (a) CGS units, (b) MKS units?

5. How is specific gravity converted to density in lb/ft³?

6. State the meaning of: (a) density, (b) specific gravity.

7. What is meant by the information "S.G. = 1.84" placed on a winchester of reagent sulphuric acid?

8. How is buoyancy used to determine the specific gravity of solids that are more dense than water?

9. (a) Name the three steps to be taken in order to find, by the buoyancy method, the specific gravity of a solid less dense than water.
   (b) How is the specific gravity calculated in this case?

10. Draw the scales for those commercial hydrometers that enable one to read the specific gravity of liquids: (a) less dense than water, (b) more dense than water.

11. Will the water line of a ship rise or fall as it passes from fresh to salt water? Explain.

12. When the Chicago breakwater was being built, many barge loads of huge stones were taken from the bottom of Georgian Bay and towed to Chicago:
    (a) Why would they want the largest stones they could handle?
    (b) Some of the chains placed around the stones by the diver broke. The cables often gave way when the rocks were being lifted out of the water. Give an explanation for this.

13. A man fishing from a rowboat in a small pond, throws out a heavy cast-iron anchor. He observes that the level of the water *falls*. Explain.

14. An ice cube floats in a glass of water. What change in the level of the water will have taken place when the ice is completely melted? Explain.

EXERCISE B

In the following problems, assume all numerical data accurate to the number of digits quoted.
Density of fresh water = 62.4 lb/ft³.

1. The earth has a mass of 5.98×10^{27} grams and a volume of 1.083×10^{27} cm³. What is the average density of the earth? The rocks of the earth's crust vary from 2.5 g/cm³

to 3.4 g/cm³. What conclusion can you come to about the density of the material that comprises the inside of the earth?

2. The specific gravity of gold is 19.3; calculate its weight per unit volume in lb/ft³.

3. Calculate the pressure in gf/cm² exerted by a column of mercury 76.0 cm high when the density of mercury is 13.6 g/cm³.

4. An open U-tube contains mercury. One limb of the tube is connected to a pressure vessel and the other limb is open to the air. The mercury in the open limb stands 12.00 in. above that in the limb connected to the pressure vessel. Calculate the pressure difference between the vessel and the air, in gf/cm².

5. In 1934 Charles Beebe looked through a circular quartz-glass window in his bathysphere off the coast of Bermuda at a depth of 3028 feet. The window had a diameter of 6 inches. Approximately what force must the window have withstood if the specific gravity of sea water is 1.03?

6. A cubical container is filled with a liquid. If the total force on the bottom is 5000 lb, what is the total force on one of its sides?

7. An empty bottle has mass 100 grams. The total mass of this bottle filled with water is 250 grams. When a quantity of metal turnings is put into the empty bottle, the combined weight is 750 grams. Finally, when the remainder of the volume is filled with water the combined mass of the metal, water, and bottle becomes 810 grams.

Find: (a) the internal volume of the bottle in cm³
  (b) the volume of the metal turnings
  (c) the specific gravity of the metal.

8. A quartz rock containing gold has a mass of 200 grams. The specific gravity of quartz is 2.60, of gold 19.3, and of the rock 6.40.
(a) What is the volume of the rock?
(b) How many grams of gold are in the rock?

9. A stone weighs 310 gf in air and 210 gf when submerged in water. What is its density?

10. A piece of metal with a volume of 20 cm³ weighs 180 gf in air. Find its weight when immersed in (a) water, (b) a liquid twice as dense as water.

11. A stone of mass 435 g has an apparent weight of 270 gf when immersed in water, and 303 gf when immersed in oil.
(a) Find the density of the stone.
(b) Find the specific gravity of the oil.

12. A block of metal weighs 120 lb in air, 105 lb when immersed in water, and 108 lb when immersed in a certain liquid. Determine:
(a) the density of the metal
(b) the density of the liquid
(c) the specific gravity of the liquid.

13. A submarine of volume 1.65×10^5 ft³ and weighing 4.83×10^3 tons, is floating at the surface of sea water of density 64.0 lb/ft³.

    (a) What is the buoyant force on the submarine?

    (b) What volume of water does it displace?

    (c) What volume of water must be admitted into the submarine so it will just submerge?

14. What is the volume of a whale that weighs 25 tons? The specific gravity of sea water is 1.03.

15. A plastic float for a fishing line has a volume of 20 cm³ and a specific gravity of 0.15. With what force must a fish pull to submerge it?

16. A glass bulb requires 3.50×10^{-1} newtons less to support it when submerged in water than when supported in air, and 5.25×10^{-1} newtons less to support it in chloroform. Calculate the specific gravity of chloroform.

17. If a block of wood floats half immersed in water, what fraction would be immersed in a liquid with a density of 2 g/cm³?

18. In the harbour of a sea port, a barge (40 ft by 16 ft) sinks 3 inches when an elephant is loaded on it. What is the weight of the elephant? The specific gravity of sea water is 1.03.

19. If a block of wood floats $\frac{1}{2}$ immersed in water and $\frac{2}{3}$ immersed in another liquid, what is the density of the other liquid?

20. A piece of wax weighs 6.0 gf in air. When it is attached to a sinker, and both sinker and wax are submerged in water, the apparent weight of the combination is 86.5 gf. When only the sinker is immersed, the weight of the combination is 95.7 gf. Determine the specific gravity of the wax.

21. A boy can lift 125 lb. If the specific gravity of stone is 2.50 what is the weight in air of a stone that he can just lift when it is submerged?

22. A jar about half full of water is balanced on an equal-arm scale. An iron bolt weighing 37 grams is lowered by a fine thread into the water. How many grams must be added to the other side of the scales to obtain a balance once more? The specific gravity of iron is 7.6.

23. A hollow sphere made of glass (density 2.60 g/cm³) weighs 234.0 grams in air and only 39 grams in water. What is the volume of air inside the sphere? (Ignore both the weight and the buoyant force of the air.)

24. Two bodies are in equilibrium when suspended in water from the arms of a balance. The mass of one body is 280 grams and its density is 5.6 g/cm³. If the mass of the other is 360 grams, what is its density?

25. An iron weight of 400 lb, placed on top of a rectangular raft, sinks it so that its surface is level with the surface of the water.

    (a) If the specific gravity of the iron is 7.6, how many pounds of iron suspended from the bottom of the raft would do the same thing?

(b) Would 400 lb of rock (specific gravity 2.5) placed on top do the same thing as 400 lb of iron?

(c) What weight of rock suspended would keep the raft in the same position?

(d) Why is lead used in the keels of fast sailing boats rather than iron or concrete?

(e) Why is it put at the bottom of the keel?

26. A rectangular piece of styrofoam of mass 2.00 kg floats with 5.00% of its volume under water. What is the smallest mass that will just submerge it if the mass is placed on top?

27. A 400-cm³ sphere of glass (specific gravity 2.8) is dropped into a jar containing mercury (specific gravity 13.6) and water in sufficient quantities that the sphere will float on the mercury and be under the surface of the water:

(a) Will the part of the sphere under the surface of the mercury be buoyed up by the water?

(b) Will the mercury have to hold up the whole weight of the sphere?

(c) By letting the part of the sphere under the mercury be X cm³ and the part buoyed up by the water be (400-X) cm³, find how many cubic centimetres will be under the surface of the mercury.

Liquids at Rest

▶ Experiment 10

To show that an object submerged in a fluid experiences an apparent loss in weight equal to the weight of the fluid displaced.

Metal cylinder or hooked weight

Graduated cylinder(100 ml)

Retort stand

Triple-beam or platform balance

Thread

Alcohol

Overflow can

400- or 500-ml beaker

Procedure

1. Elevate the balance as indicated.

2. Suspend the metal cylinder below the scale pan by a fine thread.

3. Weigh the metal cylinder in its suspended position. Record the cylinder weight.

4. Fill the beaker ⅔ full of water and weigh the metal cylinder while it is completely immersed in the water. Do not let the cylinder touch the sides or bottom of the beaker. Record the cylinder's apparent weight.

5. Completely fill the overflow can with water, permitting excess water to flow out the spout into a sink or the beaker.

6. Slowly immerse the metal cylinder on a thread held over the overflow can and catch the overflow in the graduated cylinder. Record the volume and weight of the water displaced.

7. Refer to Figure 8-4 and compare the apparent loss in weight with the weight of the water displaced.

8. Repeat the experiment, using alcohol as the liquid. Since the specific gravity of alcohol is not unity, it will be necessary to weigh the empty graduated cylinder before starting the experiment and to weigh the cylinder with the alcohol that overflows, in order to determine the weight of the overflow.

Your conclusions should confirm Archimedes' Principle.

Experiment 11

To study the law of flotation.

Wooden block (varnished)
    with fine thread attached

Overflow can

Alcohol

Carbon tetrachloride

Triple-beam or platform balance

Beaker

Procedure

1. Weigh the wooden block and record this weight to the nearest tenth of a gram.

2. Weigh the beaker.

3. Fill the overflow can to the point of overflow, using water. When the spout has stopped dripping, place the beaker under the spout.

4. Slowly lower the block into the overflow can, using the thread. Do not allow the block to touch the sides of the can. Catch all the overflow in the beaker.

5. Weigh the beaker and its contents.

6. Empty the beaker and thoroughly dry it and the wooden block.

7. Repeat the experiment, using alcohol in place of water. If time permits, repeat once more, using carbon tetrachloride.

Analysis

1. Determine the weight of liquid overflow for each of the liquids used. Compare this weight with the weight of the floating object.

2. State your conclusions.

Question

Why is it necessary that the wooden block be varnished?

Experiment 12

To employ Archimedes' Principle in determining the specific gravity of a liquid, of a solid more dense than water, and of a solid less dense than water.

Retort stand
Triple-beam balance
Metal cylinder
Wooden cylinder (with small hook)
Sinker (hooked weight or substitute)
Methyl alcohol
2 beakers (350- or 400-ml capacity)
Hydrometer jar
Hydrometer
Thread
Distilled water (if available)

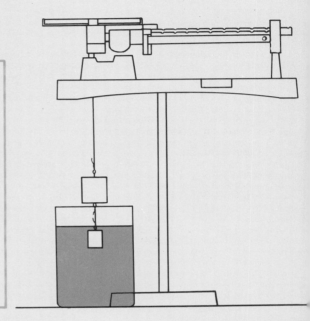

Procedure

METAL CYLINDER

1. Elevate the balance as indicated in the illustration.

2. Suspend the metal cylinder below the scale pan by a fine thread.

3. Weigh the cylinder in its suspended position.

4. Completely immerse the cylinder in alcohol contained in one of the beakers.

5. Weigh the cylinder while it is immersed in the alcohol. *Do not permit the cylinder to touch the side or bottom of the beaker.*

6. Remove the cylinder and dry it.

7. Reweigh the cylinder while it is immersed in water contained in the second beaker.

WOODEN CYLINDER

1. Weigh the wooden cylinder in the suspended position previously described.

2. Attach the sinker below the cylinder.

3. With the sinker *only* immersed in the beaker of water, weigh the cylinder-sinker combination.

4. Immerse *both* the cylinder and the sinker in the water and weigh once more.

HYDROMETER

1. Pour the alcohol into a hydrometer jar.

2. Gently introduce the hydrometer and measure the specific gravity of the alcohol as recorded on the scale.

3. Examine the hydrometer scale carefully. In which direction do the numbers increase? Do you read the scale from the bottom upward or from the top downward?

Calculations

Using the methods outlined in section 6 of this chapter:

1. Calculate the specific gravity of the metal cylinder and of the wooden cylinder.

2. By the buoyancy method, calculate the specific gravity of the alcohol and compare it with the result obtained by direct measurement.

Chapter 9

Temperature and Thermal Expansion

1. THE NATURE OF HEAT

Many phenomena involving heat were known to the earliest and most primitive of civilizations. The necessity for the warmth provided by fire and the use of clothing to preserve the heat of the human body was well recognized. It was not until the seventeenth century, however, that a systematic study of the nature of heat evolved. The study was facilitated by the invention of a device—the thermometer—by which the "degree of heat" (temperature) possessed by a body could be measured. The first such instrument was constructed by Galileo around 1593.

Until about the middle of the nineteenth century, heat was thought to be an invisible, weightless fluid called caloric. When substances burned they were assumed to lose large quantities of caloric. It was further assumed that this caloric could be transferred from one body or substance to another. When a body absorbed caloric it was warmed; when it emitted caloric it was cooled.

About 1800, Count Rumford, a military engineer working in Germany, observed the heat developed when cannon were bored in the shops. He noticed that heat was developed even when the boring tool was dull

and did not cut. The evidence of the heat developed was the boiling of the cooling water in the bore of the cannon. He therefore concluded that limitless amounts of heat could be developed from friction. About 40 years later Count Rumford's observations were established on a firm basis by the work of James Prescott Joule. By means of many careful experiments Joule showed that a given amount of mechanical energy, when dissipated, always produced the same amount of heat. Apparatus similar to that used in Joule's original experiments is shown on page 78.

Rumford's contribution to science lies in his questioning the caloric theory—a theory which, at that time, was quite acceptable in the explanation of many thermal phenomena. The work of Joule and many of his contemporaries, notably Robert Mayer in Germany, established beyond doubt the quantitative relationship between mechanical energy and heat. When further experimentation with other forms of energy yielded the same quantitative relationship, the concept of heat as a form of energy was born.

The Law of Conservation of Energy (page 79), the great unifying concept of eighteenth-century physics, stems from these findings.

2. THE KINETIC THEORY OF MATTER

In a paper published in 1847, Joule postulated that heat was a form of internal energy possessed by the molecules of a substance due to their random motion. The idea that matter consists of molecules stems from early times. The ability of a substance, such as water, to exist in three different states—solid, liquid, and gas, each with different volumes—suggests that movement of fundamental particles of the matter is responsible.

Other basic properties of matter are conveniently explained by assuming a molecular structure. The ability of a solid to retain its shape suggests that the molecules in this state cannot readily move about from one part of the solid to another. Also, the property of cohesion, whereby a great amount of work is required to pull a solid apart, suggests that the molecules exert forces of attraction upon each other. These cohesive forces are evident to a lesser degree in liquids, but are almost nonexistent in the case of gases. A similar explanation can be given for adhesion.

In the case of liquids and gases, the phenomenon of diffusion demonstrates the existence of molecular motion. If a small quantity of ammonia is introduced into a room, the gas will diffuse to every part of the room in a relatively short time. The molecules may be regarded as moving freely, and not, to any great extent, affected by forces existing between them.

If we explain the cohesion of a solid on the basis of mutual attraction of its molecules, how may we account for the tremendous resistance offered by the same substance when an effort is made to compress it? To be consistent we must conclude that as the intermolecular distance becomes smaller, the forces of attraction that exist between the molecules, become forces of repulsion. Figure 9-1 shows graphically our present concept of how the forces between molecules vary with the distance separating them.

The first direct observation of molecular motion is attributed to the English botanist Robert Brown. In 1827, while viewing minute grains of pollen by microscope, Brown observed that these particles were in very erratic motion. Brown attributed this movement to minute forms of life, but later experiment showed the same result using inorganic material. Later, this "Brownian Movement" was attributed to collisions between the suspended particles and the invisible high-speed molecules of the gas or liquid.

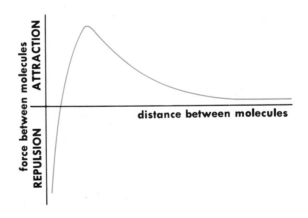

Fig. 9-1: *Force exerted between two molecules, plotted against the distance separating them. Note that the amount of separation determines whether the force is attractive or repulsive.*

3. THE KINETIC THEORY OF HEAT

In his treatise of 1847, Joule envisioned each of the closely packed molecules of a solid as vibrating about a fixed position

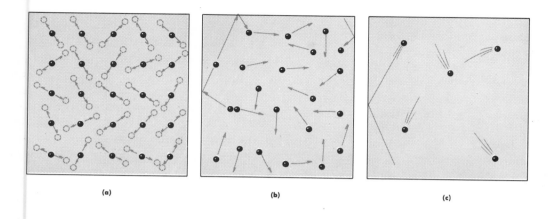

Fig. 9-2: *Representation of molecules: (a) solid, (b) liquid, (c) gas.*

(Figure 9-2). If the solid is rubbed, the work done against friction accelerates the particles on the surface, and, through collision with other molecules, the total state of vibration of the molecules comprising the solid is increased. In other words, the work done by the outside agent results in an increase in the kinetic energy of each molecule, and a rise in the temperature of the object involved. Here we associate temperature with a measure of the kinetic energy of vibration of each molecule.

Conduction of heat is explained in a similar fashion, using the kinetic theory. Molecular bombardment allows a transfer of energy from one part of the material to another. The increased kinetic energy of each molecule results in a greater amplitude of vibration for the molecule, and the cumulative result is an overall increase in volume of the substance.

The increased kinetic energy of a molecule also serves to explain the more rapid diffusion of a gas when heated, and the increased pressure on the walls of its container, due to the many collisions of the molecules with the walls.

It is well to point out at this time that there are certain thermal phenomena that cannot be explained in terms of this simple kinetic theory. These exceptions are of a much too involved nature to concern us at this stage.

4. HEAT AND TEMPERATURE

We know from experience that heat and temperature are related. They are not, however, the same thing. Figure 9-3 shows a large kettle full of water at boiling temperature and a cup of water, also at boiling temperature.

140

Fig. 9-3: *Two substances at the same temperature possess different total amounts of heat energy, even though (on the average) the kinetic energy of their molecules is the same.*

The temperatures are the same because these two objects, if put into contact, would not transmit heat to each other; but the kettle has a great deal *more* heat than the cup. The kettle has more heat because it took more time to heat the water in the kettle from room temperature to boiling temperature than it took to heat the water in the cup (the source of heat remaining constant during both operations).

When a body is hot, it has more *thermal energy* than when it is cold. We associate the thermal energy of a body with the total energy of all its molecules; whereas the temperature is a measure of the average kinetic energy of an individual molecule.

It is important at this point that we make mention of one aspect of heat and temperature, not yet touched upon, which will be considered in detail in the following chapter. When heat is added to a substance that is undergoing a change of state, no change in temperature takes place. We may conclude that the average kinetic energy of the molecules undergoes no change. Where, then, did this hidden or "latent" heat go? As we shall find, this extra heat is absorbed as a form of *potential energy.* Consequently, **we**

shall define the temperature of a substance to be the measure of the kinetic energy possessed by each molecule.

5. TRANSFER OF HEAT

Heat may be transmitted from one point to another in three ways—*conduction, convection, and radiation.* In any actual case of transmission, a combination of these methods may be operating simultaneously.

We have already touched upon the transfer of heat by conduction in our discussion of the kinetic theory. It is clear that this method requires the presence of a material medium.

Convection is the transfer of heat from one part of a fluid to another by the flow of the fluid, resulting in a mixture of the warmer parts with the cooler parts. Figure 9-4 illustrates the principle. The warm water at A expands as a result of the heat conducted to it through the glass. It floats to the top because of its decreased density, and is

Fig. 9-4: *Convection currents in a fluid.*

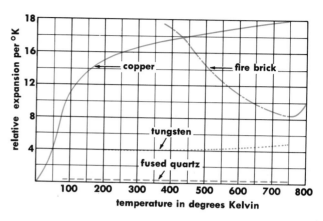

Fig. 9-5: *Relative expansion characteristics of various solids. Note that tungsten and quartz expand at an almost constant rate, while the amount of expansion of fire brick decreases with increasing temperature. Why would this latter characteristic be of advantage in a furnace system?*

replaced by the cooler water above it. In time, a fairly uniform temperature is attained throughout the liquid. This principle lies behind the operation of the home heating system, whether the medium be water or air.

In the case of the hot-water heating system, heat is carried to the radiator by convection currents of water from the furnace. The transfer of heat from the radiator to the air in contact with it, is effected by conduction. The room is heated by the resulting convection currents of air. Although air is effective in the transfer of heat by convection, it is at the same time a poor conductor of heat. Normally, the space separating the inner and outer surfaces of an exterior wall is filled with an insulating medium to prevent transfer of heat. Air, alone, does not suffice because of its ability to transfer heat from one wall to the other by convection. The use of other insulating substances, such as fiberglass, or rock wool, restricts the path of the air sufficiently that transfer of heat is minimized.

Radiation

Unlike conduction and convection, transfer of heat by radiation requires no material medium. The heat received from the sun, through 93 million miles of empty space, is a familiar example. Needless to say, transfer

of heat by this method cannot be explained in terms of the kinetic theory alone.

Heat radiation consists of electromagnetic waves, identical in character to radio waves, light waves, and X-rays. Every object has a tendency to emit radiation to its surroundings if the latter are at a lower temperature. If such is not the case, the object absorbs heat from its surroundings and an increase in the objects' temperature results. Obviously, if the temperature of the object is constant, the rate at which it radiates heat energy is equal to the rate at which it absorbs it.

The heat radiated by a given object depends upon other factors in addition to the temperature difference. Of importance are the shape of the object (its surface area) and the nature of the surface. We are aware of the greater ability of black objects to radiate heat at a greater rate than light-coloured or shiny objects, other factors remaining equal. It is also true that the best radiators of heat energy are also the best absorbers.

6. EXPANSION DUE TO THERMAL ENERGY

The expansion of solids and liquids with a rise in temperature is conveniently described in terms of the thermal energy that the molecules, or groups of molecules, of the substance acquire. We think of the mole-

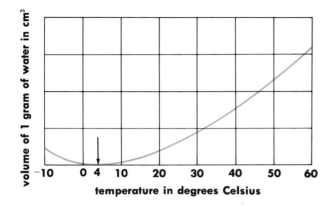

cules of solids as vibrating more and more violently as the temperature rises; in consequence, they are on the average farther apart, with the result that a given number of molecules will occupy a larger space.

The case of liquids is much the same, except that in their case not only is the energy of vibration increased but the molecules wander (move) about in the liquid with a greater speed. Thus, any given molecule requires more space when its thermal energy is great; that is, when the temperature of the body is high.

Different solids and liquids have quite different rates of expansion but the *rates of expansion for different gases are very much the same.* Moreover, the rate of expansion of any given gas is more nearly constant over a wider range of temperature than that of a solid or a liquid.

All gases have approximately the same rate of expansion because their widely separated molecules behave, in effect, as independent particles. Gas molecules are separated by distances much greater than their molecular dimensions and consequently the forces acting between them are negligibly small. This picture breaks down when the temperature and pressure of a gas are such that it is near its liquefaction point. At this point it begins to behave as a liquid.

Figure 9-5 illustrates graphically the wide variation in expansivity exhibited by different substances. In the design of equipment that is intended to undergo wide extremes in temperature, it is imperative that these variations be taken into consideration. For example, tungsten is a metal that expands in a manner similar to that of many types of glass. For this reason it is often used to seal electrodes through the glass of electric light bulbs.

The most common exception to the general rule that substances expand when heated, lies in the peculiar behaviour of water. If water at 0° C is heated, its volume diminishes steadily and reaches a minimum at 4° C. Further heating results in expansion. This behaviour, illustrated in Figure 9-6, is observed for no other liquid nor for any common solids save for a few rubberlike substances. The fact that water has its maximum density at 4° C accounts for the freezing of lakes from the surface downwards.

7. THE MERCURY THERMOMETER

Since liquids expand with an increase of temperature and the expansion is, within a reasonable range of temperature, proportional to the temperature rise, the expansion is used to measure differences in temperature.

A liquid commonly used is mercury. Mercury has the advantage that over a useful range of temperatures it remains a liquid and over this range, too, its degree of expansion is very nearly constant. In order that we may be able to observe the change in volume, the mercury is contained in a small glass bulb to which is attached a long capillary tube or stem of uniform bore. The bulb is made of quite thin glass so that heat may pass readily from the surroundings to the mercury, or the reverse. A change in volume of the mercury is made evident by a change in the length of the mercury column in the capillary. This is really a difference between the change in volume of the mercury and of the glass, the former being the greater.

8. GRADUATING THE THERMOMETER

The bulb and lower portion of the stem of the thermometer are packed in a funnel containing ice that is well mixed with water. The temperature of this mixture is constant. See Figure 9-7.

The lowest point to which the mercury in the stem falls is marked on the stem. This is known as the freezing point. The thermometer is next suspended in the steam from a boiler containing distilled water as illustrated in Figure 9-8.

When the water is boiling under pressure of 760 mm of mercury, the standard atmospheric pressure, the highest point to which the mercury in the stem rises is marked on the stem. This is the boiling point. When the two fixed points have been marked on the stem, the distance between them is divided into 100 parts for a Celsius thermometer or into 180 parts for a Fahrenheit thermometer. Graduations of the proper size, suitably numbered, are then marked on the stem of the thermometer. In the Celsius or Centigrade thermometer, the freezing point is

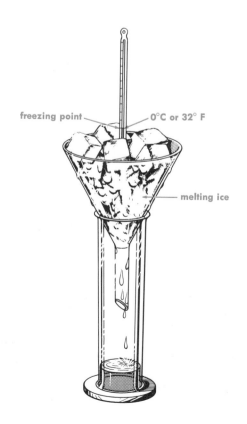

Fig. 9-7: *Determining the ice point.*

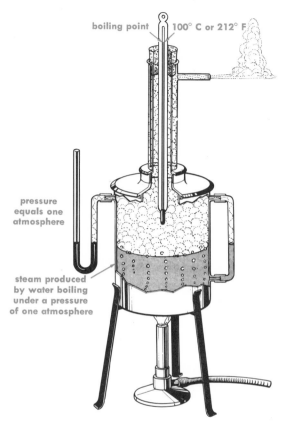

boiling point   100° C or 212° F

pressure
equals one
atmosphere

steam produced
by water boiling
under a pressure
of one atmosphere

Fig. 9-8: *Determining the steam point.*

same temperature. The temperature difference between any Celsius temperature, T_c, and the freezing point is $(T_c - 0)$ degrees. The temperature difference between any Fahrenheit temperature, T_f, and the freezing point is $(T_f - 32)$ degrees. If, then, T_c and T_f are the boiling temperatures it follows that:

$$\frac{T_c - 0}{T_f - 32} = \frac{100}{180} = \frac{5}{9}.$$

Solving, in turn, for T_c and T_f, we get:

$$T_c = \tfrac{5}{9}(T_f - 32)$$
$$T_f = \tfrac{9}{5}T_c + 32.$$

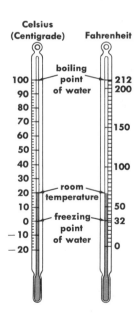

Fig. 9-9: *Corresponding temperatures on the Celsius and Fahrenheit scales.*

marked 0° and the boiling point 100°. In the Fahrenheit thermometer the freezing point is marked 32° and the boiling point 212°.

The Centigrade and Fahrenheit scales are graphically portrayed in Figure 9-9. Because these two scales are both in common use, it often becomes necessary to convert from one scale to the other. To do this, we recognize that 0° C and 32° F are the same temperature and that 100° C and 212° F are also the

EXAMPLE 1

(*a*) If the lowest temperature on a winter's night was recorded as $-5.0°$ F, what would be the recording on a Centigrade thermometer?

(*b*) What is the familiar Fahrenheit temperature that is equivalent to $37.0°$ C?

Solution:

(*a*) $-5°$ F is 37 F° below freezing

or

$37 \times \frac{5}{9}$ C° below freezing
The reading would be $-21°$ **C**.

Alternatively:
$$T_c = \tfrac{5}{9}(T_f - 32)$$
$$= \tfrac{5}{9}(-5 - 32)$$
$$= \tfrac{5}{9} \times -37$$
$$= -21° \text{ C}.$$

(*b*) $37.0°$ C is 37 C° above freezing

or

$37.0 \times \frac{9}{5}$ F° above freezing
The reading would be
$$66.6 \text{ F°} + 32.0 = 98.6° \text{ F}.$$

Alternatively:
$$T_f = \tfrac{9}{5}T_c + 32$$
$$= \tfrac{9}{5} \times 37.0 + 32.0$$
$$= 98.6° \text{ F}.$$

9. THE LOWEST TEMPERATURE POSSIBLE—THE KELVIN SCALE

In addition to the familiar Fahrenheit and Centigrade temperature scales, another scale —one devised by Lord Kelvin (Sir William Thomson, 1824-1907)—is of great value scientifically. The Kelvin scale was devised when it became evident that all gases expand the same amount for a given rise in temperature if the pressure is kept constant.

The expansion of gases can be studied when they are trapped in a capillary tube by a globule of mercury and the change in length of the enclosed gas measured as shown in Figure 9-10. If the length of the column of air is 273 mm when the capillary tube is in an ice-water mixture, it will increase to 373 mm when placed in boiling water at $100°$ C. The air column has increased $\frac{100}{273}$ of its original length when heated from $0°$ C to $100°$ C; or for each degree of temperature change, the expansion is $\frac{1}{273}$ of the volume at $0°$ C.

If the air column were cooled to $-100°$ C, it would now be only 173 mm long, and 0 mm long if the temperature could be reduced to $-273°$ C. This temperature of $-273°$ C is the lowest temperature the air column can reach: *it is at the absolute zero of temperature.*

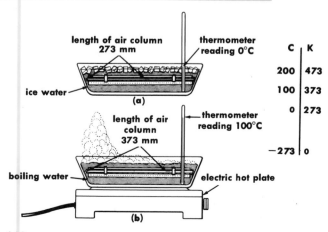

C	K
200	473
100	373
0	273
-273	0

Fig. 9-10: *Volume of a gas is proportional to its absolute temperature, if the pressure remains constant.*

Absolute zero is more accurately expressed as −273.16° C or −459.67° F. Laboratory experiments have reduced temperatures to within a few thousandths of a degree of absolute zero.

Lord Kelvin devised a temperature scale with scale divisions the same as those of the Celsius scale. Zero on the Kelvin scale is absolute zero or −273° C; hence 0° on the Centigrade scale is +273° K.

To change from Centigrade to Kelvin, add 273 degrees to the Celsius reading; or algebraically

$$T_k = T_c + 273°$$
$$-273°C = 0°K$$
$$0°C = 273°K$$
$$100°C = 373°K .$$

If the pressure is constant, the volume of a gas is directly proportional to the Kelvin temperature.

$$\frac{V}{T_k} = \frac{V'}{T'_k}$$

EXAMPLE 2

At 20.0° C a vessel contains 22.4 litres of oxygen. What will be the volume of the gas at 80.0° C, if the pressure remains constant?

Solution:

20.0° C = 293° K   80.0° C = 353° K

$$V_{293} = 22.4 \; l$$
$$V_{353} = \frac{22.4 \times 353}{293} \; l$$
$$V_{353} = 27.0 \; l .$$

THE KINETIC THEORY OF HEAT serves to give explanation to many phenomena involving heat. The overthrow of the caloric or fluid theory of heat is the result of observations by Rumford and the experimentation of nineteenth-century scientists, notably Joule.

HEAT AND TEMPERATURE differ, in that heat represents the total internal energy of all molecules in the substance (which may be of both kinetic and potential form) while temperature is a measure of the average kinetic energy of each molecule of that substance.

HEAT MAY BE TRANSFERRED by one or a combination of three methods—conduction, convection, and radiation. The first two require a material medium and can be explained in terms of our simple kinetic theory. Radiation, however, requires no material medium and requires more than the kinetic theory for satisfactory explanation.

TEMPERATURE SCALES in common use are the Celsius (Centigrade), Fahrenheit, and Kelvin (absolute).

$$T_c = 5/9 \; (T_f - 32)$$
$$T_f = 9/5 \; T_c + 32$$
$$T_k = T_c + 273$$

EXERCISE A

1. What was the evidence used by Count Rumford to indicate that heat is a form of energy?

2. List five main sources of heat on the planet Earth and some practical uses or devices stemming from these sources.

3. How can you explain that two quite different masses of water can both be at the boiling temperature under the same conditions, yet one of them possess a great deal more heat energy than the other?   How can the molecular activity of a substance measure: (a) its temperature, (b) its heat capacity?

4. When a mercury-in-glass thermometer is placed in a flame, the mercury column first descends and then rises.   Explain.

5. State what is unique about the expansion of all gases compared with that of liquids and solids.

6. What structure of gases produces the behaviour referred to in question 5?

7. What provision is made to allow for expansion in each of the following:
   (a) a concrete highway?
   (b) a steel bridge?
   (c) the piston rings in an engine?

8. A platinum wire may easily be sealed into a glass tube.   A copper wire does not form a tight seal with glass.   Explain.

9. If you examine several similar laboratory thermometers you may find that the distance between the 0° C mark and 100° C mark is not the same on all of them.   Give several possible explanations for this.

EXERCISE B

Consider all data accurate to the number of digits specified.

1. The temperature in a classroom is 77° F.   What is the Celsius reading?

2. Acetone, a colourless liquid used as a solvent, boils at 56.5° C.   What is this temperature on the Fahrenheit scale?

3. The temperature in the stratosphere is about −85° F.   Convert this to the corresponding temperature on the Celsius scale.

4. Liquid nitrogen boils at −195° C.   What is the reading on the Fahrenheit scale?

5. During a summer thunderstorm the temperature dropped 18 F°.   What was the drop in C°?

6. If water is cooled from 50° C to 10° C, what is the temperature change in F°?

7. The boiling point of liquid oxygen is −183° C. What is this temperature in K°?

8. What will be the boiling point of helium on the Centigrade scale if its boiling point is 4.1° K? (Consider absolute zero as −273.2° C.)

9. The temperature on the surface of the sun is approximately 5.75×10^{3}° K. What is this temperature on the Fahrenheit scale?

10. The temperature of Uranus is estimated as −346° F. How much is this above or below absolute zero in Kelvin degrees?

11. The mean temperature on the surface of Mars is −40° F. What is the mean Martian temperature on the Centigrade scale?

12. Some oxygen occupies a volume of 5.00 litres at 27.0° C. If the pressure is unchanged, what volume does the gas occupy at 77.0° C?

13. A certain gas occupies a volume of 250 ml at 37.0° C. What is its volume at 67.0° C if the pressure is not changed?

14. The stem of a thermometer is marked off in 150 equal scale divisions. When the bulb of this thermometer is placed in melting ice, the mercury stands at 30; and when the bulb is suspended in the steam from water boiling at standard pressure, the mercury stands at 80. To what Centigrade temperature does a reading of 125 on this thermometer correspond?

Chapter 10

Heat Units and the
Measurement of Heat

1. HEAT CAPACITY

Figure 10-1 shows blocks of five different metals, all of the same mass and the same horizontal cross-section. They have been heated in boiling water until they are all at the same temperature and then they have been placed on a block of ice. As they cool to ice temperature, they melt the ice and sink into the block. It will be seen that the aluminum sinks farther than the others, iron sinking second farthest, copper and zinc being about even, and lead coming a poor fifth.

It is evident that different materials give out or absorb different amounts of heat even though they are of the same mass and are subjected to the same temperature change. In the previous chapter it was suggested that different masses of the same material will require different amounts of heat to change their temperatures through the same range. These objects differ in *heat capacity*. Objects with a great heat capacity will require a longer time to have their temperatures raised through a given range

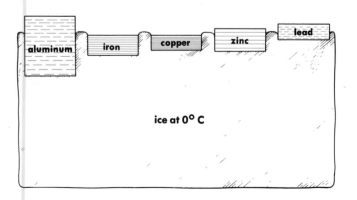

ice at 0° C

Fig. 10-1: *The metals have the same mass and diameter and have been heated in boiling water to the same temperature of 100°C. Are equal quantities of heat given out by each block?*

by the same heat source than will objects of small heat capacity.

The heat capacity of a body is the quantity of heat required to raise its temperature through one degree, or in symbols,

$$\text{heat capacity} = E_H / \triangle T,$$

where E_H is the quantity of heat required to raise the temperature of the body through $\triangle T$ deg. The Greek letter $\triangle$ (delta) is widely used to indicate the change in a quantity. Thus, $\triangle T$ indicates a temperature change.

2. HEAT UNITS AND SPECIFIC HEAT

Since heat is a form of energy, standard units are required for its measurement. It is useful to recall that mechanical energy was measured in joules (nt m) and foot-pounds.

The thermal energy E_H possessed by a material is determined by the mass and the temperature of the material since both determine the total molecular activity. Because the energy required to raise the same mass of different materials to a given temperature varies with the material used, the thermal energy will also vary with the material considered.

The kilocalorie (kcal) is the amount of heat absorbed by *one* kg of water when its temperature rises through *one* Celsius degree. This is the MKS unit of heat.

The calorie (cal) is the amount of heat absorbed by *one* g of water when its temperature rises through *one* Celsius degree. This is the CGS unit of heat.

The **British Thermal Unit** (Btu) is the amount of heat absorbed by one pound of water when its temperature rises through one Fahrenheit degree.

Table 10-1

HEAT CONSTANTS FOR VARIOUS SUBSTANCES

	Specific Heat (cal/g C°)	Melting Point (°C)	Boiling Point (°C)	Heat of Fusion (cal/g)	Heat of Vaporization (cal/g)
Alcohol, ethyl	0.58	−115	78.5	24.9	204
Aluminum	0.21	659	2057	76.8	
Ammonia	1.12	−77.7	−33.4	83.9	327
Brass	0.09	940			
Copper	0.092	1083	2336	49.0	
Glass	0.20				
Ice	0.50	0		79.71	
Iron	0.11	1535	3000	7.89	
Lead	0.031	327.4	1620	5.86	
Mercury	0.033	−38.9	357	2.8	71
Platinum	0.032	1773	4300	27.2	
Silver	0.056	961	1950	26.0	
Steam	0.48				
Tungsten	0.034	3370	5900		
Water	1.00		100		540
Zinc	0.092	419.5	907	23.0	

By the same token, when the temperature of these respective masses of water falls through *one* degree in the appropriate units, the above amounts of heat, in the appropriate units, are given out by the water.

The energy required to raise a unit mass of a material one degree is called the *specific heat capacity* or, more usually, the *specific heat* of the material. The symbol for specific heat is c; consequently c_w represents the specific heat of water.

It is evident from the three units of heat here defined that the specific heat of water has a numerical value of *one*. Appropriate units for specific heat are given in the following section. Table 10-1 lists the specific heats for several common substances. Note the relatively high value for water, in relation to the other substances. A high value of specific heat indicates that the substance is capable of absorbing or losing large amounts of heat, with a relatively small change in temperature.

3. HEAT ABSORBED BY A BODY

From the definition of the specific heat of a material, c heat units will be absorbed or given out when one unit mass of the substance changes one temperature degree. A mass m, therefore, will gain or lose mc heat units when the mass undergoes a temperature change of one degree, or $mc\Delta T$ heat units for a temperature change of ΔT.

The calculation of the heat energy transferred can now be stated as:

$$E_H = mc\Delta T$$

heat energy	mass	specific heat	temperature change
kilocalories	kg	kcal/kg C°	C°
calories	g	cal/g C°	C°
Btu	lb	Btu/lb F°	F°

152

EXAMPLE 1

(a) How much heat is lost when the temperature of 25 grams of steel ($c_s = .102$ cal/g C°) falls from 80° to 76° C?

(b) What is the heat gained by 5.0 pounds of glass ($c_g = .200$ Btu/lb F°) when the temperature of the glass changes from 20° F to 35° F?

Solution:

(a) $E_H = m_s c_s \triangle T = 25\ (80 - 76)\ .102 = 25 \times 4 \times .102 = 1.0 \times 10$ **cal lost**.

(b) $E_H = m_g c_g \triangle T = 5.0\ (35 - 20)\ .200 = 5.0 \times 15 \times .200 = 15$ **Btu**.

EXAMPLE 2

When 10 g of a substance are supplied with 50 cal of heat, the temperature of the substance rises from 40°C to 50°C. What is the specific heat of this material?

Solution:

$$E_H = mc\Delta T$$
$$\therefore\ c = \frac{E_H}{m\Delta T} = \frac{50\text{ cal}}{10\text{g} \times 10\text{C}°} = 0.50\text{ cal/g C}°.$$

---

4. THE CALORIMETER: MEASUREMENT OF SPECIFIC HEAT

If a basin of water is too hot, it may be cooled by adding cold water. The hot and cold water mix, and the final temperature of the mixture is somewhere between the temperatures of the original hot water and the added cold. If no heat has escaped from the basin, the heat that the added cold water received is equal to the heat given up by the hot water. This is really a statement of the conservation of energy. Always when two substances at different temperatures, whether solids, liquids, or gases, are brought into close contact and the mixture is heat-insulated from the surroundings, the heat given off by the substance at the higher temperature is equal to the heat received by the substance at the lower temperature. This is the *law of heat exchange* and is the basis of calorimetry, the measurement of exchange of heat from one substance to another. In symbols the law is,

$$E_H = E_H$$
$$\text{lost} \quad \text{gained}$$

A calorimetric measurement based upon this law is usually said to be carried out by the *method of mixtures*.

The method of mixtures and its use in determining heat quantities is illustrated in the following example:

EXAMPLE 3

An aluminum cylinder of mass 75 g is quickly transferred from boiling water to a beaker containing 62 g of water at 25°C. The final temperature of the mixture is 40°C. Determine the specific heat of aluminum.

Solution:

Let the specific heat of aluminum be c_{al}
Heat lost by aluminum
$$= 75 \times c_{al} \times (100 - 40) \text{ cal}.$$
Heat gained by water
$$= 62 \times 1 \times (40 - 25).$$

Assuming that all the heat lost by the aluminum is absorbed by the water, we can write

$$75 \times c_{al} \times 60 = 62 \times 15$$
$$\text{or} \qquad c_{al} = \textbf{0.21 cal/g C°}.$$

The assumption that none of the heat possessed by the aluminum escapes to the outside is, of course, invalid. A certain amount of heat will be radiated to the air during the transfer, no matter how quickly it is performed, and heat will also be absorbed by the beaker after the transfer. It is possible to take this latter factor into considera-

Fig. 10-2: *The calorimeter. Compare the photograph with the cross-sectional diagram of the calorimeter illustrated in Experiment 15.*

tion if the specific heat of the material of the beaker is known.

The specific heat of a substance is conveniently and accurately obtained by the use of a *calorimeter*. A calorimeter is essentially an insulated vessel of known specific heat in which the transfer of heat is allowed to take place. Such an instrument is illustrated in Figure 10-2. Heat loss from the inner vessel (which is usually of aluminum or copper) is minimized, owing to poor conduction through the air space separating it from the outer vessel, and also because of the polished surfaces of both inner and outer containers. The inner vessel, which contains the mixture, is supported by a fibre collar of low conductivity. Means are provided for the insertion, through the bakelite cover, of a thermometer and stirrer.

In employing the calorimeter in a situation involving heat exchange, a knowledge of the mass of the inner vessel and its specific heat enables us to determine the heat given up by the hot substance to its container. It is usual to assume that the inner vessel undergoes a temperature change equal to that of the liquid it contains. The heat lost by radiation and conduction from the inner to outer vessel is considered negligible.

The following example illustrates the calculations involved in determining the specific heat of brass, using a calorimeter.

EXAMPLE 4

The inner vessel of a calorimeter has a mass of 100 g and a specific heat of 0.100 cal/g C°. It contains 400 g of water at a temperature of 20.0°C. When 200 g of brass are transferred from boiling water to the inner vessel, the highest temperature attained by the resulting mixture is 23.5°C. Determine the specific heat of brass. (Assume the above measurements are accurate to three significant digits.)

Solution:

It is convenient to arrange the masses and their corresponding temperature on a temperature scale as shown. We then consider those quantities that lose heat, and those that absorb heat.

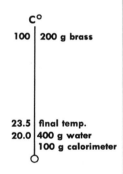

Heat lost $(mc\Delta T)$

by brass $= 200 \times c_b \times (100 - 23.5)$ cal
$\qquad = 15,300\ c_b$ cal

Heat gained $(mc\Delta T)$

by water $= 400 \times 1.00 \times (23.5 - 20.0)$ cal
$\qquad = 1400$ cal

by calorimeter $= 100 \times 0.100\ (23.5 - 20.0)$ cal
$\qquad = 35.0$ cal

Total heat gained $= (1400 + 35)$ cal $= 1435$ cal

$\qquad$ Heat lost $=$ Heat gained

$\therefore\ 15,300\ c_b = 1435$

$$c_b = \frac{1435}{15,300} = .094 \text{ cal/g C}°.$$

5. FUSION

When heat is added to a solid, its temperature rises. As we have seen, this observation is interpreted as an increase in the thermal motion of the molecules, or groups of molecules, or basic particles of the solid. As the temperature rises, there comes a time when the molecular thermal motion approaches that of a liquid, in which the motion is much freer. The solid melts, or as one says in physics, *fusion* takes place. When this point is reached, *the temperature ceases to rise until the whole of the solid has become liquid.* The heat that is added while the solid is melting, is used in breaking up the crystalline bonds uniting the molecules in the solid and hence does not go into thermal agitation. We refer to this heat as *latent* heat. Each unit of mass of a solid always requires a definite amount of heat to change it from the solid to the liquid phase; accordingly, different substances have different latent heats. The symbol for the latent heat of fusion is L_f.

$\qquad L_f = 80$ cal/g for ice at 0° C
or $L_f = 144$ Btu/lb for ice at 32° F.

Fusion is a reversible process, and when a unit mass of liquid freezes, or as we say, solidifies, it gives up its latent heat. Thus, when water freezes at 0° C, it gives up 80 cal/g to its surroundings, and when it melts, it absorbs 80 cal/g from its surroundings.

The heat of fusion may be defined as the amount of heat absorbed by a unit mass of a substance in undergoing a change from the solid to the liquid state, or the amount of heat liberated by a unit mass in changing from the liquid to the solid state.

It is important for the student to keep in mind that the absorption or loss of this latent heat takes place without a temperature change. Its absorption is to be considered an increase in the internal *potential energy* of the substance, resulting in a much greater mobility of the molecules, that is characteristic of the liquid state. On the other hand, its loss represents a decrease in this internal potential energy as a result of a reorientation of the molecules into the closely packed form that is characteristic of the solid state. In neither case is there a change in the average *kinetic energy* of each molecule of the substance, unless, of course, additional heat is gained or lost. Hence, the temperature, a measure of this average kinetic energy, undergoes no change until this change of state is complete.

The heats of fusion of some common substances are given in Table 10-1. Note the wide variation in this important characteristic, and the extremely low value for mercury: 2.8 cal/g C°. The large value for the heat of fusion of ice makes it valuable as a refrigerant—it is able to absorb large amounts of heat from its surroundings while melting.

EXAMPLE 5

25.0 g of ice at 0°C is heated until the resulting liquid is at a temperature of 20.0°C. What quantity of heat was absorbed by the ice and water?

Solution:

Heat absorbed

to melt ice $= mL_f = 25.0 \times 80$
$$= 2000 \text{ cal.}$$

Heat absorbed
by water in
rising from
0°C to 20°C $= mc\Delta T = 25.0 \times 1 \times (20.0)$
$$= 500 \text{ cal.}$$

Total heat gained $= 2000 + 500$ cal
$$= 2500 \text{ cal.}$$

(two significant digits)

The experimental determination of the heat of fusion of a substance, using a calorimeter, is illustrated in the following example:

EXAMPLE 6

A calorimeter of mass 100.0 g and specific heat 0.100 cal/g C°, contains 400.0 g of water at 40.0°C. When 90.0 g of ice at 0°C is added and completely melted, the lowest temperature of the mixture is 18.0°C. Determine the heat of fusion of ice.

Solution:

Let L_f = heat of fusion of ice

$$\begin{array}{l|l} & \text{C}° \\ \hline 40.0 & \text{100.0 g calorimeter} \\ & c = 0.100 \\ & \text{400.0 g water} \\ 18.0 & T_f \\ 0 & \text{90.0 g ice} \end{array}$$

Heat lost

by original water
$$(mc\Delta T) = 400.0 \times 1 \times (40.0 - 18.0) \text{ cal}$$
$$= 8800 \text{ cal}$$

by calorimeter
$$= 100.0 \times 0.100 (40.0 - 18.0) \text{ cal}$$
$$= 220 \text{ cal.}$$

Total heat lost $= 8800 + 220$ cal $= 9020$ cal.

Heat gained

by ice in melting $(mL_f) = 90.0 \, L_f$
by resulting water
$$(mc\Delta T) = 90.0 \times 1 \times (18.0 - 0)$$
$$= 1620 \text{ cal.}$$

Total heat gained $= 90.0 \, L_f + 1620$
Heat lost $=$ Heat gained
$$9020 = 90.0 \, L_f + 1620$$
$$L_f = 82.2 \text{ cal/g.}$$

$$\left(\% \text{ error} = \frac{82 - 80}{80} \times 100 = 2.5\%\right)$$

6. VOLUME CHANGES DURING SOLIDIFICATION

In most substances the particles are closer together in the solid phase than in the liquid phase. In these circumstances, the total volume occupied by the solid is less than that occupied by the corresponding liquid. The substance contracts upon cooling. When most metals are cast, they contract upon solidification, and consideration must be given to this fact. The contraction upon solidification may be illustrated by pouring melted paraffin into a beaker and noticing the indentation in the surface when it solidifies.

On the other hand, a few substances expand upon solidification. Water is the outstanding example. When water is frozen in a beaker, the surface is convex, since the volume of the ice is greater than the volume of the water. Bismuth and antimony are two metals which, like water, expand upon solidification. The latter metal is used as a component of type metal, since because of its expansion, it produces a type that is sharp and clear-cut. We assume that in the case of *these* substances the crystalline structure is more open or the particles are, on the average, farther apart in the solid phase than in the liquid phase.

7. EFFECT OF PRESSURE ON THE FREEZING POINT

When a substance expands upon solidification, we assume the particles of the substance to be farther apart in the solid phase than in the liquid phase. It follows that if the substance is under pressure that will tend to push or hold the particles closer together, it will be more difficult for the substance to solidify. If it has already solidified, it should melt under pressure. This process of melting under pressure, called *regelation*, is often demonstrated by putting a saddle of copper wire over a block of ice and hanging weights from the pendent ends of the wire. (See Figure 10-3.) Because of the heavy weights and the small area of cross-section of the wire, the pressure under the wire is very great; consequently, the ice under the wire melts and the water flows out to the upper side of the wire, where, the pressure being normal, the water again freezes. Thus the wire will, in time, work its way right through the block of ice. If skating ice is not too cold, the great pressure under the edge of the skates of a skater will momentarily melt the ice and the skate will slide on a smooth surface of water. One says the ice is very "fast". When the ice is very cold, this may not happen unless the skates are very sharp indeed, thus increasing the pressure under the skate.

This lowering of the freezing point when pressure is applied is partly responsible for the flow of glaciers down valleys, and the packing of snowballs when the temperature is less than 0°C.

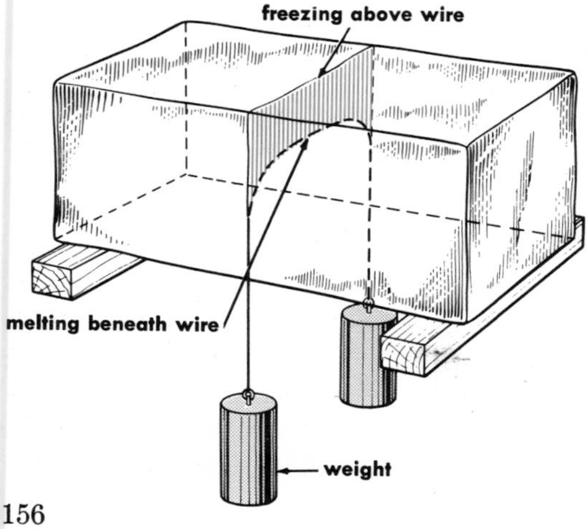

freezing above wire

melting beneath wire

weight

Fig. 10-3: *Liquids that expand upon solidification melt when subjected to pressure.*

156

In the case of substances that contract upon solidification, an increase of pressure will aid solidification and thus raise the freezing point.

8. VAPORIZATION

When a liquid such as ether or alcohol is placed in an open vessel such as a watchglass, it rapidly disappears and the odour of the substance permeates the surrounding air. The particles of the liquid evidently leave the liquid phase and move about as a gas mixed with the air. This process is called *vaporization*. A good exercise is to attempt to weigh with a chemical balance a small amount of distilled water in a watchglass when the air in the room is fairly dry. It will be found that the water evaporates so quickly that weighings must be made "on the run". On the average, the particles of the liquid have a kinetic energy that depends upon the temperature. Because of collisions, however, many molecules have a much higher energy than the average, whereas others have a lower energy. When a high-energy molecule is near the surface, it may chance to have sufficient energy to get away from the attraction of the surrounding liquid molecules and get into the air as a gas molecule. This escape process is the molecular picture of vaporization. The fact that a little ether placed in the palm of the hand will feel very cold as it evaporates, substantiates the molecular picture of vaporization, since this picture implies that the liquid is tending to lose its high-energy molecules, thereby lowering the average energy of the remaining molecules. The average energy is re-established by the taking of heat energy away from the hand in which the ether lies. It also follows from this molecular picture that the higher the temperature the more rapid will be the evaporation.

Heat of Vaporization

It has been noted that when a solid commences to melt, the heat that is being added to the solid will not raise the solid's temperature but will be used up in breaking up the crystalline formation of the solid. Similarly, when a liquid commences to boil, the further addition of heat will not raise its temperature, but the added heat will be used in changing the liquid to vapour. **The heat required to change unit mass of a substance from the liquid phase to the vapour phase is called the heat of vaporization of that substance.** The symbol for the latent heat of vaporization is L_v.

$$L_v = 540 \text{ cal/g for water at } 100° \text{ C}$$
$$\text{or } L_v = 970 \text{ Btu/lb for water at } 212° \text{ F}$$

(each to two significant digits)

The heats of vaporization for other common substances are given in Table 10-1.

EXAMPLE 7

How much heat is required to vaporize 45 g of water initially at 60.0° C?

Solution:

Heat required to raise water
  to boiling point
$$= (mc\Delta T) = 45 \times 1 \times (100 - 60.0) \text{ cal}$$
$$= 1800 \text{ cal.}$$
Heat required to vaporize this
  boiling water
$$= mL_v = 45 \times 540$$
$$= 24,300 \text{ cal.}$$
Total heat required $= 1800 + 24,300 \text{ cal}$
$$= \textbf{26,100 cal}$$
$$= \textbf{2.6} \times \textbf{10}^4 \textbf{ cal.}$$
(two significant digits)

In the following example, the method of mixtures is used to determine the latent heat of vaporization of water. It is determined by finding how much heat is given out by a quantity of water undergoing condensation.

EXAMPLE 8

A calorimeter has an inner vessel of mass 120.0 g and specific heat 0.100 cal/g C°. It contains 400.0 g of water at 6.0° C. When 22.5 g of water vapour at 100° C are introduced into the water, the highest temperature attained by the mixture is 38.0° C. Determine the heat of vaporization of water.

Solution:

Let L_v = heat of vaporization (or condensation) of water.

C°	
100.0	22.5 g steam
38.0	T_f
6.0	400.0 g water
	120.0 g calorimeter

Heat lost
by water vapour in condensing
$$(mL_v) = 22.5 \ L_v \ \text{cal}$$
by resulting water cooling to 38.0° C
$$(mc\Delta T) = 22.5 \times 1 \times (100 - 38.0)$$
$$= 1395 \ \text{cal}.$$

Heat gained
by original water
$$(mc\Delta T) = 400.0 \times 1 \times (38.0 - 6.0)$$
$$= 12,800 \ \text{cal}$$
by calorimeter
$$(mc\Delta T) = 120.0 \times 0.100 \ (38.0 - 6.0)$$
$$= 384 \ \text{cal}.$$

Heat lost = Heat gained
$$22.5 \ L_v + 1395 = 12,800 + 384$$
$$L_v = \frac{11,789}{22.5} = 524 \ \text{cal/g}.$$

$$\left(\% \ \text{error} = \frac{540 - 524}{540} \times 100\% = 3.0\% \right)$$

9. EQUILIBRIUM VAPOUR PRESSURE

Figure 10-4 shows a basin of water over which a bell jar has been placed. The air in the bell jar is at atmospheric pressure. Some of the high-energy water molecules in the liquid phase will escape from the surface of the liquid and move about among the air molecules, colliding with the air molecules,

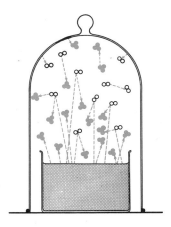

Fig. 10-4: *The equilibrium vapour pressure is reached when the rate of vaporization of the water is equal to the rate of condensation of the water vapour.*

with the sides of the bell jar, and with the surface of the water. In this latter case, a water molecule may be held by the water, thus leaving the vapour phase and re-entering the liquid phase. There will thus be a two-way process—water molecules in the liquid entering the vapour and water molecules of the vapour re-entering the liquid. Initially, many more water molecules will leave the liquid and enter the vapour than will leave the vapour and enter the liquid. As time goes on and more and more water molecules are in the vapour, the number going from the vapour to the liquid phase will become equal to the number going from the liquid to the vapour phase. The two processes balance. The water molecules in the vapour phase will exercise a pressure on the bell jar, depending upon their number, so that when the two processes of vaporization and liquefaction have balanced, or there is equilibrium, the pressure of the water vapour will become constant. This constant pressure is called the *equilibrium vapour pressure.*

This equilibrium may be upset by increasing the temperature of the water, since this addition of heat will increase the average kinetic energy of the water molecules in the liquid and thus increase the number which may escape into the vapour, or vaporize. Once again, however, equilibrium will be established, but at a higher equilibrium vapour pressure. The curve in Figure 10-5 shows the relation between the temperature and the equilibrium vapour pressure of water. It will be observed from this curve that when the temperature is 100° C, the equilibrium vapour pressure of water is 760 mm pressure, that is, one atmosphere. If the liquid is in the open air, it will then *boil*.* **Boiling occurs when the equilibrium vapour pressure equals the pressure on the surface of the liquid.** On high mountains where the atmospheric pressure is low, water boils at a lower temperature.

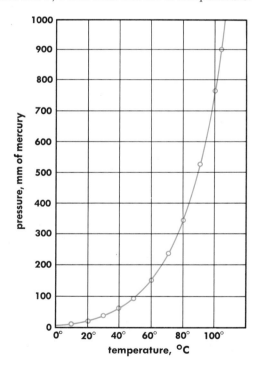

Fig. 10-5: *The curve indicates how the boiling point of water changes with pressure. What is the boiling temperature of water when the pressure is 350 mm of mercury?*

---

*If further heat is added.

As the water is heated, bubbles of water vapour appear on the side and bottom of the container, where the pressure is greater than atmospheric by reason of the depth of water, and the temperature of the bubbles will therefore exceed 100° C. If they rise to meet surface water of a lower temperature, this will tend to condense the bubbles; on the other hand, lower surface pressure (atmospheric) will have the opposite effect. Depending on which influence prevails, the bubbles may condense or may reach the surface and escape into the air above.

Fig. 10-6: *When the pressure in the flask is reduced, the water boils at a lower temperature.*

10. SUBLIMATION

When a piece of camphor is placed in the open, it will slowly evaporate. This evaporation might be suspected from the fact that a small amount of camphor vapour is in the air adjacent to the solid camphor. If the block of camphor is in a confined space in the same way as the basin of water that was surrounded by the bell jar, the pressure of the camphor vapour will build up to an equilibrium vapour pressure depending upon the temperature. Thus we see that over an appropriate range of temperature, liquid may be in equilibrium with its vapour, solid with its liquid, and solid with its vapour. When a solid evaporates directly without first forming liquid, we say that the solid *sublimes*. If atmospheric conditions are appropriate, snow on the ground may sublime, leaving the ground completely dry. The **heat of sublima-** tion is defined as the **heat necessary to change one unit mass of a solid directly to one gram of vapour at the same temperature.**

11. MECHANICAL EQUIVALENT OF HEAT

In section 4 of Chapter 6, the apparatus used by Joule to find the mechanical energy required to produce a calorie of heat energy is illustrated in Figure 6-3. The value is known as the mechanical equivalent of heat:

$$1 \text{ calorie} = 4.2 \text{ joules}.$$

Also, $$1 \text{ Btu} = 778 \text{ ft-lb}.$$

EXAMPLE 9

A snowball of mass 100.0 g, travelling at a speed of 10.0 m/sec, hits a brick wall. The outdoor temperature is 0°C.

(a) Determine the heat generated by the impact.

(b) Determine the amount of snow melted at impact, if all of the heat produced is absorbed by the snow.

Solution:

(a) Kinetic energy of the snowball $= \dfrac{1}{2} mv^2$

$$= \dfrac{1}{2} (0.100 \text{ kg}) (10.0 \text{ m/sec})^2$$

$$= 5.00 \text{ joules}$$

$$= \dfrac{5.00}{4.18} \text{ cal} = \textbf{1.20 cal}.$$

(b) 80 cal will melt 1 gram of snow

$$\therefore \text{ mass melted} = \dfrac{1.20}{80} = \textbf{.015 g}.$$

HEAT UNITS:
  The kilocalorie is the heat absorbed by one kilogram of water when its temperature rises one Celsius degree.
  The calorie is the heat absorbed by one gram of water when its temperature rises one Celsius degree.
  The British thermal unit (Btu) is the amount of heat absorbed by one pound of water when its temperature rises through one Fahrenheit degree.

SPECIFIC HEAT CAPACITY (c): the energy required to raise a unit mass of a material one degree.

HEAT ABSORBED BY AN OBJECT: $E_H = mc\Delta T$ (mass $\times$ specific heat $\times$ temperature change).

LAW OF HEAT EXCHANGE: when two quantities of matter are mixed, the heat lost by one is equal to the heat gained by the other, if the total heat is confined to the two substances.

LATENT HEAT OF FUSION (L_f): the energy absorbed when unit mass of a material changes from solid to liquid phase at its melting point.

160

LATENT HEAT OF VAPORIZATION (L_v): the heat energy required to change a unit mass of a substance from the liquid phase to the vapour phase at its boiling point.

HEAT OF SUBLIMATION: the heat required to change one unit mass of a solid directly to one gram of vapour at the same temperature.

EXERCISE A

1. Name three heat units used as standards to measure heat energy.

2. Explain the difference between the heat capacity and the specific heat of an object.

3. How can the heat energy required to change the temperature of a material be calculated?

4. In what way is the law of heat exchange related to the law of the conservation of energy?

5. Why does the *latent* heat not change the temperature of a substance?

6. Name the temperatures at which latent heat exchanges occur for water (at atmospheric pressure).

7. Give a reason for the concave surface of paraffin wax when it solidifies in a container and the convex surface of ice formed from water in a container.

8. Explain why ice melts when a pressure is applied to it.

9. What happens to the molecular structure of a liquid when subjected to the latent heat of vaporization?

10. It is dangerous to continue heating water in a boiler unless a safety pressure release is installed. Explain the danger in terms of the equilibrium vapour pressure.

11. Why does it take longer to cook potatoes at high altitudes (mountains) than at ground level?

12. "Dry ice" is frequently used to keep beverages cold. Why is it not necessary to arrange drainage for the "melted" ice.

EXERCISE B

Assume that all temperatures are measured to the nearest degree unless otherwise indicated, and that all digits in the quotation of masses are significant.

1. A cube of iron weighs 4.00 lb. How many Btu will be needed to raise its temperature from 70° F to 500° F?

2. How many calories will be needed to change the temperature of 500 g of water from 20° C to 100° C?

3. An aluminum cylinder is heated to 300° F. If the cylinder weighs 3.0 lb, how many Btu are given out as the cylinder cools to 50° F?

4. How much heat is given out when 85 g of lead cool from 200° C to 10° C?

5. If 10.0 g of water at 0.0° C is mixed with 20.0 g of water at 30.0° C, what is the final temperature of the mixture?

6. A loaf of bread contains approximately 3000 kcal. If the bread is used as a fuel with 100 per cent conversion to heat energy, calculate the number of kilograms of water that could be heated from 20° C to 80° C.

7. Calculate the heat given out at a steel company by a steel ingot weighing one ton as it cools from 900° F to 70° F. ($c_s = .107$ cal/g C°)

8. What is the final temperature of a mixture of 0.300 lb of water at 70.0° F, and 0.400 lb of silver at 210.0° F, assuming that no heat is lost to the container?

9. An aluminum calorimeter has a mass of 60.0 g. Its temperature is 25.0° C. What is the final temperature attained when 75.0 g of water at 95.0° C is poured into it?

10. A piece of tin weighing 0.50 lb and having a temperature of 210° F is dropped into 0.20 lb of water at a temperature of 50° F. If the final temperature of the mixture is 68° F, what is the specific heat of the tin, assuming that no heat is lost to the container?

11. A block of metal has a mass of 1000 g. It is heated to 300° C and then placed in 100.0 g of water at 0.0° C in a calorimeter. The mass of the calorimeter is 50.0 g; its specific heat is 0.200. If the final temperature is 70.0° C, calculate the specific heat of the metal.

12. A block of brass, mass 500.0 g, temperature 100.0° C is placed in 300.0 g of water, temperature 20.0° C, in an aluminum calorimeter, mass 75.0 g. If the final temperature is 30.0° C, what is the value of the specific heat of the brass?

13. A lump of copper has a mass of 95.3 g and a specific heat of 0.092. It is heated to 90.5° C and then placed in 75.2 g of turpentine, temperature 20.5° C. The temperature of the mixture, after stirring, is 35.5° C. Determine the specific heat of this sample of turpentine.

14. A metal cylinder, mass 450 g, temperature 100° C, is dropped into a 150 g iron calorimeter, specific heat 0.100, which contains 300 g of water at 21.5° C. If the resulting temperature of the mixture is 30.5° C, what is the value of the specific heat of the metal cylinder?

15. Calculate the mass of ice at 0° C which must be added to 400 g of water at 80° C to cool the water to 15° C, assuming all the added ice melts.

16. The specific heat of ice is 0.50. Calculate the number of calories needed to change 100 g of ice at −55° C:
    (a) to water at 100° C
    (b) to steam at 100° C
    (c) to steam at 200° C (specific heat of steam = 0.50 cal/g C°).

17. Calculate the number of Btu needed to change 10.0 lb of ice at 22.0° F:
    (a) to water at 212° F
    (b) to steam at 212° F.

18. In an experiment to determine the heat of vaporization of water (heat of condensation of steam), a 100 g calorimeter ($c = 0.09$) is filled with 290 g of water at 20° C. Steam at 100° C is mixed with the water until the final weight of the calorimeter and its contents is 400 g. The final recorded temperature is 40° C. Calculate the heat of vaporization of water from these data.

19. Ten g of ice at 0° C are added to 200 g of water at 70° C. Then, 10 g of steam at 100° C are added. Assuming no heat losses, calculate the final temperature of the mixture.

20. How many Btu are required to vaporize 50.0 lb of water at 212° F?

21. How many (a) calories and (b) joules are given off by 50.0 g of steam at 100° C when it condenses?

22. Calculate the number of Btu evolved when 10.0 lb of steam at 212° F is condensed, cooled, and changed into ice at a temperature of 32° F.

23. What is the final temperature attained by the addition of 0.025 lb of steam at 212° F to 1.50 lb of water at 75° F, if no heat is lost to the container?

24. A calorimeter contains 400 g of water at 20.0° C. How many grams of steam at 100.0° C are needed to raise the temperature of the water and calorimeter to 80.0° C? The calorimeter has a mass of 100 g; its specific heat is 0.100 cal/g C°.

25. A mixture of ice and water, mass 200.0 g is in a 100.0 g calorimeter, specific heat .0200· When 40.0 g of steam is added to the mixture, the temperature is raised to 60.0° C· Determine how many grams of ice were originally in the calorimeter.

26. An aluminum cylinder, mass 50.0 g, is placed in a 100.0 g brass calorimeter with 250.0 g of water at 20.0° C. What equilibrium temperature is reached after the addition of 25.0 g of steam at 120.0° C?

27. A copper ball weighing 10.0 lb is removed from a furnace and dropped into 3.00 lb of water, temperature 72.0° F. After the water stops boiling, the combined weight of the ball and water is 12.8 lb. What was the furnace temperature?

28. The rate of radiation from the surface of the sun is about 8.95×10^4 calories per sq. cm per minute.
    (a) What is the energy radiated in joules per sq. cm per minute?
    (b) What is the power in watts produced per sq. cm?

29. What quantity of butter would supply the energy required to enable a 160 lb man to ascend a mountain of elevation 6.3×10^3 ft? The energy contained in 1 lb of butter is 1.1×10^4 Btu.

30. A quantity of mercury falls from a height of 12 m to a nonconducting surface. By how much will the temperature of the mercury rise? (Let the mass of mercury be m kg).

31. In drilling a hole in a casting, power is supplied at the rate of 0.400 hp for 2.50 min. How many Btu of heat are developed?

32. A sliding trunk with an initial speed of 4.00 m/sec coasts to a stop along a level floor. How much heat is developed due to friction, if the mass of the trunk is 16.0 kg?

33. A lead bullet, at a temperature of 40° C, strikes a steel target. The heat produced on impact is just sufficient to melt the bullet. Determine the speed that the bullet must have possessed, assuming that no heat is lost to the surroundings. The specific heat of lead is .031 cal/g C°, its melting point is 327° C, and the heat of fusion is 5.9 cal/g.

Heat Units and the Measurement of Heat

► Experiment 13

To determine the specific heat of one or two metals.

Calorimeter

Celsius thermometer

Boiler (beaker)

Tripod

Burner

Asbestos gauze

*Metal cylinders (aluminum and copper are suggested)

Strong thread or fish line

Triple-beam or platform balance

*Note: With modified equipment and procedure, metal pellets or shot can be used in place of the metal cylinders.

Procedure

1. Fill a beaker $\frac{2}{3}$ full of water. Bring the water in the beaker to the boiling point. While the water is heating, start water running from a cold-water tap.

2. Weigh the aluminum cylinder.

3. Attach a suitable length of thread to the cylinder and lower it into the water in the beaker.

4. While the water and cylinder continue to heat, weigh the inner vessel and stirrer of the calorimeter.

5. Fill the inner vessel $\frac{2}{3}$ full of water from the cold tap and weigh the inner vessel, stirrer, and cold water.

6. Record the room temperature as indicated on the thermometer. Place the inner vessel and contents within the outer vessel of the calorimeter. Set the lid in place and insert the thermometer in the water.

7. When the boiler water is boiling, record the temperature of the cold water in the calorimeter, remove the lid, and without splashing, quickly place the hot cylinder within the inner vessel.

8. Replace the lid and stir gently as the rising temperature is observed.

9. When the temperature of the calorimeter and contents ceases to rise, record the final temperature.

10. List all measurements in a suitable table.

Using the method of Example 3 in this chapter, calculate the specific heat of aluminum.

Your instructor may decide to have you repeat the experiment using a copper cylinder as a substitute for the aluminum.

Experiment 14

To determine the heat of fusion of ice.

Calorimeter and stirring rod

Celsius thermometer

Triple-beam or platform balance

Ice cubes

Paper towelling

Procedure

1. Find the combined weight of the inner vessel and the stirrer.

2. Read the room temperature on the Celsius thermometer and half fill the inner vessel with water about 15°C above room temperature.

3. Weigh the inner vessel, stirrer, and water.

4. Place the inner vessel and contents within the outer calorimeter vessel.

5. Dry an ice cube on some paper towelling in order to remove any water. Without splashing, gently place the ice cube in the water in the calorimeter.

6. Stir gently until all the ice has melted and the temperature has fallen to the lowest point. Record this temperature.

7. Weigh the inner vessel and contents.

8. List all readings in a suitable table as your observations.

Calculations

Refer to Example 6 of Chapter 10 and calculate L_f from the data obtained in your experiment. List the value as your conclusion and, taking 80.0 cal/g C° as the true value, calculate your percentage error.

Experiment 15

To determine the heat of vaporization of water.

Steam boiler

Support and clamps for boiler

Bunsen burner

Heat shield

Steam trap

Rubber tubing and glass delivery tubing

Pinch clamp

Celsius thermometer

Calorimeter with stirrer

Triple-beam or platform balance

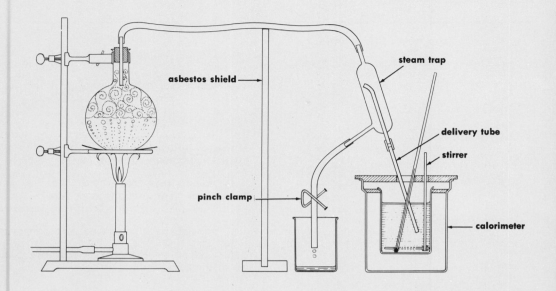

asbestos shield

steam trap

delivery tube

stirrer

pinch clamp

calorimeter

Procedure

1. Half fill the boiler with water.

2. With the pinch cock removed and the delivery tube open to the air, light the burner in order to thoroughly heat the steam trap and delivery tubing as soon as possible.

3. Start water running from a cold tap while weighing the inner vessel of the calorimeter on the balance. *Your weighing is critical: clean and zero the balance before commencing.*

4. When the delivery apparatus has been delivering steam for approximately 5 minutes, fill the inner vessel of the calorimeter about $\frac{2}{3}$ full of cold water at approximately 10°C. (Ice may be used.) Record this temperature.

5. Weigh the inner vessel, stirrer, and contents.

6. Place the vessel, stirrer, and contents within the outer calorimeter vessel.

7. Record the room temperature in °C: determine the number of C° that the cold water is below room temperature.

8. Tap the delivery tube and side tube of the steam trap in order to remove any condensed water vapour.

9. Use the pinch cock to close the side arm of the trap. Introduce the delivery tube so that it is under the surface of the cold water in the calorimeter.

10. *Gently* stir the water in the calorimeter while observing its rising temperature.

11. When the calorimeter contents have reached a temperature as far above room temperature as the cold water was below it, remove the delivery tube and shut off the burner. Record this temperature.

12. Remove the thermometer after touching it to the inside of the calorimeter to remove any liquid and reweigh the inner vessel and contents.

13. If time permits, restart the boiler with the delivery apparatus removed and

the thermometer held in the steam (by a clamp). Record the steam temperature.

If step 13 cannot be carried out, record the barometric pressure in mm of mercury and determine the boiling temperature from the equilibrium vapour pressure (Reference: Figure 10-5 page 159).

Analysis

1. Determine the mass of: (a) the cold water, (b) the water vapour used to heat the cold water, stirrer, and inner vessel.

2. Using the method outlined in Example 8 of this chapter, calculate the heat of condensation or vaporization of water.

Question

Why was T_f taken as far above room temperature as the cold water was below room temperature?

Chapter 11

Waves

1. ENERGY TRANSFER BY WAVES

When a baseball is thrown, it carries kinetic energy with it. This energy is absorbed by the person who catches the ball. A bullet from a gun carries energy which is transferred to the target; falling rain carries energy that is absorbed by the ground on which it falls. In general, we see that energy may be transmitted from place to place by the movement of particles. Another form of the transmission of energy by particles is that of heat conduction. Here we conceive of the particles—molecules perhaps—of the conducting material as being in violent agitation. This agitation is transmitted by collision to neighbouring particles, which in turn transmit their agitation to further particles, and so on. The energy transferred here is not accompanied by an actual transference of matter, but rather by a transference of molecular vibrations. Likewise we conceive of electric conduction as an activity in which electrons in the conducting material transmit their motion along the electrical conductor.

Energy may also be transmitted by waves. A familiar illustration is found in the damage which waves may do when beating against a shore or breakwater. This is another illustration of the transference of energy, not by the gross movement of matter, but rather by the transference of motion from one region of a medium to the next, and so on. We shall see that sound is propagated by a wave motion in a variety of media; that is to say, sound energy is transferred from some sound source to some sound receiver that is activated by the energy carried by the wave. Usually the energy in this case is very small, except in the case of an explosive sound. Most of us are familiar with the comparatively large amount of energy carried by the wave pulse set up when an airplane breaks the sound barrier. Energy carried by this wave has done considerable damage from time to time.

Waves on the surface of water, provided that they are small enough not to break the surface, provide an interesting example of wave motion. Watching such waves, one notices that at a given point the surface is alternately rising above normal level and falling below normal level. The observation is improved if a floating body such as a rowboat is at the point of observation. The wake of a motor boat, viewed from the rowboat as the crest of a particular wave, will be found to move across the water at a definite speed. Furthermore, if any part of a wave, crest, trough, or some intermediate point is observed, such crests, troughs, etc., will all be seen to move along the surface at the same speed. It appears that any given particle of water remains in one position, merely bobbing

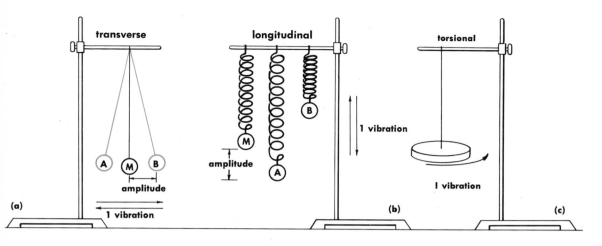

Fig. 11-1: *Some illustrations of objects in a state of vibration.*

up and down, whereas the *wave form* itself moves along the surface at a definite speed.

The water wave was associated with an oscillating motion of the particles. The bobbing motion is referred to as a vibratory motion, which is illustrated by the to-and-fro motion of a swing, the prongs of a tuning fork, or the motion of a hooked weight on the end of a spring. In each of these illustrations, a complete vibration (i.e., one that completes a cycle) is a single to-and-fro motion of the vibrating particle. Some simple illustrations of vibrating objects are shown in Figure 11-1.

As we shall see, there is much evidence for thinking of light as being transmitted by wave motion. Here we must be careful; in familiar situations a dense elastic medium is required for the propagation of a wave, and in the case of light there seems to be no medium at all. We can, however, learn much about the behaviour of light if we think of it as being transmitted by a wave. These light "waves" also transmit energy, as experience shows when objects are placed in sunlight. Indeed, the light and heat so transmitted to us from the sun form our main source of energy.

2. CLASSIFICATION OF WAVES

There are several ways in which the many varieties of wave motion may be classified. One broad classification is that of *mechanical waves*, to which our discussion in this chapter will be limited. This type of wave is most common in our everyday experience.

A mechanical wave is a disturbance which travels in an *elastic medium*. An elastic medium is simply one that can be deformed and as a result will tend to restore itself to its initial or equilibrium condition. A coil spring provides a simple example of such a medium. In Figure 11-2, the spring is deformed at the left by squeezing adjacent coils together. When released, these coils move away from each other toward their equilibrium position. In so doing, the inertia of each causes it to move beyond this rest position, and a deformation of another section of the spring is created. The result is a disturbance which travels through the entire length of the medium.

Different kinds of waves may be distinguished by considering how the particles move in relation to the direction of travel of the actual disturbance. In the coil spring of Figure 11-2, each disturbed particle of the

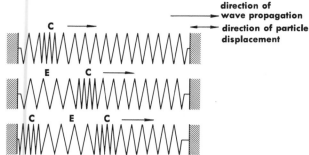

Fig. 11-2: *A disturbance passing along a coil spring creates regions of compression (C) and elongation (E). Because the particles of the medium are displaced parallel to the direction of the wave, such a wave is called a longitudinal wave.*

spring vibrates over a very restricted region on either side of its rest position, **in directions parallel to the direction in which the disturbance travels.** Such a wave is called a **longitudinal wave.**

If the motions of the particles of the medium are **perpendicular to the direction of wave travel**, the disturbance is a **transverse wave.** The simplest example of such a wave is provided by a rope supported at one end and set oscillating up and down at the other (Figure 11-3). As the wave advances, each particle of the rope moves *across* the line of propagation of the wave.

Waves may also be transmitted through an elastic medium by the application of a twisting force. Here the particles undergo angular displacements from their rest positions. Such a disturbance is called a *torsional wave.* In Figure 11-1(c) the twisting of the rope at the upper end is transferred throughout the entire length, imparting angular vibrations to each particle of the medium. A useful application of a torsional wave in studying transverse wave motion is illustrated in Figure 11-4. The bars are supported by a central backbone of stiff wire, which, when twisted, imparts its angular vibrations to each cross-member in turn.

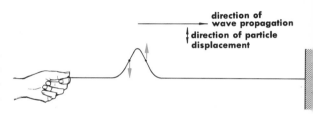

direction of
→ wave propagation
↕ direction of particle
displacement

Fig. 11-3: *In a transverse wave particle displacement is across the direction of wave propagation.*

American Telephone and Telegra

Fig. 11-4: *A torsional wave travelling along the central backbone of this wave machine makes the ends of the rods execute a transverse vibratory motion.*

170

The ends of the cross-members execute an almost completely vertical motion while the main disturbance travels horizontally. These ends can then be thought of as particles through which a transverse wave travels.

Waves may also be classified according to whether the disturbance is a single wave, called a *pulse*, or a continuous succession of waves—a *train of waves*. Considering again a rope fixed at one end, a single deflection of the hand in one direction produces a pulse which causes each particle of the medium, in turn, to move for a short time and then return to rest [Figure 11-5(a)]. If, however, this process is repeated, a train of waves results, as shown in Figure 11-5(b). Waves produced by a regularly vibrating source are called *periodic waves*.

As we progress in our analysis of wave motion, certain other broad classifications of waves will become apparent. However, before we enter into our main discussion of the similarities in behaviour exhibited by all waves, we shall find it necessary to employ certain terms defined in the following section.

3. DEFINITIONS RELATED TO WAVE MOTION

From our discussion thus far, it is evident that whenever a wave exists in a medium, the particles of that medium undergo a vibratory motion about an equilibrium position. Let us consider once more a transverse wave in a rope (Figure 11-6). In the first five situations (a to e) the hand is depicted as starting from its equilibrium position and moving toward a position of maximum upward displacement, thence downward to a point of maximum downward displacement, and finally back to its starting position. At this stage, one complete *cycle* of vibration of the source has taken place, and the wave has travelled along the rope a distance determined by the velocity of the wave in the particular rope.

Wavelength

The distance travelled by the wave during one complete cycle of the vibrating source is called one wavelength. The Greek letter λ (lambda) is universally used as a symbol for wavelength.

It is evident from Figure 11-6 that as the source executes one complete to-and-fro vibration (one cycle), each particle that has been disturbed also executes a cycle of vibration about its rest position.

Period and Frequency

The time required for each particle to complete one cycle of vibratory motion is called the period of vibration. We shall adopt the symbol T for this quantity. Closely related to the period is the *frequency* of vibration. **The frequency of vibration is the number of cycles occurring in one second.**

A simple relationship exists between the period and frequency of any vibrating particle. Let f represent the frequency of the particle. Then,

f vibrations occur in 1 sec and 1 vibration occurs in $\dfrac{1}{f}$ sec. $\quad \therefore \text{ period} = \dfrac{1}{\text{frequency}}$

$$\text{or, } T = \frac{1}{f}.$$

Fig. 11-5: *(a) A pulse.(b) A train of waves.*

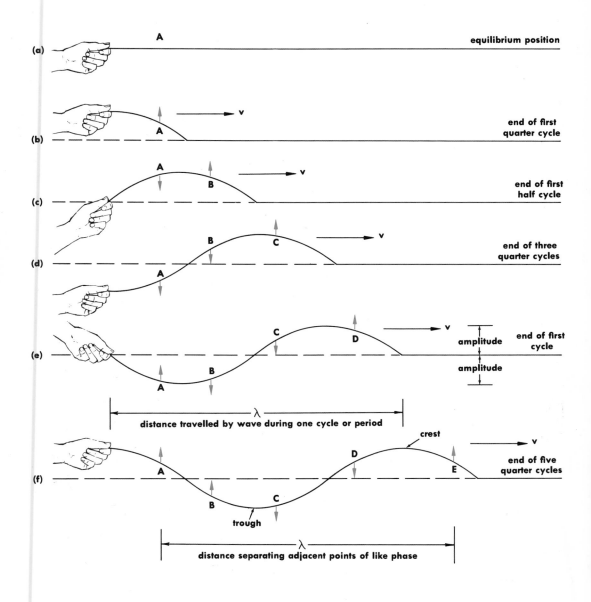

(a)   A   equilibrium position

(b)   A   v   end of first quarter cycle

(c)   A   B   v   end of first half cycle

(d)   B   C   v   end of three quarter cycles   A

(e)   C   D   v   amplitude   end of first cycle   B   amplitude   A

λ
distance travelled by wave during one cycle or period

(f)   crest   D   v   A   E   end of five quarter cycles   B   C   trough

λ
distance separating adjacent points of like phase

Fig. 11-6: *Progressive formation of a wave in a rope, and terms descriptive of the wave.*

172

The amplitude of a wave is defined as the maximum departure of any particle in the medium from its rest position. Thus, in Figure 11-6, the amplitude is shown as the distance from the equilibrium position to the peak of the crest, or to the lowest point of the trough.

Phase

It is clear from Figure 11-6 that as the particles vibrate about their position of rest, they generally reach corresponding positions in their paths at different times. For instance, in part (f) of this diagram the motion of five particular points is shown for this instant—some are moving up while others are moving down. Also some, such as point C, are about to reach their maximum displacement while others, points B and D, are about to pass through their equilibrium positions. However, further examination will show that points A and E are both displaced the same amount from rest position, and are travelling in the same direction (upward for the instant shown). Points such as these are said to be *in phase*. These points will always remain in step with each other provided, of course, that the source continues to agitate the medium in the same manner. Points A and D are not in phase because they are travelling in opposite directions (although their displacements are at the moment identical). Similarly, points B and D are not in phase, because not only is one displaced downward while the other is displaced upward, but also they are moving in opposite directions. **Two points are in phase when their displacements from rest positions are equal, and they move in the same direction.** Figure 11-6(f) illustrates that points of like phase are separated by a distance of one wavelength. Accordingly a wavelength may also be defined as the distance separating two adjacent points of like phase.

Figure 11-6 illustrates the actual contour of the rope at different instants, due to the transverse wave passing through it. Usually, in representing a transverse wave, it is more meaningful to graph the displacement of a particle as time passes, that is, to graph the displacement as a function of time. This is done in Figure 11-7.

4. THE WAVE EQUATION

A very important relationship exists for any wave motion, relating the frequency, wavelength and velocity of the wave. The velocity of a wave is defined as the rate at which the disturbance travels along the medium.

Let $v =$ velocity of the wave
$T =$ period of the vibrating particles
$\lambda =$ wavelength

Because, by definition, the wave advances one wavelength during one period of time, the velocity of the wave can be expressed as:

$$\frac{\text{distance travelled}}{\text{corresponding elapsed time}} = \frac{\lambda}{T}$$

$$\therefore v = \frac{\lambda}{T}.$$

Since $\frac{1}{T} = f$, we have $v = f\lambda$.

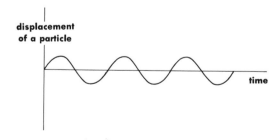

displacement of a particle

time

Fig. 11-7: A wave may be represented by a graph indicating how the displacement of a particle of the medium changes with time.

173

EXAMPLE 1

A train of waves is sent along a rope under tension. The velocity of the wave is 8.0 m/sec, and the frequency of vibration is 2.0 cycles/sec (c/sec). Determine: (a) the period; (b) the wavelength.

Solution:

(a) $T = \dfrac{1}{f} = \dfrac{1}{2.0 \text{ c/sec}} = \textbf{0.50 sec}$.

(b) $v = f\lambda \quad \lambda = \dfrac{v}{f} = \dfrac{8.0 \text{ m/sec}}{2.0 \text{ c/sec}} = \textbf{4.0 m}$.

5. PROPERTIES OF WAVES

We have used the simple device of a stretched rope to convey basic concepts related to wave motion. Waves propagated along a rope, on the surface of a body of water, and waves set up in air by a rapidly vibrating object—indeed, most waves exhibit certain common characteristics or properties, which we shall now consider.

Fig. 11-8: *A ripple tank*

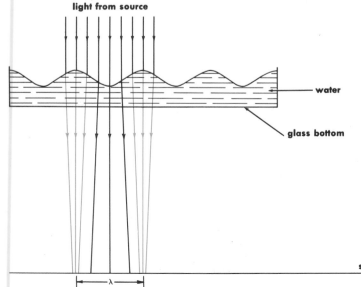

light from source

water

glass bottom

λ

screen

Fig. 11-9: *Formation of the image under a ripple tank. Each crest acts as a lens to concentrate the light.*

A basic understanding of these characteristics is essential to a fuller comprehension of the behaviour of sound and light. In describing and illustrating these characteristics, we shall at times continue to refer to our stretched rope, which may be considered a "one-dimensional" medium. In some cases, this device will be too restrictive, and a two-dimensional medium will be more useful. For our purposes, a convenient two-dimensional medium is provided by the small surface of water enclosed in a ripple tank, illustrated in Figure 11-8. The ripple tank has a glass bottom. A source of light above the tank produces an image of the water waves in the tank on a screen under the tank. How the image is formed is depicted in Figure 11-9.

Agitation of the water is accomplished by any of several methods. Figure 11-10 shows a train of *straight waves*. These were generated by a straight wooden bar on which was mounted a small motor. The vibration of the bar creates the disturbance in the wave medium. Alternatively, straight waves may be generated by rolling a wooden dowel along the bottom of the tank.

In Figure 11-11, *circular waves* are illustrated. These waves were generated by a point source consisting of a vibrating sphere that barely grazes the surface of the water.

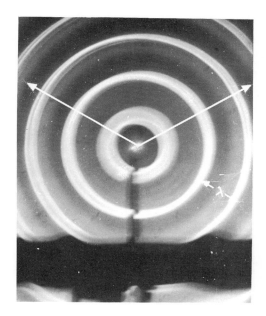

Fig. 11-11: *Circular waves in a ripple tank, with superimposed rays.*

In each of Figures 11-10 and 11-11, the continuous light portions of the pattern correspond to wave crests, and the darker areas between these correspond to troughs of the water waves. Any continuous crest, or trough, is frequently referred to as a *wave front*. All points on a wave front are of the same phase; that is, at any instant they are in the same position relative to their rest position, and are travelling in the same direction. The rate at which each wave front advances represents the velocity of the wave.

Figures 11-10 and 11-11 both show lines drawn perpendicular to the wave fronts. These lines, called *rays*, indicate the direction of propagation of the wave front at a particular point. It is obvious that for straight waves, all rays are parallel, while, for circular waves, all rays pass through the source. Another interesting aspect of circular waves is that as the wave fronts advance away from the source, their curvature becomes less and less apparent; that is, *at relatively great distances from a point source, the wave fronts are essentially straight.*

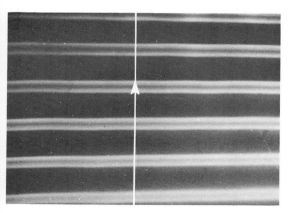

Fig. 11-10: *Straight waves in a ripple tank, with superimposed ray.*

175

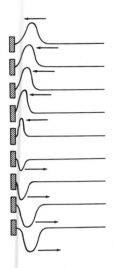

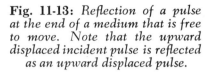

Fig. 11-12: *Reflection of a pulse at the fixed end of a rope. Note that the pulse is reflected upside-down.*

Fig. 11-13: *Reflection of a pulse at the end of a medium that is free to move. Note that the upward displaced incident pulse is reflected as an upward displaced pulse.*

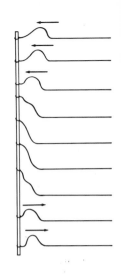

(i) *Reflection*

Whenever an advancing wave encounters a sudden change in medium, the phenomenon of reflection occurs. The simplest example of reflection is that demonstrated by a rope fixed at one end. A pulse travelling along a rope bounces back from the rigid support in the manner shown in Figure 11-12. An interesting aspect of this particular case of reflection is that an upward-displaced inci-

dent pulse gives rise to a downward-displaced reflected pulse, and a downward-displaced pulse is reflected as an upward-displaced pulse. This, however, is not true in all cases of reflection. If the reflecting end of the rope were somewhat less rigidly supported, this reversal would not take place. The concept is illustrated in Figure 11-13.

The important aspect of reflection is that it represents a return of a portion of the energy carried by the incident wave. In applications of transfer of energy by wave motion, it is usually desirable to keep this reflected energy to a minimum.

Figure 11-14 illustrates reflection of a circular wave front from a plane surface, while Figure 11-15 indicates reflection by a straight wave front from the same surface. In the latter case the wave front is shown hitting the reflecting surface obliquely. A ray for each of the incident and reflected wave fronts is shown, along with the *normal* or perpendicular to the surface at the point common to both rays. The angle between the incident ray and the normal is called the *angle of incidence*, while that between the reflected ray and the normal is called the *angle of reflection*. Do you see a relationship between these angles?

Fig. 11-14: *Reflection of circular waves from a plane surface.*

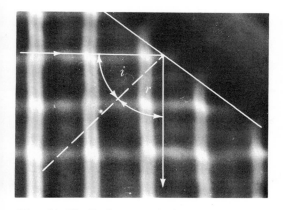 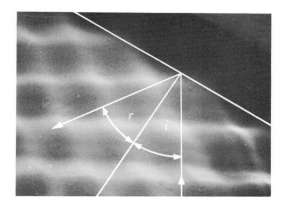

Fig. 11-15: *Reflection of plane waves from a plane surface. The angles of incidence and reflection are indicated by* **i** *and* **r** *respectively. In (a) the incident and reflected waves are perpendicular to each other.*

(ii) *Refraction*

Refraction is the bending of a wave front when it passes from one medium to another. The effect is demonstrated quite clearly using plane waves generated in a ripple tank. The velocity of waves in a body of water is dependent upon the depth of the water, if this is considerably less than the wavelength. The more shallow the water the less rapid is the advance of each wave front. Accordingly, the velocity of waves in a ripple tank may be altered by arranging one portion of the tank to be more shallow than the other. In practice this is done by supporting a glass plate just below the surface of the water.

In Figure 11-16, the water in the lower portion of the photograph is approximately one inch in depth, while that in the upper portion of the photograph is effectively about 0.1 inch, this being the portion above the supporting plate. The edge of the supporting plate is represented by the oblique line.

Two important observations are obtained from this figure. First, the wave fronts undergo bending as they enter the shallow water. The superimposed rays give an indication of the degree of bending. Once again the normal is drawn at the point of incidence. The angle made by the refracted ray and this normal is called the *angle of refraction.*

Fig. 11-16: *Refraction of water waves in passing from deep to shallow water. What changes take place in the wave?*

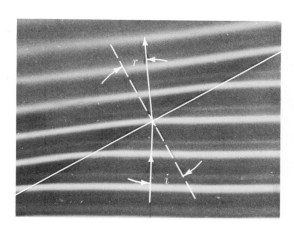

Secondly, the wavelength has undergone a change in the new medium: it has been shortened considerably. This is exactly as we would expect, because of the decreased speed of the wave in the shallow water. (Recall that wavelength is the distance travelled by the wave during one cycle of vibration of the source.)

The behaviour of these same wave fronts when the refracting surface (i.e. the edge of the shallow water) is parallel to the wave fronts is shown in Figure 11-17. Note here that no bending of the wave front takes place, but, as before, the wavelength has decreased.

In general, when a wave is refracted while entering a different medium, simultaneous reflection takes place. The amount of reflected energy depends upon the characteristics of the refracting surface. In Figure 11-18, partial reflection of the incident wave is noticeable.

Fig. 11-17: *No bending takes place when the incident wave fronts are parallel to the refracting surface.*

(iii) *Diffraction*

The term diffraction is used to describe the various effects produced when part of a wave front encounters an obstacle. One such effect is shown in Figure 11-19(a). Here straight waves of long wavelength are incident upon a solid object protruding above the surface of the water. The obstructing surface is parallel to the wave fronts. A "spilling over" of the disturbance into the region behind the obstacle is quite apparent. In Figure 11-19(b), the frequency of the wave generator has been increased, resulting in a corresponding decrease in wavelength of the straight waves. What do you notice about the "spilling over" effect?

As we have seen, waves tend to travel in a straight line, providing no change is encountered in the characteristics of the medium. Here we see that a bending *can* take place if an obstacle partially obstructs the wave fronts. The term diffraction is most commonly used to describe this tendency to bend into the region behind an obstacle.

Another interesting aspect of diffraction appears when a train of straight waves is completely obstructed, except for a small slit or opening in the obstruction. The effect is shown in Figure 11-20. A series of circular waves is seen to emanate from the

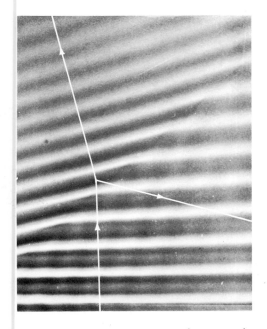

Fig. 11-18: *When a wave undergoes refraction partial reflection usually occurs, as shown here.*

Fig. 11-19: *Diffraction effects produced by an obstacle in the path of advancing waves. In (a) waves of long wavelength spill over into the region behind the obstacle. In (b) the region behind the obstacle remains undisturbed by waves of shorter wave-length.*

slit, entirely as if the slit itself were acting as a point source of circular waves. Compare this photograph with that in Figure 11-11. We shall make reference to this phenomenon in our later discussion, as well as to the effect produced when two such slits exist side by side.

In Figure 11-21, the aperture, or size of slit, has been considerably increased. The result is a decrease in the action of the slit as a source of new waves, although a slight bending around the corners of the slit is still evident.

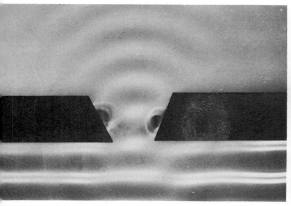

Fig. 11-20: *A small opening in an obstruction acts as a source of circular waves when straight waves are incident at it.*

Fig. 11-21: *As the width of the opening is increased, it acts less as a source of circular waves.*

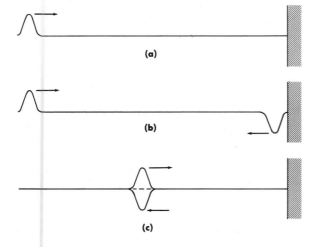

(a)

(b)

(c)

Fig. 11-22: *Destructive interference takes place at the centre of a rope if a new pulse is sent out when the previous one is reflected from the distant end.*

(iv) *Interference*

We have used the simple medium of a rope in our preliminary investigation into the phenomenon of reflection. However, refraction and diffraction effects cannot be shown using this device, because a rope is essentially a medium of one dimension only —length. To illustrate refraction and diffraction, a two-dimensional medium such as water has been employed, because both these effects have to do with the *bending* of a wave front. We now return to our rope, fixed at one end, to investigate yet another property possessed by all waves—their ability to interfere with each other.

Interference Effects in a Rope

The phenomenon of wave interference is the combined effect of two or more waves which meet at a point. A simple way to create two waves in a rope is to send a single pulse toward the fixed end, then, during its return after reflection, to send out a second pulse. The effect is illustrated in Figure 11-22. In (a) the rope has been given a single upward jerk. This pulse travels to

the right, undergoes an upside-down reflection at the rigid support, and is shown in (b) at the instant it begins its return. At this same instant, a second pulse is sent out, equal in amplitude to the initial pulse. Both pulses will meet at the centre of the rope. At the centre, the second pulse will tend to displace the rope upward by the same amount that the reflected first pulse will tend to displace the rope downward. The *combined effect* of these two pulses at the centre is to cancel displacement. This is an example of *destructive interference*.. Here, two pulses of equal amplitude, but opposite displacement, arrive simultaneously at a point in the wave medium, resulting in no net disturbance at the point.

Before we leave this particular example of interference, you may wonder what happens to each reflected pulse when it arrives back at the hand. Actually, the hand acts as a rigid support, even though it is able to initiate new pulses. Consequently the reflected pulse undergoes another reversal in displacement, and travels again to the right as an *upward* displacement, thus adding to the new pulse initiated by the hand.

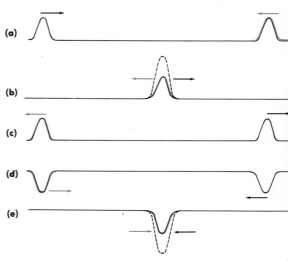

(a)

(b)

(c)

(d)

(e)

Fig. 11-23: *Pulses sent simultaneously from opposite ends of a rope will interfere constructively at the middle.*

Let us now examine Figure 11-23 to see how two waves may reinforce each other. Here, in (a), a pulse is sent out simultaneously from each end of the rope by giving each end a single upward jerk. The pulses arrive at the centre simultaneously, and the combined effect on the rope, at this point, is to displace it upward by an amount greater than would each individual pulse.

In (c), each pulse has travelled to the opposite end of the rope. Should no new jerks be given the rope, each of the pulses would be reflected, undergoing a change in displacement as shown in (d), each returning to the midpoint as a downward displacement. Here the midpoint will be displaced *downward* by an amount greater than that which would be caused by the individual pulses.

In this example, the midpoint of the rope is being displaced first in one direction and then in the other by the simultaneous arrival of two pulses which reinforce each other. This situation is called **constructive interference—the reinforcement of two waves at a point, causing a displacement greater than that caused by each wave individually.**

6. STANDING WAVES

Our analysis of interference of waves along a rope can be further extended by considering the case in which waves are continuously generated at each end of the rope. In Figure 11-24(a) two wave trains of like frequency and amplitude travel in opposite directions from each end of the rope, the black wave travelling to the right, and the red wave toward the left end. Figure 11-24(b) indicates the situation one quarter period later. At this time, each wave has advanced one quarter wavelength. Successive portions of this drawing illustrate the situation at further intervals of one quarter period; each wave advances in its own direction by a quarter wavelength. In (b) the waves are on the verge of coming in contact, and from this instant on, various parts of the

rope will be simultaneously under the influence of the two waves. At such points, the resultant effect on the rope is shown by a heavy black line. In (c), for example, the middle portion of the rope tends to be displaced downward by each of two wave trains. This part of the rope, as a result, is displaced downward by twice the amplitude of the individual waves.

In (d), each part near the centre of the rope feels an upward tug by one wave, but an equal and opposite tug by the other. Consequently the central portion of the rope is undisplaced at this instant. Somewhat the same situation exists in (f), except that almost the entire length of the rope is in its equilibrium position.

In (g) to (k) inclusive, all parts of the rope are under the simultaneous influence of the two wave trains. Note that at intervals of one half period, all parts of the rope are undisplaced. This is the situation in (h) and (j).

In (h) eleven points along the rope have been labelled, at intervals of one quarter wavelength. These are the points A to K inclusive. Observe the motion of each of these points from Figure 11-24(h) to (k). You will note that points A, C, E, G, I, K are undisplaced from their rest positions *at all times*. These points are called *nodes*. At points halfway between these nodes, maximum displacement takes place, alternating between upward and downward displacement. These points of maximum disturbance located midway between the nodes are called *loops* or *antinodes*.

In practice, the separate up and down motions of the loops cannot be distinguished; the visual effect resulting from the interference of the travelling waves is illustrated in Figure 11-24(l). The pattern appears stationary, and for this reason is called a *stationary wave* or *standing wave*. **A standing wave in a rope is produced by the interference of two waves of like amplitude and wavelength, travelling in opposite directions.**

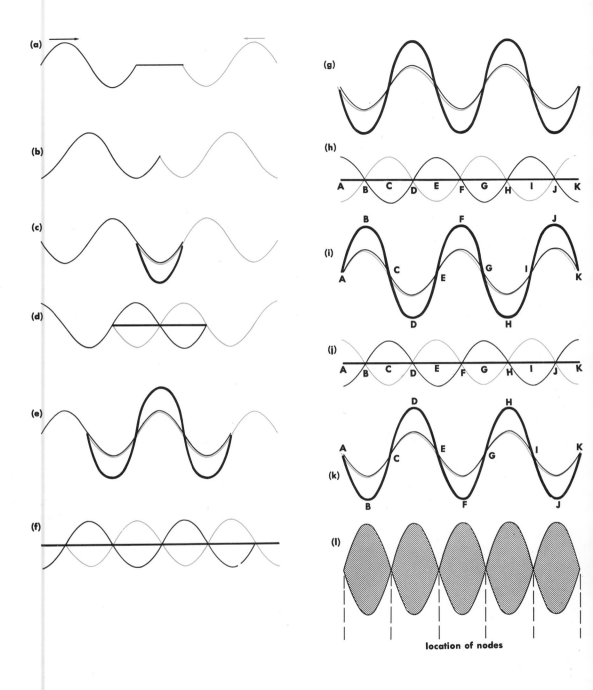

Fig. 11-24: *Interference of two wave trains of like frequency and amplitude, travelling in opposite directions along a rope. The resulting wave is shown by the heavy black line. The resulting pattern, shown in (l), is called a standing wave.*

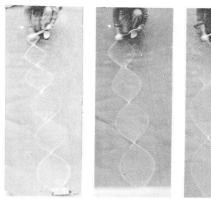

Fig. 11-25: *Standing waves in a spring.*

Figure 11-25 is a photograph of a standing wave pattern in a vibrating spring. Here the travelling waves producing the interference pattern are the waves sent out by the hand and their corresponding reflections from the fixed end of the rope. Standing wave patterns are by no means limited to vibrating ropes. They may be produced in a coil spring fixed at one end, with the other end initiating longitudinal pulses. These pulses upon reflection will interfere with new pulses to produce points of constant minimum disturbance (nodes) at regular intervals along the medium.

Practically all sounds emanating from musical instruments are the result of standing waves in the instrument. In many such cases, the vibrating medium is a column of air. We shall investigate this aspect of standing waves more fully in Chapter 12.

7. INTERFERENCE OF WATER WAVES

We shall now consider the manner in which waves in a two dimensional medium may interfere with each other. Once again the ripple tank serves as a convenient tool in our investigation.

Let us assume that two sources of circular waves, S_1 and S_2 in Figure 11-26, are generating the waves. In practice, S_1 and S_2 are two spheres, a few inches apart, mounted on

a common support which vibrates. These spheres move up and down in unison. As they move down, they graze the water's surface, and this results in circular waves being sent out from these points. An important fact is that the waves from each of the two sources are *in phase*, because both spheres hit the surface simultaneously. At the moment of contact, crests are sent out from each source and propelled across the water's surface. Each time the spheres touch the surface, new crests are formed, and we shall assume that this process continues indefinitely.

Between the formation of crests, a trough is produced at each source. This will occur when each sphere emerges from the surface. Thus a continuous succession of crests and troughs emanates from each source, and the waves sent out by each source are periodic waves of like frequency and amplitude.

Figure 11-26(a) illustrates the situation after one complete vibration of each sphere. Here the peak of a crest is indicated in red, and the lowest point of a trough in black. These are points of maximum disturbance. Between these circles, the medium is in various lesser states of agitation. Halfway between the crests and troughs the water is undisturbed. At that instant shown in (a), each sphere is about to dip into the water to produce a new crest.

In (b), the situation is shown one period later. Another new crest and trough have been generated, and the initial ones have moved out by a distance of one wavelength. Because the sources, in this example, are separated by four wavelengths, the initial crests meet at one point, A, and here a maximum upward displacement of the water will result—to produce *constructive interference*.

In (c), another period has elapsed. Three complete vibrations of each sphere have taken place, and the disturbance from each source has travelled three wavelengths, in all directions. At how many locations can you find two crests superimposed, causing constructive interference? You will note also that at certain points, a trough from S_1 arrives simultaneously with a trough from S_2. This also is a case of constructive interference. At such points we would expect maximum displacement of the water, this time in a downward direction. How many such points exist in Figure 11-26(c)?

Another important set of points exists in this illustration. At certain points, a crest from one source arrives with a trough from the other source. There are twelve such points for the instant shown. (Check this.) The combined effect is zero disturbance at these points—or *destructive interference*.

A condition for interference

Consider the nine points in Figure 11-26(c) at which crests are superimposed. Determine the distance from each of these points to the two sources, in order to find the difference in these distances. A convenient unit of measurement is a half wavelength. For example, at point B, two crests are superimposed. Its distance from S_1 is four

half wavelengths; from S_2, six half wavelengths. The difference in distances from each of the sources is two half wavelengths. Analyse each of the other points in a similar manner in order to find the difference in distance from the point to the two sources. Now repeat this procedure for points at which two troughs are superimposed, in each case determining the difference in the distances from that point to each of the two sources.

What is true of all points at which constructive interference takes place?

Consider now all the points at which destructive interference exists—points at which crests and troughs arrive simultaneously. What do you find concerning their distance from each of the sources? Formulate this into a general statement.

In Figure 11-26(d) the situation is shown for the moment that each of the original disturbances has travelled a distance of five wavelengths. Points at which crests and troughs are superimposed are indicated by dots. At all such points, the water is undisplaced. These undisturbed points form a definite geometric pattern, as indicated by the dashed lines. Although only the points where the peak of a crest meets the peak of a trough are indicated here by dots, it should be clear that *any* point on these lines is a point where the disturbance due to S_1 is equal and opposite to that due to S_2.

In Figure 11-26(e) the pattern of undisturbed points is shown a short time later. Note that the location of the pattern is unchanged from that in (d). That is, *certain points exist where the net disturbance is permanently zero*. These points are nodes. The lines joining the nodes in Figure 11-26 (d) and (e) are called *nodal lines*.

Fig. 11-26: *Interference of waves from two point sources in phase. (a) A crest (red) and a trough have been sent out from each source. (b) One period later, another crest and trough have been sent out. The initial crests are interfering constructively at point A. (c) Another period later, several points of constructive and destructive interference exist. (d) The locations of points where destructive interference exists form a geometric pattern shown by the dashed lines. These lines, joining nodes, are called nodal lines. (e) A short time later (one quarter period) each wave front has advanced one quarter wavelength from the position shown in (d). Note that the location of the nodal lines is unchanged.*

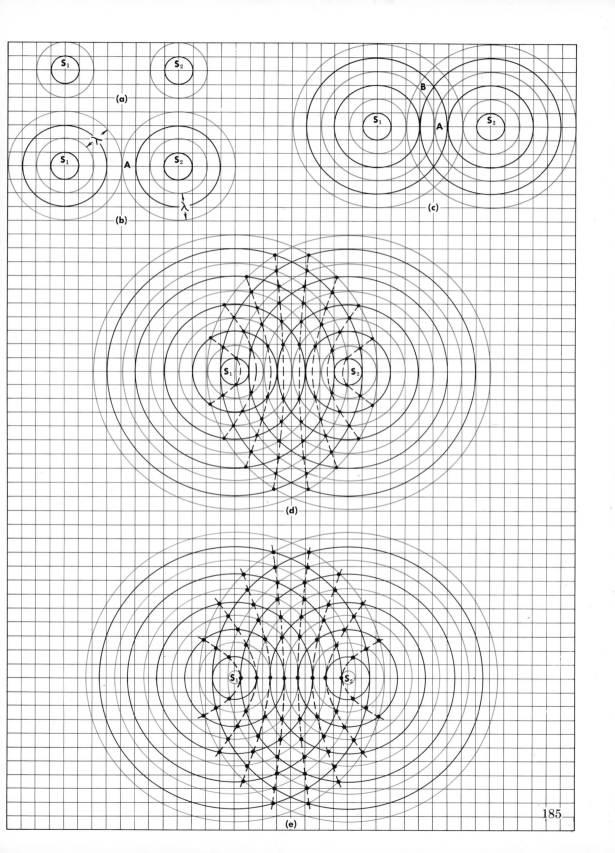

185

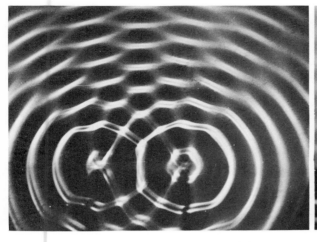

Fig. 11-27: *A photograph showing a nodal line pattern in the region surrounding two point sources.*

Fig. 11-28: *Interference effects produced by two openings in the path of obstructed waves. Each opening acts as source of circular waves.*

Figure 11-27 shows the actual nodal pattern obtained in a ripple tank when, as in our discussion, the two point sources generate periodic waves of like frequency.

You will recall that a small opening in an obstruction to a straight wave behaved as a source of spherical waves (Figure 11-20).

In Figure 11-28 two such openings exist and interference effects take place in the region beyond the slits. The two slits act as sources of spherical waves. We shall find such interference effects of great significance in our investigation into the nature of light.

In this chapter our study of wave motion has been confined to mechanical waves—disturbances transmitted in an elastic medium. These waves have been classified in various ways, the most common standard being the manner in which the particles of the medium move relative to the direction of the disturbance. In transverse waves, the particles move across the path of the wave, while in longitudinal waves the particles move small distances parallel to the path of the wave.

Certain particles will constantly move in step with each other; that is, they will be displaced by the same amount and move in the same direction at all times. Such particles are **in phase**. The distance separating adjacent particles in phase or the distance travelled by the wave disturbance in one period of vibration of the source is one **wavelength**.

The terms period, frequency and amplitude are descriptive of wave motion as well as of any vibratory motion.

The wave equation $v = f\lambda$ states an important relationship between the velocity, frequency and wavelength of any wave, and we shall use it extensively for waves other than those referred to in this chapter.

We have investigated four characteristics of waves—reflection, refraction, diffraction and interference. Both refraction and diffraction have to do with the bending of a wave.

Refraction is the bending of a wave due to a change in its velocity when entering a different medium, while diffraction is a bending or "spilling over" behind an obstruction.

Interference takes place when two or more waves arrive at a point. If the waves reinforce, we have **constructive interference**. If they tend to nullify, **destructive interference** results. Under suitable conditions, some points in a medium, called nodes, will be permanently undisturbed by the arrival of two waves. At other points, called loops, maximum displacement takes place. The disturbance pattern produced is called a standing wave or stationary wave. Stationary waves, then, are produced by the interference effects of two travelling waves.

When a point receives waves from two sources in phase, constructive interference is a maximum if the difference in distances from the point to the sources is zero, or an **even number of half-wavelengths**. Similarly, destructive interference will be a maximum if this difference of distances is an **odd number of half-wavelengths**.

EXERCISE A

1. What is common concerning a bullet shot from a gun, an electron moving in a vacuum tube, and a wave motion?

2. Explain what is meant by a complete vibration or cycle.

3. What is meant by: (a) the frequency of a vibration, (b) the period of a vibration? Describe the difference between a longitudinal and a transverse vibration.

4. When are two parts of a wave said to be in phase?

5. Where is an oscillating particle positioned when it possesses its: (a) maximum velocity, (b) minimum velocity?
Give two definitions of wavelength.

6. What distance does a crest move as each particle of the medium oscillates once?

7. How would you define a wave?

8. When a wave enters a different medium, what characteristic of the wave remains unchanged?

9. Prior to the invasion of North Africa during World War II, the velocity of water waves along the coastline was determined by aerial observation. How was this information useful in determining the location of invasion beaches?

10. Under what conditions will destructive interference exist at a point receiving waves from two sources which vibrate in phase?

11. A point is located equidistant from two sources which are out of phase; that is, as one generates a trough, the other generates a crest. What is the nature of the interference at this point? At what other locations would similar interference occur?

12. A point on a vibrating rope is, at a certain instant, in its equilibrium position. Are we justified in calling this location a node?

13. What conditions must be fulfilled in order for standing waves to exist in a medium?

14. A circular glass plate is supported in a ripple tank so that its surface is just below the surface of the water. Straight waves are sent from the deeper water to the plate. Predict what changes will take place in the image on the screen.

EXERCISE B

Consider all data accurate to the number of digits quoted.

1. A student timed a pendulum that completed 30 vibrations in 20 seconds. What was: (*a*) the frequency, (*b*) the period of the pendulum?

2. Middle C on the piano has a frequency of 256 vib/sec. Find the period of the string when C is sounded.

3. The wavelength of a sound vibrating with a frequency of 200 vib/sec is 1.72 metres. Find the velocity of the sound wave.

4. The wavelength of electromagnetic waves from a certain radio station is 2.97×10^2 m. Calculate the velocity of electromagnetic waves, if the frequency of the waves is 1.00×10^6 c/sec.

5. Cosmic rays of outer space travel at the speed of light (3.0×10^8 m/sec). Calculate the frequency of a cosmic ray of wavelength 1.0×10^{-14} m.

6. A train of waves moves along a wire with a speed of 30 ft/sec. Find the frequency and period of the source, if the wavelength is 3.0 inches.

7. A bat emits ultrasonic sound of frequency 5.5×10^4 vib/sec to aid in the location of obstacles. If the speed of the emitted waves is 1100 ft/sec, what is the corresponding wavelength?

8. The range of human hearing extends over the frequency range 20 vib/sec to about 20,000 vib/sec, depending on the individual. Taking the speed of sound as 1100 ft/sec, what is the corresponding range of wavelengths?

9. A wave is sent along a rope. The velocity of the wave is 8.0 m/sec. The wavelength of the disturbance is 4.0 m. At a given instant, one part of the rope is in its equilibrium position. What time will elapse before this part of the rope is at its point of maximum upward displacement?

10. A string is attached to the clapper of an electric doorbell, which vibrates at a frequency of 120 vib/sec. If the resulting waves are 6.0 in long, what time is required for the disturbance to travel 30 ft?

11. A rope fixed at one end is agitated at a rate of 3.0 c/sec. When the first disturbance reaches the fixed end, there are 5.0 complete waves on the rope. Determine the velocity of waves on the rope if it is 25 ft long.

12. Two fishermen sit on the edge of a bridge, 60 ft apart. Waves pass below them in such a manner that when a crest is under one of them, a trough is located under the other, with two crests located between them. The cork attached to each line bobs up and down 15 times per minute. Determine the speed of the water waves.

13. In Figure 11-6 the rope is 20 ft long and the hand vibrates at a rate of 4.0 vib/sec. What is the speed of the travelling waves?

14. A certain tuning fork has a natural frequency of 250 vib/sec. When struck, the amplitude of each prong (tine) is .050 in. What is the average speed of the tip during one complete vibration?

15. Two sources, S_1 and S_2, vibrate in phase in a ripple tank. At a certain instant, constructive interference takes place at point A, located 7.0 in from S_1 and 3.0 in from S_2.

    (a) Why can we not determine the wavelength of the ripples from this information?

    (b) Suppose that at the same instant destructive interference takes place at point B, located 6.0 in from S_1 and 3.0 in from S_2. Is this additional information sufficient to determine the wavelength?

Waves

▶ Experiment 16

To measure frequency with a hand
stroboscope.

Hand stroboscope kit

Stop watch

3 C-clamps

Recording timer

The stroboscope is a device used in studying the motion of vibrating or rotating objects. It can reduce the apparent motion of the object for the observer so that it appears stationary, or moves at greatly reduced speed.

The hand stroboscope to be used in this experiment is a cardboard disk with several slots (usually twelve) located evenly along the circumference. A handle at the disk's centre permits the disk to be rotated by one hand while the other supports the instrument. With twelve slots open, twelve glimpses at a vibrating object are obtained during each revolution of the disk. If eleven of these slots are covered by tape, then only one glimpse is obtained per revolution.

Consider the vibrating metal strip shown in the photograph. Let us suppose its frequency is 4 vib/sec. If we view it through the stroboscope with only one slot open, and rotate it at a steady rate of 4 rotations/sec, the strip will appear stationary, because as the strip vibrates once, the disk goes through one rotation. Each time we obtain a glimpse at the strip, it will be in the same location, because its period is equal to the number of glimpses we receive each second. If the disk's rate of rotation is now increased slightly, we will view the strip a little sooner during each of its cycles. It will appear to move slowly in the direction opposite to its actual motion. How will it appear to move if the disk's rate is slightly less than 4 rotations/sec?

Before we use this instrument to measure frequency, there are further considerations of importance. Suppose we rotate the disk, with one slot open, at half its former rate, that is, at one revolution each $\frac{1}{2}$ sec. How will the vibrating strip appear? It will still appear stationary because we will be allowed one glimpse at it for two complete vibrations. Similarly if the disk were rotated once each full second, it would still appear stationary (to allow one glimpse every 4 complete vibrations). In each of these cases we would be given a look at the strip at the same point on its vibrating path. Further reductions of the disk rate would produce other stationary patterns. Obviously, *in measuring the frequency of a vibrating system, the stroboscope must be rotated at the highest rate that produces a stationary image.*

Finally, what will happen if the disk, with one slot open, rotates at twice the frequency of the steel strip? Then we will be given two glimpses at it during each of its cycles, and a *double image* will appear because at each of these glimpses the strip will be at different locations. Other multiple images will appear as the speed of the disk is steadily increased.

It is difficult to rotate the disk steadily at a rate much greater than 4 rotations/sec. The same effect is produced by exposing two slots (located opposite each other). A rotation rate of 2 per second would then give us 4 glimpses per second. The greater the number of open slots, the higher the frequency we can measure for a given rate of disk rotation. What is the highest frequency we can measure with this stroboscope if we rotate it no faster than 4 rotations/sec?

Industrial stroboscopes employ a flashing lamp rather than a rotating disk. The rate of flash can be varied permitting measurement of frequencies as high as 5000 vib/sec.

Procedure

1. Clamp the steel strip to a table's edge, as shown. Load one end of the strip with another clamp, and set the system into vibration by pulling this clamp to one side and releasing it.

2. With one slot open, rotate the disk at various rates which produce a stationary image of the end of the strip. Note also the change in apparent motion of the strip when the rate of disk rotation is changed.

3. Increase the rate of rotation and obtain several multiple image patterns of the strip.

4. Rotate the disk at the highest rate which produces a single stationary image. Have your partner time a large number of the disk rotations to determine the rate of rotation.

5. Move the clamp closer to the fixed clamp, and, with two slots exposed, repeat steps 2, 3, and 4.

6. Try to "stop" the motion of a rapidly vibrating mass like the clapper of the recording timer used in the earlier experiments. This time you will probably require 12 open slots. Rotate the disk at the highest rate that produces a stationary image and once again have your partner time a large number of rotations.

7. If an electric fan is available, you will find it interesting to observe its motion using the stroboscope. Make the necessary measurements to determine its frequency.

Analysis

Use the rate of rotation of the disk, in addition to the number of open slots, to determine the frequencies of the vibrating objects.

Questions

1. In this experiment we have used the stroboscope to measure frequency. In what other way is the instrument important?

2. The end of a motor shaft has a white dot on its circumference. When the motor is running and is viewed through a hand stroboscope with 12 open slots, a stationary pattern of 3 equally spaced dots is seen. What is the speed of the motor in revolutions per minute, if the stroboscope disk makes 3.5 rotations each second?

To study waves in a one-dimensional medium.

> Coil spring wave kit
>
> Metre stick or tape-measure
>
> Stop watch

In this experiment we shall make a qualitative investigation of the properties of transverse waves in a one-dimensional medium, such as a coil spring. The velocity of these waves will also be determined. Coil springs are chosen because of the low velocity of transverse waves in such a medium.

Procedure

1. While your partner holds one end fixed, stretch the large-diameter coil along the floor, a distance of about 30 ft.

2. Initiate a transverse pulse along the spring by quickly moving one end to the side and then back to rest position. Note the manner in which the pulse is reflected.

3. Stretch the spring further, and initiate additional pulses. How does the speed of the pulses compare with that in step 2?

4. Repeat steps 2 and 3 using the stiffer coil spring.

5. With the stiffer coil spring free to move at the far end, that is, unsupported by your partner, initiate new pulses. How do these reflections differ from those in step 4?

6. Initiate a pulse on the same side of the spring as a pulse sent by your partner. Note the effect at the point where they meet. Repeat this for pulses sent on opposite sides of the spring.

7. Connect together one end of each spring. Initiate a pulse at the end of the large-diameter coil. What happens at the junction of the springs?

8. Initiate a pulse in the denser spring and note what happens at the junction. How does this differ from what occurred in step 7?

9. Produce transverse standing waves in the spring by vibrating one end with the other end fixed. Obtain several standing wave patterns by steadily increasing the rate of vibration.

10. To determine the speed of wave motion in the springs, two methods are possible. The most obvious is to initiate a pulse at one end, and time the interval required for the pulse to return to the hand. The speed of the wave is then determined by dividing twice the length of the spring by this time interval. If the pulse can make several back-and-forth reflections before dying out, the accuracy of the speed calculation will be greatly improved.
Try this method for either of the coil springs. Measure the total time interval during which it travels, and the total distance travelled.

11. The other method of determining the wave velocity makes use of the wave equation and standing waves. Recall that when standing waves exist in a medium, the distance between consecutive nodes bears a simple relationship to the wavelength of the travelling waves.

Stretch the spring by the same amount as in step 9. Produce a standing wave pattern with one loop located at the centre. You or your partner can time a large number of vibrations; this will enable you to determine the frequency of the waves. The length of the stretched spring gives the distance between adjacent nodes.

Analysis

1. From your observations of waves in the first 9 steps of the procedure, list your conclusions regarding the manner in which reflections occur at the fixed end and the free end of a spring, and at the junction of two springs.

2. Determine the speed of the wave from your observations in step 10.

3. Determine the frequency and wavelength of the travelling waves in step 11. Using the wave equation, determine the velocity of these waves. Compare it with that obtained previously.

4. Which of the two speed calculations do you consider the more accurate? Why?

Experiment 18

To study waves in a two-dimensional medium—the ripple tank.

> Complete ripple tank apparatus
>
> Stroboscope

Procedure

1. Set up the ripple tank and place water in it to a depth of about 1 cm. Level the tank until the water has equal depth at all corners.

2. Place the wire screen and gauze along the four sides of the tank. These serve to minimize undesired reflections from the sides of the tank.

3. Create a circular pulse by touching the water with a finger. What happens to the shape of this pulse as it recedes from the source? A single straight pulse may be formed by rolling a piece of wooden dowel a short distance along the bottom of the tank.

4. To observe reflection effects, set a row of paraffin blocks on edge across the path of the wave (illustration 1). Generate straight pulses at various angles of incidence to the barrier.

5. To produce a periodic train of waves, the wave generator is used. Generate straight waves of low frequency. Some adjustments of the generator may be necessary to get wave fronts that are very straight. When straight waves are being generated, the lamp filament should be placed parallel to the waves for maximum contrast in the image. Adjustment in the height of the lamp will also help.

6. Observe the straight waves through the hand stroboscope. Obtain a stationary image and make a rough estimate of the wavelength.

7. Increase the frequency of the waves by adjusting the rheostat. Observe the resulting stationary pattern given by the stroboscope. Estimate the new wavelength. How could you have predicted the manner in which the wavelength changed?

8. Repeat steps 6 and 7, this time generating circular waves.

9. To observe refraction, support a glass plate above the tank bottom using coins or rubber grommets (illustration 2). The depth of water above the glass plate will have to be very slight—just enough to cover the plate evenly. Adjust the water level accordingly. Generate straight waves of low frequency to hit the refracting surface obliquely.
Observe the pattern through the stroboscope. Does the frequency of the waves change after refraction? Does the wavelength change? Is there a change in wave velocity?

10. Adjust the glass plate so that its refracting edge is parallel to the oncoming straight waves. This can be done accurately by "strobing" the generated wave pattern and the image of the refracting edge while your partner makes fine adjustments in the position of the plate. Is there any bending in the waves as they pass from deep to shallow water?

11. Remove the glass plate and supports and place one paraffin block parallel to the wave generator, resting on its longer edge. Observe any bending into the region behind this obstacle for straight waves of various frequencies, beginning with a low frequency. Does the disturbance behind the obstacle increase as frequency increases, or does it decrease?

12. Place another block adjacent to the existing one with its edge also parallel to the oncoming waves (illustration 3). Leave a small separation between the adjacent edges. Describe the waves emerging from this slit. Increase the slit width gradually. What change takes place in the emerging waves?

Analysis

Summarize the properties of a two-dimensional wave under the headings of reflection, refraction, and diffraction.

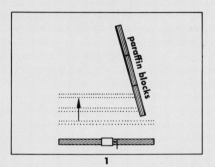

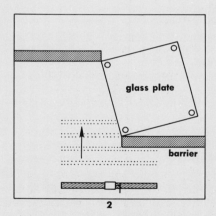

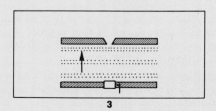

Experiment 19

To verify the wave equation.

```
Complete ripple tank apparatus
Ruler
Stop watch
Stroboscope
```

The wave equation $v = f\lambda$ can be verified using the waves on the screen of a ripple tank.

Procedure

1. Set up the ripple tank and fill it to a depth of about 1 cm. As before, make any necessary adjustments so that the depth is uniform throughout the tank.

2. To determine the velocity of waves along the screen, position a finger so that its image lies along the narrow edge of the screen. Create a circular pulse and time its travel to the opposite edge of the screen. Repeat this several times to obtain an average time of travel. Measure the length of the screen and determine the speed of the waves along the screen. Note: this is greater than the actual speed of the water waves.

3. To determine the wavelength and frequency, generate straight waves of low frequency. Before making any measurements, make sure the generator is stable enough to generate these waves at a constant rate. If it has a tendency to stop, increase the frequency slightly. The frequency of the waves must remain constant throughout the experiment.

4. To measure the frequency, rotate the stroboscope at the maximum rate that produces a stationary image. Two or four open slots should prove satisfactory. Have your partner time 20 rotations of the stroboscope.

5. To measure the wavelength of the waves on the screen, place a ruler on the screen, perpendicular to the wave fronts. Stop the motion once more with the stroboscope, and count the number of waves that lie along the length of the ruler. This measurement requires some patience in keeping a stationary image while counting the waves.

6. An alternative method for measuring wavelength is to produce standing waves in the tank, using a paraffin block as a reflecting surface. Place the block with its long edge parallel to the straight wave. Adjust its distance from the generator until a standing wave pattern is produced. Stationary waves will appear on the screen between the block and generator when this distance is properly adjusted. Make the necessary measurements to obtain the distance between consecutive nodal lines, and from this determine the wavelength of the generated waves.

Analysis

1. Evaluate the velocity, frequency, and wavelength from the measurements obtained above.

2. How closely does your calculation of speed compare with the product of frequency and wavelength?

To study the law of reflection.

Complete ripple tank apparatus

Protractor

Stroboscope

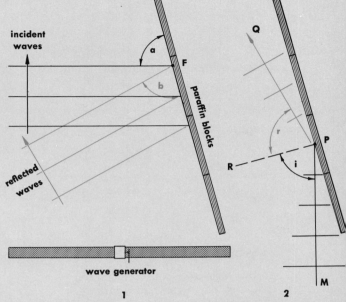

1

2

In this experiment we investigate the relationship between the angles of incidence and reflection when a wave is reflected in a two-dimensional medium.

Procedure

1. Set up the ripple tank to generate straight waves in water of uniform depth of about 1 cm.

2. Place a barrier across the path of the straight waves. A row of paraffin blocks set on edge will serve the purpose (illustration 1). Adjust the frequency of the generator so that straight reflected waves are clearly visible.

3. Mark with pencil a point on the screen that lies on the image of the reflecting edge, such as point *F*.

4. Draw a line through this point, parallel to the incident waves. This can be done accurately by stopping the wave motion with a stroboscope and having your partner, under your direction, place a ruler through the point and align it parallel to the wavefronts.

5. Repeat step 4 for the reflected waves

6. Measure the angles made by these lines and the reflecting barrier. These are the angles *a* and *b* (illustration 1). How do they compare?

7. Repeat this procedure for a different point along the barrier, and a different angle of obstruction of the barrier. Measure the new angles *a* and *b*, and compare them.

Analysis

1. What do you conclude regarding the angles made with the reflecting surface by the incident and reflected wavefronts?

2. In illustration 2 the incident ray MP and the reflected ray PQ are shown. PR is perpendicular to the reflecting surface. Using your conclusion from step 1, can you prove that angles *a*, *b*, *i*, and *r* are all equal? Angles *a* and *i* are called the angle of incidence; *b* and *r* are called the angle of reflection.

Experiment 21

To study interference from two point sources.

| Complete ripple tank apparatus |
| Metre stick |
| Stroboscope |

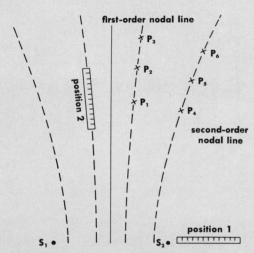

In this experiment we investigate the conditions for destructive interference at a point distant from two sources.

Procedure

1. Arrange the ripple tank as in the previous experiments, with the two point sources generating waves in phase. The source separation should be about 5 cm.

2. Note the nodal lines on the screen pattern. What does a nodal line represent? Change the frequency of the generated waves. How does the nodal line pattern change? Note the moving waves located in the area between nodal lines. You can "stop" these waves with the stroboscope. If the two sources are exactly in phase, crests will appear to "explode" simultaneously from each source when the pattern is almost stopped.

3. Increase the separation of the two point sources. How does the increased separation affect the number of nodal lines?

To make a quantitative investigation of points where destructive interference takes place, proceed as follows:

4. Mark on the screen the location of the two point sources S_1 and S_2. Mark also the location of two or three points P_1, P_2, P_3 on the first-order nodal line far

away from the sources. Indicate in addition the location of a few points P_4, P_5 and P_6 on the second-order nodal line.

5. Before the frequency of the waves changes, measure their wavelength, using a stroboscope and ruler. Place the ruler in a location where the waves do not interfere, such as position 1 in illustration 1, or alternatively at a position some distance from the sources along a nodal line. Count the number of crests along the length of the ruler.

Analysis

1. From step 5, determine the wavelength.

2. Measure the distances S_1P_1 and S_2P_2 and find their difference. Repeat for points P_2 and P_3. How are these differences related to the wavelength?

3. Join S_1 and S_2 to each of P_4, P_5, and P_6 and as before find the difference in distances from each of these points to the two sources. How are these distances related to the wavelength?

4. What do you predict about the difference in distances from any point on the third nodal line to the points S_1 and S_2?

Chapter 12 (PART A)

Sound

1. WHAT IS SOUND?

When we hear a sound and trace down its source, we find that the sound has originated from some vibrating body. In its simplest form, a source of sound might be a strip of steel or wood clamped in a vise as illustrated in Figure 12-1. When the upper end of this strip of elastic material is displaced and released, it vibrates to and fro and we hear a humming sound. We hear the bell of a locomotive. Examination reveals that the brass material of the bell is vibrating. On a warm, quiet summer day we hear a bee buzzing and discover that its wings are vibrating and causing the sound.

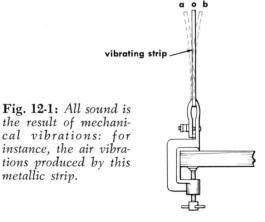

Fig. 12-1: *All sound is the result of mechanical vibrations: for instance, the air vibrations produced by this metallic strip.*

We are aware that the existence of a vibrating object is not, in itself, sufficient to ensure the sensation of sound. Figure 12-2 illustrates a familiar demonstration that no sound ensues without the presence of a medium between the vibrating object and the ear. The source of sound in this case is the electric bell inside the bell jar. As the air is evacuated, the intensity of the sound progressively diminishes, even though the amplitude of the source remains constant. Usually, when the evacuation has reached its highest degree, some sound is still perceptible, probably due to transmission of the vibrations from the bell directly through its support to the bell jar. We can conclude that not only is a medium required for the transmission of sound, but also that the intensity of the sound depends upon the density of the medium: in this case, air.

Of course, sound, as we use the term, also requires the presence of a detector—the ear. If the strip in Figure 12-1 is lengthened sufficiently and then allowed to vibrate, the ear will be incapable of detecting these vibrations because of their low frequency. The range of audible frequencies is usually taken as 20 c/sec to 20,000 c/sec. Inaudible vibrations below this range are termed *infrasonic*, while those above this range are referred to as *ultrasonic*.

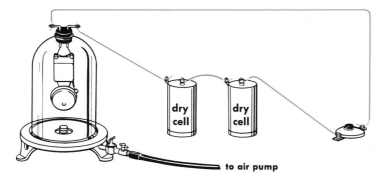

Fig. 12-2: *When air is removed from the bell jar, the ringing bell is no longer heard. What does this demonstrate about sound?*

For our purpose, then, we shall simply think of sound as the audible sensation produced by a vibrating source.

2. THE PRODUCTION OF SOUND

Let us now investigate the effect produced by a vibrating object on the surrounding air. In Figure 12-3, a column of air is enclosed in a cylinder, at one end of which a tightly fitting piston vibrates longitudinally. We may think of the vertical lines as representing layers of molecules, equally spaced when the piston is at rest, as in (a). As the piston moves forward, the adjoining layers are compressed. A *compression* or *condensation* is said to exist in this region. This compression travels down the tube as shown in (b). As the piston moves to the left, a region of low air density (and hence low pressure) results at the face of the piston. This region of rarefied air is called a *rarefaction*.

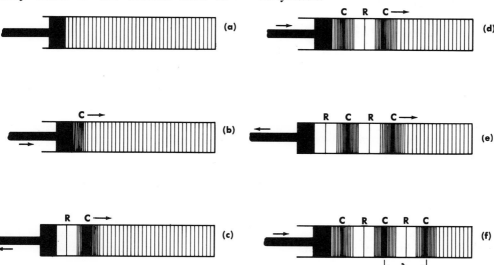

Fig. 12-3: *How a sound wave is produced. The piston, in moving forward, creates a compression, or high pressure region, indicated by the heavily shaded area. As the piston moves back, a rarefaction, or region of low pressure, is produced. These disturbances travel along the tube, although each air molecule vibrates only over a very limited region about its rest position. Here, C and R refer to compressions and rarefactions produced by the piston, and λ represents the wavelength.*

199

In (d) one vibration of the piston has been completed and another compression is being formed. The original compression has travelled some distance by now, and the formation of alternate compressions and rarefactions will continue as long as the source vibrates.

The distance travelled by the initial compression during one cycle of the piston represents the wavelength of the disturbance. Similarly the wavelength may be thought of as the distance between consecutive compressions, or consecutive rarefactions.

Clearly, the displacement of the particles constituting the medium is *parallel* to the direction of propagation, and this vibrating piston is producing a longitudinal wave in the column. Each particle, of course, vibrates over a very restricted distance about its normal position in (a). If the piston is vibrating within the approximate range of 20 to 20,000 c/sec, the wave disturbance may be referred to as a *sound wave*.

3. THE SPEED OF SOUND

The speed of sound depends on the medium used to transmit the sound. The earliest accurate determinations of the speed of sound in air were made by firing a gun and observing the time necessary for the sound to travel a known distance. The flash of the gunpowder seen by a distant observer notified the observer at what instant he was to begin the time measurement. Here the assumption is made that the light of the gunflash travels with infinite speed. This assumption, though not absolutely true, is justified by the tremendously large value of the speed of light.

The density of the medium and its elastic properties determine the speed of sound in that medium. In solids and liquids, the speed of sound is substantially independent of temperature change, while in gases, the speed increases linearly with increasing temperature.

In air, the speed of sound at 0° C is 331.4 m/sec (1087 ft/sec) and increases by 0.6 m/sec for each °C increase in temperature (1.1 ft/sec for each °F increase in temperature).

Table 12-1 gives the speed of sound in various media.

Table 12-1

Speed of Sound

	M/sec	Ft/sec
Air (0° C)	331	1,087
Alcohol	1,213	3,890
Aluminum	5,104	16,740
Brass	3,500	11,480
Carbon dioxide (0° C)	258	846
Copper	3,560	11,670
Glass	5,030	16,500
Hydrogen (0° C)	1,270	4,165
Iron	5,030	16,500
Maple, along the grain	4,110	13,470
Pine, along the grain	3,320	10,900
Steel	5,030	16,500
Water	1,461	4,794

4. REPRESENTATION OF A SOUND WAVE

In Figure 11-7 a transverse wave in a rope was represented by considering how any particle on the rope was displaced from its equilibrium position at various times. This is the usual way of representing a mechanical transverse wave motion.

In representing a longitudinal wave, the same process could be followed. Alternatively, we may represent the wave by depicting the manner in which the *density* of the medium at a particular point varies with time. This is illustrated for the vibrating tuning fork of Figure 12-4. Here, three wavelengths of the medium are shown. In a compression, the density of the medium is a maximum, while in a rarefaction it is a minimum. Midway between a compression

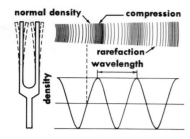

normal density
compression
rarefaction
wavelength
density

Fig. 12-4: *A sound wave may be illustrated graphically by a graph that shows how the density of the medium varies.*

and rarefaction, the medium is of normal density. This variation in air density is plotted in the accompanying graph.

5. CHARACTERISTICS OF SOUND

The ear distinguishes different sounds in any of three ways. The *loudness* of a sound is one of these. We know from experience that we associate the loudness of a sound with the strength or amplitude of vibration of the source—the greater the amplitude, the greater the loudness. Some sources may not transmit sufficient energy to create the sensation of sound, while in extreme cases, others may vibrate with sufficient amplitude that the sensation becomes one of pain rather than of hearing.

The *pitch* of a sound is a second distinguishing feature. This we associate with the rate of vibration of the source, and hence the rate at which compressions and rarefactions are received by the ear. If the vibrations are periodic, that is, regularly spaced, the effect produced is that of a musical tone. In Figure 12-5 a siren disk, containing a number of concentric rings of

Fig. 12-5: *A siren produces sound by interrupting at regular intervals the flow of air through evenly-spaced holes.*

evenly-spaced holes, is rotated at high speed. When a stream of air is directed against the outermost series of holes, a high-pitched musical tone results. Here, each time a hole passes the end of the nozzle, a compression is sent out. Because of the regular spacing of the holes and the steady speed of the motor, these compressions (and rarefactions) are transmitted at regular, short intervals. As the nozzle is moved inward to another series of holes, the pitch of the musical note decreases. Why?

The same apparatus may be used to demonstrate the result of a random series of compressions. The innermost circle contains an irregular series of holes. The resulting irregular air vibrations produce a nonmusical sound, or *noise.*

A note sounded on the piano is easily distinguished from one of exactly the same pitch sounded on an organ or any other instrument. Here the difference in the sounds is one of *tone quality* or *timbre.* This is the third feature used by the ear to distinguish among sounds. To analyze the cause of this difference in quality, let us consider the vibration of a tuning fork. If a tuning fork is struck gently with a rubber hammer, a pure tone results. Pressure or density variations caused by the vibrations

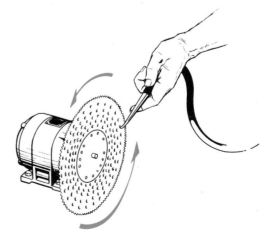

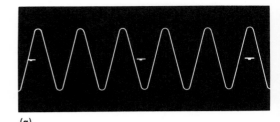

(a)

(b)

Fig. 12-6: *(a) This waveform represents the pressure variations produced by a tuning fork struck gently with a rubber hammer. (b) The waveform for the same tuning fork, after it was struck against a hard surface. The overall shape of the waveform is similar to that of (a), but the ripples denote the presence of more rapid vibrations.*

can be observed on an oscilloscope, in conjunction with a microphone and amplifier. The resulting waveform, shown in Figure 12-6(a), is typical of a pure tone, and is called a *sine curve*. If the tuning fork is struck again, but this time against a table, the quality of the sound is unmistakably different. The pitch of the sound is unchanged, but a metallic "clang" is now apparent. Viewed on the oscilloscope, the waveform would appear as in Figure 12-6(b).

A comparison of these two waveforms is instructive. The complex waveform in (b) resembles the general shape of the sine curve in (a), but with a series of rapidly fluctuating "ripples" superimposed. The fork is, in effect, vibrating at two different frequencies simultaneously. The chief frequency (called the *fundamental* frequency) is that obtained when the fork was struck lightly. The frequency producing the ripples is much higher than the fundamental, and is called an *overtone*.

It is the presence of overtones that provides the difference in quality between sounds of the same pitch. Far from being undesirable, it is this presence of overtones that contributes to the richness and variety of musical instruments, the human voice and other sound-producing devices. Indeed, if

Fig. 12-7: *The ear.*

middle ear with bones
semicircular canals
auditory nerve
cochlea
round window
stirrup
Eustachian tube to throat
outer ear
eardrum

all sounds were pure tones, we would find them very monotonous.

6. THE EAR

The ear (Figure 12-7) consists of three separate parts, called the outer, middle, and inner ear. Pressure variations enter the outer ear and pass to the middle ear by way of the auditory canal to the eardrum, a diaphragm set into oscillation by the air vibrations.

A set of three bones (anvil, hammer, and stirrup) in the middle ear are attached to the ear drum. These bones serve as a system of levers, with a mechanical advantage of approximately 30. The stirrup is attached to the oval window of the inner ear, to which the pressure variations, amplified by the lever system, are transmitted.

The inner ear contains a set of semicircular canals, which are very nearly mutually perpendicular. These canals serve the important function of preserving a sense of balance. Also in the inner ear is the cochlea, so named because its shape resembles that of a snail. This is filled with a liquid and contains a few turns of a membrane called the basilar membrane. This membrane detects and analyzes the pressure variations resulting from the sound falling on the ear by means of nerve endings attached to it from the brain.

The Eustachian tube, leading to the throat, enables pressure within the middle ear to be kept close to the atmospheric level. The ear is most sensitive to frequencies in the vicinity of 2000 c/sec, where periodic changes in pressure of the order of 10^{-8} nt/cm^2 (or 10^{-8} lb/in^2) may be detected. The ears of some individuals are also amazingly sensitive to changes of pitch. In some cases, a variation in frequency of 1 c/sec can be detected when the pitch is in the neighbourhood of 500 c/sec.

7. RESONANCE

If any of the vibrating systems shown in Figure 11-1 are set into vibration by a single push, pull or twist, they continue to oscillate at a constant rate for an appreciable length of time. The frequency of oscillation is a constant for any one of these vibrating systems.

For the simple pendulum, this frequency of vibration is determined mainly by the length of the string, while for the spring and torsion pendulums, the elastic properties of the spring and wire, and the magnitude of the suspended mass govern the frequency.

It is generally true that any system set into vibration has a tendency to vibrate at a particular frequency, called its *natural frequency*. For the systems shown in Figure 11-1, there is only one natural frequency of vibration, but, as we shall see, very often a vibrating system can have several natural frequencies or *modes* of vibration.

How does the natural frequency of a system determine the way it should be vibrated? We have all pushed someone on a swing. One push or impulse will set the swing into vibration, and the amplitude of the vibration will gradually diminish if no further pushes are applied. If, however, one impulse is given the swing at the same point of each vibration, the amplitude of the swing may be made quite large. On the other hand, if the series of impulses differs in frequency from that of the swing, the vibrations of the swing will become quite erratic and may indeed cease entirely.

When an object capable of vibrating is given a regular series of impulses of the same frequency as its natural frequency, the object is said to *resonate* with the applied impulses. We may think of resonance as **the build-up of vibrations in one system caused by the reception of impulses of the same frequency from another.**

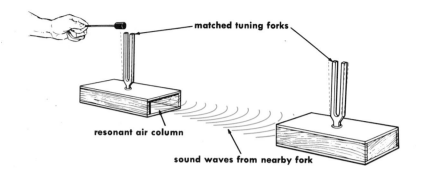

Fig. 12-8: *An example of resonance. The two tuning forks have the same natural frequency of vibration. If one is struck, its vibrations set the other vibrating. Such vibrations are called sympathetic vibrations.*

Figure 12-8 provides another example of resonance. Here, two tuning forks of like frequency are each mounted on boxes open at one end. If the boxes are properly designed, the air enclosed within them will vibrate at a frequency equal to that of the tuning fork; that is, the air will resonate with the tuning fork. If the boxes are placed some distance apart, with their open ends facing each other, the vibrations of one fork will be found to set the other fork into vibration. This can be verified by sounding one fork and then stopping it. The vibrations of the second fork are sometimes referred to as *sympathetic vibrations*. Should the frequency of the forks differ even slightly, the amplitude of the induced vibrations will be reduced considerably.

When a body is compelled to vibrate at a frequency other than its natural frequency, the resulting vibrations are called *forced vibrations*. It is extremely difficult to make a tuning fork vibrate at any frequency other than its natural frequency. The tuning fork is said to be sharply resonant.

Other devices, such as a radio loudspeaker, can be forced into vibration quite easily. A loudspeaker of good quality should be designed so that its natural or resonant frequency lies below the audible frequencies at which it is forced to vibrate. If not, it will reproduce certain frequencies unduly, by resonance.

Other examples of mechanical resonance may be cited. The design of a bridge requires careful consideration of its natural frequency of vibration to prevent traffic or winds from causing vibrations at this frequency. You can provide an interesting demonstration of resonance by singing one note into a piano while the damper pedal is depressed. The fundamental tones and overtones present in the note produce sympathetic vibrations in many of the strings, and a fair reproduction of the note is returned to you.

Although we have limited our discussion to mechanical resonance, we should be aware of other forms of resonance. Notable is that of electrical resonance. When a radio station is tuned in, the natural frequency of an electrical system within the radio is made equal to the frequency of the radio waves being received.

In all cases of resonance, a transfer of energy takes place. Indeed, we might define resonance as a situation in which an object capable of vibration extracts a maximum of energy from its surroundings.

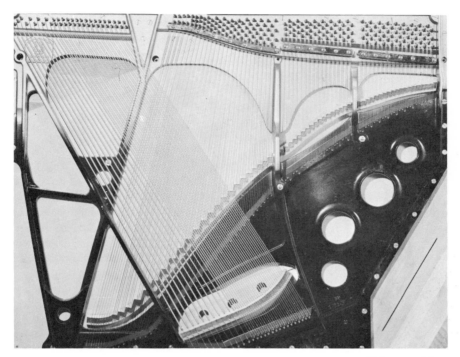

Fig. 12-9: *The strings of a grand piano. The vibrations of these strings are transferred to the sound board, a large horizontal sheet of wood that can be seen under the strings. What factors determine the pitch of these strings?*

8. VIBRATING STRINGS

If the string of a musical instrument is plucked or bowed several times in succession, the same pitch will emerge each time. This suggests that a stretched string possesses a natural frequency of vibration. The factors that determine this frequency are studied in Experiment 22, with the aid of a sonometer (Page 230).

From an examination of several stringed instruments, it would not be difficult to ascertain some of these determining factors. The steel plate containing the strings of a grand piano, Figure 12-9, provides useful information. The length of these strings diminishes steadily from the longest, the bass strings, at the upper left, to the treble strings, at the extreme right. Note also the variation in thickness of the strings. Each string is made of steel, but in the lower two octaves, copper wire is wound around the steel wire to increase not only the overall diameter of the string, but also its density.

Each string terminates at the upper end of the plate in a peg, or tuning pin. By rotating this pin slightly, thereby altering the tension in the wire, one may bring the string to the desired pitch.

The frequency of any string is dependent upon the factors touched upon in this brief description: that is, the length, diameter, density, and tension of the string. The exact dependence of pitch upon these variables is given below.

Length: The frequency varies inversely as the length, if the diameter, density, and tension are constant. For example, if the string is doubled in length, the frequency of the string will be halved, if other factors are unchanged.

Tension: The frequency varies directly as the square root of the tension. Thus, to double the frequency of a string (that is, to raise its pitch one octave), the tension would have to be increased four times if the other factors remain fixed.

Diameter: The frequency is inversely proportional to diameter. Consequently, a string of diameter 2 mm will have a frequency one half that of a string of diameter 1 mm; that is, it will be one octave lower. Here we assume that the tension, length, and density of the wires are equal.

Density: The frequency is inversely proportional to the square root of the density, other factors remaining fixed. Thus, winding copper wire around the bass strings of the piano decreases the natural frequency for two reasons—both the diameter and the density are thereby increased.

The operation of all these laws is utilized in the design of the structure in Figure 12-9. The manufacturer could obtain any range of frequencies by altering only the length of the strings. However, the frequency range encountered, 27 to 4096 c/sec, would require that the longest string be 150 times the length of the shortest. This excessive length in the bass strings is avoided by increasing their mass and diameter, as already mentioned. Also, to avoid excessive shortness in the treble strings, these strings are placed under greater tension. The total tension exerted on the steel frame by the more than 200 strings approaches 30 tons.

EXAMPLE 1

The D string of a violin is 30.0 cm long, and has a natural frequency of 288 c/sec. At what point would a violinist place his finger on it to produce the note E (320 c/sec)?

Solution:

$$\frac{l_2}{l_1} = \frac{f_1}{f_2}$$

$$\text{or } l_2 = \frac{f_1 l_1}{f_2} = \frac{288 \times 30.0}{320} = 27.0 \text{ cm.}$$

Therefore his finger should be placed **3.0 cm from the end.**

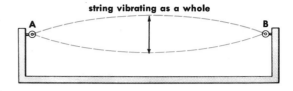

string vibrating as a whole

A · · B

Fig. 12-10: *A string vibrating in its fundamental mode.*

EXAMPLE 2

A string, under tension of 49.0 nt, produces the frequency 260 c/sec (middle C). What tension would be required to produce the note A of frequency 440 c/sec?

Solution:

Frequency varies as the square root of tension. Therefore we may write:

$$\frac{f_2}{f_1} = \frac{\sqrt{T_2}}{\sqrt{T_1}}$$

$$\text{or } T_2 = \left(\frac{f_2}{f_1}\right)^2 T_1$$

$$= \left(\frac{440}{260}\right)^2 \times 49.0$$

$$= 140 \text{ nt.}$$

9. MODES OF VIBRATION

A string is capable of vibrating in several different ways, called *modes* of vibration. The most common mode is that illustrated in Figure 12-10. Here the string vibrates as a whole, with only the fixed ends stationary. Such a pattern of vibration is called the *fundamental* mode, and is a standing wave pattern with a node at each end of the string and a loop at the centre. Plucking the string at any point along its length gives rise to this fundamental mode.

If the string is touched at its midpoint, and then plucked, it can vibrate in such a manner that a node will exist at this point as well as at the fixed ends. The pattern produced is that illustrated in Figure 12-11(b).

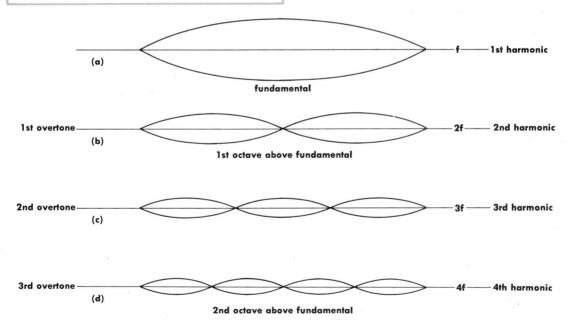

(a)
f — 1st harmonic
fundamental

1st overtone
(b)
2f — 2nd harmonic
1st octave above fundamental

2nd overtone
(c)
3f — 3rd harmonic

3rd overtone
(d)
4f — 4th harmonic
2nd octave above fundamental

Fig. 12-11: *The fundamental mode and first three overtone modes of a vibrating string.*

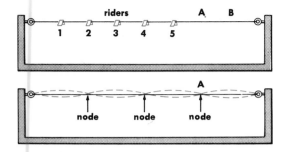

The frequency of these vibrations is twice that produced in the fundamental mode. This mode is referred to as the *second harmonic,* or *first overtone.*

Other modes may be produced by inducing nodal points at evenly spaced intervals along the string. The third and fourth harmonics (second and third overtones) are illustrated in Figure 12-11. Other modes of vibration are possible. In each case the overtone has a frequency that is a multiple of the fundamental frequency.

A violinist, by touching the string at its centre, will cause the string to vibrate at its second harmonic. If the same string is touched lightly at a point one-third of the distance from the end, it will then vibrate in three sections, producing the third harmonic with a frequency three times that of the fundamental. Hence it is only necessary to induce one node along the length of the string to produce the others automatically.

Theoretically a string has an infinite number of natural frequencies, each one a multiple of the fundamental frequency obtained when the string vibrates as a whole. These natural modes of vibration are the results of the constructive and destructive interference of the waves reflected from each end of the string, producing a standing wave pattern with evenly spaced nodes. (See Chapter 11, pages 181-183, for a detailed account of standing waves in a string.)

Figure 12-12 illustrates an interesting demonstration of nodal points in a vibrating string. This string is divided into eight equal sections, and paper riders are placed at points 1 to 5 inclusive. If point A is held fixed, and the string bowed at point B, the riders at 1, 3, 5 are thrown off, while those at 2 and 4 remain fixed. This demonstration shows that the string is vibrating in four sections as illustrated in the lower half of the drawing.

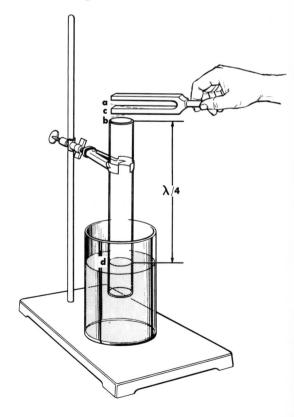

Fig. 12-13: *This air column will be set into strong resonant vibrations if its length is one quarter of the wavelength produced by the tuning fork.*

10. VIBRATING AIR COLUMN

(a) Column open at one end

Just as a string possesses a large number of natural frequencies, so also does a column of air. The vibrations of an air column may be demonstrated using the apparatus in Figure 12-13. Here, the length of the air column enclosed in a wide cylinder is adjusted by raising or lowering the cylinder in the water container.

If a vibrating tuning fork is held over the mouth of the tube while the length of the column is adjusted, the intensity of sound is found to vary, and is a maximum for a particular setting. At this particular length of the column, the air in the tube is resonant with the tuning fork. An explanation of this resonance is obtained by considering the motion of the tuning fork tines.

As the tine moves downward from position a, a compression is formed in the tube, which will move downward to the closed end d. Here it is reflected and sent back to the mouth of the tube. If this compression arrives at the mouth of the tube just as the tine is beginning its upward journey to position a, then it will reinforce the new compression that this tine is about to create by moving upward.

For this situation to exist, the length of the column must be such that the wave moves twice the length of the column (down and back) while the fork vibrates from a to b, that is, over one-half cycle. Accordingly, the disturbance travels the length of the column in one-quarter cycle, and the length of the column is a quarter wavelength of the waves initiated by the tuning fork.

If the length of the tube can be increased, other resonance points will be found. These are illustrated in Figure 12-14. All such resonance points are an indication of *standing waves* in the tube, and each standing wave pattern incorporates a node at the closed end and an antinode (or loop) at the open end. For a given tuning fork, the second resonance point will occur when the length of the tube is $3\lambda/4$, and the third resonance point when the length of the column is $5\lambda/4$. Other resonance points are obtained when the column is increased in length by intervals of $\lambda/2$.

The patterns shown inside the tubes in Figure 12-14 are a convenient way of indicating the relative amounts of air disturbance inside the tube. At the closed end of the tube the air is incapable of longitudinal motion, and hence a node exists at this end. At the open end, a region of maximum vibration (antinode) exists because of the difference in air pressure within and outside the tube.

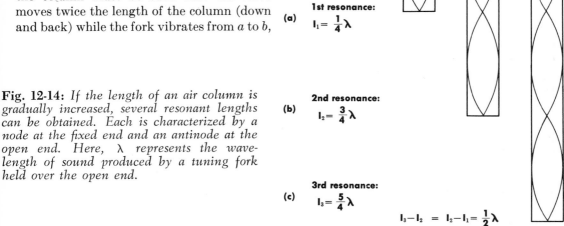

(a) 1st resonance: $l_1 = \frac{1}{4}\lambda$

(b) 2nd resonance: $l_2 = \frac{3}{4}\lambda$

(c) 3rd resonance: $l_3 = \frac{5}{4}\lambda$

$l_3 - l_2 = l_2 - l_1 = \frac{1}{2}\lambda$

Fig. 12-14: *If the length of an air column is gradually increased, several resonant lengths can be obtained. Each is characterized by a node at the fixed end and an antinode at the open end. Here, λ represents the wavelength of sound produced by a tuning fork held over the open end.*

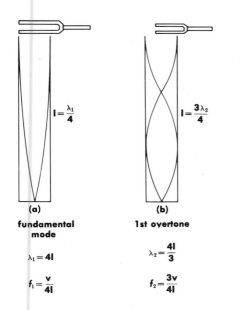

$$l = \frac{\lambda_1}{4}$$

$$l = \frac{3\lambda_2}{4}$$

(a)

**fundamental
mode**

$$\lambda_1 = 4l$$

$$f_1 = \frac{v}{4l}$$

(b)

1st overtone

$$\lambda_2 = \frac{4l}{3}$$

$$f_2 = \frac{3v}{4l}$$

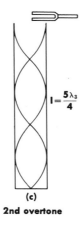

$$l = \frac{5\lambda_3}{4}$$

(c)

2nd overtone

$$\lambda_3 = \frac{4l}{5}$$

$$f_3 = \frac{5v}{4l}$$

Fig. 12-15: *Any fixed air column possesses several modes of vibration. Here, three different tuning forks are used to produce the fundamental mode and first and second overtones, respectively. What is the relationship of these overtone frequencies to the fundamental frequency? (The symbol v represents the velocity of the wave.)*

If the length of the air column of Figure 12-13 is kept fixed, several cases of resonance can be obtained by employing different tuning forks. In Figure 12-15, three cases are shown. In (a), the tube is one-quarter of the wavelength of the vibrations produced by this fork. This is the *fundamental mode* of vibration of this tube. In (b) the column is agitated by a fork whose frequency is three times that of (a), producing the *first overtone* mode (third harmonic). In (c) the *second overtone*, or fifth harmonic, is produced by a fork whose frequency is 5 times that of the fork in (a).

Hence, an air column of fixed length, closed at one end and open at the other, possesses several natural frequencies of vibration, and each is an *odd multiple* of the fundamental frequency.

Fig. 12-16: *An air column open at each end will also resonate. Its resonant lengths are different from those of the same column with one end closed.*

(b) Column open at both ends

In Figure 12-16, two tubes are supported with one slipping closely over the other. Such an arrangement constitutes an adjustable air column open at both ends.

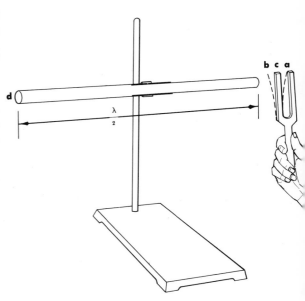

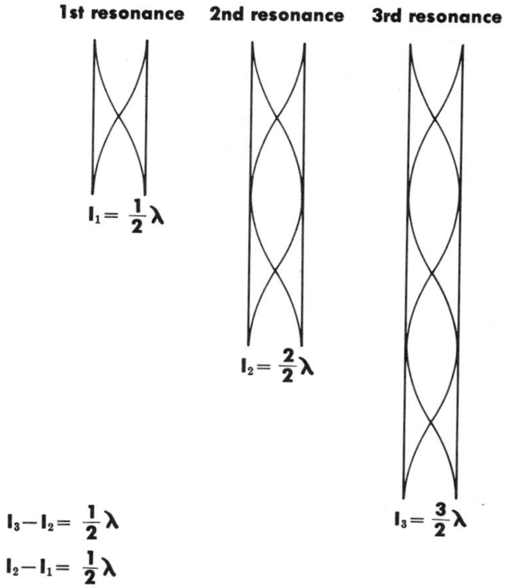

1st resonance **2nd resonance** **3rd resonance**

$$l_1 = \frac{1}{2}\lambda$$

$$l_2 = \frac{2}{2}\lambda$$

$$l_3 - l_2 = \frac{1}{2}\lambda$$

$$l_3 = \frac{3}{2}\lambda$$

$$l_2 - l_1 = \frac{1}{2}\lambda$$

Fig. 12-17: *Resonant lengths of an air column open at both ends.*

If the air column is set into vibration by the same tuning fork as was used in Figure 12-13, and the length of the column is adjusted, it will be found that resonance first takes place when the tube is twice the length that resonated when the tube was closed. Thus the length of the tube is one-half wavelength. If the tube be further extended, other resonance points will be obtained when the length is increased by intervals of a half wavelength (Figure 12-17). This was the case also with the adjustable closed column.

Why does the open tube fail to resonate at the resonant lengths of the closed tube? The answer lies in the way reflections take place at an open end. In Chapter 11 we found that reflections occur when any wave encounters a change in characteristics of the medium—for instance a change in stiffness from one spring to another. Reflections in an air column can take place if the air through which the wave passes undergoes a sudden change in pressure. A condensation in a sound wave represents a region of relatively high-pressure air. When a condensation reaches the open end of the tube surrounded by air at normal atmospheric pressure, a reflection takes place. The air comprising the condensation is forced out of the tube, creating a sudden rarefaction in the tube at this end. Thus a condensation reaching the open end of the tube is reflected back along the length of the tube as a rarefaction. Similarly, a rarefaction reaching an open end is reflected as a compression. The rarefaction comprises a region of low air density or pressure. The air outside the opening is forced into the open end, forming a sudden compression which travels back along the tube (See Figure 12-18).

As the tine in Figure 12-16 moves from *a* to *b*, a compression travels the full length of the tube to point *d* where it is reflected as a rarefaction. This rarefaction begins its return travel from *d* to *b*, and reaches *b* as the tine returns to point *a*. The rarefaction arriving at this end of the tube is now reflected back as a compression, and is reinforced by the new compression sent down the tube by the tine as it begins its travel once again from *a* to *b*. The air column and the tuning fork are resonant.

11. MEASUREMENT OF SPEED OF SOUND BY RESONANCE

The resonance of an air column provides a convenient method of determining the velocity of sound in air (Experiment 23). An adjustable air column and a tuning fork of known frequency are used, and at least two consecutive resonance points are determined.

As shown in Figure 12-14, consecutive resonance points are separated by a half wavelength.

EXAMPLE 3

A tuning fork of frequency 670 c/sec is sounded over an adjustable air column. Consecutive resonance points occur when the column is 12.4 cm and 37.6 cm in length. What is the speed of sound? (Assume the column is open at one end.)

Solution:

$$\frac{\lambda}{2} = 37.6 - 12.4 = 25.2 \text{ cm}$$

$$\therefore \lambda = 50.4 \text{ cm} \quad f = 670 \text{ c/sec}$$

$$\therefore v = f\lambda = 670 \times 50.4 \text{ cm/sec} = \textbf{338 m/sec.}$$

EXAMPLE 4

What is the shortest air column, open at one end, that will resonate at a frequency of 440 c/sec when the speed of sound is 1100 ft/sec?

Solution:

The shortest resonant air column is one which accommodates the standing wave pattern of Figure 12-15(a). Its length is $\lambda/4$.

From the wave equation

$$v = f\lambda \text{ and } \lambda = \frac{v}{f}$$

$$= \frac{1100}{440} = 2.5 \text{ ft.}$$

Thus the shortest air column is $\frac{2.5}{4}$ ft

or **0.62 ft (7.5 in).**

---

12. MUSICAL INSTRUMENTS

Organ

The operation of organ pipes is the most familiar application of vibrating air columns.

The process by which the air column is set into vibration can be understood by referring to Figure 12-19. Air under pressure flows into the pipe at A and issues at high velocity from a small opening B, called the flue. This flow of air enters the lower open end of the pipe and strikes a thin lip, labelled C in the illustration. Because of the speed of this stream of air, a pressure difference is created between the air inside and outside the opening at C (see Bernoulli's Principle, page 84). Air alternately flows into the tube and out of the tube at the opening C, producing whirlwinds on each side of the pipe, as shown. The whole process takes place very rapidly. A sound is produced, called an edge tone, whose pitch is determined by the velocity of the air jet and the shape of the lip at C, as well as the size of the opening BC, but not by the length of the pipe.

By proper design of the lip, or by adjustment of the jet velocity, the pitch of the edge tone can be made to correspond to the fundamental frequency of vibration of the air column or to one of its many overtones. Then resonance takes place, and the entire column, set into vibration, produces a musical sound of high intensity.

Organ pipes may be closed or open at the upper end. If closed, the note produced is double the frequency produced when the pipe is open. The standing wave patterns set up by the vibrations are those shown in Figure 12-20. Because of the extreme agitation of the air at the lower end, an antinode always exists at this end.

Figure 12-21 shows the wide variety of pipes comprising a typical organ installation. The lengths of pipes may range from as short as one inch to as long as 30 ft.

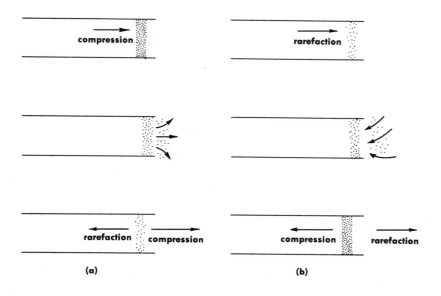

Fig. 12-18: *Reflections at the open end of an air column. (a) A compression reaching the open end is reflected as a rarefaction because of air escaping to the outside. (b) A rarefaction reaching the open end is reflected as a compression because of air being drawn into the tube.*

Fig. 12-19: *Cross-sectional view of an organ pipe.*

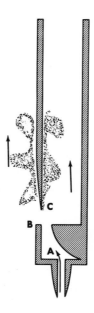

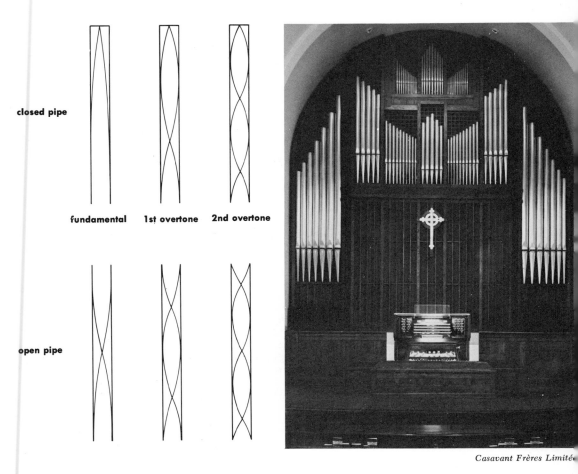

closed pipe

fundamental   1st overtone   2nd overtone

open pipe

Fig. 12-20: *Standing wave patterns for closed organ pipes and open organ pipes.*

Fig. 12-21: *A modern pipe organ.*

Other Wind Instruments

The operation of wind instruments such as the flute, piccolo, and simple tin whistle is essentially the same as that of the organ pipe. Edge tones are produced in the flute (Figure 12-22) by blowing into the mouthpiece. The effective length of air column is altered by opening or covering the holes along the column, or by activating levers. By blowing more sharply against the opening, thus changing the frequency of the edge tones, the entire scale of notes may be doubled in frequency (raised one octave).

Instruments such as the oboe, clarinet, saxophone, and bassoon also consist of an air column of variable length in which standing waves are produced. However, vibrations are initiated by a reed rather than by the flue principle of the organ pipe. The reed is a thin strip of wood set into vibration by blowing through the mouthpiece. The reed vibrates at several frequencies simultaneously, with overtones that are not exact multiples of the fundamental frequency. This imparts a tonal quality characteristic of many reed instruments. The mouth organ and accordion are other examples of reed instruments.

Fig. 12-22: *Three musical instruments: from left to right, tuba, oboe, flute.*

In brass instruments, vibrations are set up by the lips of the performer. In effect, the lips act as reeds, and their tension and the pressure of the air blown into the mouthpiece determine to a large extent the pitch of the resulting sound. In the tuba of Figure 12-22, the three valves allow the length of the air column to be changed by certain definite steps. The same can be said for the trumpet and French horn. In the trombone, however, the length of the resonating column is continually adjusted by a sliding tube, allowing the pitch to be changed by almost imperceptible degrees.

Stringed Instruments

The strings of the violin, viola, cello, and double bass are set into motion by bowing. The vibrations of the strings are transferred to the body of the instrument and the air inside it by the bridge over which the strings pass. The resulting vibrations are forced vibrations, but the body itself is resonant to some of the many overtones produced by the strings. It is these resonances that impart to a specific instrument its tonal quality. The tonal quality of the violins made by the Italian School of the late 16th century is still unsurpassed: the secret of their process has never been recovered.

The various notes are obtained by pressing the strings to the fingerboard, thus shortening their vibrating lengths.

Instruments of the guitar family operate on the same principles, but here the strings are plucked. The strings of a harp are also plucked, but transfer of sound to the air takes place directly from the strings; that is, no resonating chamber of air is used. Consequently the harp has a rather feeble, though beautiful sound.

The strings of a piano are struck by felt-covered hammers, producing a tone different from that of a bowed or plucked string. The vibrations are transferred by a wooden bridge to a long thin sheet of wood, called the sounding board. The forced vibrations of the sounding board agitate the air surrounding it, so that the instrument is capable of producing sound of high intensity.

13. TONE QUALITY

Sounds produced by musical instruments are rarely, if ever, pure tones with waveforms similar to that of Figure 12-6(a). Their complex sounds are created by the simultaneous presence of vibrations at several frequencies, usually multiples of the fundamental frequency.

It is perhaps difficult to imagine a given object vibrating at two different frequencies simultaneously. Figure 12-23(a) illustrates a string vibrating as a whole at its fundamental frequency. At the same time two nodes exist between the ends of the string, creating the third harmonic in the emitted sound. The sound produced by the fundamental vibration has a waveform indicated by *a* in Figure 12-23(b) while that produced by the third harmonic has the waveform indicated by *b*. The resulting waveform of the complete sound emitted by the string is obtained by superimposing these two components, giving the waveform *c*.

The complex waveform *c* is the combination of two simple sine curves representing two pure tones. Note that the complex wave is a periodic wave, repeating itself in a regular manner. Note also that the rate at which it repeats itself, that is, its frequency, is the same as that of the fundamental tone. Thus the pitch of the resulting sound is that of the fundamental mode of vibration, but its quality is different because of the presence of the second overtone.

It can be shown that any complex wave,

Fig. 12-23: *(a) A string vibrating simultaneously in its fundamental mode and second overtone. (b) Curve a is the waveform of sound produced by the fundamental vibration of the string of Figure 12-13. Curve b is the waveform of the string's second overtone (third harmonic). Each of these sounds is a pure tone. Curve c is the resultant waveform obtained by adding the two individual waveforms a and b. It is not a pure tone.*

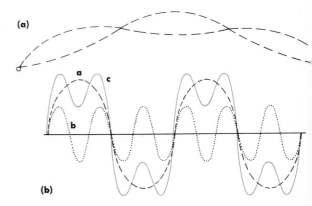

(a)

(b)

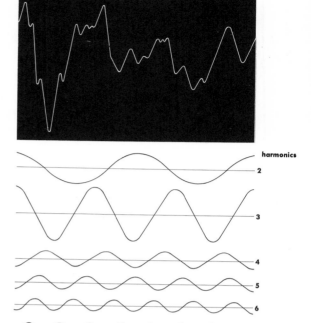

Fig. 12-24: *The complex wave-form at the top was produced by a violin. It actually consists of a number of pure tones added together. These pure tones are the seven waveforms shown ranging from the 2nd to the 17th harmonic.*

providing it is periodic, can be considered to be made up of a number of pure tones. Figure 12-24 shows an oscilloscope tracing of the sound produced by a violin at a pitch of 200 c/sec. Below the tracing, the seven harmonics present in the sound are shown, the third harmonic being the most intense.

In Figure 12-25 are shown waveforms for an oboe and clarinet producing a tone of the same pitch. Note that although their periods are the same, the rate of fluctuation for the oboe is greater, which indicates the presence of a larger number of high harmonics.

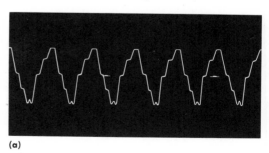

(a)

Fig. 12-25: *The waveforms of (a) a clarinet, and (b) an oboe, both playing the note middle C. What do the waveforms have in common?*

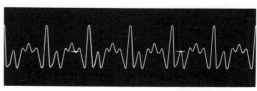

(b)

1. Explain why a window may be broken by an explosion several miles away.

2. You can estimate your distance from a lightning flash by counting the seconds to the time of hearing the thunder and dividing by five. Explain. What unit of distance is employed here?

3. Does the pitch of a sound from a circular saw rise or fall as the saw goes deeper into the wood? Explain.

4. How does a noise differ from a musical sound?

5. Marchers may find it difficult to keep in step with a band some distance away. Explain.

6. How might a motorist employ the principle of resonance to free his car from a small snowdrift?

7. What is the outstanding difference between the overtone frequencies produced by an open organ pipe and those produced by a closed pipe, even though their fundamental pitches are identical? Why are both open and closed pipes used in pipe organs?

8. A tuning fork of frequency 256 c/sec is sounded in a jar of hydrogen. Is there a change in its pitch?

9. An organ pipe has a fundamental frequency of 256 c/sec. The air in it is replaced with hydrogen. What effect, if any, does this have on the pitch of the pipe?

10. What effect would an increase in temperature have on the pitch of a wind instrument? Why?

11. What is the difference between sympathetic vibrations and forced vibrations? Sound a tuning fork and time the duration of the resulting sound. Sound the tuning fork again and hold its lower end to the surface of a table. Time the resulting sound. Would you say the table vibrations are sympathetic or forced? How do you explain the difference in the two measured time intervals?

12. Blow across the mouth of a test tube or bottle. What factors determine the pitch of the resulting musical note? How could you raise the pitch of this note? Can you produce a tone by blowing directly into the container?

13. When water is poured into a tall container, what change takes place in the resulting sound as the water level rises? Why is this?

14. An organ pipe has a fundamental pitch of 120 c/sec. When blown more strongly, it emits a note of frequency 240 c/sec. Is this a closed pipe or an open pipe?

15. A cornet has three valves. How many fundamental notes may be produced? How can a cornet player produce many more notes?

16. You can perform the following interesting demonstration of resonance at the piano.
    (a) Gently depress middle C, without sounding it. This raises the damper for this note. Momentarily sound in turn each of the C keys below middle C, while the latter key is held down. What is the result?

(b) With middle C depressed, sound a lower C sharp or B flat.

(c) With middle C depressed, sound the C one octave higher, and then two octaves higher.

(d) With middle C depressed, sound the note G above it. Repeat for the G one octave above this.

Explain your observations in terms of overtones and resonance.

17. (a) To make its first overtone most prominent, a stretched string should be plucked at a point $\frac{1}{4}$ of its length from one support, and then touched at the centre. Explain this in terms of nodes and antinodes.

(b) Where should the string be plucked, and then touched, to make its second overtone most prominent?

18. What is the frequency of a note
(a) one octave higher than 400 c/sec?

(b) two octaves higher?

(c) three octaves higher?

EXERCISE B

Use speed of sound in air at 0°C (32°F) = 331 m/sec = 1090 ft/sec (3 significant digits). Increase due to temperature = 0.6 m/sec per C°, or 1.1 ft/sec per F°.

1. What is the speed of sound in air at 60.0° F, in ft/sec? In what time would it travel 1.00 mi?

2. What time is required for sound to travel 4.00 km in air at 10° C?

3. A tuning fork has a frequency of 256 c/sec. What is the wavelength of the sound produced, when the speed of sound is 1120 ft/sec?

4. The speed of sound in sea water is 4.8×10^3 ft/sec. A sound ranging device sends an impulse to the ocean bottom and 0.80 second elapses before its return. What is the depth of the water?

5. A steamer approaches a steep precipice several miles away and sounds a short blast of its horn. The echo is heard 20.0 sec later. Twenty minutes later another blast produces an echo which returns in 6.0 sec. Determine the speed of the ship in mi/hr, if the temperature is 60° F.

6. A bullet fired at a target 0.80 km distant was heard to strike it 5.0 sec later. Determine the average speed of the bullet if the air temperature is 20° C.

7. A siren similar to that in Figure 12-5 has 50 evenly spaced holes along its periphery. What frequency will be emitted when the siren rotates at 720 rpm?

8. A string under tension is 100 cm long and has a fundamental frequency of 200 c/sec. If a bridge is placed 20 cm from one end, what will be the fundamental frequency of the longer segment?

9. Under a tension of 160 nt a string has a fundamental frequency of 256 c/sec. What is the new pitch when the tension is increased to 250 nt?

10. Two steel strings have the same thickness, but one is 10 in long and under a tension of 9 lb while the other is 14 in long and under a tension of 16 lb. Compare their frequencies.

11. A copper string has the same length, diameter, and tension as an aluminum string. If the fundamental frequency of the copper string is 440 c/sec, what is the frequency of the aluminum string?

12. Two steel strings of equal length and tension have diameters of 0.5 mm and 0.8 mm respectively. If the first has a frequency of 240 c/sec, what is the frequency of the other?

13. (a) A resonance box, similar to those shown in Figure 12-8, is to be designed for a tuning fork of frequency 256 c/sec. What should be the length of the air column in inches? Consider the speed of sound as 1120 ft/sec.

    (b) What should the length be if both ends of the box are open?

14. A closed organ pipe (that is, closed at one end) is 8.0 ft long.

    (a) What is the lowest frequency at which this pipe will resonate, if the speed of sound is 1120 ft/sec?

    (b) What are the frequencies of the first two overtones produced by this pipe?

15. It is desired that the second overtone of an open organ pipe have a frequency of 5000 c/sec. How long should this pipe be? (Speed of sound = 1120 ft/sec.)

16. For the apparatus of Figure 12-13, the sound intensity is maximum when the level of the water is 14.0 cm, 42.1 cm, and 70.2 cm below the open mouth of the tube. Determine the speed of sound if the tuning fork has a frequency of 605 c/sec.

17. The lowest note of a pipe organ has a fundamental frequency of 16.4 c/sec. Find the length of an open organ pipe that will produce this note at 72°F. Express your answer in feet.

18. A closed organ pipe is 1.0 m long. What are the frequencies of the first three overtones if the temperature is 20° C?

19. Two organ pipes, one open and the other closed at the upper end, are each 45 in long. What is the wavelength of the second overtone of each?

20. A tuning fork is held in front of a tube open at both ends. The length of the tube is adjusted until resonance occurs. At the first resonance point, the length of the tube is 39.0 cm. What is the frequency of the fork if the room temperature is 20° C?

Chapter 12 (PART B)

Sound Waves

Sound waves differ in many respects from the water waves studied in Chapter 11. Waves of sound are longitudinal, whereas water waves are essentially transverse. Furthermore, water waves travel in a two dimensional medium—the surface of the water. Sound waves in air, by contrast, are not confinable to two dimensions, and spread from the source in all directions. We could call them three-dimensional waves.

Despite these obvious differences, the properties which we found characteristic of water waves—reflection, refraction, diffraction and interference—are exhibited also by sound waves.

14. REFLECTION, REFRACTION AND DIFFRACTION OF SOUND

Reflection

A sound is seldom heard without accompanying reflections from obstacles, such as walls, ceiling or floor, and even furniture. Normally we are unaware of these reflections because the ear is unable to separate two sounds which arrive at intervals of less than about 0.1 sec. If a sound is emitted and reflected back to the ear after 0.1 sec, then an *echo* is perceptible.

The echo principle is used to advantage in *sonar*—an electronic system that sends out short pulses of ultrasonic sound and times their arrival back at the source. Such systems are used extensively at sea in determining water depth.

In Chapter 11, the reflections of periodic transverse waves on a rope were found to produce a seemingly stationary pattern along the rope, called a *standing wave* (Figure 11-25). Standing waves of sound may be produced by the reflection of sound waves and their resulting superposition with the incident sound waves.

If a loudspeaker faces a wall some distance away, regularly spaced regions of low and high intensity sound can be determined between source and wall when the source emits a note of steady pitch. This standing wave pattern is most pronounced for a particular distance between source and wall. Or, for a given distance, the pattern is most pronounced for a particular frequency.

More dramatic evidence of the existence of a standing wave pattern is obtained using Kundt's apparatus, described in Experiment 25.

Refraction

Under suitable conditions, refraction of sound can be observed. Recall that refraction is the bending of a wave caused by a

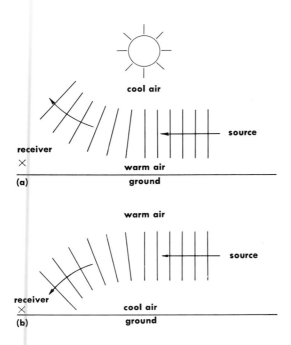

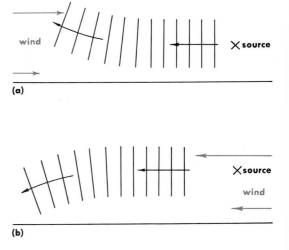

Refraction can also be caused by winds. A mass of air moving over the earth's surface usually encounters resistance or friction at the surface of the earth. Thus the air speeds are slower at the surface than in the higher levels. If a sound disturbance is sent against the wind, as in Figure 12-27(a), it will encounter less resistance at the surface, and its net speed will be greater there. The wavefront will bend upward, away from the observer. If, however, the sound disturbance is sent with the wind, the wavefront then will travel faster above the earth, and will bend downward toward the observer.

Fig. 12-26: *Refraction of sound waves due to differences in air temperature (a) on a warm day and (b) at nighttime.*

change in its speed. Figure 12-26 illustrates the principle for sound. On a warm day, the air near the ground becomes warmer than the higher layers of air. Because sound travels faster in warmer air, a wave front of sound will travel faster near the surface of the ground, resulting in a bending upwards, away from the observer.

The opposite result is produced at night, when the ground and the adjacent air give off their heat. The speed of sound at the surface is now less than in the upper layers, and the wave is bent downward toward the observer.

The result is that sound carries over greater distances at nighttime than during the day.

Fig. 12-27: *Refraction due to wind. Sound travelling against the wind is refracted upward. Why?*

Diffraction

Diffraction of sound, that is, its bending around an obstacle, is a well known phenomenon. Were it not for diffraction, we would find it difficult to hear any sound whose source did not lie in an unobstructed straight path to our ear.

In Chapter 11 we found that diffraction of water waves around an obstacle was less apparent for high-frequency waves (see Figure 11-19). The same is true for sounds of high frequency. You can obtain evidence of sound diffraction by listening to someone talk from around a corner, or through a partially-open doorway. The quality of the voice will be somewhat different from its quality when heard directly, because the higher-frequency parts of the sound do not diffract as easily as the low-frequency parts.

15. INTERFERENCE—SILENT POINTS NEAR A TUNING FORK

The simplest illustration of interference of sound waves is obtained using a tuning fork. Sound a tuning fork, and while holding it vertically, rotate it slowly about its axis. You will notice that at certain points of the rotation, corresponding to the directions

A, B, C, D in Figure 12-28(a), the sound intensity is a minimum, and may even disappear completely. At other positions (E, F, G, H), the sound intensity is a maximum.

To explain this variation in sound intensity, let us refer to part (b) of this illustration. As each prong moves outward, a compression is sent out on each side of the fork (locations p and q). The intensity of each of these compressions varies with direction, and is greatest in the direction of motion of the prong, as shown. While these compressions are being created at p and q, the air in the region r between the prongs becomes rarefied, and rarefactions travel out from r, with an intensity indicated by the red arrows in (b).

In Figure 12-29(c) the prongs are moving inward, creating rarefactions at p and q and a compression at r. We can consider p and q as two sources *in phase* with each other because at any instant they are creating the same type of disturbance. The region r is a third source of sound, but of *opposite phase* to the other sources, because at any instant the disturbance it creates is opposite in nature to that of p and q.

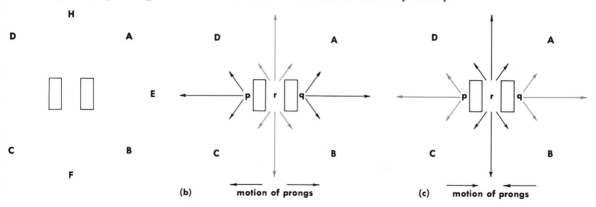

Fig. 12-28: *Interference produced by a tuning fork. (a) Location of points around a tuning fork. (b) As the prongs move outward, compressions are sent from p and q, and a rarefaction from r. (c) As the prongs move inward, p and q become sources of rarefactions and r a source of compressions. Destructive interference takes place along the directions A, B, C, D.*

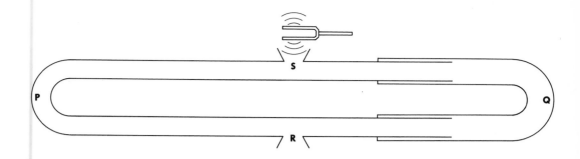

Fig. 12-29: *Interference of sound waves may be obtained using this device. Sound splits into two paths at S. The two waves are reunited at R. By adjusting the difference of path lengths, one may cause constructive or destructive interference at R.*

Directions such as A and B will receive disturbances of equal intensity from q and r which, because of their opposite phase, will tend to cancel at these points. Destructive interference will also take place in directions C and D, due to simultaneous reception of compressions and rarefactions of equal intensity from sources p and r.

Directions E, F, G and H receive disturbances from only one source, and therefore no cancellation takes place, while in other directions, such as one between A and E, the sound from one source will exceed in intensity that from the other, and partial cancellation will result.

16. INTERFERENCE FROM A SINGLE SOURCE

Interference of sound waves may be produced by a quite different method, using the apparatus of Figure 12-29. A wave emitted by a tuning fork enters the apparatus at point S, where it splits into two waves that travel different paths. One of these paths, SPR, is fixed in length, while the other, SQR, may be varied in length by extending the slide. At the opening R is located a receiver, such as the ear or a microphone. The two waves arrive at R, where they may interfere constructively or destructively.

Suppose the two path lengths are equal. Then a condensation or rarefaction passing from S and splitting into two parts will arrive at R along one path in exactly the same time as it will by the other path, and *constructive interference* will exist at R.

If the sliding tube is extended so that the path length SQR is one-half a wave length longer than SPR, then a condensation splitting up at S will arrive at R by the shorter route at the instant the *previously-sent rarefaction* arrives there by the longer route. In this case, destructive interference takes place at R. Further extension will produce other settings for which destructive interference occurs. For each of these settings, the difference in path length from S to R will be some odd number of half wavelengths.

A device such as this, in which waves from a single source are made to travel separate paths, and are then brought together, is called an *interferometer*. The optical interferometer, a device similar in principle to the acoustical interferometer of Figure 12-29, but employing light instead of sound, has been of great experimental importance in the development of modern physics.

17. INTERFERENCE OF TWO IDENTICAL SOURCES

In Chapter 11, an investigation was made of the interference pattern in a ripple tank produced by two sources of the same frequency (Figures 11-26 and 11-27).

Analagous patterns can be obtained for sound by using as sources two loudspeakers connected to the same amplifier (see Experiment 25) whose output is a sound of constant pitch. In this case, however, each source does not radiate with equal intensity in all directions. There is little sound radiated in the direction behind the speaker, although sound will be perceptible at any location because of reflections from surrounding surfaces.

At any point equidistant from the two speakers, we would expect constructive interference to exist. All of these points lie on the right bisector of the line joining the two sources. Other locations of maximum intensity also exist, where the difference of distances to the sources is a whole number of wavelengths. Where this difference is an odd number of half-wavelengths, destructive interference (minimum sound intensity) will occur.

18. BEATS—INTERFERENCE OF WAVES OF DIFFERENT FREQUENCY

In all cases of interference so far considered, the two waves involved have been of the same frequency. An interesting form of interference is produced when two sound waves of slightly different frequency are brought together.

Take two identical tuning forks, such as those illustrated in Figure 12-8, and lower the frequency of one very slightly by attaching to one of its prongs a piece of wax or a rubber band. If the forks are now sounded together, the intensity of the resulting sound will be found to vary at a slow but regular rate. The pulsating pattern of intensity so produced is called a *beat*. If additional wax is placed on the prong to lower the frequency of that fork further, the rate of the beat (that is, the beat frequency) will be increased.

Figure 12-30 illustrates how a beat is produced. Wave forms (a) and (b) represent the two interfering waves. In the time interval AE, 16 cycles of the former and 18 cycles of the latter take place. At the instant A, the two waves are of opposite phase, that is, one source is producing a compression while the other is producing a rarefaction. Because the waves are shown to be equal in amplitude, the resultant of these at this instant will be a sound of zero intensity. At instant B, the two forks are in phase—one will have "caught up" with the other, and the resultant intensity will be a maximum.

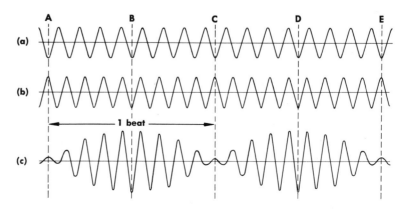

Fig. 12-30: *The production of beats. In the time interval AE wave (a) goes through 16 cycles while wave (b) goes through 18 cycles. If the two are superposed, the resulting waveform (c) pulsates slowly in amplitude. This pulsation is called a beat. Two beats occur in the time AE.*

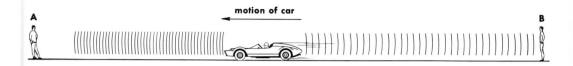

Fig. 12-31: *The Doppler Effect: to the observer at the left the pitch of the automobile's horn is higher than it is to the observer at the right.*

At instant C, the two forks are again out of phase and minimum intensity is produced. Waveform (c) is a plot of the resultant intensity produced by the superposition of the two waves of different frequency. In the time interval AC, the resultant intensity has gone from minimum to maximum and back to minimum again—a pulsation referred to as *one beat*. In the time interval CE, the above sequence is repeated and another beat is produced.

Note that in the time interval AE, 2 beats are produced during the time that the sources perform 16 and 18 cycles respectively. It can be shown that the beat frequency is always equal to the difference of the frequencies of the two sources. For example, a tuning fork of frequency 256 c/sec, sounded with a fork of frequency 261 c/sec, will produce a sound that will pulsate at the rate of 5 beats per second.

The phenomenon of beats provides a very simple and remarkably precise means of tuning two sources of sound to the same pitch. A piano tuner adjusts the tension in a string until no beat is produced by it and

the adjacent string played by the same key. His practised ear can detect beats of as low a frequency as 1 beat in 20 sec. This represents a difference in pitch between the two strings of only .05 c/sec.

The frequency of the beats produced by two sources that are of almost the same pitch has a bearing on the degree of pleasantness of the sound. If the beat frequency is of the order of 5 beats/sec or greater, the resulting sound is unpleasant. If the two sources differ in pitch by more than about 15 c/sec, the beats will occur too rapidly to be detected individually, but their presence may still prove unpleasant in overall effect.

19. THE DOPPLER EFFECT

We have all, at one time or another, observed the Doppler effect, perhaps without realizing it. As a fast moving car passes us while sounding its horn, a change of pitch is detected. This change in pitch, caused by a change in the relative motion of the source and observer, is named after the German physicist who analysed the phenomenon.

An explanation of this interesting effect is

quite simple. Let us consider an automobile that approaches an observer A and recedes from an observer B, Figure 12-31. As the car approaches A, each wave emitted by its horn is a little closer to the wave in front than would have been the case had the car not been moving. Consequently, observer A will receive a greater number of waves per second than he would had the source not been approaching, and the pitch, to him, will be higher than the pitch would be to the driver of the car.

At the same time, observer B receives waves at a *lower* rate, because the source is moving away from him, and the pitch to him is lower than that for observer A, or for the driver of the car. Similar effects are obtained when an observer moves relative to a stationary source.

In general, then, when a source and an observer approach one another, the apparent frequency of the sound increases and wavelength decreases; when the source and observer move apart, the apparent frequency decreases and wavelength increases.

The Doppler effect is displayed for any wave motion where source and observer move with respect to each other. In astronomy it is of great importance in determining the speed with which stars approach or recede from the earth. An apparent change in the wavelength of light received from the star is a result of this relative motion.

Short-range radar systems make use of the Doppler principle in conjunction with the phenomenon of beats. Police radar is an example. Electromagnetic waves from the radar transmitter are reflected from the approaching car, and arrive at the radar receiver with a frequency slightly greater than that at which they were sent out. (The car acts as an approaching source.) In the radar receiver, this reflected wave energy is mixed with the wave being transmitted and, because of the difference in frequencies, beats are produced. The number of beats per second is proportional to the car's speed. This beat frequency is determined electronically, and the speed of the car is registered on a meter.

Sound is a longitudinal wave motion, requiring a medium for its transmission. Its speed in air and other gases is dependent upon temperature. In air, the speed of sound is 331 m/sec at 0° C, and it increases by 0.6 m/sec for each degree increase in temperature.

Sounds are distinguished by three characteristics—**pitch**, determined by the frequency of the source; **loudness**, determined by the amplitude of the vibrating source; and **quality**, determined by the complexity of vibration.

The natural frequency of a stretched string is dependent upon the length, tension, diameter and density of the string. The string may be made to vibrate at frequencies other than its lowest natural frequency, or **fundamental**. These **modes** of vibration have frequencies that are multiples of the fundamental. Vibrating air columns also possess natural frequencies of vibration.

Sound waves exhibit the four main properties of water waves: reflection, refraction, diffraction and interference. The interference of sound waves of slightly different frequencies produces an audible variation in intensity of the combination, called a **beat**.

When relative motion exists between a source of sound and a listener, the pitch of the sound is altered. The pitch is higher as the source approaches the listener, and lower as it recedes.

EXERCISE A

1. A lightning flash usually lasts no longer than one or two seconds, while the accompanying thunder may persist for 10 seconds or longer. Explain.

2. It is well known that sound is heard at greater distances over water than over land. Give a reason for this.

3. A train approaching a station gives a short blast of its whistle. An observer on the station platform hears the original blast, and also its echo caused by a bridge behind the train. In what way would these two sounds differ in pitch, if at all?

4. A tuning fork is struck and then rotated slowly about its axis. Describe the changes in the sound heard.

5. A tuning fork of frequency 512 c/sec is sounded with a second fork and 20 beats are counted in 5 sec. What are the possible frequencies of the second fork?

6. How would you determine which of the two frequencies in Question 5 is the actual one,
   (a) using a third tuning fork?
   (b) using a piece of wax?

7. What is the frequency of the beats produced by the first overtone of two strings whose fundamental frequencies are 256 c/sec and 254 c/sec, respectively?

In the following problems, use the speed of sound as 1100 ft/sec or 335 m/sec.

1. What is the minimum distance a reflecting surface must be from a source of sound, if it is to produce a distinct echo?   (See section 14.)

2. Using the apparatus of Figure 12-29, and a tuning fork of unknown pitch, no sound is heard at R when the path length SQR is 16 cm longer than SPR.   The next silent point is obtained when the path difference is 48 cm.   What is the frequency of the fork?

3. Two organ pipes, open at both ends, are 10 ft and 11 ft long respectively.   When sounded simultaneously, what will be the frequency of their beats?

4. A source of sound faces a wall some distance away.   A man walking from the source to the wall notices that points of minimum intensity in the sound are located at regularly spaced points 75 cm apart.   What is the frequency of the sound?

5. A tuning fork of frequency 440 c/sec produces 10 beats in 4 sec with the first overtone of a string.   When a little wax is placed on the prongs, the number of beats is increased. What is the fundamental frequency of the string?

Chapter 12

Sound

▶ **Experiment 22**

___

To study the factors determining the frequency of a stretched string.

> Sonometer
>
> Several 1-kg and 2-kg
>   slotted masses
>
> Set of standard size masses

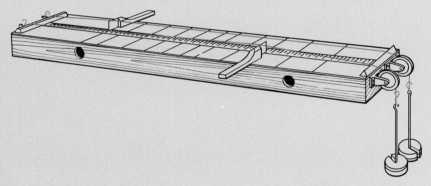

The sonometer is a large wooden box enclosing a volume of air, and strung with one or more wires. The vibrations of the wire are transferred to the sound board through a bridge. The position of the bridge determines the effective length of the vibrating string, while the total weight suspended from the string determines its tension.

Procedure

Relation between frequency and length

1. With 4 kg suspended from one end of one wire, sound the fork of lowest frequency and adjust the bridge so that when the wire is gently plucked, it sounds in unison with the fork.

Note: if you have a "musical ear", you will be able to arrive at this adjustment very quickly. If not, you can determine the proper bridge setting by placing a paper rider on the string, as indicated in Figure 12-12. Then sound the fork and press its base to the sound board. When the bridge is properly adjusted, the string will be set into sympathetic vibration, and the rider thrown off.

Record the length of the vibrating string and its frequency when unison is attained.

230

2. Repeat step 1 for the other forks in order of increasing frequency. List in a table the corresponding values of length and frequency.

Relation between frequency and tension

3. Set the tension at 4 kg, and the length of string so that its pitch is the same as that of the highest fork. Record this tension and length.

4. Keeping the length constant, reduce the tension in the string until it sounds in unison with the fork of next lower pitch. Record this tension and frequency.

5. Repeat step 4 for the remaining forks. Record corresponding values of tension and frequency in a table.

6. (Optional.) If you have strings of various diameters and densities, you can investigate the dependence of frequency upon these factors. Keeping the tension and length constant for each string, note the difference in pitch.

Analysis

1. From the table of step 2, plot a graph of frequency against length, using frequency as the ordinates (vertical axis). What is the name given to the relationship shown by this graph?

2. From the results of steps 3 and 4, plot a graph of frequency against tension. Plot also a graph of frequency against square root of tension. How would you describe the relationship between frequency and tension?

Experiment 23

To determine the speed of sound, using a resonant air column.

Adjustable air column

Metre stick

Tuning fork (approximately
500 c/sec or higher pitch)

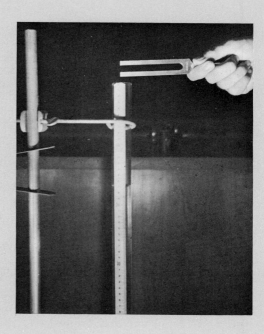

Procedure

1. Adjust the water level in the glass tube by raising the supply tank until the water is near the top of the tube.

2. Sound the tuning fork and hold it over the mouth of the tube as illustrated. Have your partner slowly lower the level of the water and listen for the first resonance point. At resonance the intensity of the sound will increase suddenly. When the approximate point of resonance has been determined, run the water level up and down around this point to determine it accurately. Record the length of air column at resonance.

3. Repeat the above procedure to locate the next resonant point, and successive resonance points as they occur. In each case determine the length of the air column.

4. Record the room temperature.

Analysis

1. Use the results of steps 2 and 3 to determine the distance between successive resonance points. Find the average separation. What portion of a wavelength does this represent?

2. Knowing the frequency and wavelength of the sound produced by the tuning fork, use the wave equation to find the velocity of sound.

3. Check the value obtained above with the accepted value using a temperature correction.

Experiment 24

To determine the speed of sound, using Kundt's apparatus.

| Kundt's apparatus |
| Metre stick |
| Audio frequency generator |
| Thermometer |

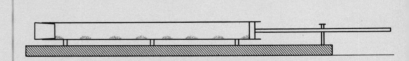

As shown in the illustration, Kundt's apparatus consists of an air column closed at both ends. Along the bottom of the tube is spread a thin layer of cork dust or lycopodium powder. One end of the tube is closed by a piston whose supporting rod is clamped at its mid-point. When this rod is stroked longitudinally, the piston is set into vibration, as is the air in the column. The frequency of the vibrations is determined by the length of the metal rod. The length of the air column is adjusted by moving it relative to the fixed rod.

As the rod is stroked, the dust in the tube moves about violently because of the air movement inside the tube. For certain lengths, the air in the tube is resonant with the rod, as indicated by the collection of dust in well-defined and evenly-spaced piles along the tube. This is a visual indication of a standing wave pattern, each pile of dust representing a region of minimum vibration, or a *node*.

By finding the separation of these nodes and using the known frequency of vibration, the velocity of sound in air may be determined.

Procedure

1. Place a thin, evenly-distributed layer of powder along the inner surface of the tube. Close one end securely with a cork.

2. Find the mid-point of the driving rod and clamp the rod securely at this point.

3. Arrange the tube and rod as shown in the illustration. Stroke the rod horizontally, using a piece of leather with resin for maximum friction.

4. While stroking with one hand, slowly adjust the length of the enclosed air column with the other until a setting is reached for which the dust collects in heaps.

5. Make the necessary measurements to determine the average separation of these nodes. For example, measure the distance separating 10 nodes.

6. Calculate the frequency from the wave equation. Look up the speed of sound in the material of the metal rod. The length of the metal rod is one-half a wavelength.

Alternative method:

Adjust the audio-frequency generator until its pitch is the same as that of the metal tube when stroked. Record this frequency.

7. Record the room temperature.

Analysis

1. Determine from step 5 the average separation of the nodes. If you measured the distance occupied by 10 nodes, divide this distance by 9 to determine the average distance between nodes. What fraction of a wavelength does this represent?

2. Using the value of frequency obtained from step 6, and the wavelength determined above, use the wave equation to find the velocity of sound in air.

3. Use the room temperature to compute the accepted value of the velocity of sound, and compare it with your experimental value.

Experiment 25

To study the interference pattern produced by two identical sources of sound.

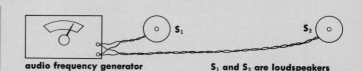

Audio frequency generator

Amplifier

Two loud speakers

audio frequency generator S_1 and S_2 are loudspeakers

Procedure

1. Connect the apparatus as illustrated in the diagram. Set the loudspeakers about 6 ft. apart, and at least waist high. Their axes should be parallel.

2. Adjust the frequency of the generator to approximately 600 c/sec. Note the intensity of sound at various points in front of the sources. Walk along the path whose points are equidistant from the sources (i.e. the right bisector of S_1S_2). Does the intensity of sound vary? Walk along a line perpendicular to this path. What do you notice about the intensity?

3. Repeat this procedure for a higher frequency, say 1500 c/sec.

Questions

1. Give an explanation for the variation in intensity from one point to another.

2. What is true of all points where the sound intensity is a maximum?

3. What is true of points where the intensity is a minimum?

4. What change, if any, occurred in the interference pattern when the source frequency was changed to the higher value?

Chapter 13

The Behaviour and Nature of Light

The problem of determining the nature of light has occupied a prominent position in the history of science. Four centuries before the Christian era, the Greeks conceived of light as a stream of particles, or corpuscles, sent forth from any light-producing or *luminous* source. This simple theory proved fairly adequate as a basis for the explanation of all the properties of light known at that time. Not until the eighteenth century did the "particle theory" come into question, when certain new discoveries concerning the behaviour of light raised serious doubts about the adequacy of this simple picture.

We shall begin our study of light by first considering those properties of light with which we are most familiar, and by seeing how we can fit them into a particle theory.

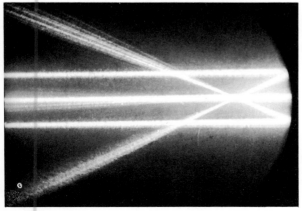

1. SOME BASIC PROPERTIES OF LIGHT

1. *Light travels at tremendous speed.*

Until only a few hundred years ago, the transmission of light from source to observer was believed to take place instantaneously. We shall discuss later the means whereby the speed of light has been accurately determined.

2. *Light travels in straight lines.*

The rectilinear propagation of light is illustrated by the formation of sharp shadows by an obstacle in the path of the light.

3. *Light is a form of energy.*

The rise in temperature brought on by the absorption of sunlight suggests that energy is associated with light. The *photoelectric effect*, whereby electrical charges are made to flow from certain materials upon exposure to light, illustrates that light is a form of energy.

Fig. 13-1: *Reflection of light. Three rays of light approach a cylindrical mirror from the left. The middle ray is reflected along its initial path while the outer rays are reflected along new paths. Would you expect particles to behave in the same manner?*

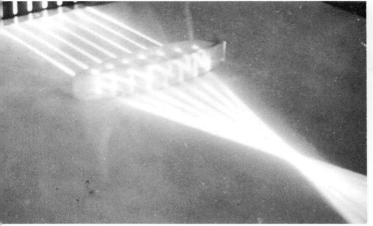

Fig. 13-2: *Refraction of light. Parallel rays of light are bent or refracted upon entering the lens. Would you expect particles to behave in this manner?*

Fig. 13-3: *Simultaneous reflection and refraction of light. Light approaching the prism from the left is partially reflected upward. Some of the light is refracted as it enters the prism and again as it leaves.*

4. *No material medium is necessary for the propagation of light.*

We are familiar with the fact that light passes through air, water, glass, and other materials that we call *transparent*. However, the fact that light is transmitted through the vast vacuum of space dispels any notion that a material medium is necessary. Unlike sound, then, light cannot consist of the vibrations of particles in a material medium.

5. *Light is regularly reflected from a smooth surface.*

6. *Light is refracted (bent) at a surface separating two transparent media.*

7. *Light may be simultaneously reflected and refracted at a surface.*

Some of these properties are illustrated by Figures 13-1, 13-2, and 13-3.

2. THE PARTICLE THEORY

The properties of light listed above form the basis upon which a particle theory of light can be founded. To accommodate the first of these properties, we must think of these particles as always travelling at extremely high speeds.

As we know, all particles are subject to gravitational forces that pull them downwards. If their speed were great enough, however, any curvature of their path would be negligible, and essentially straight-line propagation would be the case.

Even minute particles travelling at high speeds will possess kinetic energy. Upon collision with material objects, the particles would transfer some of this energy to the object in the form of heat. After collision, it is logical to assume that the particles

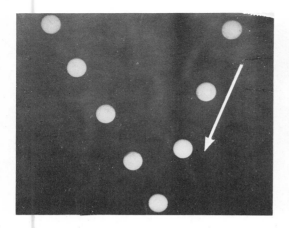

Fig. 13-4: *Reflection of a particle. A rolling ball was photographed at intervals of 1/20 sec. Compare its direction after reflection with its initial direction. What change takes place in its speed?*

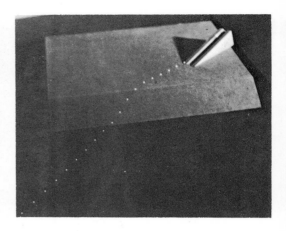

Fig. 13-5: *Refraction of a particle. The path of the rolling ball, photographed here at intervals of 1/20 sec, bends abruptly when the incline steepens. What change takes place in the speed of the ball as it enters the incline?*

would rebound, or be reflected, in much the same manner as shown in Figure 13-4.

Can a stream of particles undergo a sudden bending to account for the refraction of light? Figure 13-5 illustrates the deviation in the path of a "particle" as it undergoes a sudden increase in speed. Perhaps the bending of light in passing from air to glass is due to an increase in speed in the glass medium. The particle theory would suggest this.

It becomes somewhat more difficult to explain the *simultaneous* refraction and reflection of a beam of light particles. Why should some particles pass through the transparent medium while others reflect from this medium as though it were a mirror surface? No simple explanation suggests itself here.

3. DISPERSION OF LIGHT

If a beam of white light is allowed to pass through a triangular prism such as that shown in Figure 13-6, a dramatic spreading-out of the light into all colours of the rainbow is seen when the emerging light falls on a screen.

There is little doubt that a similar effect was observed by early philosophers when sunlight passed through jewellery or transparent crystals. Newton, however, was the first to show that these colours were not created by the substance through which they passed, but rather that they were present in the sunlight itself.

In passing through the prism, each of the coloured components of white light undergoes a separate amount of refraction and emerges as a single band of colour; this phenomenon is called *dispersion*.

As shown in Figure 13-6, red light is bent least and violet light most. The arrangement of these colours on the screen is called a *spectrum*.

Newton was a strong supporter of the particle theory of light, but he was unable to give a simple explanation of dispersion using this theory.

Perhaps we could explain dispersion by making a further assumption that there are many different kinds of particles, each kind producing a particular colour sensation. In so doing, however, we are developing a theory that no longer remains simple.

236

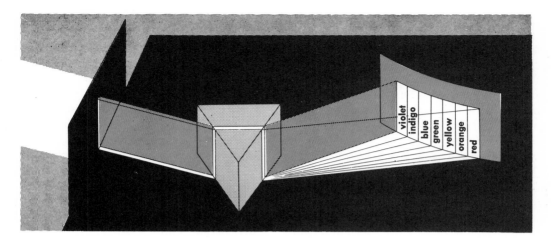

Fig. 13-6: *Dispersion of white light. White light entering the prism from the left is spread out into individual colours.*

4. THE WAVE THEORY OF LIGHT

An effect similar to the dispersion of light can be observed using waves in a ripple tank. In Figure 13-7, a difference in the amount of bending is obtained for waves of different wavelengths (and hence of different frequencies). Is it possible that other properties of light may be explained in terms of waves?

Our experiments in Chapter 11 illustrated several properties of water waves. The reflection of these waves at a barrier and their bending, or refraction, bring to mind the same general properties of light that we have mentioned at the outset of this chapter.

The idea that light is a wave disturbance was upheld by many prominent scientists of the seventeenth and eighteenth centuries. It was opposed by an almost equal number of men who favoured the corpuscular theory. Among the latter group was Sir Isaac Newton.

5. PARTICLE VS. WAVE THEORY

It is interesting to make a comparison between the two rival theories of light to discover which of the two provides a better picture of the nature of light.

A major difficulty encountered by the supporters of the wave theory was the fact that light can travel through empty space. Normally we consider a wave as a disturbance requiring a medium through which to travel. To overcome this difficulty, those favouring the wave theory developed the concept of a mysterious, invisible medium. This medium, called the *ether*, was assumed to pervade the universe. Such a drastic assumption is, of course, unnecessary in the particle theory.

Fig. 13-7: *(a) The pencil is aligned parallel to the low-frequency refracted wavefronts. (b) The frequency of the waves has been increased. What has happened to the alignment? What does this suggest about the individual colours in Figure 13-6?*

Another difficulty inherent in the wave concept of light is posed by straight-line propagation. If light is a wave motion, why does it travel only in a straight line? A voice can be heard around a corner, but the speaker cannot be seen. In Newton's own words: "If light consisted of vibrations, it would bend into the shadow and spread every way into the medium which lies beyond the obstacle." For this reason, Newton supported the particle theory.

Certain properties of light, such as reflection and refraction, are explained by either theory, but simultaneous reflection and refraction seem much more characteristic of waves than of particles.

A theory is useful as a basis both of explanations for observed phenomena and of predictions concerning other phenomena which cannot or have not been observed. For instance, as already mentioned in Section 2, the particle theory predicts that light under-goes an *increase* in speed when entering glass from air. What does the wave theory predict? If we refer to Figure 11-16, we see that a ray, which represents the direction of travel of the water waves, is bent toward the normal when undergoing a *decrease* in speed, that is, in going from deep to shallow water. This manner of bending is similar to that of a ray of light entering glass. The wave theory of light suggests then, that light *slows down* upon entering glass.

Opposing predictions such as those above provide a most important base upon which to test the validity of each of these theories. If one could but measure the speed of light in glass or water, and compare this with its speed in air, the result would be very strong evidence in favor of one or the other of the opposing theories.

These conclusive measurements were not made until more than a century and a half after Newton's time.

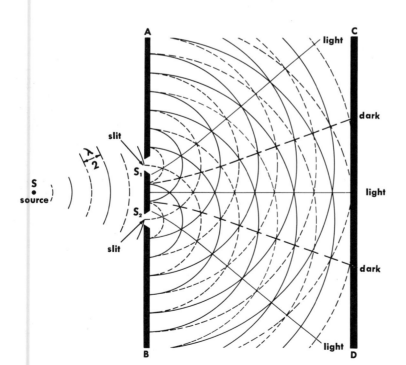

Fig. 13-8: *Thomas Young employed two small holes, S_1 and S_2, which were illuminated by a single source S. The screen CD displayed alternate regions of light and dark. What theory does this observation tend to support?*

6. INTERFERENCE OF LIGHT— YOUNG'S DOUBLE-SLIT EXPERIMENT

The wave theory was revived in the year 1802 as a result of a simple but most important experiment carried out by an English physician, Thomas Young. This experiment can be regarded as the first definite proof that light exhibits characteristics attributable only to wave motion.

In this experiment, Young allowed light of a single colour (monochromatic light) from a pinhole S to fall on a distant screen AB containing two pinholes, S_1 and S_2, separated by a fraction of one millimetre (Figure 13-8). A screen CD, held some distance from AB, exhibited alternate light and dark spots along its length. When two slits were used instead of pinholes, alternate light and dark bands, called *fringes*, were seen on each side of the central portion of the screen. This pattern is shown in Figure 13-9.

Young interpreted these fringes as direct evidence of interference of light waves. The dark fringes, he concluded, were the results of a wave from each of the sources S_1 and S_2 arriving out of phase with each other at the screen to produce destructive interference, while the bright spots were evidence of waves from these sources arriving at the screen in phase.

Figure 13-8 gives a representation of the wave picture conjectured by Young. Light emanating from S in the form of spherical wave fronts reaches the slits S_1 and S_2 simultaneously. Each of these two slits acts as a new source of spherical waves, spreading out into the region beyond AB. In this diagram the solid lines indicate crest wave fronts, and the broken lines represent troughs. Where two crests or two troughs overlap at the screen, *constructive interference* exists, and maximum light intensity results. Similarly, minimum light intensity (darkness) is produced at points where a crest and trough meet at the screen.

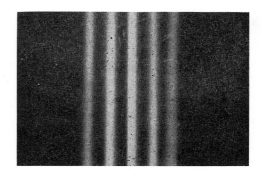

Fig. 13-9: *Interference fringes produced by a double slit.*

The corresponding effect, using water waves, is shown in Figure 13-10. Here the interference pattern is produced by two point sources. A similar pattern can be obtained using, instead, a double slit, as shown in Figure 11-28.

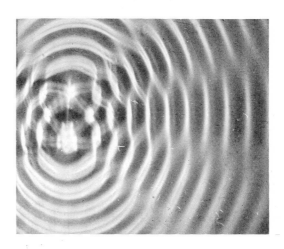

Fig. 13-10: *Interference pattern in a ripple tank produced by two point sources. Compare this with Figure 13-8.*

Fig. 13-11: *Young's experiment can be simulated by using two closely-spaced slits held to the eye. The retina of the eye serves as the screen CD of Figure 13-8.*

Young's famous experiment can be simulated quite easily without the use of elaborate equipment. The slits can be made by scratching two straight parallel lines on a piece of exposed photographic film. The slits should be as close together as possible. By holding the film close to the eye in front of a source of light S (Figure 13-11), one observes a series of parallel, coloured fringes. The best source of light in this instance is a light bulb of clear glass with a straight single-wire filament. The retina of the eye serves as the screen CD of Figure 13-8.

The significance of Young's experiment rests in the necessity of relying upon outstanding characteristics of wave motion to produce what turns out to be an exceedingly simple explanation of the fringe pattern. The first of these is *diffraction*— the spreading out of the wave disturbance into the regions behind the obstacle containing the slits. The second is *interference*—the effect produced when two waves meet at a point. Young's findings, however, did not receive general acceptance in 1802, and some years passed before this and other evidence, notably the measurement of the speed of light in water, led overwhelmingly to the acceptance of the wave theory of light. Toward the end of the 19th century, the wave theory was solidly entrenched as the explanation for all optical phenomena.

We have traced the historical development of the enquiry into the nature of light and have found that the centuries-old corpuscular theory gradually gave way to the concept of light as a wave motion.

It is typical of scientific endeavour that a theory that seems plausible one day can be placed in doubt by new and unexpected discoveries the next. At the turn of the twentieth century, undeniable evidence was obtained that light is indeed sent out in little packets or bundles of energy, and that each bundle, or *photon*, exhibits some characteristics of *both* matter and waves. To explain all the presently-known properties of light, one must refer to the idea of light *as both wave and particle*.

7. THE SPEED OF LIGHT

One of the earliest measurements of the speed of light was made in 1675 by a Dane, Olaus Röemer, in a series of observations on the times of eclipse of one of Jupiter's moons. The eclipses should take place at regularly spaced time intervals. Röemer found that there was a measurable delay in the time of eclipse when the earth, in its revolution around the sun, was nearest to Jupiter and when it was farther away. He measured this delay in time (17 minutes), and assumed it to be the time it took light to travel the diameter of the earth's orbit, (Figure 13-12). Since this diameter was known, it was possible to calculate the speed of light. Röemer found it to be about 200,000 miles per second, somewhat more than the value of 186,000 miles per second determined by others in later experiments.

At this enormous speed it is clear that it would be very difficult to set up a terrestrial experiment to measure the speed of light. Nevertheless, very precise measurements have been made. Among experimenters in this field the name of A. A. Michelson, an American, stands out. He carried out a long

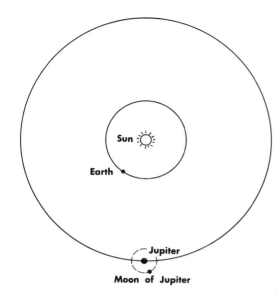

Fig. 13-12: *When a moon of Jupiter passes behind that planet, it undergoes eclipse as seen from the earth. The duration of the eclipse varies depending on the location of the earth in its revolution about the sun. Röemer correctly attributed these variations to the different lengths of time required for light to travel to earth from the moon.*

Figure 13-13 illustrates Michelson's experimental arrangement. The illuminated slit in the figure forms the source of light. The rays of light from the slit are rendered parallel by the lens shown. The beam from the lens is reflected from face 1 of the *stationary* octagonal mirror *M* in the direction of the concave and plane mirror system *M'* on Mount San Antonio, 22 miles away. From here it is reflected back to face 3 of the octagonal mirror on Mount Wilson and thence into the observing telescope. The observer will thus see a clear and steady image of the slit by means of a beam of light which has travelled from Mount Wilson to Mount San Antonio and back.

series of experiments; these culminated in a very famous experiment in which he sent a beam of light from Mount Wilson, California, to Mount San Antonio, California, whence the beam was reflected back to the observation post on Mount Wilson. The light thus travelled a distance of 44 miles, twice the distance between the two mountain stations. The principles involved in this measurement are very simple although the experiment itself is difficult.

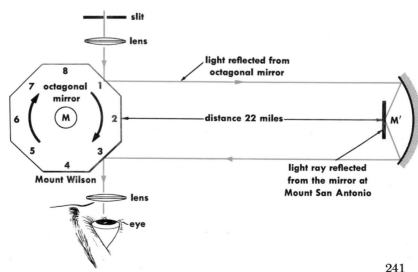

Fig. 13-13: *The first accurate determination of the speed of light was made by Michelson using a revolving mirror. Light from this mirror travelled to a point 22 miles distant, whence it was reflected back to the observer.*

The octagonal mirror M is now *rotated* in the manner shown in the figure (clockwise). The directions of the reflected beams will be disturbed, and the observer will see a flickering image. As the speed of rotation of the octagonal mirror is increased, a speed will be reached at which face 1 of the mirror will be exactly replaced by face 8 and face 3 will be replaced by face 2, in a time exactly equal to the time it takes for the light to travel from the mirror M to the mirror M' and back. At this critical speed, the image of the slit will again be steady and clear. This critical speed of rotation of the octagonal mirror is carefully measured so that the time of the fractional rotation to replace face 1 by face 8, and face 3 by face 2

can be calculated. This is clearly the time t that elapsed while the beam travelled twice the distance MM'. It follows at once that the speed of light c is given by the equation:

$$c = \frac{2MM'}{t} = \frac{\text{distance travelled}}{\text{time}}$$

As a result of this experiment and subsequent experiments by Michelson and other workers, the speed of light in a vacuum (which is very close to its speed in air) is accepted as 2.997928×10^8 m/sec. This is a very precise measurement which represents not only what we refer to as the speed of light, but also what we consider to be a most important universal physical constant. It is usually designated by the letter c.

SUMMARY:

1. As a summary of this chapter, list vertically ten properties of light that have been mentioned.

2. Beside each of these, indicate which of these theories in your own estimation provides an explanation for this property. Should you believe that both theories provide an explanation, then include both.

3. Determine which single theory seems the more suitable by awarding one point to each theory each time it has been mentioned. Total the scores and compare your score with others in your class.
   (Perhaps you will find that one of the two theories provides only a partial explanation of a particular property. In such cases, award that theory one half point.)

EXERCISE A

1. If light consisted of particles, what might you expect to observe when two flashlight beams cross each other?

2. If light consists of particles travelling in straight lines, describe the pattern that you would expect to observe on the screen in Figure 13-8 when light passes through the double slit.

3. List three similarities in the behaviour of light waves and sound waves.

4. List three ways in which light waves differ in behaviour from sound waves.

5. Some substances are opaque, others translucent and still others transparent. Consult a dictionary for the meaning of these terms, and give one example of each type of substance.

6. State two important purposes served by a theory of light, or by any theory.

7. What general requirement for wave motion hindered the acceptance of a wave theory of light?

242

8. What general property of wave motion remained unnoticed, in the case of light, until the nineteenth century?

9. What opposing predictions followed from the two theories of light concerning the speed of light in water?

EXERCISE B

Speed of light in vacuum or air $= 3.00 \times 10^8$ m/sec $= 1.86 \times 10^5$ mi/sec.
Mean distance from sun to earth $= 9.3 \times 10^7$ mi.

1. A light-year is the distance travelled by light in one year. Express this distance in miles, to three significant digits.

2. The nearest star is 4.3 light-years from earth. What distance is this in miles?

3. (a) How long does it take light to reach the earth from the sun?
   (b) Express the distance from the sun to the earth in light-minutes.
   (c) Express this distance in light-seconds.

4. The wavelength of blue light is known to be 4.0×10^{-7} m. Using the speed of light as 3.0×10^8 m/sec, determine the frequency of a source that emits blue light.

Chapter 13

The Behaviour and Nature of Light

Experiment 26

Microscope slide, one side coated black

Cellophane (red, blue)

Straight filament bulb

Two razor blades

Straight edge

To study the interference of light.

Procedure

1. Use a straight edge and two razor blades held together to produce a double slit on the precoated microscope slides. Make a single slit with one razor blade on the same slide.

2. View the vertically-placed straight filament bulb through the double slit while standing 3 or 4 metres from the bulb. Note any difference in the appearance of the outer interference fringes (nodal lines).

3. Repeat step 2 but cover the bulb with first the red and next the blue cellophane filter. How does what you see differ from what you observed in step 2? Besides the difference in colour, how does the observed pattern for blue light differ from that of red light?

4. Use the single slit to view the bulb with and without the filters. What is the outstanding difference between this pattern and that observed with the double slit?

Analysis

1. What property of light is demonstrated by this experiment?

2. How could you account for the variety of colours present when the clear bulb was observed?

3. State the chief difference in the patterns observed with the single slit and those observed with the double slit.

4. This experiment is similar in principle to an earlier one involving the ripple tank. To what are the two slits in this experiment analogous?

243

Chapter 14

Reflection of Light

One characteristic of light is the casting of reasonably sharp shadows by an object in its path. This observation is explained by the supposition that light travels in straight lines. From a little further observation, we recognize that light that encounters highly polished surfaces is reflected and forms images, depending upon the geometry of the reflecting surfaces. **A study of the rectilinear nature of light in terms of rays is known as geometric optics.**

A description of geometric optics requires an understanding of the terms *opaque*, *transparent*, and *translucent*. An opaque substance will not transmit light; a transparent material transmits light to produce clearly visible objects; a translucent material produces indistinct objects as a result of its light transmission.

Arrange a plane mirror in any convenient way, such as *MN* in Figure 14-1, and scatter a little dust about the space near the mirror in order to make rays of light visible. Allow sunlight or parallel rays from an arc lamp to pass through a small opening at *A* so that a ray of light falls upon the mirror at *D*. *AD* is called the *incident ray*. We shall see that the *reflected ray*, *DB*, is sent back in a definite direction with respect to the incident ray. In the figure, *CD* is the *normal* to the mirror's surface. (A normal is a perpendicular to the reflecting surface at the point of incidence.) By manipulating an opaque sheet so that the rays *AD* and *DB* skim along its surface, we shall see that the incident ray, the reflected ray, and the normal to the surface are all in the same plane. If we measure the angle *i* (the *angle of incidence*) and the angle *r* (the *angle of reflection*), we shall see that these are equal. If the angle *i* is changed, the angle *r* will change to maintain equality, and will remain in the same plane as the incident ray and the normal to the surface at the point of incidence.

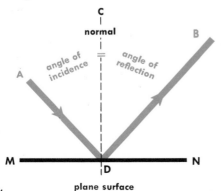

Fig. 14-1: *A ray of light is reflected from the surface MN. The angles of incidence and reflection are equal.*

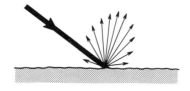

(a) negligible scattering

(b) complete scattering

Fig. 14-2: *(a) A highly-polished reflecting surface reflects a ray of light strongly in one direction with a minimum of scattering. Such reflection is termed specular. (b) A less smooth surface produces diffuse reflection.*

On the basis of this or similar observations, we can state the *laws of reflection*:

(a) The incident ray, the reflected ray, and the normal to the reflecting surface all lie in the same plane.

(b) The angle of incidence is equal to the angle of reflection.

The surface illustrated in Figure 14-1 is a highly polished surface, or mirror surface, which produces reflection called *specular reflection.* If the surface is not polished, the light is not specularly reflected but is scattered or *diffusely reflected.* Figure 14-2(b) illustrates diffuse reflection. Figure 14-2(a) shows that even a highly polished surface scatters a small fraction of the light.

Figures 14-3 and 14-4 illustrate in more detail the specular, or regular, reflection of a beam of light and the scattering of such a beam. It will be observed from Figure 14-4 that the light rays from the minute and variously orientated parts of the rough surface still follow the laws of reflection. This observation will be important when we come to discuss reflection from curved surfaces.

1. IMAGE FORMATION BY MEANS OF A SMALL APERTURE

Figure 14-5 shows how the straight-line propagation of light leads to an explanation of the formation of an image by a small aperture or pinhole. A self-illuminated object, such as a candle or an electric light,

Fig. 14-3: *A beam of light, consisting of parallel rays, will be reflected as a parallel beam by a smooth surface.*

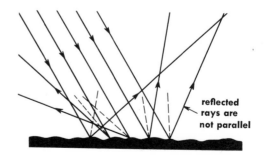

Fig. 14-4: *An irregular surface will reflect the rays of a parallel beam in various directions. This is another example of diffuse reflection. Note that the laws of reflection still hold for any individual incident ray.*

245

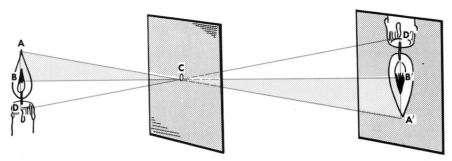

Fig. 14-5: *The formation of a real image. Three rays are shown leaving the flame, from points A, B, D respectively. After passing through the pinhole these rays meet the screen at A', B', and D' respectively, whence they are reflected to the eye. Rays leaving from all other points of the object (that is, the flame) build up the entire image on the screen. Would the image be formed if the pinhole were not used?*

is placed at ABD, and an opaque sheet with a small aperture C is positioned at some distance from it. The light which passes through the aperture falls on a screen. An inverted image, $A'B'D'$, of the candle will be observed on the screen. The formation of the image may be described by choosing from the bundle of rays which go out in all directions from the several points in the self-illuminated object (for example, the points A, B, and D) those particular rays which go toward the aperture C and pass through in straight lines to meet the screen at the respective points A', B', and D'. Thus, point by point, the image is built up. On the basis of this geometry we expect an inverted image: the image size will depend upon the relative distances of object and image, respectively, from the aperture. Since such an image, formed by rays of light originating at an object, is capable of being received on a screen, it is called a *real image*. The test of a real image is that it can be formed on a screen.

2. THE IMAGE FORMED BY A PLANE MIRROR

Probably the most familiar case of image formation is that observed in a plane mirror. Figure 14-6 shows the geometric formation of such an image. A plane mirror is fixed vertically on a large sheet of paper lying on a table top. MN in the diagram is a section of this mirror. Any figure, a triangle ABC

for example, is drawn on the paper in front of the mirror. Pins are set up at the vertices of the triangle. The image of the pin at A, that is, A', is observed from some point E; and two pins, E and D, are set up on the line of sight $EDOA'$. A second line of sight in any direction is set up, with two pins, G and F, determining the line of sight GFA'. These two lines of sight must intersect at the image of A. The line of the mirror face, MN, is marked on the paper and the mirror removed.

The lines-of-sight pins ED and GF may now be continued as dotted lines behind the mirror to meet at A', a position point of the image. In a similar way the positions of the images of vertices B and C (that is, B' and C') may be located.

Measurement will now show that the distances of A', B', and C' behind the mirror are the same as the distances of A, B, and C in front of the mirror. Furthermore, if A and A' are joined, the line joining them will be found to be normal to the mirror. The images of points formed in a plane mirror are thus *as far behind the mirror as the object is in front of the mirror, and they lie on the same normal to the mirror surface.* It follows that the image of the triangle is as large as the triangle itself. The image is also reversed with respect to the viewer, since the near vertex B of the object appears as the far vertex B' of the image.

It will be realized that the light originating

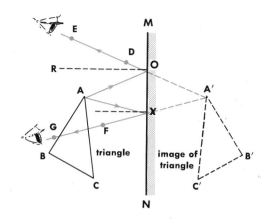

Fig. 14-6: *Locating an image produced by a plane mirror. A ray leaving point A enters the eye after reflection at O. Point A thus appears to be along the line EDO. Another ray leaving point A is reflected to the eye from point X. Point A in this case appears to lie along the line GFX. The image of A' thus lies at the intersection of these two lines. By a similar process the images of points B and C may be located.*

at the pin *A* does not go through the mirror, but is reflected at the point at which it meets the mirror, that is, at the point *O* in Figure 14-6. If the normal to the mirror (*OR* at *O*) is constructed, it will be found that the angles *EOR* and *AOR* are equal. Although the light actually seems to come from the image points *A'*, *B'*, and *C'* and the image appears to be at these points, the image of the triangle in the plane mirror cannot be obtained on a screen and is therefore not a real image by the definition of "real" already given. We therefore call it a *virtual image*.

3. CURVED MIRRORS

A curved mirror surface is usually a portion of a concave or convex spherical surface. Figure 14-7 shows the section of two such mirrors. Rays of light that fall on such mirrors obey the laws of reflection. The central line *PCV* in (a) and *PVC* in (b) is called the *principal axis*. It passes through the *centre of curvature*, *C*, of the spherical surface and through the *vertex*, *V*. The *normal* to any point on the surface will be the line drawn from the centre of curvature to the point (of the surface) in question.

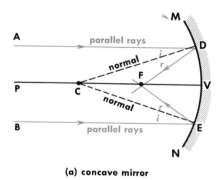

(a) concave mirror

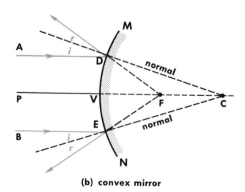

(b) convex mirror

Fig. 14-7: *The concave and convex mirrors are each a portion of a spherical surface. Point C on the principal axes PCV or PVC represents the centre of curvature of the spherical surface. A line joining point C to any point on the surface is perpendicular to the surface at that point. In the case of the concave mirror, rays parallel to and close to the principal axis are reflected through a single point called the principal focus. For the convex mirror, such rays appear to be reflected from a single point, called the virtual focus, but do not actually pass through this point. The focus lies halfway between the centre of curvature and the vertex.*

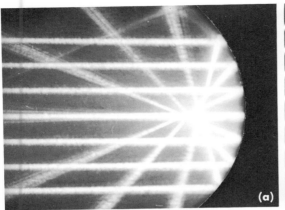

(a)

(b)

Fig. 14-8: *Reflection of rays that are parallel to the principal axis. Note that in (a) only those rays near the principal axis are reflected through a common point.*

An important property of spherical mirrors is the manner in which rays parallel to the principal axis are reflected. As shown in Figure 14-8(a), a group of rays are incident on a spherical mirror, and are parallel to the principal axis. The reflected rays cross the principal axis at approximately the same point.

Further examination shows that, except for the two outer incident rays, *the parallel rays closer to the principal axis, when reflected, pass through a single point on this axis.* This point is called the *principal focus*, and its distance from the mirror is called the *focal length*. The principal focus is located half-way between the centre of curvature and the mirror.

Similarly, *incident rays that pass through the principal focus are reflected parallel to the principal axis.*

When parallel rays meet the convex mirror, the reflected rays, if extended, would appear to meet behind the mirror at *F* [Figure 14-7(b)].

Since rays parallel to the principal axis will converge after reflection to the focal point in a concave mirror [Figure 14-7(a)], such a mirror is called a *converging mirror*. On the other hand, rays approaching a convex mirror parallel to its principal axis will diverge as though they came from the focal point of the mirror [Figure 14-7(b)]: such a mirror is therefore called a *diverging mirror*.

Rays that are not parallel to the axis are

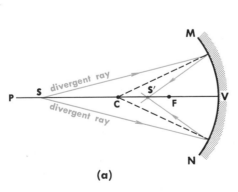

(a)

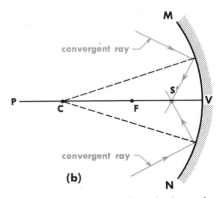

(b)

Fig. 14-9: *Rays that are not parallel to the principal axis are not reflected through the principal focus.*

248

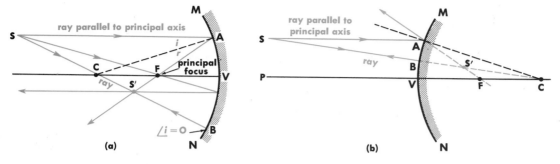

Fig. 14-10: *To determine the location of the image S' of an object S, any two rays leaving point S may be employed. For the concave mirror (a), the intersection of these rays determines the location of the real image S'. For the convex mirror (b), the location of the virtual image S' is found by determining the location of a point from which the two reflected rays appear to diverge.*

not reflected through the principal focus. Figure 14-9 illustrates two such situations. In (a), rays diverging from a point S on the principal axis are reflected through S', which is farther from the vertex than is the principal focus. In (b), rays converging toward the same mirror cross the principal axis at some point between the principal focus and the vertex.

4. IMAGES FORMED BY CURVED MIRRORS

The position of the image of an object is found by locating the image of each point in the object. In practice, it is usually necessary to establish only the position of two points in the image. To do this, we shall make use of the following:

(1) A ray parallel to the principal axis is reflected through the principal focus.

(2) A ray passing through the principal focus is reflected parallel to the principal axis.

(3) A ray passing through the centre of curvature is reflected along its incident path.

In Figure 14-10(a), three such rays are shown leaving S, a point on the object. Their intersection at S' determines the location of the corresponding point in the image. It is not necessary to draw all three rays, since the intersection of any two of them determines the point S'.

Figure 14-10(b) shows the corresponding construction for the case of a diverging (convex) mirror. In this situation, S' is a point in the virtual image.

In Figure 14-11, the construction lines are shown which locate the image of an object BA, represented by an arrow. The object in this case is outside the centre of curvature of the mirror. The image is inverted, is smaller than the object, and lies between

14-11: A ray diagram illustrating the ...tion of an image A'B' of an object AB ...ed beyond the centre of curvature of a ...cave mirror. The image is real, inverted, and smaller than the object.

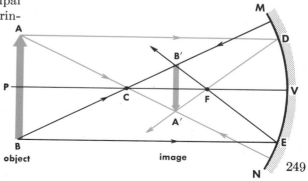

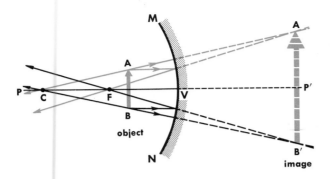

object

image

the centre of curvature and the focal point. A little consideration, or several more reconstructions with the object farther and farther from the mirror, will show that as the object recedes from the mirror, the image approaches nearer and nearer to the plane passing through the focal point.

Figures 14-12 and 14-13 respectively show the construction to locate the image when the object is within the focal point and when it is between the centre of curvature and the focal point. In the former case the image is seen to be a virtual image. The method of construction is the same in all cases.

The image construction in the case of a convex, or diverging, mirror is shown in Figure 14-14. Here a virtual image is formed, and the construction rays must be artificially projected behind the mirror in order to locate the points of the virtual image.

5. THE MIRROR EQUATION

By using simple principles of geometry, it is possible to determine the position of the

image produced by a curved mirror without the necessity of a ray diagram.

Consider first the ray diagram in Figure 14-15. The two black-shaded triangles are similar, and the ratios of corresponding sides are equal. Thus $FC/PA = BC/FA$. In terms of the algebraic symbols shown in the diagram, $\dfrac{H_i}{H_o} = \dfrac{f}{S_o}$ where H_i and H_o are the sizes of the image and object respectively, and S_i and S_o are their respective distances from the principal focus.

Also, from the coloured triangles, $\dfrac{H_i}{H_o} = \dfrac{S_i}{f}$.

Equating these two ratios for $\dfrac{H_i}{H_o}$ we obtain the simple relationship $\dfrac{f}{S_o} = \dfrac{S_i}{f}$,

or $S_i \cdot S_o = f^2$.

Hence, if the focal length of the mirror is known, the position of the image can be determined for any value of the object's distance from the focus.

Let us see how this equation may be employed to confirm many of the properties of curved mirrors that we already know from our previously constructed ray diagrams. As the object is moved further from the mirror, thus increasing the value of S_o, the corresponding value of S_i must decrease proportionally to preserve their constant product f^2. In effect, this means that the image will move closer to the principal focus.

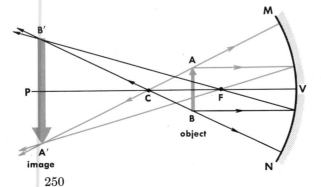

object

image

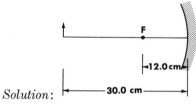

Fig. 14-15: *Ray diagram used in the derivation of the mirror equation.*

In the limiting case, when the object is at an extremely large distance from the mirror, the image will be located at the focus.

Similarly, when the object approaches the principal focus, the image will recede. In the limiting case, when the object is located at the focus, no image is formed. In fact, this is so because all rays from any point on the object will be reflected parallel to each other, and will therefore not intersect to form an image. Our interpretation of this from the equation would be that when S_o is zero, no value of S_i will satisfy the equation.

When the object moves to a position between the principal focus and the mirror, we know from Figure 14-13 that the image is located *behind* the mirror. The above equations allow us to determine the locations of the virtual images as well.

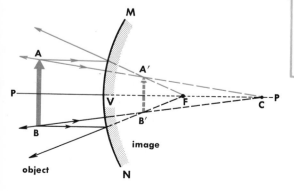

Fig. 14-14: *The image formed by a convex mirror is virtual, upright and smaller than the object.*

EXAMPLE 1

An object is placed 30.0 cm from a concave mirror of focal length 12.0 cm. Determine the position of the image and compare its size with that of the subject.

Solution:

Here, $S_o = 30.0 \text{ cm} - 12.0 \text{ cm}$
$\qquad = 18.0 \text{ cm}$
$\qquad f = 12.0 \text{ cm}$
$\qquad S_i S_o = f^2$
$\therefore \quad 18.0 \, S_i = 144$
$\qquad S_i = \dfrac{144}{18.0} = 8.0 \text{ cm}.$

Thus the image is located 8.0 cm from the focus, or **20.0 cm from the mirror**.

$$\frac{H_i}{H_o} = \frac{f}{S_o} = \frac{12.0}{18.0} = 0.667$$

The image is **0.667 times the size of the object.**

EXAMPLE 2

If the object in Example 1 is placed 9.00 cm from the mirror, what is the location and size of the image?

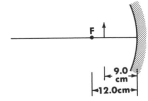

Solution:

$$S_o = 12.0 \text{ cm} - 9.00 \text{ cm} = 3.00 \text{ cm}$$
$$S_i S_o = f^2$$
$$\therefore 3.00 S_i = 144$$
$$S_i = \frac{144}{3.00} = 48.0 \text{ cm}$$

We know that for concave mirrors an object placed between the focus and mirror produces a virtual image behind the mirror.

This image will be located 48.0 cm from the focus, or **36.0 cm behind the mirror.**

$$\frac{H_i}{H_o} = \frac{f}{S_o} = \frac{12.0}{3.0} = 4.00$$

The image will be **4.00 times greater than the object.** (It will be virtual and upright.)

EXAMPLE 3

An object is placed 36 cm in front of a convex mirror of focal length 12 cm. What is the position and size of its image?

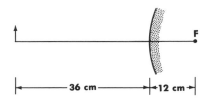

Solution:

$$S_o = 36 + 12 = 48 \text{ cm}$$
$$f = 12 \text{ cm}$$
$$S_i = \frac{f^2}{S_o} = \frac{144}{48} = 3.0 \text{ cm}$$

The image will be 3.0 cm from the focus, or **9.0 cm behind the mirror.** (Convex mirrors always produce images that lie between the mirror and focus.)

$$\frac{H_i}{H_o} = \frac{f}{S_o} = \frac{12}{48} = 0.25$$

The image is **0.25 times the size of the object.**

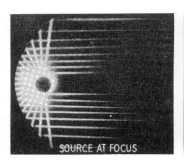
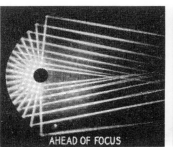

Fig. 14-16: *If a source of light is placed at the focus of a parabolic mirror, all rays are reflected parallel to the principal axis. If it is placed ahead of the focus, the reflected beam is convergent.*

GEOMETRIC OPTICS: This is the study of the formation of images, using the fact that, in a given medium, light is propagated in straight lines.

THE LAWS OF REFLECTION: These state that at a point on a reflecting surface, an incident ray and its path of reflection make equal angles with the normal to the surface at that point. Also, the incident and reflected rays, together with the normal at that point, lie in the same plane.

REFLECTION: There are two types, specular and diffuse. Specular reflection takes place at a smooth surface. There is negligible scattering in such cases. Diffuse reflection takes place from less smooth surfaces, but the laws of reflection are still obeyed by each individual ray of light.

Objects are seen when light leaving the object enters the eye directly, or is reflected from some intermediate surface. When light from an object is reflected from a mirror into the eye, what it sees in the mirror is called the image of that object.

IMAGES: Two types exist: virtual and real. If light, after reflection, actually passes through the points where the image is located, then the image is said to be real. Such an image can be seen on a screen placed at the proper location. If the light only *appears* to come from the points where the image is located, the image is said to be virtual.

PLANE MIRRORS: These form virtual images that are located behind the mirror at a distance equal to the object's distance in front of the mirror.

SPHERICAL MIRRORS: There are two types, concave and convex. Their surface is very nearly parabolic in the region close to the principal axis. Their focus lies midway between the mirror and its centre of curvature.

Concave mirrors: These produce real images, except when the object is located between the mirror and the principal focus. The real images are inverted. The closer the object is to the principal focus, the greater the size of the real, inverted image and the greater its distance from the mirror. No image is formed when the object is located at the focus.

Convex mirrors: These produce virtual, erect images of the object, regardless of the latter's location. The image is located behind the mirror, somewhere between the mirror and principal focus.

PARABOLIC MIRRORS: These will reflect all rays parallel to the principal axis through a common point called the principal focus. Similarly, rays passing through the focus will be reflected parallel to the principal axis.

THE MIRROR EQUATION: This expresses a simple relationship between the object and image distances, as measured to the principal focus.

$$S_i S_o = f^2$$

where S_o = object's distance from focus
S_i = image distance from focus
f = focal length.

Also, $\dfrac{H_i}{H_o} = \dfrac{f}{S_o} = \dfrac{S_i}{f}$

where H_i = image size
H_o = object size.

EXERCISE A

1. In Figure 1, M is a man in front of a mirror AB, and P and Q are objects located as shown.
   (a) Will the man be able to see himself in the mirror?
   (b) Will the man be able to see object P by looking at the mirror?
   (c) Will he be able to see object Q in the mirror?
   (d) Where will the image of P be located?

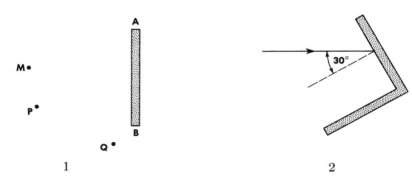

1   2

2. A ray of light strikes one of two plane mirrors that are at right angles to each other, as shown in Figure 2. Determine the subsequent path of this ray.

3. In Figure 1, will the image of P change position when the man M walks toward the mirror?

4. In Figure 3, a candle is placed in front of two perpendicular mirrors, such as those shown in Figure 2. The camera records three images. Show by means of a ray diagram why three images of the candle appear. (Your solution to Question 2 should help.)

5. A man stands 6 ft in front of a plane mirror.
   (a) How far is he from his virtual image?
   (b) If he steps back 1 ft, what distance will now separate him from his image?
   (c) If he walks away from the mirror at a speed of 3 ft/sec, what will his speed be relative to his image?

3

6. A distant object is brought toward a concave spherical mirror. Describe the changes in size of image as the object is brought from far away to the centre of curvature.

7. What change takes place in the image when the object in Question 6 approaches the focus?

8. Under what conditions will the concave mirror of Question 6 produce an upright image?

9. Where should an object be placed so that its image, as formed by a concave mirror, is upright and as large as possible?

10. You are given a concave spherical mirror. Suggest a method whereby you could determine its focal length.

11. What kinds of mirrors could be used, and where should the object be placed to produce the following images:
    (a) an enlarged real image
    (b) a reduced real image
    (c) a real image the same size as the object
    (d) an enlarged virtual image
    (e) a reduced virtual image.

12. A concave mirror has a focal length of 24 cm. What is its radius of curvature?

EXERCISE B

Note: Ray diagrams should be used wherever possible in the solution to the following problems. The diagrams must be drawn accurately to scale. Always choose a metric scale.

1. A man 6.00 ft tall stands 8.00 ft in front of a vertically-placed plane mirror. His eyes are 5.70 ft above floor level. If the man is to see an image of his entire self, determine:
   (a) the minimum size of the mirror
   (b) its height above the floor.

   Draw a ray diagram accurately to scale. (Hint: If the mirror is to be of minimum length, light reflected from the man's shoes should be reflected to the man's eyes from the bottom of the mirror.)

2. How would your answer to Question 1 be altered if the mirror were placed 4.00 ft from the man?

3. An object is located four times farther from a concave mirror than is the focus. Draw a ray diagram to show how the image is formed.

4. Repeat Question 3, using instead a convex mirror.

5. Light from a distant star is collected by a concave mirror whose radius of curvature is 6.00 ft.
   (a) What is the focal length of the mirror?
   (b) Where will the image be located?

6. An object is placed 45.0 cm from a concave mirror whose focal length is 15.0 cm.
   (a) Determine by scale drawing the position of the image.
   (b) Is the image larger or smaller than the object? By what factor?

7. An object and its image in a concave mirror are the same size when the object is 18.0 cm from the mirror. What is the focal length of the mirror?

8. A candle 5.0 cm high is placed at the 0.0 cm end of a metre stick. A convex mirror is located at the 50.0 cm mark on the ruler. The focal length of the mirror is 20.0 cm.
   (a) At what point on the metre stick will the image be formed?
   (b) How tall will the image be?

9. A concave mirror of radius 3.50 m is used to form an image of the moon. The rays from the moon that reach the mirror may be considered as parallel.
   (a) Where will the image of the moon be located?
   (b) The distance from earth to the moon is 3.8×10^8 m. What will be the ratio of image size to object size?
   (c) If the diameter of the moon is 2.16×10^3 miles, what will the size of the image be?

10. An object is placed 42.0 cm from a concave mirror, and the real image appears at 21.0 cm from the mirror.
    (a) Determine the focal length of the mirror. (Here S_o and S_i are unknown, but each may be expressed in terms of f.)
    (b) If the image is 3.0 cm high, what is the height of the object?
    (c) Check your answer to (a) by an accurately constructed ray diagram.

11. The relationship $S_i S_o = f^2$ is true for convex as well as concave mirrors. Try to prove this relationship using a ray diagram for a convex mirror.

12. The convex rear-view mirror in an automobile has a radius of curvature of 6.4 m.
    (a) What is the focal length of the mirror?
    (b) Another car is located 45 m from this mirror. Determine the location of its image, using a ray diagram. Check your answer using a formula.
    (c) If the trailing automobile is 1.5 m high, what is the size of the image?

Reflection of Light

Experiment 27

To determine the location of an image produced by a plane mirror, and to verify the laws of reflection.

Plane mirror

Unruled paper

Pins

Procedure

1. Draw a straight line AB across the mid-section of a sheet of unruled paper.

2. Place a plane mirror vertically in its holder with the reflecting surface along AB.

3. Place a pin as an object approximately 10 cm in front of the mirror at O.

4. Draw an identifying mark in the form of a circle on the paper at the base of the pin.

5. Place a pin at D, and by sighting, place a pin at E so that D and E are on a line of sight with the image in the mirror.

6. Repeat step 5 by placing two pins F and G, to the right of the object so that they are in a line of sight with the image of pin O.

7. Remove the mirror and draw a straight line through ED to continue behind the mirror position AB.

8. Draw a straight line through FG to meet ED extended at I. The point I is the location of the image of pin O.

Analysis

1. Measure the distance from the mirror of the object pin at O, and also the distance of its image from the mirror. How do they compare?

2. Join point O to points P and Q respectively as shown in the diagram. OP and OQ then represent the incident rays by which the image of the pin was seen by reflection along the paths PE and QG respectively. Measure the angles of incidence and reflection for each case.

What conclusions do you reach?

Experiment 28

To locate an image by the parallax method.

Plane mirror
Object, such as a candle
Upright wire supported by a cork
Ruler

A lighted candle is positioned behind the mirror so that parallax between it and the image of the other candle is non-existent. In such a location one appears to be the extension of the other.

In Experiment 27, the image of a pin was located by establishing two lines of sight, each line of sight including the image. The intersection of the lines of sight then determined the location of the image. In this experiment, we shall locate the image of an object by a process known as the *parallax method*.

Parallax is the apparent change in position of one object relative to another when they are viewed from different locations. You can observe parallax by holding up one finger of each hand and sighting along them. When you move your head from side to side, one finger appears to move relative to the other. Continue this motion as you move the fingers closer to each other. You will notice the apparent shift, or parallax decrease. What do you notice when the fingers are touching?

The location of the image produced by a plane mirror can be found by making use of parallax.

Procedure

1. Place an object in front of an upright plane mirror.

2. Position behind the mirror another object, such as an upright wire supported on a cork. Adjust its location until no parallax is observed as you view the image and the wire from different positions.

When no shift is observed, the wire is located at the position of the image.

3. Measure the image and object distance from the mirror.

Analysis

What do your measurements suggest about the location of an image produced by a plane mirror?

258

Experiment 29

To study the properties of a concave mirror.

> Concave mirror
>
> Flashlight bulb and socket, with battery
>
> Metre stick
>
> Modelling clay to support mirror
>
> Parallax indicator
>   (straight wire, or pin in a cork)

Procedure

1. Support a concave mirror on a metre stick, as shown, locating it at the 10 cm mark.

2. Place the lighted flashlight bulb at a distance of a few metres from the front of the mirror. Locate the image of the bulb by moving a small white card between the object (the flashlight bulb) and the mirror. (Be careful not to block the entire path of light between image and mirror.) When the image is properly located, it will be sharply formed on the screen. Record the location of the image. Its distance to the mirror is the *focal length* of the mirror. Why? The image is now located at the *principal focus* or *focal point*.

3. With the object in this position, try to locate the image in Experiment 28, using the upright pin supported by a cork as a parallax indicator.

4. Move the object to the end of the metre stick, and obtain the image on the screen. Record in a table the location of the object and of the image, as measured from the previously determined focal-point. Record these measurements as S_o and S_i respectively. Record also the nature of the image, and its approximate size as compared to the object size.

5. Note particularly the location of the object that coincides with the location of the image.

6. Note what happens to the image as the object nears the principal focus. Can you locate the image when the object is at the principal focus?

7. Locate the image for two positions of the object between the principal focus and the mirror. To do so, you must use the method of parallax. What change do you note in the appearance of the image? As before, record S_o and S_i, the distances of object and image from the focus.

Analysis

1. From your table of corresponding values of S_o and S_i, determine their product. What do you notice about it? How is it related to the focal length? Express the relationship by a formula.

2. Under what circumstances is the image in the concave mirror inverted?

3. At what distance from the principal focus did object and image coincide? How is this distance related to the focal length?

Chapter 15

Refraction of Light

Much was learned about waves from our experiments in Chapter 11. When plane waves encountered a shallow section of the ripple tank, the speed of the waves was noticeably reduced. Perhaps more striking was the sudden change in direction taken by the wavefronts when they met obliquely the line separating the deep from the shallow water (see Figure 11-16).

Accompanying the decrease in speed was a decrease in wavelength, or distance between adjacent crests. This we could predict from the wave equation $v = f\lambda$: a decrease in speed, v, will be accompanied by a proportional decrease in wavelength, provided the frequency remains unchanged from the deep to the shallow water.

That the frequency *is* unchanged is easily verified by stopping the waves with a hand stroboscope. A viewing rate that stops the deep-water waves also stops those in the shallow portion. This is to be expected: the number of waves leaving the deep water each second must equal the number entering the shallow water each second.

We are aware that light bends when it encounters a change in medium. Two simple illustrations of this appear in Figures 15-1 and 15-2. In this chapter we shall investigate in some detail this bending of light caused by a change in its speed. The term *refraction* is employed to describe such bending. We shall use our concept of light as a wave disturbance as outlined in Chapter 13.

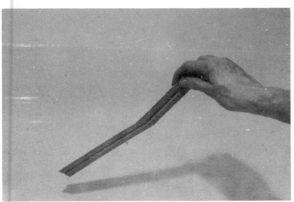

Fig. 15-1: *A familiar effect produced by the refraction of light. Light leaving the submerged portion of the ruler bends in such a manner that its depth appears less than it actually is.*

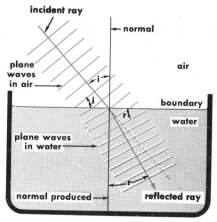

Fig. 15-2: *Another illustration of refraction. At the left, a coin is located at the bottom of the tumbler. When covered with water, the coin appears.*

1. REFRACTION AND THE SPEED OF LIGHT

One of the most important experiments of the nineteenth century was carried out by the French physicist Jean Foucault. In 1850, he successfully demonstrated that the speed of light is lower in water than in air. His findings gave conclusive evidence of the wave nature of light and were contrary to what had been predicted by the particle theory.

Mindful of this fact, we would expect a train of plane waves of light entering water from air to be bent in the manner shown in Figure 15-3. It is convenient to indicate the direction of propagation of the waves by a straight line called a *ray*, drawn perpendicular to the wave fronts. The portion of each wave front that first enters the water undergoes a decrease in speed, which results in a bending of the ray toward the normal at the point of incidence.

It is convenient to define the directions of the incident and refracted rays by the angle that each makes with the normal to the surface. These are the angles i and r in the figure. Note that each is respectively equal to the angle made by the corresponding wavefront and the surface of the refracting medium.

The term *optical density* is often used in describing the relative speed of light in a medium. The slower the speed in a particular medium, the greater is its optical density. Thus a medium of high optical density provides a higher degree of refraction than does a medium of low optical density. Optical density has no relation to the weight density or mass density studied in earlier chapters.

Fig. 15-3: *Plane waves entering water from air. A ray perpendicular to the wavefronts indicates the direction of travel of the waves. The angles of incidence and refraction are indicated by i and r respectively.*

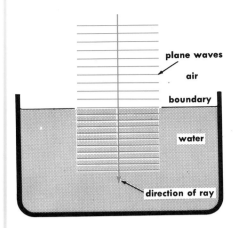

plane waves

air

boundary

water

direction of ray

Figure 15-4 illustrates the absence of bending when the wave fronts are parallel to the refracting surface (see also Figure 11-17).

2. INDEX OF REFRACTION

The apparatus shown in Figure 15-5, called an optical disk, may be used to study the refractive properties of glass or other transparent solids. At the centre of the disk, a semicircular piece of glass is mounted with its flat edge along one diameter of the disk. The graduated circumference of the disk permits us to read directly the angle of refraction for various angles of incidence.

Fig. 15-4: *No bending of wavefronts occurs when the wavefronts are parallel to the boundary. A change in wavelength takes place, as before.*

In the particular case shown, the angle of refraction is 18° for an angle of incidence of 30°. No bending occurs when the ray of light re-enters air from the semicircular block because it is travelling perpendicular to the surface at that point.

Experiments similar in principle to this were carried out by Snell in the seventeenth century. Snell found that a simple relationship existed concerning the angles of incidence and refraction for a given medium.

In Experiment 30 we shall investigate this relationship, but reference to it will be made at this point. Figure 15-6 illustrates a semicircular block of glass ABC with incident ray PO and refracted ray OQ. Point O represents the centre of the circle of which the block is a part, and GOC is the normal to the surface at that point. AGB is a semicircular arc of the same radius and centre as the glass block; MN and RS are perpendicular to the normal, drawn from points M and R of the resulting circle, and are semichords of this circle.

Fig. 15-5: *The optical disk is helpful in studying the reflecting and refractive properties of materials. Note the simultaneous reflection and refraction here. Are the laws of reflection obeyed?*

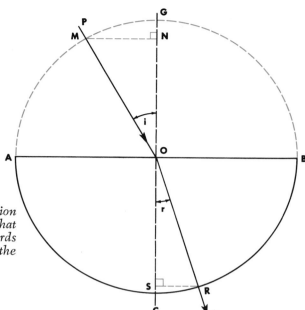

Fig. 15-6: *A ray PO is bent in the direction OQ by a glass block ABC. Snell found that for a given material the ratio of semichords MN and RS was constant, regardless of the angle of incidence.*

Snell found that, regardless of the direction of the incident ray *PO*, the *ratio* of the semichords was constant. We may state this relationship as follows:

If a circle be drawn about the point of incidence, the ratio of semichords of this circle, drawn from the incident and refracted rays, is a constant. This constant is called the *index of refraction* of the material and is dependent upon what incident medium is used. Unless otherwise stated, the incident medium is assumed to be air. For water, the index of refraction is 1.33, and for glass, 1.5.

Stated as such, the above relationship, known as Snell's Law, involves only indirectly the angles of incidence and refraction. A statement of this law using angles rather than semichords requires an understanding of what is meant by the *sine* function (abbreviated *sin*) of an angle, but it is much more useful in this form. The meaning of the sine function is outlined on page 264.

An equivalent statement of Snell's Law then becomes:

For any two media, the ratio of the sines of the angles of incidence and refraction is a constant: sin *i* / sin *r* = a constant. This constant is the index of refraction from the first to the second medium. The symbol used for index of refraction is *n*.

A most important interpretation of the index of refraction involves the speed of light in the incident and refracting media. Using the concept of light as a wave motion, it is easily shown that the index of refraction is equal to the ratio of speeds in the two media. That is,

$$\frac{\text{speed of light in incident medium}}{\text{speed of light in refracting medium}}$$

$$= \frac{v_1}{v_2}$$

= index of refraction from first to second medium.

This relationship is derived on page 264.

1. **Trigonometry** is a branch of mathematics that deals with the ratios of the sides of a right triangle. In Figure 15-7, for the triangle ABC, we could state three such ratios; a/c, b/c, a/b. Including their reciprocals, c/a, c/b, b/a, there are six ratios in all. Each is given a specific name, but in this chapter we need only concern ourselves with one of these. This is the *sine* ratio, or sine function.

For the right triangle ABC, the sine of angle A is defined as the ratio of the opposite side to the hypotenuse, i.e. a/c.

$$\sin A = a/c$$

If we make the same angle A part of a larger right triangle, such as $AB'C'$, the ratio a'/c' is identical to a/c, because the two triangles are similar.

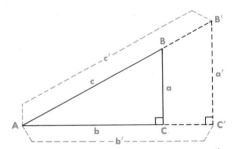

Fig. 15-7: *For angle A, $\sin A = \dfrac{a}{c} = \dfrac{a^1}{c^1}$*

Returning to Figure 15-6, we see that $\sin i = \dfrac{MN}{MO}$ and $\sin r = \dfrac{SR}{OR} = \dfrac{SR}{MO}$ (because OR and MO are radii of the same circle).

Hence $\dfrac{\sin i}{\sin r} = \dfrac{MN}{MO} \div \dfrac{SR}{MO} = \dfrac{MN}{SR}$.

Thus, index of refraction $= \dfrac{\sin i}{\sin r}$.

Sine ratios for acute angles are tabulated in the appendix.

2. The relationship between the velocities of light in two media and the index of refraction of the refracting medium may be obtained by making the following analysis:

In Figure 15-8, wavefronts AA' and BB', are shown approaching obliquely an air-to-glass surface. Point C of wavefront CC' is just entering the glass, while part DO of wavefront DD' is already in glass, and has been bent because of its reduced speed. The portion OD' of this wavefront has travelled the distance EO in the same time that the part of the wave at point D has travelled the distance CD.

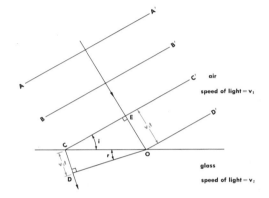

Fig. 15-8: *Construction used in showing that index of refraction is equal to the ratio of speeds in the two media.*

If we represent this time by t, then

$$EO = v_1 t \text{ and } CD = v_2 t.$$
(distance = speed × time)

$$\sin i = \frac{v_1 t}{CO} \text{ and } \sin r = \frac{v_2 t}{CO}$$

$$\therefore \frac{\sin i}{\sin r} = \frac{v_1 t}{CO} \div \frac{v_2 t}{CO} = \frac{v_1}{v_2}$$

Thus, **the index of refraction is equal to the ratio of the speeds in the two media.**

Furthermore, from the wave equation $v = f\lambda$ we may state that $\dfrac{v_1}{v_2} = \dfrac{f\lambda_1}{f\lambda_2} = \dfrac{\lambda_1}{\lambda_2}$, where λ_1 and λ_2 are the wavelengths of light in the first and second medium respectively.

In summary, we may state four equivalent interpretations of the index of refraction, n.

$$n = \text{ratio of semichords} = \frac{\sin i}{\sin r} = \frac{v_1}{v_2} = \frac{\lambda_1}{\lambda_2}$$

Table 15-1.

Index of Refraction

Air	1.00
Alcohol, ethyl	1.36
Benzene	1.50
Carbon disulphide	1.63
Carbon tetrachloride	1.46
Diamond	2.42
Glass, crown	1.52
Glass, flint	1.61
Water	1.33
Water vapour	1.00

EXAMPLE 1

In Figure 15-5, a ray of light enters glass from air at an angle of incidence of 30°. The angle of refraction is 18°. What is the index of refraction from air to glass?

Solution:

Two methods are possible. The first employs a circle diagram similar to that in Figure 15-6. The semichords are drawn, and the ratio MN/RS is found to be **1.60.**

The second method involves finding the ratio $\sin i/\sin r$, employing a table of sines.

$$\sin 30° = 0.500$$
$$\sin 18° = 0.309$$
$$\sin 30°/\sin 18° = \mathbf{1.62.}$$

EXAMPLE 2

The speed of light in air is 3.00×10^8 m/sec. What is its speed in water if the index of refraction of water is 1.33?

Solution:

$$\frac{v_{\text{air}}}{v_{\text{water}}} = 1.33$$

$$v_{\text{water}} = \frac{v_{\text{air}}}{1.33} = \frac{3.00}{1.33} \times 10^8 \text{ m/sec}$$

$$= \mathbf{2.26 \times 10^8 \text{ m/sec.}}$$

3. PATH OF A RAY THROUGH A RECTANGULAR PRISM

In Figure 15-9, EO is a ray of light incident at an angle i at point O of a rectangular prism of glass. Upon entering the glass, the ray is bent toward the normal, making an angle of refraction r. On leaving the glass, the ray is bent away from the normal by an amount equal to that by which it was bent toward the normal, and emerges from the glass at point R in a direction parallel to its initial direction. Note, however, that the path of the ray RQ is displaced from the original path EO.

Consider now a ray QR incident at point R of the block. The path of this ray through the glass will be the same as that shown in Figure 15-9, and the ray will emerge along the path OE. Thus, **the path taken by a ray of light is unchanged when its direction of travel is reversed.** The student can verify this by placing two pins on one side

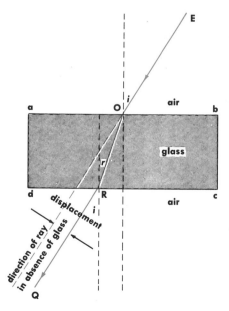

Fig. 15-9: *A ray of light passing through the parallel surfaces of a medium emerges in a direction parallel to its initial direction.*

ab of the block, at points such as O and E, and two pins on the other side *cd* in such a position that the four pins appear aligned when viewed from the side *cd*. If the four pins are then viewed from side *ab*, they will still appear to be aligned.

4. PATH OF LIGHT THROUGH A TRIANGULAR PRISM

If the refracting surfaces are not parallel, the direction of the ray on emerging will not be parallel to its initial direction. Such is the case for the triangular prism in Figure 15-10. Here, as before, the ray is bent toward the normal on entering the glass, and away from the normal on emerging. The angular displacement of the ray, as indicated by the angle θ, is called *deviation*. Figure 13-3 is a photograph of refraction produced by a right triangular prism.

In Chapter 13, reference was made to the ability of a triangular prism to separate the components of white light (Figure 13-6). It is found that for a given angle of incidence, deviation is least for red light, and greatest for violet light. This would suggest that the speed of violet light in glass is lower than that of red light, and accordingly that the index of refraction of the material is somewhat dependent upon the colour of light being considered.

5. TOTAL INTERNAL REFLECTION

A ray of light entering glass from air is, as we have seen, refracted toward the normal. When emerging from the glass into air, the ray is bent away from the normal. Figure 15-11 illustrates four such rays entering air from an optically denser medium, such as water. As the angle of incidence increases, the direction of emergence becomes closer to the surface separating the water from air. For ray 3, the angle of refraction is 90°: that is, the refracted ray will skim along the surface of the water. The angle of incidence i_3 is called the *critical angle* for a water-to-air surface. For a ray such as 4, whose angle of incidence is greater than the critical angle, no refraction takes place and the ray is totally reflected at the point of incidence.

This phenomenon is called *total internal reflection*; it can occur only when light meets a medium of an optical density lower than that in which it is travelling, at an angle greater than the critical angle.

The critical angle for any substance may be determined by experiment or by the method shown in the following example.

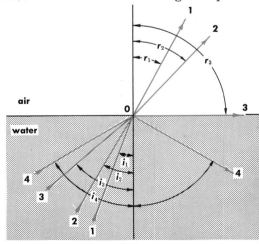

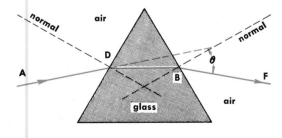

Fig. 15-10: *When the refracting surfaces are not parallel, as for this triangular prism, the direction of the ray is changed. The angle θ is called the deviation of ray AD.*

Fig. 15-11: *When light enters air from a denser medium, it is bent away from the normal. If the angle of incidence is greater than a certain value, no refraction takes place and the ray is totally reflected at the surface. Ray 4 is such a ray.*

EXAMPLE 3

Find the critical angle for light entering air from glass (index of refraction 1.5)

Solution:

We shall solve this problem in two ways, each making use of the fact that the path of a ray of light is reversible. Thus we shall consider a ray of light that *enters* glass at an angle of incidence of 90°.

1. Draw a circle with its centre at the point of incidence. The radius of this circle will be the semichord for a ray AO whose angle of incidence is 90°. Suppose this semichord is 5.0 cm in length. Then the semichord for the ray in glass will be $\frac{5.0}{1.5}$ cm = 3.3 cm. This semichord may be located by trial. It is the line PQ in the diagram. The ray OP can then be drawn. The angle of refraction r for the refracted ray OP is found to be 42°. Thus the critical angle for light entering air from glass is about **42°**.

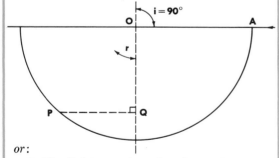

or:

2. For light entering glass from air,

$$\frac{\sin i}{\sin r} = 1.5.$$

If the angle of incidence, i, is 90°, $\sin i = 1.00$ and $\sin r = \frac{1.00}{1.5} = 0.67.$

From the table of sines (see appendix) we discover that the angle whose sine is 0.67 is 42°.

Thus when the ray is reversed, the critical angle in glass is **42°**.

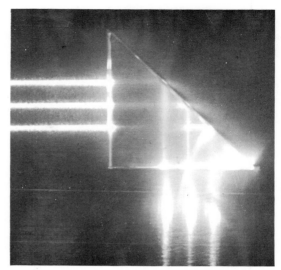

Fig. 15-12: *Light entering this right triangular prism is totally reflected at the oblique surface. Many optical instruments employ this principle.*

An important application of total internal reflection is shown in Figure 15-12. Here a right triangular prism is used to change the path of light by 90°. The angle of incidence at the oblique surface is 45°, slightly greater than the critical angle for glass, and total internal reflection takes place at this surface. A mirror could be used to serve the same purpose, but the polished surface of a mirror absorbs more light than does the prism.

A novel example of total internal reflection is shown in Figure 15-13. Here light is conveyed from one end to the other of a "light pipe" by several internal reflections. A minimum amount of light is lost through the walls of the tube.

The high brilliance of a diamond is due to total internal reflection. In this material, the critical angle is very low—about 24°. Light entering a properly-cut diamond from any side undergoes reflection from the internal surfaces and passes out through the top surface.

E. I. du Pont de Nemours and Company, Inc.

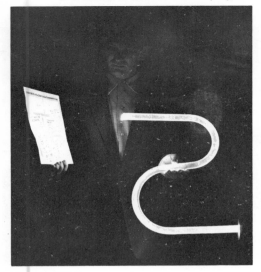

Fig. 15-13: *A further illustration of total reflection. Light entering this "light pipe" from the right is totally reflected by the walls, and emerges at the left.*

6. LENSES

In Figure 15-10, we observed that a ray of light passing through a triangular prism is bent toward the thicker portion of the prism. If two such prisms are placed with their bases in contact, the effect on parallel rays is to make them cross one another's paths in two groups of parallel rays, as shown in Figure 15-14(a). If the surfaces of these prisms are rounded to produce spherical surfaces, the incident parallel rays now converge to a point after leaving the refracting device. This effect is shown in Figure 15-15(a). The device is called a *converging*

lens, and the point at which the rays converge is called the *principal focus* of the lens.

If the two prisms are positioned as in Figure 15-14(b), the emerging rays diverge in two groups of parallel rays. If the surfaces of the prisms are then made spherical, the rays do not emerge parallel to each other, but appear to diverge from a single point, as shown in Figure 15-15(b). This is a *diverging lens,* and the point from which the rays appear to diverge is called the *virtual focus.* The term "virtual" signifies that the diverging rays do not actually pass through this point.

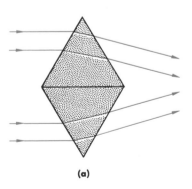

(a)

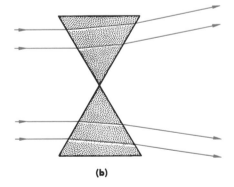

(b)

Fig. 15-14: *(a) Parallel rays, incident upon two prisms positioned as shown, are refracted into two groups of parallel rays that cross each other's path. (b) Prisms positioned as shown create two groups of parallel rays that diverge.*

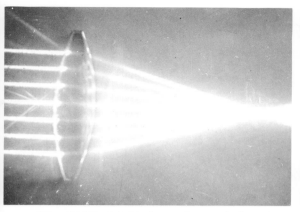 

Fig. 15-15: *(a) If the surfaces of the prisms of Figure 15-14 are made spherical, parallel rays entering the resulting lens are refracted by different amounts, and converge to a point called the principal focus. (b) When the surfaces of the prisms are made inversely spherical, parallel rays entering the resulting lens appear to diverge from a single point in front of the lens. This point is called the virtual focus. Note the reflection at the front surfaces of each lens. These surfaces act as mirrors.*

7. CONVERGING LENSES

The converging property of a lens can be investigated by considering a train of plane waves incident upon it. In Figure 15-16, plane waves approaching the lens from the left slow down when they enter the glass. The portion of each wave front near the axis of the lens is retarded by an amount greater than the rest of the wavefront because it has the greatest distance to travel in glass. The result is a permanent bending of the wavefront. If the surfaces of the lens are spherical, the emerging wavefronts are spherical

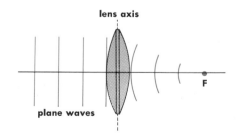

Fig. 15-16: *That part of a plane wave that passes through a converging lens is retarded the most, resulting in a spherical wavefront with the principal focus as centre.*

in shape and converge to the principal focus at *F*.

A similar effect can be observed in a ripple tank by using a glass lens on the bottom of the tank to form a shallow region of water. The shallow region serves as a medium of decreased wave velocity. Plane waves passing over this shallow region become curved, as illustrated in Figure 15-17. Note also the decrease in wavelength in the low-velocity medium.

It is evident that any lens that is thicker in the middle than in the extremities will be a converging lens. Three types of converging lenses are illustrated in Figure 15-18.

8. FORMATION OF IMAGES BY CONVERGING LENSES

The widest application of the refraction of light makes use of the ability of a lens to produce an image of an object placed in front of it. By this is meant that any ray of light leaving a point in the object will, after emerging from the lens, pass through, or appear to pass through, a fixed point called the image of that point. The images of all points making up the object constitute the image of the object.

269

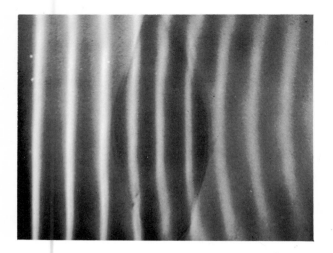

Fig. 15-17: *Waves from a straight wave generator in a ripple tank, after passing over the shallow region indicated, assume the curvature typical of that produced by a converging lens. Note the decrease in wavelength in the shallow region.*

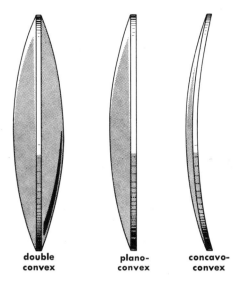

double convex   **plano-convex**   **concavo-convex**

Fig. 15-18: *Three types of converging lens. Note that each is thickest along its axis.*

In discussing how the image can be located, we shall make use of two rays whose paths are directly predictable. In Figure 15-19, ray *1* is parallel to the axis of the lens. As we have seen, this ray, after being refracted, passes through the principal axis at the principal focus *F*. Ray *2* is a ray leaving the object in a direction that takes it through the centre of the lens. If the lens is thin,

this second ray undergoes no refraction because the lens surfaces near the axis are almost parallel, causing only a lateral displacement of a ray, as shown in Figure 15-9. This displacement is very small if the lens is thin.

The intersection of these two rays determines the location of the image of the point from which the rays were drawn.

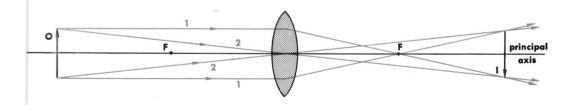

Fig. 15-19: *In determining the location of the image produced by a lens, only two rays need be constructed. These are ray 1, parallel to the axis and refracted through the focus, and ray 2 which passes through the centre, unchanged in direction. The intersection of these rays determines a point in the image.*

270

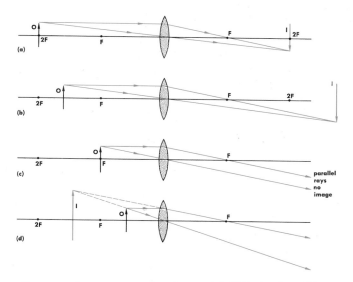

Fig. 15-20: *Ray diagrams for a converging lens. (a) When the object is located away from the lens by a distance equal to twice the focal length, the image is similarly located on the other side of the lens. The image is real, inverted, and the same size as the object. (b) When the object approaches the principal focus, the image becomes larger and recedes. (c) When the object is located at the principal focus, no image is formed. (d) For an object located between focus and lens, a virtual image, upright and magnified, is formed on the same side of the lens. What is the description of the image when the object is located at a greater distance than that shown at (a)?*

Figure 15-20 illustrates how the location of the image is determined for various positions of the object. In (a) and (b) a *real image* is formed; that is, the image can be seen on a screen placed at the proper location. In (d), a *virtual image* is formed. Here the image can be seen by looking through the lens from the opposite side. Rays leaving a point of the object then appear to diverge from a corresponding point of the image.

In (c), no image is formed: the rays emerge parallel to each other.

9. A FORMULA FOR LENSES

In Figure 15-21, three rays are employed to locate the position of the image produced by a converging lens. In addition to the two rays used in the previous section, a ray is shown leaving the object and passing through the focus that lies on the object side of the lens. These three rays intersect at a point.

Considering the similar coloured triangles, we find that $\dfrac{H_i}{H_o} = \dfrac{S_i}{f}$.

Also, from the two other shaded triangles,

$$\frac{H_i}{H_o} = \frac{f}{S_o}.$$

Combining these, we obtain

$$\frac{S_i}{f} = \frac{f}{S_o}, \text{ or } S_i S_o = f^2.$$

Note that these relationships are identical to those derived for spherical mirrors. However, the values of S_i and S_o are determined somewhat differently. S_o is the distance from object to focus on the object side of the lens, whereas S_i is the distance from the image to the other focus. It is important to remember that object and image are located on opposite sides of the lens, except when the object lies between the lens and principal focus (see Figure 15-20).

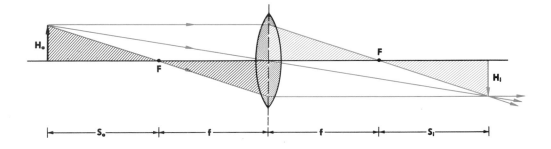

Fig. 15-21: *Diagram used in deriving the lens equation.*

EXAMPLE 4

An object is placed 14.0 cm from a convex lens of focal length 10.0 cm. Determine the location of the image, and its relative size.

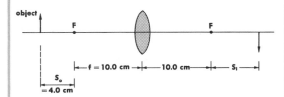

Solution:

$$S_o = 4.0 \text{ cm}$$
$$f = 10.0 \text{ cm}$$
$$S_i S_o = f^2$$
$$\therefore S_i = \frac{100}{4.0} \text{ or } 25 \text{ cm.}$$

Thus the image is located 25 cm from the focus on the other side of the lens: that is, **35 cm** from the lens.

The relative size of the image may be determined from

$$\frac{H_i}{H_o} = \frac{f}{S_o} = \frac{10.0}{4.0} = 2.5.$$

The image is **2.5 times the size of the object.**

EXAMPLE 5

An object is placed 6.0 cm from the convex lens in the previous example. Determine the location and magnification of the image.

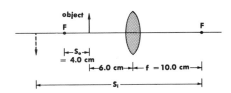

Solution:

Because the object is between lens and focus, we know that a virtual image will be formed.

Again, $S_o = 4.0$ cm
$$f = 10.0 \text{ cm}$$
$$S_i S_o = f^2 \quad \therefore S_i = \frac{100}{4.0} \text{ or } \textbf{25 cm.}$$

This **25 cm** is measured from the focus behind the lens in a direction toward the object. This locates the image 9.0 cm behind the object, that is, 15 cm from the lens, on the same side as the object.

$$\frac{H_i}{H_o} = \frac{f}{S_o} = 2.5$$

Thus the magnification is **2.5**, as in the previous example.

10. DIVERGING LENSES

In Figure 15-22, a train of plane waves approaches a lens. All parts of each wave front are slowed down while passing through the lens. Because the part of each wavefront near the axis of the lens is the last to enter the lens, and the first to leave it, the emerging wavefronts are curved in the manner indicated. The emerging wavefronts are now spherical, and appear to emanate from a point F in front of the lens. F is the *virtual focus* of the lens.

It is evident that any lens thinner in the middle than elsewhere will produce curved wavefronts that appear to be sent from a virtual focus that is located in front of the lens. Such lenses are called diverging lenses; three common examples are illustrated in Figure 15-23.

A ray diagram for a diverging lens enables us to determine the location of the image of an object placed in front of the lens. An example is shown in Figure 15-24. The two rays used to determine the image of each point are as follows: a ray parallel to the axis, which, on passing through the lens, appears to emanate from the virtual focus, and a ray passing through the centre of the lens, which, for reasons previously stated, continues in its original direction. The image thus formed is a virtual upright image, and is located between the lens and the virtual focus.

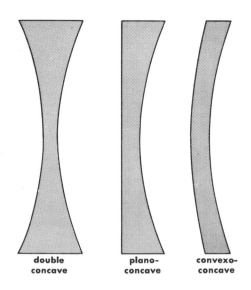

double concave   **plano- concave**   **convexo- concave**

Fig. 15-23: *Three types of diverging lens. How do they differ from converging lenses?*

A study of Figure 15-24 will show that if the object AB moves toward the lens, so will the image. Thus the image is always located between object and lens.

The equation $S_i S_o = f^2$ is true for diverging lenses provided the object distance S_o is measured to the focus on the other side of the lens. The image distance S_i is measured to the focus on the image side of the lens (which, for diverging lenses, is the same side as that of the object).

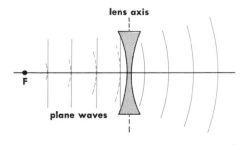

Fig. 15-22: *When the plane waves approach this lens, the central part of each wavefront is retarded the least. The wave emerges with a curvature that makes it appear to emanate from a point in front of the lens.*

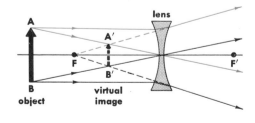

Fig. 15-24: *A diverging lens produces a virtual image. The image of object AB can be seen by looking through the lens from the right. Rays entering the eye appear to come from points along the line A' B'.*

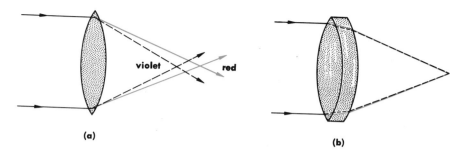

(a)

(b)

Fig. 15-25: *Chromatic aberration is the inability of a single lens to focus all colours at a single point. It is minimized by combining a converging lens with a weak diverging lens.*

EXAMPLE 6

In Figure 15-24, the virtual focus is located 10.0 cm from the lens. If the object is placed 15.0 cm from the lens, where is the image?

Solution:

The problem may be solved by drawing a ray diagram or by using the equation $S_i S_o = f^2$. Here, $S_o = 15.0 + 10.0 = 25.0$ cm

$$f = 10.0 \text{ cm}$$

$$S_i = \frac{f^2}{S_o} = \frac{100}{25.0} = 4.00 \text{ cm}.$$

Thus the image will be **4.00 cm from the focus (on the object side) between the focus and lens.**

11. CHROMATIC ABERRATION

We know that white light is composed of individual components of different wavelengths, each component giving a particular colour sensation after entering the eye. The index of refraction of each component differs slightly from that of the other components, and, accordingly, each is bent by a slightly different amount when entering glass.

In Figure 15-25(a), white light enters the lens from the left. The components of the white light will be brought to a focus at slightly different places on the principal axis. The violet light will focus nearest the lens, while the longer wavelengths of orange and red light focus farther from it. This effect, called *chromatic* or *colour aberration*, produces colour fringes in the image, undesirable in photographic and other optical work.

Chromatic aberration can be minimized by employing two lenses, one a converging lens and the other a diverging lens. The two lenses, each made of different glass, are placed in contact, as in Figure 15-25(b). The diverging lens diverges the violet light to a greater extent than it does the red, and as a result the two cross the principal axis at a common focus. This combination of lenses, called an *achromatic lens*, is said to be *colour-corrected*.

REFRACTION: This refers to the change in direction of travel undergone by a ray of light when entering a different medium.

SNELL'S LAW: The statement that for two given media, the angles of incidence and refraction are related according to the formula sin i/sin r = a constant. This constant is called the index of refraction from the first to the second medium, and may also be interpreted as the ratio of speeds in the two media, or the ratio of wavelengths in these media.

TOTAL INTERNAL REFLECTION: This may take place when light enters a medium of lower optical density, that is, one in which its speed increases. If the angle of incidence in the optically-denser medium is greater than a certain value, called the *critical angle*, the incident light will be entirely reflected.

CONVERGING LENSES: These are capable of refracting a bundle of parallel rays to a point, called the principal focus. The distance from the principal focus to the centre of the lens is called the focal length. Every converging lens has two principal foci, and for thin lenses, they are equidistant from the lens centre, on the principal axis of the lens.

DIVERGING LENSES: These cause a bundle of parallel rays to diverge as though they passed through a point in front of the lens, called the *virtual focus*.

Either type of lens can form an image. A converging lens may form either a real image that can be seen on a screen, or a virtual image. Diverging lenses form virtual images only.

RAY TRACING: This technique may be employed to locate the position of an image formed by a lens. To locate the image, only two rays need be traced from the object: one parallel to the principal axis and the other in a direction that takes it through the lens centre.

THE LENS FORMULA: This may also be used to determine the image location:
$$S_i S_o = f^2$$
For converging lenses: S_o = distance from object to the focus on the object side of lens
S_i = distance from image to the other focus.
For diverging lenses: S_o = distance from object to focus on the other side of lens
S_i = distance from image to focus on the object side of lens.

MAGNIFICATION: This may be obtained from the relationship
$$\frac{H_i}{H_o} = \frac{S_i}{f} \quad \text{and} \quad \frac{H_i}{H_o} = \frac{f}{S_o},$$
where H_i and H_o are the size of image and object respectively.

EXERCISE A

1. Describe the direction of bending for a ray of light entering glass from air. How does it bend when re-entering the air?

2. What is meant by the term optical density?

3. Define the term index of refraction.

4. Would you expect a ray entering glass from water to be bent toward the normal, or away from the normal?

5. A ray of light enters a transparent medium at an angle of incidence of zero. What is the angle of refraction?

6. Suppose a bundle of rays converges to a certain point. If a thick piece of plate glass is placed in the path of the rays, would the rays converge to the same point, to a point closer to the source, or to a point farther from the source?

7. The sun viewed from the earth appears higher than it actually is (except when directly overhead) because of refraction by the earth's atmosphere. Indicate in a sketch the manner in which light must bend to create this effect. Figure 15-1 illustrates a situation analagous to that existing at sunrise.

8. What effect would the refraction by the earth's atmosphere have on the duration of daylight?

9. A hunter wishes to shoot a fish whose image can be seen in clear water. Should he aim above or below what he sees?

10. Suppose the prism of Figure 15-10 is immersed in water. Would the deviation of the ray be the same, less, or greater than shown in the illustration? Explain in terms of the speed of light in the two media.

11. What two conditions must be fulfilled in order that a ray be totally reflected at a transparent surface?

12. Why is a right triangular prism a better reflector than a plane silvered surface?

13. (a) Place an object such as a coin on a table beside a glass or beaker that is full of water. Try to observe the coin by looking through the surface of the water.

    (b) Try to observe the coin by looking up through the glass at the underside of the surface of the water.

    Explain your observations by means of a ray diagram.

14. A ray passing through the centre of a thin lens continues in its initial direction. Explain why.

15. How would you determine the focal length of a converging lens?

16. One half of a lens is covered with paper. Will the lens form a complete image of an object? Try it.

17. What change in plane waves is produced by
    (a) a double convex lens?
    (b) a double concave lens?

18. The text suggests that a lens thicker at the centre than at the edges is a converging lens. Can you suggest a situation in which such a lens would be a diverging lens?

19. In the illustration, the location of an object is indicated for each of five cases, *I, II, III, IV, V*. Select the corresponding image location for each from *a, b, c, d* and *e*.

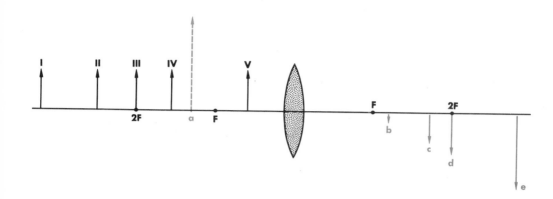

EXERCISE B

Speed of light in air $= 3.00 \times 10^8$ m/sec.

1. A ray of light travelling in air strikes a transparent solid material at an angle of incidence of 30°. The refracted ray makes an angle of 22° with the normal at the point of incidence. Using a circle diagram, find the index of refraction for this material.

2. The angles of incidence and refraction for a certain ray are 50° and 30° respectively. What is the index of refraction of the refracting medium?

3. (*a*) What is the speed of light in the transparent solid medium of Question 1?
   (*b*) What is the speed of light in the medium of Question 2?

4. The index of refraction of a plastic material is 2.00. What is the speed of light in this medium?

5. The speed of light in a certain liquid is 2.1×10^8 m/sec. What is its index of refraction?

6. The wavelength of orange light in air is 6.0×10^{-7} m. What is its wavelength in glass of index of refraction 1.6?

7. (*a*) Determine the sine of each of the following angles by making each angle part of a right triangle and then finding the ratio of appropriate sides.
   (*i*) 30°   (*ii*) 18°   (*iii*) 54°   (*iv*) 90°
   (*b*) Check your answers to (*a*) by referring to the table of sines in the appendix.

8. Each of the following numbers is the sine of an acute angle. Determine the angle to the nearest degree using tables.
   (*i*) 0.210   (*ii*) 0.707   (*iii*) 0.425   (*iv*) 0.928

9. (a) the angle of refraction of a ray entering glass from air is 35°. Using a circle diagram, determine the angle of incidence. The index of refraction of the glass is 1.60.

   (b) Check your answer to (a) by using another method.

10. Repeat Question 9 for a ray whose angle of refraction is 20°.

11. (a) An object located underwater appears closer than it actually is when viewed from above the surface. Consider a coin at the bottom of a beaker that is filled to a depth of 10.0 cm. Locate the image of a point on the coin by drawing two rays—one from the point and travelling vertically upward, and another at an angle of incidence (in water) of, say, 5.0°. The angle of refraction for this latter ray will be 6.5°. What is the apparent depth of the coin when viewed from above?

    (b) Suppose you are fishing from a rowboat, and a fish is looking straight up at you. To the fish, does your fishing rod appear farther away or closer than it actually is?

12. Show, by any method, that the critical angle for a ray entering air from diamond is 24°.

13. The critical angle for a certain material is 35°. Determine its index of refraction.

14. Using Snell's Law in the form $\sin i/\sin r = n$, determine:

    (a) the index of refraction if the angle of incidence in air is 50° and the angle of refraction 30°

    (b) the angle of incidence in air for a ray whose angle of refraction is 30°, in a medium of refractive index 1.40

    (c) the angle of refraction in a medium of refractive index 1.40, if the angle of incidence in air is 60°

    (d) the index of refraction of a medium whose critical angle is 38°

    (e) the angle of incidence in air of a ray whose angle of refraction in water is 30°.

15. The sides of a triangular prism are each 6.0 cm in length. A ray of light enters the mid-point of one of the sides at an angle of incidence of 45°. The refractive index of the material is 1.50. Using an accurately-drawn diagram, determine the deviation of this ray.

16. In each of the following situations, a thin converging lens of focal length 10.0 cm is employed. Determine for each case the location of the image by constructing, accurately to scale, a ray diagram. State whether the image is real or virtual, erect or inverted, if:

    (a) object is located 30.0 cm from the lens

    (b) object is located 20.0 cm from the lens

    (c) object is located 15.0 cm from the lens

    (d) object is located 5.0 cm from the lens.

17. (a) Using the lens formula, determine the image locations for each of the situations in Question 16.

    (b) Determine, in each of the above cases, the magnification of the image.

18. (a) A thin diverging lens of focal length 10.0 cm is used to form an image of an object placed 15.0 cm from the lens. Determine by ray diagram the location of the image.

278

(b) Check your result in (a) by employing the lens equation. What is the relative size of the image?

19. A convex lens has a focal length of 10.0 cm. What size of image will it form of a building 50 m tall located 100 m from the lens?

20. A slide projector has a converging lens of focal length 4.0 in, and the screen is located 10.0 ft from the lens.

    (a) How far from the lens should the slide be placed?
    (b) What magnification will be produced?

Refraction of Light

▶ Experiment 30

To study the path of light through a rectangular prism and to use this path to determine the index of refraction of the prism.

Rectangular prism

4 pins

Compass, ruler and protractor

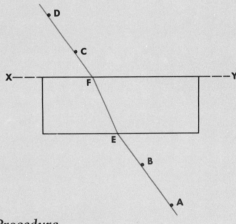

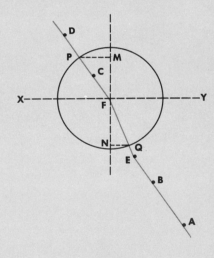

Procedure

1. Draw a straight line XY across a sheet of paper. Place the glass block on the paper with one edge coinciding with XY. Using pencil, outline on paper the four edges of the block.

2. Place pins A and B on one side of the block as illustrated.

3. Look through the opposite side of the block so that you see pins A and B through the glass. Place pins C and D so that all four pins appear in a straight line. Now observe the alignment from the side of the block that lies along XY. It is important that all pins be placed vertically.

4. Remove the block and pins and draw a straight line through AB and CD to meet the outline of the sides at E and F respectively. Join EF.

5. Repeat the above procedure for other locations of pins A and B on a new line XY. In each case draw in the path DCFEBA.

280

Analysis

1. With *F* as centre, draw a circle of radius slightly less than *FE* so that it intersects the incident ray and refracted ray. Call these points of intersection *P* and *Q* respectively.

2. Draw a straight line through *F* perpendicular to *XY*, and construct the semichords *PM* and *QN*.

3. Measure the semichords and find their ratio.

4. Measure the angle that rays *BA* and *DC* make with the face of the block (the line *XY*).

5. Repeat these steps for each set of positions of the four pins.

6. State three major conclusions derived from this experiment.

Experiment 31

To study the path of a ray of light through a triangular prism, and to measure the deviation of this ray.

Triangular prism

4 pins

Ruler and protractor

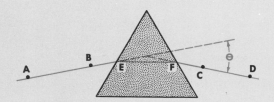

Procedure

1. Place the prism on a sheet of paper and outline with pencil the edges of the prism.

2. Place pins *A* and *B* at least 5 cm apart, as shown in the diagram.

3. Sight pins *A* and *B* through another edge of the prism and locate two pins *C* and *D* on this side of the prism so that *ABCD* appear in line when viewed through the glass. Now sight the pins through the first edge of the prism.

4. Remove the prism and pins and join *A* and *B*, continuing this line to meet the prism outline at *E*. Join *C* and *D* and project this line to meet the prism outline at point *F*. Join *E* and *F*.

5. Extend the lines representing the incident and refracted rays in order to determine the deviation. Measure this angle.

Question

How does refraction by a triangular prism differ from that by a rectangular prism?

281

To determine the index of refraction of a liquid and the critical angle for this liquid.

Semicircular plastic box

2 pins

Protractor

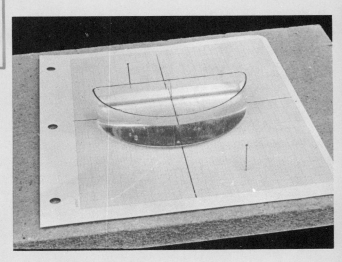

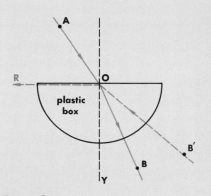

Procedure

Index of Refraction

1. Scratch a vertical line across the straight edge of the plastic box at its centre, if such a line does not already exist. This is point O in the diagram.

2. Place the box on a sheet of paper, fill it two-thirds with water and outline on the paper with pencil the edges of the box.

3. Place pin A at some location opposite the flat edge of the box and view through the curved edge of the box. Place pin B so that the two pins and the vertical scratch appear in alignment. Record in pencil the positions of pins A and B.

Critical angle

4. Remove pins A and B. Now, sighting through the flat edge of the box, slowly re-position pin B away from the normal at point O while keeping it in line with the scratch at O as seen through the box. Continue this until the line of sight lies along the flat edge of the box. Record the positions of pin B (shown in the diagram as B') that produce a line of sight B'OR.

5. Remove the pins and plastic box.

6. Steps 1 to 4 may be repeated using another liquid and sheet of paper.

Analysis

1. Join AOB and determine the index of refraction of the liquid, using either a circle diagram or ratio $\dfrac{\sin i}{\sin r}$.

2. Measure the critical angle B'OY.

Questions

1. Why do we use a box that is semi-circular in cross-section?

2. How would a thick-walled box affect the results of this experiment?

Experiment 33

To study the formation of images by a converging lens.

> Converging lens
>
> 1 or 2 metre sticks
>
> Illuminated object (flashlight bulb)
>
> Small white screen

Procedure

1. Support the lens in a vertical position on the table, using putty or modeling clay. Place the lens beside the metre stick at the 50.0 cm mark.

2. Locate the image of an object that is several meters away by allowing the sharply-focused image to fall on a screen. The rays from this object incident on the lens may be considered parallel. The screen location is then at the principal focus. Record the locations of lens and principal focus. Is the image erect, or is it inverted?

3. Turn the lens around and form the image of the same object. Is the image located at the same place as in step 2?

4. Place the lighted bulb at one end of the ruler and locate its image on the other side of the lens. Record in a table the distances from lens to object and lens to image as d_o and d_i respectively.

5. Move the object closer to the lens and locate the image. Obtain at least four sets of values of d_o and d_i. As the object moves closer to the principal focus, how does the image move? What other change takes place in the image? An additional metre stick may be helpful in recording the image location.

6. Try to locate the image when the object is about 2 cm from the principal focus. Can you locate it when the object is at the principal focus?

7. Move the object past the principal focus. Can you find its image by using the screen? Look through the lens from the side opposite to that of the object. You can locate the image position by parallax. How has the image changed?

8. Record a few corresponding values of d_o and d_i with the object between lens and principal focus.

Analysis

1. From step 2, determine the focal length of the lens.

2. From the table of values of d_o and d_i, calculate for each case the distance of the object from the principal focus on the object side and the distance of the image from the other principal focus. Call these distances S_o and S_i.

3. Evaluate the product $S_o S_i$ for each case, and compare it with f^2.

Questions

1. Under what circumstances does a converging lens produce an enlarged image?

2. Under what circumstances does this lens produce an upright image?

Chapter 16

Optical Instruments

1. THE EYE

The eye is almost spherical in shape and about one inch in diameter. Some idea of its construction and functioning may be obtained from Figure 16-1. The *cornea* is a transparent protective membrane covering the front portion of the eye; behind this is located a water-like substance, the *aqueous humour*. The *lens* is suspended by ligaments which, through muscular action, are capable of changing the shape (and hence focal length) of the lens. The region behind the lens is filled with a jelly-like transparent substance, the *vitreous humour*.

In front of the lens is the *iris*, an opaque muscular membrane with a central opening, the *pupil*. The pupil contracts and dilates to automatically control the amount of light entering the eye.

Light passing through the lens forms a real inverted image on the light-sensitive portion at the rear called the *retina*. Many millions of light receptors, called *rods* and *cones*, form one layer of the retina. These rods and cones connect to a smaller number of nerve fibers which, from all over the inner surface of the retina, converge at one spot, passing out through the eyeball as the *optic nerve*. The sensations produced in the rods and cones are relayed by way of the optic nerve to the brain, where the complete image is interpreted as upright.

The retina is not uniformly sensitive to light. At the region where the optic nerve leaves the eye, the retina is completely insensitive, due to the absence of rods and cones at this point. Accordingly, a "blind spot" is located here. A short distance away from this blind spot is the region of maximum sensitivity indicated in Figure 16-1 by a small indentation in the inner surface. This region, called the *fovea*, is less than 0.5 mm in diameter. In focusing an object, the eye automatically adjusts so that the image falls on this part of the retina.

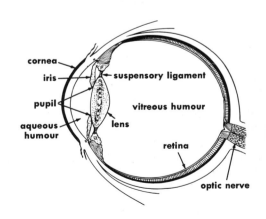

Fig. 16-1: *The eye.*

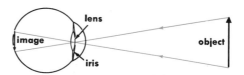

Fig. 16-2: *Formation of an image on the retina of an eye.*

The indices of refraction of the transparent portions of the eye are very nearly uniform, ranging from 1.34 to 1.44. Accordingly, the greatest refraction of light takes place at the cornea, where the change in optical density is greatest. The comparatively high curvature of the cornea adds to this effect.

A normal eye, when its muscles are relaxed will focus on the retina the image of a distant object. For focusing objects that are closer, the curvature of the lens is increased by muscular action. This ability of the eye to adjust to different object distances is called *accommodation*. Figure 16-2 shows the formation of an image on the retina.

It may happen that the eye lens cannot be relaxed to such an extent that the image is focused on the retina unless these rays are already divergent as they enter the eye. This is the nature of the malfunction leading to *nearsightedness*. Figure 16-3(a) illustrates this situation. A correction to such an eye may be provided by placing in front of it a divergent lens that will correct the incoming rays sufficiently to bring them to a focus on the retina. The action of such a lens is depicted in Figure 16-3(b).

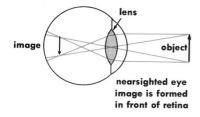

nearsighted eye
image is formed
in front of retina

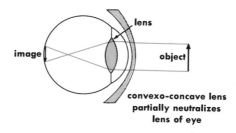

convexo-concave lens
partially neutralizes
lens of eye

Fig. 16-3: *(a) Nearsightedness is characterized by a tendency of the eye to form images in front of the retina. (b) The malfunction is corrected by a diverging lens placed in front of the eye.*

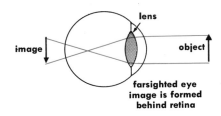

farsighted eye
image is formed
behind retina

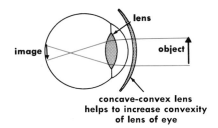

concave-convex lens
helps to increase convexity
of lens of eye

Fig. 16-4: *Farsightedness is characterized by a tendency of the eye to form images behind the retina. Correction is accomplished by means of a converging lens in front of the eye.*

At the other extreme is the so-called *farsighted* eye, the lens of which is not capable of shortening its focal length sufficiently to bring parallel rays to a focus on the retina, but focuses them behind the retina. Such an eye lens requires an additional lens to aid it in converging the rays. This is illustrated in Figure 16-4.

Our judgment of the size of objects at which we look and their distance from us involves more than optics. In general we judge the size of an object by the angular size of the image formed on the retina. This is not an absolute judgment, but it is aided by some additional knowledge of what the object is or by comparison with some other object in the same vicinity: that is, an object

whose size we know from other considerations. If we focus our eye on a distant object and its image gradually becomes larger, we conclude that the object is approaching us. If it slowly becomes smaller, we say that it is receding. This is one criterion by which we judge the approach or recession of objects. Figure 16-5 illustrates the relation between distance and image size.

Judgment of distance is aided by the fact that we have two eyes. They are both focused upon the same object, and so must be swivelled toward a central line, as illustrated in Figure 16-6. When an object is close, and this swivelling is quite marked, we are conscious that the object is close to our eyes.

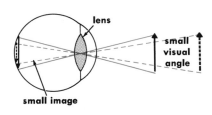

small visual angle

small image

Fig. 16-5: *The angle subtended by an object is an important factor in our judgment of distances and sizes of objects.*

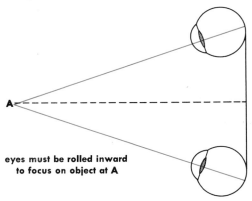

eyes must be rolled inward
to focus on object at A

Fig. 16-6: *Binocular vision (the viewing of an object by both eyes) is another key factor in our judgment of distances.*

286

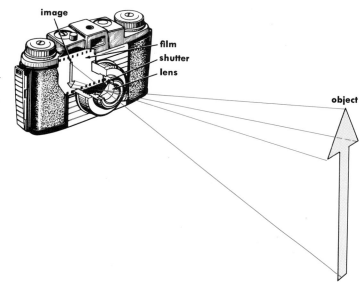

Fig. 16-7: *The key elements of a camera include a light-tight box, a lens to admit light and provide a well-focused image, a shutter to control the amount of light entering the box, and a light-sensitive film on which to record the image.*

2. THE CAMERA

The camera, Figure 16-7, functions in many respects like the human eye. A converging lens forms a real image on a light-sensitive surface, the photographic film, contained in a light-sensitive box. The amount of light reaching the lens is controlled by an adjustable diaphragm situated in front of or behind the lens. This diaphragm corresponds to the iris of the eye. An additional control of the amount of light exposure given the film is provided by the shutter, normally closed, which can be opened for any of several lengths of time, the number of which depends upon the individual camera.

Whereas focusing in the eye results from muscular action which changes the lens curvature, this function is accomplished in a camera by moving the lens away from or toward the film. In some box or "fixed-focus" cameras, the lens is fixed in position, but because of the short focal length of the lens, any object distance greater than about 6 ft will produce a sharply-focused image on the film.

Fig. 16-8: *A modern camera. The lens system comprises six individual components. The mirror and five-sided prism permit viewing the scene as it will be recorded on the film. When the picture is taken, the mirror flips up, and the shutter, located behind the mirror, opens to expose the film.*

Asahi Pentax

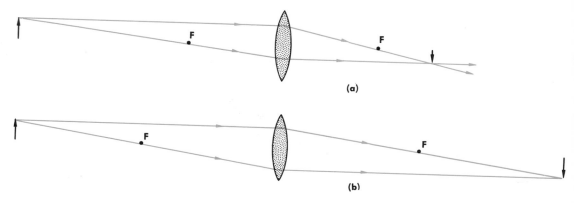

Fig. 16-9: *The field of view recorded on a given area of film depends on the focal length of the lens. Here, two identical objects are viewed by a lens of short focal length (a) and by a lens of long focal length (b). The latter produces a larger image, and the field of view is accordingly smaller. The resultant effects are shown in Figure 16-10.*

The lens system in a high-quality camera may be quite complex if the many types of lens distortions are to be minimized. The camera in Figure 16-8 is equipped with a six-element lens with the adjustable diaphragm located in the middle of this lens system. In this type of camera, known as a reflex camera, a plane mirror is located between lens and the shutter. This mirror, in conjunction with the five-sided prism located above it, allows the photographer to view the exact image that will be focused on the film. The totally-reflecting prism serves the additional function of erecting the image formed by the lens, while the object is being viewed. When the picture is taken, the plane mirror moves out of the path of the light, and the shutter opens, exposing the film located behind the shutter.

The size of the image produced on the film depends on the object's distance and on the focal length of the lens. The greater the focal length, the larger this image. This dependence upon focal length is illustrated by the ray diagrams of Figure 16-9. Accordingly, the "angle of view" is increased by using a lens of short focal length. A comparison of the images obtained from lenses of long and short focal lengths is illustrated in Figure 16-10.

The amount of light entering the camera depends upon the size of the opening of the adjustable diaphragm in the lens system. This opening is called the *aperture*. Figure 16-9 illustrates two lenses of equal diameter, but different focal length. In a given period of time, these lenses would allow the same amount of light into the camera. However, for the lens of short focal length, light from the object is concentrated over a smaller area of the film than is the case for the lens of longer focal length. Thus, it is not the diameter of the lens itself, but rather the combination of diameter and focal length that determines the exposure per unit area.

The *relative aperture* of a lens is the ratio of the diaphragm opening to the focal length of the lens. A relative aperture of $f/16$ indicates that the diameter of the diaphragm opening is one-sixteenth the focal length. The relative aperture becomes $f/8$ if the opening is doubled (in diameter). In so doing, one increases the *area* of the opening by a factor of *four*, allowing four times the amount of light into the camera. In a typical camera, the diaphragm is calibrated in steps that progressively double the area of the opening: $f/22$, $f/16$, $f/11$, $f/8$, $f/5.6$, $f/4$, $f/3.5$, $f/2.8$, $f/2$. The smaller the $f/$ number, the greater the "speed" of the lens; that is,

Fig. 16-10: *These photographs were taken from the same position by the same camera, using a lens of focal length 55 mm in (a) and 135 mm focal length in (b). The lens of longer focal length produces a narrow field of view, but the objects in the scene occupy a larger area of film.*

the greater the amount of light allowed through the lens.

The other factor determining the exposure of the film is the time during which the shutter is open. A relative aperture of $f/4$ for $\frac{1}{100}$ second is equivalent to a relative aperture of $f/8$ for $\frac{1}{25}$ second. Why?

The photographic film consists of minute crystals of silver bromide, embedded in gelatine, or coated on a transparent base. When exposed to light, part of each exposed silver bromide crystal reduces to silver. The film now holds a latent image of the object. When the film is developed, the developer solution attacks only those silver bromide crystals that contain some pure silver, that is, only those crystals that have been exposed to light.

A second solution, called the fixer, dissolves the unexposed silver bromide crystals so that the film will no longer be light-sensitive. Because of the fineness of the silver grains, they appear black, and the developed film now exists in the form of a "negative", on which original bright areas of the object are represented in black.

3. THE PROJECTOR

A standard form of slide projector is shown

in Figure 16-11. The transparent slide is placed close to the principal focus of a converging *objective* lens. An inverted enlarged image is produced on the screen placed several feet away. A high-powered source of light illuminates the slide from behind. This light source is located at the principal focus of the condensing lens which renders the light passing through it into a parallel beam before it passes through the slide.

The similarity between a projector and a camera is obvious. In fact, a light source, in conjunction with a camera, can be used to project pictures.

The photographic enlarger is identical in principle to the slide projector.

4. THE MAGNIFIER

When an object is to be examined in detail, it is usually brought as close to the eye as is consistent with comfort. The closer the object, the greater is the visual angle that the object subtends, and accordingly, the larger the image produced on the retina (see Figure 16-5). In the normal eye, the object distance that produces most distinct vision is about 10 in (25 cm). Object distances shorter than this usually produce eye strain.

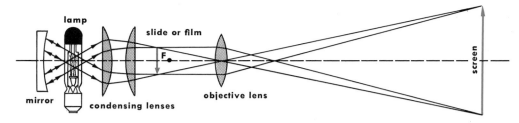

Fig. 16-11: *In a projector, the slide or film is placed just outside the principal focus of the objective lens. The slide is illuminated by a lamp in conjunction with a condensing lens system. What purpose is served by the mirror? Where should it be located relative to the filament? Why should the slide be positioned upside down?*

One instrument by which an object may be made to appear larger is the simple magnifying glass illustrated in Figure 16-12. Here a converging lens is positioned so that the object lies between the lens and the principal focus. An upright virtual image *I* of the object is formed, and its distance from the eye may be adjusted by moving the lens. For most distinct vision, the image should be located about 25 cm from the eye.

We can employ the lens relationships outlined in the previous chapter to determine the magnification produced by this magnifier.

$$\text{Thus, } \frac{H_i}{H_o} = \frac{S_i}{f}.$$

Here, as before, S_i is the distance from image to the focus on the side of the lens opposite to that of the object. In the illustration, this distance is $d+f$.

$$\frac{H_i}{H_o} = \frac{d+f}{f} = 1 + \frac{d}{f}$$

Hence the ratio of image size to object size (the magnification) increases as the focal length is made smaller.

Fig. 16-12: *The simple magnifier produces an enlarged, upright virtual image of an object* ⟶ *placed inside its principal focus.*

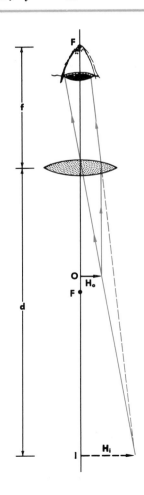

290

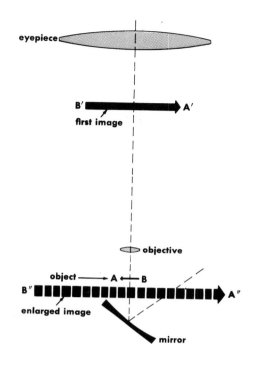

Fig. 16-13: *The compound microscope employs two systems of lenses. The objective lens produces a first image, which serves as an object for the eyepiece lens, which acts as a simple magnifier.*

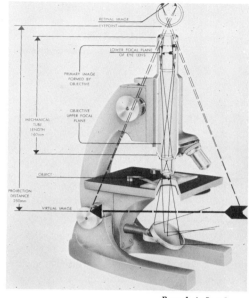

Bausch & Lomb

Fig. 16-14: *A commercial microscope.*

5. THE COMPOUND MICROSCOPE

The compound microscope consists of two lenses, or systems of lens, as illustrated in Figure 16-13. The object AB is placed just beyond the principal focus of the lower lens, which is called the *objective*. This forms an inverted, enlarged image $A'B'$. This image is not formed on a screen, but does exist at the intersection of rays from the object. The image $A'B'$ is used as an object for the upper lens, or *eyepiece*. The eyepiece serves as a simple magnifier, because the image $A'B'$ lies just inside its principal focus.

Accordingly, an enlarged virtual image $A''B''$ is formed.

The objective and eyepiece are mounted in a tube which can be extended or contracted to bring the first image $A'B'$ to the proper position for focusing. In practice, the objective consists of several lenses in order to reduce chromatic aberration. Typical magnification for the objective is 75, and for the eyepiece is 10. The result is an overall magnification of 750. The mirror at the bottom serves to illuminate the object.

A commercial microscope is illustrated in Figure 16-14.

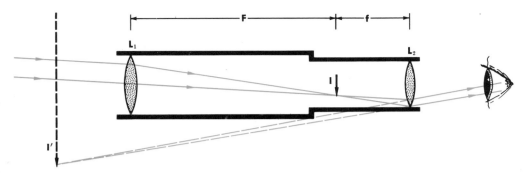

Fig. 16-15: *A refracting telescope. Note the similarity to the microscope of Figure 16-13. The objective lens L_1, however, is of long focal length. Why?*

6. THE TELESCOPE

Telescopes are employed to bring the images of distant objects close. They fall into two broad classifications: refracting telescopes, which employ lenses as the image-forming device, and reflecting telescopes, which produce images by means of a mirror.

Refracting telescope

The refracting telescope is similar in principle to the microscope. Whereas the objective lens of a microscope produces an image that is larger than the object, in general the telescope objective produces an image that is smaller than the object, and an eyepiece is used to magnify this image.

In Figure 16-15, the objective lens L_1 is of long focal length to produce as large an image I as practicable. Because the instrument is used to view only distant objects, the incoming rays from the object are essentially parallel, and the image I is formed at the focal plane of L_1. This image is, of course, inverted.

The eyepiece L_2 produces an enlarged virtual image of I, indicated in the figure as I'.

The magnifying power of a telescope is defined as the ratio of the angle subtended at the eye by the image I', to the angle that the object subtends at the eye. As already mentioned in connection with Figure 16-5,

it is this visual angle that determines the size of the image produced on the retina. This angular magnification should be distinguished from the *linear magnification* $\dfrac{H_i}{H_o}$, which compares actual sizes of image and object.

It can be shown that the angular magnification produced by the telescope of Figure 16-15 is $\dfrac{F}{f}$, where F and f are the focal lengths of the objective and eyepiece respectively.

The refracting telescope in Figure 16-15 produces an inverted image. This feature would be undesirable when viewing terrain. Any one of several methods may be employed to provide an erect image — the simplest being shown in Figure 16-16. Here the eyepiece is a diverging lens placed between the objective and the principal focus of the objective. The image is located at I'. This is the form of the original telescope constructed by Galileo in 1609. Low-power binoculars, or "opera glasses", consist of one of these systems for each eye.

The inverted image produced by the telescope in Figure 16-15 may also be made erect by inserting a converging lens between the objective and eyepiece. This has the disadvantage of requiring a longer tube. Yet another method is employed in high-power binoculars (see Section 7).

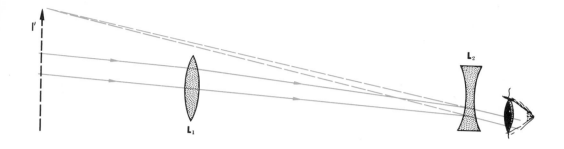

Fig. 16-16: *The Galilean telescope produces an upright image by means of a diverging lens as eyepiece.*

Reflecting Telescope

Most of the large telescopes used in astronomy employ reflection from a concave mirror, rather than refraction by a lens to form an image.

A reflecting telescope is illustrated in Figure 16-17(a). Here, parallel rays from the distant object, a star, incident on the concave mirror at the lower end of the tube, are reflected back up the tube to a plane mirror which, in turn, reflects the light to an eyepiece in the side of the tube. This is but one of several possible arrangements. For instance, the plane mirror may be dispensed with, and the image produced by the concave mirror, in this case, allowed to fall on a photographic plate located at the principal

focus of the concave mirror, as in Figure 16-17(b).

There are several reasons why, in many cases, a reflecting telescope is preferable to the refracting telescope. Light does not go through the mirror, and the problem of providing optically perfect glass is non-existent. Also, the mirror is much easier to support, being braced at several points at the lower end of the tube. Consequently, large mirrors are more practicable than large lenses because similar bracing of the lens would interfere with the passage of light through the lens. Finally, because light does not pass through a mirror, chromatic aberration is not present in the reflecting telescope.

Fig. 16-17: *Reflecting telescopes. In (a) light from a distant star falls on a concave mirror. Rays converging to its principal focus are reflected by a plane mirror to an eyepiece. In (b) the star may be photographed if a photographic plate is placed at the principal focus.*

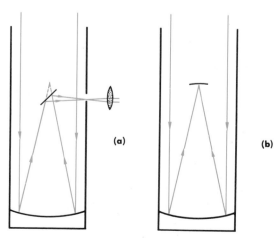

Fig. 16-I8: *The 200-inch Hale telescope, showing an observer working at the prime focus of the mirror, which is 55 feet beneath him. The light from the stars passes down to the surface of the mirror and is reflected back to the observer in the cage, where it comes to a focus on the photographic plate. Some light is intercepted by the cage so that the full aperture of the mirror is not used.*

A large mirror is desirable because of the greater amount of light it collects from the distant star. The world's largest reflecting telescope has a mirror diameter of 200 inches, and weighs over 14 tons. It is located at the Palomar Observatory in California. What is to be Canada's largest reflecting

Fig. 16-19: *Prism binoculars are refracting telescopes that employ prisms to provide an upright image.*

telescope is in the early stages of construction on Mount Kobau near Penticton, B.C. This telescope will have a mirror 150 inches in diameter, and will be designed along the lines of the instrument at Palomar.

7. PRISM BINOCULARS

This instrument (Figure 16-19) is actually a pair of refracting telescopes mounted side by side, one for each eye. In addition to the objective lens and eyepiece, each of the telescopes contains a pair of prisms that serve to invert the rays, thus providing an erect image.

THE EYE AND THE CAMERA: The similarity between the two is that each forms a real image on a light-sensitive surface. They differ in focusing arrangements in that, for the eye, the shape of the lens is changed while, for the camera, the position of the lens is changed.

THE PROJECTOR: This is essentially a camera with image and object positions reversed.

THE SIMPLE MAGNIFIER: A single convex lens, positioned so that it forms an enlarged virtual image, constitutes a simple magnifier.

THE TELESCOPE: This is similar to the microscope in construction, the real image produced by the objective being smaller than the object. In astronomy, the reflecting telescope offers advantages, employing a concave mirror to form a real image that may be viewed or photographed in any of several ways.

THE PRISM BINOCULARS: This instrument is composed essentially of two telescopes, one for each eye.

THE COMPOUND MICROSCOPE: This device is a simple magnifier, used in conjunction with an objective lens of short focal length. The objective produces an inverted real image of the object, which serves as an object for the eyepiece. The image produced by the eyepiece is enlarged and virtual.

EXERCISE A

1. State three similarities between the eye and a photographic camera.

2. In what way do the focusing arrangements in a camera and eye differ?

3. List two common eye defects. By what means is each corrected?

4. What is meant by the term "relative aperture"?

5. Which has the greater relative aperture, a lens of diameter 60 cm and focal length 180 cm, or a lens of diameter 20 cm and focal length 40 cm?

6. State two factors that determine the amount of light received by a photographic film.

7. What factors determine the size of the image produced on a photographic film?

8. If a certain camera lens is changed from relative aperture $f/2$ to $f/8$, how is the size of the image affected? How is the required exposure time affected?

9. (a) Should the focal length of a lens used as a simple magnifier be long or short?
   (b) Answer part (a) for the case of a microscope objective.
   (c) Answer part (a) for the case of a telescope objective.

10. Suppose you are looking at the moon through a telescope when someone covers half of the objective lens. In what way would the appearance of the moon be affected?

11. What determines the magnification produced by a simple magnifier? What determines this magnification in the case of a compound microscope?

12. What are the principal advantages of a reflecting telescope in astronomy?

EXERCISE B

1. A certain camera lens has a diameter of 5.0 cm and a focal length of 20.0 cm. What is the f/number (relative aperture) of this lens?

2. A picture is taken with a shutter speed of 1/100 sec and a relative aperture of $f/11$. If the picture is to be retaken with a relative aperture of $f/22$, what should the corresponding shutter speed be in order to expose the film to the same amount of light?

3. A projector slide 2.0 in wide is to be projected onto a screen 40 ft away (from the lens) by means of a lens of focal length 8.0 in. What width of screen would be required to show the entire picture? (Hint: use an appropriate equation from Chapter 15.)

4. Bacteria were discovered by the Dutch biologist Leeuwenhoek in 1675, using a simple magnifier of focal length 1.2 mm. What was the magnifying power of this instrument?

5. The lens from a camera is 4.0 cm in diameter and is $f/2$. If the lens is removed from the camera and used as a magnifier, what maximum magnification would you obtain from it?

6. A refracting telescope has an objective lens of focal length 60 in and an eyepiece of focal length 1 in. What angular magnification can be obtained from it?

295

Chapter 17

Electrostatics

1. ELECTRIFICATION

The sensation you feel as you walk across a rug to turn on a lamp, the dry hair attracted to a comb, the rubber balloon clinging to the wall—these are examples of electrification. Electrification is the production of an electric charge on an object.

If a charge remains on an object, the object is said to possess an electrostatic charge; a comb or other object charged in this manner can pick up small pieces of paper, or sawdust, or other lightweight materials.

The Greeks recorded that amber, a fossilized resin, if rubbed with wool, would attract many lightweight objects. Accordingly, the word *electricity* was obtained from *elektron*, the Greek word for amber.

Electrostatic charges are produced by friction, as when two dry objects are rubbed together; the hair's "standing on end" is a common example. What changes to the comb and to the hair can account for this behaviour?

2. THE ELECTROSCOPE

Objects possessing electrostatic charges can be studied by means of a device called an electroscope. In its simplest form, (Figure 17-1) it consists of a small ball of wood pith attached to a silk thread. When the silk thread is suspended, our device becomes a pith-ball electroscope.

When an ebonite (hard rubber) rod is rubbed with fur and brought near the pith ball, the ball is first attracted to the rod; however, after touching it, the ball is repelled by the rod. We would assume that the ball received some of the charge from the rod at contact, and that both became similarly charged.

If the pith ball is now approached by a glass rod rubbed with silk or paper, the ball is attracted. Hence we conclude that the rubbed glass rod had a charge which differed from that on the ebonite rod.

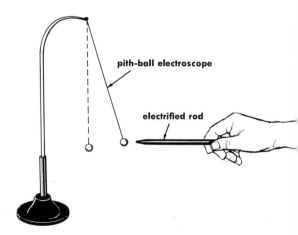

Fig. 17-1: *A known charge placed on the electroscope can be used to detect an unknown charge on another object.*

296

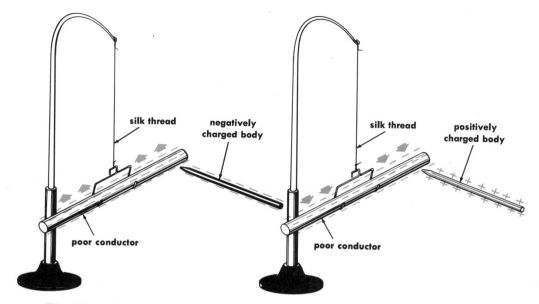

Fig. 17-2: *An illustration of the repulsion between like charges and the attraction between unlike charges.*

The charge given to an ebonite rod rubbed
with fur is called a *negative* charge, while
that given to a glass rod rubbed with silk is
called a *positive* charge.

The behaviour of these charges can be
investigated with the equipment illustrated
in Figure 17-2.

When a negatively charged ebonite rod is
placed in the stirrup, and a similarly charged
rod brought close to it, the rod in the stirrup
is repelled. If a glass rod rubbed with silk is
the approaching body, the negatively charged
rod in the stirrup is attracted.

These observations, especially those
derived from experiments involving the pith
ball, illustrate a basic law of electrostatics:
**objects of like charge repel each other;
objects of unlike charge attract each other.**

Considering the hair and comb once more,
we conclude that the hair has a different
charge from that on the comb, and that this
difference explains the attraction. A discussion of the structure of matter will reveal
the charging process.

3. THE LEAF ELECTROSCOPE

The electroscope shown in Figure 17-3 is
quite sensitive compared to the pith-ball
electroscope. It consists of a thin foil of
gold attached to a metallic conducting rod
flattened at the attachment end. Other

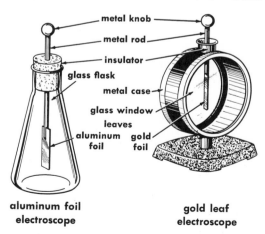

Fig. 17-3: *The leaf electroscope can be used
to study and detect electrostatic charges.*

Fig. 17-4: *The soda straw and support provide the detecting device in this type of electroscope.*

models have two strips of aluminum foil secured at one end of the rod. The other end of the rod is threaded to hold a small metal sphere. A soda-straw electroscope (Figure 17-4) is satisfactory for most student experiments.

The leaf system, the functional part of the instrument, is protected from air currents by a glass, or metal-and-glass container. The functional area is insulated from the container at the neck by means of an insulating stopper.

4. THE ELECTRICAL THEORY OF MATTER

Many experiments have indicated that all matter is composed of atoms which may or may not be combined to form molecules. The atom consists of *electrons*, which are negatively charged, *protons*, which are positively charged, and *neutrons* (with the exception of hydrogen), which are neutral.

The protons and neutrons are confined to a dense mass called the nucleus: as it contains protons and neutral particles, it is positively charged. The number of protons in the nucleus determines the positive nuclear

charge, and this number gives the *atomic number* of the element.

The negatively charged electrons orbit the nucleus at various distances and form a negatively charged "cloud" about the nucleus (Figure 17-5). As the charge on the electron is equal and opposite to that on the proton, an uncharged atom has an equal number of electrons and protons.

A tremendous mutual force binds the protons and neutrons together in the nucleus. In contrast, the electrons revolving at high speeds about the nucleus (which provides a centripetal force by virtue of its positive charge) can be easily moved from one orbiting level to another, or some can be removed or added.

When an atom has lost some of its electrons, it will no longer be neutral, but will be left with a net positive charge. On the other hand, as well as being able to lose electrons, an atom may gain some and thus become negatively charged.

Since the protons are held within the nucleus by powerful forces, *an object can obtain a positive charge only by losing electrons and a negative charge only by gaining electrons.*

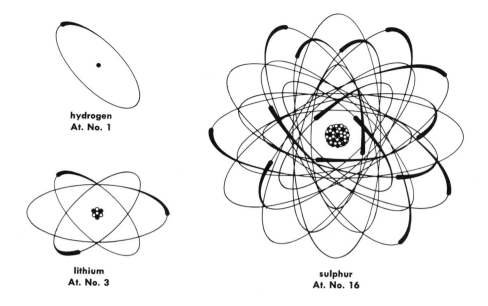

Fig. 17-5: *A neutral atom contains the same number of positive protons in the nucleus as it has of negative electrons revolving about the nucleus. A neutral atom of lithium possesses three protons (Atomic Number 3) and three electrons.*

When an ebonite rod is rubbed with fur, the ebonite captures electrons at the expense of the fur; it thus becomes negatively charged, whereas the fur becomes positively charged.

Accordingly, a negative charge may now be considered as an excess of electrons.

What kind of test can you devise to show that there is a charge on the comb you use and also a charge on your hair?

The mass of an electron is 9.11×10^{-31} kilograms, and the mass of a proton or neutron is approximately 1800 times as great. Thus the mass of an atom is almost entirely confined to the nucleus.

5. CONDUCTORS AND INSULATORS

The atoms of solid materials are arranged in patterns characteristic of each material.

The atoms of metals are closely packed in a crystal lattice (repetitive) structure. The electrons close to the nuclei of these atoms are firmly held, but those in the outer orbits are loosely held and can be easily detached. Electrons having been removed in this fashion are called *free electrons.*

Free electrons have random motion; however, when they collide with neutral atoms they may be retained as a result of displacing other electrons. Mutual repulsion among electrons and their attraction by positively charged atoms will cause any local concentration of charge to spread throughout the metal. The number of free electrons in a given material determines the ease of charge transfer within it.

A *conductor* is a material which can transfer charges easily. It contains a large number of free electrons.

An *insulator* is a material which does not transfer charges easily. Insulators are considered to have few free electrons. The electrons of the atoms comprising the insulator are rigidly held by the nuclei. Therefore any local charges placed on an insulator remain relatively immobile, as few electrons are free to move and spread the charge evenly.

6. CHARGING BY INDUCTION

In earlier sections of this chapter we noted that an object obtains an electric charge by being rubbed with another object. By this process, electrons are made to leave one object, giving it a negative charge, while the other object, now deficient in electrons, is left with an overall positive charge. In this section we shall investigate a quite different process of charging, called *induction*.

Suppose we bring a negatively charged ebonite rod close to an electroscope knob,

as shown in Figure 17-6. We note that the leaves diverge, indicating that they are repelling each other and hence are similarly charged. If this procedure is repeated using a positively charged rod, such as a glass rod rubbed with silk, a similar divergence of the leaves is noted. When the rods are removed, the electroscope returns to normal. In both cases, no actual contact has been made between the leaf system and the charged rods. How can we explain these results?

It is natural to assume that in the first case the negative ebonite rod repelled electrons from the knob to the leaf system, causing an excess of electrons to exist in this area. This can be verified by bringing the positively charged glass rod close to the knob while the negatively charged rod is still in proximity. The leaves are seen to collapse, indicating the return of the electrons from the leaf system.

In the second case, the positively charged glass rod has the effect of attracting electrons

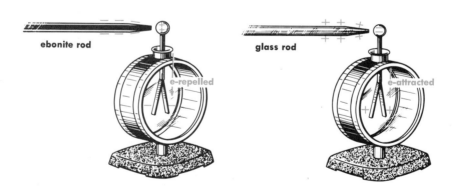

Fig. 17-6: *A charged rod brought near a neutral leaf electroscope provides a force which alters the electron-proton balance. The negative ebonite rod repels electrons from the knob to the leaf system; the positive glass rod attracts electrons to the knob from the leaf system. In both cases, the leaves diverge because of the repulsion produced by similar charges. The leaf system is said to be charged by induction.*

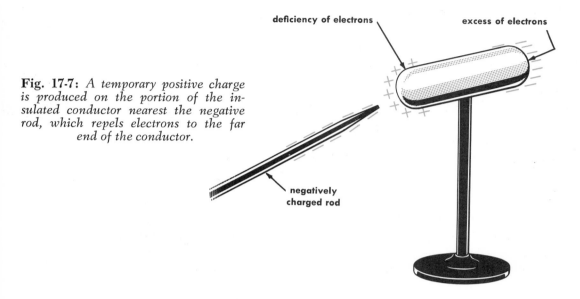

Fig. 17-7: *A temporary positive charge is produced on the portion of the insulated conductor nearest the negative rod, which repels electrons to the far end of the conductor.*

negatively
charged rod

from the leaf system to the knob, leaving a net positive charge in the leaf system.

It is important to note that in this induction process, the total number of charges in the electroscope has remained unaltered—none have been added or removed. The proximity of the electroscope to a charged object (the ebonite rod or the glass rod) has caused only a *redistribution* of the individual charges on it.

Any conductor, such as that shown in Figure 17-7, may be charged by induction simply by bringing close to it a previously charged object. The distribution of charges returns to normal when the charged object is removed.

The induction process can be modified to provide a conductor with a *permanent* charge. The procedure is illustrated in Figure 17-8. Again, for convenience, we use an electroscope as the object to be charged. The initially uncharged electroscope leaf system

is charged negatively, as before, by the nearby ebonite rod. In the third illustration, a finger placed in contact with the knob causes the leaves to collapse. Evidently, electrons have left the leaf system, and have flowed from the electroscope to the finger. In the fourth illustration, the finger has been removed, but the negatively charged rod is still close to the knob. At this stage, the electroscope is deficient in electrons. When, as in the final illustration, the rod is removed, the leaves diverge, indicating a permanent charge on the leaf system. That this charge is a positive charge may be verified by approaching the electroscope with a positively charged rod: when so affected, the leaves diverge further.

The foregoing procedure may be employed to produce a permanent negative charge on the electroscope as well. What single change in procedure would be necessary?

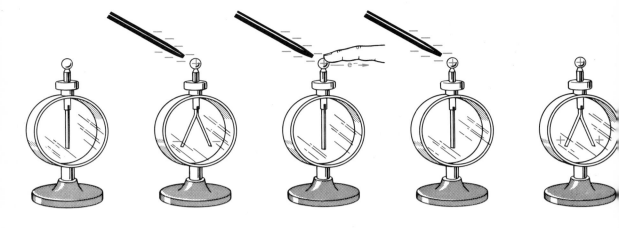

Fig. 17-8: *Charging an electroscope by induction. Compare the charge left on the electro-scope with the charge on the ebonite rod. How could you charge an electroscope negatively by induction?*

7. CHARGING BY CONTACT

A previous example of contact charging was the creation of electrostatic charges on insulators by friction. A conductor can be charged by contact as follows.

Let us suppose that, rather than merely approaching it, we *touch* the knob of a neutral electroscope with a charged ebonite rod. (Figure 17-9). The leaves again move apart. This time, however, when the rod is removed, the leaves do not collapse but remain apart, showing that the electroscope has retained a charge. The question arises, "What kind of charge does it possess?"

To answer this question, we approach (but do not touch) the electroscope with the rod a second time, and see the leaves move still farther apart. However, if a glass rod rubbed with silk is brought close to the electroscope, the leaves collapse. These

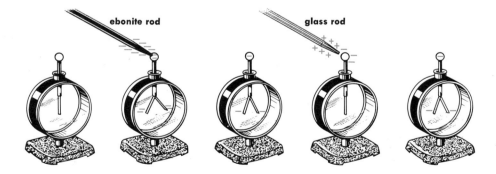

Fig. 17-9: *When the negatively charged rod touches the electroscope, some electrons leave the rod to place a negative charge on the electroscope. The charged glass rod, when brought near, attracts the electrons from the leaf system to the knob to collapse the leaves. After removal of the glass rod, the leaves regain their negative charge and diverge again.*

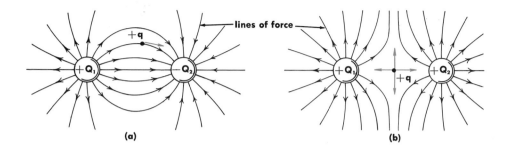

Fig. 17-10: *The electric field produced by two equal but opposite charges (a) and two equal but like charges (b). + q, equidistant from + Q₁ + Q₂, would not move.*

observations indicate that the electroscope has obtained a negative charge by *contact*.

Since the leaves separated more widely as the negatively charged rod was approaching the knob, the electrons repelled toward the leaves must have increased the negative charge on the leaves. The positive charge on the glass rod attracted electrons to the electroscope knob, and, since the leaves collapsed, the charge they possessed must have been due to an excess of electrons.

A positive charge can be placed on a neutral electroscope by touching the knob with a positively charged glass rod, and the nature of the charge transferred can be determined by the method indicated here.

In general, we may state that *when an electroscope is charged by contact, it receives a charge of the same kind as that of the charging object*.

8. A UNIT OF CHARGE—THE COULOMB

The amount of charge on an object depends upon its excess or deficiency of electrons with respect to its number of protons. The practical unit of charge is the coulomb, named after French physicist Charles Augustin de Coulomb.

$$1 \text{ coulomb} = 6.24 \times 10^{18} \text{ electrons}$$

The coulomb is defined later in terms of an electric current as the quantity of charge passing a point in a wire when the current is one ampere.

9. CONCEPT OF THE ELECTRIC FIELD

When a charged object is placed near another charged object, it will be subjected to a force. The region around a charged body where this force is located is called the *electric field* (Figure 17-10). If a single or unit positive charge that is free to move is placed near the surface of a positively charged object, it will be repelled by an electric force; the path it traces is called a *line of force*. If this positive test charge should

303

be brought near a negatively charged object, it would be attracted and would move toward the object. By convention, the path traced out by a positive test charge in such an electric field is an electric line of force.

When a stronger field exists, more lines of force per unit area are present, and the force per unit charge determines the *field strength* or *intensity*.

The electric field for two equal positive charges and for two equal but opposite charges is indicated in Figure 17-10. The net force on a positive charge in the field would be a tangent drawn to the lines of force at that point. A test charge placed midway between two equal like charges would have a balanced force acting on it, and hence it would not move.

ELECTROSTATIC CHARGES: These are electric charges in a stationary state. They may be produced by friction, a process whereby the positive and negative charges are separated, or by induction.

THE ELECTROSCOPE: A device used to detect or identify an electrostatic charge. The pith ball, gold leaf and soda-straw devices are three types of electroscopes.

LAW OF ELECTROSTATICS: Objects possessing like charges repel each other; those with unlike charges attract each other.

TYPES OF CHARGES: The electrical theory of matter considers a negative charge to be an excess of electrons and a positive charge a deficiency of electrons.

MATERIALS OF TRANSFER: Conductors, or materials which readily transmit electric charges, possess a large number of free electrons. The reverse condition holds true for insulators.

THE CHARGING PROCESS: When a neutral object is touched by a charged material, the charge received is the same type as that possessed by the charged material. The charge obtained by induction is opposite in quality to that of the charging object.

THE UNIT OF CHARGE: The unit of charge, the coulomb, is equivalent to an excess or deficiency of 6.24×10^{18} electrons.

ELECTRIC FIELD: This is the region in the vicinity of a charged object where an electric force acts.

EXERCISE A

1. Record at least five examples illustrating electrification produced by friction.

2. Why do some teachers gently heat electrostatic materials before demonstrating electrostatic principles?

3. After combing your hair, how could you use a pith-ball electroscope to find the charge on the comb?

4. Describe a method of showing that there are two kinds of electricity and explain the basic law of electrostatics stated on page 297 from the observations made.

304

5. Using the electrical theory of matter, explain the changes to the glass and silk molecules when a glass test tube is rubbed with silk.

6. By means of a series of diagrams indicating the functional portion of a leaf electroscope, show how to charge the electroscope negatively by induction.

7. Why are metals good conductors of electricity and waxes poor conductors?

8. How can a leaf electroscope be charged positively by contact?

9. The type of charge that an object receives by friction depends on the material with which it is rubbed. Some common substances are listed below in an electrostatic series. A material receives a negative charge when rubbed with a substance preceding it in the list, and a positive charge when rubbed with a substance following it.

    glass, wool, fur, lead, silk, paraffin wax, ebonite, copper, brass, sulphur

    (a) What type of charge will fur receive when it is rubbed against (i) glass (ii) paraffin?

    (b) Would you use fur or silk to give lead a negative charge?

    (c) How would you determine where to place vinylite, acetate and cotton in the list?

Electrostatics

▶ **Experiment 34**

To study the behaviour of electric charges.

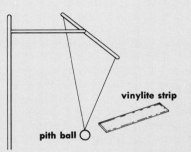

Electrostatic apparatus

Ring stand

Woollen cloth

Cotton cloth

Scrap paper, sawdust, or iron filings

Masking tape

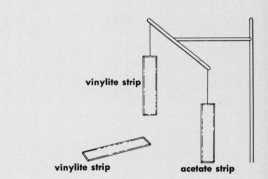

Procedure

1. Suspend a vinylite and an acetate strip from a ring stand so that they can swing freely without twisting.

2. Rub the vinylite strip briskly with a dry woollen cloth (a coat sleeve will do); rub the acetate strip with a dry cotton cloth. Do not touch the surfaces that have been rubbed.

3. Rub a second vinylite strip with wool and then bring it close to each of the suspended and charged strips. Record the results.

4. Rub a second acetate strip with cotton and then bring it near each of the suspended and charged strips. Record the results.

5. Try charging some common articles, such as a comb, pen or plastic ruler, by rubbing them on the woollen cloth and test their charges by bringing them close to the suspended and charged strips. Record the results.

6. Remove the vinylite and acetate strips and suspend a pith ball from the ring mount, using a polyethylene insulator and thread to hold the pith ball.

7. Charge the vinylite strip as before and bring it close to but not into contact with the pith ball. Note all movements.

Analysis

1. Using the information that a vinylite strip, if rubbed with wool, receives a negative charge, account for all your observations.

2. Your conclusions should state the distribution of charges that occurs when (a) a negatively charged object and (b) a positively charged object is brought close to a neutral object.

Note

The experiment can be performed by using a stirrup for a holder and a charged ebonite rod and glass rod instead of the vinylite and acetate strips. Ebonite receives an excellent positive charge when rubbed with saran wrap in contrast to the negative charge produced with fur. A test tube briskly struck on the free end of a piece of paper receives a good positive charge.

Experiment 35

To study induction with an electroscope.

Electrostatic apparatus

acetate strip

electroscope

Procedure

1. Charge the acetate strip by rubbing it with a cotton cloth. Bring the acetate strip near the neutral electroscope disk but not near enough to allow a transfer of charge. Observe the reaction of the leaf system and any change as you withdraw the strip.

2. To produce a permanent charge by induction, proceed as follows: bring the re-charged acetate strip close to the disk, and while it is in this position touch the disk momentarily with a finger. When you withdraw the strip, the leaf should indicate that the electroscope is charged.

3. Test the reaction of the leaf system of the charged electroscope when (a) a charged acetate strip is brought near but not into contact with the disk and (b) a charged vinylite strip is brought near the disk. Record the results.

4. Charge the electroscope in the same manner as in step 2, but use a charged vinylite strip in place of the acetate. Test and record as in step 3.

Analysis

A vinylite strip rubbed with wool receives a negative charge. Using this information, account for all your observations.

Question

How is the charge on the electroscope related to that on the charging object when (a) the electroscope is charged by conduction, (b) the electroscope is charged by induction?

Chapter 18

Potential Difference

1. MEANING OF ELECTRICAL POTENTIAL DIFFERENCE

In mechanics, an object gains potential energy when work is done to raise it against the force of gravity. Thus a skier increases his potential energy as he climbs the ski slope, by doing work against the force of gravity. On the downhill journey, the gravitational force performs work on the skier as he loses potential energy. If the ski slope ended at sea level, the skier might be considered to have returned to a position of zero potential energy. Two points of different elevation may be considered to be at different levels of potential, and the difference in elevation may be considered the difference in levels of potential.

Similarly, when two insulated conductors are charged to different levels of potential with respect to ground or earth potential, we say that a potential difference exists between them. An electric field exists between two charged conductors that are at different potentials; hence, if another charged object is placed in the field, it will experience an electrical force. If, like the skier moving *up* the slope, the object is moved *against* the force, work is done and the object increases its electrical potential. If the charge is free to move, it will move *in the direction of the force* and work will be done by the field.

In mechanics, potential energy can be measured as the work done per unit of mass when an object is raised from one level to another. If a 100-lb boy climbs up a 50-ft slope (measured vertically), he performs 5000 ft-lb of work, or *fifty foot-pounds of work per pound.*

In electricity the potential difference (V) between two points is the amount of work done (W) per unit of charge (Q) when the charge is moved from one point to the other.

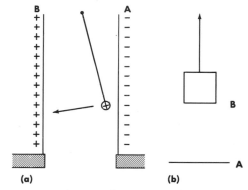

Fig. 18-1: (a) *Work is required to transport the small positive charge from the region near plate A to that near plate B. In the process, the charge acquires electrical potential energy, and plate A is said to be at a higher level of potential than plate B. (b) A gravitational analogy to (a). Work is required to lift a mass from level A to level B. This work is absorbed as gravitational potential energy, and level B is said to be at a higher level of potential than level A.*

308

In symbols:

$$V\text{(potential difference)} = \frac{W \text{ (work)}}{Q \text{ (charge)}}$$

or:

$$W = QV$$

The unit of potential difference is the volt.

The potential difference between two points is one volt if one joule of work per coulomb of charge is done in moving a charge from one point to the other.

$$1 \text{ volt} = \frac{1 \text{ joule}}{1 \text{ coulomb}} = \frac{1 \text{ newton-metre}}{1 \text{ coulomb}}$$

The earth is such a vast reservoir for electric charges that the normal addition and removal of charges from it does not measurably alter its potential. It is useful to consider its constant potential as zero. Any charged conductor, when grounded, will quickly lose its charge to become neutral. In this event it has returned to ground or zero potential.

The human body can also be considered a large reservoir to which the addition or removal of small quantities of charge does not appreciably change the electric field surrounding it, and hence its level of potential.

2. ELECTROSTATIC GENERATORS

Electrostatic generators are devices used to separate large quantities of charge.

Electrophorus

As would be expected, electrostatic generators operate by the formation of electrostatic charges produced by friction. The simplest type is the electrophorus (Figure 18-2). This device consists of a metallic base with a shallow circular top filled with ebonite, wax, or sulphur. A negative charge may be established on the top surface of the ebonite base by rubbing it with fur; this remains there for a considerable time, owing to the insulating quality of the material used. A thin brass plate held by an insulating handle is placed upon the base.

The charging process is accomplished by "grounding" the brass plate with the finger and then removing it by means of the insulating handle. The plate, when tested, is found to be positively charged. This can be explained in the following manner.

The electron excess on the base repels electrons in the brass plate to the top surface of the plate, and these electrons are conducted to ground via the finger. These electrons are not replaced, for the insulating material of the base is a poor conductor. As the charged insulator will lose few electrons during each operation, the plate charge can be renewed many times without recharging the ebonite, wax, or sulphur.

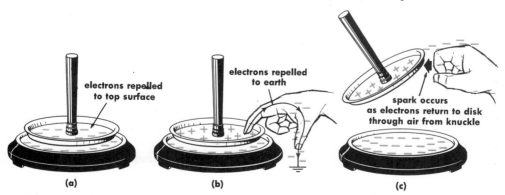

(a) electrons repelled to top surface

(b) electrons repelled to earth

(c) spark occurs as electrons return to disk through air from knuckle

Fig. 18-2: *The Electrophorus. One may charge the metal plate repeatedly by induction without recharging the ebonite cake. The electrons repelled to the upper surface in (a) are sent to the ground in (b), leaving the plate with a positive charge (c).*

Fig. 18-3: *The Wimshurst Machine. The two storage capacitors can be seen at the ends. Spark discharges can be produced between the two metallic balls when they are separated by a gap of up to 6 or 7 centimetres. For these discharges to occur, a potential difference of approximately 30,000 volts is required for each centimetre of gap.*

Wimshurst Machine

This machine consists of two circular insulating disks of glass, placed back to back with strips of metallic foil uniformly spaced and glued near the circumference of each disk (Figure 18-3). In operation, the disks rotate in opposite directions.

Any foil possessing a charge induces the opposite charge as it passes the foil strips of the adjacent disk; then, in turn, the opposite foils induce charges in the same way. This interchange results in the accumulation of like charges on one set of foils, but opposite charges on the two disks.

During the rotation, the charges are carried by the strips to two metallic collector combs—one for each disk. The charge from the combs is conducted to two storage capacitors, where the charges of opposite sign can be built up to ionize an adjustable air gap between two brass balls, causing a spark discharge.

Van de Graaff Generator

By a belt made of insulating material, charges are conveyed from the base of the generator (Figure 18-4) to a hollow metallic sphere at the top. The charges are placed on the belt by friction as the belt passes over a fleece-lined pulley in the base; in larger models the charges are sprayed on by a corona discharge from needle points attached to a generator. The sphere at the top is insulated from the base by a nonconducting cylindrical support. The charges carried to the top are collected by a metallic comb and

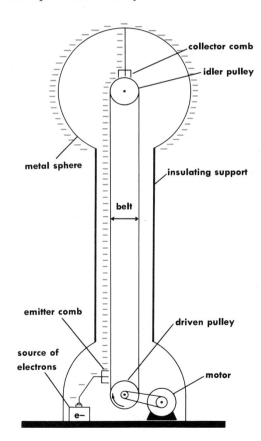

Fig. 18-4: *The Van de Graaff Generator. The potential of millions of volts can be used as an atom-smashing device.*

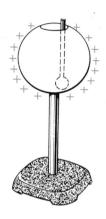

Fig. 18-5: *The charging of a hollow metal sphere to show that charges reside on the outer surface of conductors.*

conducted to the inside of the sphere, where by mutual repulsion they disperse to the outer surface. Large charges at potentials of millions of volts can be built up in this way.

3. SHAPE OF A CONDUCTOR AND THE DISTRIBUTION OF CHARGES

From Section 1 it will be seen that potential is related to the amount of work done in moving a charge in an electric field. Since unit charges mutually repel each other, a charge placed on a spherical conductor will reside on the *outside* of the conductor and the charge distribution will be uniform on the outer surface. On an irregularly-shaped conductor, however, the charge distribution will not be uniform. These conclusions can be illustrated as follows:

Distribution of Charge on Insulated Hollow Conductors

A hollow metallic sphere (Figure 18-5), open at the top and mounted on an insulating

stand, can be charged on contact by an electrophorus disk, or charged from the inside by a conductor suspended from one terminal of a Wimshurst machine. The charge distribution is tested by a "proof plane" and a leaf electroscope. The proof plane is a small flat metal plate attached to an insulating handle.

When a neutral proof plane is touched to the inside of the conductor and its charge tested on a neutral electroscope, the leaves indicate that no charge was picked up. When, however, the outside of the charged conductor is touched with a neutral proof plane and the latter is tested for charge as before, the leaves diverge, indicating that the charge given to the conductor resides on the outside surface.

Distribution of Charge on Irregularly-Shaped Conductors

A pear-shaped metal conductor mounted on an insulating stand is charged with an electrophorus. The charge density is investigated with the aid of a proof plane and a leaf electroscope. The charge on the proof plane is found to be largest when the proof plane is touched to the point of greatest curvature. (The conductor charge should be sufficiently large that the proof plane does not alter the charge distribution by its presence.)

Charge distribution on irregular shapes can also be tested on an insulated aluminum cooking pan or pie plate. The charge is greatest at the corners and edges and least on the flat surfaces.

To show discharge from a point, an electric whirl (see Figure 18-6) is connected to one terminal of a Wimshurst machine. This device rotates on its pivot owing to reaction forces produced by ions repulsed from the points. This observation leads to the following discussion.

311

4. DISCHARGING EFFECT OF POINTS

On a pear-shaped conductor, the charge distribution is uneven; the greatest concentration occurs at the end of greatest curvature. A conductor with a pointed end would have a still greater charge density at the point; also, the electric field about the point would possess a greater concentration of lines of force. This charge concentration can become large enough to *ionize* or charge the air molecules near it. Since dry air usually has a few charged molecules, those of like charge will be repelled, and those of unlike charge will be attracted to the point. These moving charges collide with neutral molecules and particles to produce further ionization. The ions of opposite charge are attracted to the points of an electric whirl and, receiving a like charge as they touch, are repelled. The stream of charged particles leaving the points produces a recoil force, thus causing the whirling action. The leakage of charge from sharp edges or points can produce a glow known as St. Elmo's fire, often seen at the trailing edges of aircraft wings. Charge removal is aided by the attachment of conducting streamers at the edges of the wings.

Benjamin Franklin designed lightning rods to help discharge clouds as they pass over buildings. The metallic rods are pointed and are joined to the ground by metallic conducting cables of low resistance. Electrons stream from the network of rods to neutralize positive clouds or in the opposite direction to neutralize negative ones. When the exchange increases to produce a strong ionization of air, the potential difference of millions of volts causes a lightning discharge in the space between. The rods and conductors provide a low-resistance path to the ground and prevent fires by minimizing the heating effect. The paths of low resistance thus protect the building and the adjacent areas. The lightning discharge produces a rapid air expansion and the sound shock-wave that results is the familiar thunder.

Fig. 18-6: *The electric whirl.*

5. CAPACITANCE

The potential of a conductor is determined by the work required to place a unit charge on it. During the charging period, as the charge on the conductor increases, the work required to add additional charge becomes greater. Thus the potential of a conductor is proportional to the charge on it, or, for a given conductor, the ratio $\dfrac{Q}{V}$ is a constant (C). This constant is called the *capacitance* of the conductor.

Transforming the symbols:

$$Q = CV$$

Quantity of charge Capacitance Potential

The unit of capacitance is called the **farad, which is the capacitance of a conductor when**

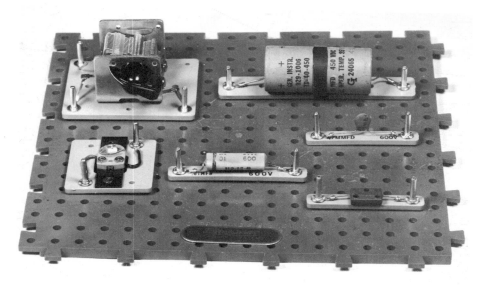

Fig. 18-7: *Illustration of different types of capacitors. Can you pick out the variable air-dielectric capacitor?*

the potential changes by one volt as its charge is altered by one coulomb.

Other units of capacitance are the micro-farad and the micro-microfarad.

$$1 \mu f \text{(microfarad)} = 10^{-6} \text{ f (farads)}$$
$$1 \mu\mu f \text{(micro-microfarad)} = 10^{-12} \text{ f}$$

A circuit component designed to store charge is called a *capacitor*. A capacitor consists of two conducting plates separated by an insulator known as the *dielectric*. From the above equation it may be seen that a conductor that can hold a large charge at a given potential has a high capacity.

The student should examine the construction details of several types of commercial capacitors, some of which are depicted in Figure 18-7.

EXAMPLE 1

The potential difference between the cathode and plate of a radio tube (diode) is 90 volts. How much work is required to move 100 microcoulombs of positive charge from the cathode to the plate?

Solution:

$$W = QV$$
$$W = 100 \times 10^{-6} \times 90 \text{ joules}$$
$$W = 9000 \times 10^{-6} \text{ joules}$$
$$W = 9.0 \times 10^{-3} \text{ joules}$$

The work required is **9.0×10^{-3} joules.**

EXAMPLE 2

When a capacitor is connected to a 120-volt source, the charge builds up to 480×10^{-8} coulombs. Calculate the capacitance of the capacitor.

Solution:

$$Q = CV$$
$$C = \frac{Q}{V}$$
$$C = \frac{480 \times 10^{-8}}{120} \text{ farads}$$
$$C = 4.00 \times 10^{-8} \text{ farads}$$
$$C = 4.00 \times 10^{-2} \text{ microfarads}$$

The capacitance is **$4.00 \times 10^{-2} \mu f$.**

313

POTENTIAL DIFFERENCE: The potential difference V between two points is equal to the amount of work done, W, per unit of charge, Q, when the charge is moved from one point to the other. Algebraically, $V = \dfrac{W}{Q}$.

UNIT OF POTENTIAL: One volt is the amount of potential difference existing between two points if one joule of work is required to move one coulomb of charge between the points.

$$1 \text{ volt} = \frac{1 \text{ joule}}{1 \text{ coulomb}}.$$

DISTRIBUTION OF CHARGES: Charges reside on the outside surface of conductors and are concentrated at points of greatest curvature.

CAPACITANCE: Conductors that can hold a large charge at a given potential have a large capacitance. The unit of capacitance is the farad.

EXERCISE A

1. (*a*) Name the two quantities used in the definition of potential difference.

   (*b*) What are the units used in the MKS system for these two quantities?

2. From the definition of potential difference, what criterion is used for stating that two points are at the same potential?

3. When is a conductor said to possess zero potential?

4. Charges escape at various rates from an irregularly-shaped conductor. How does an electric whirl make use of this fact?

5. State what must occur before a spark discharge will bridge an air gap.

6. Explain how buildings can be protected by lightning rods.

EXERCISE B

Charge on electron $= 1.60 \times 10^{-19}$ coulombs

1. 3.20×10^{-1} microcoulombs of charge is moved through a potential difference of 1.60×10^{2} volts. Find the work done.

2. Find the potential difference between points a and b if 920 joules of work are required to move 5.0 coulombs of positive charge from a to b.

3. To move a charge between two points with a potential difference of 120 volts requires 6.00×10^{-4} joules of work. Calculate the quantity of charge.

314

4. A capacitor, the capacitance of which is 5.00×10^{-5} microfarads, is connected to a 120-volt source. Calculate the charge on the capacitor.

5. A 250-μf capacitor has a charge of 5.00×10^{-6} coulombs. What is the potential difference across the plates of the capacitor?

6. What is the energy acquired by an electron subjected to 100 megavolts?

7. Find the potential difference between points a and b if it takes 950 joules of work to move 6.0 coulombs of charge from a to b.

8. The values of three capacitors are 0.15 μf, 0.22 μf, and 0.47 μf. When they are connected in parallel and charged to a potential of 240 volts, find:

   (a) the charge on each capacitor

   (b) the total charge acquired

   (c) the total capacitance of the combination.

   (Note: When capacitors are wired in parallel, their combined capacity is the sum of the individual capacities.)

Chapter 19

Direct-Current Circuits

1. CURRENT, ELECTROMOTIVE FORCE, AND RESISTANCE

In the previous chapter, the object of study was electricity in conductors insulated from nearby objects—a circumstance which permitted placing on the conductors charges that would remain on them for some time. The study of such electric charges at rest is termed electrostatics, whereas the study of electric charges in motion is called *current electricity*.

As is illustrated in Figure 17-9 on page 302, the leaves of an electroscope diverge when the system receives a charge, but immediately collapse when the knob is grounded. Since the leaves are an indicator of potential and potential is proportional to charge, the voltage must have returned to zero as a result of a flow of charge. In this instance, the charge movement was of short duration because the charges were not replaced and the potential was not maintained. When the charges are replaced as fast as they are lost, a continuous current can be produced. Charge replacement requires a source of electrical energy, which works to maintain the potential. Any device which maintains the potential difference is called a source of *electromotive force* (emf). Potential difference and emf are usually measured in volts by an instrument called a voltmeter.

In addition to a constant emf, a closed conducting path is required between the positive and negative terminals of the emf source to provide a constant path for the current. The components of this path are termed the *electric circuit*. When the path is broken there is said to be an *open circuit;* when it is continuous there is said to be a *closed circuit*.

From a closed circuit and a constant source of emf, a constant flow of charge results. The rate of flow is called the **current**, which is defined as **the rate of flow of charge past a given point in an electric circuit**.

The MKS unit of current is the ampere. **The current is one ampere when one coulomb of charge passes a point in the circuit in one second.**

$$\text{Current } (I) = \frac{\text{Quantity of charge } (Q)}{\text{Time } (t)}$$

$$1 \text{ ampere} = \frac{1 \text{ coulomb}}{1 \text{ second}},$$

$$\text{i.e., } \left[\frac{6.24 \times 10^{18} \text{ electrons}}{1 \text{ second}}\right].$$

With a constant emf, the current is altered by the amount of hindrance or *resistance* (R) to the electron flow. The MKS unit of resistance is the *ohm*, which is discussed under the heading of Ohm's Law (Section 3).

2. SOURCES OF CONTINUOUS CURRENT

Chemical: The emf required to produce a current is provided by chemical activity in a cell consisting of two different conductors, called electrodes, that are immersed in a liquid conductor called an electrolyte. Electrolytic cells are classed as either primary or secondary. The life of a primary cell is limited, since it ceases to function when either electrode is exhausted; in contrast, the effectiveness of a secondary cell can be lengthened by recharging, a process that renews the electrodes.

The Voltaic Cell—a Primary Cell

When a zinc and a copper plate are placed in a dilute solution of sulphuric acid, the zinc becomes negative by gaining electrons and the copper positive by losing electrons. The zinc becomes the *cathode* (negative terminal) and the copper becomes the *anode* (positive terminal).

The emf supplied by a zinc-copper cell in an open circuit is approximately 1.1 volts. In a closed circuit some of the energy supplied by the cell is used up, mainly as heat

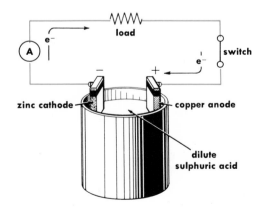

Fig. 19-1: *The voltaic cell provides a source of electromotive force by the chemical action between the electrodes and the electrolyte.*

energy. The components using the electrical energy are referred to as the *load*.

The conventional symbols for most load components are shown on the following page.

The Dry Cell—a Commercial Voltaic Cell

Practical considerations lead to the use of a moist paste as the electrolyte rather than a liquid. The zinc case becomes the cathode and a carbon rod the anode in a paste containing ammonium chloride as the electrolyte. To prevent loss of moisture the cell is sealed at the top.

Secondary Cells—the Storage Cell

Secondary cells, like primary, are voltaic cells, but they can have their energy restored by a recharging process. The most common type of secondary cell is the lead-acid storage cell.

As the name indicates, the electrolyte is an acid, usually sulphuric acid. The anode consists of lead peroxide, obtained by chemically altering the lead or, in commercial cells, by filling the grids of a lead plate with oxides of lead.

When in use, the cell is said to be discharging—the chemical process of turning both electrodes into lead sulphate and diluting the electrolyte by producing water. When the cell is fully charged, the specific gravity of the acid is 1.3, but during the discharging process it may fall as low as 1.1.

The energy is restored by passing a direct current from a generator in the reverse direction to that in the cell during use. During this charging process, the lead peroxide of the anode is renewed; the cathode returns to a spongy lead; the water in the electrolyte is used up; and the specific gravity of the sulphuric acid is returned to approximately 1.3.

A fully charged storage cell provides 2.2 volts when not under load. However, the emf falls during discharge.

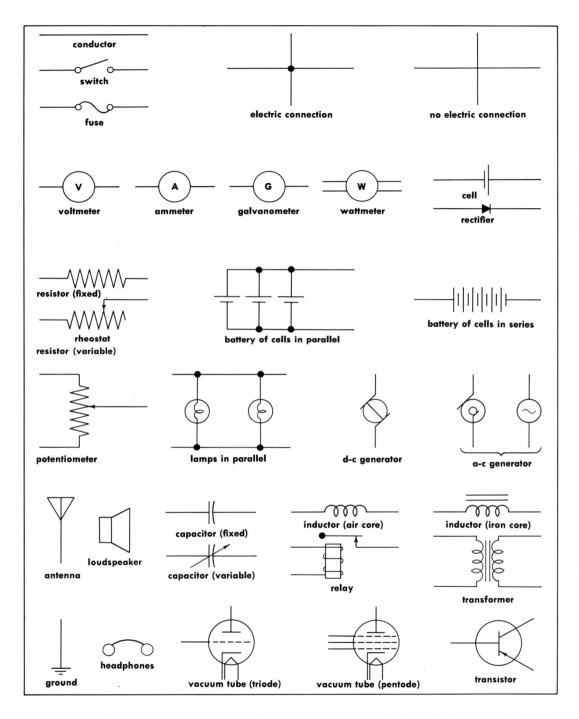

Fig. 19-2: *The components of electrical circuits have standard symbols, some of which are pictured here.*

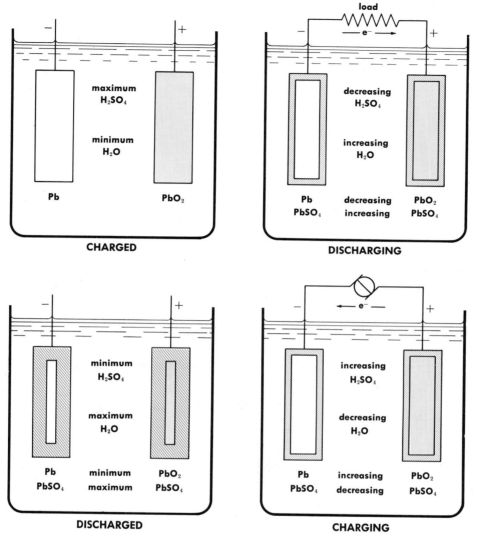

Fig. 19-3: *A secondary cell has its energy restored by a charging process. An external source of emf connected to reverse the e flow increases the concentration of the electrolyte and renews the chemical characteristics of the electrodes.*

Combinations of Electric Cells

The emf supplied by a single cell cannot be kept constant if the energy consumption of the load is too great. In addition to this difficulty, certain load devices are designed to operate using voltages other than those which can be supplied by a single cell.

As a solution to this problem, several cells are used in series or parallel or in series-parallel combinations. Such a group of two or more cells is called a *battery*.

Series Combination

To connect cells in series, the negative terminal of one cell must be joined to the positive terminal of the next. As more cells are added, this process is repeated; thus

319

the unconnected terminals of the first and the last cells will have opposite *polarity*. Each additional cell increases the energy level, thereby raising the emf to any value desired (Figure 19-4).

The current flow through each cell in this type of combination is the same: the emf is the sum of the voltages supplied by the respective cells, and the resistance of the combination is the sum of the resistances of the individual cells (see Ohm's Law).

The 6-volt storage battery consists of three lead-acid cells connected in series, and the 12-volt of six lead-acid cells in series.

Both batteries are constructed in such a way as to create the advantage of a parallel cell combination. This advantage is that of increased energy, obtained by an increase in electrode area. In a parallel hookup all the negative terminals are joined together and the positive terminals are likewise joined. The combination of the negative electrodes creates, in effect, one large

negative electrode; the connected positive electrodes, one larger positive electrode.

The storage cell attains a large plate area by the connection of several parallel plates together by means of a metallic strip.

Storage batteries and electric cells do not store electrical energy; they store chemical energy, which is changed into electrical energy when the source is connected to a closed circuit.

Photoelectricity: Light energy may be transformed into electrical energy. When incident light of sufficiently short wavelength is shone on a metallic surface, each photon of light energy increases the energy of the surface electrons. As the energy of the electrons increases, they reach a level of energy at which they can overcome the forces binding them together; the result is emission of electrons by the metal.

Photoelectricity will be discussed in greater detail in a later section of this text.

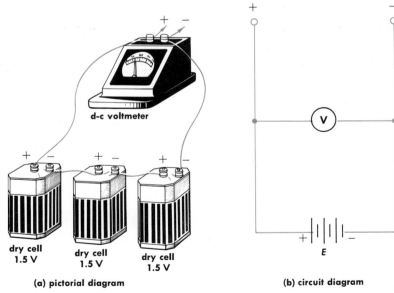

(a) pictorial diagram   (b) circuit diagram

Fig. 19-4: *The three cells have been connected in series. Note that the positive terminal of one cell is connected to the negative terminal of the neighbouring cell. The potential difference created by the combination is the sum of the potential differences provided by the individual cells.*

Thermoelectricity: If two wires made of dissimilar metals, such as copper and iron, are joined at both ends, and the ends maintained at different temperatures, an electron flow takes place around the loop. A device such as this is called a thermocouple.

Piezoelectricity: When subjected to alternating mechanical pressures, crystals of certain materials, such as quartz or Rochelle salt, generate a minute amount of alternating electric voltage. The potential produced varies according to the pressure applied. This transformation and its reverse (crystal oscillation by electrical stimulus) is known as the *piezoelectric effect*.

The crystal pickup of a phonograph generates voltages determined by the degree of pressure produced upon the needle travelling along the record groove.

If the phonograph needle is replaced by a diaphragm actuated by sound waves, the device becomes a piezoelectric-crystal type of microphone.

Electromagnetism: This source of energy will be studied in greater detail in Chapter 22 (Electromagnetism). The movement of a conducting wire in a magnetic field produces an emf in the wire. This method of electrical production is known as *electromagnetic induction*.

3. OHM'S LAW

In Section 1 of this chapter, electric current was expressed as the rate of flow of electrons. The practical unit of current is the ampere, that is, a flow of one coulomb, or 6.24×10^{18} electrons per second. Under a constant emf, the current flow is determined by the amount of opposition or resistance in the conductor.

The German physicist Georg Ohm tested this relationship and found that **in a closed metallic circuit, the ratio of the emf applied to the circuit to the current in the circuit is constant if the temperature remains constant.**

For any conductor, this ratio of emf to current is called the *resistance* of the conductor. Ohm's Law states that, for metals, the resistance of a particular conductor is constant. This is not true, in general, for other types of conductors, as discussed on page 324.

$$R \text{ (resistance)} = \frac{V \text{ (emf)}}{I \text{ (current)}}$$

The unit of resistance is the ohm, and its symbol is the Greek letter Ω(omega). **An ohm**

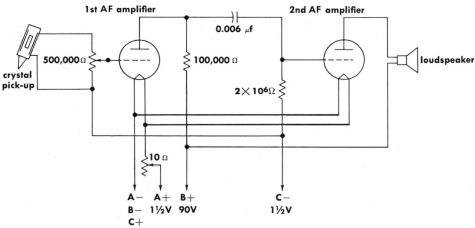

Fig. 19-5: *The crystal pickup illustrates the piezoelectric effect. The variations in pressure picked up by the needle are transformed into variations of electrical potential which can be amplified to provide sufficient energy to operate the loudspeaker.* 321

is defined as **that resistance which allows one ampere of current flow through a potential difference of one volt.**

Hence $1\Omega = \dfrac{1\text{ V}}{1\text{ amp}}$. This is a unit in the MKS system and can be expressed in other forms:

$$1\Omega = \frac{1\text{ V}}{1\text{ amp}} = \frac{1\,\dfrac{\text{joule}}{\text{coul}}}{1\,\dfrac{\text{coul}}{\text{sec}}} = \frac{1\text{ joule-sec}}{1\text{ coul}^2} = \frac{1\text{ nt-m sec}}{1\text{ coul}^2}$$

Students should frequently expand all MKS units in this way to understand their relationship.

Ohm's law for d-c circuits can be applied to the entire circuit or to any part or branch of it.

For example, consider a device that is connected across a potential difference of 100 volts, resulting in a current of 2.0 amperes. By definition, the resistance of the device is $\dfrac{V}{I} = \dfrac{100\text{ V}}{2.0\text{ amps}} = 50\Omega$.

4. RESISTANCES IN SERIES AND IN PARALLEL

Series: Since all conductors and electrical devices offer some opposition to the current flow, they can each be termed resistances. Two or more resistances connected in an arrangement providing only one path for the current flow are said to be connected *in series.* Because of the single path, the current flows through each resistance in turn, producing a corresponding drop in potential. As observed in Example 1, the sum of the potential drops equals the emf provided by the source.

A series hookup has characteristics which can be summarized as follows:

1. As there is only one current path, *the current is the same in all parts of the circuit.*

2. An open circuit in any part of the single path stops the current in all parts of the circuit.

3. Each resistance opposes the current flow; consequently their effect is accumulative. Thus the total resistance is the sum of the individual resistances.
$$R\text{ (Total)} = R_1 + R_1 + R_3, \text{ etc.}$$

4. The sum of the separate potential drops across the resistances is equal to the emf applied.
$$V\text{ (Total)} = V_1 + V_2 + V_3, \text{ etc.}$$

EXAMPLE 1

In the diagram the resistors R_1, R_2, and R_3 are connected in series to a 110-volt supply. Calculate the potential drop across each resistor and the total current in the circuit.

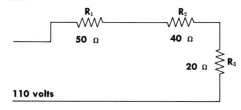

Solution:

$$R = \frac{V}{I} = \text{Total resistance} = R_1 + R_2 + R_3$$

$$I = \frac{V}{R} = \frac{110}{110} \text{ amps} = 1 \text{ amp.}$$

Voltage drops

across $R_1 = R_1 I = 1 \times 50$ V = **50 volts**
across $R_2 = R_2 I = 1 \times 40$ V = **40 volts**
across $R_3 = R_3 I = 1 \times 20$ V = **20 volts**
                                    110 volts

Note: The voltage drops across the respective resistors obtained by Ohm's Law, when added together, yield the emf applied.

Parallel: When a light bulb burns out in the home, the TV, the radio, the hair-drier, and the toaster on the same circuit will still operate. Such continued operation in spite of a circuit break is characteristic of parallel, but not of series circuits.

A parallel circuit provides an alternate route or branch for the current. Alternate paths for the current arise when the components of a parallel circuit are connected to points of common potential. Since each branch has a common potential, the current through each resistor will depend on the value of its resistance.

EXAMPLE 2

Let us connect in parallel the three resistors of Example 1, as illustrated in the diagram.

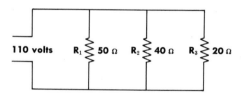

110 volts R_1 ⩾ 50 Ω R_2 ⩾ 40 Ω R_3 ⩾ 20 Ω

Calculate:

(a) the current in each branch: R_1, R_2, and R_3

(b) the total current in the circuit and the total resistance of the circuit: that is, the value of the *single* resistor which, connected across the source, would allow the same current to flow.

Solution:

Ohm's Law can be used for each branch. A common potential of 110 V is applied across each resistor.

∴ The current in the R_1 branch

$$= I_1 = \frac{V_1}{R_1} = \frac{110}{50} = 2.2 \text{ amps.}$$

The current in the R_2 branch

$$= I_2 = \frac{V_2}{R_2} = \frac{110}{40} = 2.75 \text{ amps.}$$

The current in the R_3 branch

$$= I_3 = \frac{V_3}{R_3} = \frac{110}{20} = 5.5 \text{ amps.}$$

Since the total current must split when entering the branches and rejoin when leaving, the total current I_T in the external circuit must be the sum of $I_1 + I_2 + I_3$.

$$\therefore I_T = I_1 + I_2 + I_3 = 10.5 \text{ amps.}$$

Applying Ohm's Law for the entire circuit:

$$R \text{ (Total)} = \frac{V}{I} = \frac{110}{10.5} = 10.5\Omega = R_T.$$

Note that the total resistance of the circuit is *less* than that of any of the individual resistors.

Alternate solution for R_T:

Let V be 1 volt instead of 110 volts.

Then
$$I_T = \frac{V}{R_T} = \frac{1}{R_T}$$

$$I_1 = \frac{V_1}{R_1} = \frac{1}{R_1}$$

$$I_2 = \frac{V_2}{R_2} = \frac{1}{R_2}$$

$$I_3 = \frac{V_3}{R_3} = \frac{1}{R_3}$$

But
$$I_T = I_1 + I_2 + I_3$$

∴
$$\frac{1}{R_T} = \frac{1}{R_1} + \frac{1}{R_2} + \frac{1}{R_3}$$

$$R_T = \frac{1}{\frac{1}{50} + \frac{1}{40} + \frac{1}{20}}$$

$$R_T = \frac{1}{.02 + .025 + .05}$$

$$R_T = 10.5\Omega.$$

The above equation will be true for any combination of resistors.

The characteristics of a *parallel* circuit can now be summarized as follows:

1. The total current in the circuit is the sum of the currents from each branch.

2. The potential across every component of a parallel circuit is the same.

3. The total resistance is less than the smallest branch resistance and can be calculated from the parallel-circuit equation; namely,

$$\frac{1}{R_T} = \frac{1}{R_1} + \frac{1}{R_2} + \frac{1}{R_3}.$$

4. Ohm's Law can be applied to the entire circuit or to any branch of the parallel circuit.

5. FACTORS AFFECTING THE RESISTANCE OF A CONDUCTOR

Temperature: Since temperature changes molecular agitation, it is reasonable to suspect that temperature will also affect the conductivity of solids. Nearly all metals, metallic compounds, and alloys show an increase in resistance as their temperatures are raised. The increased resistance is the result of an increase in thermal molecular agitation. Since the thermal agitation decreases as the temperature is lowered, the resistance decreases steadily and becomes nearly zero when the temperature approaches absolute zero (0°K).

Semiconductors—carbon, glass, and many electrolytes—behave in an entirely different way. In these materials, the resistance decreases as the temperature increases. This behaviour has been attributed partially to an increase in free electrons at the higher temperatures. The increase in free electrons can be due in part to the impurities present.

Length: When resistors are connected in series, the overall resistance increases and is found to be the sum of the individual resistances. For a uniform conductor such as copper wire, resistance increases uniformly with the increase in length used.

Cross-sectional area: With an increase in diameter, the cross-sectional area of a wire increases, providing a larger space for free-electron movement. As expected in this event, the resistance is lowered.

Type of material: As compared with insulators, good conductors have many free electrons; hence clearly the resistance and the conductivity depend on the nature of the material used for the conductor. In general, metals are good conductors.

6. MEASUREMENT OF RESISTANCE

Voltmeter-Ammeter Method: A very simple illustration of a d-c circuit is the voltmeter-ammeter method of measuring the resistance of a conductor. The moving coil galvanometer measures small d-c currents, but by using suitable series or parallel (shunt) resistors, the same instrument can be used as a voltmeter or an ammeter to measure voltages or larger currents.

To measure the potential drop across a resistance, a voltmeter must be connected in parallel with the resistance. An ammeter, however, must be connected in series with the resistance in order to measure the current.

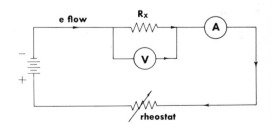

Fig. 19-6: *The use of the voltmeter (V) and the ammeter (A) to measure the value of an unknown resistor (R$_x$).*

An appropriate circuit for such a measurement is shown in Figure 19-6. In this circuit, the ammeter measures the sum of the currents through the resistor and the voltmeter. The latter current, however, is negligible in comparison to the relatively high current through the resistor. The value of the resistance is obtained by dividing the voltmeter reading by that of the ammeter.

ELECTRICAL CURRENT: A continuous flow of charge in a curcuit will occur if an electromotive force is maintained by a source of electrical energy. $1 \text{ ampere} = \dfrac{1 \text{ coulomb}}{1 \text{ second}} \left(I = \dfrac{Q}{t} \right)$.

OHM'S LAW: In a closed circuit, the ratio of the emf applied to the current produced is a constant called the resistance. $R = \dfrac{V}{I}$. The unit of resistance (the ohm) $= \dfrac{1 \text{ volt}}{1 \text{ ampere}}$.

SERIES CIRCUIT:

$$R_T = R_1 + R_2 + R_3$$

$$V_T = V_1 + V_2 + V_3$$

$$I_T = I_1 = I_2 = I_3$$

PARALLEL CIRCUIT:

$$R_T = \dfrac{1}{\dfrac{1}{R_1} + \dfrac{1}{R_2} + \dfrac{1}{R_3}}$$

$$V_T = V_1 = V_2 = V_3$$

$$I_T = I_1 + I_2 + I_3$$

RESISTANCE: The resistance of a conductor decreases when its temperature is reduced. The resistance of a wire is directly proportional to its length and inversely proportional to its cross-sectional area.

EXERCISE A

1. Diagram a circuit which could be used to measure the value of an unknown resistance.

2. Explain the difference between emf and voltage drop.

3. Write the formula for Ohm's Law in terms of emf and in terms of voltage drop across a resistance.

4. State the relationship between coulombs and amperes.

5. What is the fundamental difference between a primary cell and a secondary cell?

6. State the advantages of a battery composed of cells connected: (*a*) in series, (*b*) in parallel.

7. List five sources of emf which differ in the method of energy exchange.

8. What arrangement identifies a series circuit as compared with a parallel circuit?

9. State the characteristics of series and parallel circuits.

10. Write the equations for the total resistance in both a series and a parallel circuit.

11. Define the ohm.

12. List four factors that determine the resistance of a piece of conducting material.

13. How does temperature affect the resistance of a metal?

EXERCISE B

Consider all values correct to the number of digits quoted.

1. Calculate the quantity of charge transferred by a current of 0.25 ampere in a period of 15 minutes.

2. Calculate the emf of a battery composed of 30 dry cells connected: (*a*) in series, (*b*) in parallel. A dry cell has an emf of 1.5 volts.

3. An automobile battery composed of 6 cells each of emf 2.2 volts and resistance 0.10 ohm is connected in series to a load of resistance 5.20 ohms.
   (*a*) Draw a circuit diagram.
   (*b*) Calculate the current in the circuit.
   (*c*) Find the potential difference across the load and across the battery.

4. A current of 2.0 amperes produces a voltage drop of 6.0 volts. Calculate the energy used in joules during a period of 25 seconds.

5. A miniature lamp draws 200 milliamps when connected to a 1.5-volt dry cell. Find the resistance of the lamp filament.

6. A series set of 8 Christmas-tree lamps connected to a 110-volt source draws a current of 0.50 ampere. Calculate:
   (*a*) the total circuit resistance
   (*b*) the resistance of each lamp
   (*c*) the potential drop across each lamp.

7. Express the following equation in terms of R:
$$\frac{1}{R}=\frac{1}{R_1}+\frac{1}{R_2}+\frac{1}{R_3}.$$

8. Prove the following equation for two resistances connected in parallel: $R=\dfrac{R_1R_2}{R_1+R_2}.$

9. Four resistors rated at 20, 40, 60, and 80 ohms respectively are connected in parallel. Find the total resistance of the combination.

10. How many 220-ohm resistors must be connected in parallel to draw a current of 5 amperes on a 110-volt circuit?

11. Find the rating of a resistance connected in parallel with a 40-ohm resistor, which will make the total resistance 20 ohms.

12. Determine the net resistance, or total resistance, between points A and B for each of the following circuits:

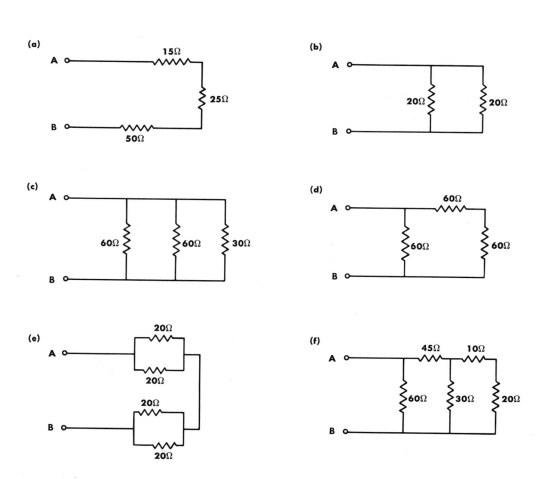

327

Direct-Current Circuits

▶ **Experiment 36**

To determine the relation between the potential difference across the ends of a conductor and the current through it.

Power supply (6 volts)

Rheostat (50 watt, 4 ohm)

D-c voltmeter (0-5 V range)

D-c milliammeter

Single-pole, double-throw (SPDT) switch

Resistors (15, 22, 100 ohms suggested)

Connecting wires (fast clips)

Mounting board (optional)

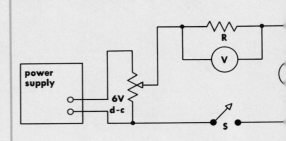

Procedure

1. Wire the circuit as indicated in the diagram.

2. Close the switch S and adjust the rheostat until the voltmeter records one volt. Read and record the current in milliamperes.

3. Read and record the corresponding current in milliamperes as the rheostat is adjusted to produce voltmeter readings of 2, 3, 4, 5, and 6 volts.

4. Repeat the experiment for each of the two remaining resistors. List the current readings corresponding to each

of the six voltmeter readings for each resistance.

Analysis

1. Plot a curve of potential difference in volts vs current in milliamperes for the six observations obtained for each resistor. Plot the current on the horizontal axis and the potential difference on the vertical axis to obtain three curves on a single graph, one for each resistor.

2. What is the type of variation obtained for each of the plots? What does the slope of each plot represent?

Experiment 37

To study the current through parallel resistors.

Power supply (6 volts)

Rheostat

D-c voltmeter

D-c milliammeter

2 SPDT switches

2 resistors (15 and 100 ohms suggested)

Connecting wires (fast clips)

Mounting board (optional)

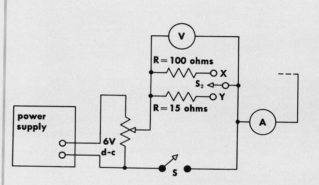

Procedure

1. Wire the circuit as indicated in the diagram.

2. Connect S_2 to the X position and the free ammeter lead to the Y position. Read and record the current in the 15-ohm circuit as you close switch S and then adjust the rheostat until the voltmeter records one volt.

3. Obtain five more current readings for settings of the rheostat which alter the voltmeter readings in turn to 2, 3, 4, 5, and 6 volts.

4. Open switch S and connect S_2 to the Y position. Disconnect the Y connection of the ammeter and reconnect it to the X position.

5. Close switch S; read and record the current in the 100-ohm circuit for volt-meter readings of 1, 2, 3, 4, 5, and 6 volts obtained by adjusting the rheostat.

6. Open switch S and S_2, and by means of a connecting wire connect X to Y. Leave the ammeter connection on the X position.

7. Close switch S; read and record the current in the circuit for the same six voltmeter readings as before.

Analysis

1. Make a table of your observations, listing the current in the 15-ohm and 100-ohm resistors, and the total current for each of the six voltmeter readings.

2. Find a relationship between the current in the 15-ohm and 100-ohm resistors and the total current. What do you conclude?

329

Chapter 20

Electric Power

1. ENERGY DELIVERED BY AN ELECTRIC CURRENT

When the sources of continuous current were studied in Chapter 19, electric current was found to be maintained by an emf supplied by chemical, light (photoelectric), heat (thermoelectric), mechanical (piezoelectric), and electromagnetic means. Each of the sources mentioned involved a conversion of another form of energy into electrical energy. The five energy sources each produced an emf which could maintain a current in a circuit.

We now turn to the consideration of an energy transformation in reverse: the formation of heat energy (thermal) from electrical energy.

The language of mechanics describes energy as the ability to do work. The ability of electrical energy to do work can be established by a re-examination of potential (Chapter 18). Here potential was defined as the amount of work per unit of charge required to move the charge from one point to another, or mathematically $V = \dfrac{W}{Q}$. In terms of work or energy:

$$W = QV = \text{Electrical energy}$$

joules   coulombs   volts

$\therefore$ E (electrical energy) $= QV$;
but in current electricity,

$$Q = It \ \ (\text{see page 325});$$

hence $E = VIt$.

electrical energy   volts   amperes   time in
in joules   seconds

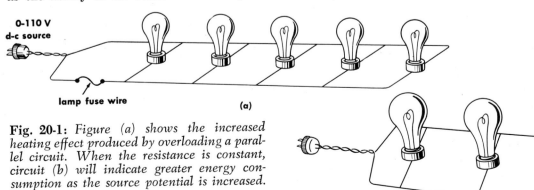

0-110 V d-c source

lamp fuse wire

(a)

(b)

Fig. 20-1: *Figure (a) shows the increased heating effect produced by overloading a parallel circuit. When the resistance is constant, circuit (b) will indicate greater energy consumption as the source potential is increased.*

330

From this expression of energy it can be seen that the electrical energy will increase if: (a) the potential is increased, (b) the current is increased, or (c) the circuit is closed for a longer time. Finally, let us consider the practical aspects of $E = VIt$ by discussing electric circuits. If equipment is available the discussion can be illustrated as follows:

Consider the circuit connections illustrated in Figure 20-1(a). All the lamps except one are unscrewed, and the circuit plugged into the 110-volt d-c source. If the remaining lamps are then screwed in one by one, the fuse wire will be observed to become very hot and finally to break.

In Figure 20-1(b), the circuit has been unplugged and the fuse replaced with a connecting wire. All the lamps except one are unscrewed and the circuit plugged into the source set at 0 volts. Then, as the source potential is increased, the remaining lamp will be found to glow more brightly.

The result of adding resistances in parallel was studied in Chapter 19. As each lamp becomes part of the circuit, the circuit resistance becomes progressively lower. In a parallel circuit, the potential across each lamp is the same as that of the source, in this instance, 110 volts. With a constant voltage and decreasing resistance, the current increases proportionately. When the heating effect produced by the increased current raises the fuse wire's temperature to its melting point, the circuit becomes open and the lamps go out.

In the second demonstration above, the increased glow of the lamp as the source potential is raised is the result of an increased current, which in turn heats the lamp filament to a greater degree, indicating an increase in expended energy.

Thus it has been shown that an increase in current or in potential increases the electrical energy used. If the lamp were placed in a beaker containing water, the temperature of the water would increase as time passed, thereby demonstrating the third factor that determines the amount of electrical energy used.

2. DISSIPATION OF ELECTRICAL ENERGY AS HEAT IN A RESISTOR

The apparatus used to study electrical energy showed that as the current increased, the heat produced by the current in the fuse wire became sufficient to melt it.

Let us consider a toaster and its attachment cord. When the cord is joined to the toaster and plugged into an outlet, the same current must flow through both the cord and the toaster. Nonetheless, there is a marked difference in the heat generated by each. The toaster element is made of nichrome wire, which offers a high resistance to the current flow, whereas the toaster cord is made of copper, which presents a low resistance to the flow of electricity.

In Section 1 of this chapter, the formula for electrical energy was developed from known equations and found to be $E = VIt$. In this formula V stands for the potential drop across a resistance. By Ohm's Law V can be expressed as $R \times I$.

$$\therefore E = RIIt \text{ or } E = I^2Rt \text{ joules}$$

Thus the electrical energy dissipated in a circuit is directly proportional to the square of the current times the resistance times the period of time over which the current flows.

When a battery is connected to a circuit, the battery delivers energy to the circuit. This delivery begins when kinetic energy of motion is transmitted to the electrons flowing in the wire. Since the electrons frequently collide with the atoms of the conducting wire, their energy of motion is transformed into heat energy. When the electrons pass through a motor or electromagnet in the circuit, their energy is transformed into other forms of energy, one of which is heat.

3. JOULE'S LAW

As noted in Chapter 6, James Joule studied the conversion of mechanical energy into heat energy. He also studied the conversion of electrical energy into heat energy; the result of his work, the equation $E = I^2Rt$, is therefore known as Joule's Law.

Joule's Law: The heat developed in a conductor is directly proportional to the product of the square of the current, the resistance of the conductor, and the time that the current flows.

This law states the means of calculating the electrical energy in a circuit and offers another method of finding the mechanical equivalent of heat.

In the circuit of Figure 20-2, the energy input is electrical. This energy is used to heat the water in the calorimeter together with the container and stirrer used. If the heat lost to the room is negligible, the input of electrical energy is equal to the output of heat energy. Thus by equating the input and output energies, the energy in joules equivalent to a calorie (heat) can be found.

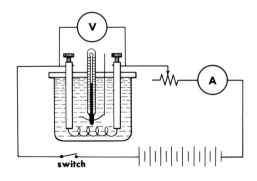

Fig. 20-2: *The electrical method used to determine the mechanical equivalent of heat.*

The measurements and calculations follow. For convenience, symbols are used in listing these.

$M_{(c)}$ = mass of dry inner vessel and stirrer of the calorimeter (grams).

$M_{(c+w)}$ = mass $M_{(c)}$ plus the mass of water (below room temperature) which is added to the vessel (grams).

$I_{(av)}$ = average of the current taken every minute and kept relatively constant by slight alterations of the rheostat setting (amperes).

$V_{(av)}$ = average of the voltmeter readings taken every minute (volts).

T_1 = water temperature at the beginning of the experiment (°C).

T_2 = water temperature at the end of the experiment when T_2 has become as far above room temperature as T_1 was below room temperature (°C).

t = time taken for the experiment (seconds).

$c_{(c)}$ = specific heat of the calorimeter and stirrer (cals/g. deg).

$c_{(w)}$ = specific heat of water (1 cal/g. C°).

The rheostat is used in the circuit to adjust the circuit resistance and so maintain a relatively constant current. What are the factors that can account for the current fluctuation?

The experiment is continued until the calorimeter and its contents reach a temperature as far above room temperature as they were below room temperature at the beginning of the experiment. How is the experimental result improved by the adoption of this procedure?

The mechanical equivalent of heat, J, named in honour of Joule, is expressed as:

$$1 \text{ cal} = 4.18 \text{ joules}$$

Calculations

Input electrical energy: $E = VIt$ (see Section 1) $= V_{(av)} \times I_{(av)} \times t$ joules

Output heat energy: H (see Chapter 10, Section 4)

$$= M_{(c)} [T_2 - T_1] c_{(c)} + [M_{(c+w)} - M_{(c)}] [T_2 - T_1] c_{(w)} \text{ cals}$$

mass of   temp.   sp. heat of   mass of   temp.   1 cal/g
cal.+stirrer   change   calorimeter   water   change

$E = H$ and $\dfrac{E}{H} = J$ (the number of joules of energy equivalent to one calorie of heat energy)

EXAMPLE 1

Express the energy liberated in heat units when a current of 0.25 ampere flows through a device connected to a 120-volt supply for a period of 5.0 minutes.

Solution: $E = VIt$

$E = 120 \times \tfrac{1}{4} \times 5 \times 60$ joules

$E = 9.0 \times 10^3$ joules

Since 1 calorie $= 4.18$ joules,

$$E = \frac{9.0}{4.18} \times 10^3 \text{ calories}$$

$$= 2.2 \times 10^3 \textbf{ calories.}$$

EXAMPLE 2

An immersion heater connected to a 120-volt supply has a resistance of 24 ohms. Assuming no heat losses to the surroundings, calculate:

(a) the heat produced by the heater for a period of ten minutes

(b) the mass of water that could be raised from room temperature (20°C) to boiling point in the ten minutes.

Solution:

(a) $E = VIt = V \times \dfrac{V}{R} \times t = \dfrac{V^2 t}{R}$

$\therefore E = \dfrac{120^2 \times 10 \times 60}{24}$ joules

$= \dfrac{120^2 \times 10 \times 60}{24 \times 4.18}$ cals

$= 8.6 \times 10^4 \textbf{ cals.}$

(b) $E = H = 8.6 \times 10^4$ cals.

$H = M_{(w)} [T_2 - T_1] c_{(w)}$

$$M_{(w)} = \frac{H}{[T_2 - T_1] c_{(w)}}$$

$$= \frac{8.6 \times 10^4}{[100 - 20] 1} = 1.1 \times 10^4 \textbf{ g.}$$

4. POWER IN AN ELECTRIC CIRCUIT

In Chapter 6, on page 87, power is defined as the rate of doing work, or consuming energy.

Electrical power can be determined by considering the relationship

$$\frac{P}{t}.$$

Thus,

$$P = \frac{VIt}{t} \qquad \frac{\text{joules}}{\text{sec}}$$

$$= VI \qquad \text{watts}$$

1 watt $= 1$ joule/sec

Hence, $P = V \times I$

watts   volts   amperes

The conversion units for power are as follows:

1 hp $= 746$ watts $= 550$ ft-lbs/sec

$= 33,000$ ft-lbs/min

5. APPLIANCE RATING

Electrical appliances are usually rated according to the power they deliver. Electric motors are generally rated in horsepower.

333

However, most appliances are rated in watts (60-watt bulb, 1500-watt heater). Some electric drills are rated according to the current they draw at a given voltage; thus the marking on a drill, 115V a-c 60~3 amps, means that it must be operated using a 60-cycle alternating current and that its power rating is approximately 115×3 watts, or 345 watts.

The power delivered by several appliances on the same circuit is additive. Hence the total power of the above appliances amounts to $1500+345+60$, or 1905 watts. Thus if the above-mentioned drill were used in a basement workshop together with a 1500-watt heater for comfort and a 60-watt bulb for light, from $P = VI$, $I = \frac{1905}{120}$ amps, or 15.9 amps, representing the amount of current required. If the circuit were properly equipped with 15-amp fuses, the fuse link would melt, thus producing an open circuit and some inconvenience. The circuit in this example is said to be *overloaded*.

One cure for the overloaded condition would be to replace the 15-amp fuse with a 20-amp fuse, but this is not recommended. House-wiring codes provide proper fuse ratings for circuits in order to prevent fires resulting from overheated wires. It is well to remember that the heat developed in conductors increases according to the square of the current. A procedure safer than over-loading the circuit would be turning the heater off while using the drill.

6. COST OF ELECTRICITY

The cost of electricity is calculated from the energy consumed. The charge is based on the kilowatt-hour (kw-hr or KWH); hence the energy used is measured in this unit. A reappraisal of electrical energy will clarify the meaning of this new electrical unit.

Electrical energy $E = VIt$

joules volts amps secs

From Section 4, volts $\times$ amps $=$ watts (a unit of power). Hence, E (in joules) $=$ watt-secs, and thus it follows that 1 *watt-sec of energy is equivalent to a joule of energy.*

The magnitude of the watt-second, or joule of energy, is too small for calculating electrical energy consumption; hence, the practical unit, the kilowatt-hour, is used.

$$1 \text{ joule} = 1 \text{ watt-sec} = \frac{1}{1000} \text{ kw-sec}$$

$$= \frac{1}{1000 \times 60} \text{ kw-min} = \frac{1}{1000 \times 3600} \text{ kw-hrs}$$

$$\text{or } 1 \text{ joule} = \frac{1}{3.6 \times 10^6} \text{ kw-hrs.}$$

$$1 \text{ kw-hr} = 3.6 \times 10^6 \text{ joules.}$$

EXAMPLE 3

Calculate the cost of running a 5-ampere toaster on a 120-volt circuit for 20 minutes a day for 30 days at the rate of 6 cents per kw-hr.

Solution:

$$E = VIt$$

$$E = 120 \times 5 \times \frac{20}{60} \times 30 \text{ watt-hrs}$$

$$E = \frac{120 \times 5 \times 20 \times 30}{1000 \times 60} \text{ kw-hrs}$$

$$= 6 \text{ kw-hrs.}$$

$$\text{Cost} = 6 \times 6 = \textbf{36 cents.}$$

EXAMPLE 4

The following appliances were operated for a 30-day month on a 120-volt circuit: a coffee percolator (resistance 20Ω) for $\frac{1}{2}$ hour per day; a 250-watt electric drill for 2 hours per day; a toaster drawing 5 amps for a period of 15 minutes per day. Calculate:

(a) the energy used by these devices in a month

(b) the bill for the month at 4 cents per kw-hr.

Solution:

(a) Percolator

$$I = \frac{V}{R} = \frac{120}{20} = 6 \text{ amps.} \quad E = Pt = VIt$$

$$= \frac{120 \times 6}{1000} \times \tfrac{1}{2} \times 30 = 10.8 \text{ kw-hr.}$$

Drill

$$E = Pt = \frac{250}{1000} \times 2 \times 30 = 15.0 \text{ kw-hr.}$$

Toaster

$$E = VIt = \frac{120 \times 5}{1000} \times \frac{15}{60} \times 30 = 4.5 \text{ kw-hr.}$$

Total energy consumed = **30.3 kw-hr.**

(b) Cost at 4 cents per kw-hr = 30.3×4
= 121 cents = **\$1.21.**

EXAMPLE 5

A hoist operated by a d-c electric motor drawing 20 amperes from a 220-volt source lifts $\tfrac{1}{2}$ ton of scrap metal at the rate of 132 feet per minute. Calculate:

(a) the power in watts supplied to the motor

(b) the hoist output in horsepower

(c) the efficiency of the system

(d) the cost of operation for 8 hours, at a rate of 5 cents per kilowatt-hour.

Solution:

(a) Input power $P = VI = 220 \times 20$ watts
= **4.4×10^3 watts.**

(b) Output power $P = \dfrac{\text{work done}}{\text{time}} = \dfrac{Fs}{t}$

$$= \tfrac{1}{2} \times 2000 \times \frac{132}{1} \text{ ft-lbs/min}$$

$$\therefore P = \frac{2000 \times 132}{2 \times 33,000} \text{ hp} = \textbf{4.0 hp.}$$

(c) Efficiency $= \dfrac{\text{Output power}}{\text{Input power}} \times 100\%$

$$= \frac{4.0}{4.4 \times 10^3/746} \times 100\% = \frac{4.0 \times 746}{4.4 \times 10^3}$$

= **68%.** (1 hp = .746 kw.)

(d) Cost at 5 cents per kw-hr

$$= \frac{4.4 \times 10^3}{1000} \times 8 \times 5 = 176 \text{ cents} = \textbf{\$1.76.}$$

ELECTRICAL ENERGY: The electrical energy supplied to a circuit is the product of the charge moved and the potential supplied to the circuit. $E = VIt$ where E is the energy in joules, V the potential in volts, I the current in amperes and t the time in seconds. The energy E can also be expressed by Joule's Law as I^2Rt joules.

THE MECHANICAL EQUIVALENT OF HEAT: Joule's Law provides a means of calculating the electrical energy supplied to a circuit. If the energy is used to heat a known quantity of water, the heat received can be calculated from the equation $E_H = mc\triangle T$. 1 calorie is the equivalent of 4.18 joules of energy.

ELECTRICAL POWER: Developing Joule's Law further, power, the rate of consuming energy or doing work, becomes $E/t = VI$. Power in joules/sec is thus the product of potential in volts and current in amperes. A power rating in joules/sec is usually expressed in watts, because 1 watt = 1 joule/sec.

COST OF ELECTRICITY: This is based on the energy consumed in kilowatt hours.

1 kw-hr $= 1 \times 10^3 \times 3.6 \times 10^3$ watt-secs $= 3.6 \times 10^6$ watt-secs, or joules

EXERCISE A

1. State the three factors which determine the electrical energy used in a circuit. Express the relationship in a formula indicating the MKS units for each term.

2. Explain the function of a fuse. Why is it dangerous to increase the fuse rating of a circuit?

3. State why a much greater amount of heat is produced in an electric element than in the conducting wires.

4. Write Joule's Law as a statement and then express this statement in the form of an equation.

5. What does the letter J stand for in this chapter? State the value of J to three significant figures.

6. How is power expressed in electricity? Name an equivalent unit for a joule/sec.

7. Name three ways in which electrical appliances are rated.

8. How many newton-metres are equal to one kilowatt-hour?

9. What unit of energy is used on your electric bill to state electrical consumption? What contributes more to the size of the bill: an electric kettle or a TV set operated for the same period of time?

EXERCISE B

1. An electric heater connected to a 115-volt source draws a current of 8.0 amperes. Find:
   (a) the quantity of electricity flowing through the heater in 15 minutes
   (b) the energy consumed in watt-sec
   (c) the power delivered by the source.

2. A heater is rated at 1725 watts at 115 volts. Calculate:
   (a) the resistance of the heater
   (b) the heat generated in calories when the heater is turned on for 10 minutes.

3. Find the resistance of an electric broiler connected to a 110-volt source if the broiler produces 7260 calories per minute. Assume that no heat losses occur.

4. A heating coil rated at 620 watts at 120 volts is used to convert 500 grams of water at room temperature (20°C) to steam. Find the time in minutes required to change all the water to steam.

5. An aluminum calorimeter and stirrer (c = 0.22) weigh 50 grams when empty, and 450 grams when filled with water at 10°C. Drawing 2.0 amperes at an average voltage of 30, a heating coil takes 9.0 minutes, 35.4 seconds to heat the water to 30°C. From this data calculate the mechanical equivalent of heat.

6. In 8 minutes a hot plate heater can raise 800 grams of water from room temperature (20°C) to boiling point and boil away 50 grams of water. If the current is 10 amps when the hot plate is connected to 110 volts, find the efficiency of the hot plate.

7. Assuming that an electric kettle has an efficiency of 78%, how much water can be raised from 20°C to 100°C in a period of 6 minutes if the kettle draws 10 amperes on a 120-volt circuit?

8. A voltmeter across an arc lamp connected in series with a 3.0Ω resistor reads 35 volts when the circuit is connected to a 110-volt source.   Calculate:

    (a) the current in the circuit

    (b) the rate of energy consumption for the resistance, in watts

    (c) the cost of operating the arc lamp for 20 hours at a rate of 4 cents a kilowatt-hour.

9. The oil burner connected to a furnace is operated by a $\frac{1}{2}$ hp motor.   On the average, the motor runs 40 times a day for an average of 4 minutes each time.   Calculate the cost for a period of 60 days if electricity costs 3 cents a kilowatt-hour.

10. A pump operated by a d-c motor drawing 20 amperes from a 220-volt line delivers 1100 pounds of water per minute to a storage tank 120 feet high.   Calculate:

    (a) the cost of operation at 2 cents a kilowatt-hour if the pump is operated 8 hours a day for 30 days

    (b) the efficiency of the pump.   (Note: 1 ft-lb of work = 1.36 joules.)

Electric Power

▶ **Experiment 38**

To find the mechanical equivalent of heat by the electrical method.

> 6-12 volt d-c supply
>
> D-c voltmeter (0-15 V range)
>
> D-c ammeter (0-10 amp range)
>
> Rheostat (0-20 ohms)
>
> Electric calorimeter
>
> Knife switch
>
> Celsius thermometer
>
> Balance
>
> Connecting wires (fast clips)
>
> Stop watch or sweep-hand timing device

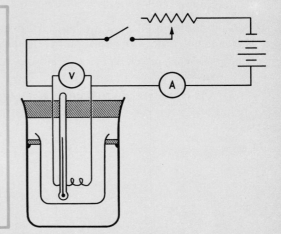

Note

If the calorimeter used has different electrical characteristics from those required, your instructor will alter the apparatus.

Procedure

1. Open the tap of a cold-water supply and have the water running as you proceed with the rest of the experiment.

2. Wire the circuit as indicated in the diagram.

3. Weigh the inner vessel of the calorimeter and the stirrer. Record.

4. Fill the calorimeter $\frac{3}{4}$ full of cold water (approximately 10 °C lower than room temperature). Record the room temperature in °C.

5. Reweigh the inner vessel of the calorimeter, which now contains the stirrer and cold water. Record this weight.

6. Assemble the calorimeter: the thermometer bulb should be in the water but positioned to permit temperature recordings.

7. Close the switch. Adjust the rheostat to give a current of approximately 2.0 amperes. Open the switch immediately.

8. Stir the water gently. Record the temperature to 0.1 °C. Close the switch as you start the timer.

9. As soon as possible, read and record the ammeter and voltmeter values: stir the water occasionally and record the

voltmeter and ammeter readings every minute.

10. When the water temperature becomes as far above room temperature as it was originally below room temperature, stop the timer (or record the time) and open the knife switch.

11. Gently stir the water to check if the temperature has not risen above that recorded during step 10. Record the highest temperature of the water. (It is difficult to mix the water thoroughly without spilling it. Usually the temperature of the water is found to be higher after the final stir. Therefore, to achieve good results, this final temperature should be used.)

Calculations and Analysis

1. The input energy was electrical. Refer to Section 3 and calculate the input energy in joules. Use the average values of the ammeter and voltmeter recordings when calculating this result.

2. The output energy was received as heat by the water and its container. Calculate this energy in calories.

3. Assuming that all the input electrical energy was received by the water and its container, input energy may be equated to output energy. Calculate the number of joules that are equivalent to one calorie.

4. State your experimental error as a percentage of the accepted value stated on page 332.

5. Account for any energy losses.

Chapter 21

Magnets and Magnetic Fields

1. MAGNETIC AND NONMAGNETIC SUBSTANCES

The study of electric currents must be interrupted at this point in order to consider another aspect of electricity.

In the early 19th century, Hans Oersted, a Danish scientist, discovered that a magnetic needle was influenced by a wire carrying an electric current. Before this discovery, magnetism was considered a subject separate from electricity.

The Greeks observed that some ores were unusual because they could attract and pick up certain articles. The iron ore exhibiting this property was later given the name *magnetite*: hence materials possessing this property are called magnets.

When it was observed that some pieces of magnetite always pointed in the same direction, the name *leading stone* or *lodestone* was applied to them. The word lodestone is reserved for nonartificial magnets, or *natural* magnets obtained from the earth.

After these earlier observations, it was found that the elements iron, cobalt, and nickel, as well as some of their compounds and alloys, were capable of being magnetized. Such substances are termed *magnetic substances* and are said to have *ferro-magnetic* properties.

The term *nonmagnetic* is usually applied to materials which do not possess the ferro-magnetic properties of the iron-cobalt-nickel group; however, if even these substances are placed in a strong magnetic field, some are slightly repelled and some slightly attracted.

2. THE DOMAIN THEORY OF MAGNETISM

The phenomenon of magnetism has been investigated since the seventeenth century; only within the last twenty years, however, have physicists begun to comprehend the true nature of magnetism. The discovery by Oersted that a current of electricity has a magnetic field associated with it provided a clue to the understanding of magnetism, as well as the variations in magnetic condition of different materials. Guided by the discoveries of Oersted and others, theorists developed the domain theory, which attributes magnetism to the movements of electrons within materials.

There are two modes of electron motion within an atom:

1. An electron orbits about the central nucleus.

2. In the course of this orbit, it spins about its own axis.

The domain theory uses these facts as the basis of an explanation of magnetism.

The most significant magnetic properties have been attributed to the second mode of motion mentioned above: the spinning of an electron about its axis. By convention, one direction of spin is designated as clockwise or +, the other as counterclockwise, or −. Two electrons, one of + spin and the other of − spin, are considered to be of opposite polarity. It is obvious that two such electrons in close proximity would have no composite magnetic effect, since each cancels the other's force. On the other hand, atoms containing two or more electrons that are spinning in the same direction and are unbalanced by electrons of opposite spin exhibit strong magnetic characteristics.

The strong magnetic properties of the atoms of the ferro-magnetic group may now be explained. In Figure 21-1, the M energy level of the iron atom, typical of the group, may be seen to have four more electrons of + spin than of − ; these electrons in millions of iron atoms may be aligned by an external magnetic influence. Regions of atoms aligned in this manner to exhibit like polarity are called *domains*.

3. INDUCED MAGNETISM

An iron nail or knitting needle dipped into some tacks and withdrawn slowly will not lift any of the tacks.

Suppose we hold the nail vertically with one end in the tacks, and hold a bar magnet within half an inch of the other end, as shown in Figure 21-2. If the nail and magnet are raised together while the space between them is maintained, some tacks are lifted with the nail; when the magnet is removed, the tacks drop to the table.

With the bar in place, the nail, because of its high permeability, has, in effect, extended the field of the magnet. The magnetic field is removed when the magnet is removed; in this event, the nail loses nearly all of its ability to pick up the tacks.

The magnetism produced in the nail by the influence of the magnet's field is known as *induced magnetism*. The residual magnetism left in the nail when the magnetizing influence has been removed is quite weak; the nail has therefore become a temporary magnet, since its magnetic properties will not last long.

The polarity of induced magnetism can be investigated by means of the arrangement

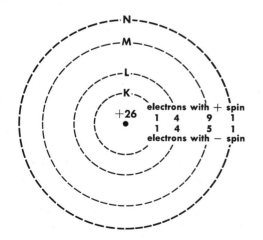

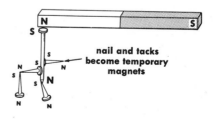

Fig. 21-2: *An illustration of induced magnetism.*

Fig. 21-1: *The iron atom possesses strong magnetic properties because of the unpaired electrons of the M energy level.*

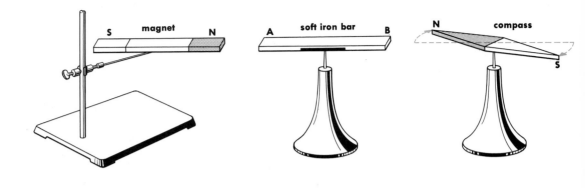

Fig. 21-3: *The needle movement indicates the induced polarity of A and B. Can you designate them as either N or S?*

shown in Figure 21-3. As indicated, the south pole of the needle will be attracted to B. If the magnet is reversed and the S pole placed nearest A, end B of the iron bar will attract the N pole of the needle.

The needle deflection indicated the polarity of the magnetism induced in the soft-iron bar. Students should formulate a rule for discovering the polarity produced by induction and draw a diagram to show the magnetic field for the combination of the bar magnet and the soft-iron bar.

Magnetization by contact is essentially the same as that by induction; the magnetising effect, however, is more pronounced, since the air gap is replaced by iron. A needle stroked in the same direction repeatedly by the same pole of the permanent magnet will become magnetized.

4. FORCE BETWEEN MAGNETIC POLES

The region in the vicinity of a magnet in which its magnetic force acts is called the magnetic field of the magnet. This field can be explored by sprinkling iron filings on a paper held over the magnet. The field of

the magnet acts on the current loops of the domains in each sliver to turn it parallel to the field (see Figure 22-5, page 347).

When a field is mapped with iron filings in this way, the filings are found to be concentrated in two regions, called the *poles*. If the magnet is freely suspended by a thread, or is pivoted, it will align itself in a north-south direction. The magnet in this case has turned to line up parallel to the earth's magnetic field.

The end of the magnet which points in a north direction is called a *north-seeking pole* and is labelled N. The end pointing to the south is called the *south-seeking pole* and is labelled S.

When two magnets are brought near each other, it is discovered that a North pole repels a North pole and attracts a South pole. Similarly, it is found that a *South pole repels a South pole and attracts a North pole.* These reactions are summarized in the **Law of Magnetism,** which states that **unlike magnetic poles attract, and like poles repel.**

The student should be aware of the distinction between electrical and magnetic forces. They both influence a charged par-

342

ticle like an electron, but not in the same way. Also, positive and negative electrical charges can be isolated, but north and south poles cannot. If a magnet were cut and recut into infinitesimal pieces, each piece would still possess a north-pole and a south-pole region.

5. MAGNETIC FIELD

It was noted that the magnetic field about a magnet can be explored and mapped with the aid of iron filings. When the filings are sprinkled on a sheet of paper held over a magnet and allowed to move freely, they arrange themselves in paths to produce a definite pattern. The field near the two similar and the two dissimilar poles of a pair of magnets can likewise be examined to discover the pattern characteristic of each field.

The field patterns appear to consist of many "paths" (see Figures 21-4, 21-5 and 21-6). Each path is called a **flux line**; this can be defined theoretically as **the path traced out by a free north pole in a magnetic field.** This definition can be tested practi-

cally by moving a small magnetic needle in the field of a magnet. The needle will be found to align itself with the paths described by the iron filings; the N pole of the needle will follow the path leading to the S pole of the magnet. By the definition given above, flux lines have a direction: namely, from the N to the S pole of the magnet. Accordingly, it is customary to place an arrow on flux lines to indicate this direction.

The characteristics of flux lines (loosely called lines of force) can be indicated as follows:

(*a*) Flux lines form complete paths proceeding from the N to the S pole outside the magnet and from the S to the N pole inside the magnet.

(*b*) Flux lines mutually repel one another; hence, they never cross.

(*c*) Flux lines, because of the forces exerted by neighbouring lines, cannot take a direct path between N and S poles.

(*d*) The concentration of flux lines at any point (the flux density) determines the field strength at that point.

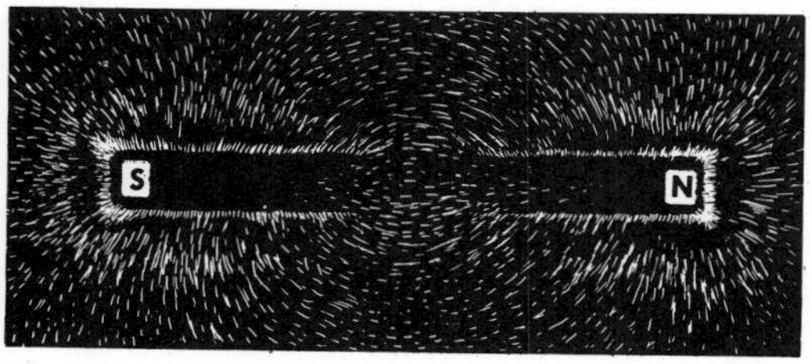

Fig. 21-4: *The field of a single bar magnet* ← *as indicated by a sprinkling of iron filings on a piece of paper placed on top of the magnet.*

Fig. 21-5: *The magnetic field has been revealed by sprinkling iron filings on a piece of paper resting on two unlike poles placed about 1 inch apart.* →

Fig. 21-6: *The field between two like poles* ← *indicates that the fields of the two poles mutually repel.*

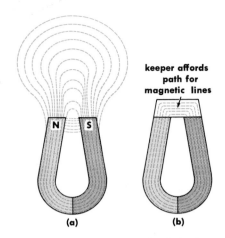

keeper affords
path for
magnetic lines

(a)   (b)

Fig. 21-7: *The pole strength of the horseshoe magnet is best maintained by placing a soft iron keeper across the poles.*

6. MAGNETIC PERMEABILITY

As noted above, the strength of a magnetic field is determined by the concentration of the flux lines within it. This concentration of lines may be altered by introducing into the field a magnetic substance, which offers little resistance to the force of the magnet. The flux density of the magnetic field is thus altered, in the sense that the concentraton of lines within the substance is denser than that within the surrounding area. **The ability of a material to alter the flux density of a magnetic field is called its permeability.**

The permeability of materials can be tested by placing some tacks, small nails, or iron filings on a nonmagnetic surface and attempting to pick them up with a magnet while interposing sheets of different materials between the magnet and the tacks. Sheets of glass, tin, cardboard, copper, and other nonmagnetic materials do not alter the magnet's ability to pick up the tacks. On the other hand, a sheet of iron or steel effectively shields the area beneath the magnet by turning the flux lines of the magnet's field away from the tacks. A flattened "tin" can (soft steel) works well as a shield in this way.

Since soft iron has a high permeability rating, soft-iron "keepers" are placed between the poles of horseshoe magnets (Figure 21-7). These keepers concentrate the field of the magnet, thus aiding in the maintenance of domain orientation. The strength of bar magnets is likewise preserved by storing them in pairs, with opposite poles touching, and soft-iron keepers between the poles.

Because the steel plates of a submarine effectively shield a compass needle from the earth's magnetic field, the compass is of little use in submarines. A ship's compass, however, may be shielded from the effect of the steel structure of the vessel by a permeable substance, thereby enabling the needle to respond to the earth's magnetic field.

MAGNETIC SUBSTANCES: The elements iron, cobalt and nickel, as well as their alloys, comprise a group of materials which are attracted by magnets.

DOMAIN THEORY: The magnetic properties of materials are attributed to electron movement. The strongest magnetic properties are related to the spinning of electrons. Domains are regions consisting of many atoms whose unpaired spinning electrons have the same direction of spin.

MAGNETIC FIELD: This is the region near a magnet or group of magnets where their magnetic influence can be detected. The field consists of lines of flux. A line of flux is the path that a free north pole would trace out while under the influence of a magnetic field, and the concentration of such lines determines the strength of the field.

MAGNETIC PERMEABILITY: This is determined by the ability of a material to alter the flux of a magnetic field. Materials of high permeability are used as keepers for magnets.

EXERCISE A

1. What did Oersted discover regarding the link between electricity and magnetism?

2. State two other names for lodestone.

3. What are alnico and permalloy? (A dictionary description will help.)

4. Name three elements which possess ferro-magnetic properties.

5. What unique characteristic of the atoms of ferro-magnetic substances accounts for their magnetic properties?

6. Describe a domain. What change comes over the domains when magnetic substances are placed in a strong magnetic field?

7. State the essential difference between a temporary and a permanent magnet.

8. Explain the mechanism by which iron filings become arranged in a pattern when they are sprinkled on a paper held over a magnetic field.

9. State the meaning of:
   (a) a north-seeking pole
   (b) a south-seeking pole.

10. Because the proximity of one magnet affects the field of another, sometimes magnetic needles in storage have their polarities reversed. Devise a test to check the accuracy of the N and S markings on a needle.

11. State the Law of Magnetism and explain why this law appears to be contravened when a magnetic needle is placed in the earth's magnetic field.

12. Why is one end of a surveyor's compass needle made heavier than the other? Which end would be made heavier in the northern hemisphere?

13. Aerial magnetic surveying was used in 1964 to disclose an ore body at Timmins, Ontario. Explain the operation of an airborne magnetometer. Be prepared to discuss how you would use a magnetic needle for this purpose.

14. State four rules concerning flux lines.

15. How is the density of flux lines in a space affected when a substance of high permeability is placed in the space?

16. Describe the difference between magnetization by contact and magnetization by induction.

Chapter 22

Electromagnetism

1. MAGNETIC FIELD SURROUNDING AN ELECTRIC CHARGE IN MOTION

The discussion concerning the domain theory of magnetism (Chapter 21 Section 2) was based on the work of the Danish scientist Oersted. When he placed a compass needle close to a wire carrying a current (Figure 22-1), he found it to be deflected as indicated. Moreover, when the needle was placed on the other side of the wire (Figure 22-2), it was deflected in the opposite direction, thereby suggesting that a magnetic field encircled the wire. The field can be shown as follows:

A conductor is arranged to stand vertically above the lecture table, preferably by mounting a U-shaped conductor on a wooden box. Iron filings are sprinkled in the area surrounding the conductor while a magnetic needle mounted on a pivot is placed farther away. One terminal of a storage battery is connected to the vertical conductor: the box is tapped while the remaining terminal is momentarily connected to the other end of the conductor.

Fig. 22-1: *The movement of the magnetic needle from the position shown in black (circuit open) to that shown in red (circuit closed) indicates that there is a magnetic field about a wire carrying a current. The needle moves in the opposite direction when the flow is reversed.*

The battery connections are reversed, and the field explored as before.

The direction taken by the N pole of the needle is indicated in Figure 22-3. The concentric circles obtained by sprinkling iron filings on a piece of cardboard or top of the box through which the wire passes represent the magnetic field around the wire.

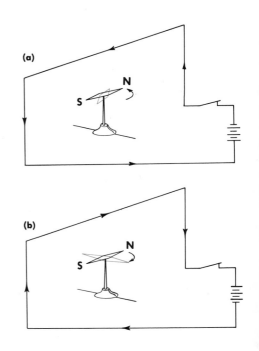

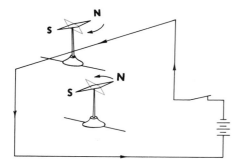

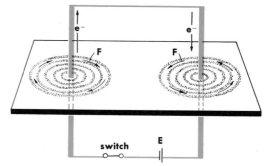

Fig. 22-2: *Above the wire, the N pole of the needle moves towards the viewer; below the wire, the N pole of the needle moves away from the viewer.*

Fig. 22-3: *The magnetic field about a straight wire carrying a current. The arrows indicate the direction taken by the north pole of a small compass.*

The observations made above obey a rule known as Ampère's rule for determining the field about a wire carrying a current. The rule is illustrated in Figure 22-4 and is stated as follows:

Ampère's rule for a straight conductor: Grasp the conductor with the left hand, thumb pointing in the direction of the electron flow: the fingers will encircle the wire in the direction of the magnetic flux lines.

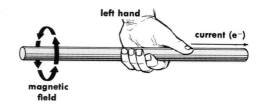

Fig. 22-4: *How to determine the field direction about a straight wire carrying a current. When the thumb of the left hand points in the direction of the e flow, the fingers encircle the wire in the direction of the magnetic field.*

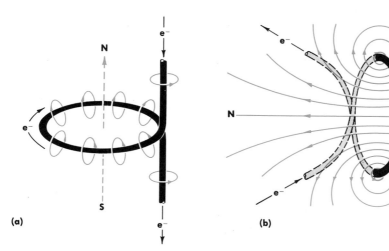

Fig. 22-5: *When a straight wire is bent into a loop, the field (a) can be found by the use of the Ampère's rule for a straight conductor. The fields combine to produce the field indicated in (b).*

2. THE FIELD ABOUT A CURRENT IN A CONDUCTING LOOP

In order to strengthen the magnetic field of a wire carrying a current, the wire is bent into a series of loops. If the wire is bent in the form of a single loop (Figure 22-5), the direction of the field about the wire, as indicated, can be determined by Ampère's rule for a straight conductor. The diagram shows that the flux lines all have the same direction, i.e., upwards through the centre of the loop. If the field of the loop is compared with that of a bar magnet, where the lines have a south-north direction inside the magnet, it becomes apparent that the field in the loop is similar to that within the magnet; that is, a north pole exists above the loop and a south pole below.

When several loops of wire are formed into a coil, the coil is termed a *helix*. When the helix conducts a current, each field created about each coil has the same direction, and this provides a concentration of flux lines which pass through the cylindrical core formed by the loops (Figure 22-6). The similarity of the helix field to the field about a bar magnet is readily apparent.

A helix designed for magnetic purposes consists of many tightly-wound turns of wire. An arrangement such as this is called a *solenoid*. The core of a solenoid usually consists of soft iron, which creates a further concentration of flux lines throughout its length to augment the strength of the magnetic field.

The polarity of the magnetic field about a solenoid might be found by applying Ampère's rule for a straight conductor. The rule has been modified as follows, however, to provide an easier determination:

Ampère's rule for a solenoid: Grasp the solenoid in the left hand with the fingers circling the coil in the direction of the electron flow. The pointed thumb will now indicate the N pole of the solenoid.

3. THE ELECTROMAGNET

Electromagnets used in electrical equipment are solenoids designed for a particular function. The core of electromagnets is made of soft iron of high permeability in order to concentrate the magnetic field. In addition to the core material, two other factors can increase the magnetic strength—the number of turns in the conducting coil and the strength of the current in the conducting wire.

The last two factors are often combined as the *number of ampere-turns*. An electromagnet with 500 turns of wire carrying a current of 1.0 amperes would have 500×1.0 ampere-turns, a strength equivalent to that of a magnet consisting of 5000 turns and conducting a current of 0.1 amperes. The strength of the electromagnet cannot be increased indefinitely by increasing the ampere-turns, for the effect is diminished when the core becomes saturated. When the size of the core is increased to offset the saturation effect, the field strength per unit area remains constant, but the magnet becomes capable of lifting heavier loads.

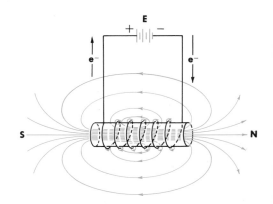

Fig. 22-6: *The magnetic field about a helix carrying a current. Note the similarity between this field and that about a bar magnet. Check the field polarity by the use of Ampère's rule for a solenoid.*

Electromagnets have many uses, some of which are listed as follows:

1. Large magnets are often installed in overhead cranes to load and unload steel beams or scrap iron from railway flatcars.

2. Strong electromagnetic fields are used in the manufacture of permanent magnets.

3. Electromagnets are used to record television programs on magnetic tape.

4. Surgeons remove steel splinters from wounds by this means.

5. Ribbon and dynamic types of microphones use electromagnets.

6. Electric generators and motors depend on electromagnetism.

General Electric Research Laboratory

Fig. 22-7: *The lines of force in the field around two superconducting magnets, demonstrated with iron nails. The coils of the magnets become superconducting at extremely low temperatures, which are maintained by immersion in liquid helium (in this case at −452°F).*

THE MAGNETIC FIELD SURROUNDING A WIRE CARRYING A CURRENT: The field consists of concentric circles. The direction of the field can be determined by Ampère's rule.

AMPÈRE'S RULE FOR A STRAIGHT CONDUCTOR: If the conductor is grasped with the left hand, with the thumb pointing in the direction of the electron flow, the fingers will encircle the wire in the direction of the magnetic field.

AMPÈRE'S RULE FOR A SOLENOID: If the solenoid is grasped with the left hand, fingers encircling the wire in the direction of the electron flow, the thumb will indicate the north pole of the solenoid.

ELECTROMAGNETS: These are solenoids designed for a particular function. The strength of an electromagnet of a given core material is determined by the number of ampere-turns around it.

EXERCISE A

1. Draw two straight lines side by side to represent conducting wires. By the use of arrows indicate reversed electron flow on the two wires. Predict the direction of the flux lines about each wire.

2. When the field about a wire carrying a current is examined, the current is permitted to flow for only a very short time if the resistance of the circuit is low. Why?

3. A conducting wire is placed in a north-south direction, the electron flow being from south to north. Make diagrams indicating how a magnetic needle will be deflected when the needle is placed:
   (a) under the wire
   (b) over the wire.

4. State Ampère's rule for:
   (a) a straight wire carrying a current
   (b) a solenoid.

5. State the number of ampere-turns for each of the conditions listed:
   (a) 10^4 turns, current 100 microamperes
   (b) 10^5 turns, current 10^3 microamperes
   (c) 5000 turns, current 10 amperes.

6. List four ways to increase the strength of an electromagnet.

7. List as many applications of electromagnets as you can.

8. Suggest a method which could be used to remove "tramp" iron from coal ore as it passes along a conveyor belt.

9. What role is served by electromagnetism in the operation of a cyclotron? See page 421.

10. How would a circuit breaker operate?

Chapter 23

Induced Electromotive Force

1. FARADAY'S INDUCTION EXPERIMENTS

The connection between electricity and magnetism was established by Oersted, who found that a magnetic field was produced around a wire carrying a current. A discovery of equal importance was made by Michael Faraday, an English scientist. Faraday found a method to produce an electromotive force utilizing a magnetic field. The basic experiments in the production of an emf by a magnetic field are known as Faraday's induction experiments.

A conducting wire is connected to a sensitive galvanometer, which records slight cur-

rents. The galvanometer needle at the upright or zero position indicates that no current is flowing in the circuit. When the conductor is moved downward between the poles of a horseshoe magnet as shown in Figure 23-1(a), the galvanometer needle moves to one side of zero. When the conductor is stationary, the needle returns to zero, but when the conductor is moved upward through the field as illustrated in Figure 23-1(b), the needle moves in the opposite direction, indicating that the current is the reverse of the current produced by the downward movement.

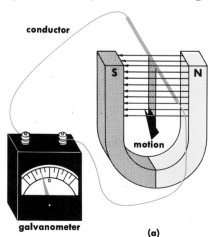

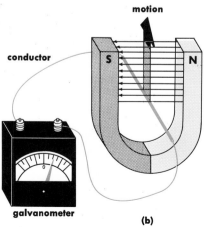

Fig. 23-1: *The current recorded on the galvanometer indicates that an emf must be produced when the wire is moved in the magnetic field. What change in current is indicated when the wire is withdrawn from rather than inserted into the magnetic field?*

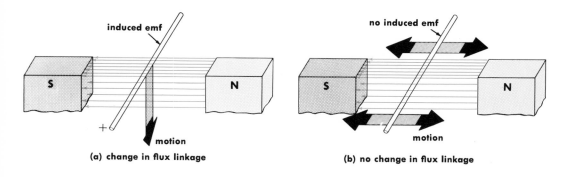

(a) change in flux linkage   **(b) no change in flux linkage**

Fig. 23-2: *An electromotive force is produced only when the conductor is moved at right angles to the magnetic field.*

When the conductor is moved rapidly downward or upward through the field, the current produced, as indicated by the galvanometer, becomes greater. Apparently an emf is induced in the conductor as a result of its movement through the magnetic field. Faraday's experiments showed that *the emf remains constant if the movement rate is not changed.*

Faraday also discovered that results similar to those produced by movements of the conductor were obtained when the conductor was held stationary while the magnet was moved across the wire. Thus a general conclusion can be formed: *an induced emf is produced in a conductor when the conductor cuts magnetic lines of flux.*

This conclusion can be tested by moving a conducting wire *parallel* rather than *perpendicular* to magnetic flux lines. When this is done no current results, proving that the conductor must cut across flux lines to produce an induced emf (Figure 23-2).

Since the galvanometer indicated an increased current when the conductor movement was rapid, it is apparent that the magnitude of the emf stems from the number of flux lines that the wire crosses in a given time. The crossing rate can be increased in several ways. The first involves coiling the conductor in the form of a helix (Figure 23-3).

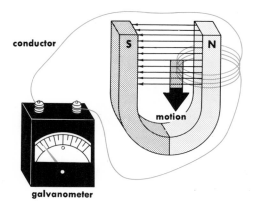

Fig. 23-3: *The galvanometer records a larger current when a helix rather than a straight wire is moved perpendicular to the magnetic field.*

From the diagram it is evident that each turn of the helix cuts an equal number of flux lines; *hence the current increase is proportional to the number of turns in the helix.* Another way to increase the emf would be to *increase the strength of the magnet,* thus providing more lines in a given area. A third way is to *increase the movement rate of the helix,* a procedure usually accomplished by the use of a motor. When the efficiency of the arrangement is improved in this way, the device becomes a practical generator.

2. DESCRIPTION OF THE PROCESS OF INDUCING AN EMF

By experiment it may be discovered that the inverse of Faraday's discovery is true: namely, if a conductor is supplied with a current and held in a magnetic field, a force will be exerted upon it. Consider Figure 23-4. When the knife switch is closed, the conductor is forced either up or down. If the current direction or the polarity of the magnet be reversed, the direction of force is reversed. Force production requires that a current flow exist in the conductor; hence, the magnetic force must act on the free electrons moving in the wire. Also, the magnetic force acts at right angles to the current direction.

We have now been provided with the clues pertinent to the understanding of production of an induced emf. Let us return to

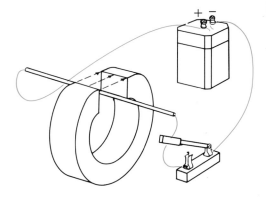

Fig. 23-4: *When the knife switch is closed, the magnetic field created by the current reacts with the field of the permanent magnet to force the wire either up or down. If either the permanent magnet's field or the current direction is reversed, the force direction is reversed and the wire moves in the direction opposite to that of the first movement.*

Faraday's results. In the conductor shown in Figure 23-5, the flow results from a force on the free electrons of the conductor acting in a direction at right angles to the flux lines of the field (force *F* in the diagram). When the movement and field directions correspond to those shown in the diagram, the electrons will move as indicated until the emf built up at the ends of the conductor provides a counterforce equal to the force on the electrons produced by the conductor movement. Of course, if the conductor were connected to a closed circuit and the movement were continuous, a steady current would flow in the conductor.

Fig. 23-5: *The force F moving the free electrons in the conductor ab creates an electron flow in a direction such that the field produced by it opposes the motion v.*

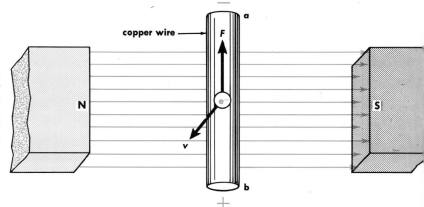

354

3. DIRECTION OF THE INDUCED EMF—LENZ LAW

If the potential energy of an object is to be increased, the object must be moved against a force. Thus the skier and the electric charge of Section 1, Chapter 18, were moved against the force of gravity and an electrical force respectively in order to increase their potential energy. Accordingly, the electrons that are starting from rest in Figure 23-5 must have increased their potential energy by moving *against* the electromagnetic force.

Let us consider a copper wire moving downward in a magnetic field as illustrated in Figure 23-6(a). The plus sign on the end of the conductor indicates that the electrons are moving away (through the page).

If the electrons flowed away from us as the wire was pulled downward, according to Ampère's rule the flux lines about the conductor would run in a counterclockwise direction. This counterclockwise field would oppose and *diminish* the permanent magnetic field *above* the conductor while augmenting the field below; consequently, the flux lines attempting to take a direct path from N to S would exert a net force upward on the conductor to produce the electron flow indicated. Since the downward motion of the wire

opposes this upward force, the potential energy of the electrons increases. The opposite electron flow would occur during an upward movement of the conductor, as illustrated in Figure 23-6(b).

The German physicist Lenz performed similar experiments and summarized his conclusions concerning the induced emf produced in a conductor within a magnetic field. **Lenz Law: The field of the current produced by an induced emf will oppose the motion inducing the emf.**

When the wire provides a closed circuit, the wire section moving in the magnetic field is a source of emf, and the remainder of the wire is an external circuit. The potential energy of the electrons in the external circuit can be utilized to perform work such as heating a coil, driving a motor or charging a battery.

4. THE SIMPLE ELECTRIC GENERATOR

An application of Faraday's induction experiments as described in Section 1 would be a practical generator consisting of a helix moved rapidly within a strong magnetic field. The helix is mounted on a shaft, which is rotated in the field to attain this rapid motion.

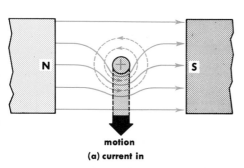

motion

(a) current in

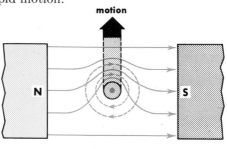

motion

(b) current out

Fig. 23-6: *In (a) the direction of the dotted field (discovered by Ampère's rule) opposes that of the permanent magnet field above the wire and decreases the field strength there; the dotted field reinforces the field below the wire. The net result is an upward force, which works to prevent the downward movement of the wire. (b) The reverse situation occurs when the wire is withdrawn.*

The terms to be used henceforward should be defined; the rotating shaft on which the coil is wound is called the *armature*: this term refers to both coil and shaft. The coil itself is the *armature winding,* and the shaft the *armature iron.* To simplify the processes involved, let us consider the turning of a single loop of the helix in the generator.

In order that a current be produced, the loop must be connected to a closed circuit. Contact with an external circuit is maintained with an arrangement of slip rings and brushes (Figure 23-7). The slip rings are mounted on an extension of the armature iron, and the stationary brushes make a

wiping contact with the rotating slip rings to conduct the current to the external circuit. The current in this form of generator is produced by the rotation of a conductor in a magnetic field.

As an alternative to the method described, the generator current may be produced by rotating the permanent magnet about a stationary armature. Some generators are constructed so that they function by the latter method.

The current direction from an induced emf can be determined as illustrated in Figure 23-7. However, it is more convenient to find the direction of the electron flow with the aid of a rule:

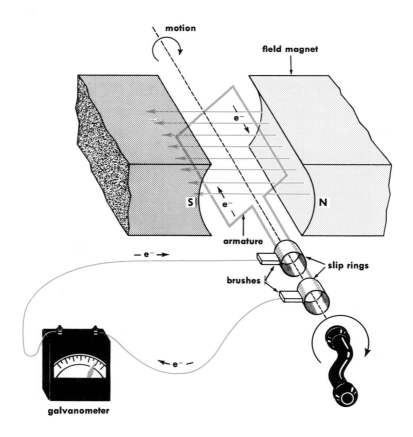

Fig. 23-7: *A simplified drawing of a generator to illustrate its various parts.*

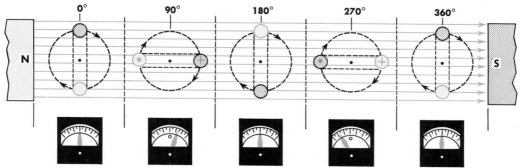

Fig. 23-8: *At the 0, 180 and 360-degree turn positions shown, the conductor moves parallel to the field, and no current results. In the 90 and 270 degree positions, the loop is moving perpendicular to the field, which creates maximum e flow. The direction of the movement is reversed in the two positions: hence the reversal of e flow direction indicated on the galvanometer.*

The Left-Hand Generator Rule: Extend the thumb, forefinger, and the centre finger of the left hand in a three-dimensional manner at right angles to one another. If the thumb (toward) now points toward the direction in which the conductor is moving, the forefinger (field) in the direction of the field, then the centre finger (current) will point in the direction of the electron current.

The A-c Generator

One aspect of the current direction has not as yet been considered. By referring to a sectional cut of our simple generator (Figure 23-8), we can make the following observations:

(1) When the loop is at the vertical position during rotation, it is moving parallel to the flux; hence no current is produced.

(2) As above, the dot represents an electron flow toward the reader, whereas a plus indicates an electron flow away from the reader. After a 90° rotation, application of the generator rule will affirm the current indicated, as the left side of the loop moves upward through the field and the right side downward.

(3) At $\frac{3}{4}$ of a cycle (270°), the movement in the left and right side of the loop has been reversed and, as indicated, so has the current.

These observations reveal that in a single cycle (or 360° revolution) of the loop, the electron flow therein reverses direction twice, and diminishes to zero between these reversals. A current that reverses cyclically in this manner is known as an *alternating*, or *a-c* current.

The a-c current produced in the generator was initiated by the emf induced during the rotation of the loop. When all the voltages are plotted for the emf produced during one cycle, the result is a sine curve (Figure 23-9). If the current strength resulting from the emf is plotted for the progressive time intervals during one cycle, an analogous sine curve is produced. The characteristic sine curve for a-c voltage and current is the basis of the familiar symbol $\sim$ used on many appliances to restrict their use to alternating current only.

The terms applied to simple generators are frequently at variance with those used for commercial generators.

The term *magneto* is applied to small generators used to start some lawn mowers and outboard motors, to ring the bell for army field telephones or to light bicycle lamps. Since the a-c generator produces alternating current, it is frequently called an *alternator*.

Large output voltages may be obtained from alternators by rotating the field magnets

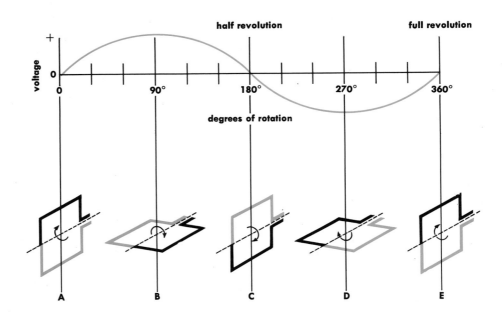

Fig. 23-9: *A graph of the emf produced by the simple generator for the loop positions A, B, C, D, E: namely, voltage vs time as degrees of turn. Relate the positions and emf produced with the currents indicated in Figure 23-8.*

around a stationary armature. The armature in this case is called the *stator*; the rotating magnet, the *rotor*. The rotor is usually an electromagnet whose voltage is low compared to the output voltage of the stator.

A generator consisting of a single magnetic field and coil produces a complete sine wave for each cycle: such a generator is spoken of as a *single-phase generator*. When two or more fields are used, each field produces a sine curve alternation for each cycle. The stator coils must be suitably spaced around the stator. The common multiphase generator is a three-phase generator, with fields evenly-placed at intervals of 120 degrees about the rotor. The output frequency of a multiple-phase generator is given by the following equation: $f(cps)$ = number of fields $\times$ rotation speed (rps).

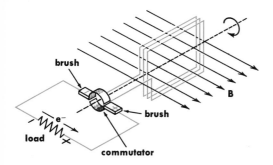

Fig. 23-10: *In a d-c generator, a split ring commutator is used. Its purpose is to ensure that electron flow to the load is unidirectional. Note that one brush is always connected to an upward-moving conductor, and the other to a downward-moving conductor.*

The D-c Generator

The construction of a simple d-c generator is the same as that of the simple alternator, the only exception being the method of current transfer to the external circuit. The slip rings of the a-c generator are replaced by a *commutator*. The commutator, mounted on an extension of the armature iron, consists of a single conducting sleeve ring split into two halves, with each half joined to a terminal of the armature winding.

Each time that the armature coil is at right angles to the field (zero current), the current direction is about to reverse in the two arms of the loop (Figure 23-10). At this

point in the cycle, the commutator halves reverse their respective brush connections; hence each brush is always in contact with a commutator section of the same polarity.

The commutator described is referred to as a *split-ring commutator*. The induced emf and current sent by the split-ring commutator to each of the brushes varies from a value of zero to a maximum and again back to zero. Thus, although the commutator provides unidirectional current and voltage to the brushes, the values fluctuate. The output in this case is called a *pulsating or fluctuating d-c current or voltage.*

The simple d-c generator output is shown in Figure 23-11. A comparison of the graph of this output with that of the alternator output (Figure 23-9) reveals that the second half of the cycle is the mirror image of the first. **This alteration of the a-c output into a direct fluctuating output is called rectification.**

D-c fluctuation can be minimized by the use of a multi-pole field within which the armature is rotated. The output obtained from a commutator connected to an armature turning within three magnetic fields per cycle is illustrated in Figure 23-12. The multifield output shown has been improved to the point where the value is nearly a constant approximately equal to the maximum

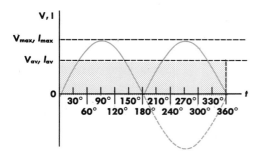

Fig. 23-11: *The fluctuating d-c output of the simple generator when a split-ring commutator is used.*

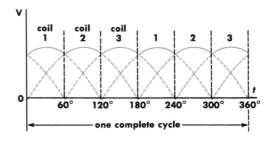

Fig. 23-12: *The fluctuating output potential is smoothed when three coils are wound on the armature. How would the commutator be constructed in this case?*

359

value of a single field. The multi-pole field not only increases output, but reduces the pulsations to a slight ripple, a process referred to as *smoothing* the fluctuation. A smoothed, rectified output, like that illustrated above, is suitable for most d-c requirements.

5. THE INDUCTION COIL

Faraday's induction experiments showed that an induced emf is produced when flux lines cross a conductor. This condition can be met by moving a conductor in a magnetic field or by moving the field about a conductor. In both cases the *essential* condition is a *changing* field strength (flux lines) in the vicinity of the conductor.

Let us consider the apparatus illustrated in Figure 23-13, in which a smaller coil connected by a knife switch to a battery can be placed inside a second coil connected to a galvanometer. The smaller helix connected to the input source is known as the *primary coil*, while the larger coil becomes the *secondary*. If the primary is plunged into the secondary with the key closed, the galvanometer needle moves to one side, but returns to zero when the primary is held stationary within. When the primary is removed, the needle moves to the opposite side, but once more returns to zero when the primary becomes stationary or moves some distance away.

When the primary coil is placed inside the secondary coil with the switch open, the galvanometer records zero, since there is no current in the primary, and hence no associated magnetic field to influence the secondary. If the switch is now closed, the galvanometer needle swings rapidly to one side and then returns to zero. When the switch is opened, the needle swings to the opposite side before returning to zero.

The conclusions to be drawn are as follows: in both cases an emf, together with its resultant current, was produced in the sec-

ondary circuit when a changing magnetic field or moving flux lines cut across the field of the secondary. When Ampère's rule for a solenoid is applied in the first instance, the discovery is made that the current direction in the secondary is such as to produce a field which opposes the primary field (Lenz Law). The primary field in the second case increases from zero flux to a maximum and back to zero as the switch is closed; the same occurs when the switch is opened, but in this case, the field has the opposite direction. The achievement of similar results by the two methods proves that no mechanical movement is necessary to induce an emf in the secondary: the only requirement is a changing field consisting of moving flux lines. This is called **mutual inductance, which is the production of an induced emf in one circuit by a changing current in the other.**

An important aspect of inductance is the effect produced in a single coil. Since mutual inductance results from the field variations produced by one coil crossing a second, it follows that a changing field in a single turn of a coil will produce an induced emf in

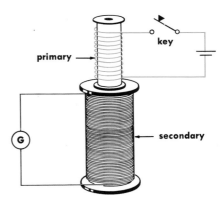

Fig. 23-13: *An interrupted current to the primary coil creates an emf in the secondary coil. The direction of the emf in the secondary when the current is stopped (broken) is the reverse of that when it is started (made). The emf created in the secondary is comparable to that obtained by inserting and withdrawing the energized primary.*

adjacent turns. The term *self-inductance* is used to distinguish this type of inductance from mutual inductance. The designation *inductance* is customarily used for *self-inductance*.

The self-inductance of a coil opposes any change in the flux caused by a change in the current in the coil in question. This is just an aspect of Lenz Law. Thus a coil offers a greater apparent resistance to an alternating current than to a steady current. In the case of a steady current, the resistance is equal to the ratio of the potential drop in the coil to the current in the coil. This ratio is usually referred to as the d-c resistance. The resistance opposing an alternating current in the coil is called the *impedance*. This term includes both the ohmic resistance and the effect due to the induced emf developed by the self-inductance.

6. APPLICATIONS OF MUTUAL INDUCTANCE

For practical use, mutual inductance is applied in two ways.

When high voltages are required in d-c circuits, the induction coil is used. Since an increase in voltage is desired, the secondary of the induction coil has more turns than the primary. However, a stepped-up voltage in the secondary does not imply an increase in energy; the increase in voltage is accompanied by a corresponding decrease in the secondary current to maintain the same power rating of voltage times current.

A requirement of mutual inductance is a fluctuating field in the primary. Since a steady d-c source does not supply a field variation, the current supplied to the primary circuit is interrupted by a make-and-break vibrator. This mechanism consists of an electromagnet with an accompanying spring vibrator, which produces automatic circuit interruption (Figure 23-14). A comparison of Figures 23-13 and 23-14 reveals that the make-and-break circuit replaces the

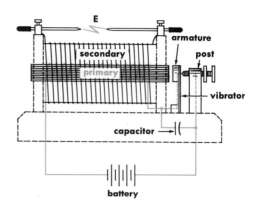

Fig. 23-14: *The induction coil. The vibrator provides a periodic intermittent current in the primary coil.*

knife switch. The emf of the secondary coil is commonly used to bridge a spark gap, E, as illustrated. The spark discharge in the spark plugs of an automobile engine is a well-known application of the induction coil. In this case, the secondary coil is joined to the distributor, which arranges the correct timing sequence to insure that the spark will explode the gas mixture in the cylinders.

A second application of mutual inductance is found in the *transformer*. If an alternating current were supplied to the primary of the circuit in Figure 23-13, the device would be a transformer. By the employment of an a-c source, the primary field is automatically varied in a cyclical manner. It follows that the changing primary field produces a corresponding a-c emf in the secondary.

The magnitude of the secondary emf depends on the ratio of the number of secondary to primary turns. Should the primary consist of 500 turns to the secondary's 5000, the emf induced in the secondary would ideally be ten times as large. A transformer operated to increase the secondary emf is a *step-up transformer*. Since the requirements of alternating current are often the reverse, a step-down transformer with more turns on the primary than on the secondary is used.

The discussion of the ratio of the number of primary to secondary turns implied a direct relationship between the turns ratio and the voltage ratio. In practise this does not follow, since energy is lost in the transfer. The energy losses may be classed as follows:

Hysteresis: Each reversal of primary current (which occurs 120 times a second in 60-cycle current), produces a corresponding reversal in the domains of the material of the transformer core. However, because the core material is a temporary magnet, reversal of magnetization occurs slightly later than the reversal of primary current; this condition results in heat production in the core. This consumption of energy in magnetization reversal is known as *hysteresis*.

Eddy Currents: These are currents set up by the primary field in the core material, which cause it to act as an undesirable secondary. These represent a loss of energy.

Resistance Losses: This energy loss is the familiar heat loss involved in the normal transmission of electricity through a resistance. Resistance losses are often referred to as *copper or I^2R losses*.

7. TRANSFORMER CONSTRUCTION

Energy losses are kept to a minimum by certain modifications in transformer and ignition-coil construction. The problem of hysteresis is reduced when the core is constructed of material which magnetizes readily. Alloys of silicon and steel have been developed for this function. Eddy currents are minimized when the cores are laminated and each lamination is insulated from the one next to it. The laminations are tightly bound to prevent humming noises that stem from core vibration.

The primary and secondary coils of transformers are wound about the same core to facilitate the energy exchange. When high-energy exchanges are to be made, the core used is a completely closed unit of ferromagnetic materials about which are wound the primary and secondary. By means of this arrangement the current necessary to force the required flux through the magnetic circuit is reduced. Transformers operate with an efficiency of 90% or better.

8. USE OF TRANSFORMERS

Transformers are used to alter the voltage in a-c circiuts when it is not suitable. For example, step-down transformers are required for doorbells and electric trains. On the other hand, step-up transformers are used for the transmission of electric power. Energy

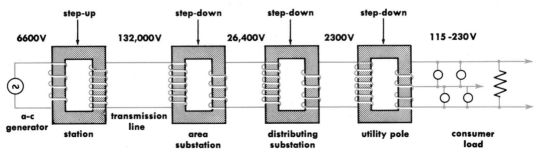

Fig. 23-15: *Step-up and step-down transformers are used to transmit energy from the generating station to the consumer.*

transmission at levels of up to 500,000 volts or more minimizes I^2R losses, since the current becomes correspondingly lower. The voltage is reduced at the consumer end by stepdown transformers. A simplified system is illustrated in Figure 23-15.

EXAMPLE 1

A transformer connected to a 115-volt outlet has 50 turns on the primary and 600 turns on the secondary. Find the output voltage.

Solution:

Let N_p and N_s respectively be the number of primary and secondary turns, and V_p and V_s the respective voltages.

Then $\dfrac{V_p}{V_s} = \dfrac{N_p}{N_s}$. Substituting, $\dfrac{115}{V_s} = \dfrac{50}{600}$.

$\therefore V_s = \dfrac{115 \times 600}{50} = 1.38 \times 10^3$ **volts.**

EXAMPLE 2

A step-down transformer with a primary-to-secondary ratio of 20 to 1 draws a current of 1.0 amperes when connected to a 120-volt line. Calculate the output current if the transformer efficiency is 95%.

Solution: $\dfrac{V_p}{V_s} = \dfrac{N_p}{N_s} = \dfrac{20}{1}$, or $\dfrac{120}{V_s} = 20$

$$V_s = \dfrac{120}{20} = 6.0 \text{ volts.}$$

Efficiency $= \dfrac{\text{Power Output}}{\text{Power Input}} \times 100 = \dfrac{V_s I_s}{V_p I_p} \times 100$

$$\therefore 95 = \dfrac{6 \times I_s}{120 \times 1} \times 100$$

$$I_s = \dfrac{95 \times 120}{6 \times 100} = 19 \text{ amps.}$$

Note: The voltage ratio is proportional to the turns ratio, as the flux linkage can be considered ideal. However, the output power is not equal to the input power.

INDUCED ELECTROMOTIVE FORCE: This is an emf produced in a conductor by a magnetic field. The emf is induced in the conductor when magnetic lines of flux cut the conductor as the result of a changing magnetic field in the vicinity of the conductor, or a movement of the conductor within a magnetic field.

LENZ LAW: The direction of the current produced by an induced emf was studied by the physicist Lenz. He stated his findings in the form of a law: namely, the field of the current created by an induced emf will oppose the motion producing it.

THE GENERATOR: The simple generator consists of a single loop of wire that is rotated in a magnetic field. Electrical contact with the loop is provided by slip rings and brushes: the rotating portion of the generator is called the armature.

The direction of the electron flow created by a generator can be predicted by the Left Hand Generator Rule. The rule predicts an alternating emf and current in the form of a sine curve fluctuation. A generator that employs slip rings and brushes provides alternating emf and current to the circuit: a generator employing a commutator generates fluctuating direct emf and current. Multiphase d-c generators smooth the fluctuations to a ripple.

THE INDUCTION COIL: A changing or fluctuating magnetic field in the vicinity of a conductor produces an emf in the conductor; a fluctuating field can be provided by a direct current if the current is interrupted by a make-and-break circuit. The induction coil consists of two coils concentrically wound, with one inside the other; a make-and-break circuit interrupts the current sent to the inner coil, called the primary coil. The emf induced in the outer, or secondary coil, may be greatly increased by employing a large ratio of secondary to primary coil turns. Two terminals attached to the secondary supply a spark discharge through the intervening air.

SELF INDUCTANCE: Current fluctuations in a coil are responsible for undesirable induced emf between adjacent turns of the coil. The emf produced in this way is termed self inductance; it increases the pure or ohmic resistance of a coil to the passage of alternating current.

TRANSFORMERS: Like the induction coil, the transformer uses a primary and secondary coil to alter the emf. The primary of a transformer is connected to an alternating source that periodically reverses the magnetic field created by the current. The changes in the primary field induce an alternating emf in the secondary. A large secondary-to-primary turns ratio steps up or increases the secondary emf; a large primary-to-secondary turns ratio reduces the secondary emf.

EXERCISE A

1. What condition is required to induce an emf in a conductor?

2. List three ways of increasing the rate at which flux is cut by a conductor in a magnetic field.

3. What bearing has Newton's second law on the production of a current in a conductor moving in a magnetic field?

4. Explain the increase in potential energy of electrons in the production of an induced emf.

5. How did Lenz summarize the method of determining the direction of an induced current?

6. State the purpose of slip rings and brushes in a-c generators and motors.

7. Describe the function of the generator armature.

8. State the left-hand generator rule.

9. Describe the current produced in each of the following:
   (a) the armature
   (b) the slip rings
   (c) an external circuit connected to the commutator of a simple d-c generator
   (d) an external circuit connected to the commutator of a three-phase d-c generator.

10. Describe each of the following: (a) a magneto, (b) an alternator, (c) a stator, (d) a rotor.

11. What relationship exists between: (a) the motion of a simple pendulum and an a-c current, (b) a complete vibration and a cycle?

12. Explain the meaning of a hexa-phase generator.

13. What is the function and structure of a split-ring commutator?

14. Describe the output from a simple d-c generator.

15. Explain the meaning of: (a) rectification, (b) smoothing of a current.

16. State the meaning of the primary and secondary terms applicable to electrical circuits.

17. Describe how the essential condition is met for an induced emf when a knife switch is operated in a d-c circuit.

18. Explain the meaning of: (*a*) mutual inductance, (*b*) self-inductance.

19. Explain the meaning of the term *impedance*.

20. Describe the function of the make-and-break circuit of the induction coil.

21. What method is used to increase the voltage output of an induction coil or transformer?

22. Explain the meaning of the terms *step-up* and *step-down* as applied to transformers.

23. Describe the meaning of each of the following: (*a*) hysteresis, (*b*) eddy currents, (*c*) I^2R losses.

24. In simplified form explain the use of transformers by the Ontario Hydro-Electric Commission in the transmission of energy from the Niagara plant to the industrial heart of Ontario.

EXERCISE B

The loads of Questions 3, 4, 5 and 6 are assumed to be non-inductive.

1. Draw a circle of about 2 in diameter on the left side of a sheet of graph paper to represent a rotating generator coil.   Divide the circle into 30° segments in an anticlockwise direction, beginning at 3 o'clock.   To the right of the circle plot a curve to represent the induced emf.   The *x* axis represents the time for each 30° of rotation: the *y* axis represents the induced emf indicated by the vertical components of the segment radii.

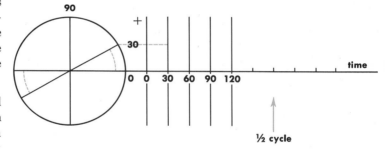

2. Plot the output of a 2-coil d-c generator using a graph similar to that shown in Figure 23-12.

3. The primary-to-secondary turns ratio of a transformer is 50 to 1.   The output current is 10 amperes and the voltage 2 volts.   Calculate:
   (*a*) the primary current if the transformer is ideal
   (*b*) the primary current if the transformer is 95% efficient
   (*c*) the efficiency if the primary current is 0.22 amperes.

4. A transformer connected to a 110-volt outlet produces 2200 volts emf in the secondary. Find: (*a*) the number of secondary turns if the primary has 200 turns (*b*) the primary current if the power output is 300 watts with a 95% efficiency.

5. A generating station develops 20,000 hp.   Assuming 100% efficiency, calculate the current flow in a transmission line at 400,000 volts potential.

6. A transformer is used to operate a 12-volt electric train from a 120-volt line.   The secondary current is 1.5 amperes.   Calculate:
   (*a*) the power output in the secondary
   (*b*) the primary current if the transformer is 90% efficient
   (*c*) the cost of operating the train for 30 hours at 4 cents per kwh.

Chapter 23

Induced Electromotive Force

▶ ## Experiment 39

To study electromagnetic induction.

Induction coil

Rheostat

Galvanometer

Magnet (cylindrical recommended)

A small solenoid which fits inside a larger one

Connecting wires (fast clips)

Power supply (6 volts)

SPST switch

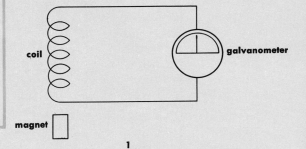

1

Suggestions

Suitable solenoid sets can be made by winding insulated copper wire around a 4-inch nail for a primary, and around the barrel of a Bunsen burner for a secondary. Alternatively, the wire can be wound around a small-diameter test tube for the primary and a large-diameter test tube for the secondary.

Procedure

1. Connect the apparatus as indicated in illustration 1.

2. Quickly insert the N pole of the magnet into the centre of the coil and note the deflection of the galvanometer. Rapidly withdraw the magnet and note the direction of the galvanometer's deflection. Reverse the magnet and repeat the magnet movement, inserting the S pole first, and noting the deflection of the galvanometer.

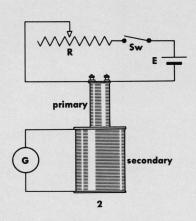

2

3. Insert and withdraw the magnet at different rates while noting the galvanometer's deflection.

4. Using a coil with more turns, insert and then withdraw the magnet. Note the effect on the galvanometer. The rate of insertion and withdrawal of the magnet should be constant when comparing coils.

5. Connect the apparatus as indicated in illustration 2. Set the rheostat to offer maximum resistance. Connect the primary to the 1.5 volt supply.

6. Carefully insert the primary into the secondary with the switch closed; withdraw the primary. Note the movements of the galvanometer needle. If satisfactory results are not obtained, reduce the rheostat resistance and repeat. If still greater primary current is required for satisfactory results, use the 6-volt supply. Check the e flow in the primary, and from it, the pole of the primary coil that was inserted and withdrawn. Repeat the procedure with the primary current reversed.

7. With the switch open, place the primary coil inside the secondary. Follow the precautions described in step 5 before closing the switch. Open the switch. Note the galvanometer's movements. Reverse the primary e flow and repeat step 7.

Analysis

1. A magnetic field is produced around the induction coil when the magnet is inserted. Determine if the induced field of the coil repels or attracts the magnet from a consideration of the direction of e flow in the coil-galvanometer circuit. Does the induced field attract or repel the magnet as it is withdrawn?

2. Use the Law of the Conservation of Energy to explain the galvanometer's reaction when the magnet is stationary within the coil.

3. Compare the insertion of the primary coil to the insertion of a permanent magnet.

4. When the primary switch is closed in step 7, do the results obtained from the secondary e flow and field produced resemble the results from the insertion or from the withdrawal of the permanent magnet? Also compare with the latter the results obtained when the switch is opened.

5. How is the primary field changed when (a) the primary current is increased, (b) the number of coil turns is increased, (c) an iron core rather than air is used?

6. Your conclusions should confirm Lenz Law and determine the factors that increase the strength of an electromagnet.

Chapter 24

The Electric Motor

1. FORCE ON A CONDUCTOR IN A MAGNETIC FIELD

Electrical energy is converted into mechanical energy by a device called a motor. The simple electric motor and the generator have essentially the same structure: in both, a loop of wire turns in a magnetic field. The motor, however, starts with an electron flow in the wire, whence it develops mechanical energy; the generator, on the other hand, uses mechanical energy supplied to it to *create* a flow of electrons in the loop.

As described in Chapter 23, a magnetic field exerts a force upon a conductor carrying a flow of electrons. It will be recalled that the direction of this force is related to the direction of electron flow in the conductor (Figure 24-1). Figure 24-2 illustrates that the current in either arm of the loop travels in a direction opposite to that in the other arm. Consequently, forces of opposite direction are exerted upon the two arms of the loop. If the loop is wound about an armature pivoted between the poles, these two forces will combine to impart a turning action, or *torque*, to the armature. Hence, mechanical energy has been derived from electrical and magnetic energy.

Although the generator rule cannot be applied to predict the direction of torque in the motor, a similar guide, the *right-hand motor rule*, can be substituted.

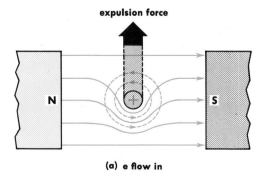

(a) e flow in

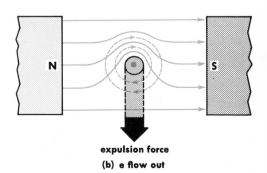

expulsion force

(b) e flow out

Fig. 24-1: *The armature of a motor is subjected to a force produced by the interaction of two magnetic fields.*

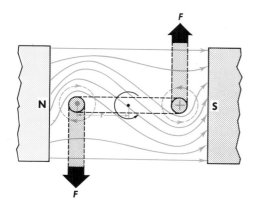

F

F

The Right-Hand Motor Rule: Extend the thumb, forefinger, and centre finger of the right hand in a three-dimensional manner at right angles to one another. If the first finger (field) points in the direction of the field, the centre (current) finger in the direction of the electron current, then the thumb (toward) will point toward the direction of motion (Figure 24-3).

2. BACK EMF IN A MOTOR

If the armature of a motor could turn without carrying a current, the motor would act as a generator; consequently, the rotating armature in a magnetic field would gain an induced emf that would oppose the motion producing it. Since the generator effect cannot be eliminated, as the motor armature turns in the magnetic field by virtue of its current and associated field, an induced emf opposes the applied voltage, thus reducing the current in the armature. Because the induced emf acts in the direction opposite to the applied voltage, it is called the *back emf* of the motor.

Fig. 24-2: *The forces on a single coil rotating on a plane with the page provide a turning motion, or torque, in the direction indicated.*

The size of the induced emf is determined by the number of flux lines cut by the armature coil in a given time; accordingly, the faster the armature turns, the greater the back emf becomes. When the motor is not connected to a load, the rapidly rotating armature produces a back emf nearly equal to the voltage applied. Conversely, when the motor is starting up under load, the slow build-up of induced emf momentarily permits a large current flow. At full speed the value of the back emf is in the neighbourhood of 90% of the applied voltage. Hence, if the motor were connected to a 100-volt supply, approximately 10 volts would remain to produce the armature current.

The amount of back emf in the rotating coil varies during each rotation for the same reasons as induced emf in the generator varies, resulting in a fluctuating torque. In practical motors, a smooth torque is obtained by the use of multiple armature coils. Also, the inertia of the armature tends to maintain smoothness of rotation.

Fig. 24-3: *Illustration of the Right-Hand Motor Rule.*

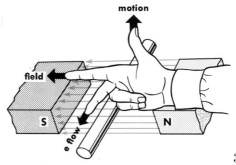

motion

field

S   N

e flow

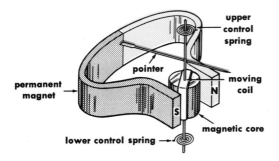

upper
control
spring

pointer

permanent
magnet

moving
coil

N

S

magnetic core

lower control spring

Fig. 24-4: *The basic d-c meter is known as the d-c galvanometer, a device used to measure small currents.*

3. MOVING COIL GALVANOMETER, AMMETER, AND VOLTMETER

The d-c meter is basically a d-c motor consisting of a permanent horseshoe magnet that acts as the field; a few turns of wire wound around a magnetic core provide the "armature". The "armature" is mounted on a shaft which turns against the opposing force of two coiled springs fixed to the top and bottom, respectively, of the shaft (Figure 24-4). [Henceforth the word "armature" will be used to describe the moving part of d-c meters (the magnetic core and the helix surrounding it), although its use in this sense is not customary.] The spring mechanism limits the degree of armature rotation, which is indicated by a pointer fixed to the shaft. Electrical contact is made to the armature via the two control springs; in this way, the armature current energizes the coil to provide a field opposing the field of the horseshoe magnet. Since the field of the permanent magnet remains constant, the pointer torque (armature rotation) is determined by the current flowing in the armature.

D-c Galvanometer

The d-c galvanometer has the basic d-c meter mechanism of Figure 24-4. It is a sensitive instrument used to indicate small currents and voltages.

The current direction determines the polarity of the armature electromagnet in accordance with Ampère's rule for solenoids. The pointers of some types of galvanometers indicate currents to the right or left of a centre zero marker. In the operation of this type of meter, however, a reversal of the current direction to the meter will reverse the deflection direction from zero, and with a correct initial alignment on zero, the pointer will indicate currents of equal magnitude in both directions.

In the event that the galvanometer scale begins with zero on the left and moves to the right only, care must be taken when the meter is connected in the circuit. Should a connection be made with incorrect polarity, the pointer will turn to the left of zero against the meter case, and the meter may become damaged. Accordingly, this type of meter should be connected with the terminal marked −, toward the negative side of the voltage source.

D-c Ammeter

A galvanometer is too delicate for the measurement of the current in most circuits. Consequently, it is modified to the form of the ammeter for use in these cases. A galvanometer or an ammeter must be connected in series to indicate the current. A galvanometer used for larger current determination would be permanently damaged by the I^2Rt heat energy in the armature. A full-scale galvanometer deflection is obtained with a current of approximately 2.5 milliamperes; hence a 0-10 milliamp meter must permit only

2.5 milliamps of armature current when the meter is used in a circuit carrying 10 ma. Therefore, to convert the galvanometer to a 0-10 millammeter, a low resistance must be connected in parallel with the armature terminals. This parallel resistor used in d-c ammeters is called the *shunt*.

The value of shunt required to convert the above galvanometer to a 0-10 milliammeter is calculated as follows: $10 - 2.5$, or 7.5 ma, of current must be carried through the shunt. If the internal resistance of the galvanometer is 10Ω, the voltage across both the shunt and armature resistances for maximum current would be $R_m I_m = 10 \times 2.5 \times 10^{-3}$ volts $= 25$ mV. Thus the resistance of the shunt for a current range of 0-10 ma can be found by the use of Ohm's Law:

$$R_s = \frac{V_s}{I_s} = \frac{V_m}{I_s} \qquad \therefore R_s = \frac{25 \times 10^{-3}}{7.5 \times 10^{-3}}\Omega = 3\frac{1}{3}\Omega$$

To convert the meter to other ranges, shunts of suitable resistances are used. In each case the shunt resistance is lower than the internal resistance of the meter, while the higher the range required, the lower the shunt resistance becomes, since more current must be bypassed away from the meter (Figure 24-5).

When shunts of various resistance values are interchangable between the armature terminals, the instrument becomes a multirange ammeter. In some instruments, multiple terminals marked for the range desired are provided, whereas in others, the shunt resistances are changed by a switch with the range position marked to correspond with the shunt. A multirange scale is usually supplied for a multirange meter. When a multirange meter such as this is used, care must be

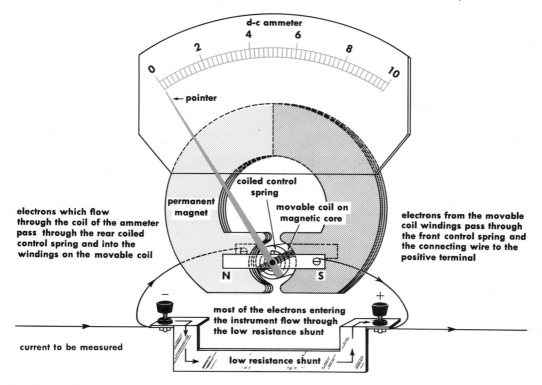

Fig. 24-5: *The construction of a d-c ammeter. What is the function of the low resistance shunt?*

exercised in reading the scale, for a gross error is introduced if the scale corresponding to the range is not used.

Demonstration meters for several ranges of current may be provided with shunts for insertion between the galvanometer terminals, or may incorporate the correct shunt for the scale indicated when the scale is replaced.

When one scale only is supplied for a multirange ammeter, the value recorded must be multiplied by a factor. Let us suppose that the shunt has altered the scale range from 0-10 amperes to 0-100 amperes: a reading of 3 amperes on the scale would be 30 amperes in this example. The multiplying factor was obtained from

$$\frac{I_2}{I_1} = \frac{100}{10} = 10.$$

EXAMPLE 1

Find the shunt value required to convert a galvanometer with an internal resistance of 10Ω and full-scale deflection for 2.5 ma into a 0-100-ampere d-c ammeter.

Solution:

The voltage across the shunt (V_s) is equal to that applied to the armature (V_m).

Hence,

$$V_m = V_s = R_m I_m = 10 \times 2.5 \times 10^{-3} \text{ volts.}$$

By Ohm's Law:

$$R_s = \frac{V_s}{I_s} = \frac{25 \times 10^{-3}}{100 - .0025}$$

Negligible value

$$= \frac{25 \times 10^{-3}}{100}$$
$$= 2.5 \times 10^{-4}\Omega$$
$$= 250\mu\Omega.$$

D-c Voltmeters

To measure the potential difference between two points in a circuit, one must connect a voltmeter to these two points. A d-c voltmeter incorporates the delicate moving coil, which deflects to full scale with only a few milliamperes passing through it. A larger current would seriously damage the meter by overheating the coil and by mechanical shock. It is therefore generally necessary to connect a high value of resistance in series with the moving coil to prevent excessive current. Such a series resistor, suited to the magnitude of the voltage to be measured, is termed a *multiplier* (Figure 24-6).

The value of a multiplier required to convert a basic d-c meter for a given range can be calculated as follows. Let us, as before, consider the basic meter to carry 2.5 ma for a full-scale deflection, the internal resistance being 10Ω.

EXAMPLE 2

Calculate the multiplier value which will convert the meter above to a voltmeter with a range of 0-10 volts.

Solution:

The total resistance $= R_T = \dfrac{V_T}{I}$

$$\therefore R_T = \frac{10}{2.5 \times 10^{-3}}\Omega \qquad = \frac{10 \times 10^4 \Omega}{25}$$

$$= 4000\Omega$$

The value of the multiplier $= 4000 - 10$

$$= 3990\Omega.$$

Analogous to the multirange ammeter is the multirange voltmeter, which alters the value of the multiplier for the range desired.

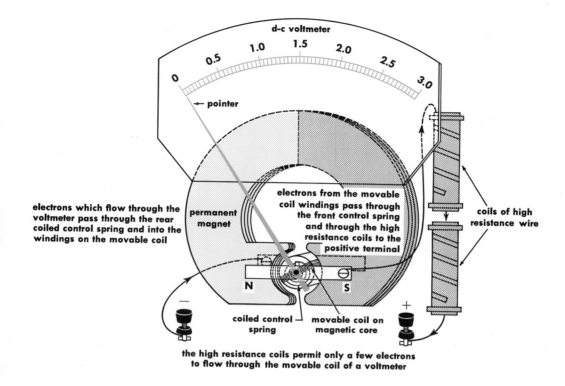

d-c voltmeter

0   0.5   1.0   1.5   2.0   2.5   3.0

← pointer

electrons which flow through the voltmeter pass through the rear coiled control spring and into the windings on the movable coil

permanent magnet

electrons from the movable coil windings pass through the front control spring and through the high resistance coils to the positive terminal

coils of high resistance wire

N   S

coiled control spring

movable coil on magnetic core

the high resistance coils permit only a few electrons to flow through the movable coil of a voltmeter

Fig. 24-6: *The d-c voltmeter. What is the function of the multiplier (coils of high resistance wire)?*

The multiplier is selected by the method described for the selection of the ammeter shunt (page 371).

4. METER SENSITIVITY

The word "sensitivity", when applied to meters, refers to their ability to respond to small changes in current. The more sensitive the instrument, the smaller the current required to move the pointer a given distance across the scale. It is customary to give the sensitivity rating of ammeters and milli-ammeters by the amount of current in the meter coil which will give a full-scale deflection. Thus a meter of sensitivity 0.1 ma will produce a full-scale deflection if $\dfrac{1}{10,000}$ of an ampere flows through the armature.

Sensitivity as applied to voltmeters does *not* refer to the response of the meter to low voltages, but to the current required by the instrument in order to make the measurement. The same moving-coil current is required by a meter to measure the range 0-1000 volts as is necessary to measure voltages in the range 0-10 volts. In the former case, the multiplier has limited the current through the moving coil to the same values as those required for the 0-10 range.

The sensitivity of voltmeters is usually expressed in ohms per volt. Thus a meter of sensitivity 1000Ω/ volt would have an internal resistance of 1000×1000 ohms, or 1 megohm, when used in the 0-1000 volt range, but would have an internal resistance of 1000×10, or 10^4 ohms, when used in the 0-10 volt range. The sensitivity of the voltmeter indicates its suitability for use in a given circuit. Should the meter require a comparatively significant amount of current for a full-scale deflection, the meter would alter the characteristics of the circuit.

The meter range selected should conform to the values to be read. Thus, a voltmeter connected to the 0-1000 volt range would not be suitable for recording voltages up to 100 volts, as the readings would be confined to a few scale divisions at the left of a meter unable to record small variations in voltage. On the other hand, the range selected should be slightly larger than the maximum potential difference to be measured in order to protect the meter from a sudden variation.

THE ELECTRIC MOTOR: A motor is a device that converts electrical energy into mechanical energy. Its operation is based on the principle that electrons flowing perpendicular to a magnetic field in which they are located are subjected to a force. The direction of this force is perpendicular to both the magnetic and electric field.

D-C METERS: A d-c meter is basically a d-c motor in which the "armature" rotation is opposed by coiled springs. The degree of rotation is determined by the magnitude of the current passing through the meter and is indicated by a pointer attached to the rotating coil.

D-C GALVANOMETER: The pointer moves to either side of a middle, or zero position; the direction of rotation is determined by the direction of the meter current, and the amount of rotation by the magnitude of the current. The galvanometer is used to measure small currents.

D-C AMMETER: This is a galvanometer altered in order to permit the meter to measure larger currents. A low resistance shunt carries most of the circuit current and permits a safe current to enter the basic galvanometer system. The resistance value of the shunt determines the range of currents that the meter can record.

D-C VOLTMETER: The voltmeter, which is connected in parallel with circuit components, must be protected from large current conduction by a high resistance operating in series with the galvanometer movement; consequently the meter constitutes a high resistance path, and the circuit components carry most of the circuit current. The series resistor is called a multiplier; its value determines the range of emf that the meter can record.

EXERCISE A

1. Explain the meaning of torque. Describe how a torque is obtained in a d-c motor.

2. State the law used to find the turning direction of a d-c motor.

3. What is back emf and how is it produced?

4. Explain the wide current variation in the armature during the starting process.

374

5. Describe the mechanism of the basic d-c meter.

6. Why are some galvanometers equipped with a scale that reads zero at the centre?

7. What is the purpose of a shunt and its operation in a multirange meter? What value remaihs constant in a multirange meter for full-scale deflections?

8. State the function of a multiplier.

9. What is the meaning of the term "sensitivity" as applied to d-c ammeters and voltmeters?

EXERCISE B

1. A 0-1 ma milliammeter has an internal resistance of 49Ω. Determine the shunt resistance when the meter has a 0-50 ma range.

2. An ammeter with an internal resistance of 1870Ω has a sensitivity of $100\mu a$. Calculate the shunt resistance which will convert the meter for use in the 0 to 10 ma range.

3. The internal resistance of a 0-50 milliammeter is 1350Ω. If the meter is shunted by a 150Ω resistor, what should the meter readings be multiplied by in order that the correct current values be obtained?

4. Fifty milliamperes produces a full-scale deflection for a galvanometer with an internal resistance of 10 ohms. Calculate the value of the multiplier which will change the range to a maximum of 200 volts.

5. A 0-200 voltmeter has a sensitivity of $100\Omega/volt$. The meter is connected across R_2 in the following circuit:

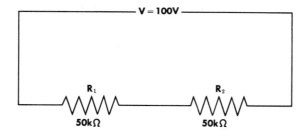

(a) What should the meter indicate?
(b) What is the internal resistance of the meter?
(c) What is the voltage drop across R_2 with the meter in place?

Chapter 25

Conduction in Gases and Vacuum Tubes

1. IONIZATION IN AIR— THE SPARK DISCHARGE

When charged conductors of various shapes were investigated (Section 3, Chapter 18), it was found that charge accumulated at the points or sharp edges of the conductors. In dry air, the potential difference between such a sharp point and another conductor must be greatly increased to charge, or *ionize* the intervening air sufficiently for the production of a spark discharge. The magnitude of the potential gradient required to ionize the air between two charged conductors is approximately 30 kV/cm. A spark discharge of this nature can be demonstrated between the terminals of a Wimshurst machine or by the use of a Tesla coil near metallic conductors.

A positively charged electroscope is rapidly discharged when a copper wire attached to the negative terminal of a Wimshurst machine is used to ionize the air in its vicinity.

It is evident, then, that under normal conditions, gases are only slightly ionized by cosmic rays from outer space and the ever-present radioactive materials in the atmosphere. Thus, a charged electroscope, if well insulated, will retain its charge for an appreciable interval of time: even when the electroscope case is grounded and the stem system charged, ionization of the air will be in-

sufficient to rapidly discharge the leaf system. However, should a beam of X rays fall on the air surrounding the system, the electroscope will be quickly discharged, indicating that the air was ionized by the X rays.

Air can also be ionized by a flame when it liberates electrons from nearby molecules. The effect can be demonstrated by holding a lighted match close to a positively charged electroscope. The ionized air soon neutralizes the positive charge and the leaves collapse.

Since the conduction of electricity by gases is poor under ordinary conditions of temperature and pressure, high potentials or other impractical means would be required for gas ionization, were it not for a discovery made in the last century.

2. LOW-PRESSURE CONDUCTION —CATHODE RAYS

Towards the turn of the century, during the investigation of conduction through gases, air was placed in a glass tube fitted with two electrodes, a positive *anode* and a negative *cathode*. When a high potential of 10,000 volts was applied to the electrodes, a discharge did not result, but as air was removed from the tube, there was a flow of charge between the electrodes. In addition to the current, the air inside the tube glowed initially; but as the pressure was reduced further by air removal, the glow disappeared, and the glass tube itself began

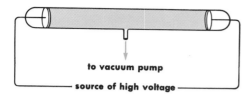

to vacuum pump

source of high voltage

Fig. 25-1: *The discovery of the electron just before the turn of the century occurred as a result of studies involving conduction in evacuated tubes.*

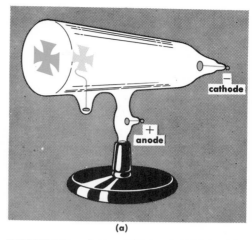

(a)

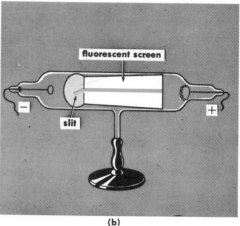

(b)

to exhibit a green fluorescence. Since the emanations producing the fluorescence were found to have their origin in the negative electrode, they have been called cathode rays.

If a metallic plate is placed between the electrodes while the rays impinge on a fluorescent material at the end of the tube, the shape of the plate will appear as a dark silhouette against the fluorescent material. The silhouette indicates that the rays follow a linear path between the electrodes.

Another characteristic of the rays is revealed when a magnet is used to deflect a narrow beam of cathode rays passing through a slit in a metal screen close to the cathode. A beam may be readily produced by connecting the electrodes with suitable polarity to the secondary terminals of an induction coil: it becomes visible when it falls on a fluorescent screen parallel to itself. When this device is used, the direction of beam deflection caused by the magnet indicates that the ray particles are negatively charged (see Section 3, Chapter 23).

Fig. 25-2: *Investigation of conduction in vacuum tubes revealed that: (a) the emanations started in the cathode and travelled in straight lines, (b) cathode rays made certain materials fluoresce, (c) cathode rays consisted of negatively charged particles which would be deflected in a magnetic or electric field.*

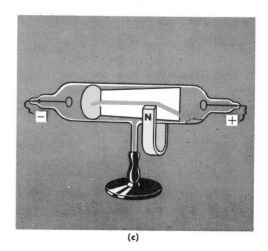

(c)

Professor J. J. Thomson investigated many different cathode-gas combinations to discover that the properties of the cathode ray were the same regardless of materials used. These observations proved that cathode rays consist of electrons with characteristics common to all atoms.

3. VACUUM TUBES— THE EDISON EFFECT

Thomas Edison found that his early electric light bulbs failed when the carbon filament burnt out at the positive end. To investigate the trouble, Edison sealed a metal plate in the evacuated bulb and connected it in series through a galvanometer to the filament of the bulb. With the plate connected to the positive terminal of the filament battery, the galvanometer indicated a current; when the plate was made negative, however, no current was indicated. Edison merely recorded these observations: they were explained later, when J. J. Thomson discovered the negative electron. Edison had constructed a primitive vacuum tube,

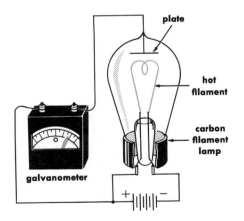

Fig. 25-3: *Edison constructed a primitive vacuum tube when investigating trouble with his early electric lightbulbs. What did the galvanometer read when the plate was connected to the negative side of the filament battery?*

in which the hot filament emitted electrons that were attracted by the positive plate to produce a current in the external circuit.

Vacuum tubes were investigated and improved through many years of research to develop an assortment of tubes for various functions. All types of vacuum tubes provide a source of electrons, which emanate from a negative electrode. The electrons emitted by the cathode are attracted to the positive anode, sometimes called the *plate*. In its simplest form, the tube consists of the cathode and plate enclosed in a glass or metallic envelope from which the air has been extracted.

The vacuum tube just described is the *diode*. When further electrodes are added to the evacuated tube between the cathode and the plate, the tube becomes a *triode* (3 electrodes), a *tetrode* (4 electrodes), or a *pentode* (5 electrodes).

4. PHOTOELECTRICITY

The current in Edison's primitive vacuum tube was produced when electrons emitted by a hot filament were attracted to the positive electrode of the tube. Figure 25-4 illustrates a vacuum tube in which electrons are emitted by the action of light incident on a negative electrode. The negative electrode is coated with a material such as caesium that will emit electrons when visible light falls on it: the shape of the electrode provides a large area for the incident light. The electrons freed from the cathode by the action of the light are attracted to the positive wire-like electrode called the anode. The vacuum tube in this case becomes a photoelectric cell: **the emission of electrons from certain materials due to incident light is referred to as the photoelectric effect.**

Although the photoelectric effect can be demonstrated using a phototube with its associated circuit, classroom observation of the effect has customarily been shown as indicated in Figure 25-5. A large zinc plate freshly cleaned with steel wool is connected to a sensitive electroscope mounted on an insulating stand. The electroscope-plate system is first charged negatively by induction. When ultraviolet light from a carbon arc is placed a few inches from the plate the electroscope is soon discharged. Evidently negative particles have been emitted from the electroscope system. This conclusion is further substantiated when the experiment is repeated using a positively charged system, since, in this case, no noticeable change in leaf deflection occurs. The carbon arc has a negligible effect in either case when the lens is used in the projector.

The "bare" carbon arc has sufficient energy to cause electron emission from the zinc, but when the plate and electroscope system have a negative charge, the electrons on the plate repel those emitted by the

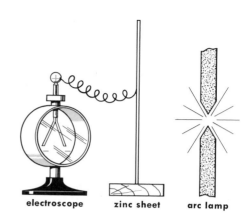

electroscope   **zinc sheet**   **arc lamp**

Fig. 25-5: *Demonstration of the photoelectric effect with an electroscope system.*

action of the light and, as the system is losing electrons, the electroscope is discharged. When charged positively, the electrons freed by the ultraviolet light are attracted back to the plate and since there is no net change in the charge, the electroscope is not discharged.

The photoelectric cell or phototube has many applications; a familiar one is the sound track of a motion picture. The sounds produced in the studio are converted in a microphone to electrical waves of the same frequency. After amplification, the current from the microphone is used to vary the intensity or the width of a light incident on the edge of the film where the sound track is provided. When the track passes in front of the projector light, the light transmitted will vary to provide a light pattern that can be used to reproduce the original studio sound.

The phototube can be employed to turn street lights on and off automatically when the light intensity shining on the tube either provides a current large enough to close a relay or diminishes enough to allow the relay to open. A light beam falling on such a tube can be interrupted to open doors, start burglar alarms, etc.

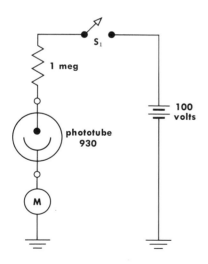

Fig. 25-4: *Diagram showing a photoelectric cell in circuit.*

5. THERMIONIC EMISSION

A prerequisite for the operation of any vacuum tube is the efficient emission of electrons from the cathode of the tube. The electrons are the charged particles that provide the current bridging the space between the two electrodes. This is an essential function: one which cannot be performed by the few ions of the rarefied air inside the tube.

The cathode surface is a material possessing many free electrons. Heating the cathode increases the agitation, and hence the kinetic energy of the electrons on its surface. As the temperature rises, the electron energy becomes sufficient to overcome the attractive forces at the surface, and the electrons escape from the cathode. The analogy between this process and the boiling of water should be apparent.

Since the agent releasing the electrons is heat, **the process of electron emission from a hot body is called thermionic emission**.

The temperature required for electron emission is quite high; hence, tungsten or alloys of tungsten are used to carry the cathode current. When the conductor itself is the emitter, the cathode is called a *directly heated cathode* (Figure 25-6). On the other hand, some cathodes are *indirectly heated* by a separate heater circuit. Metallic oxides, which are efficient sources of electrons, are often used as coatings on such cathodes.

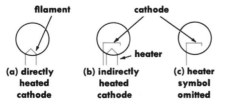

(a) directly heated cathode   **(b) indirectly heated cathode**   **(c) heater symbol omitted**

Fig. 25-6: *Vacuum tube cathodes consist of (a) a hot filament alone as the emitter, or (b) a cathode coated with a metallic oxide and heated indirectly by means of a filament.*

6. THE DIODE—RECTIFICATION

The hot cathode of a diode produces a cloud of electrons by thermionic emission. The electron cloud close to the cathode is known as a *space charge*. Since the space charge consists of negatively charged electrons, the charge will be attracted to the plate when the latter is at a positive potential, but no current will flow when the plate is negative. The diode, by virtue of this unidirectional current, acts as a valve to stop the current when the plate is negative or to permit a current to flow when the plate becomes positive.

The one-way flow of electrons from the diode is the characteristic used in the process of rectification. In Figure 25-8, the input signal consists of an alternating plate potential V_p plotted horizontally below the origin O as a sine curve, the amplitude of which varies with time. No current will flow in the plate circuit I_p during the alternate half cycles when the plate voltage is negative. Thus the output current consists of unidirectional half cycles occurring during the intervals when V_p is positive. The magnitude of the output current for a given input is determined by the diode characteristic curve (characteristic of the diode used).

This transformation of alternating current into direct fluctuating current is called rectification. When diodes are used to rectify alternating power supplies such as 120 volts a-c into direct current for d-c components, they are called *power diodes* (power tubes).

Diodes can also handle weak signals in the same manner to provide a weak output that varies unidirectionally according to the input signal. A diode used in this way takes over the function of a crystal detector; hence, it is known as a *diode detector* or *signal diode*.

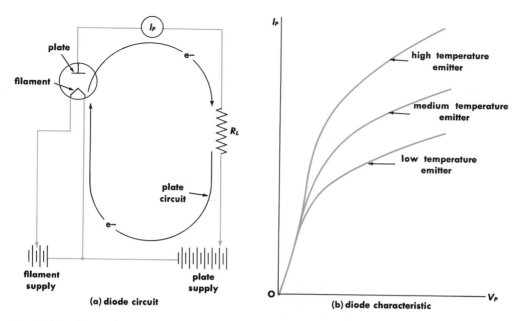

(a) diode circuit

(b) diode characteristic

Fig. 25-7: *A simple diode circuit. The tube acts as a valve, in that electron flow (e flow) occurs only when the plate has a positive potential with respect to the filament. Variations in performance occur for different types of diodes.*

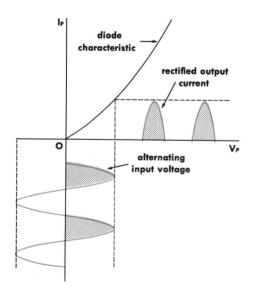

Fig. 25-8: *Only the positive half-cycle of the input potential permits the diode to conduct. Since the electron flow is in one direction only and is not steady, the type of current produced is termed a rectified current.*

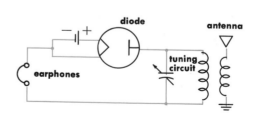

Fig. 25-9: *A simple diode circuit used as a radio. Alternating potential from the antenna is induced into the plate-to-cathode circuit. The plate conducts during the positive half-cycles only to produce a weak fluctuating d-c current which actuates the earphones.*

7. THE TRIODE—AMPLIFICATION

The diode, when rectifying a signal, does not increase the signal strength. This low-energy output can be used only with earphones. The rectified signal of both the diode and the triode is used in radio work to obtain audio signals (detection), as described in Chapter 26.

De Forest improved diode performance by introducing an additional electrode between the cathode and the plate. This electrode consists of an open meshwork of wire which presents little mechanical hindrance to the flow of electrons between the cathode and the plate. When the potential of the new electrode is negative with respect to the cathode, it repels electrons, thus decreasing the cathode-to-plate electron flow. Indeed, the negative potential of the third electrode can be increased to the extent that no electrons are permitted to reach the plate.

In electronics, the potential between the new electrode and the cathode has become known as the *bias*, hence the term *cut-off bias* is used to describe that bias high enough to prevent a current flow in the tube. A positive bias will increase the tube current rather than decrease it. Since the bias controls the e flow from the cathode to the plate, and the structure is a mesh or grid, the new electrode is called *the control grid.*

The new tube, with its three electrodes, becomes a *triode*. It should be emphasized that the control grid does not provide the tube current in the triode, since the cathode and the plate function in the same manner as those of the diode. However, when a weak signal of alternating potential is placed between the control grid and the cathode, the grid alters a large cathode-to-plate e flow according to the signal placed between the grid and the cathode. Thus, the triode provides unidirectional current; in addition, the signal is amplified when a weak grid signal varies a large tube-current to faithfully reproduce the input.

When the grid is positive, the grid can attract electrons to produce a grid current. The grid is customarily operated at a potential which is zero or slightly negative with respect to the cathode.

The **amplification factor** of a triode is **a ratio expressing the amplifying ability of the tube.** Should a one-volt alteration in bias provide the same plate-current change as would a change of 20 volts in the plate-to-cathode potential, then the amplification factor of the tube would be 20.

8. MULTIELECTRODE TUBES

The term multielectrode is frequently applied to tubes containing more electrodes than the triode. A multielectrode tube essentially performs the amplifying and rectifying functions of the triode. However, the cathode-to-plate electron flow is influenced by the potential placed on the additional electrodes. The additional electrodes make the vacuum tube more efficient for some purposes: tetrodes and pentodes extend the frequency range of tube operation and are capable of producing greater amplification.

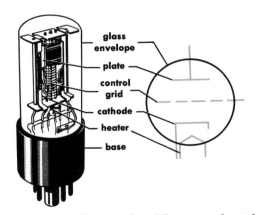

glass envelope
plate
control grid
cathode
heater
base

Fig. 25-10: *The triode. The control grid, which is close to and surrounds the cathode, carries the signal as potential fluctuations. A weak signal on the grid produces large fluctuations in the cathode-to-plate e flow.*

9. THE CRYSTAL DIODE

Before the development of the vacuum diode, early radio accomplished rectification by means of galena or silicon crystals. Rectification can also be obtained with artificial wafers of silicon or germanium, which operate more efficiently than the early crystals.

A thin wire *catwhisker* with its *pigtail* connection provides the anode; the tiny wafer of silicon or germanium provides the cathode of the crystal diode. The device offers low resistance to current flow in one direction, but a high resistance in the opposite direction—the essential requirements to operate a diode.

10. THE TRANSISTOR

Transistors were developed by the Bell Telephone Laboratories to replace vacuum tubes for many purposes. These are small solid packets of semiconducting materials, such as germanium or silicon, which contain small traces of impurities. These impurities contribute characteristics which permit the transistor to replace the vacuum tube for most functions, such as rectification and amplification.

Both germanium and silicon are composed of atoms with *four* valence electrons bonded to neighbouring atoms in a cubic crystal lattice network. This bonded electron structure makes pure germanium and silicon poor conductors, but they receive the ability to conduct from their impurities, known as *donors* or *acceptors*.

Donor-material atoms have *five* valence electrons, four of which can be bonded in the semiconductor lattice, leaving one electron free to move in much the same way as do free electrons in metallic conductors. These free electrons may be *donated* to acceptor materials under suitable conditions. This structure is known as an *N-type* (negative) semiconductor.

Acceptor atoms possess *three* valence electrons, which can be bonded in the crystal lattice only by *receiving* an electron from a neighbouring germanium atom. Introduction of acceptor elements thus leaves lattice structures requiring electrons for a stable condition. Each such lattice in need of an electron provides a *hole* or *trap* into which an electron can fall. The holes are free to move about the semiconductor in much the same way that free electrons move. Semiconductors of this type are called *P-type* (positive) semiconductors.

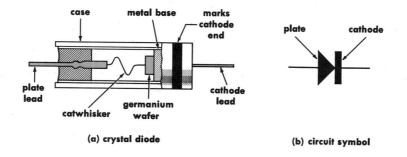

(a) crystal diode   (b) circuit symbol

Fig. 25-11: *Since the crystal diode passes current in one direction only, it can be used as a rectifier.*

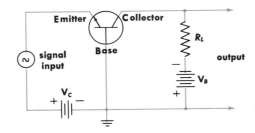

Fig. 25-12: *The N-P-N transistor circuit.*

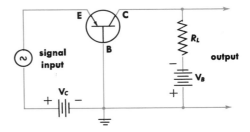

Fig. 25-13: *The P-N-P transistor circuit.*

Diode Functions

Both the P- and N-type semiconductors can transmit current in two directions, but when joined together at a *P-N junction*, the N electrons cannot pass through to the holes of the P structure unless a small potential difference across the pair permits a uni-directional current (when the N side is negative with respect to the P side). Thus a P-N junction has the requirement for recti-fication.

Triode Functions

The P-N junction can be used to amplify when two different combinations of junc-tures are employed. These combinations are the result of sandwiching one type of semi-conductor between two wafers of the other type; hence, the arrangement constitutes the N-P-N type or the P-N-P type of transistor.

The centre semiconductor is the *base*, the materials flanking it the *emitter* and the *collector* (see Figures 25-12 and 25-13).

The centre semiconductor is the *base*, the materials flanking it the *emitter* and the *collector* (see Figures 25-10 and 25-11).

The emitter circuit functions in much the same way as the cathode-grid circuit of the triode; the collector circuit, as the cathode-plate circuit. Thus, a weak signal intro-duced into the emitter circuit effects a large current in the collector circuit, which pro-vides amplification. The polarity and cur-rent directions of the N-P-N emitter and collector circuits are opposite to those of the P-N-P emitter and collector circuits.

11. THE CATHODE-RAY TUBE

The cathode-ray tube is a vacuum tube modified to produce a *visual* interpretation of a signal for use in test equipment, radar, and television transmission.

The parts of the tube providing electron production and control are similar to those of a triode; collectively they are called the *gun* of the tube. An efficient, indirectly heated *cathode* is the source of electrons for the gun. A *control grid* assumes the function of altering the cathode-to-anode (plate) e flow, but at this point the gun differs from the triode. The gun anode consists of two portions, the *focusing anode* and the *acceler-ating anode*. Both anodes have a high posi-tive potential with respect to the cathode; they attract electrons with great vigour to create a concentrated beam of electrons through the holes at their centres. Electron inertia keeps the beam moving past the horizontal and vertical deflecting systems to impinge finally on a coating of fluorescent material on the inside of the tube face. The fluorescent chemicals used for this purpose are called *phosphors*. These materials emit light when struck by electrons.

Deflecting Systems

The electron stream, or beam, initiated by the gun is deflected by either an electro-static or an electromagnetic method.

Electrostatic deflection: The electron beam passes by two sets of deflecting plates set at right angles to each other. The electrostatic field of one set deflects the beam to and fro in a horizontal direction, hence the designation *horizontal deflection plates*. The horizontal sweep of the electrons changes the afterglow light of the phosphor from a dot to a line. (Owing to the persistence of vision, the retina of the eye retains an image for approximately $\frac{1}{25}$ of a second; hence, a cycle of more than 25 sweeps per second produces a line image.)

A cathode-ray (C-R) oscilloscope permits signal interpretation by placing the signal as potential alterations on the vertical deflection plates to deflect the beam vertically during the horizontal sweep. These characteristics of the oscilloscope can be illustrated as follows:

When the oscilloscope has had time to warm up, a horizontal sweep of approximately 60 cps is selected. The *horizontal amplitude* is *momentarily* (to prevent damage to the phosphor) reduced to zero, and a spot image appears. The horizontal sweep frequency can also be reduced to the point where individual sweeps are evident. The deflection of the electron beam in this case is electrostatic, but magnetic deflection can also be used as indicated in the description of low-pressure conduction—cathode rays (Section 2).

(With the horizontal sweep turned to 60 cps, a 60 cps signal may be placed on the *vertical plates* via the fingers if sufficient pickup can be obtained from the chassis, or via an audio generator if not.)

Electromagnetic deflection: X and Y deflection of the electron beam is accomplished by means of a magnetic field provided by two sets of electromagnets set at right angles to each other. The electromagnets are constructed in the form of a yoke or sleeve placed outside the neck portion of the tube. The beam is moved in the same manner as for electrostatic deflection, but electromagnetic deflection permits a clearer trace when used with larger tubes; hence, this is the method employed for television-receiver tubes.

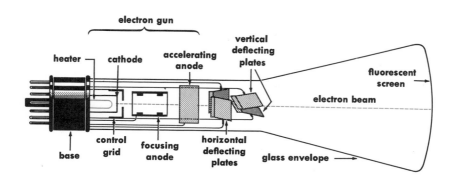

Fig. 25-14: *The cathode-ray tube. The control grid potential alters the number of electrons in the beam and hence the intensity of the image on the face of the tube. The signal is placed on the vertical deflecting plates.*

12. THE TELEVISION-RECEIVER TUBE—THE KINESCOPE

The television picture tube is merely a special cathode-ray tube equipped with a similar gun, but with electromagnetic deflection.

The phosphor used as a coating on the inside face of the tube emits white light when activated by the electron beam. The colour or wavelength produced on the face can be varied by the use of different phosphors. The characteristic green afterglow of the phosphor in C-R oscilloscopes is designed to reduce eye strain. Coloured picture tubes are coated with three separate phosphors which give off the three primary colours, each phosphor being separately excited by one of the three guns in the tube.

Signal analysis with a C-R oscilloscope is accomplished by placing the input signal on the vertical deflection plates. Signal presentation on a TV-receiver tube is more complex and may be explained as follows:

The horizontal (X) and the vertical (Y) deflection systems cause the electron beam to scan the tube face with 525 separate lines, commencing at the top, as illustrated in Figure 25-15, and ending at the bottom. The entire 525 lines are completed and replaced 30 times a second, although the electron beam scans the screen 60 times a second. Alternate lines are scanned on one downward sweep of the beam and the remaining lines on the next downward sweep.

At the end of each line the beam is returned across the tube but is pulled down. During the return time or *fly-back time*, a large negative voltage is applied to the control grid, cutting off the beam to eliminate the trace. (The return trace is not seen.)

During the scanning period the signal voltage is applied between the control grid and cathode. As signal variations of potential occur, similar variations are produced in the beam current; hence the beam excites the phosphor in accordance with the signal received during the scanning period.

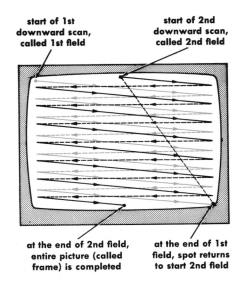

Fig. 25-15: *The television receiver. Thirty frames per second are placed on the tube face. During the scanning, signal variations on the control grid alter the electron beam intensity to produce variations in light intensity given off by the phosphor.*

start of 1st downward scan, called 1st field

start of 2nd downward scan, called 2nd field

at the end of 2nd field, entire picture (called frame) is completed

at the end of 1st field, spot returns to start 2nd field

13. THE TELEVISION CAMERA TUBE—THE ICONOSCOPE

The production of a video or light signal in a television camera involves the photoelectric effect, the scanning action of an electron gun and the use of a capacitor. Figure 25-16 is a diagram of the iconoscope, one of the camera tubes used in television studios.

In the iconoscope, scenes viewed by the camera lens are focused on a capacitor of special design. The mosaic plate of the capacitor consists of an outer layer of minute droplets of metal approximately one molecule in thickness. Each droplet of the mosaic is insulated from its neighbouring droplets so that, in effect, each drop is a separate island functioning as a single electrical unit. The mosaic side of the capacitor transforms variations in light intensities of the scene into corresponding degrees of positive charge resulting from the electron emission of each photoelectric droplet. The "light image" is thus changed to an "electrical image" that faithfully reproduces the light intensities of the scene.

An electron gun scans this electrical image in the same manner as described for the television receiver tube. During the scanning, the positive charge for each photoelectric droplet is removed by the electrons from the gun. As each individual charge is removed, a corresponding charge intensity is induced on the back or signal plate of the capacitor. The charge variations become alterations in potential across the resistance R of Figure 25-16 and the variations in potential are imparted to a carrier wave sent from the transmitting antenna.

Thus, the scenes are not transmitted in "bulk form" but are sent point by point in a definite time sequence as the gun scans the electrical image.

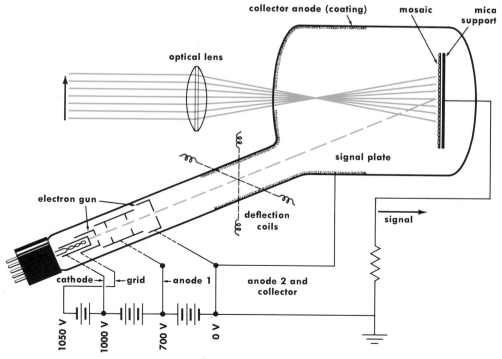

Fig. 25-16: *The iconoscope.*

CATHODE RAYS: Conduction between electrodes is greatly improved when the electrodes are placed in an evacuated tube. When first observed in the late 19th century, the discharge was found to start from the cathode: hence the emanations were called cathode rays. Later investigation showed that the rays consisted of negatively charged particles common to all atoms.

PHOTOELECTRIC EFFECT: Light sensitive materials emit electrons when exposed to incident rays of wave length characteristic for each material.

VACUUM TUBES: When the cathode is heated, either directly or indirectly, an electron cloud called a space charge is formed. The space charge is attracted to the plate, or anode, of a diode only when the plate is positive. Consequently, when alternating potential is applied across a two-electrode tube, or diode, it will conduct only during the positive half-cycle periods. The output of the diode is direct fluctuating current, and the process of producing it from an alternating source is known as rectification.

THE TRIODE: The triode incorporates an additional electrode, in the form of a *control grid*. Weak signals on the control grid produce large fluctuations in the cathode-to-plate flow. Thus, in addition to rectification, the triode is capable of amplification of a signal.

THE TRANSISTOR: Certain semiconductors that contain impurities have characteristics that permit them to perform functions similar to those of vacuum tubes. Donor materials constitute N-type (negative) semiconductors; acceptor materials, P-type (positive) semiconductors. A P-N junction permits unidirectional current only, and can perform the diode function of rectification. N-P-N or P-N-P combinations can be used for the triode function of amplification.

THE CATHODE-RAY TUBE: The triode portion, or gun, provides a high-velocity beam of electrons which passes through horizontal and vertical deflecting systems. In response to external impulses, the horizontal deflecting plates sweep the electron beam back and forth horizontally; the signal is then applied to the vertical plates to move the beam up and down during the horizontal sweep. This beam activates a phosphor placed on the face of the tube and causes it to glow, producing a graphic interpretation of the signals it receives.

TELEVISION RECEIVER TUBE: This is a sophisticated cathode-ray tube in which an electron beam is made to scan the face of the tube to place 525 lines upon it during two scans of 1/60 sec duration each. The complete scan of 525 lines is known as a frame, and 30 frames a second are provided. Variations in light intensity are produced by the signal applied to the control grid.

TELEVISION TRANSMITTER TUBE: The iconoscope converts a video scene into an "electrical image" when light falls on a mosaic composed of minute photoelectric cells. The electron emission from the mosaic creates variations of positive charge that are removed by the scanning action of an electron gun. The induced charges on the signal plate of the mosaic-capacitor arrangement are transmitted as variations in potential.

EXERCISE A

1. What magnitude of potential difference is required to provide a spark discharge?
2. What are cathode rays and how are they produced?
3. Describe the method used to show that the cathode ray particles are negatively charged
4. What did Thomas Edison construct when investigating electric-light bulbs?
5. Name the parts used in the construction of: (a) a diode, (b) a triode.
6. Explain the meaning of the words *tetrode* and *pentode*.
7. What is meant by the term *thermionic emission*?
8. Describe two types of cathodes used in vacuum tubes.
9. Explain the process known as rectification.
10. What is the function of the control grid used in the triode?
11. What function is provided by the triode that cannot be provided by the diode?
12. In what way is a crystal diode similar to a vacuum-tube diode?
13. What is the purpose of donors and acceptors used in the manufacture of transistors?
14. What characteristics make a P-N transistor junction suitable for use as a diode?
15. Name the parts comprising the "gun" of a cathode-ray tube and describe the action of each part.
16. Describe the action of the X and Y plates of a C-R-T (cathode-ray tube).
17. Describe the scanning process used in a TV picture tube.
18. How does the screen of a colour TV tube differ from that of a black-and-white tube?
19. What is the meaning of the term, "fly-back time"?
20. The energy required to liberate free electrons from the surface of a metal is known as the work function of the metal. The energy of a photon = a constant $\times \dfrac{c \text{ (velocity of light).}}{\lambda \text{ (wave length)}}$ The work function of caesium is 2.9×10^{-19} joules; zinc, 6.5×10^5 joules. Which of the two metals is more sensitive to visible light and why? Should the metal used to produce the mosaic of the iconoscope have a large or small work function?

Conduction in Gases and Vacuum Tubes

▶ **Experiment 40**

To show rectification of a-c voltage to d-c voltage by a diode.

Mounting board

Mounted octal socket

Mounted SPDT switch

DPDT switch

A-c line, fused

Mounted potentiometer (50kΩ)

6J-5 tube

D-c milliammeter

Mounted 2 neon bulbs

Connecting wires (fast clips)

Power supply

Procedure

1. Join pin 5 of the 6J-5 tube to pin 3 to connect the grid to the plate and thus convert the triode to a diode.

2. Connect the circuit as indicated in the diagram. Only one side of the DPDT switch is used.

Be sure that the full resistance of the potentiometer is used (50,000 ohms) to protect the neon bulb.

3. Close switch S_1. If the two electrodes of the neon bulb N_1 glow, an alternating current is indicated.

4. Close S_2. If only one electrode of the neon bulb N_2 glows, a direct current is indicated.

5. Read the plate current on the d-c milliammeter.

Analysis

1. What did N_1 indicate regarding the kind of potential applied to the tube between the cathode and the plate?

2. What indication was given by N_2 and A regarding the type of current flowing in the plate circuit?

3. How would you describe the output or plate current obtained from the diode?

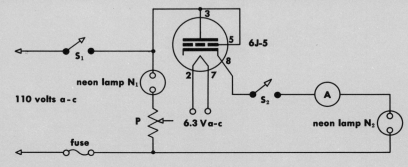

Experiment 41

To study thermionic emission of electrons in a vacuum tube.

Mounting board

Power supply (200 volts)

Power supply (6 volts)

D-c voltmeter

D-c milliammeter

Mounted octal socket

6J-5 tube

Switch

Mounted potentiometer (50kΩ)

Rheostat

Connecting wires (fast clips)

Procedure

1. Complete the circuit as indicated in the diagram. To use the 6J-5 triode as a diode, connect pin 5 to pin 3 (the plate).

Do not touch any bare terminals once the power has been turned on.

2. Adjust the rheostat P_1 to make the voltmeter record 6.00 volts. Read the plate current indicated on the ammeter; adjust the potentiometer P until the plate current reads 10 milliamperes.

3. Read and record the plate current for rheostat settings that alter the potential to 1.00; 1.25; 1.50; 1.75; 2.00; 2.25; 2.50; 2.60; 2.70; 2.75; 3.00; 4.00; 5.00, and 6.00 volts.

4. Make a graph marking the filament voltage on the horizontal axis and the corresponding plate currents in milliamperes on the vertical axis, then plot the resulting curve.

Analysis

1. What conclusion may be reached about the minimum filament potential required to produce electron emission?

2. Is there a limit to the number of electrons that can be emitted from the cathode? Does the curve indicate that such a limit exists?

3. What is the optimum filament voltage for production of nearly maximum plate current?

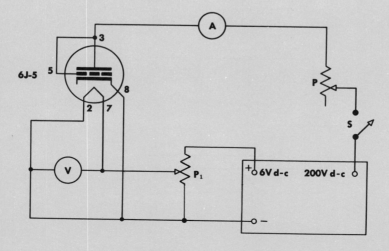

To show variation of the current flow in a diode with respect to the cathode-to-plate potential.

Mounting board

Power supply (200, 150 V)

Power supply (6.3 V a-c)

D-c voltmeter

D-c milliammeter

Mounted octal socket

6J-5 tube

Two switches

Mounted potentiometer (50kΩ)

Connecting wires (fast clips)

---

terminal. Close S_1: read and record the current in milliamperes. *Do not alter the setting of P.*

4. Repeat step 3 to obtain plate potentials of 100 and then 50 volts. Read and record the corresponding plate currents. Repeat the 50-volt trial, but *momentarily* open S_2 as you observe A.

5. Open S_1 and S_2. Reverse the connections on the power supply to pin 8 and to the switch. The switch should now be connected to the negative terminal and the cathode (pin 8) to the positive.

6. Close S_2. Momentarily close S_1 and observe the milliammeter.

7. Close S_1 and S_2. Momentarily open switch S_2 while you observe the milliammeter.

8. Graph the results as plate current in milliamperes on the vertical axis vs plate potential in volts on the horizontal axis.

Procedure

1. Connect the circuit as indicated in the diagram. Close S_2.

2. Close S_1 and adjust P until a maximum deflection of 10 milliamperes is recorded on the meter.

3. Open S_1 and change the connection from the 200-volt terminal to the 150-volt

Analysis

1. Your observations should lead to conclusions regarding the conditions required to successfully operate the diode.

2. What type of variation does your graph indicate regarding the relationship between plate potential and plate current for the range of potentials examined?

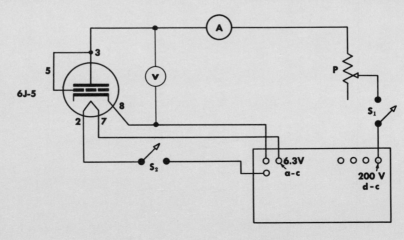

Chapter 26

Vacuum Tube Application

1. AMPLIFIER CIRCUITS

Amplification is the process of increasing the strength of a signal with transistors or vacuum tubes and their associated circuits. The basic amplifier circuit consists of a single tube or transistor and its components. Figures 26-1 and 26-2 illustrate a basic amplifier circuit for a triode and an N-P-N transistor.

From Chapter 25 it will be recalled that the control grid of the triode has the ability to alter the cathode-to-plate e flow in response to the signals placed upon it. Such an alteration, if the grid is negative with respect to the cathode, provides an amplification of the grid signal. The grid potential with respect to the cathode should be negative for amplification. In the circuit of Figure 26-1, the magnitude of this voltage depends on the values of input voltage V_g and the resistor R_C. The variations in potential produced across R_L constitute the amplified signal passed on to the next stage of the circuit.

Since weak signals require more than one stage of amplification, the output of one stage is connected to the input of the next stage. The grid signal of each succeeding stage must be isolated from the plate potential of the preceding stage by a *coupling* device (Figure 26-3).

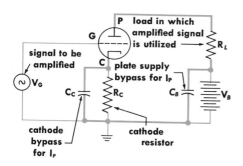

Fig. 26-1: *A triode amplifier circuit. The changes in potential across* R_L *produced by the plate current are sent on to the next stage of the circuit.*

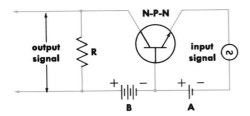

Fig. 26-2: *A circuit hookup for an N-P-N transistor used for amplification. Variations in output current produce corresponding potential variation across R to provide the output signal.*

Functions of Amplifiers

Multistage amplification provides an increase in potential variations, current variations, or both.

The basic function of the early stages of amplification is to increase the signal voltage variations from each stage to the next. The greatest gains in potential are achieved when the resistance of the load is increased to the highest practical level; under these conditions, large voltage fluctuations are applied to the grid of each succeeding stage. If the amplifier is intended to operate a loudspeaker, current amplification must be used in the last stage. This increased current is required to produce vibration of the diaphragm of the speaker.

2. OSCILLATING CIRCUITS

A simple pendulum pulled to one side and released will move to and fro, or oscillate, until friction finally stops the motion by decreasing the amplitude. However, if the pendulum is gently pushed in phase, the energy lost because of friction in the system is replaced, and a continuous movement of the pendulum maintained.

An oscillating circuit in radio can be compared to the simple pendulum. The circuit consists of a coil and a capacitor connected in parallel, between which is set up an oscillating electron flow. The natural frequency of this system is the rate of oscillation of the e flow between the plates of the capacitor as determined by the setting of the capacitor.

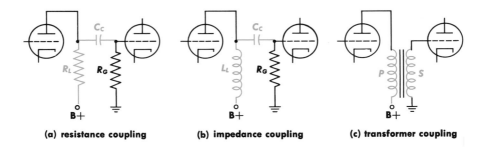

(a) resistance coupling **(b) impedance coupling** **(c) transformer coupling**

Fig. 26-3: *Fluctuations in potential across the resistance R_L, the coil L_L and the primary P are sent on to the grid of the next stage. Coupling devices are used to isolate the grid of the second stage from the high B+ potential of the first stage. The capacitor C_C will transmit a-c current, but will not transmit d-c.*

394

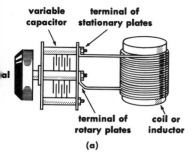

variable capacitor — terminal of stationary plates

terminal of rotary plates — coil or inductor

(a)

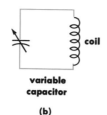

coil

variable capacitor

(b)

Fig. 26-4: *The oscillating circuit. The capacitor and coil values determine the natural frequency of the oscillations. The variable capacitor permits a range of natural frequencies to be set.*

When this circuit is actuated by a potential supplied by a spark discharge or other means, electrons flow back and forth as the capacitor charges and discharges through the coil. The coil offers to the e flow of the system a resistance or impedance, the degree of which is determined by its impedance value; by means of the capacitor setting, one may vary the potential built up between the capacitor plates as well as the time of build-up. Thus the coil and capacitor values establish the period and natural frequency of oscillation.

Since energy is lost in the circuit as a result of the resistance, an oscillation will soon stop unless energy is returned in phase with the electron flow. The frequency of the energy required to maintain oscillation must be a harmonic of the natural frequency of the circuit.

Oscillating circuits have two applications in radio: in transmitters, they are termed tank circuits, in receivers, tuning circuits.

The Tuning Circuit

In the operation of a tuning circuit, as shown in Figure 26-5, the natural frequency of the tuner is adjusted by means of the capacitor setting to equal that of an incoming signal. This maintains an oscillation which is fed to the control grid of the first stage of amplification.

The Tank Circuit

The energy built up in a tank circuit is too weak to transmit a signal at the oscillating frequency: to produce an oscillation strong enough to send a radio signal, the tank circuit must receive additional energy. Since the tank circuit influences the plate current via the control grid, the fluctuations in the plate circuit mutually respond to those in the tank circuit. The energy of these fluctuations is returned to the tank circuit via a "feedback circuit", the coil of which resonates with that of the tank circuit. This mutual fluctuation between the two coils builds up the oscillations of the tank circuit to transmittable proportions. The circuit by which this energy build-up is accomplished is shown in Figure 26-6.

Fig. 26-5: *The tuning circuit. The natural frequency of the tuning circuit can be varied by means of the variable capacitor. When the natural frequency is the same as the signal desired, the signal received via the antenna will actuate the circuit in phase to build up the intensity of the signal desired.*

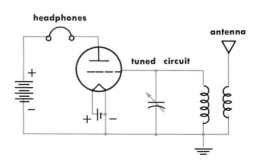

headphones

antenna

tuned circuit

395

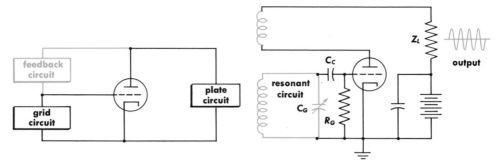

Fig. 26-6: *The oscillating circuit of a transmitter. The amplitude of the input signal is increased when the output oscillations are coupled with the resonant circuit.*

Early radio receivers employed a feedback circuit to activate their tuning circuits in order to build up the incoming signal. When the feed-back energy became too large, the first amplifying stage of the receiver acted as a transmitter, emitting a signal squeal which could upset radio reception in the vicinity.

3. BEAT FREQUENCIES— HETERODYNING

If a given signal is to be selected from other signals transmitted in the radio band, a tuning circuit is used, consisting of a coil and a variable capacitor. When the capacitor setting has selected for the circuit a natural frequency that is identical with that of the station desired, the signal activates the tuning circuit in phase to maintain an oscillation which is amplified in later stages.

Since most amplifiers require several stages of amplification, or cascade amplification, the tuning circuit of each stage requires separate capacitor settings to provide natural frequencies identical with those of the station selected. To overcome the need for several tuning circuits, an oscillating circuit, known as the local oscillator, is maintained inside the receiving set. The frequency of this circuit is varied in relation to that of the incoming signal by a ganged variable capacitor operated by the tuning knob of the set. Those two frequencies are then mixed, and a beat frequency, or intermediate frequency (IF) is produced. (You will recall

that, when two audible frequencies are mixed, the resultant frequency, or beat frequency, is the difference between the two.) The IF is constant in any given radio receiver.

This process of "beating" the two radio frequencies together is called *heterodyning*, and receivers employing the heterodyning principle are called *superheterodyne* receivers. Since the IF stages of the superheterodyne receiver can be tuned accurately by the use of preset capacitors, the set becomes more selective. The tube where heterodyning occurs, together with its associated circuits, is called the *mixer stage*.

4. DETECTION

The signal received by a tuning circuit is a composite wave pattern consisting of a radio-frequency (RF) carrier wave that has been combined with the audio-frequency (AF) transmission.

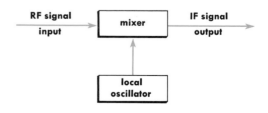

Fig. 26-7: *Heterodyning: the process of combining an oscillation formed within the receiver with the input signal to produce an intermediate frequency.*

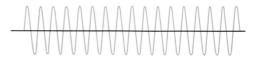

unmodulated carrier signal

Fig. 26-8: *Modulation—the process of mixing a radio frequency and an audio frequency. When the audio signal is used to produce variations in the RF amplitude, the modulation is termed AM (amplitude modulation); when it is used to produce variations in the RF frequency, the modulation is called FM (frequency modulation).*

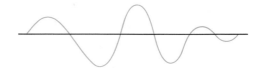

audio signal

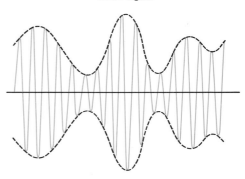

amplitude-modulated carrier signal

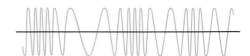

frequency-modulated carrier signal

The necessity for this composite wave becomes apparent when one considers that the range of any sound is relatively limited. Long-distance radio transmission of audio frequencies therefore requires a second wave of more extensive range: the RF carrier wave.

These waves are combined in the transmitter by *modulation*. By this process, the steady oscillations of the RF wave are altered, or modulated, to conform to either the frequency or the amplitude of the irregular audio signal (see Figure 26-8). A carrier signal modulated in frequency is known as an FM (frequency-modulated) signal; one modulated in amplitude, an AM signal. The standard broadcast band uses an AM signal.

At the receiver end, a radio receiver must separate this combined wave back into its original components. The process of deriv-

ing an audio signal from its carrier wave is known as *detection*.

A circuit used for detection is illustrated in Figure 26-9. The capacitor C has a value such that it functions with an AF signal but has a charging and discharging rate that is much too slow to respond to the rapid RF fluctuations. The capacitor charges during the half cycles when the tube conducts, then it discharges through the resistance R during the alternate half cycles. Thus the output is sent on as an audio signal: the RF portion has been eliminated (bypassed to ground).

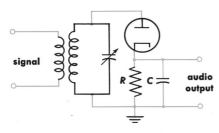

Fig. 26-9: *A circuit used for the detection of audio frequencies from the radio frequency. What is the function of capacitor C in the circuit?*

397

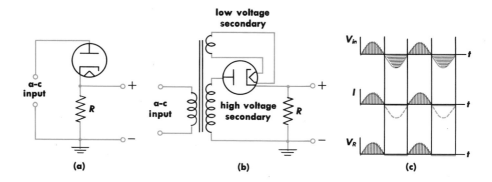

Fig. 26-10: *Half-wave rectification as accomplished by a single diode.*

The detector circuit described is only one of several which can be employed for the formation of an audio output.

5. POWER SUPPLY

All vacuum tubes in radio work require a d-c source for their operation. Since standard household current is a-c, radio circuits must incorporate some means of rectification. As outlined in Chapter 25, diodes may be used to rectify an a-c power source.

A single diode output provides half-wave rectification, as shown in Figure 26-10(c). The low voltage a-c supply from the secondary in (b) is used as a power source for the indirectly-heated cathode, but a rectified d-c source is required by the plate-cathode circuits in the load R. The pulsating d-c output shown in (c) is unsuitable for this purpose, but the violent d-c fluctuations can be smoothed out by a capacitor filter system, as illustrated in Figure 26-11.

The potential build-up across the capacitor as the tube conducts is maintained at nearly maximum level while the capacitor slowly discharges through the resistance. This sluggish behaviour of the capacitor thus diminishes the fluctuations.

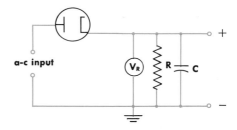

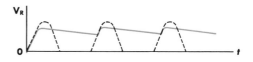

Fig. 26-11: *The fluctuating d-c output can be smoothed by connecting a large filter capacitor C across the load R. The resultant voltage across R is shown in red on the graph.*

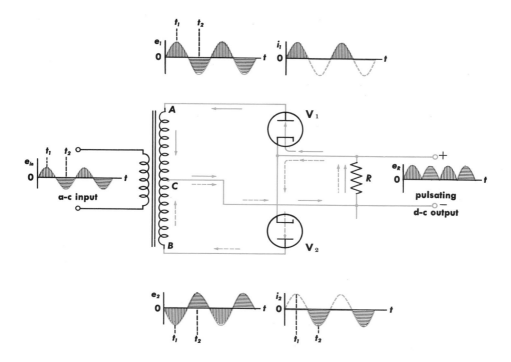

Fig. 26-12: *Full-wave rectification is accomplished when two diodes are employed in a circuit such as this. When A is positive with respect to C, electron flow takes place through V_1 (solid arrows). When B is positive the flow is through V_2 (dashed arrows).*

Several capacitor-resistance hookups connected in parallel can provide a steady non-fluctuating d-c output.

Half-wave rectification is an inefficient use of the a-c source, since only half the energy supplied to the circuit is used. Therefore, most radio circuits employ full-wave rectification.

In this operation, shown in Figure 26-12, the diodes V_1 and V_2 are synchronized in such a way that they operate during alternate half-cycles, so that the load R receives a current almost continuously. The timing device in the circuit is the secondary that is centre-tapped at C.

In essence, full-wave rectification is double half-wave rectification.

6. TELEVISION BROADCASTING

Both the video and audio signals from the studio are sent simultaneously but by independent means. The sound signals are sent by frequency modulation and the video signals by amplitude modulation.

Timing pulses originating in the synchronizing generator of Figure 26-13 ensure that the scanning sweeps of the transmitter and receiver coincide. The video signal after amplification is combined in the modulator with the radio frequency carrier wave as shown in the block diagram. Each station uses a band of frequencies about 6 mc/sec wide in the region 54 to 216 mc/sec.

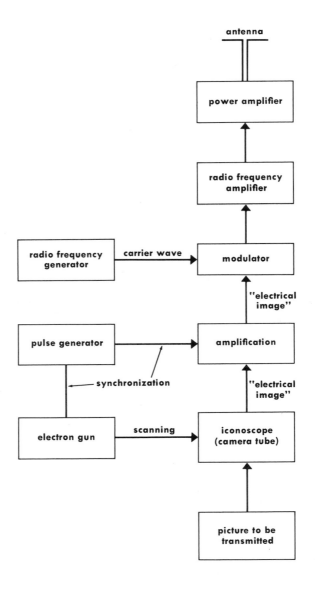

Fig. 26-13: *A block diagram of a video transmitter. The audio signal is sent simultaneously but independently.*

Fig. 26-14: *A schematic interpretation of the stages of transmission and reception of radio signals outlined in this chapter.*

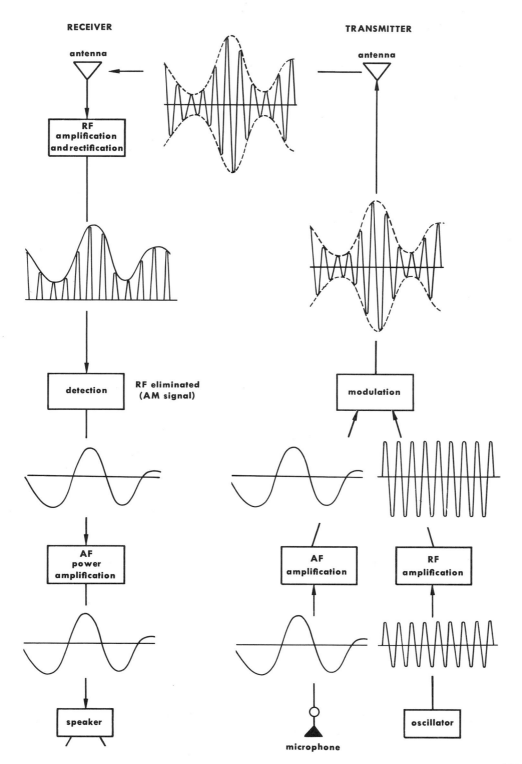

RECEIVER

TRANSMITTER

antenna

antenna

RF
amplification
and rectification

detection   RF eliminated
(AM signal)

modulation

AF
power
amplification

AF
amplification

RF
amplification

speaker

microphone

oscillator

401

AMPLIFIER CIRCUITS: Simple amplification can be accomplished by means of a triode or an N-P-N or P-N-P transistor. Most signals require more than one stage of amplification; a coupling device is used when the amplified signal is transmitted between stages.

OSCILLATING CIRCUITS: A capacitor-coil hook-up will oscillate electrically when energized If oscillation is to be maintained, the circuit must be activated periodically in phase.

THE TANK CIRCUIT: This oscillating circuit increases the energy output of a transmitter to transmittable proportions.

THE TUNING CIRCUIT: This oscillating circuit employs a variable capacitor to tune the frequency of the receiver circuit to that of a desired incoming wave.

HETERODYNING: Superheterodyne receivers produce an oscillation within the receiving set which is mixed with the incoming signal to produce an intermediate frequency.

DETECTION: This refers to the process of separating an audio signal from its radio frequency carrier.

POWER SUPPLY: D-c power can be obtained from an a-c source by half-wave rectification with a single diode circuit. The resultant fluctuating d-c output can be smoothed by the use of a capacitor filter system.

EXERCISE A

1. Explain the meaning of amplification applicable to electronics.

2. Name the electrode to which a weak signal is applied in order to produce amplification. What type of tube is used for this purpose?

3. Name the basic components of a tank circuit. What oscillates in the circuit?

4. How can the natural frequency of a tuning circuit be varied?

5. When producing an oscillating circuit for a large energy increase, energy must be returned in phase with the grid tank circuit. Explain how this is accomplished.

6. Using sound-wave theory, explain the meaning of heterodyning.

7. What is: (*a*) the intermediate frequency, (*b*) the local oscillator?

8. Explain the meaning of the term *detection* as used in radio theory.

9. What is meant by: (*a*) AM, (*b*) FM?

10. Detection is accomplished by the use of a capacitor. Explain how this is done.

11. How are d-c fluctuations removed after rectification in order to provide a suitable power supply?

12. Draw a graph to illustrate full-wave rectification.

Vacuum Tube Application

Experiment 43

To study the triode as an amplifier.

> Mounting board
>
> Power supply
>
> D-c milliammeter
>
> D-c voltmeter
>
> Mounted octal socket
>
> 6J-5 tube
>
> SPDT switch
>
> DPDT switch
>
> Mounted potentiometer (50kΩ)
>
> Rheostat
>
> Connecting wires (fast connectors)

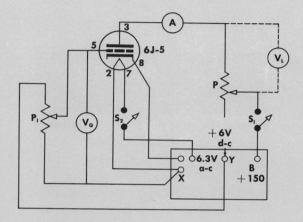

Procedure

1. Wire the circuit according to the illustration. Connect S_1 to the 150 volt terminal and adjust P_1 to make the grid voltage on V_G read 6 volts. Alter P to where a full scale reading of 10 milliamperes is recorded on A (S_1 and S_2 closed).

2. Adjust P_1 to change the grid voltage as recorded on V_G in one-volt steps from +6 volts to −6 volts. Negative potential is obtained by reversing the 6-volt X and Y connections on the power supply. Read and record the plate current from A and the line potential drop across P on V_L. V_L is shown dotted in the circuit diagram to indicate that V_G is disconnected and used to measure V_L each time.

If a second voltmeter is available it can be used as V_L.

3. Make a suitable table listing V_G and the corresponding values for I_P and V_L.

4. Graph V_G on the horizontal axis from −6 to +6 volts and I_P on the vertical axis.

5. Plot a second curve of V_G on the horizontal axis from −6 to +6 and V_L on the vertical axis.

Analysis

1. The straight portion on the V_G vs I_P curve is the range where minimum distortion occurs when a signal placed on the grid is amplified. Record the V_G voltage range that can be used for undistorted amplification.

2. From the V_G vs V_L curve, determine the amount of variation of load potential that is produced by the 12-volt grid range.

The ratio of $\dfrac{V_L}{V_G}$ gives a measure of the amplification ability of the tube.

Chapter 27

The Electromagnetic Spectrum

1. OTHER ELECTROMAGNETIC WAVES

A superficial consideration of light, electricity, heat, or other forms of energy does not seem to indicate any interrelationship between them. James Maxwell (1831-79), when studying the transmission of electric and magnetic forces, developed a set of equations indicating that electric and magnetic transmissions travel at the speed of light. We have already become familiar with some of the waves that travel with the speed of light in our study of thermionic emission, the thermo-electric effect, fluorescence, and the magnetic effect of an electric current. All radiations travelling at the speed of light have been combined into what is called the electromagnetic spectrum, which includes electric waves, radio waves, infrared rays, visible light, ultraviolet rays, X rays (Röntgen rays), gamma rays, and cosmic rays.

2. RADIO WAVES— ELECTROMAGNETIC RADIATION

Radio waves (waves of low frequency but long wavelength) occupy one end of the electromagnetic spectrum. Any electric current will transmit energy in the form of a wave motion, but quite inefficiently, since the wavelength at a frequency of 60 cycles is

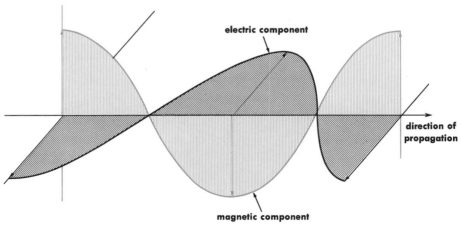

Fig. 27-1: *The electromagnetic wave. The energy of the electric component travels at right angles to that of the magnetic component, and both are at right angles to the direction of propagation. Are the waves longitudinal or transverse?*

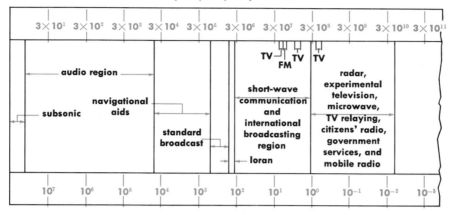

Fig. 27-2: *The lower end of the electromagnetic spectrum. The bands set aside for commercial and government use have been allocated by international agreement. For any transmission, what is the product of the frequency and the wavelength?*

approximately 3100 miles. The radio wave, as predicted by Maxwell, consists of an electric component set at right angles to a magnetic component, while both are perpendicular to the direction of wave propagation (Figure 27-1).

As the frequency is increased, the efficiency of energy transfer becomes much greater. Thus the electrons of a conductor placed in the path of such a wave are set in motion with vibrations characteristic of the wave transmitted.

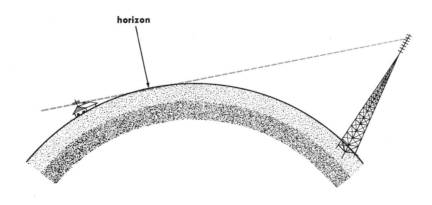

Fig. 27-3: *Line-of-sight transmission.*

405

3. TRANSMISSIONS—GROUND AND SKY WAVES

Energy produced in a transmitter is sent from the antenna in all directions unless reflectors are used. The energy that spreads out along the ground is termed the *ground wave*. Since this wave sets up induced currents over the area it traverses, the ground-wave energy rapidly diminishes. This energy loss increases as the transmission energy increases.

Ground-wave transmission is effective for a radius of 50-200 miles about the transmitting station for transmissions in the broadcast band (535-1605 kc). At higher frequencies the ground wave can be sent only 15-20 miles.

The energy transmitted upward is called the *sky wave*. When the sky wave reaches the ionized layer of air known as the ionosphere, about 60-200 miles above the earth, some of the energy passes through this layer, some is absorbed, and the remainder is reflected back to the earth. At frequencies lower than 30 megacycles, the sky wave can transmit for thousands of miles.

In the case of the transmission of frequencies above 30 megacycles, the waves penetrate the ionosphere so well that sky-wave transmission becomes ineffective. Since the ground-wave attenuation is also extreme at these frequencies, *line-of-sight transmission* between the transmitter and receiver must be used. Line-of-sight transmission is employed in television.

4. RÖNTGEN RAYS—X RAYS

As the frequencies of electromagnetic radiations are increased, the behaviour of the transmissions gradually changes. Radiations in the infrared band of frequencies transmit energy in the form of heat; the visible spectrum sends out energy waves that can be seen by the human eye; ultraviolet rays "tan" the skin.

Waves of frequencies higher than ultraviolet were first studied by W. K. Röntgen in 1895. Since these rays possessed new and exciting properties, they were called X rays. While studying a Crookes tube, Röntgen discovered that rays were produced which could penetrate the glass envelope to excite a fluorescent screen held outside the tube.

Modern X-ray tubes produce Röntgen rays by bombarding a metallic anode with high-speed electrons in a vacuum tube. The electrons are produced by an indirectly heated cathode; electron velocity is obtained by means of a large potential difference between the cathode and the anode.

Nearly everyone is familiar with the use of X rays for the detection of lung ailments, breaks or flaws in bone structure, foreign materials in the body, or metallic strains in castings.

5. GAMMA AND COSMIC RAYS

Gamma rays were discovered during the course of the investigation of radioactive material. This study disclosed the fact that

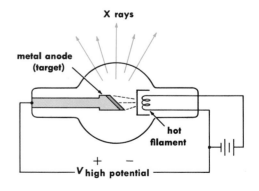

Fig. 27-4: *The X-ray tube. X rays penetrate flesh (but not bone) to disclose abnormalities or cell damage.*

natural disintegration of the nuclei of such elements as uranium and radium is accompanied by the emission of energy capable of affecting photographic film. Unlike the alpha and beta emissions of radioactive matter, gamma radiation was found not to be influenced by a magnetic field. Further investigation disclosed that gamma rays are high-frequency X rays possessing even more penetrating power than the other radioactive emissions.

Radiations of higher frequency and still shorter wavelength than gamma rays complete the electromagnetic spectrum. Since these rays are produced by particles entering our solar system from outer space, they are called *cosmic rays*.

Cosmic rays slowly discharge electroscopes that are not near radioactive materials; indeed, it was the observation of this phenomenon that revealed their existence. Most of the radiation from cosmic sources stems from secondary emanations produced when the high-velocity cosmic particles enter the earth's atmosphere.

Cosmic ray intensity increases with altitude; hence, one objective of the satellite programme is to gather information concerning variations of cosmic ray intensity.

6. INVESTIGATION OF ELECTROMAGNETIC WAVES

Radio Waves

High-frequency oscillators and equipment available from supply houses can be used to study some characteristics of radio transmission.

(a) *Radio transmissions may be exhibited as standing waves*: A dipole antenna attached to a high-frequency oscillator emitting radio waves acts as a medium for the waves. Therefore, a neon lamp will glow when held at the ends of the antenna (voltage loops), but will remain unlit when held at the centre (a voltage node).

The energy from the transmissions sent to a wire conducting system (lecher wires) creates standing waves on the wires. The presence of the waves may be confirmed by means of the neon bulb, as above.

(b) *Radio waves are polarized*: A simple receiver, consisting of a dipole antenna connected to a miniature neon lamp, is used to demonstrate polarization (the confinement of transmission to one plane of vibration). The lamp glows when the receiver antenna is held a few feet away from, and parallel to, the transmitter antenna, but goes out when the antennae are at right angles to each other.

(c) *Radio signals may cause a receiver to resonate*: A receiver equipped with a signal light or wavemeter will resonate when tuned to the frequency of the radio emissions. The resonance point is indicated by the glow of the lamp or maximum deflection of the wavemeter needle.

X Rays

X-ray tubes suitable for classroom demonstrations can be excited by an induction coil. Care must be taken that the target or anode of the tube is positive and the cathode negative. *Students should not be overexposed to X-ray radiation because of its adverse physiological effects.*

The presence of X rays can be demonstrated with a charged electroscope. When the electroscope is placed on an insulating stand, it discharges slowly; but when it is placed in the path of X rays from the tube, it becomes quickly discharged. The electroscope undergoes equal rates of discharge under X-ray bombardment for both positive and negative charges.

A viewing apparatus equipped with a fluorescent screen (fluoroscope) may be used to demonstrate the presence of X rays. When a hand is placed on the outside of the fluoroscope between the screen and the X-ray source, the bone outlines can be seen.

The absorptive ability of such materials as cardboard, paper, wood, copper, lead, etc., can be tested by placing sheets of the materials between the fluoroscope and the X rays while viewing the screen.

Since X rays are radiations of short wavelength, they are capable of penetrating glass, paper, flesh, and many other materials. Thus, the rays penetrate the glass envelope of the tube and ionize the air in the vicinity to discharge a positively or negatively charged electroscope.

X-ray excitation causes fluorescent materials to glow with a colour characteristic of the substance being X-rayed. Lead acts as a shield, but wood, paper, flesh, etc., allow the X rays to pass through to excite the fluorescent screen. The bones of the hand absorb most of the radiation; hence they are outlined inside the flesh.

The light transmitted by fluorescent materials is of low energy compared to light from other sources; hence it is desirable that the observer acclimatize his eyes for 5 to 10 minutes in the darkness before viewing fluorescence.

7. THE DUALITY OF MATTER AND LIGHT

At first sight, the original description of cathode emission in vacuum tubes, *as rays* seems absurd when we know that it consists of a stream of electrons of known mass—a stream of particles. However, this idea is not only acceptable today, but essential to the understanding of the nature of matter. When electrons are speeded up in an accelerator *they emit light*; electrons are used to photograph molecules in an electron microscope; at high speeds, electrons can be assigned a predictable wave length. In addition to possessing these wave properties it should be emphasized that they are negatively charged particles of known mass: they are deflected by a magnetic or electric field in a predictable fashion. In effect, we have atomic billiard balls behaving as waves when travelling at high speeds.

Conversely, it can be demonstrated that X rays also exhibit particle-like behaviour. A. H. Compton discovered that X rays bounce off or "recoil" when they meet electrons. In the collision between X rays and electrons, energy is conserved and a mass must be assigned to the X rays in order to express the energy conservation in the collision.

Many of the wave properties assigned to X rays have been previously discussed. They can penetrate wood, glass, flesh, etc.—useful properties which are employed in medicine and industry. Refraction and diffraction effects of X rays are used to investigate the crystal structure of many materials.

ELECTROMAGNETIC WAVES: This designation covers all transmissions with the speed of light. Electric, radio, infrared, visible light, ultraviolet, Röntgen, gamma and cosmic transmissions are all electromagnetic waves.

TRANSMISSION OF RADIO WAVES: The energy that spreads out along the ground is called the ground wave, the energy transmitted upward, the sky wave. Ground wave transmission has a range of up to 200 miles for the broadcast band.

HIGH-FREQUENCY WAVES: As the frequency of electromagnetic waves becomes greater, their penetrating ability increases. X rays can penetrate glass, flesh and wood; cosmic rays from outer space penetrate the earth's atmosphere.

1. Explain the contribution made by James Maxwell to the understanding of electromagnetic wave transmission.

2. List the radiation groups usually included in the electro-magnetic spectrum.

3. State whether electromagnetic waves are transverse or longitudinal and give a reason for your choice.

4. How is energy transmitted by the ground wave lost?

5. Name the principle, studied earlier in connection with light, that explains the return of the sky wave to the ground.

6. What are line-of-sight transmissions? Name the frequencies that require this type of transmission.

7. State the observation which resulted in the discovery of X rays.

8. List four applications of Röntgen rays.

9. What is the basic nature of gamma radiation?

10. Name one function of the satellite programme that aids in the study of the electro-magnetic spectrum.

11. The collision of X rays and electrons is known as the Compton Effect. The electron microscope produces "light" photographs. What is unusual about the roles of X rays and electrons in these two situations?

Chapter 28

Investigating the Atom

Our present knowledge of the basic constituents of matter has its beginnings in the work of the chemists of the eighteenth and nineteenth centuries. Little progress toward an understanding of matter had taken place from the time of Aristotle, who conceived of all substances as composed of four basic elements—earth, fire, water and air, to the Middle Ages when alchemists labored in vain to change or "transmute" base metals to gold. Two thousand years of speculation had produced virtually nothing in atomic theory.

1. THE ATOMIC THEORY OF JOHN DALTON

Atomic theory, as we know it, had its beginnings with the bold concepts put forth by the English schoolmaster John Dalton in 1800. At that time, about thirty chemical elements had been discovered (the list of elements, interestingly enough, still included "caloric"). The term *element* here refers to substances which at that time could not be broken down into other substances. On the basis of his research with these elements, Dalton postulated the following:

(1) All matter consists of atoms that are indivisible

(2) Each element is composed of its own kind of atom, distinguishable from the atoms of all other elements

(3) The atoms of each element are unchangeable

(4) The atoms of individual elements combine to form compounds. The smallest part of a compound is composed of a grouping of a number of atoms of the elements comprising the compound. This smallest part of the compound is a *molecule*.

(5) During chemical reactions, a rearrangement of the atoms takes place, but the atoms themselves remain unchanged.

Dalton's theory allowed chemistry to progress on a quantitative basis. Investigations by chemists in the nineteenth century disclosed the manner in which elements combined. The simplicity of these relationships afforded great support to Dalton's theory, and provided the means of determining the *relative weights of the atoms of the various elements*. A determination of the *atomic weights* of the elements was a most important task if further developments in chemistry were to take place.

2. THE PERIODIC SYSTEM OF THE ELEMENTS

By the year 1870, over sixty chemical elements had been discovered. Many of these elements bore properties amazingly similar to those of other elements. For example, lithium, sodium and potassium are all light metals which react strongly with water. Also, gold, copper and silver are heavy metals, and each a good conductor of electricity. As more and more elements were discovered, it became desirable to arrange them in some kind of order.

The Russian chemist Mendeleeff arranged the elements in sequence according to their atomic weights. In doing so, he found that every eighth element had somewhat similar properties, chemically and physically. This grouping by atomic weight had been done before with no important consequences. Mendeleeff, however, was wise enough to leave spaces for elements which might exist, and which might yet be discovered. Table 28-1 illustrates his grouping for the first twenty-one elements with the chemical symbol and atomic weight of each of these elements.

Note the space left by Mendeleeff after the element calcium. The element with the next higher atomic weight, at that time was titanium, with properties akin to those of carbon and silicon. The space next to calcium was left vacant, and Mendeleeff predicted that an element yet to be discovered would fill it. He predicted it would have properties similar to those of boron and aluminium, and he estimated its atomic weight. Years later such an element, scandium, was discovered. In his original table, over twenty such blank spaces were left, and have since been filled.

A table such as this, in which elements similar in properties occur periodically, is called a *periodic table*. Mendeleeff's findings brought system and order to the study of chemistry.

Figure 28-1 gives an idea of the periodic variation of a physical property, namely the melting points of several elements, again arranged in order of atomic weight.

We shall return to a more detailed study of the periodic table in later chapters.

Table 28-1

Group 1	Group 2	Group 3	Group 4	Group 5	Group 6	Group 7
Hydrogen H 1						
Lithium Li 7	Beryllium Be 9.4	Boron B 11	Carbon C 12	Nitrogen N 14	Oxygen O 16	Fluorine F 18
Sodium Na 23	Magnesium Mg 24	Aluminum Al 27.3	Silicon Si 28	Phosphorus P 31	Sulphur S 32	Chlorine Cl 35.5
Potassium K 39	Calcium Ca 40		Titanium Ti 48	Vanadium V 51	Chromium Cr 52	Manganese Mn 55

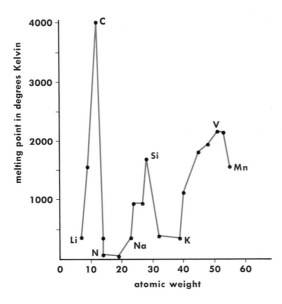

Fig. 28-1: *The melting points of the elements are shown here as a function of atomic weight. Note how the melting point rises and falls with increasing atomic weight. This is an example of the periodic nature of a physical property. The symbols represent chemical elements which you can identify from page 426.*

3. DISCOVERY OF THE ELECTRON

Conclusive evidence that atoms were electrical in nature was obtained through the investigation of electric conduction in gases by the eminent British physicist J. J. Thomson. The name *cathode rays* was given to the mysterious phenomenon occurring in the evacuated tube (pages 376-7). Prior to Thomson's investigations, much controversy arose concerning the nature of these rays, but Thomson was convinced that the rays were streams of electrified particles moving at high speeds from cathode to anode, rather than some form of radiation similar to light.

Thomson demonstrated the electrical nature of these rays using the three experimental set-ups shown in Figure 28-2. In

(a) the cathode rays were made to pass through an electric field produced by two parallel plates that were connected to a source of high voltage. The deflection of the beam toward the positive plate indicated that the beam consisted of negatively-charged particles. This was substantiated by their deflection in a magnetic field, illustrated in (b). Thomson was also able to deflect the beam to a receptacle in the tube that was connected to an electroscope. As a result, the electroscope became negatively charged, as shown in (c).

Other experiments performed by Thomson demonstrated that the "rays" possessed not only electrical charge, but also the property of mass, characteristic of all particles. One convincing demonstration was the motion imparted to a light-weight paddle-wheel free to move on a track, as illustrated in Figure 28-3. The kinetic energy of the particles, imparted to the paddle-wheel, set it in motion along the track.

The apparatus employed by Thomson was not sufficient in itself to allow a determination of the actual mass of the moving particles, nor of the magnitude of their electrical charge. Of great significance, however, was the calculation by Thomson of the *ratio* of these two quantities, which we shall denote by m/e. The value obtained by Thomson was of the order of 5×10^{-9} g/coulomb, and he obtained a *constant value for this ratio regardless of the kind of gas in the tube.*

Thomson's conclusions were threefold: evidently these charged particles were constituent parts of the atoms comprising the gas in the tube. No longer could the atom be thought of as indestructible. Furthermore since identical results for the ratio m/e were obtained regardless of the nature of the gas in the tube, these particles must be *elementary particles common to all atoms.* Finally, the extremely small value of the ratio m/e (about 2,000 times smaller than

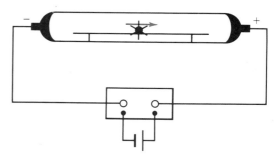

Fig. 28-3: *This apparatus demonstrates that the cathode ray possesses energy. The impact of the ray causes the paddlewheel to move down the tube.*

that ratio obtained in experiments carried out with the hydrogen atom) led to the tentative conclusion that these elementary particles possessed mass 2,000 times smaller than the lightest atom encountered—the hydrogen atom.

To these elementary particles Thomson gave the name "electron".

4. POSITIVE RAYS

With the apparatus shown in Figure 28-4, convincing proof was obtained that atoms contained positively charged particles. This apparatus is a modified version of a cathode ray tube, with an opening in the negative electrode, or cathode, and the partially evacuated tube extended to the left, beyond the cathode.

With a high potential difference applied between the electrodes, a visible beam is seen in the left section of the tube. This beam can be deflected, as shown, by the external magnetic field. The direction of the deflection indicates that the beam is *positively* charged. Apparently positively charged particles are being accelerated from the anode to the cathode, into the left portion of the tube. The deflection, however, is much less than that obtained for cathode rays indicating that the mass of these particles is much *greater* than that of the electron

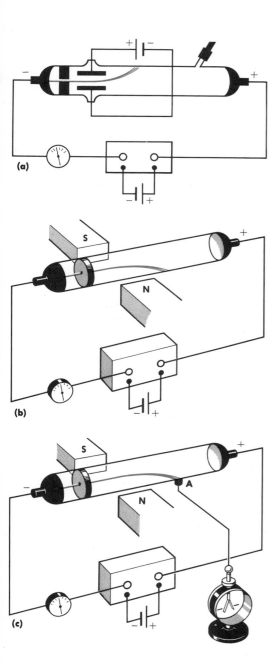

Fig. 28-2: *J. J. Thomson demonstrated the electrical nature of cathode rays. In (a) the rays are deflected by an electric field; in (b) by a magnetic field; and in (c) collected at A charging the electroscope negatively.*

(assuming the charge on these particles is comparable in magnitude to that of the electron).

Experiments similar in principle to those carried out by Thomson and employing hydrogen gas in this apparatus, allowed a determination of the ratio m/e for these positively charged particles. This value was about 1800 times greater than that found by Thomson for the electron.

Here was rather convincing evidence that the hydrogen atom contains two charged particles—the electron, a negatively charged particle common to all atoms, and a positively-charged particle much more massive. The name *proton* was given to this positive portion of the hydrogen atom.

When gases other than hydrogen are placed in the tube, the "positive" rays bend by amounts differing from that for hydrogen, and split into two or more paths. Evidently atoms of these other elements possess mass and charge different from that of the proton.

An explanation of conduction in a gas can now be formulated. The normally neutral atoms of the gas under the stress of the intense electric field between anode and cathode, have one or more electrons stripped from them. The electrons accelerate toward the anode, colliding on the way, with atoms. These collisions are apparently the cause of the emission of light from within the tube. At the same time, the atoms which have lost electrons (called *ions*) now possessing a net positive charge, are propelled toward the cathode. In the apparatus of Figure 28-4, some of these will pass through the opening in the cathode into the extended portion of the tube.

5. THE THOMSON ATOM

By the end of the nineteenth century evidence from chemistry and electricity pointed overwhelmingly to the electrical nature of matter. These findings led to the formulation by Thomson of a model of the atom. Thomson envisaged the atom as composed of a jelly-like positively-charged substance, in which electrons were imbedded. Since the atom usually is electrically neutral, the total negative charge of the electrons would neutralize the electrical effect of the positive jelly. Grossly magnified, the cross-section of an atom would, according to this model, resemble the cross-section of an orange, with the seeds representing the electrons (Figure 28-5).

Fig. 28-5: *J. J. Thomson envisaged the atom as composed of electrons imbedded in a positively charged substance. This cross-section of an orange would be analogous to that for an atom, with the seeds representing electrons.*

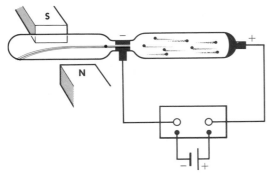

Fig. 28-4: *An apparatus to produce positive rays. Particles are accelerated toward the cathode and pass into the portion of the tube at the left. This ray, too, can be bent by a magnetic field.*

As we shall see in the next chapter, this concept of the atom was not able to stand up to the vigorous test put to it by Rutherford and his associates in 1911.

6. DISCOVERY OF RADIOACTIVITY

Towards the end of the nineteenth century, startling new discoveries made it necessary to change many fundamental notions which hitherto had formed the basis of physical science. The first of these, the discovery of X rays by Röntgen in 1896, has already been described in Chapter 27. Only a few months later, Henri Becquerel, a French scientist, discovered an equally amazing phenomenon —radioactivity.

Becquerel was investigating the phosphorescence of various materials, that is, their ability to glow for a period of time after exposure to sunlight. Some of this material, a uranium ore, had been put away in a drawer beside an unopened package of photographic plates. When the plates were later developed, he was surprised to find they had been badly fogged. Becquerel was shrewd enough to relate this fogging to the presence of the uranium ore. Further investigation showed that indeed some invisible radiation constantly emanated from this material. Such materials were said to be "radioactive".

Investigations of the mysterious radiation during the next few years showed that a portion of it could be deflected in a magnetic field, indicating the presence of charged particles. Three distinct types of rays were identified, named alpha (α), beta (β) and gamma (γ) respectively. All three rays affected photographic plates. The bending of the α rays and β rays by a magnetic field indicated they were charged positively and negatively respectively (Figure 28-6). The α rays possessed relatively little energy, with the ability to penetrate only a few centi-metres of air. The β rays, apparently travelling at much higher speed, were able to penetrate solids such as wood and paper.

By comparison, the γ rays could penetrate thick slabs of lead and were undeflected by magnetic fields. In these respects, they resembled the newly-discovered X rays.

The β rays were identified in 1900 as a stream of high-speed electrons. Pierre and Marie Curie made this identification by bending the stream of β rays in a magnetic field and measuring the ratio of mass to charge for these particles, much in the manner performed by J. J. Thomson a few years earlier. The Curies obtained values of m/e identical to that for the electron.

Experiments similar to this were performed on the α rays by the English physicist Ernest Rutherford. The ratio m/e for the α-particles was found to be exactly twice that found in gas-discharge experiments for the charged hydrogen atom, and to be exactly that of the charged helium atom in similar experiments. The α-particle was thus identified as a helium atom with a positive charge.

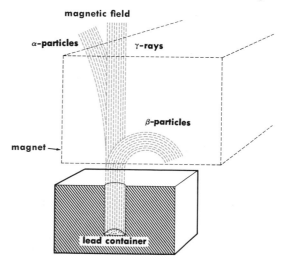

Fig. 28-6: *Deflection in a magnetic field shows that three kinds of emanation from a radioactive source are possible.*

7. DETECTION OF RADIOACTIVITY

Methods presently employed to detect radioactivity are based upon the ability of this radiation to produce fluorescence, to ionize surrounding gas molecules, or to affect a photographic plate.

(a) *Fluorescence*—When alpha or beta particles fall upon a screen coated with zinc sulphide, they produce a momentary flash of light. When the screen is in the dark, these may be observed through a microscope. This was the earliest-employed method of detecting the presence of these particles.

(b) *Ionization*—A charged electroscope left standing in air will be discharged because of the presence of ions in the surrounding gas. The amount of ionization will depend upon the intensity of the radiation; thus the rate of discharge of the electroscope will be a measure of the radioactivity present (see Experiment 44).

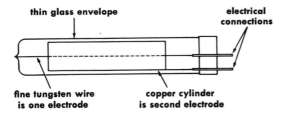

thin glass envelope · electrical connections

fine tungsten wire is one electrode · copper cylinder is second electrode

Fig. 28-7: *The Geiger-Müller tube. An outside source maintains a potential between the electrodes at a level close to the ionization level of the gas in the chamber.*

The Geiger-Müller counter tube (Figure 28-7) is a much more sensitive device. This tube contains a gas at low pressure. Inside the glass envelope is a hollow copper cylinder which acts as one electrode, and a fine wire running along the axis of the tube, acting as the other electrode. A potential difference is maintained between these electrodes. When a particle enters the tube, ionizing some gas molecules, a flow of charge passes between the electrodes. This is translated into an audible click, and the rate of the clicks is a measure of the intensity or radioactivity.

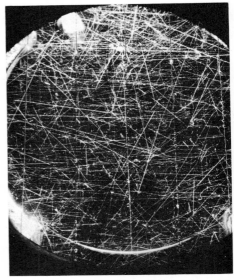

Brookhaven National Laboratory

Fig. 28-8: *A photograph of particle paths in a cloud chamber.*

(c) *Cloud chamber*—A cloud chamber gives a visible indication of the path taken by α- and β-particles. In this device, liquid droplets condense on the ions produced by charged particles moving through the chamber. The tracks may be photographed. One such photograph is shown in Figure 28-8. Cloud chambers are of two types—expansion type and diffusion type.

The Wilson cloud chamber is an expansion-type chamber. A simple form is shown in Figure 28-9. Water containing a black die fills most of a specially-constructed vessel. by means of a rubber bulb, the level of the

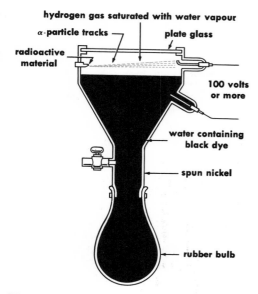

Fig. 28-9: *The Wilson cloud chamber. In a manner similar to that of the production of the vapour trail of an aircraft, radioactive particle paths become visible when the particles collect moisture in the saturated hydrogen gas vapour.*

water surface may be raised or lowered at will. Enclosed in the narrow space between the water and the glass cover is hydrogen saturated with water vapour. If the water surface is suddenly lowered by means of the

bulb, the sudden expansion of the gas causes it to cool. Water vapour will then condense on any ions present in the enclosed region.

In the diffusion chamber, Figure 28-10, a volatile liquid, such as methyl alcohol, diffuses into the air in the chamber. If one end of the chamber rests on dry ice, with the top end at room temperature, somewhere between the top and bottom the air becomes supersaturated with vapour. In that region, droplets will then condense on ions present in the gas. Light reflected from the droplets makes the particle track visible.

8. THE MILLIKAN EXPERIMENT

It is appropriate to consider now an important experiment conducted by R. A. Millikan of the University of Chicago, around 1911. At that time it was known that matter contains a large number of positive and negative charges, and Thomson had determined the ratio m/e for the small negatively-charged particle called the electron. However, it was not firmly established whether all electrons were identical—that is whether all electrons possessed the same mass, and the same charge. Only the ratio m/e for these particles was known to be constant.

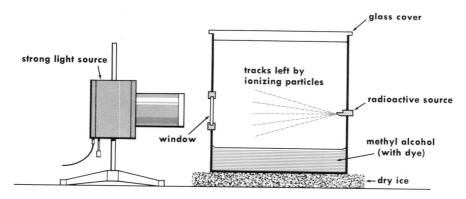

Fig. 28-10: *The diffusion cloud chamber. The cold air above the alcohol becomes supersaturated with alcohol vapour. Particles from the radioactive source produce ionization of the vapour, causing droplets to condense on these ions, and making the particle path visible.*

Millikan employed the apparatus shown in Figure 28-11. The box (thick lines) contains two parallel metal plates a fraction of a centimetre apart. The plates are charged by connecting them to a series of batteries. Fine oil droplets are sprayed into the space above the upper plate. A few of these droplets will find their way through the hole in the upper plate, and fall into the region between the plates. A light source (not shown) illuminates this region, allowing the droplets to be observed through the window, by means of a telescope.

The oil droplets pick up electrical charges by friction during the spraying process or by contact with free electrons or gas ions that are always present in the air. With the batteries disconnected, and the plates short-circuited, the droplets fall at a constant speed,—their terminal velocity (Chapter 3, section 5). However, with the plates charged, the electric force exerted on the charged drop will cause it either to fall at a greater rate or to rise, depending on the nature of the charge on the drop, and the polarity of the plates. If the battery voltage is adjustable, the charged oil drop can be held stationary, indicating a balance between the weight of the drop and the upward electrical force.

Millikan calculated the mass and hence the weight of each drop by observing its terminal velocity in free fall. By balancing each drop, he then knew the electrical force on the drop, and could calculate the amount of charge on it. In many cases, observation of a single drop would last for hours.

Over a period of years with observations on thousands of drops, the data indicated that the quantity of charge on the drops was always a multiple of the smallest value obtained, convincing proof that there is such a thing as a "smallest amount" of electricity and that all electrical charge is a collection of these identical "packages". This smallest amount of charge, the charge on the electron, was found by Millikan to be 1.6×10^{-19} coulombs. As a result, the mass of the electron could now be calculated, using the already established ratio m/e. Accurate measurements of the mass of the electron give it as 1.1×10^{-31} kg.

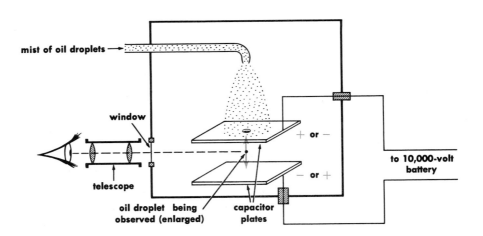

Fig. 28-11: *Millikan's oil-drop experiment. In the illustration, the forces on the oil drop are balanced. How are the upward and the downward forces produced?*

MENDELEEFF'S PERIODIC TABLE: This was the first successful attempt to arrange the elements by atomic weight in a sequence which showed the periodic nature of their properties. In his table Mendeleeff was also able to predict the discovery of unknown elements.

THE ELECTRON: Conduction in low-pressure gases reveals that the electron possesses a negative charge, travels in straight lines, and is identical in all atoms. The size of the electronic charge (as determined by Millikan's oil-drop experiment) is 1.609×10^{-19} coulombs.

THE PROTON: A modified cathode-ray tube demonstrated the existence of positively charged particles with mass greater than the electron. These particles are protons, and the hydrogen atom contains one electron and one proton.

RADIOACTIVITY: Becquerel discovered that a uranium ore, pitchblende, gave off emanations that affected a photographic plate. The naturally-occurring radiations were found to consist of positive alpha particles (having a mass four times that of the proton and carrying two electronic charges), negative beta particles (electrons), and neutral gamma rays.

RADIATION DETECTION: Active materials can be detected by the ability of alpha and beta particles to produce flashes of light (scintillating effect) when they fall on a fluorescent screen. The radiation, by ionizing the air, can discharge an electroscope with a discharge rate proportional to the radiation intensity. The Geiger-Müller tube is a special application of the ionization effect, in which the radiations ionize a gas between two electrodes to produce a "click" sound in an amplified circuit. The Wilson cloud chamber provides a visible trace of the radiations when water drops condense on them in a moisture-saturated hydrogen gas that has been supercooled.

EXERCISE A

1. (a) How would you prove that the "rays" in a highly evacuated discharge tube are electrically charged?
   (b) How would you prove that this charge is negative?
   (c) How could you prove that the "rays" consist of particles carrying energy?

2. The motion of the electrons in the discharge tube depends upon many factors. In each of the following cases, one of these factors is considered. What is the effect on
   (a) the speed, if the potential difference between anode and cathode is increased?
   (b) the amount of bending, if the mass were greater?
   (c) the amount of bending if the charge were greater?
   (d) the amount of bending if the speed were greater?
   (e) the amount of bending if the magnetic field were stronger?
   (f) the m/e ratio if the magnetic field were stronger?

3. (a) Why can we conclude that all atoms contain the same kind of negative particles (electrons)?

(b) What evidence is there that atoms differ in the amount of positive charge they contain?

4. How would you demonstrate experimentally that the negative particles in gold atoms were the same as those in hydrogen?

5. What aspect of Dalton's theory of the atom were disproved by Thomson's experiments with gas discharge tubes?

6. Name the three kinds of radioactive rays and describe the nature of each.

EXERCISE B

1. Millikan found that the elementary electric charge was 1.6×10^{-19} coulombs. Find the number of elementary charges in 1 coulomb.

2. A situation analogous to that of determining, from a large set of data, the magnitude of the elementary charge, is contained in the following problem: you are given several sealed paper bags each containing a number of identical balls. The weights of some of the bags and contents are respectively 2.5 lb, 7.0 lb, 8.5 lb, 1.5 lb, 0.75 lb.

(a) What is a possible value of the weight of each ball?

(b) Can you be certain that this is the weight of each ball?

(c) Without weighing an individual ball, what could you do to increase your certainty?

3. From one set of data, Millikan obtained the following measured charges on an oil drop:

6.6×10^{-19} coul, 8.2×10^{-19} coul, 16.5×10^{-19} coul,
11.5×10^{-19} coul, 13.1×10^{-19} coul, 18.1×10^{-19} coul,
19.7×10^{-19} coul, 26.1×10^{-19} coul, 16.5×10^{-19} coul.

From these results, what value for the elementary electric charge can be deduced?

420

Investigating the Atom

Experiment 44

To study the electroscope as a detector of radioactivity.

Electroscope
Glass rod and silk
Ebonite rod and wool
Source of α-radiation
Source of β-radiation

3. Repeat steps 1 and 2 using this time a source of β-radiation.

4. Investigate the effect on electroscope discharge, of interposing barriers such as paper and tin foil, between the source and the electroscope knob.

Procedure

1. Charge an electroscope negatively by induction. Place a source of α-radiation near the electroscope knob, and note any change in the leaf deflection.

2. Repeat this procedure, this time with a positively-charged electroscope.

Analysis

1. Was there any difference in the way in which the electroscope was affected by the sources?

2. Which of the two kinds of radiation seemed to have greater penetrating power?

Chapter 29

The Nuclear Atom

1. THE RUTHERFORD EXPERIMENT

In 1911, Ernest Rutherford, a New Zealander who for a time performed valuable research at McGill University in Montreal, became interested in probing the inner structure of the atom. Much of his earlier research dealt with radioactivity, and led to the study of the penetration of α-particles through very thin metal foils. The results of this research led to an entirely new understanding of the structure of the atom.

The apparatus used by Rutherford, and his associates Geiger and Marsden, is shown in Figure 29-2. A radioactive substance is contained within a narrow opening of a lead block, permitting α-particles to stream from the block in essentially one direction. A short distance from the opening a thin gold foil is located. A fluorescent screen is placed behind and also beside the gold foil to make visible any impacts by the high-energy alpha particles (see section 28-7).

Most of these impacts with the fluorescent screen took place at a point directly in front of the radioactive source. This in itself was surprising, because it indicated that the α-particles passed through the metal foil, undeviated by the atoms of the foil. The

Bettmann Archive

Fig. 29-1: *Ernest Rutherford, one of the outstanding scientists of the twentieth century, performed experiments that revealed much about the structure of the atom.*

thickness of the foil was of the order of 10^{-5} cm, but a knowledge of the approximate size of the atom indicated that this contained at least 1,000 layers of gold atoms. Could this mean that the atoms consisted mostly of empty space?

Much more surprising were the results found at the screen placed at the side and in

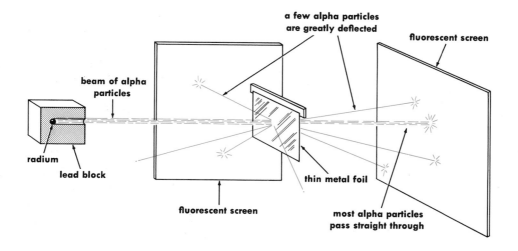

Fig. 29-2: *Rutherford's alpha-scattering experiment.*

front of the foil. An occasional bright spot on the screen in these locations indicated wild deflections of the particles sometimes almost straight back along their incident path.

A study of the distribution of this scattering involved many months of patient observation by Geiger and Marsden. The culmination of this research was the conclusion that the scattering could only be accounted for if the actual bulk of the atoms in the foil occupied a very limited space. Thus it was suggested that the material portion of the atom was not spread over the volume of the atom but formed a very densely concentrated region called the *nucleus*. The occasional backward flight of an α-particle must be the result of a direct encounter between it and the nucleus. Furthermore, the analysis of the scattering of these particles indicated that *the entire positive charge of the atom must be contained in the nucleus*. The deflections of the α-particles were accounted for by the repulsive forces between the positively charged particles and the nucleus, as indicated in Figure 29-3.

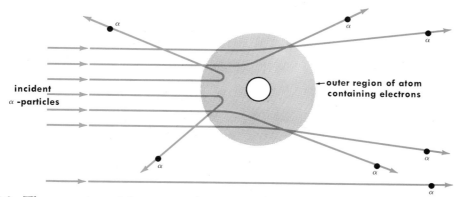

Fig. 29-3: *The scattering of the α-particles suggested that the positive charge in an atom was not uniformly distributed throughout the atom.*

2. THE RUTHERFORD ATOM

The results of the α-scattering experiments, performed on thin foils of many different metals, led to a convincing picture of the atom far different from Thomson's "jelly" model (section 28-5).

An important conclusion concerned the size of the nucleus. The mathematical analysis based on their observations of the α-scattering, indicated that the nucleus was extremely small in relation to the overall-size of the atom—about 1/10,000 times as large. Yet, because it was already known that the mass of electrons within the atom was negligible in relation to the entire mass of the atom, almost all of this mass must be contained in this nucleus.

And what of these electrons? What would prevent the electrons of the atom from falling into the positively-charged nucleus? Rutherford conjectured that the electrons in the atom must move in orbits around the nucleus, with the attractive force acting to keep them in orbit—much as the force of gravity keeps the planets in orbit about the sun. In fact, the Rutherford picture of the atom represented the atom as a miniature solar system. (See Figures 1 and 2, pages 3 and 4).

3. STRUCTURE OF THE NUCLEUS

With an entirely new concept of the atom brought about by the α-scattering experiment, one question became of great importance: what is the nucleus made of?

The experiments had shown that the nucleus was positively charged. Perhaps the nucleus consisted of positively-charged particles such as the α-particles, or the positive particles encountered in the experiments with positive rays. Experiments with various gases in gas discharge tubes had shown that the hydrogen atom possessed the smallest amount of positive charge (equal in magnitude but opposite in sign to the electron charge) and also the lowest mass (about 1800 times larger than the electron.) Could it be that all atomic nucleii were combinations of the hydrogen nucleus?

The α-particle itself helped provide the answer to this question. The positive charge of the α-particle was double that of the hydrogen positive ion (the proton), yet its mass was greater by a factor of four. Rutherford had found the α-particle identical in all respects to the positive helium ions in gas discharge tubes. Thus the helium nucleus possessed four times the mass of the hydrogen nucleus, but only twice its charge. This suggested that the helium nucleus contained four protons, to give it four times the mass of the hydrogen nucleus, and two electrons which would essentially neutralize the electrical effects of two of these protons.

Thus Rutherford concluded that nuclei are composed of protons, and neutral particles made up of an association of a proton and electron. The neutral particle was named the *neutron*. Experimental evidence of the existence of the neutron, however, was not obtained until some years later, in 1933. (See chapter 31).

The protons and neutrons in the nucleus, taken collectively, are called *nucleons*. These nucleons account for the weight of the nucleus, and practically the weight of the entire atom, since the mass of the electrons outside the nucleus is negligible by comparison. The positive charge of the nucleus is determined by the number of "free" protons, that is, those not associated with an electron to form a neutron. Beyond the nucleus are the electrons, in orbit about it. Because an atom is normally neutral, the number of electrons outside the nucleus must be equal to the number of "free" protons in the nucleus, since experiments had already shown the charge on electron and proton to be numerically equal. Rutherford's concept of the helium atom is shown in Figure 29-4.

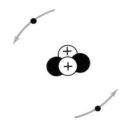

Fig. 29-4: *Rutherford envisaged the atom as consisting of a nucleus of protons and neutrons, with electrons revolving around the nucleus. A helium atom is pictured here.*

4. MASS NUMBER AND ATOMIC NUMBER

Long before the year 1915, when the concept of the nuclear atom became firmly established, various means were available for determining the atomic weight of the various elements. Since almost all the weight of an atom is concentrated in a nucleus composed of protons and neutrons of equal mass, we would expect that the atomic weight of any given element would be some multiple of the weight of the lightest atom—hydrogen. Precise measurements of atomic weights show this to be almost, but not exactly, the case.

In specifying the mass of an atom, a reference mass is required. This is arbitrarily taken as the mass of a particular form of carbon called carbon-12. The mass of this atom is taken as precisely 12 *atomic mass units* (12 amu). On the same scale, the hydrogen atom's mass is 1.00798 amu and that of uranium 238.03 amu.

Of importance to us is the **mass number** of an element. This represents the total number of nucleons (neutrons and protons) in the nucleus. Thus the mass number of hydrogen is one, since its nucleus is made up of one proton. The mass number for the form of carbon mentioned above is 12, since we now know its nucleus comprises 6 protons and 6 neutrons.

By 1920, experimental methods had been found for determining the positive charge on the nuclei of the various elements. As we would expect, this charge is a multiple of the charge on the hydrogen nucleus, the proton. This is called the *atomic number* of the nucleus. Thus the atomic number of hydrogen is 1, that of carbon-12 is 6 (since its nucleus contains 6 protons). The atomic number of uranium is 92, indicating that its nucleus contains 92 protons.

A knowledge of the mass number and atomic number of an element allows us to determine the number of neutrons in its atoms. Thus, uranium-238 with 238 nucleons, and atomic number 92 contains 146 neutrons.

5. THE PERIODIC TABLE

A knowledge of the positive charge on the nucleus gives new meaning to the periodic table of the elements. You will recall from Chapter 28 that Mendeleeff had arranged the elements in order of increasing atomic weight noting a resulting periodicity in the properties of the elements. Now if we assign a number to each of the elements, in order of increasing atomic weight, we find that with very few exceptions that number is also the atomic number of the element. A modern form of the periodic table (Figure 29-5) illustrates this.

Note, for instance, that carbon is the sixth element, in order of atomic weight. This indicates that its atomic number is 6 as mentioned above.

The periodic table is essentially a listing of the elements in terms of their chemical properties. But because this automatically lists them in order of the amount of charge on the nucleus, we are led to the important conclusion that *the charge on the nucleus determines the chemical properties of the element.* Or, expressed in a different manner, the chemical properties of the element are determined by the number of electrons outside the nucleus of that element's neutral atom.

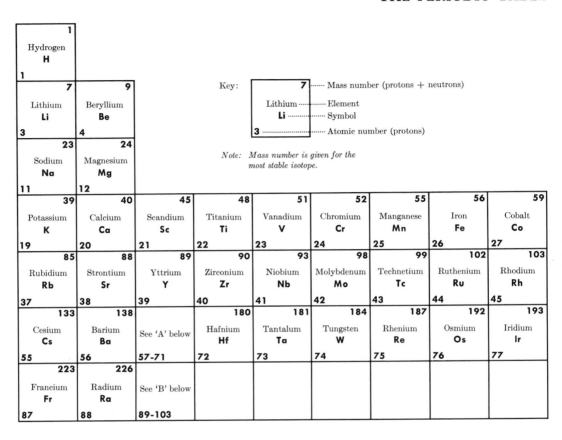

1 Hydrogen **H** 1								
7 Lithium **Li** 3	**9** Beryllium **Be** 4							
23 Sodium **Na** 11	**24** Magnesium **Mg** 12							
39 Potassium **K** 19	**40** Calcium **Ca** 20	**45** Scandium **Sc** 21	**48** Titanium **Ti** 22	**51** Vanadium **V** 23	**52** Chromium **Cr** 24	**55** Manganese **Mn** 25	**56** Iron **Fe** 26	**59** Cobalt **Co** 27
85 Rubidium **Rb** 37	**88** Strontium **Sr** 38	**89** Yttrium **Y** 39	**90** Zirconium **Zr** 40	**93** Niobium **Nb** 41	**98** Molybdenum **Mo** 42	**99** Technetium **Tc** 43	**102** Ruthenium **Ru** 44	**103** Rhodium **Rh** 45
133 Cesium **Cs** 55	**138** Barium **Ba** 56	See 'A' below 57-71	**180** Hafnium **Hf** 72	**181** Tantalum **Ta** 73	**184** Tungsten **W** 74	**187** Rhenium **Re** 75	**192** Osmium **Os** 76	**193** Iridium **Ir** 77
223 Francium **Fr** 87	**226** Radium **Ra** 88	See 'B' below 89-103						

Key:

7	.... Mass number (protons + neutrons)
Lithium	.... Element
Li	.... Symbol
3	.... Atomic number (protons)

Note: Mass number is given for the most stable isotope.

A
The Rare Earth Series

139 Lanthanum **La** 57	**140** Cerium **Ce** 58	**141** Praseodymium **Pr** 59	**142** Neodymium **Nd** 60	**147** Promethium **Pm** 61	**152** Samarium **Sm** 62	**153** Europium **Eu** 63

B
The Actinide Series

227 Actinium **Ac** 89	**232** Thorium **Th** 90	**231** Protactinium **Pa** 91	**238** Uranium **U** 92	**237** Neptunium **Np** 93	**244** Plutonium **Pu** 94	**245** Americium **Am** 95

Fig. 29-5: *A modern form*

									4
									Helium **He** 2

			11	12	14	16	19	20
			Boron **B** 5	Carbon **C** 6	Nitrogen **N** 7	Oxygen **O** 8	Fluorine **F** 9	Neon **Ne** 10
			27	28	31	32	35	40
			Aluminum **Al** 13	Silicon **Si** 14	Phosphorus **P** 15	Sulphur **S** 16	Chlorine **Cl** 17	Argon **Ar** 18

58	63	64	69	74	75	80	79	84
Nickel **Ni** 28	Copper **Cu** 29	Zinc **Zn** 30	Gallium **Ga** 31	Germanium **Ge** 32	Arsenic **As** 33	Selenium **Se** 34	Bromine **Br** 35	Krypton **Kr** 36
106	107	114	115	120	121	130	127	132
Palladium **Pd** 46	Silver **Ag** 47	Cadmium **Cd** 48	Indium **In** 49	Tin **Sn** 50	Antimony **Sb** 51	Tellurium **Te** 52	Iodine **I** 53	Xenon **Xe** 54
195	197	202	205	206	209	209	210	228
Platinum **Pt** 78	Gold **Au** 79	Mercury **Hg** 80	Thallium **Tl** 81	Lead **Pb** 82	Bismuth **Bi** 83	Polonium **Po** 84	Astatine **At** 85	Radon **Rn** 86

158	159	164	165	168	169	174	175
Gadolinium **Gd** 64	Terbium **Tb** 65	Dysprosium **Dy** 66	Holmium **Ho** 67	Erbium **Er** 68	Thulium **Tm** 69	Ytterbium **Yb** 70	Lutetium **Lu** 71

248	249	249	252	253	256	254	257
Curium **Cm** 96	Berkelium **Bk** 97	Californium **Cf** 98	Einsteinium **Es** 99	Fermium **Fm** 100	Mendelevium **Md** 101	Nobelium **No** 102	Lawrencium **Lw** 103

of the periodic table.

6. REPRESENTATION OF ATOMIC NUCLEI

It is convenient to represent the composition of nuclei by means of the chemical symbol for that element, in conjunction with its mass number and atomic number. For instance Carbon-12 is represented as $_6C^{12}$, and the helium nucleus (the α-particle with a mass number 4 and atomic number 2) as $_2He^4$.

EXAMPLE 1

Using the periodic table of Figure 29-5, write symbols for the nuclei of the following elements: hydrogen, aluminum, chlorine, uranium. From this, determine the number of neutrons in each nucleus.

Solution:

hydrogen $_1H^1$, **no neutrons**

aluminum $_{13}Al^{27}$

    number of neutrons $= 27 - 13 = 14$

chlorine $_{17}Cl^{35}$ number of neutrons $= 18$

uranium $_{92}U^{238}$ number of neutrons $= 146$

---

7. ISOTOPES

A brief study of the atomic weights of the elements in Figure 29-5, reveals that in many cases these weights are far from being whole numbers. In the case of chlorine, for instance, how can we explain the value 35.453 for the atomic weight? If its nucleus is composed of the protons and neutrons that we assume are common to most elements, should not the atomic weight be very close to 35 or to 36?

A solution to this perplexing problem was obtained by J. J. Thomson in 1912 while performing experiments with the positive rays in a neon gas discharge, using apparatus depicted in Figure 29-6. Thomson found that the beam of neon ions split off into two groups, under the action of the magnetic field.

Such an occurrence could be explained by assuming that some of the ions possessed a stronger nuclear charge than the others, or by assuming that some of the ions were different in mass. Further development of the apparatus, by Thomson and his associate F. W. Aston, showed that the difference in deflections was due to a difference in *masses* of the neon ions. A determination of the mass revealed that some of the ions had a weight 20.00 times that of the proton, while the others were slightly heavier with a weight 22.00 times that of the proton.

Evidently then there are two kinds of neon atoms, each differing slightly in mass from the other. As far as their chemical properties are concerned, however, analysis showed these were alike in all respects. Similar experiments were performed on other elements and of the 92 elements that occur in nature, about two-thirds of them have now been found to contain atoms of more than one weight. The term *isotope* is used in reference to each of these various forms of a given element. This word is derived from the Greek, and means "same place", referring to its position in the periodic table.

The concept of isotopes was a startling reversal of thought from the early Dalton theory of the atom. For a century the

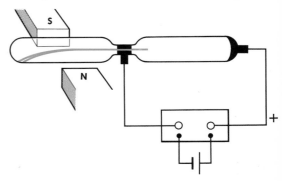

Fig. 29-6: *Using a positive-ray apparatus, a beam of positive neon ions divides into two portions under the influence of a magnetic field. What does this suggest concerning the neon atom?*

belief was firmly held that the atoms of any given element were alike in all respects. Now most of the elements are known to contain atoms that differ slightly in mass, although having the same nuclear charge, and hence the same number of electrons in the neutral atom (thus accounting for the identical chemical properties of the various isotopes of a given element).

We are now able to see why the atomic weight of an element is not necessarily an exact multiple of the weight of the proton. Consider the two isotopes of neon that were discovered by Thomson. Thomson found that the relative abundance of the heavy neon atom (22.00 amu) was only one-tenth that of the lighter one (20.00 amu). In any sample of neon, then, there are 10 heavy atoms for each lighter one, and the average of these is $\dfrac{10 \times 20.00 + 1 \times 22.00}{11}$ which gives 20.2. (A third isotope of neon, of extremely low abundance, was undetected by Thomson)

EXAMPLE 2

Chlorine is made up of two isotopes $_{17}Cl^{35}$ and $_{17}Cl^{37}$. The relative abundance of the lighter atom is 75.5%. What is the atomic weight of chlorine, using this data?

Solution:

atomic weight

$$= \frac{75.5}{100} \times 35 + \frac{24.5}{100} \times 37$$

$$= 35.5$$

---

8. RADIOACTIVE DISINTEGRATION

We are now in a position to pursue in somewhat more detail the phenomenon of radioactivity discussed in Chapter 28. Madame Curie, a Polish scientist working in Paris examined many materials for the property of radioactivity and found that pitchblende, a mixture known to contain uranium was extremely radioactive, more so even than an equal amount of uranium. A suspicion that this could be accounted for by an unknown radioactive element in the pitchblende led to many months of laborious work which culminated in the separation from the pitchblende of two hitherto unknown elements, each extremely strong in radioactivity —*polonium*, named after her native country, and *radium*, so named for its intense radiation.

A study of the new element radium under isolated conditions revealed that a new gaseous element formed in its presence, as well as the gas helium. The new element was named *radon*.

Continued study indicated that still other materials were forming. The element polonium was identified, in addition to an increased amount of helium, while at the same time the amount of radon *diminished*. Apparently radium was changing spontaneously into helium and radioactive radon, the latter in turn changing into helium and polonium, as depicted below:

$$Ra \xrightarrow{\quad} Rn \xrightarrow{\quad} Po$$
$$\nearrow He \qquad \nearrow He$$

The presence of helium near the radioactive substances is easily accounted for if we recall the emanation of α-particles from these radioactive substances, and the identification, some time later, of these particles as nuclei of helium atoms, by Rutherford.

The spontaneous transformation of one element into another, in the radioactive process shook yet another cornerstone of accepted atomic theory—the basic indestructibility of atoms. Rutherford in 1902 postulated that an atom of a radioactive substance when emitting an α-particle (or a β-particle) breaks into two parts—the emitted particle and an atom of a different substance.

The radioactive decay depicted above does not stop with the formation of polonium. The polonium itself is radioactive, emitting an α-particle to form lead-214, an unstable isotope of lead. The radioactive decay continues with the emission of α- or β-particles to form, in turn, unstable isotopes as follows: bismuth-214, polonium-214, lead-210, bismuth-210, polonium-210 and finally lead-206, a stable isotope of lead. The entire sequence is depicted in Figure 29-7 beginning with radium-226. In this diagram the nucleus of each isotope is shown, with the number of protons and neutrons it contains. Note that the emission of an α-particle (possessing a positive charge of 2 units and a mass of 4 units) results in a new nucleus whose atomic number is less than that of the previous nucleus by 2 units and whose mass number is less by 4 units. On the other hand, the emission of a β-particle (an electron of charge −1 unit, but of negligible

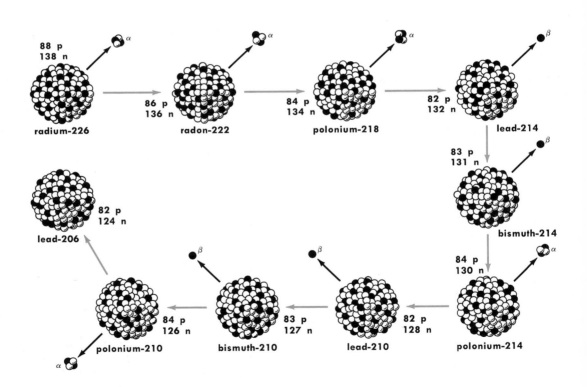

Fig. 29-7: *Radium eventually becomes lead in a sequence of disintegrations illustrated here.*

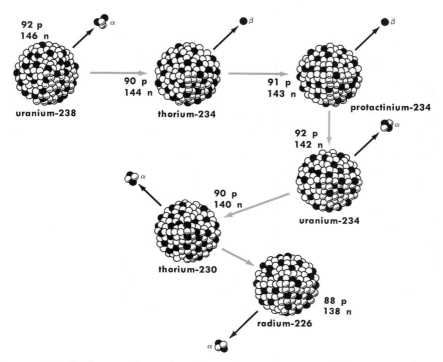

Fig. 29-8: *Radium is formed as the result of radioactive decay of uranium.*

mass) *increases* the net positive charge of the nucleus and hence its atomic number by 1 unit, while leaving the mass number unchanged.

Presumably all of the radium in a sample of pitchblende would, in time, decay to the stable form of lead of mass number 206, changing during the process to the progressively lighter unstable atoms depicted in the illustration. This led Rutherford to conjecture that the radium itself results from the decay of heavier elements in the ore. An investigation showed that this indeed was the case. This progressive decay, beginning with uranium-238, and progressing through thorium-234, protactinium-234, uranium-234, thorium-230, to radium-226, is shown in Figure 29-8.

The entire transformation from uranium to the stable, non-radioactive form of lead, is shown in Figure 29-9.

EXAMPLE 3

Write a nuclear equation to illustrate the transformation of:

(a) radium into radon

(b) the unstable isotope lead-214 into bismuth.

Solution:

(a) $_{88}Ra^{226} \rightarrow {}_{86}Rn^{222} + {}_{2}He^{4}$

Note that the total numbers of mass units and charge units on each side of the equation must balance.

(b) As a symbol for the β-particle (i.e. the electron) we can choose $_{-1}e^{0}$, indicating that its mass is virtually zero, while its charge is -1 unit.

Thus: $_{82}Pb^{214} \rightarrow {}_{83}Bi^{214} + {}_{-1}e^{0}$

As before, mass and charge are conserved on both sides of the equation.

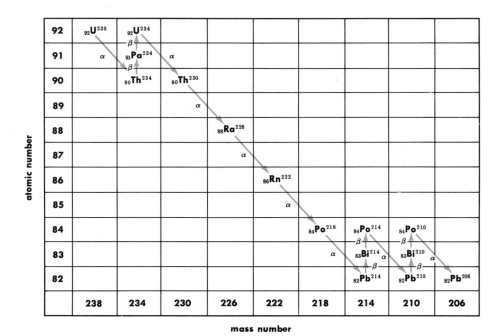

Fig. 29-9: *The decay chart of uranium 238. All α emanations reduce the mass number by 4, the atomic number by 2.*

Note that in the process of transmutation from uranium to lead-206, two other kinds of lead appear. These three forms of lead were found to be chemically indistinguishable, and led to the concept of isotopes in a manner quite different from the experiment of Thomson's described in the previous section.

9. RATE OF DECAY

In the study of radioactive elements, it soon became apparent that each element gives off particles at a definite rate, characteristic of that element. The rate of decay of the atoms is quite independent of any external conditions applied to the element, such as extreme heat or pressure, and independent of whether the element is in the free state or combined with other elements as chemical compounds.

In describing the rate at which these atoms decay, a convenient way is that of expressing the time in which *half* of the existing atoms will decay. This time is called the *half-life* of the element. The half-life of radium is 1620 years. This means that of a sample of 1 gram of radium, exactly half of it will remain as radium after 1620 years. In the succeeding 1620 years, one-half of this amount, one-quarter gram, will still remain, and so on.

The half-lives of the radioactive elements discussed so far vary enormously. Uranium for example has a half-life of 4.6 *billion years*, while that of polonium-214 is only of the order of 10^{-5} seconds. A general curve depicting the rate at which a radioactive element decays, is shown in Figure 29-10. In any sample of the substance, it is impossible to predict for any single atom, at what

432

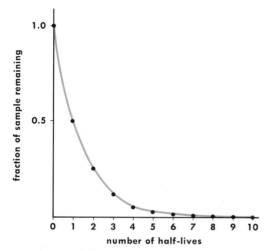

Fig. 29-10: *This graph indicates the fraction of a sample of a radioactive element remaining after a length of time specified in half-lives.*

time it will decay by emitting an α- or β-particle. However, for the many millions of atoms within the sample, one can state with a high degree of accuracy the proportion of atoms that will remain unchanged at any given time.

The measurement of half-life has very important practical applications that will be discussed in the next section.

10. RADIOACTIVE DATING

The age of geological formations of various types can be accurately estimated by determining the relative amount of uranium-238 and lead-206 contained in a sample of the rock. This important application arises from our knowledge that any quantity of uranium-238 will ultimately decay to lead-206, and that this decay occurs at a constant rate with half-life of 4.6 billion years.

As an example, consider a piece of uranium ore which, when analyzed, is found to contain a relatively small amount of lead-206 in relation to the amount of uranium-238. Obviously the uranium within the rock has had a relatively short time in which to disintegrate—the rock may have

been formed only a few million years ago. On the other hand, a rock found to contain equal amounts of uranium-238 and lead-206 could be classified as being 4.6 billion years old because half of the original uranium has decayed. Measurements such as this give the age of the oldest geological formations as 5 billion years, a figure which agrees with the age of the earth as determined from other considerations.

This method of geological dating hinges of course, upon the presence of trace amounts of uranium, or some other radioactive element, at the time of the rock's formation from a molten state.

Of equal interest is the manner by which the age of once-living organic material may be determined. Here the key element is an isotope of carbon—carbon-14.

Carbon-14 is produced in small quantities in the upper atmosphere as a result of the impact of cosmic rays on the nitrogen in the air. It becomes incorporated in the carbon dioxide of the air, and as a result is absorbed by plants and other living matter. Because carbon-14 is radioactive, with a half-life of 5700 years, all living matter exhibits a small degree of radioactivity. It is estimated that of the normal content of carbon in living matter, only one atom of carbon-14 is present for every 10^{12} atoms of the stable carbon-12.

When the plant dies it no longer absorbs carbon dioxide, and the amount of radioactive carbon in the plant gradually decreases. This decay will continue for many thousands of years. By measuring the ratio of carbon-14 to carbon-12, the time interval since the organism ceased living can be accurately established.

The age of important archaeological findings such as the Dead Sea Scrolls (2,000 years), and the coffins of Egyptian Pharaohs (up to 5,000 years) have been accurately established by this method.

433

THE NUCLEUS: Rutherford's alpha-scattering experiment demonstrated that positively charged particles were concentrated within the atom. The concentrated part of the atom is called the *nucleus*. The nucleus contains protons, which are positively charged, and neutrons, which are neutral particles with a mass slightly larger than that of the proton

MASS NUMBER AND ATOMIC NUMBER: The mass number represents the total number of nucleons (neutrons and protons) in the nucleus; the atomic number represents the number of protons in the nucleus.

THE PERIODIC TABLE: The elements are arranged in order of atomic weight. If numbers are assigned in that order it is found that, with few exceptions, these correspond with the elements' atomic numbers. As the table groups the elements according to their chemical properties, the conclusion is that it is the charge on the nucleus that determines those properties.

REPRESENTATION OF ATOMIC NUCLEI: Atomic nuclei are represented in the form $_aX^b$, where $_a$ is the atomic number, X is the symbol for the element and ^{b} is the mass number.

ISOTOPES: Isotopes of an element are forms of the element that differ only in the number of neutrons in the atoms. The chemical properties of the isotopes are the same.

RADIOACTIVE DECAY: A radioactive element decays by emitting α-particles or β-particles Emission of an α-particle (with a positive charge of 2 units and a mass of 4 units) results in a new nucleus whose atomic number is less by 2 units and whose mass number is less by 4 units. Emission of a β-particle, (a negatively charged electron with negligible mass) increases the atomic number by 1 unit and leaves the mass number unchanged.

EXERCISE A

1. Describe the chief differences in the atomic models of Rutherford and Thomson.

2. What chief observations led to the Rutherford model?

3. How do we account for the fact that the helium nucleus, with four times the mass of the hydrogen nucleus, has only twice the amount of charge?

4. There are seven isotopes of mercury. What does this statement mean?

5. For each of the elements nitrogen-14, oxygen-16, sodium-23, sulfur-32, and copper-63, state:
   (a) the atomic number   (b) the mass number
   (c) the number of protons in the nucleus
   (d) the number of neutrons in the nucleus
   (e) the number of nucleons in the nucleus
   (f) the number of electrons outside the nucleus.

434

6. How would the scattering of α-particles, due to a nucleus with a positive charge, differ from scattering that would be caused by collision with a stationary uncharged nucleus?

7. In what way are the isotopes of an element similar? In what way do they differ?

8. What experiment could you perform to show that there are two isotopes of chlorine?

9. Two isotopes of uranium have mass number 235 and 238 respectively.
   (a) What is the atomic number of each?
   (b) How many neutrons are contained in the nuclei of each?
   (c) How many planetary electrons are there in the atoms of each isotope?

10. What aspect of an atom determines the chemical properties of that element?

EXERCISE B

1. Determine the number of (i) protons (ii) neutrons (iii) planetary electrons for each of the following atoms:
   (a) $_{11}Na^{23}$ (b) $_{94}Pu^{242}$ (c) $_{82}Pb^{207}$ (d) $_{17}Cl^{35}$ (e) Ge^{70} (f) Ge^{72} (g) U^{235}

2. There are two isotopes of copper. These are copper-63, of relative abundance 69.1%, and copper-65, of relative abundance 30.9%. Using this data, calculate the atomic weight of copper and compare your answer with that value shown in the table on page 468.

3. Write a nuclear equation to illustrate the transformation of radium to another element by the emission of an α-particle. What is this other element?

4. Use the periodic table to determine which of the following indicated transmutations contain errors?
   (a) $_{90}Th^{232} \rightarrow _{88}Ra^{228} + _2He^4$
   (b) $_{82}Pb^{212} \rightarrow _{83}Bi^{208} + _{-1}e^0$
   (c) $_{84}Po^{216} \rightarrow _{82}Pb^{212} + _2He^4$

5. For the following radioactive transformations, supply the missing symbols.
   (a) $_{92}U^{235} \rightarrow ? + _2He^4$
   (b) $_{90}Th^{231} \rightarrow ? + _{-1}e^0$
   (c) $_{89}Ac^{227} \rightarrow _{90}Th^{227} + ?$
   (d) $_{84}Po^{215} \rightarrow _{82}Pb^{211} + ?$
   (e) $? \rightarrow _{82}Pb^{207} + _2He^4$
   (f) $Pb^{212} \rightarrow Bi^{212} + ?$

6. Taking the half-life of polonium-240 as 140 days, and considering one gram of this element, how much of it will remain (a) after 140 days
   (b) after 280 days
   (c) after 420 days
   (d) after two years?

Chapter 30

The Outer Structure of the Atom

1. DIFFICULTIES ARISING FROM THE RUTHERFORD MODEL

In the previous chapter we have seen how the results of Rutherford's experiments indicated that the atom was largely empty space with the mass concentrated in the central nucleus, of extremely small volume. Outside the nucleus a number of electrons are located, equal in number to the number of protons in the nucleus, resulting in an atom with no net electrical charge.

The arrangement of the electrons around the nucleus now becomes of importance to us. We know that the electrons must be in rapid motion around the nucleus; otherwise the attraction between the electrons and the nucleus would cause them to fall into the nucleus. Thus we picture the electrons in orbit about the nucleus in much the same way the planets revolve about the sun.

The solar-system model of the atom was an intriguing one to a young Danish physicist named Niels Bohr, who worked for a time with Rutherford. To Bohr, the new models while solving some problems, created many new ones.

According to electrical theory at the time (1911), whenever a charged particle *accelerates*, a portion of its energy is radiated away. This fact had been adequately demonstrated and was accepted. An electron in orbit about the nucleus is an accelerating charge, and hence should radiate its energy. This loss of energy would require its moving continuously into a smaller orbit. Eventually the electron would fall into the nucleus, as depicted in Figure 30-1.

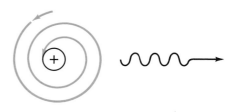

Fig. 30-1: *According to classical theory, a revolving electron should radiate energy in the form of a wave as shown. As a result of this loss of energy, the electron would soon fall into the nucleus.*

At this time, the nature of light as an electromagnetic radiation was fairly well understood, and believed to be the radiation emanating from accelerated charges in the atom. Thus, according to this new model of the atom, as the electron continued its inward spiral toward the nucleus, losing energy all the time, a continuous spectrum of light of constantly-changing wavelength should be emitted by it while it spirals toward the nucleus. This view, however, was not consistent with the observed spectra of the various elements. Each element emits its own characteristic spectrum—light of certain wavelengths, a set of wavelengths characteristic of that element alone (Figure 30-2).

Bohr was convinced that a key to understanding the atom lay in a study of these spectra, and an exhaustive study of the hydrogen spectrum led to a theory of atomic structure that was to destroy many long-held basic concepts of physics.

2. THE BOHR THEORY OF ATOMIC STRUCTURE

In developing a theory that would explain completely the particular wavelengths of light emitted by hydrogen, Bohr made the following assumptions:

1. An electron revolving about the nucleus can do so only in certain orbits. Each of these possible orbits represents a certain amount of energy possessed by the electron. The electron has the smallest amount of energy when it is in the innermost orbit, and progressively higher energy as the radius of the orbit increases.

2. While the electron is in one of its "allowed" orbits, it cannot radiate energy.

3. An electron can "jump" from an outer orbit to an inner orbit. In so doing, a portion of its energy is radiated, the amount being the difference in energy it possesses in each of the two orbits. Similarly, an electron can jump to a higher orbit if some external agent such as a colliding atom gives it the additional energy required in the higher orbit.

4. When an electron jumps to a lower orbit, or "energy level", the difference in energy is emitted as a "package" of light, called a "photon", or "quantum".

3. THE QUANTUM THEORY

The theory evolving from the idea that radiation consists of "packages" of energy is referred to as the *quantum theory*. It was first proposed by a German physicist, Max Planck, in 1900 to explain the relative amounts of electromagnetic energy of different wavelengths radiated from hot substances.

The quantum theory states that all electromagnetic radiations occur not in continuous streams of energy, but in packages of a

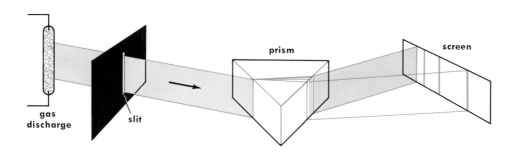

Fig. 30-2: *The nature of the light emitted by a substance in an excited state may be analyzed using a spectroscope, shown here in principle. Light from the source at the left passes through a narrow slit and then through a prism. The components (colours) of the light will be refracted by differing amounts, each producing an image of the slit on a screen.*

definite size, the size of the package depending on the wavelength of the radiation. Mathematically, the energy in each package or "photon" is *proportional* to the wavelength of the radiation: that is

$E = h f$ where E = energy of photon in joules
  f = frequency in c/sec
  h = a constant 6.63×10^{-34} joule-sec (called *Planck's constant*)

Also, since $c = f\lambda$
(where c = speed of light
  λ = wavelength of light)
we may alternatively write this equation as

$$E = h \frac{c}{\lambda}.$$

EXAMPLE 1

Yellow light from a sodium flame has a wavelength of 5890A (5.890×10^{-7}m). What is the energy of a photon of this light?

Solution:

$$E = h \frac{c}{\lambda} = 6.63 \times 10^{-34} \text{ j-sec} \times \frac{3.00 \times 10^8 \text{m/sec}}{5.89 \times 10^{-7}\text{m}}$$

$$= 3.37 \times 10^{-19}\text{j}$$

In describing exchanges of energy within the outer structure of the atom, the joule is too large a unit. It is convenient to use a smaller unit of energy, the electron-volt (ev).

EXAMPLE 2

Find the number of joules equivalent to an electron-volt.

Solution:

$W = QV$ or $E = QV$ (page 309)
$\therefore$ 1 ev = electronic charge $\times$ 1 volt

$$= 1.60 \times 10^{-19} \text{ coulomb} \times 1 \frac{\text{joule}}{\text{coulomb}}$$

$$= 1.60 \times 10^{-19}\text{j}$$

Bohr's use of the quantum concept enables us to sketch a model of the hydrogen atom somewhat as shown in Figure 30-3. The nucleus of the atom is at the centre of the five allowed orbits that are shown in the diagram. The first orbit, closest to the nucleus, represents the "ground state", or lowest energy-level that the electron can possess. Three possible transitions from higher energy states are shown, each one accompanied by a radiation of energy.

In a normal hydrogen atom, the electron would be found in its lowest energy level, orbit 1 in Figure 30-3. When the atom becomes "excited", by heating the gas, for instance, or by passage of an electrical discharge through the gas, the electron absorbs energy, raising it to a higher energy level. The electron almost immediately falls back to a lower energy level, radiating all or part of this absorbed energy.

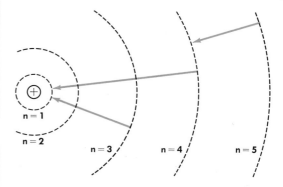

Fig. 30-3: *According to Bohr's theory of the hydrogen atom, the electron can occupy any of several "energy levels", or orbits without radiating energy. Five such orbits are shown here, and three possible transitions from higher to lower energy states, during which electromagnetic energy is radiated.*

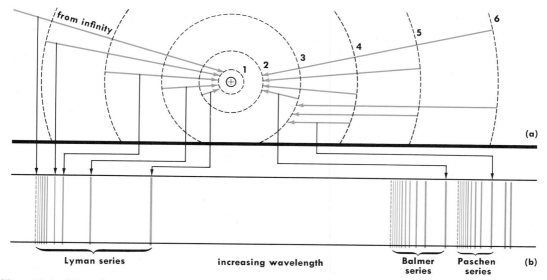

Lyman series   increasing wavelength   Balmer series   Paschen series   (b)

Fig. 30-4: *This diagram relates the electron jumps of the hydrogen atom to the wavelength of light emitted as a result of that jump. Three series of wavelengths exist, corresponding to jumps to the first, second, and third energy levels respectively, and named after the scientists who investigated them.*

In Figure 30-4 are shown the spectral lines for the hydrogen atom. Bohr was able to relate the wavelength of each of these lines to a corresponding loss of energy when an electron jumps back to a lower energy level. The ability of his theory to predict with complete accuracy the wavelengths of the various lines in the spectrum was impressive enough to warrant complete acceptance of the theory and the bold assumptions on which it was based.

4. IONIZATION ENERGY AND ELECTRON SHELLS

By studying the ionization energy of each element, a key to the electron structure of the other elements may be found. The ionization energy is simply the energy required to remove an electron from the atom so that it is no longer under the influence of the nuclear charge of that atom (Figure 30-5). This process creates a positive ion of the formerly neutral atom. The energy required to do so can be measured quite accurately.

The ionization energy of several elements is illustrated in Table 30-1 in the order in which these elements occur in the Periodic Table. As the charge on the nucleus (atomic number) increases, the energy required to remove an electron from the atom varies in the same periodic fashion as do many of the other physical and chemical properties of the element. (Compare this with Figure 28-1).

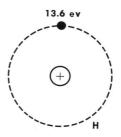

Fig. 30-5: *The amount of energy required to remove an electron from an atom is called the ionization energy for that element. For hydrogen it is 13.6 ev.*

Table 30-1

The Ionization Energies of the first Twenty Elements

H	He						
13.6	24.6						
Li	Be	B	C	N	O	F	Ne
5.4	9.3	8.3	11.2	14.5	13.6	17.4	21.6
Na	Mg	Al	Si	P	S	Cl	Ar
5.1	7.6	6.0	8.1	11.0	10.3	13.0	15.8
K	Ca						
4.3	6.1						

If the hydrogen atom contains one electron in orbit around the nucleus, our theory suggests that the helium atom, with atomic number 2, contains two such electrons, as indicated in Figure 30-6. Because of the double charge on the nucleus, however, the

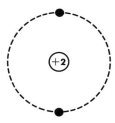

Fig. 30-6: *The ionization energy of helium is about double that for hydrogen, as we would expect because of the double nuclear charge.*

electrons are held more firmly than in the case of the hydrogen atom. This is verified by the fact that the ionization energy for helium, the amount of energy required to remove one electron, is almost double that for the hydrogen atom.

The next element in the periodic table is lithium with atomic number 3. At first glance we would place the third electron in the same orbit as that of the electrons in the hydrogen and helium atoms, as suggested in Figure 30-7 (a). But the ionization

energy of lithium, 5.4 ev, is much less than that of either hydrogen or helium. How can we account for this? The simplest solution is to picture the third electron as being farther away from the nucleus, that is, in an orbit farther removed from the nucleus than the first two electrons, as shown in Figure 30-7(b).

Successive applications of this reasoning allow us to place additional electrons in this second "shell" to construct models for the atoms of beryllium, boron, carbon, nitrogen, oxygen, fluorine, and neon. This is shown in part in Figure 30-8.

For the next element, sodium, with atomic number 11, the ionization energy takes another dramatic drop in value, suggesting that it has one electron in a still more remote orbit. Successive additions of an electron to this shell give us the elements magnesium aluminum, silicon, phosphorus, sulphur, chlorine and argon (Figure 30-9).

With reasoning similar to this, we are able to construct a model of each atom in the periodic table. The complete analysis, however, is much more complicated than this. We might assume for instance, that the third shell is complete with 8 electrons, just as the second shell was. This is to some extent justified, as we can see by considering the ionization energy of potassium (4.3 ev) the next element in the periodic table. This suggests that potassium has one electron in the fourth shell. Soon, however, we find that before the fourth shell becomes complete, additional electrons are added to the third shell. The true maximum number of electrons in the third shell is 18, and in the fourth shell 32.

Interestingly, the maximum number of electrons in a shell is given by a simple mathematical formula, $2 n^2$, where n is the number of the shell. Thus, for the third shell ($n=3$), the maximum number of electrons is 2×3^2 or 18.

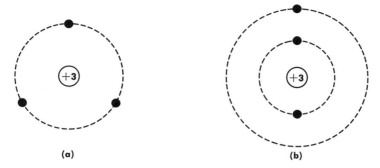

Fig. 30-7: *Because the ionization energy of lithium is much less than that for hydrogen, we picture the lithium atom as in (b) rather than (a). Why?*

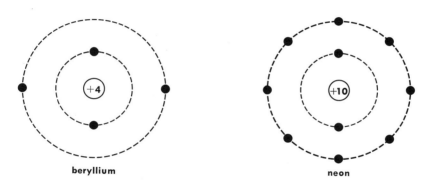

Fig. 30-8: *What is the atomic number of each of the atoms shown here? What elements are represented?*

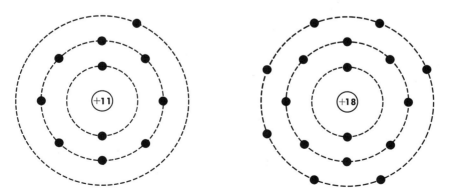

Fig. 30-9: *The ionization energy of sodium is much less than that for neon, suggesting that it has an electron in a more distant orbit. What other element is represented here?*

RUTHERFORD-BOHR ATOM: Theories current in 1911 were unable to explain why electrons could continue to orbit a nucleus without radiating their energy as electromagnetic waves and ultimately falling into the nucleus. Bohr postulated that electrons travel in certain orbits and only when electrons jump from one orbit to another would energy be emitted or absorbed by the atom. He confirmed this by applying the *Quantum Theory* to analysis of the hydrogen spectrum.

QUANTUM THEORY: The Quantum Theory, originated some years earlier by Max Planck, states that electromagnetic energy is radiated in "packages" or *photons* rather than a continuous stream. The energy of the photons is proportional to the frequency of the radiation according to the formula $E = hf$, where h is Planck's constant.

IONIZATION ENERGY: The ionization energy of an atom is the amount of energy required to remove an electron from the atom. A study of the ionization energy of the elements leads to the concept of electron shells.

RADIOACTIVE DATING: As the half-lives of all the radioactive isotopes are accurately known, it is possible to determine the age of an object by determining the proportion of isotopes of a given element in it. By this method, the age of the oldest geological formations is 5 billion years.

EXERCISE A

1. What was the chief difficulty arising from the Rutherford model of the atom?

2. State the assumptions made by Bohr concerning that part of the atom outside the nucleus.

3. What is a photon?

4. What is meant by the term "ionization energy"?

5. Why do we suspect that there are two electron "shells" for the lithium atom?

6. The atomic number of nitrogen is 7.
   (a) How many electrons exist outside the nucleus of the nitrogen atom?
   (b) How are these electrons distributed about the nucleus?
   (c) If you were able to remove, in turn, each of these electrons, what pattern would you expect to find in the successive ionization energies?

7. How do we know that there can be as many as eight electrons in the second shell?

1. Determine the amount of energy in one photon of electromagnetic energy radiated by a radio station at a frequency of 1 million cycles per second.

2. Determine the amount of energy in one photon of X rays, of wavelength 1.0×10^{-8}m.

3. Draw diagrams to illustrate the electron structures for the following elements:
   (a) boron   (b) fluorine   (c) aluminum   (d) chlorine

Chapter 31

Nuclear Transformation

1. THE FIRST TRANSMUTATION

The first artificial transmutation was performed by Rutherford in 1919, using apparatus illustrated in Figure 31-1. **Transmutation is the process of changing one element into another.** It requires that the nucleus of that element be altered in some respect, and this is accomplished by using a high speed projectile with enough energy to penetrate the nucleus. Rutherford employed as projectiles the α-particles given off by radioactive polonium.

In his apparatus, a small quantity of polonium was placed in a chamber containing nitrogen gas. At the other end of the chamber, a screen S gave off flashes of light when hit by atomic particles. However, the screen was placed far beyond the range of the α-particles from the source. During prolonged observation of the screen, a few flashes indicated that indeed some particles other than α-particles from the source were reaching the screen. Rutherford attributed these flashes to impacts by protons, particles much lighter than the α-particles.

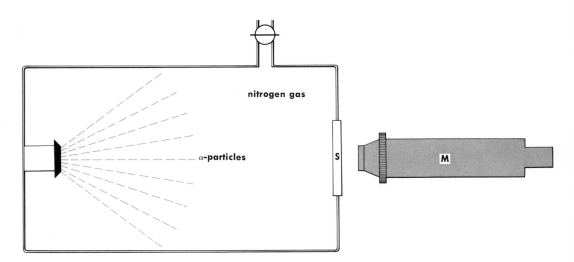

Fig. 31-1: *Apparatus used by Rutherford in the transmutation of nitrogen into oxygen.*

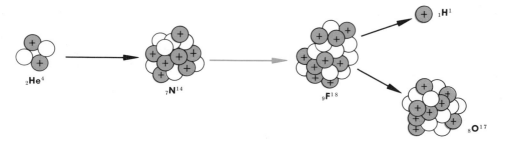

Fig. 31-2: *The α-particle and nitrogen nucleus form a nucleus of fluorine which immediately ejects a proton to become an oxygen nucleus.*

Figure 31-2 illustrates the result of the collision between the α-particle and the nitrogen nucleus. When the α-particle enters the nitrogen nucleus, a new nucleus is formed of atomic number 9 and mass number 18. The new nucleus immediately ejects a proton and a nucleus of atomic number 8 remains—the element oxygen. The nuclear reaction may be written

$$_2He^4 + {_7N^{14}} \rightarrow [\,_9F^{18}] \rightarrow {_8O^{17}} + {_1H^1}$$

Not long after Rutherford's transmutation of nitrogen into oxygen, the process was

Fig. 31-3: *A cloud-chamber photograph of the transmutation of nitrogen into oxygen. Can you identify the path of the α-particle? The proton? The oxygen nucleus?*

photographed in a cloud chamber. One such photograph is shown in Figure 31-3.

2. DISCOVERY OF THE NEUTRON

Although the existence of a neutral atomic particle was suspected many years earlier, it was not until 1932 that the existence of the neutron was demonstrated experimentally. This discovery was made by James Chadwick, a co-worker of Rutherford.

Chadwick used a radioactive source to project α-particles toward a target of beryllium (Figure 31-4). A thin sheet of paraffin wax was situated beyond this target. A detector indicated the presence of α-particles in the region A, and protons in the region C, but no charged particles in the region B.

Apparently the beryllium was blocking the flow of α-particles, but something in region B was responsible for the emission of protons from the wax. Chadwick was able to show that neutral particles had been driven from the beryllium by the impact of the α-particles, and that these neutral particles were in turn responsible for the dislodging of the protons from the wax. A determination of the mass of these particles showed they were almost identical to the mass of a proton. The name neutron was given to this newly discovered particle.

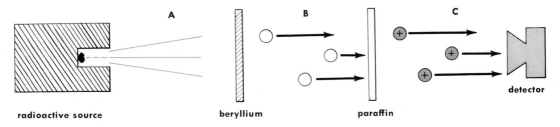

radioactive source   beryllium   paraffin

Fig. 31-4: *A schematic of the apparatus used by Chadwick in the discovery of the neutron.*

3. PARTICLE ACCELERATORS

Until 1930, alpha-particles from naturally-radioactive elements were the main "probes" used to study transmutations. The need for atomic particles of much greater energy led to the development of particle accelerators of which the best known is the cyclotron (Figure 31-5).

The main components of the cyclotron are two dees (so named because of their resemblance to the letter D) and a pair of electro-magnets. The dees are hollow, metallic, semi-cylinders, separated by a short gap and housed in an evacuated non-metallic cylinder. Hydrogen, as a source of protons, can be introduced at the centre of the gap where an electrically-heated filament will cause some of the atoms to ionize.

An alternating high-frequency potential difference of perhaps 50,000 volts, exists between the dees. When dee 1 is positive, a proton at the centre of the gap will start moving toward dee 2, but in a circular path because of the magnetic field perpendicular to its motion. If as it enters the gap, the polarity of the dees reverses, then the acceleration of the proton will continue and the radius of the spiral will increase because of its increased speed. Once in operation, the period of each orbit of the proton is constant, with a gain in energy of the proton of 50,000 ev during each orbit.

The protons that emerge from the apparatus through an opening in the periphery are deflected toward the target by a negative

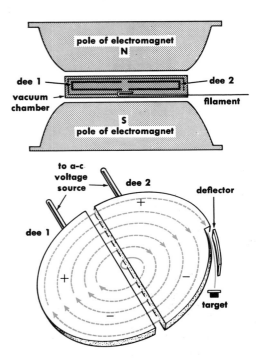

Fig. 31-5: *The cyclotron. The diameter of the magnet poles in the largest cyclotrons is in the vicinity of 180 ft. The energy acquired by a particle as it travels many miles in a tightly wound spiral becomes several million electron volts.*

electrode and strike the target with an energy of several hundred Mev.

Other particles, such as deuterium (heavy hydrogen), or helium nuclei may be accelerated to high energies by introducing the proper gas into the vacuum chamber.

446

Fig. 31-6: *The linear accelerator of the University of Toronto.*

One alternative to the cyclotron is the linear accelerator shown in Figure 31-6. In this device the particles are moved along a straight path between many electrodes.

4. THE TRANSURANIC ELEMENTS

The heaviest element occurring in nature is uranium. Beginning in 1940, it was discovered that new elements could be artificially created through bombardment of uranium with atomic particles. The first "transuranic" element, or element beyond uranium in the periodic table, was produced as the result of neutron bombardment of uranium 238. This new element was called neptunium, after the planet beyond Uranus.

$$_{92}U^{238} + _{0}n^{1} \rightarrow _{92}U^{239} \rightarrow _{93}Np^{239} + _{-1}e^{0}$$

As shown in the above equation, the nucleus U^{239} emits an electron to form the new element neptunium. This element is radioactive, its nucleus emitting another electron to form yet another element, plutonium of atomic mass 94, as shown in the following reaction:

$$_{93}Np^{239} \rightarrow _{94}Pu^{239} + _{-1}e^{0}$$

By bombardment of these heavy elements with neutrons, or with the nuclei of the lighter elements, the periodic table has been extended to element 103. All of these trans-uranic elements are radioactive and, with the exception of plutonium which has been detected in extremely minute amounts, they have no occurrence in nature. Because they are radioactive, it is possible that at one time, they did exist in nature.

5. ENERGY IN THE NUCLEUS

In the reactions arising from the bombardment of nuclei by particles, a release of energy during the reaction was apparent. The source of this energy was obviously within the nucleus. That the nucleus was a storehouse of energy had been suspected as the result of early observations of natural radioactivity—radioactive sources remained at higher temperature than their surroundings, and emitted particles of high energy.

A precise determination of the amounts of energy released in nuclear reactions revealed the nature of this source of energy, while at the same time verifying the equivalence of matter and energy postulated by Einstein in his Special Theory of Relativity. In this theory, Einstein ascribed to any mass m an amount of energy E, according to the relationship $E = mc^2$, where c is the speed of light, 3.00×10^8 m/sec. One kilogram of matter, then, is equivalent to 9.00×10^{16} joules of energy.

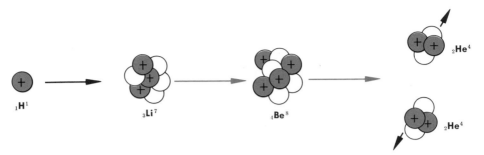

Fig. 31-7: *When a lithium nucleus is bombarded by protons, two α-particles are formed of total mass less than that of the proton and lithium nucleus. The difference is accounted for by an increase of energy.*

On an atomic scale, the amount of energy associated with a nucleon (a proton or neutron) is of importance to us. This determination is made in Example 1.

EXAMPLE 1

The mass of a proton is 1.66×10^{-27}kg (approximately one atomic mass unit, amu). What is the energy equivalent of this mass?

Solution:

$E = mc^2$
$= 1.66 \times 10^{-27}\text{kg} \times (3.00 \times 10^8 \text{m/sec})^2$
$= 14.9 \times 10^{-11}$ joules
$= \dfrac{14.9 \times 10^{-11}}{1.6 \times 10^{-19}}$ electron-volts $= \mathbf{9.3 \times 10^8}$ **ev**

or 930 million electron-volts (Mev)

Recall that 1 electron-volt $= 1.6 \times 10^{-19}$ joules (Example 2, Chapter 30).

Experimental evidence that matter is indeed converted into energy in a nuclear reaction was obtained in 1932, when lithium was bombarded by protons (Figure 31-7). In this reaction, the new nucleus splits into two α-particles which move away with high energy:

$_3\text{Li}^7 + _1\text{H}^1 \quad \longrightarrow$
$(7.104 + 1.006)\text{amu} \longrightarrow$
$\quad [_4\text{Be}^8] \rightarrow _2\text{He}^4 + _2\text{He}^4 \quad +\textbf{16.8 Mev}$
$\quad (4.001 + 4.001)\text{amu} + 16.8 \text{ Mev}$

The mass of each nuclei is shown below the nuclear equation. Note that the total mass before the reaction is greater than the total mass of the particles after the reaction, by an amount 0.018 amu. This "mass defect" is accounted for by the appearance of 16.8 Mev of energy, and agrees closely with the conversion rate predicted by Einstein.

The verification of the convertibility of matter into energy destroyed one of the basic cornerstones of nineteenth-century physics—the law of conservation of mass. Today this law must be generalized (as was done in Chapter 6, page 79), to include conservation of mass and energy collectively.

Important conclusions can be derived from a study of the mass of the nuclei of the various elements. These masses have been obtained experimentally by means of an instrument called a mass-spectrograph, which in principle is similar to that of the positive-ray tube (page 413). From this a graph of mass per nucleon can be derived (Figure 31-8). This graph indicates that the mass of protons and neutrons vary, depending on how many of them are grouped together. For example, the average mass of a proton or neutron in the nucleus of uranium-235, is 1.000 amu, but in the nucleus of nickel, or iron is 0.999amu. If by some process, the nucleons comprising uranium-235 could be rearranged to form a nucleus of nickel or iron, or any element in this region of the periodic table, a loss in mass of about 0.001 amu per nucleon would occur. This would result in a release of energy of approximately 1 Mev per nucleon, or about 200 Mev in total. **The splitting of a nucleus to form two lighter nuclei is called fission.**

For the lighter elements, the mass per nucleon differs even more markedly from their mass in the medium-weight elements. In heavy hydrogen, the mass per nucleon is 1.007 amu. If these nucleons could be brought together to form the nucleus of a heavier element, the loss of mass per nucleon, and resultant energy release would be many times greater. **The process of bringing two nuclei together to form a heavier nucleus is called fusion.**

6. NUCLEAR STABILITY

Although we can now account for the energy released by a nucleus when undergoing change, the reason for the stability of

most nuclei under ordinary conditions is still somewhat of a mystery. Let us consider the α-particle as an example, since it represents a particularly stable nucleus. Composed of two protons and two neutrons, we would expect that the two protons would violently repel each other at such close range. We can only conjecture that at such short distances, this electrostatic force of repulsion gives way to a much stronger new force—a *nuclear force.*

There is reason to believe that the neutrons act as a sort of "nuclear cement." In the lighter elements, the number of neutrons in the nucleus tends to be equal to the number of protons. As the number of protons increases, the number of neutrons required for stability becomes proportionately greater. In gold, for example, there are 118 neutrons and 79 protons. In the very heavy elements, the number of protons is sufficiently large that neutrons are unable to counteract the electrostatic repulsive forces of the protons, and part of the nucleus is emitted thus accounting for natural radioactivity.

The earlier notion that a neutron consists of a proton and electron combination had to be abandoned in the light of new evidence. Some radioactive emanations consist of particles of the same mass as that of electrons, but positively charged. These particles, called *positrons,* result from the conversion of nuclear protons into neutrons. We could represent the conversion in the following manner:

$$\text{nuclear proton} \rightarrow \text{neutron} + \text{positron}$$
$$_1\text{H}^1 \quad \rightarrow \quad _0\text{n}^1 \quad + \quad _1\text{e}^0$$

Outside the nucleus, the proton is stable. The neutron, however, outside the nucleus has a half-life of the order of twelve minutes, decaying to form a proton plus electron:

$$\text{neutron} \rightarrow \text{proton} + \text{electron}$$
$$_0\text{n}^1 \quad \rightarrow \quad _1\text{H}^1 \quad + \quad _{-1}\text{e}^0$$

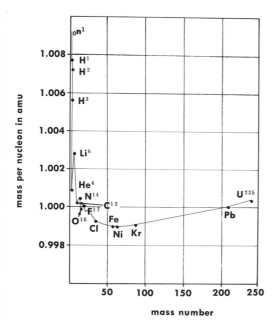

Fig. 31-8: *The mass of each nucleon is shown here as a function of the mass number of the element. For which element is the mass per nucleon the least?*

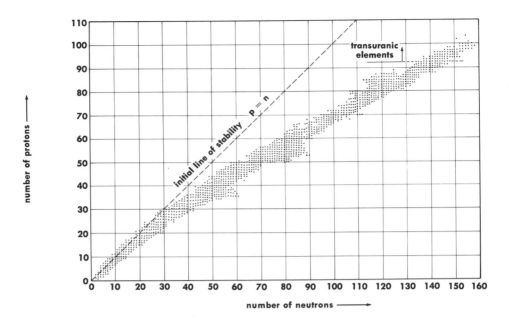

Fig. 31-9: *This chart indicates the number of neutrons and the number of protons for the nuclei of the stable elements. For the lighter elements, the numbers of neutrons and protons are about equal. For the heavier elements, the neutrons substantially exceeds the number of protons.*

7. NUCLEAR FISSION

A discovery of boundless significance took place in Germany in 1939, when Hahn and Strassman studied the effects of bombarding of natural uranium with neutrons of various speeds. Natural uranium is made up of two isotopes, the abundant uranium-238, and the much less abundant (0.7%) uranium-235 The vast majority of the uranium atoms absorb a neutron, forming a new nucleus (uranium-239), as shown in Figure 31-10(a). The U²³⁵ atoms in absorbing a neutron, behave most unexpectedly. The new nucleus, uranium-236, breaks apart almost immediately into two fragments of approximately equal mass. The reaction is accompanied by a release of energy in the form of heat, kinetic energy of the fragments, and radiation.

This breaking up of a heavy nucleus into two parts of approximately equal size is called nuclear fission. The fission of the uranium-235 nucleus is depicted in Figure 31-10(b). The possibility of fission created a stir in the scientific community for two reasons: first, the amount of energy released far exceeded that observed in any previous nuclear reaction; secondly, the fission was accompanied by the release of two or three extra neutrons which could be used to initiate fission in neighbouring atoms. A "chain reaction" was conceivable, with accompanying release of fantastic amounts of energy—about 200 Mev per fission. The concept of "chain reaction" is indicated in Figure 31-11.

Achieving a chain reaction, however, presents more difficulties than are at first apparent. The fissile uranium is the rare isotope uranium-235, and *slow* neutrons are most

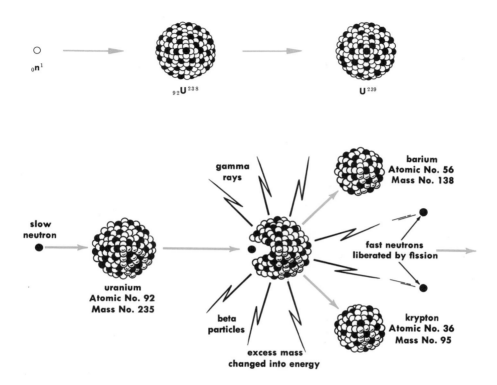

$_0n^1$

$_{92}U^{238}$

U^{239}

gamma rays

barium
Atomic No. 56
Mass No. 138

slow neutron

fast neutrons
liberated by fission

uranium
Atomic No. 92
Mass No. 235

beta particles

krypton
Atomic No. 36
Mass No. 95

excess mass
changed into energy

Fig. 31-10: (a) A U^{238} nucleus absorbs a neutron, becoming a U^{239} nucleus. (b) A U^{235} nucleus absorbs a neutron, becoming a U^{236} nucleus, which immediately fissions into two lighter nuclei, accompanied by a release of energy and additional neutrons.

effective in causing its fission. By "slow" is meant speeds of the order of 1 mile per second, with corresponding energies of about 0.1 electron-volt. Uranium-238 atoms have a tendency to "capture" neutrons of energy greater than this. In achieving a chain reaction, then, we must ensure that neutrons released as a result of fission will not be absorbed by the uranium-238 atoms.

Furthermore, even with pure uranium-235, the success of a chain reaction will depend

upon at least one neutron released from the first fission colliding with another nucleus, in turn causing another fission, and so on. If the uranium sample is too small, the neutrons released as a result of fission may pass through without hitting a nucleus. Increasing the size of the sample increases the chance that a neutron will cause fission. The minimum size of a fissionable material necessary to ensure a chain reaction is called the "critical size".

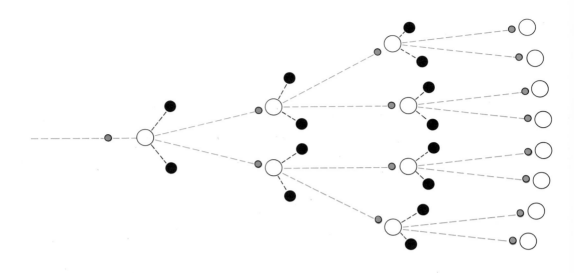

Fig. 31-11: *A chain reaction. On the average, each fission is responsible for producing another fission.*

8. NUCLEAR REACTORS

A nuclear reactor makes use of the heat energy derived from controlled fission to make steam and ultimately to produce electricity. In a sense, it may be considered an "atomic furnace". The first controlled fission reactor was put in operation at Chicago in 1942, under rigid wartime security. Since then hundreds of reactors have been successfully operating in various parts of the world. Reactors contain four essential elements—a fuel, moderator, control device, and coolant.

Without exception, the reactor fuel is uranium, either in its natural form in which the percentage of fissile uranium-235 is only 0.7%, or in a somewhat enriched form. In order to undergo fission, the uranium-235 atoms must capture neutrons. As discussed in the previous section, this will only occur when the neutrons are travelling at relatively slow speeds. The problem is complicated by

the fact that the neutrons released as a result of fission are themselves fast. Accordingly, steps must be taken to slow down the neutrons produced by fission. This is the function of the moderator.

The moderator is a substance whose atoms are of low mass so that they absorb a maximum amount of energy when in collision with the high-energy neutrons. In the first reactor, the moderator was carbon. Water would be effective as a moderator but it has a tendency to absorb neutrons. This absorption is undesirable if the supply of neutrons to sustain fission is not over-abundant. Most efficient as a moderator is "heavy" water—a form of water containing the hydrogen isotope deuterium, $_1H^2$—present in small quantities (0.02%) in all water. Reactors of Canadian design employ heavy water as the moderator, and natural uranium as the fuel.

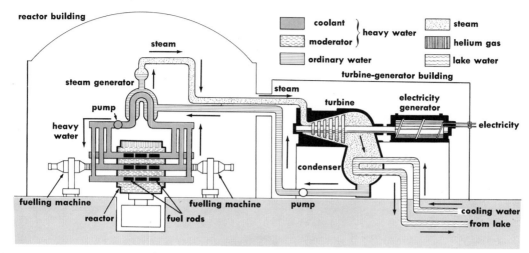

Fig. 31-12: *A simplified diagram of the nuclear power station located at Douglas Point on Lake Huron. Control rods, although not shown, are employed. See also Figure 32-1.*

Fission within the reactor produces a steady flow of heat accompanied by intense radiation. The rate of heat production must be controlled within narrow limits. If the fission proceeds too slowly, the sustained chain reaction may cease, while too-rapid fission may literally melt the reactor. Control of the reaction is effected by inserting control rods composed of substances possessing a great ability to absorb neutrons. Boron and cadmium are efficient in this respect. When the control rod is inserted, neutrons are absorbed by the rod, reducing the rate of fission. Conversely, removing the control rods will speed up the reactor's energy output to any desired value.

The coolant, which can be heavy water or light water, or a gas such as carbon dioxide, absorbs the heat produced by the fission reactions, and delivers it to a boiler for the production of steam which then drives electric generators. A diagram of the reactor is shown in Figure 31-12.

An important class of reactors can produce their own fuel. In these reactors the design is such that in addition to the sustained fission of uranium-235, an appreciable degree of neutron-capture by uranium-238 nuclei takes place. This latter isotope tends to capture those neutrons whose energy is too great to cause fission of uranium-235. In so doing, uranium-239 is formed, decaying to neptunium and ultimately to plutonium according to the reactions already described in Section 4 of this chapter. But plutonium is fissile by neutrons of moderate energy. Quite ironically, then, the reactor produces fuel. In fact, the energy that can be derived from the fissile plutonium is greater than the energy used in its production, partly because in fission, the plutonium nucleus releases more neutrons than does uranium-235. Reactors of this type are called "breeder" reactors. The first nuclear reactor was set into operation, not so much to deliver useful heat energy as to demonstrate the possibility of a sustained chain reaction, and to manufacture, by this breeding process, plutonium for use in the first fission bombs.

453

9. FUSION

In Section 5, it was suggested that an energy release would be obtained from the joining together, or fusion, of light nuclei. As an example, a helium nucleus could be formed by bringing together two protons and two neutrons. The difficulty here is that of overcoming the electrostatic forces of repulsion as the nucleons approach. Extreme temperatures of the order of millions of degrees Celsius can accomplish this fusion.

There is ample evidence to conclude that the tremendous amount of energy released continuously by the sun is the result of nuclear fusion. The primary element in the sun is hydrogen of which there are three isotopes—ordinary hydrogen $_1H^1$, deuterium $_1H^2$, and tritium $_1H^3$. Under extreme temperatures, there are many ways in which the nuclei of these elements can react. One example is the fusion of the two heavier isotopes of hydrogen to form a helium nucleus and a neutron, with release of energy, as follows:

$$_1H^2 + _1H^3 \rightarrow _2He^4 + _0n^1 + \text{energy}$$

The deuterium and tritium nuclei taking part in this reaction are formed by the earlier encounter of protons. For example, deuterium nuclei (called deuterons) are formed by the fusion of two protons, one of these protons then decaying to a neutron by emitting a positron. Tritium is then formed as the result of an encounter between a proton and a deuterium nucleus. The net effect of all such reactions is the formation of a helium nucleus from four protons, with an energy release of about 25 Mev.

Reactions such as these are called "thermonuclear" because of the high temperatures required to effect them. In the sun, these fusion reactions are self-sustaining because of the high temperature and pressure existing there. In the hotter stars, nuclei of mass number beyond that of helium are formed as a result of fusion, and play an important part in the formation of still more helium.

10. NUCLEAR WEAPONS

The first nuclear reactor demonstrated that a chain reaction resulting from the fission of uranium was possible. In this controlled reaction the release of neutrons by fission was adjusted so that on the average, one neutron from a fissioning atom caused a further fission.

If the concentration of fissile atoms is dense enough that on the average each fission will result in two or more further fissions, the reaction runs out of control and an avalanche of energy is released. Such is the principle of the fission bomb, or so-called atomic bomb.

The requirement for such a device, then, is a *supercritical* mass of uranium-235, or plutonium. Prior to detonation, the fissile material is separated in subcritical amounts. These are then brought together swiftly at the desired time. A stray neutron, always available from cosmic ray effects, can produce the first fission, leading almost instantaneously to a rapid chain reaction and violent explosion. The elements of such a device are shown in Figure 31-14(a).

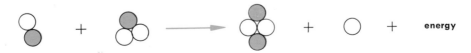

Fig. 31-13: *An example of nuclear fusion. Two isotopes of hydrogen fuse to form helium. A neutron, and energy, are released.*

The fission bomb was born of necessity during the Second World War. It provided the means for a yet more powerful device—the fusion bomb, or hydrogen bomb. The release of energy through nuclear fusion is even more dramatic than that derived from fission, but fusion of nuclei requires fantastically high temperatures—temperatures of the order of 50,000,000 degrees. Such temperatures are produced by the fission bomb which, therefore, serves as the trigger for the fusion bomb. Figure 31-14(b) shows one design for a fusion bomb.

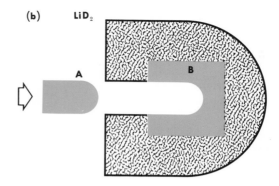

(b) LiD$_2$

A   B

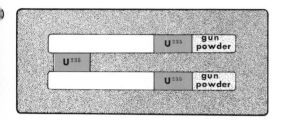

U^{235} | gun powder

U^{235}

U^{235} | gun powder

Fig. 31-14: *(a) The elements of an atom bomb. The fissile material is kept in subcritical masses. When brought together, uncontrolled fission results.*

(b) A hydrogen bomb. A subcritical mass of plutonium (B) is surrounded by a packing of lithium deuteride. For detonation, an additional mass of plutonium (A) is shot into (B). A fission explosion results, producing temperatures sufficiently intense to cause fusion of the elements composing the packing.

Lookout Mountain Laboratory, U.S.A.F.

Fig. 31-15: *An atomic detonation at the Nevada Test Site. The photograph was taken at a distance of about seven miles.*

TRANSMUTATION: Transmutation is the change of one element into another as a result of nuclear bombardment, or radioactive disintegration.

PARTICLE ACCELERATORS: A well-known type of accelerator is the *cyclotron* which accelerates particles in a spiral manner by means of a high-frequency alternating current and a powerful electromagnet. The particles can attain an energy of several hundred Mev.

TRANSURANIC ELEMENTS: Uranium is the heaviest naturally-occurring element. Elements of greater atomic number can be created by bombardment of uranium with atomic particles. These elements are called *transuranic* and are radioactive.

NUCLEAR STABILITY: The stability of the nucleus is attributed to the neutrons acting as a sort of "nuclear cement". In the lighter elements, the number of neutrons tends to be equal to the number of protons in the nucleus. As the number of protons increases, the number of neutrons required for stability becomes proportionately greater. Eventually, with elements of high atomic number, neutrons within the nucleus are unable to maintain stability resulting in radioactivity.

THE POSITRON: Some radioactive emanations consist of particles with the mass of an electron but a positive charge. These particles, called positrons, are released in the conversion of nuclear protons to neutrons.

NUCLEAR FISSION: When a heavy nucleus splits up into two parts of nearly equal mass the process is called nuclear fission. The reaction produces large amounts of energy and extra neutrons. The latter can trigger off more fissions and so on, producing a chain reaction.

NUCLEAR FUSION: When light nuclei are joined together to form heavier nuclei the process is called *fusion*. The amount of energy released in the process is much greater than in fission, but extremely high temperatures are required for fusion to occur. Reactions that require large quantities of heat energy are called *thermonuclear reactions*.

EXERCISE A

1. What is meant by artificial transmutation?

2. What products were formed as a result of Rutherford's bombardment of nitrogen by α-particles?

3. Describe the nuclear reaction in which neutrons were first discovered.

4. (*a*) What is the purpose of a cyclotron?
   (*b*) Name four main components of the cyclotron and briefly describe its operation.

5. What is meant by the term "trans-uranic elements"?

6. Can you give a reason why we think elements heavier than uranium at one time existed on earth?

7. What information is conveyed by the equation $E = mc^2$?

8. What products are formed when lithium is bombarded with protons?

9. Why must the law of conservation of mass be revised in the light of twentieth-century physics?

10. Distinguish between the terms fission and fusion.

11. What is a positron? In what way is it similar to an electron? In what way does it differ?

12. (a) How is fission of uranium produced?
    (b) State the important properties of a fission reaction.

13. State three requirements for a chain reaction.

14. What is meant by "critical mass"?

15. (a) What is the purpose of a moderator in a nuclear reactor?
    (b) How do the control rods perform their function?

16. (a) What is a "breeder" reactor?
    (b) State some ways in which the breeder reactor differs from the conventional reactor.

17. What is a "thermonuclear" reaction?

EXERCISE B

1. In Chapter 29, reference was made to the formation of carbon-14 in the atmosphere, and its usefulness as a tool for dating certain specimens.
   (a) Write an equation to illustrate that carbon-14 is formed by the absorption of a neutron in a nitrogen-14 nucleus, with the simultaneous release of a proton.
   (b) Carbon-14 is radioactive, emitting β-particles (electrons) and forming nitrogen again. Write an equation to illustrate this reaction.

2. Using Figure 31-8 we can find the total energy released in building an oxygen nucleus.
   (a) What is the total mass of the 8 protons and 8 neutrons before they are brought together to form the oxygen nucleus?
   (b) What is their total mass in the nucleus.
   (c) Find the difference in mass. To how much energy does this correspond?

3. Suppose two oxygen nuclei ($_8O^{16}$) are brought together to form a sulphur nucleus, $_{16}S^{32}$.
   (a) What is the name for this type of reaction?
   (b) Would energy be given off, or would it be absorbed?
   (c) Determine the amount of energy involved in part (b).

457

4. Use Figure 31-8 to answer the following questions:
   (a) You are given 88 protons and 138 neutrons. What is their total mass?
   (b) Suppose you bring these nucleons together to form a radium nucleus $_{88}Ra^{226}$. What is the total mass of the nucleus?
   (c) From the mass difference, find the total energy released in forming this nucleus.

5. When uranium-236 fissions, several pairs of fission products are possible. In each of the following cases one of these products is given, as well as the number of released neutrons. Using the periodic table given in Chapter 30, determine the other product:
   (a) tellurium-137 plus 2 neutrons.
   (b) rubidium-97 plus 2 neutrons.
   (c) krypton-92 plus 3 neutrons.
   (d) xenon-143 plus 3 neutrons.

6. Write nuclear equations for each of the reactions of Question 5.

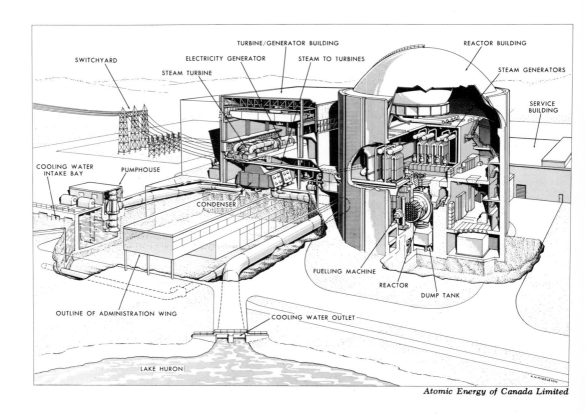

Atomic Energy of Canada Limited

Chapter 32

The Atomic Age

1. ENERGY IN THE NUCLEAR AGE

It has been estimated that, were the world to rely solely on its conventional sources of energy (coal and oil) a serious shortage of supply would exist before the year 2030. Accurate as this forecast may be, the continued development of nuclear reactors for the production of electricity has assured man of an abundant source of energy for centuries to come.

By 1967, nuclear power had become economically competitive with coal and oil when used in large installations, located near areas of high demand. The advantages inherent in nuclear fuel arise from the low transportation costs when compared with the fossil fuels. One pound of uranium, for example, contains the energy equivalent of almost three million pounds of coal. This factor makes fission fuel very attractive to

Atomic Energy of Canada Limited

Fig. 32-1: *Douglas Point, Canada's first full-scale nuclear power station, was designed and built by Atomic Energy of Canada Limited with the co-operation of Ontario Hydro. It is located on the shore of Lake Huron, between Kincardine and Port Elgin. The station has a 200,000 kilowatt capacity and went into service in January, 1967. It is powered by a single reactor fuelled with natural uranium and is moderated by heavy water.*

underdeveloped countries which lack hydro-electric facilities and complex transportation systems.

Nevertheless it is probable that a shortage of fissile uranium will develop in the next century, in which case man may then depend on *breeder reactors* for his energy supply (see Chapter 30). Recent studies indicate that if the breeding process is used on the trace amounts of uranium and thorium present in the granite of the continents, an almost inexhaustible source of energy will be available to us. Man may be entering a second Stone Age.

The ever increasing reliance on nuclear energy brings with it a major problem of waste disposal. The spent fuel from nuclear reactors is intensely radioactive. Although a portion of the highly radioactive fuel can be re-processed for future use the remaining radioactive ash, containing isotopes of varying half-lives, is of no value. For a time, radioactive wastes in the United States were placed in large concrete lined steel drums and dumped in the Atlantic. This method of disposal is being replaced and now the waste will either be placed in underground vaults of steel and concrete or stored in abandoned salt mines.

Many scientists now regard *fusion* as the ultimate solution to the world's energy problems. The fuel for fusion is available in inexhaustible quantities in the form of heavy water (deuterium). There is sufficient deuterium in the oceans of the world to meet man's energy demands for millions of years. The fusion process has a further advantage in that it produces no radioactive waste and hence avoids the major disposal problem associated with fission reactors.

Although much current research is being directed toward the attainment of controlled thermonuclear fusion, opinions are divided on the possibilities of success. The central problems are: the 100,000,000 degree temperature that must exist to fuse the nuclei, and the "container" that would be required to hold particles at that temperature.

2. RADIO-ISOTOPES

Another important function of nuclear reactors is the production of radio-isotopes—isotopes which are radioactive. Some of these isotopes are produced as a natural by-product of the fission reaction, while others can be manufactured deliberately by placing various elements in the reactor and subjecting them to neutron bombardment. Radio-isotopes have various applications in medicine, agriculture and industry.

(i) Medicine

Radio-isotopes are in widespread use as *tracers*. In medicine, for example, they can be used to *trace* the movement of various compounds through the human body. The movement of sugar, a carbon compound, can be followed throughout the body if it contains small quantities of carbon-14. Carbon-14 is a radio-isotope of carbon which cannot be distinguished chemically or physically from the more abundant carbon-12. Because of its radioactivity, a few carbon-14 atoms in a sample of carbon act as tiny radio transmitters. As the carbon moves from one place to another a suitable detector, such as a Geiger counter, permits an accurate study of all the chemical and biological processes.

In a similar manner the functioning of the thyroid gland may be studied through the use of radioactive iodine-131. Iodine in the bloodstream is absorbed by the thyroid, which in turn, regulates body metabolism. The amount of iodine-131 absorbed can be determined by holding a Geiger counter under the neck, where the thyroid is located. In yet another application, the circulation of the blood can be studied by injecting into it minute amounts of radioactive sodium.

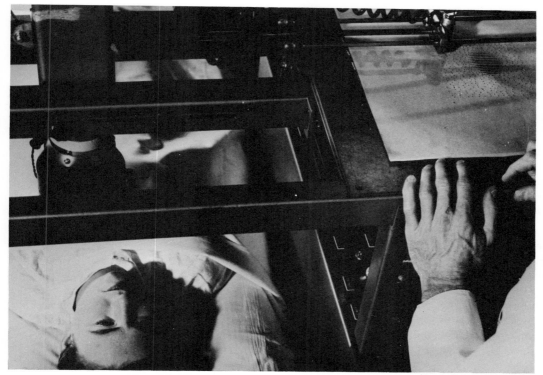

Fig. 32-2: *The pattern of the thyroid gland is traced on paper (upper right) by a scanner that detects the radiation emitted by radioactive iodine as it moves back and across the thyroid area.*

(ii) Agriculture

In agriculture, radioactive tracers have been used to advantage in gaining detailed knowledge of the food-absorbing processes of plants. Using tracers, agricultural scientists have determined that the key elements for plant growth are absorbed as effectively through the foliage and bark as through the root system. This discovery, followed by the decision to apply fertilizer directly to plant foliage, has resulted in enormous savings, since more than half the fertilizer applied to the ground is washed away before the plants can absorb it.

(iii) Industry

In industry too, radio-isotopes find a myriad of applications as tracers and control devices. Determining the location of a leak in an underground pipeline is one example of how many man hours of labour can be saved through tracer techniques. Minute amounts of radio-isotopes incorporated in the piston rings of automobile engines allow a study of engine wear. Such wear will impart radioactive particles to the lubricating oil.

Radio-isotopes are used for thickness measurement in the production of paper and thin metal sheet. In the manufacture of paper

Dunlop Tire & Rubber Co.

Fig. 32-3: *The thickness of the rubber sheeting is being continually measured by a gauge which uses a source of β-particles.*

the thickness can be observed and controlled by placing a source of β-particles, such as strontium-90 on one side of the moving paper and a detector on the other side. In gauging the thickness of sheet metal, a γ ray source is used. The great advantage of this method is that no contact is made with the product, so the control is carried on without necessitating a shutdown of the manufacturing process.

3. BIOLOGICAL EFFECTS OF RADIATION

Nuclear radiations present a hazard to living organisms because of their tendency to ionize any matter through which they pass. In ionization, electrons are knocked out of the atoms of the material. In an organism, this disruption of many atoms can lead to chemical reactions that alter the basic function of the organism. Where an entire biological system becomes impaired because of a severe overdose of radiation, death will result.

No less serious are the effects of radiation in the reproductive organs. Radiation will kill some of the germ cells within the organs immediately, while others may be damaged to an extent that will become apparent only in future generations. This damage can be transmitted from one generation to another.

An important factor concerning these genetic effects of radiation is that the overall effect of radiation on the germ cells is cumulative. A large overdose is not required to set these effects in motion.

The unit of radiation exposure dose is the *röntgen*, named after the discoverer of X rays. The röntgen is defined as that amount of radiation which will produce 1.6×10^{12} ions in 1 gram of dry air. The average person receives, from natural sources, a total of 5 to 6 röntgens during his lifetime. The additional exposure (due to medical Xrays, luminous watch dials, etc.) may raise this total to 10 röntgens.

Single doses of the order of 100 röntgens while not necessarily fatal, can prove so indirectly since they may cause leukemia or cancer. A dose of 800 röntgens is lethal. In a few instances, lethal doses have been accidentally received by workers at reactor installations, but generally speaking, the exposure received by these workers is not significantly greater than the average value because of the extreme precautions taken to shield the radioactive materials.

Another important source of radiation prior to the nuclear test ban was radioactive fallout from atmospheric nuclear explosions. Although the level of radiation produced by these tests was not significant in comparison with the natural sources such as cosmic rays, the real danger is that much of the fallout consists of substances that are taken into the body—isotopes of strontium, iron, carbon, caesium, iodine and calcium, and remain in the body during the lifetime of the individual. Some of these isotopes did not exist prior to the nuclear age. Their long-term effects on the body are unknown.

Medical science has made good use of the lethal effects of strong radiation in its fight against cancer. Cancerous cells which multiply abnormally fast can be killed by strong radiation, just as healthy cells can. The danger of irradiating healthy tissue in order to destroy the cancerous growth sets a limit to the use of this therapy. The radioisotope cobalt-60, many times more active than pure radium, is widely used in this application.

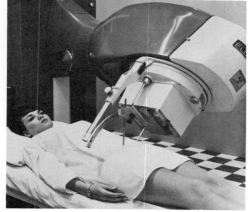

Atomic Energy of Canada Limited

Fig. 32-4: *A cobalt-60 cancer therapy machine developed by Atomic Energy of Canada Limited.*

4. PRESENT AND FUTURE

On January 21, 1954, the United States launched the U.S.S. Nautilus—the world's first nuclear-powered submarine. The nuclear reactor is an excellent source of energy for the propulsion of submarines since it does not require oxygen for its maintenance as does the diesel engine. Submarines powered with nuclear fuel have the ability to remain submerged for months on end, thus making possible the long polar passages under the Arctic ice.

It has been suggested that airplanes as well might be built with nuclear power plants. The difficulties however are formidable. Airplanes must obviously be constructed of light weight metals. At the same time, if they use atomic fuel, they must contain heavy walls of shielding materials to protect the passengers and crew from radiation.

For space travel the problems are less acute. In outer space, free from gravitational pull, heavy walls of steel, lead, and concrete present no serious disadvantages. The problem of transportation over inconceivable distances for impossible lengths of time may only be solved using atomic energy.

Controlled underground explosions have proved the feasibility of atomic blasting in order to shift vast quantities of rock and rubble. The significance of such a method for large construction projects is obvious. Proposals have been advanced for the construction of an additional Panama Canal by atomic blasting.

We live in exciting times, and atomic physicists, along with their colleagues in other areas of this fundamental science, form the vanguard of our scientific age.

U.S. Navy

Fig. 32-5: *The world's first nuclear-powered ship, U.S.S. "Nautilus" in New York Harbour.*

Appendix

Table 1
Useful Numbers—British System

12 in = 1 ft	9 ft² = 1 yd²	60 mi/hr = 88 ft/sec
3 ft = 1 yd	1728 in³ = 1 ft³	7000 grains = 1 lb avoirdupois
5280 ft = 1 mi	27 ft³ = 1 yd³	16 oz = 1 lb
1760 yd = 1 mi	231 in³ = 1 gal	2000 lb = 1 short ton
144 in² = 1 ft²	277.42 in³ = 1 gal (Imperial)	1 ft³ of water weighs 62.4 lb

Table 2
Metric-British Equivalents

1 in = 2.54 cm exactly	1 in³ = 16.3872 cm³	
1 ft = 30.48 cm exactly	1 cm³ = 0.0610 in³	
1 yd = 91.44 cm exactly	1 qt (Imperial) = 1.14 l	
1 mi = 1609.3 m	1 l = 0.88 qt	
1 mi = 1.6093 km	1 grain = 0.06480 g	
1 mm = 0.03937 in	1 oz = 28.3495 g	
1 cm = 0.3937 in	1 lb = 453.592 g	at sea
1 m = 39.37 in	1 lb = 0.4536 kg	level
1 m = 3.2808 ft	1 gr = 15.4324 grains	and 45°
1 m = 1.0936 yd	1 g = 0.03527 oz	latitude
1 in² = 6.4516 cm²	1 g = 0.002205 lb	
1 cm² = 0.1550 in²	1 kg = 2.2046 lb	

Table 3
Fundamental Constants

Electron mass = 9.11×10^{-31} kg	1 coulomb = 6.24×10^{18} electrons
Electronic charge = -1.60×10^{-19} coul	Planck's constant $[h]$ = 6.63×10^{-34} joule-sec
Proton mass = 1.67×10^{-27} kg	

Table 4
Specific Gravity of Solids

Aluminum	2.7	Gold	19.3	Nylon	1.09–1.14
Bakelite	1.25–2.09	Gold, 18k	14.88	Oak	0.60–0.98
Brass	8.2–8.7	Granite	2.65	Paraffin	0.87–0.91
Brick	1.4–2.2	Graphite	2.25	Pine	0.37–0.64
Bronze	8.8	Human body	1.07	Platinum	21.37
Butter	0.87	Ice	0.917	Porcelain	2.38
Carbon	1.9–3.5	Iron, cast	7.1–7.7	Silver	10.5
Chestnut	0.45	Iron, steel	7.6–7.8	Silver, sterling	10.38
Coal, anthracite	1.4–1.8	Iron, wrought	7.8–7.9	Sulfur	2.0
Coal, bituminous	1.2–1.5	Lead	11.34	Tin	7.3
Copper	8.9	Limestone	2.7	Tungsten	19.3
Cork	0.24	Lucite	1.16–1.20	Velon	1.68–1.75
Diamond	3.53	Magnesium	1.74	Vinylite	1.2–1.7
Glass, crown	2.5	Maple	0.51–0.75	Zinc	7.1
Glass, flint	2.9–5.9	Marble	2.6–2.8		

Table 5

Specific Gravity of Liquids

(Room Temperature)

Alcohol, ethyl	0.789	Mercury	13.56
Alcohol, methyl	0.793	Milk	1.029
Carbon disulfide	1.29	Nitric acid, 68%	1.42
Carbon tetrachloride	1.60	Oil, castor	0.969
Chloroform	1.50	Oil, cottonseed	0.926
Ether	0.74	Oil, linseed	0.942
Gasoline	0.66–0.69	Oil, olive	0.918
Glycerin	1.26	Sulfuric acid	1.84
Hydrochloric acid	1.20	Turpentine	0.87
Kerosene	0.82	Water, sea	1.025

Table 6

Specific Gravity of Gases

(Air Standard, at 0° C and 760 mm of mercury)

Acetylene	0.907	Helium	0.138
Air	1.000	Hydrogen	0.0695
Ammonia	0.596	Hydrogen chloride	1.268
Argon	1.380	Methane	0.554
Carbon dioxide	1.529	Neon	0.696
Carbon monoxide	0.967	Nitrogen	0.967
Chlorine	2.486	Oxygen	1.105
Ethane	1.049	Sulfur dioxide	2.264

Table 7

Density of Water

°C	g/cm^3	°C	g/cm^3	°C	g/cm^3
0	0.99987	15	0.99913	60	0.98324
1	0.99993	20	0.99823	65	0.98059
2	0.99997	25	0.99707	70	0.97781
3	0.99999	30	0.99567	75	0.97489
4	1.00000	35	0.99406	80	0.97183
5	0.99999	40	0.99224	85	0.96865
6	0.99997	45	0.99025	90	0.96534
8	0.99988	50	0.98807	95	0.96192
10	0.99973	55	0.98573	100	0.95838

Table 8

Index of Refraction

($\lambda = 5900$ Å; Temperature 20° C except as noted)

Air, dry, 0°	1.00029	Diamond	2.42
Alcohol, ethyl	1.36	Glass, crown	1.52
Benzene	1.50	Glass, flint	1.61
Carbon dioxide	1.00045	Quartz, fused	1.46
Carbon disulfide	1.63	Water	1.33
Carbon tetrachloride	1.46	Water vapor	1.00025

Table 9
Heat Constants

	Specific Heat	Melting Point	Normal Boiling Point	Heat of Fusion	Heat of Vaporization
	(cal/g °C)	(°C)	(°C)	(cal/g)	(cal/g)
Alcohol, ethyl	0.581	−115	78.5	24.9	204
Aluminum	0.214	659.7	2057	76.8	
Ammonia	1.125 (liq.)	−77.7	−33.35	83.9	327.1
Brass (Cu 60, Zn 40)	0.0917	940			
Copper	0.0921	1083	2336	49.0	
Glass	0.1988				
Ice	0.5	0		79.71	
Iron	0.107	1535	3000	7.89	
Lead	0.0306	327.43	1620	5.86	
Mercury	0.0332	−38.87	356.58	2.82	70.613
Platinum	0.0324	1773.5	4300	27.2	
Silver	0.0558	960.8	1950	26.0	
Steam	0.48				
Tungsten	0.0336	3370	5900		
Water	1.00		100		539.55
Zinc	0.0925	419.47	907	23.0	

Table 10
Equilibrium Vapor Pressure of Water

Temp. °C	Pressure mm of Hg	Temp. °C	Pressure mm of Hg	Temp. °C	Pressure mm of Hg
0	4.6	25	23.8	90	525.8
5	6.5	26	25.2	95	633.9
10	9.2	27	26.7	96	657.6
15	12.8	28	28.3	97	682.1
16	13.6	29	30.0	98	707.3
17	14.5	30	31.8	99	733.2
18	15.5	35	42.2	100	760.0
19	16.5	40	55.3	101	787.5
20	17.5	50	92.5	103	845.1
21	18.7	60	149.4	105	906.1
22	19.8	70	233.7	110	1074.6
23	21.1	80	355.1	120	1489.1
24	22.4	85	433.6	150	3570.5

Table 11
Speed of Sound
(Approximate)

	m/sec	ft/sec		m/sec	ft/sec
Air	331.5	1,087	Hydrogen	1,270	4,165
Alcohol	1,213	3,890	Iron	5,030	16,500
Aluminum	5,104	16,740	Maple, along grain	4,110	13,470
Brass	3,500	11,480	Pine, along grain	3,320	10,900
Copper	3,560	11,670	Steel	5,030	16,500
Glass	5,030	16,500	Water	1,461	4,794

Table 12

Natural Trigonometric Functions

Angle	Sine	Cosine	Tangent	Angle	Sine	Cosine	Tangent	Angle	Sine	Cosine	Tangent
0.0	0.000	1.000	0.000								
0.5	0.009	1.000	0.009	30.5	0.508	0.862	0.589	60.5	0.870	0.492	1.767
1.0	0.017	1.000	0.017	31.0	0.515	0.857	0.601	61.0	0.875	0.485	1.804
1.5	0.026	1.000	0.026	31.5	0.522	0.853	0.613	61.5	0.879	0.477	1.842
2.0	0.035	0.999	0.035	32.0	0.530	0.848	0.625	62.0	0.883	0.470	1.881
2.5	0.044	0.999	0.044	32.5	0.537	0.843	0.637	62.5	0.887	0.462	1.921
3.0	0.052	0.999	0.052	33.0	0.545	0.839	0.649	63.0	0.891	0.454	1.963
3.5	0.061	0.998	0.061	33.5	0.552	0.834	0.662	63.5	0.895	0.446	2.006
4.0	0.070	0.998	0.070	34.0	0.559	0.829	0.674	64.0	0.899	0.438	2.050
4.5	0.078	0.997	0.079	34.5	0.556	0.824	0.687	64.5	0.903	0.431	2.097
5.0	0.087	0.996	0.087	35.0	0.574	0.819	0.700	65.0	0.906	0.423	2.145
5.5	0.096	0.995	0.096	35.5	0.581	0.814	0.713	65.5	0.910	0.415	2.194
6.0	0.104	0.995	0.105	36.0	0.588	0.809	0.726	66.0	0.914	0.407	2.246
6.5	0.113	0.994	0.114	36.5	0.595	0.804	0.740	66.5	0.917	0.399	2.300
7.0	0.122	0.992	0.123	37.0	0.602	0.799	0.754	67.0	0.921	0.391	2.356
7.5	0.131	0.991	0.132	37.5	0.609	0.793	0.767	67.5	0.924	0.383	2.414
8.0	0.139	0.990	0.141	38.0	0.616	0.788	0.781	68.0	0.927	0.375	2.475
8.5	0.148	0.989	0.149	38.5	0.622	0.783	0.795	68.5	0.930	0.366	2.539
9.0	0.156	0.988	0.158	39.0	0.629	0.777	0.810	69.0	0.934	0.358	2.605
9.5	0.165	0.986	0.167	39.5	0.636	0.772	0.824	69.5	0.937	0.350	2.675
10.0	0.174	0.985	0.176	40.0	0.643	0.766	0.839	70.0	0.940	0.342	2.747
10.5	0.182	0.983	0.185	40.5	0.649	0.760	0.854	70.5	0.943	0.334	2.824
11.0	0.191	0.982	0.194	41.0	0.656	0.755	0.869	71.0	0.946	0.326	2.904
11.5	0.199	0.980	0.204	41.5	0.663	0.749	0.885	71.5	0.948	0.317	2.983
12.0	0.208	0.978	0.213	42.0	0.669	0.743	0.900	72.0	0.951	0.309	3.078
12.5	0.216	0.976	0.222	42.5	0.676	0.737	0.916	72.5	0.954	0.301	3.172
13.0	0.225	0.974	0.231	43.0	0.682	0.731	0.932	73.0	0.956	0.292	3.271
13.5	0.233	0.972	0.240	43.5	0.688	0.725	0.949	73.5	0.959	0.284	3.376
14.0	0.242	0.970	0.249	44.0	0.695	0.719	0.966	74.0	0.961	0.276	3.487
14.5	0.250	0.968	0.259	44.5	0.701	0.713	0.983	74.5	0.964	0.267	3.606
15.0	0.259	0.966	0.268	45.0	0.707	0.707	1.000	75.0	0.966	0.259	3.732
15.5	0.267	0.964	0.277	45.5	0.713	0.701	1.018	75.5	0.968	0.250	3.867
16.0	0.276	0.961	0.287	46.0	0.719	0.695	1.036	76.0	0.970	0.242	4.011
16.5	0.284	0.959	0.296	46.5	0.725	0.688	1.054	76.5	0.972	0.233	4.165
17.0	0.292	0.956	0.306	47.0	0.731	0.682	1.072	77.0	0.974	0.225	4.331
17.5	0.301	0.954	0.315	47.5	0.737	0.676	1.091	77.5	0.976	0.216	4.511
18.0	0.309	0.951	0.325	48.0	0.743	0.669	1.111	78.0	0.978	0.208	4.705
18.5	0.317	0.948	0.335	48.5	0.749	0.663	1.130	78.5	0.980	0.199	4.915
19.0	0.326	0.946	0.344	49.0	0.755	0.656	1.150	79.0	0.982	0.191	5.145
19.5	0.334	0.943	0.354	49.5	0.760	0.649	1.171	79.5	0.983	0.182	5.396
20.0	0.342	0.940	0.364	50.0	0.766	0.643	1.192	80.0	0.985	0.174	5.671
20.5	0.350	0.937	0.374	50.5	0.772	0.636	1.213	80.5	0.986	0.165	5.976
21.0	0.358	0.934	0.384	51.0	0.777	0.629	1.235	81.0	0.988	0.156	6.314
21.5	0.366	0.930	0.394	51.5	0.783	0.622	1.257	81.5	0.989	0.148	6.691
22.0	0.375	0.927	0.404	52.0	0.788	0.616	1.280	82.0	0.990	0.139	7.115
22.5	0.383	0.924	0.414	52.5	0.793	0.609	1.303	82.5	0.991	0.131	7.596
23.0	0.391	0.921	0.424	53.0	0.799	0.602	1.327	83.0	0.992	0.122	8.144
23.5	0.399	0.917	0.435	53.5	0.804	0.595	1.351	83.5	0.994	0.113	8.777
24.0	0.407	0.914	0.445	54.0	0.809	0.588	1.376	84.0	0.994	0.104	9.514
24.5	0.415	0.910	0.456	54.5	0.814	0.581	1.402	84.5	0.995	0.093	10.38
25.0	0.423	0.906	0.466	55.0	0.819	0.574	1.428	85.0	0.996	0.087	11.43
25.5	0.431	0.903	0.477	55.5	0.824	0.566	1.455	85.5	0.997	0.078	12.71
26.0	0.438	0.899	0.488	56.0	0.829	0.559	1.483	86.0	0.998	0.070	14.30
26.5	0.446	0.895	0.499	56.5	0.834	0.552	1.511	86.5	0.998	0.061	16.35
27.0	0.454	0.891	0.510	57.0	0.839	0.545	1.540	87.0	0.999	0.052	19.08
27.5	0.462	0.887	0.521	57.5	0.843	0.537	1.570	87.5	0.999	0.044	22.90
28.0	0.470	0.883	0.532	58.0	0.848	0.530	1.600	88.0	0.999	0.035	28.64
28.5	0.477	0.879	0.543	58.5	0.853	0.522	1.632	88.5	1.000	0.026	38.19
29.0	0.485	0.875	0.554	59.0	0.857	0.515	1.664	89.0	1.000	0.017	57.29
29.5	0.492	0.870	0.566	59.5	0.862	0.508	1.698	89.5	1.000	0.009	114.1
30.0	0.500	0.866	0.577	60.0	0.866	0.500	1.732	90.0	1.000	0.000	......

Table 13

A List of Elements with Atomic Numbers, Weights and Masses

Element	Symbol	Atomic number	Atomic weight[a]	Mass numbers of naturally occurring isotopes[bc]
Actinium	Ac	89	[227]	227†, 228†
Aluminum	Al	13	26.9815	27
Americium	Am	95	[243]	243‡
Antimony	Sb	51	121.75	121, 123
Argon	Ar	18	39.948	36, 38, 40
Arsenic	As	33	74.9216	75
Astatine	At	85	[210]	210†, 215†, 216†, 218†
Barium	Ba	56	137.34	130, 132, 134, 135, 136, 137, 138
Berkelium	Bk	97	[249*]	247‡
Beryllium	Be	4	9.0122	9
Bismuth	Bi	83	208.980	209, 210†, 211†, 212†, 214†
Boron	B	5	10.811	10, 11
Bromine	Br	35	79.909	79, 81
Cadmium	Cd	48	112.40	106, 108, 110, 111, 112, 113, 114, 116
Calcium	Ca	20	40.08	40, 42, 43, 44, 46, 48
Californium	Cf	98	[251*]	249‡
Carbon	C	6	12.01115	12, 13
Cerium	Ce	58	140.12	136, 138, 140, 142
Cesium	Cs	55	132.905	133
Chlorine	Cl	17	35.453	35, 37
Chromium	Cr	24	51.996	50, 52, 53, 54
Cobalt	Co	27	58.9332	59
Copper	Cu	29	63.54	63, 65
Curium	Cm	96	[248]	248‡
Dysprosium	Dy	66	162.50	156, 158, 160, 161, 162, 163, 164
Einsteinium	Es	99	[254]	254‡
Erbium	Er	68	167.26	162, 164, 166, 167, 168, 170
Europium	Eu	63	151.96	151, 153
Fermium	Fm	100	[253]	253‡
Fluorine	F	9	18.9984	19
Francium	Fr	87	[223]	223†
Gadolinium	Gd	64	157.25	152, 154, 155, 156, 157, 158, 160
Gallium	Ga	31	69.72	69, 71
Germanium	Ge	32	72.59	70, 72, 73, 74, 76
Gold	Au	79	196.967	197
Hafnium	Hf	72	178.49	174, 176, 177, 178, 179, 180
Helium	He	2	4.0026	3, 4
Holmium	Ho	67	164.930	165
Hydrogen	H	1	1.00797	1, 2
Indium	In	49	114.82	113, 115
Iodine	I	53	126.9044	127
Iridium	Ir	77	192.2	191, 193
Iron	Fe	26	55.847	54, 56, 57, 58
Krypton	Kr	36	83.80	78, 80, 82, 83, 84, 86
Lanthanum	La	57	138.91	138†, 139
Lawrencium	Lw	103	[257]	257‡
Lead	Pb	82	207.19	204, 206, 207, 208, 210†, 211†, 212†, 214†
Lithium	Li	3	6.939	6, 7
Lutetium	Lu	71	174.97	175, 176†
Magnesium	Mg	12	24.312	24, 25, 26
Manganese	Mn	25	54.9380	55
Mendelevium	Md	101	[256]	256‡
Mercury	Hg	80	200.59	196, 198, 199, 200, 201, 202, 204
Molybdenum	Mo	42	95.94	92, 94, 95, 96, 97, 98, 100

Element	Sym-bol	Atomic number	Atomic weight[a]	Mass numbers of naturally occurring isotopes[b][c]
Neodymium	Nd	60	144.24	142, 143, 144†, 145, 146, 148, 150
Neon	Ne	10	20.183	20, 21, 22
Neptunium	Np	93	[237]	237‡
Nickel	Ni	28	58.71	58, 60, 61, 62, 64
Niobium	Nb	41	92.906	93
Nitrogen	N	7	14.0067	14, 15
Nobelium	No	102	[253]	253‡
Osmium	Os	76	190.2	184, 186, 187, 188, 189, 190, 192
Oxygen	O	8	15.9994	16, 17, 18
Palladium	Pd	46	106.4	102, 104, 105, 106, 108, 110
Phosphorus	P	15	30.9738	31
Platinum	Pt	78	195.09	190†, 192, 194, 195, 196, 198
Plutonium	Pu	94	[242]	242‡
Polonium	Po	84	[210]	210†, 211†, 212†, 214†, 215†, 216†, 218†
Potassium	K	19	39.102	39, 40†, 41
Praseodymium	Pr	59	140.907	141
Promethium	Pm	61	[147]	147‡
Protactinium	Pa	91	[231]	231†, 234†
Radium	Ra	88	[226]	223†, 224†, 226†, 228†
Radon	Rn	86	[222]	219†, 220†, 222
Rhenium	Re	75	186.2	185, 187†
Rhodium	Rh	45	102.905	103
Rubidium	Rb	37	85.47	85, 87†
Ruthenium	Ru	44	101.07	96, 98, 99, 100, 101, 102, 104
Samarium	Sm	62	150.35	144, 147†, 148, 149, 150, 152, 154
Scandium	Sc	21	44.956	45
Selenium	Se	34	78.96	74, 76, 77, 78, 80, 82
Silicon	Si	14	28.086	28, 29, 30
Silver	Ag	47	107.870	107, 109
Sodium	Na	11	22.9898	23
Strontium	Sr	38	87.62	84, 86, 87, 88
Sulphur	S	16	32.064	32, 33, 34, 36
Tantalum	Ta	73	180.948	180, 181
Technetium	Tc	43	[99]	99‡
Tellurium	Te	52	127.60	120, 122, 123, 124, 125, 126, 128, 130
Terbium	Tb	65	158.924	159
Thallium	Tl	81	204.37	203, 205, 206†, 207†, 208†, 210†
Thorium	Th	90	232.038	227†, 228†, 230†, 231†, 232†, 234†
Thulium	Tm	69	168.934	169
Tin	Sn	50	118.69	112, 114, 115, 116, 117, 118, 119, 120, 122, 124
Titanium	Ti	22	47.90	46, 47, 48, 49, 50
Tungsten	W	74	183.85	180†, 182, 183, 184, 186
Uranium	U	92	238.03	234†, 235†, 238†
Vanadium	V	23	50.942	50, 51
Xenon	Xe	54	131.30	124, 126, 128, 129, 130, 131, 132, 134, 136
Ytterbium	Yb	70	173.04	168, 170, 171, 172, 173, 174, 176
Yttrium	Y	39	88.905	89
Zinc	Zn	30	65.37	64, 66, 67, 68, 70
Zirconium	Zr	40	91.22	90, 91, 92, 94, 96

[a]The atomic weights of most of these elements are believed to have no error greater than ±0.5 of the last digit given. A value given in brackets denotes the mass number of the isotope of longest known half-life, or for those marked with an asterisk, a better known one.

[b]Isotopes marked † are naturally-occurring radioactive isotopes. Most of these are members of one or other of the natural radioactive decay chains. Some are present in extremely small amounts. Where an element has no naturally occurring isotope (denoted by ‡), the atomic mass of its artificially-created isotope with the longest half-life is given.

[c]Elements 43, 61 and 93-102 are sometimes referred to as the "artificial" elements. Actually, radioactive isotopes of most of these may be assumed to occur in nature, but cannot be obtained in useful amounts from natural sources due to the quantity and/or distribution in which they occur.

Index

Answers To B Exercises

CHAPTER 1 (Pp. 16-19)

1. (a) 150 dm; (b) 147 mm; (c) 2300 g; (d) 6576 mg; (e) 7800 l; (f) 9370 ml; (g) 12,500 dg; (h) 625.4 mg; (i) 23,000 cm; (j) 34,000 mg. **2.** (a) 93.7 m; (b) 0.125 l; (c) 0.23 cm; (d) 312.5 g; (e) 0.0625 kg; (f) 62.7 cg; (g) .00867 km; (h) 0.489 g; (i) 0.023 cl; (j) 5.178 $\times 10^{-6}$ kl. **3.** (a) 7.9×10^2 in or 66 ft; (b) 500 in; (c) 4.05 qt; (d) 0.500 lb; (e) 4.8 lb. **4.** (a) 3.8 cm or 0.038 m; (b) 0.50000 m; (c) 3.010 l; (d) 1.6×10^3 g; (e) 7.00 kg. **5.** (i) (a) 5.6×10; (b) 7.89×10^2; (c) 4; (d) 3.210×10^3; (e) 1.86×10^5; (f) 3×10^{10}; (g) 7.0×10^{-1}; (h) 1.2×10^{-3}; (i) 4.03×10^{-4}; (j) 9.107×10^{-28}; (ii) (a) 50; (b) 6200; (c) 7.4; (d) 910; (e) 436,870; (f) 0.1; (g) 0.043; (h) 0.0000894; (i) 0.003076; (iii) (a) 10^2; (b) 10^5; (c) 10^3; (d) 10^{-3}; (e) 10^2; (f) 10^2; (g) 10^{-7}; (h) 10^{-1}; (i) 10^4; (j) 3.6×10^3; (k) 5×10; (l) 1.8×10^{-5}; (m) 2×10^3; (n) 2×10^2; (o) 8×10^6. **6.** (a) $5.432 \times 10^{-1}\mu$; (b) 2.82×10^{-5} Å; (c) 2.8×10^{-9} cm; (d) 2.25×10^{-8} m; (e) 7.40×10^{-1} mc/sec. **7.** (a) 4.50×10 Å; (b) 7.7×10^4 f; (c) 9.25 $\times 10^2 \mu$; (d) 9.11×10^{-28} g; (e) 1×10 f. **8.** (a) 6; (b) 15; (c) 70; (d) 9.6; (e) 2.2; (f) 0.0966; (g) 22; (h) 98. **9.** (a) 12; (b) 60; (c) 56; (d) 27.6; (e) 18; (f) 7.92; (g) 0.322; (h) 0.0322; (i) 0.116. **10.** (a) 25; (b) 13.2; (c) 14.2(5); (d) 0.6; (e) 0.778; (f) 1.42; (g) 8.44; (h) 2.25; (i) 2.74; (j) 0.313; (k) 77.4; (l) 0.229; (m) 0.741; (n) 32.3. **11.** (a) 8.0; (b) 12.5; (c) 280; (d) 222; (e) 40.2; (f) 0.565; (g) 16.0; (h) 2.59; (i) 19.04; (j) 210; (k) 388. **12.** (a) 2.97; (b) 0.558; (c) 558; (d) 15.4; (e) 16.3; (f) 0.0160; (g) 21.8; (h) 24,500; (i) 133; (j) 506. **13.** (a) 9; (b) 256; (c) 15,100; (d) 5.76; (e) 0.0121; (f) 49.7; **14.** (a) 2; (b) 2.65; (c) 7; (d) 8.78; (e) 16; (f) 0.505; (g) 0.80; (h) 0.447; (i) 0.224.

CHAPTER 2 (Pp. 33-37)

1. (c) 3.3×10^2 m/sec. **2.** (b) B; (c) (i) A; (ii) A; (d) A and B; (e) 367 sec (approx.); (f) 90 sec and 505 sec. **3.** (a) 37 mi; (b) (i) 19 mi/hr; (ii) 7.4 mi/hr N6°W. **4.** (a) 87 mi; (b) S9°E; (c) 87 mi S9°E; (d) (i) 58 mi/hr, 19 mi/hr; (ii) 58 mi/hr S9°E, 14 mi/hr S9°E. **5.** 4.0 mi/hr, 10.0 mi/hr. **6.** 3.3 mi/hr/sec N, or 4.9 ft/sec² N. **7.** 9.78 m/sec². **8.** (a) (i) 34 knots; (ii) 26 knots; (iii) 30 knots; (b) (i) 29 knots; (ii) 21 knots; (iii) 24 knots. **9.** (a) N30°E, 24 knots N30°E; (b) (i) N99°E; (ii) 12.5 knots N99°E; (c) N53°E; (d) 31 knots N53°E. **10.** 15 sec. **11.** (a) 133 ft.; (b) Upstream at 48° to shoreline. **12.** (a) 0.43 mi; (b) 1.1 mi; (c) Upstream at 65° to shoreline. **13.** (a) E11°N; (b) 204 nautical miles. **14.** (a) N14°W; (b) (i) N9°W; (ii) N13°W. **15.** (a) (i) 39 nautical miles; (ii) 18 nautical miles; (b) Approx. 4 nautical miles; (c) Port; (d) Starboard; (e) Collision. **16.** (a) 22 mi North of harbour; (b) 17.7 mi E; (c) 5:46 p.m.; (d) 7.8 mi North of harbour; (e) 3.1 mi South of Plucky. **17.** (a) 70 mi; (b) 1.2 mi; (c) (i) 39°N latitude; (ii) 3.0×10^2 mi/hr; (iii) N8°W.

CHAPTER 3 (Pp. 46-47)

1. -5.5 mi/hr/sec (-8.0 ft/sec²). **2.** (a) 50 mi/hr, 73 ft/sec; (b) 3.6×10^2 ft; (c) 5.9 ft/sec². **3.** (a) 176 ft/sec; (b) 5.5 sec; (c) 4.8×10^2 ft. **4.** -7.5×10^2 m/min² (-0.21 m/sec²). **5.** 31 m. **6.** (a) 11 sec and 7.3 sec; (b) 30 mi/hr. **7.** 25, 20, 15, 10, 5, 0 mi/hr. **8.** Never, Non-uniform. **9.** (a) 40.0 cm/sec²; (b) 51.2 m. **10.** (a) 4.00 sec; (b) 256 ft; (c) 128 ft/sec downward. **11.** (a) 29 sec; (b) No. **12.** 1.2×10^3 cm. **13.** 1.00×10^2 ft. **14.** 20 cm/sec left and 120 cm left; 0 cm/sec and 160 cm left; 20 cm/sec right and 120 cm left. **15.** (a) 6.10×10^3 cm/sec downward; (b) 324 m. **16.** 256 ft (78.4 m). **17.** (a) -1.25 m/sec²; (b) 1.60×10^2 m; (c) 26.7 sec; (d) 267 m. **18.** 224 ft (68.4 m). **19.** (b) 250 ft E.

CHAPTER 4 (Pp. 62-63)

1. 10.0. **2.** 2.50 kg. **3.** 48 nt W. **4.** 64 m/sec² right. **5.** (a) 1.0 nt; (b) 1.00×10^5 dynes; (c) 1.00×10^5 dynes (exactly). **6.** 125 nt. **8.** 25 nt. **9.** 8.9×10^2 nt. **10.** (a) 4.1×10^3 nt; (b) 5.1×10^3 nt; (c) 6.1×10^3 nt. **11.** (a) 1.18 nt; (b) 0.580 nt. **12.** 7.7×10^2 nt. **13.** (a) No. Rope will break; (b) 3.04 m/sec². **14.** (a) 9.8 nt; (b) 1.6 nt. **15.** (a) 6.00 slugs; (b) 2.0 ft/sec². **16.** (a) 110 lb E17°N; (b) 18 ft/sec² E17°N. **17.** (a) 3.9 m/sec² upward; (b) 1.2×10^2 nt upward; (c) 1.2×10^2 nt downward. **18.** 4.00×10^3 nt S. **19.** (a) 500 nt N; (b) 500 nt S.

CHAPTER 5 (Pp. 72-73)

1. (a) 6.0 nt; (b) 3.7 kg. **2.** 6.67×10^{-7} nt. **3.** 3×10^5. **4.** 2.8 lb. **5.** 64 ft/sec². **6.** 800 lb. **7.** (a) 2 times; (b) 250 lb. **8.** (b) 3.7×10^2 nt; (c) 3.7 m/sec². **9.** 28 ft/sec². **10.** 8.3 $\times 10^2$ ft/sec (2.5×10^2 m/sec). **11.** (a) 3.2 ft/sec²; (b) 8.0 ft/sec². **12.** 3.63×10^{-47} nt.

CHAPTER 6 (Pp. 90-93)

1. 9.0×10^2 ft-lb. **2.** (a) 1.5×10^2 ft-lb; (b) 7.5×10^2 ft-lb. **3.** 1.997×10^6 ft-lb. **4.** (a) 1.5 $\times 10^{-5}$ j; (b) 4.9×10^{-4} j; (c) 4.9×10^{-4} j. **5.** (a) 2.8×10^3 ft-lb; (b) 1.4×10^2 ft-lb/sec. **6.** 2.08 $\times 10^5$ ft-lb. **7.** (a) 9.8×10^{-2} j; (b) 9.8×10^{-2} j; (c) 1.4 m/sec. **8.** (a) 2.9×10^4 j; (b) 7.7 m/sec; (c) 2.9×10^4 j; (d) 5.9×10^5 nt. **9.** 4.6×10^{-23} j. **10.** 3.9 j. **11.** 1.3×10^4 m. **12.** (a) 2.8×10^6 j; (b) 9.3×10^5 nt. **13.** 4.4 m/sec. **14.** 0.24 watts. **15.** (a) 239 kw; (b) 2.2×10^8 j; 1.6×10^8 ft-lb. **16.** (a) 24.2 hp; (b) 97 hp. **17.** (a) 2.68 hp; (b) 7.20×10^6 j. **18.** 27 sec. **19.** $3.00. **20.** $v = \sqrt{2\,gh}$. **21.** (a) 2.0×10 j; (b) 9.8 j; (d) 2.6 m/sec. **22.** 9.00×10^{16} j. **23.** 1.8×10^{47} j. **24.** 2.75×10^{-6} j.

CHAPTER 7 (Pp. 112-115)

1. 6.0 ft. **2.** 2.40×10^2 g. **3.** 3.6×10^3 lb, 2.6×10^3 lb. **4.** 6.3 ft from unloaded end. **5.** 3.2 ft from father's end. **6.** (a) 4.00; (b) 97.0 lb. **7.** (a) 2nd class; (b) 5; (c) 2×10^2 lb. **8.** (a) 2nd class; (b) 2.67; (c) 23.4 lb. **9.** (a) 3rd class; (b) 0.57; (c) 18 lb. **10.** (a) 1; (b) 1; 100% if no friction. **11.** (a) 2.00; (b) 1.79; (c) 0.8 lb; (d) 1.00 ft. **12.** (a) 32 lb; (b) 32 lb; (c) 50 in. **13.** (a) 40.0 lb; (b) 40.0 lb; (c) 40 in. **14.** 5 or more. **15.** (a) 5.00, 6.00; (b) 83%. **16.** (a) 2.0 hp; (b) 75%. **17.** 60%. **18.** (a) 64; (b) 32. **19.** 9.4×10^2, 1.0×10^2, 11%. **20.** 0.11 hp. **21.** (a) 30 lb; (b) 60%. **22.** (a) 24; (b) 17; (c) 71%. **23.** 64%. **24.** (a) 1.20×10^2; (b) 6.9 lb. **25.** 1.2×10^4 lb. **26.** (a) 1.5×10^2; (b) 6.0; (c) 9.0×10^2; (d) 2.26×10^2; (e) 25%.

CHAPTER 8 (Pp. 130-133)

1. 5.52 g/cm³. **2.** 1.20×10^3 lb/ft³. **3.** 1.03×10^3 gf/cm². **4.** 415 gf/cm². **5.** 4×10^4 lb. **6.** 2500 lb. **7.** (a) 150 cm³; (b) 90 cm³; (c) 7.2. **8.** (a) 31.2 cm³; (b) 137 g. **9.** 3.10 g/cm³. **10.** (a) 1.60×10^2 gf; (b) 1.40×10^2 gf. **11.** (a) 2.64 g/cm³; (b) 0.800. **12.** (a) 4.99×10^2 lb/ft³; (b) 5.0×10 lb/ft³; (c) 0.80. **13.** (a) 4.83×10^3 tons (9.66×10^6 lb); (b) 1.51×10^5 ft³; (c) 1.41×10^4 ft³. **14.** 7.8×10^2 ft³. **15.** 17 gf. **16.** 1.50. **17.** $\frac{1}{4}$. **18.** 1.03×10^4 lb. **19.** 0.75 g/cm³. **20.** 0.65. **21.** 208 lb. **22.** 4.9 g. **23.** 186 cm³. **24.** 2.8 g/cm³. **25.** (a) 4.6×10^2 lb; (c) 6.7×10^2 lb. **26.** 38.0 kg. **27.** (c) 57 cm³.

CHAPTER 9 (Pp. 148-149)

1. 25°C. **2.** 134°F. **3.** −65°C. **4.** −319°F. **5.** 10 C°. **6.** 72 F°. **7.** 90°K. **8.** −269°C. **9.** 9.87×10^3°F. **10.** 63 K° above 0°K. **11.** −40°C. **12.** 5.83 l. **13.** 274 ml. **14.** 190°C.

CHAPTER 10 (Pp. 161-163)

1. 1.9×10^2 Btu. **2.** 4.0×10^4 cal. **3.** 1.6×10^2 Btu. **4.** 5.0×10^2 cal. **5.** 20.0° C. **6.** 50 kg. **7.** 1.78×10^5 Btu. **8.** 79.6°F. **9.** 85.0°C. **10.** 0.051 Btu/lb F°. **11.** 0.0335 cal/gC°. **12.** 0.0902 cal/gC°. **13.** 0.43 cal/gC°. **14.** 0.091 cal/gC°. **15.** 2.7×10^2 g. **16.** (a) 2.1×10^4 cal; (b) 7.5×10^4 cal; (c) 8.0×10^4 cal. **17.** (a) 3.29×10^3 Btu; (b) 1.3×10^4 Btu. **18.** 5.4×10^2 cal/g. **19.** 89°C. **20.** 4.8×10^4 Btu. **21.** (a) 2.7×10^4 cal; (b) 1.1×10^5 j. **22.** 1.3×10^4 Btu. **23.** 93°F. **24.** 44 g. **25.** 139 g. **26.** 73°C. **27.** 8.8×10^2 °F. **28.** (a) 3.8×10^5 j; (b) 6.2×10^3 watts. **29.** 0.12 lb. **30.** 0.85 C°. **31.** 42.5 Btu. **32.** 30.6 cal. **33.** 3.4×10^2 m/sec.

CHAPTER 11 (Pp. 188-189)

1. (a) 1.5 vib/sec; (b) 0.67 sec. **2.** 3.91×10^{-3} sec. **3.** 344 m/sec. **4.** 2.97×10^8 m/sec. **5.** 3.0×10^{22} vib/sec. **6.** 1.2×10^2 vib/sec; 8.3×10^{-3} sec. **7.** 2.0×10^{-2} ft. **8.** 55 ft to 0.055 ft. **9.** 0.12 sec or 0.38 sec. **10.** 0.50 sec. **11.** 15 ft/sec. **12.** 6.0 ft/sec. **13.** 53 ft/sec. **14.** 50 in/sec.

CHAPTER 12 (Part A) (Pp. 219-220)

1. 1.12×10^3 ft/sec, 4.2 sec. **2.** 11.9 sec. **3.** 4.38 ft. **4.** 1.9×10^3 ft. **5.** 4.5 mi/hr. **6.** 3.0×10^2

m/sec. **7.** 600 vib/sec. **8.** 250 vib/sec. **9.** 320 vib/sec. **10.** Ratio 21:20. **11.** 8.0×10^2 vib/sec. **12.** 150 vib/sec. **13.** (a) 13.1 in; (b) 26.2 in. **14.** (a) 35 c/sec; (b) 105 c/sec, 175 c/sec. **15.** 4.0 in. **16.** 340 m/sec. **17.** 34.6 ft. **18.** 260 c/sec, 430 c/sec, 600 c/sec. **19.** 30 in and 36 in. **20.** 440 c/sec.

CHAPTER 12 (Part B) (P. 229)

1. 55 ft or 17 m. **2.** 1.05×10^3 c/sec. **3.** 5.0 c/sec. **4.** 2.2×10^2 c/sec. **5.** 221 c/sec.

CHAPTER 13 (P. 243)

1. 5.87×10^{12} mi. **2.** 2.5×10^{13} mi. **3.** (a) 5.0×10^2 sec; (b) 8.3 light-minutes; (c) 5.0×10^2 light-seconds. **4.** 7.5×10^{14} c/sec.

CHAPTER 14 (Pp. 255-256)

1. (a) 3.00 ft; (b) 2.85 ft. **2.** No change. **5.** (a) 3.00 ft; (b) At focus. **6.** (a) 22.5 cm in front of mirror; (b) 0.5 times size of object. **7.** 9.0 cm. **8.** (a) 64.3 cm mark; (b) 1.4 cm. **9.** (a) At focus, 1.75 m in front of mirror; (b) 4.6×10^{-9}; (c) 0.63 in or 1.6 cm. **10.** (a) 14.0 cm; (b) 6.0 cm. **12.** (a) 3.2 m; (b) 3.0 m behind mirror; (c) 10 cm.

CHAPTER 15 (Pp. 277-279)

1. 1.33. **2.** 1.53. **3.** (a) 2.25×10^8 m/sec; (b) 1.96×10^8 m/sec. **4.** 1.50×10^8 m/sec. **5.** 1.43. **6.** 3.8×10^{-7} m. **7.** (i) 0.500; (ii) 0.309; (iii) 0.809; (iv) 1.00. **8.** (i) 12°; (ii) 45°; (iii) 25°; (iv) 68°. **9.** 67°. **10.** 33°. **11.** (a) 7.5 cm. **13.** 1.74. **14.** (a) 1.53; (b) 44°; (c) 38°; (d) 1.62; (e) 41°. **15.** 42°. **17.** (a) 15 cm behind lens; 20 cm behind lens; 30 cm behind lens; 10 cm in front of lens; (b) 0.5; 1.0; 2.0; 2.0. **18.** (b) 6.0 cm in front of lens. Relative size 0.40. **19.** 5.0 cm. **20.** (a) 4.1 in; (b) 29.

CHAPTER 16 (P. 295)

1. $f/4$. **2.** $\frac{1}{25}$ sec. **3.** 118 in. **4.** About 210. **5.** 4.1. **6.** 60.

CHAPTER 18 (Pp. 314-315)

1. 5.12×10^{-5} j. **2.** 184 volts. **3.** 5.0×10^{-6} coulombs. **4.** 6.00×10^{-9} coulombs. **5.** 2.00×10^{-2} volts. **6.** 1.6×10^{-11} j. **7.** 1.6×10^2 volts. **8.** (a) 3.6×10^{-5} coulombs, 5.3×10^{-5} coulombs, 11×10^{-5} coulombs respectively; (b) 20×10^{-5} coulombs; (c) 0.84 μf.

CHAPTER 19 (Pp. 326-327)

1. 2.2×10^2 coulombs. **2.** (a) 45 volts; (b) 1.5 volts. **3.** (b) 2.3 amps; (c) 12 volts in each case. **4.** 3.0×10^2 j. **5.** 7.5Ω. **6.** (a) 220Ω; (b) 28Ω; (c) 14 volts. **9.** 9.6Ω. **10.** 10. **11.** 40Ω. **12.** (a) 90Ω; (b) 10Ω; (c) 15Ω; (d) 40Ω; (e) 20Ω; (f) 30Ω.

CHAPTER 20 (Pp. 336-337)

1. (a) 7.2×10^3 coulombs; (b) 8.3×10^5 watt-sec; (c) 9.2×10^2 watts. **2.** (a) 7.7Ω; (b) 2.48×10^5 cal. **3.** 23.9Ω. **4.** 30.5 min. **5.** 4.2 j/cal. **6.** 72%. **7.** 1.0×10^3 g. **8.** (a) 25 amp; (b) 1.9×10^3 watts; (c) $2.20. **9.** $1.80. **10.** (a) $21; (b) 68%.

CHAPTER 23 (P. 365)

3. (a) 0.2 amp; (b) 0.21 amp; (c) 91%. **4.** (a) 4,000; (b) 2.9 amps. **5.** 37 amps. **6.** (a) 18 watts; (b) 0.17 amp; (c) 2.4 cents.

CHAPTER 24 (P. 375)

1. 1.0Ω. **2.** 18.9Ω. **3.** 10. **4.** 3.99×10^3Ω. **5.** (a) 50 volts; (b) 20,000Ω; (c) 22.2 volts.

CHAPTER 28 (P. 420)

1. 6.2×10^{18} elementary charges. **3.** 1.6×10^{-19} coulomb.

CHAPTER 29 (P. 435)

1. (a) (i) 11, (ii) 12, (iii) 11; (c) (i) 82, (ii) 125, (iii) 82; (e) (i) 32, (ii) 38, (iii) 32;

(g) (i) 92, (ii) 143, (iii) 92. **2.** 63.6 **4.** (b) is in error. **5.** (a) $_{90}Th^{231}$; (c) $_{-1}e^{0}$; (e) $_{84}Po^{211}$. **6.** (a) 0.50 g; (b) 0.25 g; (c) 0.125 g; (d) about 0.015 g.

CHAPTER 30 (P. 443)
1. 6.6×10^{-28} j. **2.** 2.0×10^{-18} j.

CHAPTER 31 (P. 457-8)
1. (a) $_{7}N^{14} + _{0}n^{1} \rightarrow _{6}C^{14} + _{1}H^{1}$ **2.** (a) 16.134 amu; (b) 15.997 amu; (c) 0.137 amu; (d) about 127 Mev. **3.** (c) about 21 Mev. **4.** (a) 227.92 amu (b) 225.77 amu (c) about 2.0×10^{3} Mev. **5.** (a) zirconium-97; (c) barium-141. **6.** (a) $_{92}U^{236} \rightarrow _{52}Te^{137} + _{40}Zr^{97} + 2_{0}n^{1}$; ($c$) $_{92}U^{236} \rightarrow _{36}Kr^{92} + _{56}Ba^{141} + 3_{0}n^{1}$.